Queen Elizabeth II

Hugo Vickers is a writer, lecturer and broadcaster, and an acknowledged expert on the British Royal Family. He has written biographies of the Queen Mother, Cecil Beaton, Vivien Leigh, Princess Andrew of Greece and the Duchess of Windsor. His book *The Kiss* won the 1996 Stern Silver Pen Award for Non-Fiction. His recent bestsellers have included *Malice in Wonderland* and *The Sphinx* – the life of Gladys, Duchess of Marlborough. He collaborated with HRH The Duke of Kent on *A Royal Life*. He is a Deputy Lieutenant for Berkshire.

Also by Hugo Vickers

We Want the Queen
Gladys, Duchess of Marlborough
Debrett's Book of the Royal Wedding
Cocktails and Laughter
Cecil Beaton
Vivien Leigh
Royal Orders
Loving Garbo
The Private World of the Duke and Duchess of Windsor
The Kiss
Alice, Princess Andrew of Greece
The Unexpurgated Beaton: The Cecil Beaton Diaries
Beaton in the Sixties
Alexis, the Memoirs of the Baron de Redé
Elizabeth, The Queen Mother
Horses and Husbands
St George's Chapel, Windsor Castle
Behind Closed Doors
Cecil Beaton: Portraits and Profiles
Coronation
The Quest for Queen Mary
The Sphinx
The Crown Dissected
Malice in Wonderland
A Royal Life (with HRH The Duke of Kent)
The Queen and Windsor
Elstree 175
Pining in Paradise
Clarissa

QUEEN ELIZABETH II

A Personal History

HUGO VICKERS

HODDER &
STOUGHTON

First published in Great Britain in 2026 by Hodder & Stoughton Limited
An Hachette UK company

The authorised representative in the EEA is Hachette Ireland, 8 Castlecourt Centre, Dublin 15, D15 XTP3, Ireland (email: info@hbgi.ie)

1

Copyright © Hugo Vickers 2026

The right of Hugo Vickers to be identified as the Author of the Work has been asserted by him in accordance with the Copyright, Designs and Patents Act 1988.

Text copyright notices can be found on pp. 571-2.

All rights reserved. No part of this publication may be reproduced, stored in a retrieval system, or transmitted, in any form or by any means without the prior written permission of the publisher, nor be otherwise circulated in any form of binding or cover other than that in which it is published and without a similar condition being imposed on the subsequent purchaser.

A CIP catalogue record for this title is available from the British Library

Hardback ISBN 9781529355178
Trade Paperback ISBN 9781529355208
ebook ISBN 9781529355185

Typeset in Bembo MT Pro by Palimpsest Book Production Ltd, Falkirk, Stirlingshire

Printed and bound in Great Britain by Clays Ltd, Elcograf S.p.A.

Hodder & Stoughton policy is to use papers that are natural, renewable and recyclable products and made from wood grown in sustainable forests. The logging and manufacturing processes are expected to conform to the environmental regulations of the country of origin.

Hodder & Stoughton Limited
Carmelite House
50 Victoria Embankment
London EC4Y 0DZ

www.hodder.co.uk

For Arthur, Alice and George
who each met The Queen twice
when they were little.
May they carry the memory through many decades.

Contents

Family Tree — viii

Introduction — 1

1. The Royal House of Windsor — 9
2. Childhood, 1926–30 — 18
3. And Then There Were Two, 1930–6 — 31
4. The Year of Three Kings, 1936 — 44
5. The Pre-War Years, 1937–9 — 54
6. The War, 1939–45 — 67
7. Enter Prince Philip, 1941–6 — 83
8. South Africa and Engagement — 98
9. The Wedding, 1947 — 112
10. Married Life, 1948 — 117
11. Anxious Years, 1949–51 — 126
12. Demise of the Crown, 1951–2 — 136
13. Accession, 1952 — 143
14. The New Reign, 1952–3 — 153
15. The Coronation, 1953 — 166
16. The Coronation Summer — 176
17. The Commonwealth Tour, 1953–4 — 187
18. Churchill and Eden, 1952–7 — 202
19. The Family in the 1950s — 215
20. Diplomacy, 1954–9 — 228
21. Harold Macmillan, 1957–63 — 245
22. The Family in the 1960s — 256
23. Diplomacy, 1960–9 — 267
24. Home Politics, 1965–6 — 281
25. Changing Times — 290
26. The Early 1970s — 303

27. The State Visit to Paris, 1972	316
28. Politics and Family, 1972–6	325
29. Australia, 1975	341
30. The Silver Jubilee, 1977	346
31. The Later 1970s, 1978–9	355
32. Royal Engagement and Wedding, 1980–1	370
33. Enter William and Harry, 1981–6	379
34. Critical Times, 1986–8	388
35. Dark Days, 1987–90	399
36. The Early 1990s, 1989–91	409
37. Annus Horribilis	418
38. The Mid 1990s, 1993–6	429
39. A Very Bad Experience, 1997	442
40. Regrouping, 1998–2000	453
41. The Golden Jubilee, 2002	465
42. Resolution, 2003–7	478
43. Challenging Times, 2007–11	489
44. The Diamond Jubilee, 2012	503
45. Fictional Representations	518
46. Prince Harry and Prince Andrew	528
47. The Road to Covid	535
48. Prince Philip	546
49. The Platinum Jubilee, 2022	554
50. The Last Days	561
Personal Postscript	569
Acknowledgements	570
Source Notes	575
Index	627

The British Royal Family – Part 1

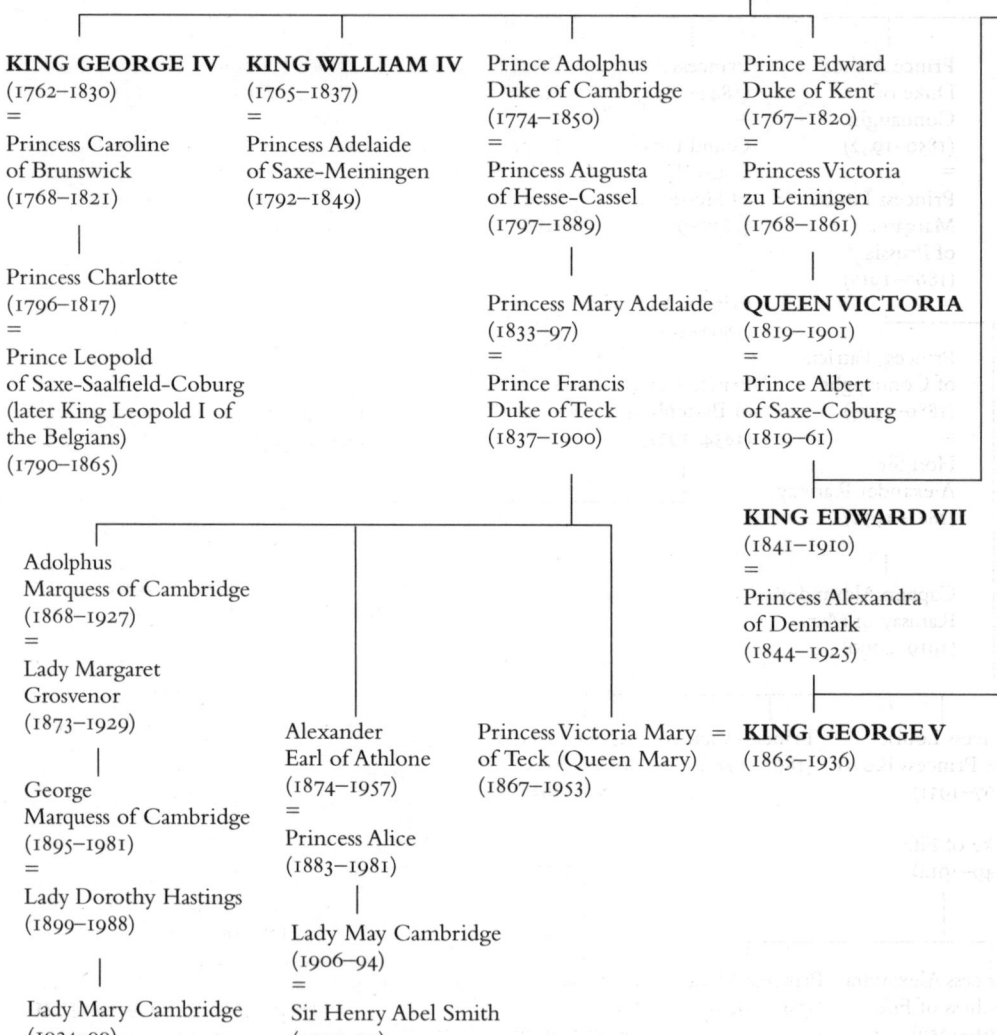

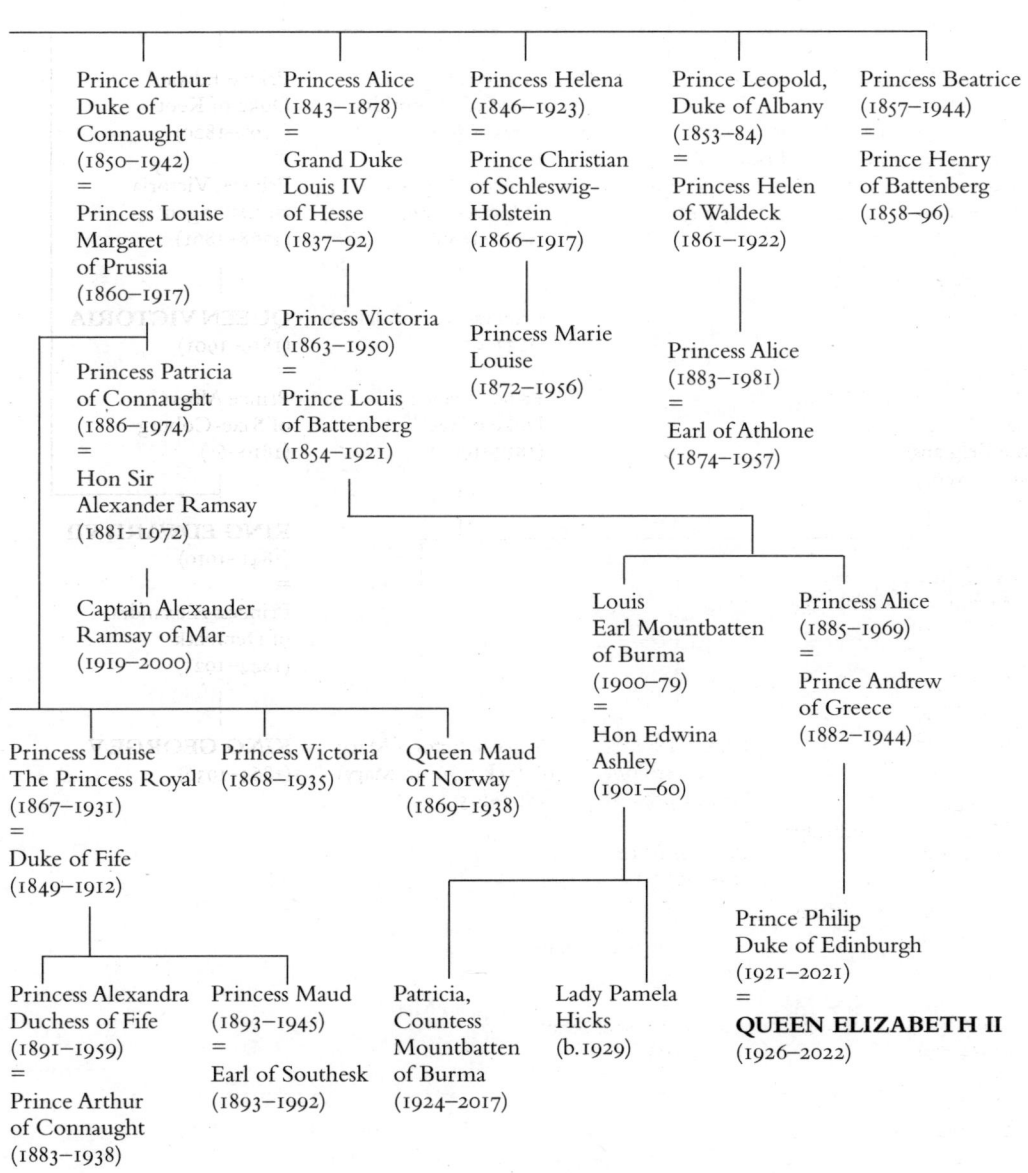

The British Royal Family – Part 2

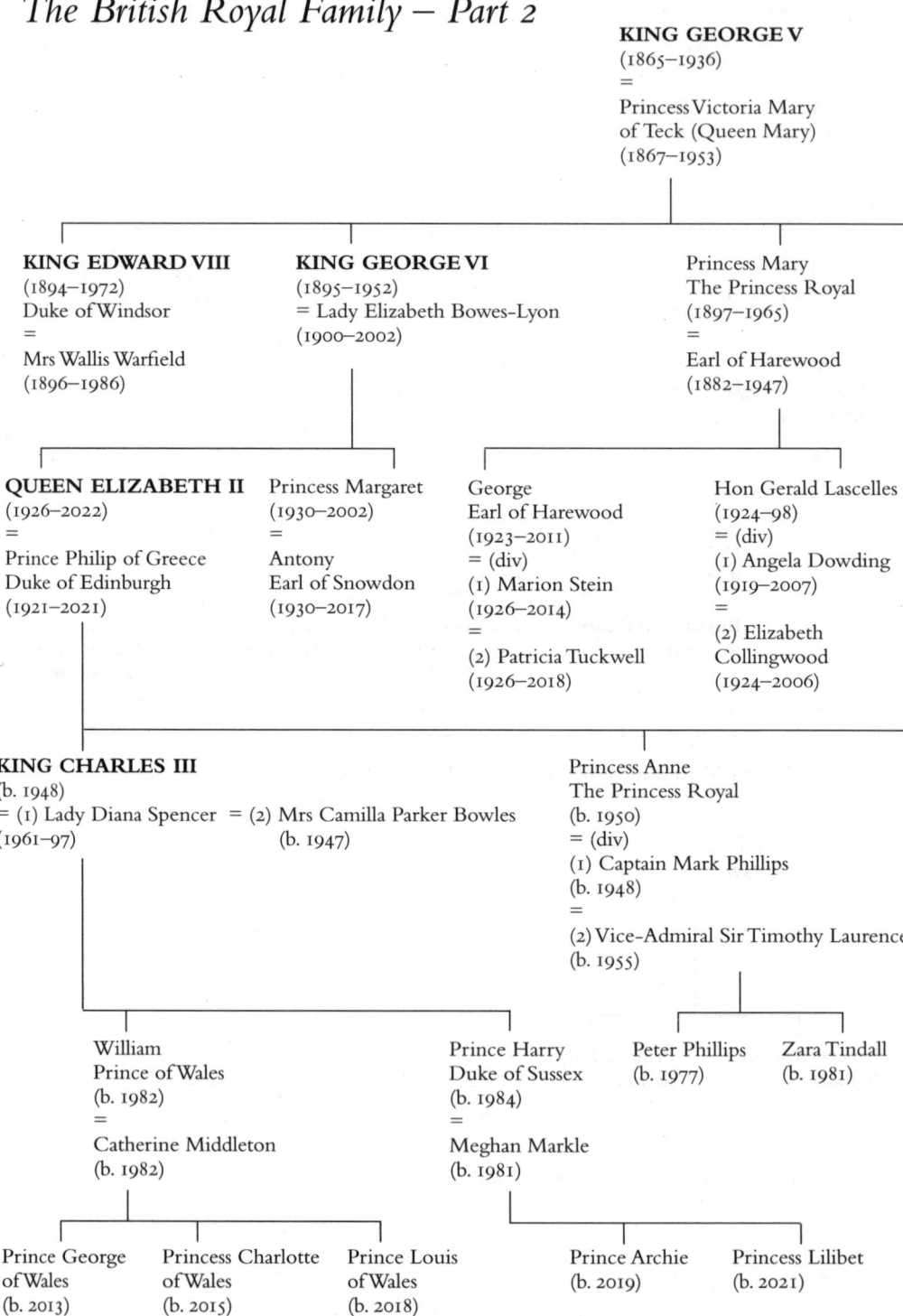

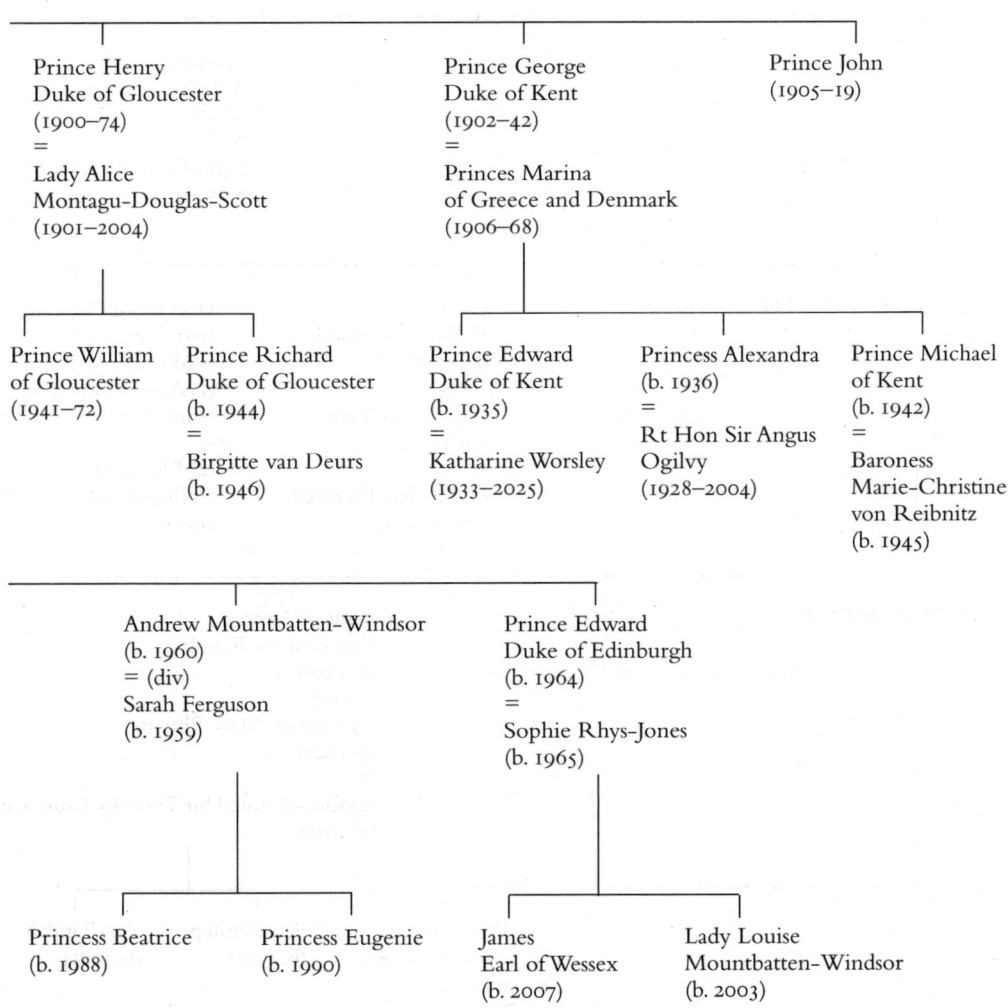

Introduction

All my life I longed to write about the Queen. As long ago as 1977 her Private Secretary, Sir Martin Charteris, read a piece I had produced to mark her Silver Jubilee, and said: 'I know you will write about the Queen again.' It is therefore a total joy to write this book to mark her centenary, on 21 April 2026.

I have no hesitation in saying that I cannot think of a reign in history in which I would have preferred to live, under any economic or political circumstances. It was a golden age, and my generation was exceptionally lucky.

She was the longest-reigning monarch in history, serving for seventy years and 214 days. King Louis XIV of France (1638–1715) reigned longer in total years – seventy-two years and 110 days – but for ten of those (between 1643 and 1653), he was a minor, so he is disqualified. Our Queen was an active monarch from the moment of her accession. On 9 September 2015, she outreigned Queen Victoria. On 13 October, she overtook King Bhumibol of Thailand (1927–2016), who reigned for seventy years and 126 days. On 1 July 2022, she became the longest ever holder of the Order of the Garter, overtaking her great-great-uncle and godfather, the Duke of Connaught. She aspired to none of these records, but they happened.

Kings and Queens sometimes have a sobriquet, such as 'Alfred the Great'. Queen Elizabeth II should be 'Elizabeth the Steadfast', as she had such a clear vision of what it was to be our Queen. She never wavered, whatever was thrown at her. One of the most iconic images of her is Cecil Beaton's Coronation portrait in 1953 – an assured young woman with the royal regalia, not in the least over-awed by them, on the brink of one of the greatest reigns in history. In common with Prince Philip and Princess Anne, she cared not a jot what people thought about her – she got on with the job.

And yet I don't know why it took me so long to realise that the leitmotif of her reign was conciliation. She could equally be remembered as 'Elizabeth the Conciliator'. Her message was consistent: 'We cannot change the past. We *can* build bridges to the future.' There are so many examples – Germany, Japan, Ireland. In the House of Lords after she died, she was hailed as 'Elizabeth the Good'.

The first time I am conscious of having seen the Queen was in the state procession for the Shah of Iran in the Mall in 1959. It was at that time that I attached myself by a thin, invisible thread to her coat tails and flew along behind her. She did not know I was there. And then there were a few times when I was allowed to fly along beside her (between 1968 and 2022). So this book is based on observation and research carried out for over sixty years, at first from afar (rather like a trainspotter or stamp collector) but gradually closer to the centre and more focused. In the absence of an official biography, I do my best to tell her story.

As a reigning Queen, she was determined to be a good successor to her father. If he met her in an afterlife, she could look him square in the eyes, confident that he would confirm that she had done a good job for him. At the age of twenty-one in 1947, she made a promise to serve and she kept that promise faithfully for seventy-five years. We will never see that again even if we live for a thousand years.

The Queen's philosophy was simple – do your best every day and say your prayers at night. Her lifetime of discretion is reflected in her favourite line in the bible – St Luke, Chapter 2, verse 19: 'But Mary kept all these things, and pondered them in her heart.'*
I would love to know when she worked out that she had more to gain by saying nothing than in revealing what she was thinking. She was the master of that. The difference between Queen Victoria and the Queen was that Queen Victoria commanded while Queen Elizabeth II obeyed. She took advice from whosoever was placed

---

* A cleric was once asked about the Queen's concept of religion, which was important to her. The answer was: 'It was not high church. It was not low church. It was short church.' The Queen had to attend many church services and preferred that they did not last longer than 40–45 minutes.

in a position to give it. Sometimes she would ask her advisers: 'What should the Queen do?' Not 'What should I do?' She was two different people – The Queen and the woman inside the Queen.

Her inherent modesty was such that she never thought the cheers and adulation were for her, they were for the person she represented – or inhabited, if you prefer. I bet that, after the Diamond Jubilee in 2012, when the crowds were thronging the Mall from one end to the other, her reaction next day was: 'Well, that was very nice. What's on the agenda for today?'

It was hard to catch the Queen out, but she liked catching others out. One of her favourite lines, delivered with great theatrical timing was: 'Are you sure?'

The Queen had a good sense of humour, all too often contained (certainly in public). It is said that if someone's mobile telephone went off when she was talking to them, she would say: 'You'd better answer that. It might be someone important.' Dick Griffin spent thirty years at Buckingham Palace, fourteen of them as the Queen's personal protection officer. Outside St Paul's Cathedral on the day of the Platinum Jubilee service in 2022, he related how he was walking with the Queen in the hills, near Craigowan Lodge, in Scotland when two American hikers approached. They did not recognise her, but asked: 'And where do you live?' She replied that she lived in London, but had a holiday home just across the hills. She said she had been coming here for eighty years. One of them then asked: 'But if you've been coming up for eighty years, you must have met the Queen?' Quick as a flash, she replied that she hadn't, but 'Dick meets her regularly.' The hiker turned to Griffin and asked what she was like. Knowing he could get away with it, he said she could be cantankerous at times, but had a lovely sense of humour. The American then gave his camera to the Queen and asked him to photograph them together. Griffin then took one of them with the Queen. After they moved on, she said: 'I'd love to be a fly on the wall when he shows the photos to friends in America and hopefully someone tells him who I am!'[1]

In the days before the kidnap attempt on Princess Anne in 1973 and yet more seriously the assassination of Lord Mountbatten in 1979, after which royal security was greatly tightened, the Queen could move about much more freely. She and Prince Philip would drive to dinner with friends near Windsor, such as the Maharajah of Jaipur, or General Sir Rodney Moore. Once the Queen was driving in Norfolk, without a detective, and her car broke down. She was near Anmer Hall, then occupied by Bill Fox. She rang the doorbell. The scene turned into the card game – *Woodland Happy Families*. The door was answered by Bill's sister, Miss Fox. The Queen asked (as in the game): 'Is Mr Fox at home?' She needed to be picked up. The plan was to call Sandringham, though she didn't know the number since she had never had to dial it. She was rescued.

Prince Philip provided robust and provocative support throughout their long marriage. He loved an argument, because by arguing you could reach an agreement. He could be abrupt. He was impatient, realising that even if you live for a hundred years there is so little time to get it done. To talk to him in his office was to have an easy and free-ranging conversation. Out on engagements he was sharper, but he wanted to get the story. If he was asked to look at a picture someone had painted, he could say: 'What a nice picture', but more likely he would ask: 'Why the hell did you paint the sky green when we patently know it's blue.' If you shrugged, he would walk away. But if you said: 'Well, the sun hits the wall at 6 p.m. and the sky then appears green,' he had engaged with you and learned something of your technique. As such he was a great back-up act.

His cousin, Crown Prince Pavlos of Greece, made the point that if he said to you: 'What the devil are you doing here?' that was his way of saying: 'How extremely nice to see you.' He had a technique in a line-up when people were trooping by. He shook the hand and then almost propelled it to the right. If he asked a question, the person would be some way away by the time they attempted to answer it.

There was a subtle difference between the Queen and her more thespian mother. If you made the Queen Mother laugh, you would be wrong to assume you had necessarily amused her. If you could make the Queen laugh, you could be sure you had, because otherwise she wouldn't. That I preferred. You knew where you were with her. And more importantly, because her role in public life came to her by hereditary descent, she had not climbed the greasy

INTRODUCTION

pole of politics. We could be absolutely sure she was totally on the side of Great Britain. The same cannot always be said of others in public life.

I never wanted this to be a 'Queen and I' book, but I should perhaps explain how I came to be involved. I was lucky to have first met the Queen in 1968, when she came to look at the King George VI Memorial Chapel being built in a corner of the North Quire Aisle of St George's Chapel. When I think back to that day, she is fixed in my mind as a young mother of forty-two, with auburn hair and a blue coat, her young son, Prince Edward, held by the hand. I have always been an observer, and I monitored her from a very early age – from 1963 onwards. I must have met her forty times over a period of fifty-five years. Sometimes these were just formal meetings, but at other times there was a chance to talk.

Undoubtedly the most memorable was the privilege of sitting next to her at dinner with the Carnarvons at Milford Lake House in April 1999. I was writing the authorised life of Princess Alice, mother of Prince Philip, at the time, and found myself explaining the exact nature of her illness to the Queen, in addition to the travails of Queen Louise of Sweden's early love life, when she had fallen in love with a homosexual artist. The Queen liked facts and information. She listened intently to this, and we then had an interesting discussion about Prince Philip's relationship with his father. The Queen said: 'Philip never talks about his father', and I replied: 'Well, he would hardly have known him,' and explained that he hardly ever saw him. He was lucky to get a three-day holiday with him once a year and that did not always happen.

I had recently had talks with Princess Anne and Prince Charles about Princess Alice (their paternal grandmother). The conversation with Princess Anne had been brilliant. I had a less easy time with Prince Charles. The Queen said: 'I know why that was. He was frightened of her. All that family have an extraordinary ability to compartmentalise their brains, while Charles has never compartmentalised his brain in his life.'

At that dinner I had the chance to see how extensive the Queen's preoccupations were. She had to think of so many things the rest of us did not have to concern ourselves with. The conversation ranged over Tonga and the King there fighting a rearguard action against the traffic light. 'Well, there isn't much need,' said the Queen. Kosovo was on the agenda too, the Queen saying she thought Milošević worse than Hitler, 'because he was a little man'. She was surprised that Yeltsin was still hanging on in Russia, thought the best television coverage was CNN (lately installed at Sandringham), and did not like Sky. 'Murdoch,' she said, with an expression I thought spoke volumes. The conversation veered to retired generals such as Michael Rose and Peter de la Billière, who went on television to say how they would handle the (second) Iraq war. The Queen said: 'I don't think the Prime Minister finds it very helpful' and 'We may finally be able to have a use for the Parachute Regiment.'

She spoke of the new Royal Family website: 'We cottoned on to it rather late in the day.' Prince Andrew's journal was proving popular.* Later the Queen looked at photos I had taken of the presentation of Lord Lewin's Garter banner in St George's Chapel. She said she didn't know any of the Military Knights, only Tommy Thompson, who used to help Prince Philip in his early carriage driving days: 'It's a bad time when you don't know any of the Military Knights,' she said.[2]

Prince Philip's sister Sophie and her husband, Prince George of Hanover, invariably came over for the Windsor Horse Show and then gravitated to Buckingham Palace for a few days. If free, the Queen would lunch with them. As Princess George said: 'If she is with other people she makes conversation, but if she is alone she *really* talks.'[3] The interesting thing about talking to The Queen was that, when you were with her, it was as if you saw her often. But these meetings were rare. When I wasn't there, in a sense I did not exist.

She was generous in making you feel special. When, in 1995, I introduced my fiancée to her, who happened to be my second cousin, I said I would be a modern man and allow her to keep her maiden name, also Vickers. 'I know that. I read that in the paper,'

---

* I did not have an internet connection at that time, but the next day I accessed the royal website. There was a section called 'Visitor's Book'. When I hit on it, it said you could leave your name and a message. Then it asked: 'Who told you about the website?' I thought: 'No, I can't!'

said the Queen. When the Foreign Minister in Malta tried to present me on the quayside in Valletta in 2015, she said: 'He turns up all over the place.' Then, when I was writing an un-authorised biography of the Queen Mother, Sir Michael Oswald agreed to help me about the racing side. I went to stay with the Oswalds in 2005. Sir Michael said he had told the Queen I was coming and she had said: 'Help him in whatever way you can.'

I will never forget waiting to meet her in Windsor Castle in 2017, when she agreed to be photographed with the Lay Stewards. I was designated to meet the Queen in the long corridor. Her arrival was not quite like Omar Sharif in the film of *Lawrence of Arabia*, but she was a long way away before I could talk to her. It was a very hot day. The first thing she said to the Superintendent was to tell him to get a sentry under cover. She had seen him in the sun, outside the George IV Gate on her way back from church. Later she told the Lay Stewards that several guardsmen had fallen at the Birthday Parade the day before, and three choristers had had to go out during the church service that morning. After the photograph we had a short talk. She was aware that some of the stewards came a long way to do their duty. I said that Alastair Bruce had come from the Falklands. Unlike me, the Queen had never been to the Falklands, but she immediately said: 'I feel so sorry for him, returning to Tumbledown.' How was a remote battlefield in the Falklands like Tumbledown so accessible in her mind? She had lately been to Grenfell Tower, she said: 'They're sending me all over the place at the moment.'

Many say that they cannot bear to think that the Queen's reign is over. I am one of them. The Queen's Gallery has become the King's Gallery. CIIIRs replace EIIRs wherever they can be changed, but I am happy when I pass an EIIR post box or spot EIIR on Rachel Reeves' budget despatch box. This book will succeed if I can bring the Queen back to life for those who read it. I for one – I for many – miss her, and have to remind myself that we were lucky that she reigned over us for so long.

Hugo Vickers
Dominica – December 2025
(and she is still on the bank notes here)

1
THE ROYAL HOUSE OF WINDSOR

Children brought up on the *Babar* books by Jean de Brunhoff will remember that while Babar the King Elephant was waiting for his child to be born, he took an anxious walk. In his case he heard not one *boom* from the Palace, but three and discovered that Queen Celeste had given birth to triplets. He was the father of three. That is how the news was given in days of old.

On the morning of Wednesday, 21 April 1926, one hundred years ago, George Gage, rejected suitor of the Duchess of York, came bounding into the room of the inveterate (and sleepy) diarist 'Chips' Channon, to tell him that the guns were booming. 'Do you know what that is?' he said sadly. 'It has arrived.' They rang Buckingham Palace to learn that a princess had been born at 2.40 a.m. at 17 Bruton Street, the London home of the Earl and Countess of Strathmore, the Duchess's parents. Channon noted: 'I have a feeling the child will be Queen of England and perhaps the last sovereign. The baby becomes first lady* in the land and third heir to the Crown.'[1] There was no reason to suppose that she would be called to a greater destiny, but as the Prince of Wales was showing no inclination to find a wife, the distant prospect became one of hope as the York family showed themselves sound and stable, and the child born in every way admirable.

The House of Windsor had been anxious that the Duchess of York should conceive. None of King George V's other sons were married so the immediate succession was: the Prince of Wales, the Duke of York, Prince Henry, Prince George, Princess Mary, then her two sons, George (born in 1923) and Gerald Lascelles (in 1924).

---

* The Princess was surely fourth lady in the land after Queen Mary, the Duchess of York and Princess Mary.

After them came King George V's sisters and their children, with no fear of them succeeding.

The Yorks had remained childless since 1923. They were sent on safari to Kenya, Uganda and the Sudan, from December 1924 until April 1925. 'Is there anything else one can do to make her have a baby?' asked Colin Buist, their equerry. To which the lady-in-waiting, Lady Annaly, longed to reply: 'Well, if you don't know what it is, I'm not going to tell you.'[2] But no baby came.

When the Duchess conceived at the end of 1925, after consultations with Sir Henry Simson,[*] the British court was considerably relieved. But there was almost a disaster. On 27 January she was being driven back to her temporary London home, Curzon House,[†] from Hampstead when a car cut in beside hers, causing it to crash into a stationary autobus. The Duchess was thrown to the floor.[3] News of this was hastily played down in an authoritative statement issued to the Press Association to the effect that a bus had skidded, caught the wing of the Duchess's car 'and crumpled it rather badly'. There had been 'no serious damage, and Her Royal Highness did not suffer in any way'.[4] Lord Gage heard that there had been fear of a miscarriage. Had that happened, there would have been no Princess Elizabeth.

The labour and the birth were difficult. 'A certain line of treatment'[5] was carried out – euphemism for Caesarean section. The Duke of York might have preferred a son, but he told his mother: 'I know Elizabeth wanted a daughter.'[6]

Therefore, there were many reasons for rejoicing, not to say relief, that the House of Windsor now had an heir in the next generation.

---

* Sir Henry Simson, KCVO (1872–1932), an eminent obstetrician, who had attended the Princess Royal and the Duchess of York at the birth of their children. He was surgeon to the Hospital for Women in Soho Square, and obstetric surgeon to the West London Hospital. He worked with Dr S. J. Aarons, to whom desperate wives turned when pregnancy eluded them. Simson died suddenly when about to perform an operation on a female patient.

† The family had moved from White Lodge to Curzon House, and were to move again, but that plan went wrong, so around 7 April 1926 they went to live at 17 Bruton Street, which belonged to the Duchess's parents, the Earl and Countess of Strathmore. The house was demolished in July 1937.

King George V and Queen Mary were woken at 4 a.m. to be told the news. They saw the child later that day, Queen Mary pronouncing her 'a little darling with a lovely complexion & pretty fair hair'.[7] Queen Mary was delighted that the baby was 'blessed with large blue eyes, tiny ears set close to a well-shaped head, and a skin almost as white as the pillow on which she lay'.[8] To the wider public her birth was greeted with the fervour and enthusiasm traditionally bestowed on the first granddaughter of the monarch. As Queen Mary's lady-in-waiting, Mabell, Countess of Airlie, put it, her birth represented 'something of continuity and of hope for the future'.[9]

Prince Albert, Duke of York, was the second son of George V, born in 1895. He did not have an easy early life. He was often ill, suffered from knock knees for which he was forced to wear splints. Naturally left-handed, he was forced to write with his right hand. The victim of a serious stammer in early life, he had joined the Royal Navy and served in the Battle of Jutland in 1916. After the war he spent a year at Trinity College, Cambridge.

Initially close to his elder brother, the Prince of Wales, he never moved comfortably in that zippy nightclub world. He had a romance with Sheila, Lady Loughborough.* When he terminated this, his father rewarded him by creating him Duke of York. With this new status, he metaphorically straightened his tie and the very same day happened to meet Lady Elizabeth Bowes-Lyon at a ball given at his house in Grosvenor Square by the seemingly rich peer Lord Farquhar (exposed after death as a bankrupt). It is greatly to the new Duke's credit that he pursued Lady Elizabeth from June 1920 to January 1923, when many times his quest seemed hopeless. She turned down two proposals, but accepted the third in a state of some panic. Marrying her was the best decision of his life. Their wedding took place in Westminster Abbey on 26 April 1923.

Lady Elizabeth Bowes-Lyon was one of the stars of her generation. Born in 1900, she was brought up in a family of ten children, the

---

* Sheila Chisholm (1895–1969), a beautiful Australian, who later married Sir John Milbanke, and Prince Dimitri of Russia. In later life George VI liked to reminisce about the good times they had. had. Aware that Queen Elizabeth had a beady eye on her, she said: 'And when you think, Sir, how innocent it was ...' To which he replied: 'Innocent. I don't know what the devil you mean!'

youngest daughter and close to her brother David, a year or so younger than her. She was well raised by her mother, the Countess of Strathmore, with a strong sense of duty instilled in her, and grew up quickly in the company of older brothers and sisters. She honed the skills she would later put to such good advantage by cheering up the wounded soldiers who recuperated at Glamis Castle in Scotland, the First World War having begun on her fourteenth birthday in 1914. She bought them cigarettes and helped them write letters to their loved ones.

She emerged from the war as the debutante of her year, dancing well, riding to hounds, with a winning smile and sparkling blue eyes, which she used to good purpose. Many hearts were broken. She was reluctant to marry the Duke of York, but her mother saw the possibilities. Given that she might be steered to a royal marriage, it would be more than understandable that she might prefer the Prince of Wales, a man altogether more charismatic than his nervous, stammering younger brother. At the time of Prince Bertie's first interest in her, she was in love with James Stuart, though he let her down by indulging in something more than a flirtation with Mollie Lascelles, a highly promiscuous girl who presently married the Duke of Buccleuch, and later became known as 'Midnight Moll' due to her numerous affairs.

Three things happened when Queen Mary descended on Glamis Castle in the summer of 1921. Young James Stuart was offered an enticing job in the oil fields of Oklahoma and removed from the equation. Despite in no way being a friend of hers, Lady Elizabeth was selected as a bridesmaid to Princess Mary at her wedding to Viscount Lascelles in February 1922. And it became clear that Lady Elizabeth needed to take the Duke of York more seriously.

On 27 October 1922 Lady Elizabeth attended a ball at Wilton House, Salisbury, for the coming-out of Lady Patricia Herbert. She sat out with the Prince of Wales and one who saw them together detected proximity so that you could suppose romance was in the air.[10] As it happens, it was not. The Prince returned to his hunting and Lady Elizabeth to London. But the press got wind of the idea and she was greatly upset by a piece in the newspaper suggesting the Prince of Wales was about to marry a Scottish aristocrat.

She panicked and when the Duke of York proposed for a third

time, she accepted him. The engagement was announced without further delay, for fear she might change her mind. She was whisked to Sandringham to stay at York Cottage with George V and Queen Mary, and presented to the elderly Queen Alexandra in the Big House. The bride-to-be told her brother: 'I could hear the door clanging behind me – never to open again.'[11]

Being the dedicated person she was, she threw herself into being a good wife to the Duke of York, giving him confidence, producing Lionel Logue to help with his stammer and creating for him a happy home, which, arguably, he had not enjoyed before.

It was into this happy home that Princess Elizabeth arrived. There is every indication that she enjoyed a blissful childhood, at least until the beginning of 1936, so for nearly a decade she acquired sound grounding for her later responsibilities. From Anne Ring,* we learn that the Princess was surrounded by a host of devoted grandparents, uncles and friends, that she started life as 'the World's best known baby',[12] albeit oblivious to this fact.

The Royal Family was presided over by King George V. He was the latest in a long line of British monarchs who traced their history back a thousand years or more. Queen Mary, the Queen's grandmother, descended from the Cambridge line, her enormously fat mother, Princess Mary Adelaide, being a daughter of the 1st Duke and therefore a granddaughter of George III. When considering her marriage prospects, Lord Clarendon pronounced: 'No German prince will venture *on such a vast undertaking.*'[13] But the impoverished Duke of Teck, a morganatic Württemberg, did and produced four children, including Queen Mary and Alexander, Earl of Athlone. Queen Mary therefore came from what was called the old Royal Family.

Queen Victoria had been one of Britain's greatest Queens,

---

* In 1930 Anne Ring (real name Beryl Poingand, 1887–1965) wrote perhaps the first life story of Princess Elizabeth and her sister. She succeeded in filling 126 pages. The book was reprinted twice and there was a second edition in 1932, again reprinted. Anne Ring had been governess and confidante to Lady Elizabeth Bowes-Lyon, and was later attached to the Duchess of York's household. She wrote her book with the sanction of the child's parents. Queen Elizabeth invited her as a special guest to the Coronation in 1937.

marrying the energetic, inspired if somewhat misunderstood Prince Albert of Saxe-Coburg. Together they laid the foundation for a charitable monarchy. By the time Princess Elizabeth was born, Edward VII, the King who followed Queen Victoria, had been dead for sixteen years. His beautiful Danish Queen, Alexandra, had died at Sandringham but five months before her birth, in November 1925. Frail, deaf and with make-up so strong that she was described as 'enamelled', Queen Alexandra was the last adornment to the Edwardian age. Her epithalamium* had been written by Lord Tennyson.

King George V, Edward VII's son, converted the House of Saxe-Coburg into the House of Windsor in 1917, subtly removing the unpopular German titles and anglicising the Tecks, Battenbergs and Schleswig-Holsteins. He steered Britain through the First World War, keeping his throne while many of his European counterparts lost theirs. Generally thought of as a gruff and unimaginative man, he was a great deal softer with his grandchildren than he had been with his own children. He was to be particularly fond of Princess Elizabeth. He told Lady Algernon Gordon-Lennox: 'I pray to God that my eldest son will never marry and have children, and that nothing will come between Bertie and Lilibet and the throne.'[14]

Queen Mary deferred to her husband during his lifetime. Queen Elizabeth II used to say that her grandmother only really blossomed after he died. The King was solid and unimaginative. She was culturally aware. Eric Maclagan, Director of the Victoria and Albert Museum, used to say that 'Any gallery in Europe would be glad to give her a job as their buyer.'[15] She did sterling work with the royal collections, hanging pictures well, uniting furniture from the different royal residences, and under a rather stern exterior there beat a kind heart. While Queen Alexandra had epitomised Edwardian elegance, Queen Mary was stately and formidable. She wore long dresses; she had perfectly good hair, but wore a silver wig by day and a gold wig by night. She sported stylish toques. When it became clear to her that Princess Elizabeth was to be Britain's Queen, her grandmotherly interest in her became more pronounced.

There were other key members of the Royal Family. Uncle David –

---

* A poem composed for a marriage.

Edward, Prince of Wales – was already feeling the strain of royal life. Popular, charismatic, charming and modern, he had survived his grim childhood to serve as well as allowed (in fact better than allowed) in the First World War. No one ever knows what to do with the heir to the throne while he waits in the wings, so this one they sent travelling. From 1919 until the early 1930s he was in almost perpetual orbit round the world, proving a tremendous hit in the United States, Canada, India, Australia and New Zealand.

While the Empire loved him, he was frequently berated by his father, and suffered from depression, ruminating on his plight. In the letters to his long-term mistress Freda Dudley Ward, there is evidence of his wish to escape the ultimate fate of being King. In 1931 he met Mrs Simpson who fascinated him to the point that he could not exist without her. Did he subconsciously see in her a means of escape? Though he would never have admitted it, he must have realised that she could never be accepted as Queen. By pressing the issue, he sealed his fate.

Genuinely fond of him – as what niece would not have been – in time the Queen would later refer to him as 'my silly uncle'. When he was King all too briefly and she knocked on his door, he would reply in light jest through pipe-clenched teeth: 'Don't forget your bloody curtsey.'

The other uncles were Prince Henry, later Duke of Gloucester, an essentially military man, who has been passed down into history rather unkindly as a stolid, unimaginative figure and yet, as was well demonstrated by James Pope-Hennessy, he made a fascinating study in his own right.* He was to be a prominent figure in the early years of the Queen's reign until his health broke down. In 1935 he married the shy but wry Lady Alice Montagu-Douglas-Scott, daughter of the Duke of Buccleuch. His ambition to command his regiment was killed by the Abdication. The Gloucesters then devoted themselves to royal duties, far from what either of them wished, but serve they did. They had two sons, Prince William (born in 1941 but killed when he turned his plane too sharply in a flying race in 1972) and Prince Richard, the present Duke of Gloucester (born in 1944).

---

* See *The Quest for Queen Mary*, pp. 168–202.

The next uncle, Prince George, Duke of Kent, was to be killed in a flying accident in 1942, when the Queen was sixteen. A man of good looks and mercurial charm, his death was a considerable blow to the family. His young widow, Princess Marina, was another key figure in the Queen's life. Being exceptionally popular and glamorous, she was to be sent round the world on significant royal tours overseas. Living at Coppins in Iver, and raising her young family on her own, she was also close to her cousin Prince Philip, who stayed there often before his marriage, a union she encouraged. Princess Marina was the mother of Prince Edward, Duke of Kent (born in 1935), Princess Alexandra (born in 1936) and Prince Michael (born in 1942).

The Queen was deeply fond of her aunt, Princess Mary, the Princess Royal. When Queen Mary died, the Duke of Wellington said that there were now no members of the Royal Family interested in the arts. He overlooked the Princess Royal, who was interested though made no impact. Cynthia Gladwyn described her as 'extremely shy', having had 'a wretched youth: strictly brought up, bullied, and without even the chance of the occasional emancipation enjoyed by her brothers when they could escape from their parents' vigilant eyes'.[16] In 1922 she married Viscount Lascelles, later Earl of Harewood. He was much older than her, rich, and had wonderful possessions. Some said he was horrible to her, others that she was happy with him. Princess Mary was widowed in 1947, and spent much time in Yorkshire. Some thought her dull. She was the mother of George, Viscount Lascelles (later 7th Earl of Harewood) and of Gerald Lascelles.

The royal side was balanced by the Scottish side, thanks to a significant decision taken by King George V. Previously royal brides were invariably found in German royal families. In 1917 the King's Private Secretary, Lord Stamfordham, informed A. J. Balfour 'that some time ago he and the Queen had decided that the Prince of Wales and his other children should be allowed to marry into British Families'.[17] Princess Elizabeth's maternal grandfather, the Earl of Strathmore, was a Scottish peer of inflexible habit, who moved between his various estates according to which birds were in season to be shot. He had flowing moustaches, which he separated before kissing his offspring. He was a knowledgeable forester. As he grew older, he became extremely deaf, which made him hard work as a neighbour in the dining room. He liked to bowl Christmas puddings down the table towards his wife. He was generally considered to be delightful.

His wife, Cecilia, was the stronger of the two. She loved the piano, was an expert needlewoman and created a Dutch garden at their Scottish home, Glamis Castle. Under a veneer of gentle domesticity, there beat a heart of steel. A friend wrote of her: 'She seemed to sail through life like a swan on a mirrored lake ... She was the directing force of the family.'[18] That she needed to be, since of her ten children, the lives of her sons were shattered in the First World War, in which they served, several of them wounded, and some falling victim to alcohol.

David, the very youngest son, was to be quite a fixture in the life of his sister Elizabeth, and of Princess Elizabeth, albeit not always a good influence. Of the three daughters, two others survived – Mary, Lady Elphinstone and Rose, Countess Granville. But it was Elizabeth who was strengthened by the experiences of the First World War – something of a star as she emerged into adult life. By the time her daughter was born, she was quietly established as the Duke of York's wife.

2
CHILDHOOD, 1926–30

Reams have been written about the childhood of Princess Elizabeth, much of it saccharine and unreliable. There emerges a picture of a childhood that was supremely content until a series of events intervened to turn a happy-go-lucky, unassuming child into one facing destiny with reserve, an element of gravitas if not indeed of some gravity.

The values instilled in her served her well. The Duchess of York was determined that her daughter's upbringing should be as normal as possible, which in those days was by no means as normal as it would be a century later. When preparing his memoirs in the late 1940s, the Duke of Windsor observed a little spikily:

> Bertie lived with his wife and two children in London. They spent their vacations with my parents who doted on the two little girls ... Bertie got bored with the court etiquette after a while but he enjoyed the shooting and spent much longer under the family roof because his wife being a commoner loved to bask in the glow of [being] a regal favourite ... At least he had his family to keep him company for these long sojourns at home – away from his 'princing'.[1]

The Duke of York asked his father's permission to call the child Elizabeth Alexandra Mary, and he 'quite' approved, mentioning in passing to Queen Mary that there was no 'Victoria' in the names, adding: 'I hardly think this necessary.'[2] The daughter of one of the other doctors present, Dr Walter Jagger, hoped to see the infant Princess so the Duchess of York sent the baby round to her house, one of her first social engagements.[3] She was known in the family as Lilibet.

The Princess was christened in the royal chapel at Buckingham Palace on 29 May, the private ceremony being performed at 3 p.m. by the Archbishop of York. The Lily Font was brought from Windsor

Castle and Jordan water was provided by Field Marshal Lord Plumer. The Palace florist, Mr Goodyear, was asked to be modest with flowers, so simply placed a coronet of white lilies, with a tinge of pink and some heather for luck, on the altar. The Princess wore the same christening robe as Edward VII, her grandfather, her uncle and her father. It was noted that there were three other well-known Elizabeths in British history – Elizabeth I (1533–1603), Elizabeth Stuart, Queen of Bohemia (1596–1662, daughter of James I) and Elizabeth, Landgravine of Hesse-Homburg (1770–1840), seventh child of George III.[4]

As princesses could fundamentally do no wrong in those days, the romantically inclined journalists reported that she cried lustily throughout the proceedings, thus expelling 'Old Adam', while her mother's 'attempts to soothe the child were not entirely successful'.[5]

Hardly had she been born than her name was being put to use, raising money for charity and hospitals. In November 1926 a 'university woman' called Miss Adamson gave £1,000 for a room to be named after Princess Elizabeth at Crosby Hall, on Cheyne Walk in London, then to be used as a residential hall for university women. In July 1927 Helen Hardinge, a childhood friend of the Duchess of York, obtained the Duchess's permission to name a new hostel 'The Princess Elizabeth of York Hostel' for the Mothercraft Training Society in the hope of raising the requisite £25,000 to build it in the grounds of Cromwell House in Highgate. A doll was made resembling her and carried by the Duchess at a ball, with the comic actor Leslie Henson as celebrity guest. The ball raised £2,700. A new infirmary was opened by the Duchess at Stirling in 1928 with another cot dedicated in Princess Elizabeth's name. The East London Hospital in Glamis Road, Shadwell, was renamed the Princess Elizabeth of York Hospital for Children in 1932. *The Princess Elizabeth Gift Book*, edited by Lady Cynthia Asquith, assisted by Eileen Bigland, raised funds to build a new hospital in Banstead, Surrey, in 1935. A site was bought, but the hospital was never built there, due to the Second World War.* Princess Elizabeth was being useful from birth onwards, without having to do a thing.

---

* It remained in Shadwell, merged with the Queen Elizabeth Hospital in Hackney, and a branch was opened in Banstead in 1946. The Shadwell hospital closed in 1960, and the chain was dissolved in 1975.

Dolls

Hospitals were one thing. Dolls soon became an occupational hazard for the Duchess of York. Many of her engagements involved touring charity fairs, where she made small purchases – on one occasion a baby toothbrush, on another a frame with feathers, a bib and some reins. And everywhere she went she was presented with a doll or a teddy bear for the Princess, who soon amassed an inordinately large collection. In desperation, when yet another teddy bear was presented at the naming of a cot at the Crippled Children's Hospital in Exeter in December 1927, the Duchess of York said: 'Elizabeth has plenty of toys. Teddy will be reserved for future occupants of this cot.'[6]

The Yorks brought home some three tons of toys, ornaments, knick-knacks and gewgaws from their 1927 visit to the Antipodes, most of which were given away to less fortunate children or auctioned for charity. There were dolls, a doll's tea set (from the children of the outback in Australia), a cot, a battalion of giant teddy bears, two singing canaries and twenty squawking macaws. In August 1928 Princess Elizabeth paraded some of these in her doll's pram at Glamis.[7]

* * * * *

Princess Elizabeth's early life was divided between the homes of her parents, her Strathmore grandparents and those of the King and Queen. She began life in a large nursery in Bruton Street, overlooking Grafton Street in Mayfair. An early visitor declared that she was 'a most darling baby, with fine limbs, and I should think perhaps she will be tall [she wasn't], she has big blue eyes and tiny ears set close to her head, and the whitest skin in the world'.[8] She had fair, curly hair.

From her earliest days, she was looked after by Mrs Clara Cooper Knight, known as 'Alah'. She was the daughter of a yeoman farmer on the St Paul's Walden Bury estate of the Duchess of York's father, was first an under-nursery maid, and then looked after the young Lady Elizabeth Bowes-Lyon. Alah went on to look after both Princess Elizabeth and Princess Margaret, with particular attention to orderliness and tidiness. A beloved servant, she stayed on with the Royal

Family until her sudden death at Sandringham just after Christmas 1945.*

Princess Elizabeth was taken to St Paul's Walden Bury, Hertfordshire, in June 1926 and paid her first visit to Glamis Castle when she was three months old, residing in the old castle nursery. She would be carried into the morning room or Oak Room after breakfast, and doze in the Dutch Garden in the afternoon. Glamis was a romantic castle for a child, a great medieval house, set on high ground, cleverly modernised inside, the family living in the oldest part, where the internal stone walls were now plastered and partly panelled. There was much needlework by Lady Strathmore, Oriental bowls filled with pot-pourri, and oranges tightly stuffed with cloves.[9] The Princess was often left there when her parents visited their friends.

During the Yorks' six-month tour of New Zealand and Australia, the Princess was moved between grandparents. Christmas 1926 had been spent at Sandringham, by which time she was sitting up. In January 1927 she moved into Buckingham Palace with the King and Queen, and they took her to Windsor Castle in April.

In May 1927, she was at St Paul's Walden Bury, moving around, sitting 'almost upright on one leg', sculling 'vigorously with the other'.[10] In the afternoon, she played with Lady Strathmore's two Chinese dogs, Brownie and Blackie, developing at this point a lifelong love of animals. When her parents returned to London on 27 June, Queen Mary had her brought from 145 Piccadilly as a surprise. The Royal Family appeared on the balcony, the Duchess guiding the little Princess's fingers in the first of many a royal wave from that august vantage point.†

After that trip the family made their home at 145 Piccadilly, a four-storey mansion, one of seven houses between the Duke of Wellington's Apsley House and Hamilton Place. 145 Piccadilly was a Crown property, much rented out, and in the early 1920s it had been used as Poppy Day headquarters. Queen Mary oversaw the preparation of the house for the Yorks. It had a dining room on the ground floor that could seat thirty guests, a study for the Duke,

---

* When she died at Sandringham on 2 January 1946, Princess Elizabeth described her to Lady Desborough as 'a wonderful person in every way'. (Letter from Sandringham, 6 January 1946 – Hertfordshire County Archives).

† The last would be ninety-six years later at the Platinum Jubilee.

a library and fifteen bedrooms. On the first floor was the Duchess of York's room and the nursery suite was on the top floor. A large dome gave sunlight to a circular landing and sweeping staircase. At the back of the house there was a small garden.

Well-off neighbours included Viscount Allendale, later to be one of the Garter Knights to carry the anointing canopy at the 1953 Coronation. The Allendales had children of the same age as the York princesses. Ela Beaumont,* their daughter, was Princess Elizabeth's particular playmate. 145 Piccadilly was the Yorks' London home until February 1937.

Some time after Princess Margaret was born in 1930, Princess Elizabeth was assigned her own bedroom on the top floor, which overlooked the garden and more distantly Hyde Park and Hamilton Gardens, with an 1880 bronze statue of Lord Byron. On the circular landing, when they were able, the princesses could play horses or trains and they could observe the grown-ups downstairs. Later the house was used for an exhibition of historical items, in aid of the Heritage Craft School for Crippled Children at Chailey, Sussex, staged there in July 1939, just before the war. The King and Queen were shown round it by Nesta Obermeyer and her girlfriend, Gluck, the painter. In September 1940 a bomb fell nearby in Park Lane. The house itself was bombed in December that year, and much of its front façade collapsed in July 1941. It was finally pulled down in October 1959. All seven houses in what used to be Piccadilly Terrace were demolished in the redevelopment of Hyde Park Corner, making way for the seven-lane road into Park Lane and for the Intercontinental Hotel.

Another home was Naseby Hall† in Northamptonshire, situated between Rugby and Kettering, rented by the Duke of York for three

---

* The Hon. Ela Beaumont (1925–2002), later Countess of Carlisle.

† Naseby was famed in history for the Civil War battle in 1645, in which Charles I's royalist army was decisively defeated. The hall's later history was chequered. It was bought by Captain (later Colonel) Sir Roland Findlay, Bt (1903–79). The hall was badly damaged by fire in 1948, the Findlays escaping from the first floor by a rope of sheets. It was rebuilt from the ground using old materials. Findlay was the father of Jane, Countess of Westmorland (1928–2009), whose husband served as Queen Elizabeth II's Master of the Horse from 1978 to 1991.

hunting seasons between 1928 and 1930. The hall had been built in 1818 for the Fitzgerald family, in a high woodland setting over a lake, with an Adam-style dining room and a ballroom in the Louis XVI style. There was stabling for nineteen horses, and a covered squash racquets court with a gallery. Until 1937 it belonged to Major Leslie Renton, former Liberal MP for Gainsborough, who tended to winter abroad. The Duke would hunt with the Pytchley. It was here that Princess Elizabeth developed her interest in horses, visiting the stables every morning and feeding the hunters sugar lumps.

George V

It was while staying with the King and Queen that Princess Elizabeth forged a strong and lasting bond with her grandfather, King George V. When he wrote of her, she was 'our sweet little grandchild' or 'dear little Elizabeth'.[11] The relationship was further strengthened by summer visits to Balmoral, the first in 1927, when she was exhibited to guests at the King's garden party, wheeled in her perambulator, and again at a fair where the Royal Family were selling in person in aid of Crathie Hall. There were Christmas visits to Sandringham, the Princess travelling there in a compartment of the royal train, converted into a fairy saloon, with cushions illustrating fairy stories, holly and silver foil, a huge cracker on the ceiling, all done by Harrods.

She spent every Easter and birthday until 1935 at Windsor Castle, with the King and Queen, the Court Circular recording her first official arrival there on 4 April 1928, just before her second birthday. She would stay for a month while her parents visited friends on the Continent.

Here, as elsewhere, her childhood companions were her cousins, George, Viscount Lascelles, and his brother Gerald. They were often at Windsor Castle and they shared birthday parties. George* was to grow up as a considerable expert on opera, but as children, he and

---

* George was in Windsor Castle on 2 April 1928, aged five. He held his grandmother's hand to witness the arrival for lunch of King Amanullah of Afghanistan, his wife and their entourage, the first time he had ever seen a man of colour.

his brother somewhat bullied her (and later Princess Margaret) largely because they were girls.* This was not forgotten.

In his memoirs, George volunteered that when at Windsor the children had to be downstairs punctually at 9 a.m. for breakfast. They had already eaten but their grandfather liked to see them playing quietly. The King's parrot Charlotte was a dominant presence in the breakfast room. George rather feared 'those pinching claws and that awesome beak', not helped by the King warning him that the parrot could smell fear. One of the things George dreaded was having to kiss his grandfather: 'The ritual good morning and good night peck had to be offered to a beard of astonishing abrasiveness.'[12] His abiding memory of his visits was the formality, combined with the fear of being late or doing something wrong, as inevitably happened.

With the Lascelles boys, Princess Elizabeth stayed in the Victoria Tower, in a nursery that had been used by Queen Victoria's children in the 1800s, and they drove out in the park together in carriages. She went out to see the changing of the Guard, and learned to salute. She liked to keep in time with the conductor of the band. In 2022 when the present author mentioned to the Queen that no one ever seemed to have written about these castle stays, she recalled Easter visits and said: 'There's a picture of me saluting.'[13] There is moving footage of her doing just that in the Quadrangle. And saluting clearly appealed to her. She saluted at every opportunity, be it the Royal Tournament or the rehearsal for the Aldershot Tattoo, both of which became regular annual outings.

On her first birthday, the King had given her a rocking horse, and when she was old enough a Shetland pony. She was exhibited to French First World War heroines, tried to say 'Mummie' with the help of George and was taken down to witness the arrival of Captain Lindbergh† in 1927. When the King opened the East Terrace Gardens to the public around five thousand people came to hear

---

* She was also somewhat bullied by a maternal cousin, James Leveson-Gower (later Earl Granville), born in 1918. In later life he lived at North Uist on the island of Mull and used to hide when *Britannia*, with the Queen on board, loomed into view on the Western Isles cruise.

† Captain Charles Lindbergh (1902–74), had just made the first successful non-stop flight from New York to Paris – 20–21 May.

the bands of the Life Guards and the Coldstreams playing. The infant princess 'waved her hand to the thousands of people who looked down at her'.¹⁴ She was animated during a concert at the castle with the Royal Welsh Ladies' Choir conducted by Madame Clara Novello Davies,* who had performed before Queen Victoria years before. She toddled across and presented herself to Madame Davies and Dr Leigh Henry, the musical adviser. But she forgot to shake hands with Robert Judge, the manager. When the King remonstrated with her, she at once rectified the oversight.

As she grew older, she and the Lascelles boys would sit on three golden chairs listening to the band, the Princess imitating the conductors and cornet players. When her uncle, Prince George, showed her how the blind on the window worked, she had fun bringing it up and down until her mother intervened. She would tear along the castle corridors, sweeping the King's food off his plate to give it to her dog, with 'Grandpapa England' scrambling on the floor with her looking for her hair-slide. In 1931 J. H. Thomas, Secretary of State for the Dominions, who had a good relationship with the King, was impressed when Queen Mary interrupted state business at 6 p.m. to say: 'Would you mind? We want the Princess to wish Grandpa good night.'¹⁵

★ ★ ★ ★ ★

While at Balmoral in September 1928 Queen Mary bought her a Spanish doll at a stall in Aberdeen. Winston Churchill was staying. He observed 'Princess Elizabeth – aged 2. The last is a character. She has an air of authority and reflectiveness astonishing in an infant.'†¹⁶ The young Princess Cécile of Greece was another guest

---

* Clara Novello Davies (1861–1943), Welsh singer and mother of Ivor Novello, who also took part in the concert.
† Churchill almost certainly set eyes on her again at royal garden parties in 1931 and 1935. They were certainly both present at the same time. By 1937 he had realised that, with her mother's blood, two royal houses were united. This excited him: 'In the heir presumptive to the Crown, the Princess Elizabeth, the Houses of Stuart & Hanover both find a representative of their blood, cheering even to the White Rose League, and reconciling in the fullness of

at the castle;* Princess Elizabeth left with her on 26 September. George V gave her biscuits for his little dog and she began to mouth the words 'Grandpa' and 'Granny'. She played a game with bricks with Lord Claud Hamilton, and when the nurse came to fetch her 'made a perfectly sweet little curtsey to the King and Queen and then to the company as she departed'.[17]

It was due to the beneficial effect she had on her grandfather that she was sent to Bognor the following year to join him as he recuperated from grave illness. In November 1928 he had fallen ill with septicaemia, which was deemed 'always dangerous, and it is usually fatal'.[†18] Sixty-four days of serious illness followed, during which the young Princess was often at Buckingham Palace with her grandmother, and though she did not see the King, she would bring a lump of sugar for his parrot, Charlotte.

On 8 February 1929 the King was well enough to be sent to Craigweil House,‡ at Aldwick, a suntrap amid the pines, about a mile and a half west of Bognor, to profit from the sea air and the lawns that stretched down to the sea shore. Lord Dawson of Penn, the King's doctor, suggested that Princess Elizabeth's presence would have a salutary effect on him. She spent ten days with him, and the King's diaries were soon peppered with references to 'sweet little Lilibet'.[§19] She arrived with her nurse on the 5.20 p.m. train

---

time one of the most prolonged & poignant quarrels of British history.' (*Strand Magazine*, May 1937).

* Princess Cécile (1911–37) was the daughter of Prince and Princess Andrew of Greece. In happier circumstances she would have been Princess Elizabeth's sister-in-law. She was killed with her family in an air crash at Ostend.

† Specifically streptococcus appeared in small clots of blood the King coughed up. Later plastic pleurisy appeared over the right lung. This was followed by 'an increasing toxaemia'.

‡ Craigweil House was put at his disposal by Sir Arthur du Cros, 1st Bt (1871–1955), a businessman and politician, not wholly free from impropriety. As a director of Dunlop, he had used company funds for personal use. He had helped George V before, by giving Daisy, Countess of Warwick, £64,000 to pay off her debts and thus securing her love letters from Edward VII.

§ Meanwhile her parents went to Norway for Crown Prince Olav's wedding on 21 March.

on 13 March, waving as ever to the crowd. She chatted with her grandfather or played on the shingle with her two nurses. Queen Mary bought her some sand moulds. She enjoyed playing with her spade, but did not like the sea. She did not always behave well. One day she misbehaved so badly that the King said to her: 'If you won't behave properly I'll leave the room.' She made no amends so he walked away. Hardly had he gone than she cried out for him in an agitated voice. The King hastened back, thinking she might have hurt herself. 'You forgot to shut the door after you,' she said.[20]

On 26 March Queen Mary took her back to London by train. When the King had recovered, he made a ceremonial carriage drive through London. Princess Elizabeth was joined by her Lascelles cousins to watch from the balcony at 145 Piccadilly. The delighted King spotted that she waved a Union Flag. Later she appeared on the Buckingham Palace balcony in his arms.

The King and Queen introduced her to public life. On 1 July 1934 they took her to the Cathedral Pilgrimage at Westminster Abbey, in aid of the unemployed in distressed and derelict areas. A small chair was placed between their thrones. As Bishop Hensley Henson recorded: 'When the Queen reached her appointed place, she looked with evident disapproval at the arrangement, sate [sic] herself in the humble seat prepared for the princess, and placed the latter on her own "throne"!'[21] So the Princess sat timidly on the throne, her feet hardly touching the floor. As the King struggled with ill health and political issues, she – and later Princess Margaret – provided what his biographer called 'gleams of sunshine in a rather grim record'.[22]

★ ★ ★ ★ ★

The Queen's main playmates were her cousins. When Alexander 'Sandy' Ramsay (grandson of the Duke of Connaught), born in December 1919, came to play, Princess Elizabeth would await the lift that brought him to her nursery. Yet another cousin, Lady Mary Cambridge, born in September 1924, daughter of the 2nd Marquess of Cambridge, and thus Queen Mary's niece, was often at tea with her aunt when the Princess visited Buckingham Palace.

Lady Mary was to be a close companion. She and Princess Elizabeth climbed over the red boxes sent by the Government to be asked if they had been good girls and were rewarded with a whiskery kiss. Known as 'the Buttercup Fairy', she was invited to Sandringham every Christmas with her parents up to 1939. Mary was more intellectually inclined than Princess Elizabeth, fond of the historical family portraits she inherited, and loved opera and ballet. Later she ran her own pack of Beagles, and was involved with Princess Anne with Riding for the Disabled. She and Princess Elizabeth were frequently bridesmaids together as children. Lady Mary was a bridesmaid when her cousin married Prince Philip.*

Lady Cynthia Asquith

Lady Cynthia Asquith materialised in the life of the Yorks in 1927, writing about the Duchess. Born a Charteris,† she was a child of that intellectual group at the end of the nineteenth century, the Souls, described by Lord David Cecil as 'a person of extraordinary and unique fascination'.[23] She had married Herbert Asquith, poet son of the Prime Minister. Invariably short of money, the chance to write about the Duchess gave a rare boost to her ever dismal finances. It was no easy task as she soon discovered because, while the Duchess was charming and gave her photographs, she imparted little information.[24] Neither did Lady Strathmore nor other sources, who were all 'lyrical in their praise' but not 'gifted either with

---

* In 1951 she married Peter Whitley (1923–2003) and after that saw less of the Queen, though she was invited to Trooping the Colour and to the Royal Box at Royal Ascot. In later life she suffered a serious stroke and could no longer speak. She was placed in a nursing home, Wick House at Stogumber, near Taunton, where she died in 1999. Her daughter called Buckingham Palace and was told that she could either wait to talk to Her Majesty or the man to whom she spoke would pass on the message. A few days later the Queen rang Peter Whitley to say she had read of the death in *The Times*. No one had told her.

† Lady Cynthia Charteris (1887–1960) was the aunt of Martin Charteris, who was later the Queen's Private Secretary.

memories more retentive or with imaginations more fertile!' Fortunately her readers were happy with anodyne anecdotes.

Lady Cynthia turned her attention to Princess Elizabeth. At 145 Piccadilly, a 'radiant and courteous' baby tottered into the room, took possession of her handbag and within minutes 'spectacles were promptly perched on tiny nose; pennies pocketed; the mirror opened and powder deftly applied'.[25] She heard the Princess say: 'Lilibet walk self; Lilibet thut door self.'[26] Lady Cynthia observed that the child loved impersonating the grown-ups, her mother at her dressing-table with hairpins and powder puff. And from an early age she learned to spot abnormalities of dress – an unfastened hook, an untied shoelace, or a safety pin protruding, a trait she retained in later life.

The Duchess taught her daughter to read, write and speak French, and in turn read to her from the Bible. Lady Cynthia was impressed:

> In repose her resolute little face has a distinct resemblance to Queen Mary, but when she smiles, her mother looks out of the friendly, candid eyes ... She is a singularly promising child, and her many natural gifts have been well cultivated. She has been beautifully brought up [by her mother] ... This can have been no easy task. To make her eldest daughter aware of her great obligations, and yet keep her unselfconscious and natural, must have needed much loving vigilance. To the Queen's lasting credit be it said that in this dedicated child we do see qualities not often found together.[27]

Soon after this the Duchess of York told journalists at Streatham:

> 'Well I have to spend nearly all day looking after her, because she is all over the place. She is a sweet little thing! But she is so active that I am always having to run after her and look after her. She is getting on so nicely. She is talking well and walking and is full of little ways. She is a most interesting child and is a perfect companion to me.'[28]

At Birkhall Princess Elizabeth rode a pony called Daisy every day for six weeks. She was much with her Elphinstone cousins 'showing the happy effect of being with a family of children in a homely atmosphere – instead of being a rather isolated personality in a Royal nursery'.[29] On a stormy day, she and these cousins got themselves blown about. Princess Elizabeth 'settled her frock with the slightest suspicion of a frown and then, turning to the little group, said in her most grown-up manner: "How tiresome the wind is. It blows one's skirts about terribly!"'[30]

★ ★ ★ ★ ★

As 1930 dawned, the Prince of Wales gave his niece a Cairn terrier called Hamish, which proceeded to eat her stuffed Airedale.[31] That year she bumped into a girl while playing in Hamilton Gardens and spontaneously made friends with her. She was Sonia Graham-Hodgson, whose father, Dr Harold Graham-Hodgson, was an authority on the diagnostic use of X-rays. He was based at King's College Hospital and had attended George V during his 1928 illness. The family lived nearby.

The children played French cricket together, skipped, played hopscotch and took dancing lessons. They were Girl Guides. They met most afternoons when the Princess was in London, and when she was away, Princess Elizabeth wrote to her friend with news of her activities. Sonia recalled later that Elizabeth was 'a thoughtful and sensitive child, and naturally well-behaved. She never seemed aware of her position and paid no attention to the people who stood by the railings to watch her play.'*[32] Until now, Princess Elizabeth had been an only child. Later that year Princess Margaret arrived.

---

* In 1934 the Princess handwrote a novel in a small book and gave it to her friend.

3
AND THEN THERE WERE TWO, 1930–6

The impending birth of another York child was heralded by the Duchess cancelling all her engagements on 16 April 1930. On 15 July the York family arrived at Glamis, the Duchess celebrating her thirtieth birthday quietly on 4 August. Her gynaecologist, Sir Henry Simson, accompanied by Frank Reynolds, obstetric surgeon, took up residence and, as ordained by law, J. R. Clynes, the Home Secretary, took the train to Scotland to be officially present at the birth.* Clynes and his stooge, Mr Boyd, were stuck at Airlie Castle for the next sixteen days, eventually daring to go no further than the garden for fear of missing the birth. Eventually news came through from Glamis on the evening of 21 August, by which time the hapless Boyd was in his blue kimono for the night. The men reached Glamis with an hour to spare.[1] Princess Margaret finally deigned to appear at 9.22 p.m. The villagers at Glamis had been hoping for a boy.

Princess Margaret Rose's birth completed the family. A magnificent bonfire raged on Hunter's Hill, convincing Princess Elizabeth that this new arrival was more important than a new puppy or a pony. She brought some of her favourite toys to the cot to present them to her baby sister, carrying them in her petticoats. She called her sister 'Bud', explaining: 'Well, she's not a real rose yet, is she? She's only a bud.'[2] Running into a tenant on the Glamis estate, she said: 'She is so lovely, and I am very, very happy to have her.'[3] She was

---

* The need for the Home Secretary to be 'present' referred to the famous warming-pan incident, in which it was suggested that a boy child had been smuggled into the bedchamber of Mary of Modena, wife of James II in 1688, thus potentially heralding a generation of Catholic monarchs. The Home Secretary was obliged to be present from 1894 but this practice was discontinued before the birth of Prince Charles in 1948.

soon accompanying the baby's pram to the Italian garden. Meanwhile she had two Elphinstone cousins to play with – Elizabeth and Jean.

On 6 September Princess Elizabeth was sent over to Balmoral, where Ramsay MacDonald was a guest. She told the Prime Minister that she had seen him in *Punch* – 'but you were a gander leading some ducks'.*[4] Back at Glamis, she particularly loved the herb garden with its varied scents. They went south by the overnight train in time for Princess Margaret Rose's christening in London on 30 October.

As they grew up, the two sisters were invariably dressed identically, but their characters were different. Princess Elizabeth was responsible and diligent. The little one was quick-witted. As early as January 1933 the reasonably well-informed social columnist of the *Daily Telegraph*, Marianne Mayfayre† (a pseudonym of course), had got the point:

> Princess Margaret is far more mischievous than her elder sister was at her age, and just now her nurse spends half her time putting things out of the little one's reach.
>
> Such an agile little Princess is bound to get through a great many clean frocks, and the Duchess of York solves this problem by having the nurseries equipped with labour-saving devices so that they can be washed at home.[5]

Sir Frederick Ponsonby, lately eased out of Birkhall, told his daughter, '*Méfiez-vous*' whenever Princess Margaret was around.[6] Princess Elizabeth kept her little sister in check. Anne Glenconner recalled the sisters staying at Holkham Hall in Norfolk and how Princess Elizabeth was infinitely more serious and would tick Princess Margaret off for rushing about the hall at Holkham on her tricycle or jumping out to surprise footmen carrying huge silver trays from the kitchen: 'Please don't do that, Margaret.'[7]

When the Duchess loaned some of the children's bricks (each made from a different Empire wood) to an exhibition at the Forum Club, Princess Margaret's teeth were in evidence on some. When she failed to curtsey to her grandmother, meeting her at a Friends

---

* On another occasion she introduced a playmate to Stanley Baldwin, commenting: 'Quite nice, isn't he?'

† Queen Mary was said to read her daily.

of the Poor Event, Princess Elizabeth 'pulled her arm and told her what to do'.⁸ At Princess Marina's wedding in 1934, Princess Elizabeth was a bridesmaid and Princess Margaret was fidgeting. The elder sister looked at her and shook her head. At that point 'all exuberance was quelled'. Despite an age difference of four years, a strong bond was forged between them, which lasted all their lives. Lady Cynthia Asquith wrote that the elder one's mission was 'to warn, to comfort and command' and the younger's 'to haunt, to startle and waylay'.⁹

In the summer of 1931 Princess Elizabeth took her place in a large family group at Glamis, at the Golden Wedding celebrations of her Strathmore grandparents. And on 24 October that year she was a bridesmaid – and the star attraction – at the wedding of her father's maternal cousin, Lady May Cambridge, to Captain Henry Abel Smith.*

Princess Elizabeth's quality of restrained calm was in evidence at annual events such as the Royal Tournament and the rehearsal for the Aldershot Tattoo, or when seated between King George V and Queen Mary on their way to Crathie Church for Sunday matins. During these years the York family played a game called Three Bears. The Duke was Very Big Bear, the Duchess was Rather Big Bear, Princess Elizabeth was Little Bear. The game now became Four Bears – Princess Margaret was Very Little Bear.

The Duke drew strength and confidence from his wife and great happiness from his two daughters. 'Lilibet is my pride,' he used to say, 'and Margaret my joy.' He greatly admired his elder daughter's character. With Princess Margaret, it was a case of sheer astonishment that he had created this beautiful creature. That she adored him and, on growing up, teased him playfully, resulted in him spoiling her to bad advantage.

---

* Lady May (1906–94) was the daughter of the Earl of Athlone and Princess Alice, Countess of Athlone. (Sir) Henry Abel Smith (1900–93) was later Governor of Queensland, Australia. The wedding took place at Balcombe, Princess Elizabeth wearing a Victorian frock of blue velvet. Other bridesmaids included Princess Ingrid of Sweden (later Queen of Denmark), Lady Alice Montagu-Douglas-Scott (later Duchess of Gloucester) and, as so often, Lady Mary Cambridge. The Prince of Wales proposed the health of the couple. The crowds were wild with excitement at seeing Princess Elizabeth, who became slightly bashful. The crowd even burst through the police cordon.

There are occasional vignettes of Princess Elizabeth. Aged about five, she announced one day with surprise: 'Sometimes strangers speak to me as if they knew me,' and she was quoted as saying: 'If ever I am Queen, the first thing I shall do will be to make a law forbidding people to ride or drive on Sunday. Horses *must* have a holiday.'[10] She took lessons in French, and when she visited Titania's Palace, an attraction due for the British Empire Exhibition in Buenos Aires, she was shocked by the untidiness of the fairy children's nursery. 'They must have a very bad Nannie to allow them to leave their toys on the floor like that. I have to put my toys away when I have finished with them.'[11]

As early as 1931 the infant Princess Margaret joined her sister on her Windsor visits. Princess Elizabeth opened her birthday presents in the Oak Room, above the Grand Entrance. She saluted the Irish Guards, ran around the Quadrangle and cantered on her pony. On 10 June she climbed onto her mother's knee at Buckingham Palace to watch her great-great-uncle, the Duke of Connaught, in a plumed hat, inspect the Yeomen of the Guard in the Palace garden. Throughout this she retained her innate modesty. Lady Helen Graham,* lady in waiting to Queen Elizabeth, first met the Princess, then aged five, in 1931:

> A lively, trim little figure in a green wool jersey and a kilt of Royal Stewart tartan, with hair shading from gold to darker tints, and eyes that were always observing, like those of a bird. She noticed everything; but in those days she never thought that she herself was being noticed. Why should she? No one had put ideas of future importance into her head and it just seemed great fun, when she drove in a car with her parents, then Duke and Duchess of York, to wave to people out of the window and for them to wave back. This ignorance of her own importance had its drawbacks. She never could understand why photographers, on going to a children's party, would pick her out for their attentions, and she was apt to frown upon them with very obvious disapproval.[12]

---

* Lady Helen (Nelly) Graham (1879–1945), elder daughter of the 5th Duke of Montrose, KT, spinster, tall and gaunt, deeply Presbyterian, had to write lots of letters about the infant princess on behalf of the Duchess of York, President of the YWCA. Sister of Lady Cameron of Lochiel. Her papers are in the Cameron of Lochiel archives at Lochaber.

At one of the Royal Tournaments Lady Helen noted: 'Princess Elizabeth remained at the front of the box – a tense, immovable little figure in a pale blue coat, hatless, entranced by the musical ride of the Household Cavalry, and quite oblivious to what anyone else in the box was saying and doing. She has always loved the tradition and pageantry of the British Army, and her sense of rhythm found great satisfaction at that age in marching round the room to music.'[13]

Lady Helen thought that Princess Elizabeth was aware from infancy 'that her parents lived a different kind of life from other children's parents; that their frequent journeys to carry out public engagements were in some mysterious way connected with the idea of service for others, but I doubt if at that time she gave her own future much thought'.[14] Soon the Princess was reading letters from children from remote spots in the world – Australia and farms in Africa – and learned that she held importance in the Empire.

★ ★ ★ ★ ★

Princess Margaret and Princess Elizabeth at the Royal Lodge

Princess Elizabeth at the Welsh house

The Duke of York gave up hunting in the autumn of 1932, and took a cut in his annual grant to help the economy. The family moved into Royal Lodge, in the grounds of Windsor Great Park, at Easter 1933. This soon became their favourite home, the Duke creating his own garden. For Princess Elizabeth (as for successive generations of youngsters in the Royal Family) a particular attraction was the little Welsh house in the grounds. This was a gift from the people of Wales, accepted by the Yorks in Cardiff on 16 March 1932. The Duke accepted Y Bwythyn Bach, saying: 'I cannot imagine any more delightful or interesting model for a child than the Little House with the Straw Roof.'[15] With six rooms, it had been designed by Morgan Willmott, and was to be exhibited at the *Daily Mail* Ideal Home Exhibition at Olympia in 1932. Horrifically, the thatched roof was destroyed by fire and the exterior walls badly charred, but it was restored in time to go on exhibition (raising a thousand pounds for a Princess Elizabeth cot at Cardiff Royal Infirmary). Princess Elizabeth was presented with its key on her sixth birthday. Besides the fun, it taught the Princesses how to lead a domestic life in miniature. Queen Mary gave a set of 172 pieces of tableware for the cottage.*

---

* Eventually £5,061 8s 10d was raised by the exhibition of the house in London,

Sister Catherine Black,* who came to nurse the King following his serious illness of 1928, was impressed by how the Princesses looked after the miniature cottage and how their mother taught them to be independent, dressing themselves. After 1932 she saw them often at Sandringham and in Scotland. Her verdict was that they were 'two of the most human, unspoiled and unaffected little girls imaginable, for although they are taught Court etiquette and manners and deportment, they are never allowed to feel anything but ordinary children'. She noted how Princess Elizabeth mothered Princess Margaret, judging her 'the stronger character, already thoughtful and unselfish. She reminds one vividly of Queen Mary sometimes.'[16]

The family also borrowed Birkhall, just along the road from Balmoral, past Abergeldie Castle, for their summer holidays. For many years this small eighteenth-century house, built in 1715, had been occupied by courtiers. The Duke and Duchess made it their summer home, redecorated it and replanted the garden, the Duke in particular relishing the physical work clearing woodland. The Princesses would ride over to Balmoral to see the King or to play with the daughters of Sir Alec Hardinge at Altnaguisach, in a pony trap pulled by a stalking pony. They played 'Kick the Tin', built moss huts in the woods, and had to rebuild them each year as they were knocked down by deer, snow and winds.[17]

This pattern of moving between the various houses continued as the Princesses grew up. The original 'Alice' – Mrs R. G. Hargreaves† – gave Princess Elizabeth a signed copy of *Alice's Adventures in Wonderland* before going to America for her eightieth birthday. They were given Welsh terriers and later Corgis. At Sandringham for

---

Cardiff, Bristol and Swansea. £525 was given to Bristol charities and cots were 'named' (sponsored) in Cardiff, Newport, Swansea and Blaina hospitals; 250,000 people saw that little house.

* Sister Catherine Black (1878–1949), an Irish nurse from Donegal.

† Alice Liddell (1852–1934), who was photographed by 'Lewis Carroll' as a child, and to whom he read stories, one becoming *Alice's Adventures in Wonderland*. She caught the eye of Queen Victoria's son, the Duke of Albany, and he named his daughter Alice after her. That Princess Alice (1883–1981) became Countess of Athlone, and was the last surviving granddaughter of Queen Victoria.

Christmas in 1932 they sat in another room to hear their grandfather give his first Christmas broadcast.

They skated at Grosvenor House. They were spotted out in a pair-horse barouche in Hyde Park. They were able to walk in public places in a way that would be concerning in the twenty-first century. The press knew that they emerged between 11.30 a.m. and 12 p.m. into St James's Park, Hyde Park and elsewhere, Princess Elizabeth being described as 'a dignified little maiden walking sedately and watching the playfulness of her younger sister'.[18]

Crawfie

The Princesses with Crawfie in the scaled down Citroën C4 toy car

At Easter 1933 Marion Crawford joined the household as governess, and stayed with the princesses until 1947. She was a Scottish girl, born in Ayrshire in 1909, who studied at the Moray House Training College in Edinburgh and worked in the poorer parts of the city. She went down the path of child psychology but then worked for the Earl of Elgin's family. Everyone she worked with liked her, but few were impressed by her academic skills. She was a great favourite of the Princesses and their friends and a trusted member of the household until Princess Elizabeth married, but fell from favour by publishing intimate details of the lives of her young charges in *The Little Princesses*.

A. N. Wilson went so far as to describe Crawfie as 'probably the most important Royal writer of the century'[19] due to her privileged access. It would be tempting to agree with him, except that not a word of her reminiscences was written by her.

Crawfie was impressed by how much the parents participated in the lives of their daughters. Princess Elizabeth loved games that involved imaginary horses; she had a high IQ and was quick to learn. She probably had something of a temper – her father certainly did – but did she really tip an inkpot over the head of her French governess? The press thought she loved knitting, but Crawfie's line was that she was hopeless with a needle.

When Princess Elizabeth was seven, the press noted her 'unaffectedness and naturalness of demeanour', how she was 'utterly unspoiled' and 'a typical British child'. It described the 'simple manner in which the Duchess of York brings up her daughters', commended the Princess's 'excellent progress at her lessons', how she could now 'read and spell well', praised the 'considerable advance in her writing' and her enjoyment of music and dance, in particular the reels and Scottish dances taught to her by her mother. There was a hint that her general education was not being hurried, rather a thorough grounding was the plan. She was afforded fresh air and relaxation and her days 'systematically arranged no matter where she is staying'. Riding was her favourite pastime and her pony, Peggy, was now kept at Windsor. Her next challenge would be to get off the leading rein. The report also highlighted the Duchess of York's stipulation that she should not stay up late or eat rich food. And it emphasised the Princess's huge affection for her grandfather, considering him the 'fount of all knowledge'.[20]

If Crawfie's accounts are to be mistrusted, Louis Wulff, Court Correspondent of the Press Association, was given privileged access, and can therefore be trusted. He was on the South Africa tour in 1947 and his book *Queen of Tomorrow* was advertised as an 'authentic study'. He related that at the end of one of the Royal Tournaments with Queen Mary, as the Royal party were about to leave she said to her grandmother how pleased the crowds would be to see her. Queen Mary jumped on this, instructing a footman: 'Take the Princess out through the back, put her in a taxi and take her home.' Another rule of royal behaviour was sharply learned.[21]

Princess Elizabeth was concerned to see her father turn pale during the 1933 Birthday Parade on Horseguards. In considerable heat, he wheeled his horse round and left the parade ground, remaining out of view on the other side of the arch for fifteen minutes.

That summer, on 20 August, the Duke and Duchess of York took the princesses from Glamis to Balnaboth in the Cairngorms, to have tea with J. M. Barrie. Princess Elizabeth had met him before with Lady Cynthia Asquith who, on this occasion noted: 'Very gay tea, with crackers and cake. Duke very nice and easy and the children enchanting. Barrie's court manners very queer. He kept sweeping in front of the Duke ... We played darts, and went into the garden, and all ate raspberries.'[22]

The next day was Princess Margaret's third birthday. Lady Cynthia brought Barrie to Glamis and he sat next to the little Princess. There were some light and friendly exchanges between Barrie and Princess Margaret, as a result of which Princess Margaret declared soon afterwards: 'I know that man. He is my greatest friend, and I am *his* greatest friend,'[23] a line Barrie slipped into one of his plays. Lady Cynthia's publishers were aghast that she had failed to photograph this significant meeting.*

The Princesses went to the theatre, to pantomimes and to a performance of *Peter Pan*. Lady Astor often invited them to fancy-dress parties and they visited Bekonscot, the model village at Beaconsfield. They swam at the Bath Club, Princess Elizabeth complaining: 'Margaret Rose is more like a limpet than a fish. She *will* cling to the side of the swimming-bath!'[24] At dance lessons, Madame Vacani said: 'She has never had any pupil quicker at picking up a new step than Princess Elizabeth, or one who showed more unflagging vitality and greater zeal to learn.'[25] They attended their first garden party on a very hot day on 26 July, Princess Elizabeth being 'the heroine of the occasion, since everyone wanted to see her'.[26]

---

* In 1935 Lady Cynthia Asquith produced *The Princess Elizabeth Gift Book* in aid of the Princess Elizabeth of York Hospital for Children, assisted by Eileen Bigland (1898–1970). Lady Cynthia cajoled her distinguished friends in the world of art and literature to contribute. The young Princess took a personal interest in the idea of a rural hospital, sketching what it should look like – 'a triumphant rural edifice' – for J. M. Barrie, when she was four (in 1930). She visited it a few times between 1934 and 1941. More than a hundred thousand copies were subscribed before publication, an additional twenty thousand being printed four days before publication. George Robey bought twenty-five copies and gave them to the Princess Elizabeth of York Hospital for Children in Shadwell.

AND THEN THERE WERE TWO, 1930–6

Princess Elizabeth with her grandparents on the balcony of Buckingham Palace for the Silver Jubilee 1935

Princess Elizabeth was bridesmaid to Princess Marina of Greece when she married Prince George, Duke of Kent at Westminster Abbey on 29 November, her most prominent public role to date. With her cousin Lady Mary Cambridge, she carried the bride's long train, some five yards of white and silver lamé. Because George V disliked young girls in long dresses, they had to wear short ballet-style ones that prickled their legs. The girls gave each other 'horrified looks' as they climbed down the steep steps. The Archbishop, Cosmo Gordon Lang, patted their heads and told them they had been 'good little girls'.[27]

Back at the Palace the Princess gave a tea party for the children and was then prominent among the confetti throwers as the bridal couple left by carriage. The occasion has extra significance since Princess Marina's first cousin, Prince Philip of Greece, was in the Abbey. He was thirteen years old at the time, and it is suggested that this was the first time Princess Elizabeth saw him, although she wrote later that she had no recall of this.

On Princess Elizabeth's ninth birthday, a record crowd of ten thousand turned out to hear the bands on the East Terrace of Windsor Castle. Flags were flown on public buildings, and tea was served in the Oak Room, the King's sister, Princess Victoria, joining the party from Coppins in Iver. Presently the Vicomtesse de Bellaigue arrived to teach Princess Elizabeth French.

The Silver Jubilee, 1935

King George V marked the Silver Jubilee of his reign in 1935. The York family processed to St Paul's Cathedral in a carriage, with a Captain's Escort of the Royal Horse Guards. In the cathedral, the Princesses, in their pale pink coats, were described as 'pictures of propriety, and behaved perfectly'. Princess Elizabeth followed the service but jumped up too soon for one of the hymns, and promptly sat down again. Princess Margaret wanted to talk to the Boy Scouts. They gazed admiringly at the Gentlemen-at-Arms. The younger Princess was somewhat alarmed by the crowds, 'a shade taken back by all the noise'.[28] Both sisters sent donations to the newly formed King George's Jubilee Trust, inspiring a child from Huthwaite in Nottinghamshire to write: 'I was told that Princess Elizabeth and Princess Margaret each sent 5s; but we can only send our halfpennies, which we hope will be acceptable.'[29]

George V and his granddaughter had the charming habit that she would wave from 145 Piccadilly and he would wave back from Buckingham Palace. They could not see each other but they knew they were doing it. There was a lot of interaction between Princess Elizabeth and her grandfather that summer. On Sunday 12 May she joined the King and Queen for lunch at Buckingham Palace, running up the Palace steps to the delight of the cheering crowd outside.[30] In June she was taken by Queen Mary to Sandringham to join the King, who was resting there with bronchitis after the rigours of the Jubilee celebrations. Again she was much in evidence at Balmoral in the late summer, seated between her grandparents in a horse-drawn carriage on their way to Crathie Church.

Princess Elizabeth was again bridesmaid in November, this time to Lady Alice Montagu-Douglas-Scott, daughter of the Duke of Buccleuch, when she married Prince Henry, Duke of Gloucester. This does not appear to have been an overwhelming love match. Prince Henry proposed, just muttering an aside on a walk, and the bride accepted as she was thirty-four, had had 'a very good innings' and felt it was time to do 'something more useful with her life'.[31]

The wedding was set to take place in Westminster Abbey on 6 November, but the illness and death of the Duke of Buccleuch meant that it took place in the private chapel at Buckingham Palace instead. The King was ailing, tended to fall asleep at dinner and was 'no less likely to die',[32] so they did not delay the wedding. Most of the two thousand guests bidden to Westminster Abbey were disinvited, with only a select two hundred chosen for the private service. The only person not wholly disappointed by the reduced service was the bride, since she was preternaturally shy. 'I was only too glad not to have a grand wedding,'[33] she wrote. After the ceremony the Princesses appeared on the Palace balcony in ermine coats, and Princess Elizabeth flung confetti over her uncle and aunt as they left in a carriage. She held another tea party at 145 Piccadilly, with the other child bridesmaids, Lady Mary Cambridge (again), and the Duchess of Gloucester's niece, Anne Hawkins (later to be a long-serving Assistant Press Secretary to Queen Elizabeth II).

This wedding brought two arbiters of style into the royal orbit. Lady Alice had chosen Norman Hartnell to design her wedding dress and those of the bridesmaids, which led him to design the dresses of the Maids of Honour for the 1937 Coronation and later to dress Queen Elizabeth the Queen Mother, the Queen and many members of the Royal Family. Cecil Beaton had already photographed the Duke and Duchess of Kent, who were his first serious royal patrons. Lady Alice asked him to take her engagement photographs. So the new Duchess of Gloucester can be credited for advancing these two men (who had somewhat disliked one another when at Cambridge in the mid-1920s). They transformed the image of Queen Elizabeth the Queen Mother with the iconic white Winterhalter wardrobe and the iconic 1939 Buckingham Palace photo session, after which they collaborated in their different fields for many decades.

On 9 October a son was born to the Duke and Duchess of Kent – the young Prince Edward (the present Duke of Kent). Princess Elizabeth took an interest in him from the start and a strong cousinly bond was established. She was present at his christening.

Up to this point the lives of the two Princesses had not been tinged with sadness. When they spent three hours at London Zoo on 5 July that year, they held a baby alligator, observed the cobras and heard the Abyssinian lions roaring. It was symbolic of their carefree happiness that they could 'shriek with laughter' as Percy the Penguin waddled behind his keeper 'doing what looked like a grotesque imitation of his walk'.[34] Lady Cynthia Asquith wrote: 'He waddled with such perfect pomposity.'[35]

Their happiness was to prove fragile.

4
THE YEAR OF THREE KINGS, 1936

King George V had been upset by the death of the Duke of Buccleuch, an old naval friend, especially so soon before the Gloucester wedding. But worse was to come. Princess Victoria was his favourite sister. She lived not far from Windsor at Coppins, near Iver. She and the King talked every day on the telephone. She used to greet him: 'Hallo, you old trout.' On one occasion the operator had to say: 'I'm sorry, Your Royal Highness, His Majesty is not yet on the line.' Queen Mary disliked her intensely. She ruined their Mediterranean cruise of 1925 with her banal comments belittling the fine sites they visited. As James Pope-Hennessy wrote, Princess Victoria aroused 'philistine tendencies' in her brother, and spoiled Queen Mary's sightseeing with 'a cataract of chaff and jokes'.[1]

She had been present in St Paul's Cathedral for the Silver Jubilee service, soon after which her health declined. On 2 December she suffered from a severe haemorrhage from the stomach and was given a blood transfusion. Lord Dawson of Penn remained with her (for better or for worse) until she died early the following morning.

The King backed out of the State Opening of Parliament and missed a week's holiday at Sandringham. The funeral in St George's Chapel exhausted him. Six weeks of mourning, the court remaining in half-mourning until 14 January 1936 – a mere six days before the King himself died. Princess Elizabeth was spared attending her great-aunt's funeral. It is unlikely that it affected her much, other than observing the effect on her grandfather.

On 21 December 1935 the Princesses took the train to Sandringham where the traditional house party consisted of the Prince of Wales, the newly married Gloucesters, the Kents and their baby, Prince Edward, as well as the Athlones, the Cambridges and their daughter

Mary. The Duchess of York was not there, confined to Royal Lodge, under the watchful eye of Lord Dawson of Penn, suffering from influenzal pneumonia. The Duke of York stayed with her, but it was thought that the Princesses would have more fun at Sandringham, while allowing their mother to relax and recover.

In Norfolk the Royal Family went to church, the King walking from the Big House, with the Kents and the Princesses. He managed his fourth and final Christmas broadcast, clearing his throat before speaking,* and the traditional Norfolk turkey, beef and plum pudding were served. By 27 December rumours were circulating about his health; these were briefly denied.

Over the Christmas holiday, the Princesses played in the little tea room added onto the dairy, but the weather prevented them spending much time outdoors. The King again walked to church on 29 December, 5 and 11 January. He rode his pony on 15 January. He was affected by the death of Rudyard Kipling on 18 January, but enjoyed a number of films, shown in the ballroom, including *Top Hat*, *Anna Karenina*, *The Thirty-Nine Steps* and *Mutiny on the Bounty*. However, the serenity did not last. While the Princesses played outside, anxiety fell over the Big House.

On 17 January it was announced that the King was suffering from bronchial catarrh with 'some signs of cardiac weakness which must be regarded with some disquiet'.[2] Lord Dawson hastened to Sandringham, hot from the deathbed of Princess Victoria and the sickbed of the Duchess of York, to assist Sir Frederick Willans, the Surgeon-Apothecary at Sandringham, and Sir Stanley Hewett, who had attended the King throughout his 1928 illness. Sir Maurice Cassidy arrived and examined the King.

As pressmen gathered outside, the Princesses were spotted making a snowman. Their faces were flushed and they were shouting excitedly.

---

* The King spoke of the 'rejoicing not merely respect for the Throne, but a warm and generous remembrance of the man himself who, may God help him, has been placed upon it'. He spoke of 'the common joys and sorrows, as when this year, you showed your happiness in the marriage of my son, and your sympathy in the death of my beloved sister'. He sent his 'truest Christmas wishes, and those of my dear wife, my children and grandchildren who are with me today'. (*Daily Telegraph*, 27 December 1935).

Then, suddenly, they were called inside to bid farewell to their ailing grandfather and dispatched home to London on the 2.40 p.m. Wolferton train on the Saturday afternoon, along with Sir Maurice Cassidy. When something on the platform amused Princess Margaret, her sister gently rebuked her: 'We must not laugh just now. Poor Grandpa is ill.' As the report put it: 'So ended, somewhat sadly, their joyous Christmas holiday.'[3] As Princess Elizabeth boarded the train, so ended her joyous childhood.

Bulletins stated that the King had held his own for forty hours and eaten a few grapes. World leaders expressed concern – Roosevelt, Hitler, Mussolini and Emperor Hirohito of Japan among them – figures who would loom ominously in the reign of George VI. Counsellors of State were appointed, and Queen Mary was seen walking in the grounds with the Princess Royal. At 5.30 p.m. a depressing bulletin announced: 'The condition of His Majesty the King shows diminishing strength,' followed at 9.25 a.m. by the famous one: 'The King's life is moving peacefully to its close.' He died on 20 January at 11.55 p.m. in the presence of Queen Mary, the Prince of Wales, the Duke of York, the Princess Royal and the Duke and Duchess of Kent.

As is now known,* that peaceful death came with the aid of Lord Dawson's needle as he injected a lethal dose of ¾ gram of morphia and a gram of cocaine into the neck of the King, to spare the family a long vigil and to make sure that the death was announced in the early editions of *The Times* and not in the evening papers. Not for nothing was the rhyme repeated:

> Lord Dawson of Penn
> Has killed many men
> That's why we sing
> 'God Save the King'.

The Princesses were with their mother at Royal Lodge and at an appropriate moment they were told. Due to the strong mutual bond

---

* Kenneth Rose revealed this in a revised edition, published in 2000, of his 1983 biography of King George V, deriving it from the account by Lord Dawson's biographer, Francis Watson, in *History Today*.

that had formed between George V and his granddaughter, Crawfie was particularly worried about 'Lilibet' attending the funeral.

Crawfie reassured her charges that it was all right to play in the days after their grandfather's death. At the Lying-in-State, Princess Elizabeth was impressed by the stillness of the scene, how 'Uncle David' stood guard over the catafalque and never moved: 'And everyone was so quiet. As if the King were asleep.'[4] It was the first time she had seen her grandfather's coffin. With them were the King and Queen of Norway, the Kings of Denmark and the Belgians, and members of other royal houses.

On the day of the funeral, Princess Margaret curtseyed from the balcony as the funeral cortège passed 145 Piccadilly. Princess Elizabeth watched from a window, left by a back door and was driven with a police escort to Paddington Station. There she stood with Crawfie and her Lascelles cousins, watching the royal coaches arrive. The long wait was alleviated by the dexterity with which a sailor who fainted was replaced. She accompanied the family mourners on the train to Windsor, and sat with Queen Mary, Queen Maud, the Princess Royal and her mother in a lone glass coach in the procession to St George's Chapel from the station. Dressed in a black coat with black beret, she held her mother's hand as she entered the chapel. She sat in the quire, 'her face a picture of childish grief'[5] and saw the King's coffin descend into the Royal Vault, so recently deployed for Princess Victoria. Lady Cynthia Asquith described her as 'a pathetic little figure in black, controlled, but very pale and awe-struck' as she curtseyed to the King's coffin in St George's Chapel. Lady Cynthia marked this moment in Princess Elizabeth's life as the time when gravity descended:

> With the death of her devoted grandfather something irreplaceable went out of Princess Elizabeth's life. It may be said to have ended the first happy phase of her childhood, to have challenged and for ever destroyed that sense of personal immunity which blesses a sheltered infancy. Someone she loved had vanished. Her little world no longer seemed secure.[6]

Lady Cynthia, pressed at times to fill the pages demanded of her in her many books about the York family, wrote that after George V died: 'She said very little about her feelings. It was as though she could not bear to speak of him; but for some time her health was seriously affected by her grief.'[7]

* * * * *

Weeks of royal mourning followed, as the family came to terms with the implications of a new reign. Towards the end of February Princess Elizabeth was spotted walking her dog in the park, dressed in black for her grandfather, and her friend Sonia Graham-Hodgson came over to a party.

On 1 March the Yorks and the Princesses listened as the new King made a St David's Day broadcast, heard by 500 million people spread across the world. He was photographed at the microphone, a picture often erroneously used as the Abdication broadcast photo (on which occasion none was taken). The King paid generous tribute to his father and pledged to carry on his work.[8]

The York family retreated to Compton Place in Eastbourne for a quiet holiday to enable the Duchess to throw off the aftermath of her pneumonia, the parents arriving first, the children on 5 March. From there the Duchess of York wrote to Lord Dawson, about 'the effects of a family break-up, which always happens when the head of a family goes. Though outwardly one's life goes on the same, yet everything is different ...'[9] She put it slightly differently from Lord David Cecil, telling him that 'patience and anger' were the qualities needed for royal life.[10]

There were walks on the headland of Seven Sisters or on the Downs, the children playing in a chalet on the seafront. On the Sunday they went to morning service at St Mary's Church, the Duchess and Princess Elizabeth still wearing black. Princess Elizabeth continued her studies and they visited St Thomas's Church, Winchelsea, dedicated to St Thomas à Becket. They returned to London on 1 April, visiting the Gainsborough exhibition at Sir Philip Sassoon's house.

That year there was no Easter court at Windsor Castle. The Yorks spent it at Royal Lodge. It was glacially cold. Queen Mary and Princess Helena Victoria came to stay. Easter Sunday fell on 10 April and King Edward came over from Fort Belvedere. They drove down the Long Walk to Windsor Castle for morning service in the private chapel, conducted by the Dean of Windsor, Albert Baillie. The King returned briefly to Royal Lodge before heading back to the Fort for his own weekend party.

In the next days Queen Mary again took her granddaughters to the model village, Bekonscot, and to Hampton Court, resplendent with spring flowers. One day they explored the gardens at Frogmore and in the castle's moat. Back in London Queen Mary, the Duchess of York and the Princesses visited Kew Gardens.

Princess Elizabeth reached her tenth birthday on 21 April. Court mourning precluded much public celebration, but now the Princesses were allowed to dress in grey. Princess Elizabeth received a small electric motor-car from her parents and a bicycle from Queen Mary. King Edward was unable to join the party but he popped in at 7 p.m. to wish her well.

As early as May 1936, Joan Woollcombe, an intelligent journalist who had been at Miss Goff's kindergarten in London with the then Elizabeth Bowes-Lyon, wrote in the *Toronto Star* that she had been ticked off by 'a certain notable woman' for suggesting that Princess Elizabeth was 'a future Queen'. This notable woman (almost certainly Lady Astor) wrote: 'We still hope that the Prince of Wales [by then the King] may marry.'[11] Joan Woollcombe compared the Princess squatting on a red carpet outside Olympia, pulling her socks up not long before, with her new 'poise and sedateness'. She praised the Yorks for not having taken the Princesses on luxury holidays, like some children, and concluded with prescience:

> Watch this child very carefully during these important years of her adolescence; her parents will evolve a special training for her in consultation with the King whom, possibly, her father may succeed.[12]

George Bernard Shaw also had his eye on her. On board the newly launched *Queen Mary*, he was asked on camera whether or not King Edward VIII should marry. He said that he hoped nothing would get in the way of the throne and that 'lovely Princess Elizabeth'.[13]

Oblivious to that prediction, Princess Elizabeth accompanied her parents to Birkhall in August. She saw something of her uncle at Balmoral in the summer. The Archbishop of Canterbury undertook his habitual peregrination to Scotland but the new King did not invite him to Balmoral. The Yorks invited him to Birkhall, greatly irritating the King. Already concerned about the antics of Edward VIII, the Primate had the opportunity to observe Princess Elizabeth:

> The children – Lilliebet [sic], Margaret Rose and Margaret Elphinstone – joined us. They sang some action-songs most charmingly. It was strange to think of the destiny which may be awaiting the little Elizabeth, at present second from the Throne! She and her lively little sister are certainly most entrancing children.[14]

If that summer was relatively carefree for the children, it was quite the opposite for their parents. Mrs Simpson was a guest at Balmoral, the Duchess of York somewhat put out to find her acting as hostess. The Mrs Simpson issue was not widely known to the general public but it was of intense interest to the King's relations. She had caught the eye of the Prince of Wales in 1931. He had become besotted by her. Concern was expressed when the names of Mr and Mrs Simpson appeared in the Court Circular and they became frequent guests at Fort Belvedere. King Edward liked nothing more than to go to their Bryanston Square apartment for cocktails or to arrange dinners there. Unseemly as this relationship was, it was not a matter of gravity until Mrs Simpson instituted divorce proceedings against her husband. Until then there could be no question of marriage with the King. After that it became an affair of state.

There are many contradictory views about the Abdication. It was usually women who made sacrifices for men, but here the King-Emperor was prepared to give up reigning over two-thirds of the world's population for the sake of a twice-divorced American woman. Whereas it is traditional to think of Mrs Simpson as the woman who stole the King, this does not hold up. She enjoyed being 'the King's friend', with whatever connotation that implies, but she had no wish to cause a constitutional crisis or to find herself the wife of an exiled monarch and one of the most hated women in the world. On the other hand, there is plenty of evidence of the King not wishing to be king and it would seem that, whether he admitted it or not (and he did not), he was seeking a means of escape. He must have known deep in his heart that Mrs Simpson would never be accepted as Queen. He made this an issue, and he abdicated.

In Scotland during that summer, the Yorks had to squash rumours that Princess Elizabeth might attend St Leonard's School in St Andrews, or any other such school. Still up there, Princess Elizabeth sent her young cousin, Prince Edward of Kent, some picture books for his first birthday. They spent some time at Glamis, where Lady Strathmore, then seventy-four, took to her room with a cold. They came south on 20 October.

The crisis duly came and was resolved by King Edward VIII abdicating on 11 December 1936 and heading into voluntary exile. There was sadness at his departure, as he had been a much-loved Prince of Wales, though some shared the view of Sir Cuthbert Headlam, former Conservative minister, that he was 'obstinate and unbalanced'. Headlam thought the Yorks would do the job 'admirably' and that the episode might even 'strengthen the monarchy'. The new King and Queen gave him confidence 'and it is clear that the people are out to help them'.[15]

Needless to say the King and Queen did not initially share that view, though it would soon prove they were better equipped than they realised. The British public had not liked the brittle cocktail-shaker world of Edward and Mrs Simpson. They soon warmed to the 'walk in the park, afternoon tea' domesticity of George VI and Queen Elizabeth. So, with the Abdication, the former King dropped into the past tense.

As for the Princesses, the Duchess of York warned Crawfie that their lives would soon change: 'We must take what is coming to us and make the best of it,' she said. She warned that presently they would be moving into Buckingham Palace. The new King attended the Accession Council and was duly proclaimed by Sir Gerald Woods Wollaston, Garter King of Arms, from the balcony of St James's Palace. Crawfie told the Princesses to curtsey to their father as they had done to their grandparents. They did so, and Crawfie recorded:

> I think perhaps nothing that had occurred had brought the change in his condition to him as clearly as this did. He stood for a moment touched and taken aback. Then he stooped and kissed them both warmly.[16]

The Abdication was a considerable shock to the Duke of York, who had never seen a state paper and was suddenly obliged to take over as King. Princess Elizabeth became heiress presumptive to the throne, a situation she accepted with that rather grave sense of duty that was always a part of her character, though it was suggested that she responded to her new role by ardently praying for a baby brother.* Had a boy been born to the Duchess of York, he would have taken precedence, under the laws of succession at that time.

Two stories support her calmer response. Lady Cynthia Asquith happened to go to tea with the Princesses and Crawfie at 145 Piccadilly on the very day of the Abdication, 11 December. There were cheering crowds outside. Princess Elizabeth was drawn to the window several times to inspect them. When she escorted Lady Cynthia out, she spotted a letter on the hall table addressed: 'Her Majesty The Queen'. Lady Cynthia described her reaction:

> Her face went very solemn. 'That's Mummy now,' she said, with a tiny tremor in her awestruck voice. Beyond that one remark she made no allusion to the event that, changing the course of history, must so profoundly affect her childhood, and confront her with so formidable a future.[17]

When Princess Margaret told Lady Helen Graham that she had been 'Margaret of York' but was now 'Margaret nothing', her elder sister 'said less because she knew more'.[18] Princess Margaret also said: 'Uncle David's such a bore – I've just learned to spell York and now I am not to use it.'†[19] One of the princesses was heard explaining that Uncle David was going to marry Mrs Baldwin.

On the day of the Abdication, photos of the new King and Queen

---

* Mabell, Countess of Airlie, told Queen Mary that, during the Coronation summer, Lady Strathmore said that Crawfie had told her this. (*Thatched with Gold*, p. 205).

† The Abdication was a nightmare for Lady Cynthia too. She had to update her Duchess of York book, adding ten thousand words. She was then told it was still twenty thousand words too short. She retreated to a country clinic, reinstated a great number of previously cut adjectives and, by 'puffing and padding', elongated her sentences.

flashed up in the Lyric Theatre during a performance of *Charles The King*. There were cheers for Princess Elizabeth. As crowds gathered outside 145 Piccadilly, two little faces appeared behind twitching curtains, this time provoking a huge cheer outside. On 13 December the Royal Family went to church in the Royal Chapel at Marlborough House and later the Princesses played in the gardens of Buckingham Palace where they could have privacy.

The Archbishop of Canterbury adjusted the royal prayers, dropping the Duke of Windsor at the very moment in his life when he needed them most, and adding Princess Elizabeth. After the new King, the wording continued: 'Bless our gracious Queen Elizabeth, Mary the Queen-mother, the Princess Elizabeth, and all the Royal Family.'[20]

A different King presided over Christmas at Sandringham. Queen Mary was there with her family, as were the Gloucesters, the Athlones and Lady Mary Cambridge. A present arrived from the Duke of Windsor in Vienna. Christmas Day was enlivened by the news that the Duchess of Kent had given birth to a daughter, Princess Alexandra.

Princess Elizabeth emerged from her early childhood years as a serious, sensible young girl, not given to undue mischief, with simple and admirable loves – for her family, for dogs, ponies and horses, a grown-up companion to her more mischievous younger sister. No stories survive of wayward behaviour, and they would surely have surfaced by now. She was loved by her family and loved by the nation. Lady Cynthia Asquith observed: 'In repose her resolute little face has a distinct resemblance to Queen Mary, but when she smiles her mother looks out of the friendly, candid eyes.'[21]

5
THE PRE-WAR YEARS, 1937–9

'The bearing of the two little girls to whom the whole of the British Empire have given their hearts was perfectly charming, and will never be forgotten by those who witnessed it.'[1]
Canon Jocelyn Perkins (Sacrist)
(1870–1962)

The new reign presented publishers, authors and journalists with complex problems. Numerous books had been prepared about King Edward VIII. Some were swiftly retitled the Duke of Windsor and took their chances in the market. The *Illustrated London News* had commissioned a glorious image of Edward VIII in his Coronation robes. They simply snipped his head off and replaced it with one of George VI.

The two Princesses were in the private chapel of Buckingham Palace when the new Kent baby, Princess Alexandra, was christened on 9 February. Presently pantechnicons drew up outside 145 Piccadilly to move the new King and his family to Buckingham Palace. By 18 February the family were in, sad to have left their happy home for the sombre splendour of the Palace. The Princesses were relieved to learn that they would still use Royal Lodge at Windsor for most weekends.

The spring included its share of pony shows and fancy-dress parties, before a snowy Easter at Royal Lodge. As for Windsor Castle, not many changes were required because the Duke of Windsor had never moved in. The new King and Queen simply took over the rooms of George V and Queen Mary. The nursery needed no alteration. As his father had done, the King opened the East Terrace Gardens and on one Sunday ten thousand people turned out to listen to the bands of the Royal Horse Guards and the Coldstream

Guards. Princess Elizabeth came out into the town to witness her father unveil the Lutyens memorial to George V on St George's Day, and watched the Scouts march past on 25 April. So intense was the interest in the Royal Family that when the Princesses emerged from matins at St George's Chapel with Lord Wigram, then Deputy Constable of the Castle, they were confronted by excited crowds, some seated on walls, some even clinging to lamp-posts. They made their way on foot to the Moat Garden, and when they left by car, a number of people were hindering their progress to the quadrangle by attempting to climb onto the running boards. On her eleventh birthday, Princess Elizabeth was sent a tennis racquet and a gold wristlet watch by her uncle in his lonely Austrian exile.

The Coronation of Edward VIII had been set for 12 May. This date was retained for George VI. All the Archbishop of Canterbury had to do was to adapt the service to incorporate the crowning of Queen Elizabeth. Cosmo Gordon Lang, who had experienced serious misgivings at the prospect of placing the crown on the head of Edward VIII, was delighted to find a cooperative monarch, keen to participate fully in the ceremony.

The Princesses were excited. Their dresses were made, Garrard had created special coronets for them, and their miniature trains were embroidered by the Royal School of Needlework. On 6 May they went to a rehearsal at the Abbey with Queen Mary, the Princess Royal, and Gerald Lascelles to practise the processions. Three days later the King and Queen and their daughters paid a surprise visit to St George's Chapel for the pre-Coronation service. They had to come to London by an unusual route to avoid the crowds as the city wallowed in Coronation fever. There was an additional influx of visitors excited by the idea that the Princesses would be taking part. The crowd was universally devoted to Princess Elizabeth, and in South Africa, General Smuts commended her in a long Coronation address saying she had 'endeared herself to all'.[2]

On the day the Princesses travelled to Westminster Abbey in a carriage with their aunt, the Princess Royal. They were led into the Abbey by two grave Pursuivants and two Gentlemen Ushers, walking at either side of their aunt in the procession of the Princes and Princesses of the Blood Royal. The Princesses scarcely dared raise their eyes to look at the splendour around them. They held their hands tightly by their sides. They did their best to keep in step with their aunt. Princess Margaret Rose almost disappeared under the Princess Royal's train. Princess Elizabeth kept pace well, but Princess Margaret either dropped back or had to quicken her step.

Queen Mary had broken with tradition to be the first Dowager Queen to attend a Coronation in order to show solidarity and continuity.* The two sisters waited for their grandmother to process to the Royal Box: 'As Princess Elizabeth walked to her chair, she gave her train an expert flick out of the way before she sat down. Princess Margaret Rose tried to do likewise, but met with less success.'[3]

The first-class cricketer, René MacColl, then employed by the *Daily Telegraph* as special correspondent, was in the Abbey that day. He noted Princess Elizabeth's 'great decorum' as she shared points of interest with Queen Mary in the Order of Service. He found Princess Margaret 'more exuberant. Not only the scene before her but the people behind and on either side of her attracted her excited attention.' The Princess Royal had to answer a stream of questions. When she drew her niece's attention to the magnificent gold altar plate, Princess Margaret 'at once craned forward, her nose flattened on the ledge, and gazed in round-eyed wonder at the splendid vessels. Then she whispered volubly to the Princess Royal and finally succeeded in drawing her elder sister into the conversation.'[4]

Henrietta Bell, wife of the Bishop of Chichester, watched the arrival of Queen Elizabeth, how she entered very gravely, but then how 'a gleam of a smile' crossed her 'serious face' when she saw 'the two eager little faces' of the Princesses watching from the Royal Box. Princess Margaret, somewhat restless at the age of six, wriggled about in her seat and swung her legs. Her elder sister 'glared at her severely from the other side of the Princess Royal'.[5]

As Princess Elizabeth watched her parents being crowned, it must have been borne in on her that one day she would be sitting in King Edward's Chair as her father's successor. But on that magnificent day in 1937, it was a distant prospect.

She and her sister joined Queen Mary in the Glass Coach for

---

* Queen Alexandra had remained quietly at Sandringham at the time of the 1911 Coronation.

the procession back to the Palace. Later they appeared on the balcony with the King and Queen, and gave a tea party for some children of their own age, including Prince Edward and the baby Princess Alexandra of Kent, and late at night as the crowd cheered on, the young Princess Elizabeth could not sleep and thrilled them by appearing at the nursery window.

Many foreign princes and potentates came to London especially for the Coronation. Among those coming from overseas were the Hereditary Grand Duke (George Donatus) of Hesse and his wife, the former Princess Cécile of Greece. She was the granddaughter of the Dowager Marchioness of Milford Haven, who took the pair to lunch with Queen Mary at Marlborough House on 7 May. Also with them was Princess Cécile's brother, Prince Philip of Greece, then a student at Gordonstoun, approaching his sixteenth birthday. The young Prince was not a guest at the Abbey,* but he must surely have seen the processions outside from some vantage point.

★ ★ ★ ★ ★

On 24 May Parliament discussed the Civil List provisions (which had been set at £6,000 a year in King Edward's reign, rising to £15,000 when she became twenty-one (assuming no brother was born).† Winston Churchill proclaimed that the 'ancient constitutional monarchy' was 'the most effectual barrier against one-man power or dictatorships arising, whether from the Right or Left'. Predictably, the maverick Communist MP Willie Gallacher‡ proposed that the King should be given £8 a week and 'live in a nice council house with a bit of a garden, where people who wanted to see him could

---

* Prince Philip was then about to be sixteen. The twelve-year-old Prince Alexander of Yugoslavia (son of Prince and Princess Paul), his first cousin once removed, was in the Abbey.

† Had a brother been born, he would have become Duke of Cornwall and been entitled to the revenues of the Duchy. Princess Elizabeth was not entitled to these, but the King used the revenues to defer costs on the Civil List.

‡ Willie Gallacher (1881–1965), one of the last Communist members of the House of Commons. He could be counted on to denigrate the monarchy at every turn. He was imprisoned several times in his career.

go and see him'. The Labour MP, Frederick Pethick-Lawrence* addressed the question of Princess Elizabeth, accepting that she should have an education that would provide her 'with the best means of understanding her position in every possible way', but he hoped she would not 'associate solely with rich people' but with all sorts 'in order that she may fully fit herself to take those high responsibilities which one day may be hers'.[6]

The Coronation summer was packed with engagements, in some of which the Princesses took part – the river voyage for the opening of the National Maritime Museum at Greenwich at the end of April, a massive inspection of Overseas Troops in the garden of Buckingham Palace, the Naval Review at Spithead, the Royal Tournament, the Empire Day Service at St Paul's Cathedral and Trooping the Colour. There was the state entry to Windsor, followed that evening by a colourful pageant. They went to a children's concert arranged by Sir Robert Mayer, conducted by Malcolm Sargent.

In St George's Chapel they listened to Dr William Harris playing the organ, the nave lit, as Canon Anthony Deane put it, 'by a dim radiance from without'.[7] They attended the great, revived Garter ceremony on 14 June, which so delighted their father, pausing to greet the old Duke of Connaught, a Knight of the Garter since 1867. He watched the procession from his car, in morning dress and a stylish white top hat. Princess Elizabeth observed her grandfather, the Earl of Strathmore, the recently retired Prime Minister, Earl Baldwin of Bewdley, the Duke of Norfolk (Earl Marshal at the Coronation) and the Duke of Beaufort (Master of the Horse) in the procession, which was somewhat delayed by the old Duke of Devonshire, leaning painfully on a stick, creating large gaps between the Knights. Princess Elizabeth's cousins, Sandy Ramsay and George Lascelles, were pages to Queen Mary.

Soon afterwards they joined their parents at Holyroodhouse in Edinburgh, and in August the King enjoyed shooting grouse at Balmoral. Back in London Queen Mary emerged from widowhood and took her grandchildren's wider education in hand. She began weekly expeditions, taking the children to the Tower of London,

---

* Frederick Pethick-Lawrence (1871–1961), a keen campaigner for women's suffrage, later a peer. He was much involved with the independence of India.

and later to see the Assyrian and Egyptian monuments and the Rosetta Stone in the British Museum, the new Bank of England building, and in February 1938 the London Museum, where the mechanical toys were a particular success. In March she took them to Westminster Abbey, where the Dean, Bishop Paul de Labilliere, explained some of the national treasures to them. Next was a visit to the Science Museum to explore the working models, the ships, the museum remaining open as usual while they were there. She took them to the National Portrait Gallery where, *inter alia*, they inspected the fine 1913 Lavery family group with the King, the Queen, the Prince of Wales and the Princess Royal. Princess Elizabeth enjoyed these excursions, but there was little rapport between Princess Margaret and her grandmother.

Their exposure to national life continued as they took their places in the Royal Gallery for the State Opening of Parliament for the first time. They met King Leopold of the Belgians on his state visit in November, the Prime Minister, Neville Chamberlain, and the American Ambassador, Joseph Kennedy, when they stayed at Windsor at Easter 1938.

The Countess of Strathmore

On 23 June 1938 the Countess of Strathmore died at the age of seventy-five. She had been much in the public eye as the mother of the Queen – at the Coronation, and the ceremonies of the Orders of the Garter and the Thistle. The Princesses stayed with the Strathmores for some days in August that year, and again in October.

In December the Strathmores came south to London to spend the winter at Cumberland Mansions, in Portman Square. They moved to Woolmers Park, the large home in Hertfordshire that they had bought in the 1920s. At the end of April 1938 Lady Strathmore became seriously ill. This was defined later as a slight heart attack from which, initially, she recovered. She was meant to attend the wedding of her granddaughter, Anne Bowes-Lyon to Viscount Anson. Thereafter, Queen Elizabeth visited her mother almost every day. Lady Strathmore died with the King and Queen at her bedside.

Her coffin was taken by train to Scotland for the funeral at Glamis on 27 June. The Princesses did not go but a cross of lilies was sent in their name. Nor did they join Queen Mary and other members of the Royal Family at the memorial service at St Martin-in-the-Fields in London on the same day. A visit to the Hippodrome was cancelled, but they were allowed to visit the zoo on 30 June.

★ ★ ★ ★ ★

In 1938 the children took cooking lessons at Sandringham, including icing cakes. Back in London, they found Buckingham Palace renovated, ducks provided for the lake by Sir Philip Sassoon, and they played with the budgerigars in what had been Queen Alexandra's aviary.

They both became Girl Guides in what was called the 1st Buckingham Palace Company of Girl Guides, Princess Elizabeth in Kingfisher Patrol, and Princess Margaret a Brownie in Leprechaun Six. The Princess Royal admitted them in December 1937 and, from February, a team of sixteen girls came regularly to the Palace to join them. On 19 June Princess Elizabeth wore her Girl Guides uniform publicly for the first time at a parade at Windsor Castle at which the Princess Royal and Princess Alice, Countess of Athlone, were both present in uniform.

Prince Edward and Princess Alexandra of Kent came to play in the Palace gardens, and when the Kent children were at Windsor the Princess Royal would bring her sons, George and Gerald, to lunch as they were both at Eton. The Princesses continued their lessons with Miss Daly at the Bath Club, Princess Elizabeth winning a Royal Life Saving Certificate for swimming, diving and life-saving. A schoolroom and a swimming-pool were installed at Royal Lodge.

Princess Elizabeth was committed to riding, first with her Shetland pony, Peggy, under the supervision of H. Owen, the stud groom at Windsor Castle. When with her parents at Naseby Hall, she had enjoyed watching a meet of the Pytchley Hounds at Boughton Cover. She had been fascinated by a fox that broke cover, posed on a wall and then jumped to safety into a ploughed field. That year Horace Smith, one of the 'best-loved and best-known characters'[8] in the equestrian world, gave her riding lessons at Buckingham Palace, invited by the Crown Equerry, Sir Arthur Erskine. He had

THE PRE-WAR YEARS, 1937-9

first come to the attention of the Yorks back in 1930 when Lady Allendale asked him to bring his sleigh and a Welsh pony to entertain the children at a Christmas party. The children were duly glued to the window, watching this magical sight. Later Princess Elizabeth would go to his Cadogan Riding School at Maidenhead, arriving for an hour's lesson at 9.30 a.m. in the summer or at eleven in the winter. Smith was proud to have been a hard taskmaster, aware that Princess Elizabeth would expect that of him. He found her well above average:

> She was very conscientious and anxious to improve her horsemanship, and her standard of riding, considering the small amount of lessons she had, soon became very high. She was just as interested in the care of horses as she was in riding them, and she asked me numerous questions concerning feeding and stable management and methods of training, which were not in the curriculum at all! She was always very fond of her ponies, and never forgot to bring carrots to give her mount after the lesson was over.[9]

In the summer the King and Queen undertook the state visit to Paris that had been postponed due to the death of Lady Strathmore. The French had hoped the Princesses would come too, and in advance of it, Paul Claudel, the French poet and dramatist, issued a poem including the lines:

> *Je vous aime, Elizabeth,*
> *Je vous aime, Marguerite,*
> *La grande et la plus petite ...*[10]

The Princesses did not go to Paris but Princess Elizabeth was given illuminated books, and Madame Bonnet, wife of the Foreign Minister, inspired the gift of the famous dolls called France and Marianne, which were widely exhibited then given to the sisters in November by the French Ambassador. The dolls were exhibited at St James's Palace with their trousseaux of haute-couture clothes from famous houses such as Lanvin and Worth, their twenty pieces of miniature luggage in aid of the Princess Elizabeth Hospital and a French charity. This made an enormous impression on the twenty-three thousand visitors who saw them, raising huge sums of money. An official pronounced: 'You could not buy the dolls and their outfits for £5,000.'*[11]

The King had to interrupt his Balmoral holiday to go south for the funeral of his cousin Prince Arthur of Connaught† on 16 September, on the day after Neville Chamberlain flew to Germany to visit Hitler. The crisis and fear of impending war kept him in London. The Queen joined him on 22 September. He was advised not to go to Clydeside when she went back to launch the *Queen Elizabeth* on 27 September 1938, but her daughters accompanied her. The liner was launched with a bottle of Australian wine in the presence of a crowd of thirty thousand. After that the Princesses returned to Balmoral and Queen Elizabeth went back to London. Chamberlain appeared to have brokered some peace, and on his next return from Germany on 30 September, he made his famous 'Peace in our time' speech. The King and Queen returned to Balmoral and the family came south on 18 October. At least Britain had time to prepare itself for the eventuality of war.

There was a further state visit in November, this time by King Carol of Romania, and his son Crown Prince Michael. December still had some normality, with a huge children's party for 150 at Buckingham Palace before the Royal Family gathered in large numbers at Sandringham for what became the last peacetime Christmas for some years. The King did not broadcast but he thanked the Lord Mayor of London for his New Year greetings, mentioning that he was sure the citizens of London would enter 1939 'in a spirit of hopeful resolution'.[12]

At the end of January the King arranged a mock ARP bombing

---

* The dolls were later exhibited in Canada. They are now displayed alongside Queen Mary's Dolls House in Windsor Castle.

† Prince Arthur of Connaught (1883–1938). He died of stomach cancer on 12 September, though this was not revealed at the time due to the stigma attached to any mention of cancer. When George V came to the throne, Prince Arthur and his father were the senior male members of the Royal Family and therefore prominent. Prince Arthur served as Governor-General of South Africa from 1920 to 1924. His old father was still alive, but was advised not to attend his son's funeral in Windsor Castle, on medical grounds.

raid over Sandringham, and in April a further such exercise at Windsor Castle. The Princesses and the Duke and Duchess of Kent took refuge in a bombproof shelter and were given a demonstration of first aid and decontamination processes. Security was generally tightened at Royal Lodge and Windsor Castle.

Princess Elizabeth had a busy thirteenth birthday, the King giving her a diamond-studded bracelet and her mother a new riding habit and some silk stockings. Queen Mary gave her a silver dressing-table set, each item bearing her initials. The Duke of Windsor did not forget her: from Paris he sent the latest cine-camera and a projector with which she proceeded to film her family in the afternoon. For her tea party Prince Edward and Princess Alexandra joined her as did the Allendale children and those of Sir Alec Hardinge.

On 6 May the King and Queen left for a seven-week tour of Canada. In those days such departures included a carriage procession through the streets of London to Waterloo Station, a civic reception at Portsmouth, the Princesses and senior members of the Royal Family accompanying them and waving the ship off as it sailed away. The two daughters stood on the jetty as the National Anthem was played. It was a tense moment and they were 'so overcome by emotion that they forgot to wave their handkerchiefs'.[13]

This was their first separation from their parents for any length of time (Princess Elizabeth having been too young to be aware of the 1927 antipodean tour). They continued to live at Buckingham Palace, the King hoping that this would make their absence less acute. In the evenings they wrote to their parents. Princess Elizabeth used her new cine camera and the results were sent to the King and Queen. There was even the occasional transatlantic telephone call, though this had to be set up in advance. The first came from St Paul's Walden Bury after a fortnight, where the sisters were spending the weekend with their uncle, David Bowes-Lyon.

Queen Mary took them on more of her sightseeing expeditions in the afternoons, beginning with a river trip on the Thames to see the docks at North Woolwich. The next day Lady Halifax took them to the zoo and they had their first ride on an elephant. And the following Monday Lady Helen Graham took them on their first ever ride on the London Underground, the escalator proving an interesting challenge.

The King and Queen returned to Southampton aboard *Empress of Britain* on 22 June. The day followed a reverse pattern from the departure, with a tumultuous welcome back on British land. There were cheers all the way through Southampton to the station and again to see the King and Queen in an open landau processing from Waterloo to Buckingham Palace. A crowd of fifty thousand burst through the cordons to cheer the Royal Family on the balcony of Buckingham Palace, at the conclusion of the first ever visit by a reigning monarch to what was called the New World. Harold Nicolson was inspired to describe Queen Elizabeth as 'in truth one of the most amazing Queens since Cleopatra'.[14] At the foot of a spectacularly detailed Court Circular account of the royal return, there was a solitary line: 'The Duke of Windsor is 45 today.'[15]

After a short rest, life returned to normal, though the international situation remained tense. The Princesses won swimming prizes, and they enjoyed the Royal Show in the Great Park, held over several days in July. Prince and Princess Paul of Yugoslavia* came on a state visit, and stayed on for many days due to his dental problems. Cecil Beaton was sent by the Duchess of Kent to photograph Princess Olga, and as a result was summoned by Queen Elizabeth for the famous first session with her in the garden and the Yellow Drawing Room – in which she wore her white dresses and a Winterhalter evening dress. And then the Royal Family headed to Dartmouth on a visit that, arguably, changed the course of royal history.

Dartmouth 1939

On 22 July the King and Queen brought the Princesses to inspect the Royal Naval College and this was where Princess Elizabeth first remembered setting eyes on Prince Philip of Greece. She had been in the same room as him before, but had not focused on him.

The previous day began with a visit to their old home, 145 Piccadilly, where they inspected an exhibition of royal and historical

---

* Prince Paul (1893–1976), wartime Regent of Yugoslavia, and Princess Olga of Greece (1903–97), sister of the Duchess of Kent. They had lately been on a state visit to Hitler in Germany.

THE PRE-WAR YEARS, 1937–9

treasures, arranged for charity by Princess Alice, Countess of Athlone. They listened to a Russian musician, Sacha Votichenko, a descendant of Louis XIV's court musician, play the only surviving tympanon royale (a kind of frame drum) from 1705, which had been used at Versailles until the Revolution of 1789.

They took a special train from Paddington to Weymouth. Significantly, Prince Philip's uncle, Captain Lord Louis Mountbatten, was in attendance as a Personal Naval ADC and he travelled with them. The royal party was given a huge welcome at Weymouth, met a celebrated local centenarian, Mary Wallis, regrettably known as 'Grannie Wallis', then embarked in a pinnace, which took them to HM Yacht *Victoria and Albert*, which voyaged to Torbay.

The next day they arrived at Dartmouth, where many picturesquely adorned boats, 'rainbow fashion', were in the harbour, and the streets were gaily decorated, even though this was described as a private visit. On arrival the King was in a blue lounge suit, the Queen was in powder blue and the Princesses in coats and berets of Eton blue. The King had been at Dartmouth as a cadet between 1911 and 1913 and had undergone a further brief stay there in 1919. The plan was for the Royal Family to watch the cadets in their sporting activities but rain curtailed this. All four planted commemorative trees. When Princess Margaret planted hers, the King jested: 'You must do it at the double. You are with the Navy now.'[16] They watched some sailing races and then returned to the Royal Yacht.

There was a second visit the following day, Sunday. On this occasion the King was in the undress uniform of Admiral of the Fleet. He inspected the 502 Dartmouth cadets and the 81 special-entry ones. The King and Queen went to church. Meanwhile the Princesses were entertained in the Captain's House. The royal party returned to *Victoria and Albert* at 7 p.m. and, according to *The Times*, all the cadets in a huge flotilla of blue boats escorted the yacht into Start Bay. The King asked that summer leave be extended from 21 September to 26 September to commemorate his visit (though by then Britain would be at war with Germany).

Much in evidence throughout the two days was the young cadet, Prince Philip of Greece, detailed to look after the young Princesses. He was one of the eager rowers who escorted the yacht into the bay. The King had met him at the funeral of his uncle and guardian, the Marquess of Milford Haven, in April 1938, and earlier that year, on 2 May, Victoria Milford Haven had taken him and his sister Margarita of Hohenlöhe-Langenburg to visit the King and Queen at Buckingham Palace. The press did not notice him during the Dartmouth visit, but Princess Elizabeth certainly did. From that moment on, he was firmly fixed in her mind. To some degree the die was cast.

More significantly, Lord Louis Mountbatten, ever ambitious, had logged the possibility of a future marriage. Up to that point, contrary to what he liked people to believe, Mountbatten had taken scant interest in his nephew, though his wife Edwina had generously paid for much of his school education. Mountbatten only assumed a stronger role in the young prince's life following the death of Lord Milford Haven. He was one of those who steered Prince Philip into the British Royal Navy.

At that fateful meeting Prince Philip was eighteen and Princess Elizabeth was thirteen.

6
THE WAR, 1939–45

'The evidence and the example of their steadfastness, rooted in the serenity of a happy home life and expressed in selfless service to their people, has steadied and encouraged the whole nation all through these years ...'
Geoffrey Fisher, Archbishop of Canterbury.[1]

The Second World War dominated the lives of the Princesses during these next years rather as the First World War had done that of their mother. Princess Elizabeth matched her in age. Each war lasted through their teenage years.

The Royal Family went up to Balmoral on 1 August for their normal holiday, hoping to stay until the end of September. There was a King's camp (formerly the Duke of York's camp) at nearby Abergeldie Castle, and the Royal Family joined the boys to sing the traditional 'Chestnut Tree' song. The imminence of war caused the King to go south to inspect the Reserve Fleet at Weymouth while the Queen and her daughters went to Glamis for some days. He returned to Balmoral but was soon back in London, followed by Queen Elizabeth on the morning of 29 August. The Princesses stayed in Scotland, unaware that this was to be the start of a long separation from their parents.

On 3 September war was declared. The King looked back at his days as a midshipman in 1914: 'We were not prepared for what we found a modern war really was, & those of us who had been through the Great War never wanted another.'[2] He broadcast 'a declaration of simple faith in simple beliefs' to his people, including the words: 'Over and over again we have tried to find a peaceful way out of the differences between ourselves and those who are now our enemies ... There may be dark days ahead ...'[3]

The Princesses moved to Birkhall with cousins and friends, while Queen Mary set off to Badminton to spend the war with her niece, the Duchess of Beaufort, a plan long made. The Duke of Bedford pitied the Duke of Beaufort: 'I hear he's got Queen Mary in his house. I'm sorry for him poor fella ... It's hard lines on him.'[4] Queen Elizabeth was able to see her daughters between 20 and 26 September, but other than that, their only contact was a nightly telephone call at 6 p.m. Many children, including children of their class, were evacuated to Canada. But there was no question of the Princesses leaving. One of the reassuring messages subtly given by the King and Queen was that they were staying in London with their people. However bad things seemed, there was optimism.

The Queen referred to their separation in her first wartime broadcast, which she had run past the Archbishop of Canterbury:

> Many of you have had to see your family life broken up – your husband going off to his allocated task – your children evacuated to places of greater safety. The King and I know what it means to be parted from our children ...[5]

The Princesses continued with their lessons under Crawfie's tutelage, the house run by Sir Basil Brooke as Comptroller, and Mrs Geoffrey Bowlby, one of the Queen's ladies in waiting. There was also a French governess, Georgina Guérin, who disliked Lettice Bowlby and referred to her as *'la sale Bowlbee'*. Nor did Princess Elizabeth like Georgina. At the beginning of the war she returned to France and became a figure in the French Resistance.*

The sisters were happy to hear that they could go to Sandringham for what was the last more or less normal Christmas for some years, a relatively brave decision because Sandringham, near the Norfolk coast, was far from inaccessible to German bombers. From there they went to Royal Lodge. In January 1940, it was announced: 'Princess Elizabeth and Princess Margaret left Buckingham Palace for their new evacuation home in the country.'[6] Their precise location was never made public, though residents of Windsor used to

---

* When, years later, on a state visit to France, the Queen met her governess, she felt she was a girl of twelve all over again.

spot them riding in the Great Park, and there were occasional references in the press to Princess Elizabeth celebrating a birthday in the Windsor area. At Easter 1940 it was publicly confirmed that the Princesses were riding in the park.

On 11 May, shortly after the fall of France the Princesses were moved into Windsor Castle for their better safety. 'We went for a weekend and stayed for five years,' Princess Margaret recalled years later.[7] She made two further statements about their life there. 'It was surrounded by barbed wire, which wouldn't have kept the Germans out, but certainly kept us in.' And: 'I was brought up by the Grenadier Guards – men from *Munchester* and the Duke of Grafton.'[8]

Princess Elizabeth riding at Windsor

But they were contained in the castle. Besides riding in the Great Park, they went to Royal Lodge or Frogmore; they used to visit Alathea Fitzalan Howard* at Cumberland Lodge. Young George Hardinge, son of Sir Alec, took them to the shooting range at Eton.

Windsor Castle was a perfect base for them and the Queen said in later life that it held all her childhood memories. The Royal Family lived in the Upper Ward, with sweeping views over the East

---

* Alathea Fitzalan Howard (1923–2001), granddaughter of Viscount Fitzalan of Derwent, who lived at Cumberland Lodge. Author of *The Windsor Diaries*.

Terrace and the stretching lawns of the Home Park. Members of the Household came and went, but the housekeeper, Alice Bruce,* who was fond of the Princesses, was there throughout the war. They were drawn to the kitchen by enticing smells, and presently she taught them how to cook kippers.

The Middle Ward contained the Round Tower and the Norman Tower, home of the Deputy Constable and Lieutenant-Governor. That office was held by Lord Wigram, who lived there throughout the war, to be replaced in April 1945 by the Earl of Gowrie VC.† The King's Private Secretary was Sir Alec Hardinge. He lived in the Winchester Tower with his wife, Helen, who had been a childhood friend of Queen Elizabeth. Their children, in particular their daughters Winifred (Win) and Elizabeth (Libby),‡ were close friends of the princesses. Sir Alec was responsible for steering the new King into his role, but in July 1943 Hardinge and Alan (Tommy) Lascelles fell out. As a result, Hardinge resigned and Lascelles and his family moved into the Winchester Tower.

The Lower Ward housed the College of St George, presided over by the Dean of Windsor, Albert Baillie until 1944, known to some as 'Albertus Magnificus', sometimes seen in an astrakhan overcoat, and then by Bishop Eric Hamilton, nicknamed 'Unctuous Eric' by Tommy Lascelles, and thought not to have been the Royal Family's favourite chaplain. Three hundred guardsmen were quartered in the Mews and St George's Chapel was not big enough for them all, so Dean Baillie asked the King if he could use St George's Hall for services. The King and Queen and the Princesses worshipped there during the war.[9] There

---

* Alice Bruce (1885–1960). She had worked for Lady Desborough at Panshanger until 1939.

† The 1st Earl of Gowrie (1872–1955) won his VC for spectacular gallantry while serving in the Sudan: he had snatched a wounded Egyptian officer away from advancing Dervishes and taken him to safety. He served as Governor-General of Australia 1936–44. He was also Colonel of the Welsh Guards. He was Deputy Constable of Windsor Castle until 1953.

‡ Libby, in particular, was to be a lifelong friend. She married Lieutenant-Colonel Sir John Johnston, Comptroller of the Lord Chamberlain's Office. For many years they lived at Adelaide Cottage, and in retirement at Studio Cottage, behind Cumberland Lodge.

were three canons, Stafford Crawley (who prepared the Princesses for confirmation), Anthony Deane (who wrote the fourth leader in *The Times* on Saturdays) and Sidney Ollard (nicknamed 'Golf-bags').[10]

The castle contained its share of memorable figures. Lieutenant-General Sir Charles Kavanagh, who had commanded the Cavalry Corps at the Battle of Amiens, was Governor of the Military Knights. Another formidable presence was the outspoken Florence Carteret-Carey, widow of a previous governor, known as 'Floodlit Flo' on account of her pronounced make-up. Major-General Sir John Hanbury-Williams, the retired Marshal of the Diplomatic Corps, lived in the Henry III Tower. His painfully thin daughter, Gwladys, sometime Mayor of Windsor, ran the Girl Guides troupe in which the Princesses and their friends served. Once the Princesses received a letter from Gwladys, but could not read it, so they put it on the floor and danced around it. Mrs Lionel (May) Ford, the widowed mother of (Sir) Edward Ford,* lived at 24 The Cloisters.

The Librarian, Sir Owen Morshead, lived with his wife in Garden House. He was an erudite man, described by Dean Baillie as the 'perfect' librarian, who worked only 'for peace and goodwill',[11] unlike some of the castle community who delighted in causing dissension.†

Lord Gowrie's widowed daughter-in-law, Pamela, Viscountess Ruthven, and her two sons, Grey and Malise (Skimper), came to live with him in the Norman Tower in 1945. Although she wrote of a post-war phase, the challenges were the same. Lady Morshead warned her that she would have to choose between the world of the court and bringing up her children. She quoted Queen Victoria's words to Randall Davidson, that Windsor was 'a place of rather a gossiping nature, requiring tact and judgement'.[12]

Pamela noted how the wives of courtiers 'often came to resent the refined living their husbands enjoyed and the hours they spent away from the necessarily restricted post-war home'.[13] She cited an example of 'residual British stuffiness' when the Master of the Household, Sir Piers (Joey) Legh berated her for bringing William

---

* Sir Edward Ford (1910–2006), Assistant Private Secretary to George VI, 1946–52, and to Queen Elizabeth II, 1952–67.

† Dean Baillie's life was made miserable by the famous Canon Dalton (until he died in 1931), Eric Hamilton's by Canon Deane.

Douglas-Home to an Ascot ball, despite Princess Margaret having invited him as her escort. The future playwright had been sentenced to a year's imprisonment and hard labour for refusing to attack Le Havre when it was still full of civilians. As she wrote: 'Poor William retreated across the quadrangle, his visage blackened by rage or humiliation.'[14] Pamela's sons were corralled into Madame Vacani's dancing classes and at the end of lessons for the under-tens loved nothing more than to grab one of the Princesses 'to tread on her toes and whirl her around for a brief spin'.[15]

Living in Adelaide Cottage in the Home Park, Sir Grismond (Jackie) Philipps* was in charge of the Castle Company guarding the King during the war. He was enormously popular, one of the men telling the Dean of Windsor: 'The fact is, he's a soldier on parade and a father to us off.'[16] Philipps and his wife Joan made a point of entertaining the Princesses and their girlfriends to tea parties in the officers' sitting room or at Adelaide Cottage, where they could play games such as charades with the Grenadier Guards officers and Life Guards, stationed in the castle. While many of the girls fell for the officers, ironically it was Lady Joan Philipps who fell for a widowed Life Guard and separated from her husband.

Among the Grenadiers and Life Guards were the Hon. Robert Cecil (later 6th Marquess of Salisbury) and, among others, Hugo Waterhouse, Philip Profumo, Francis Legh, Francis Wigram and Michael Farebrother. There were plenty of girlfriends too, including Diana Legh, Anne Crichton, Zelda Loyd, Barbadee Knight, Lady Elizabeth Lambart, Sarah Dashwood and Mary Morshead. Later in the war, Louise Cockcraft and Dawn Simpson† joined the Girl

---

* Sir Grismond Philipps, CVO (1898-1967), a former Captain in the Grenadier Guards, then Lieutenant-Colonel Commanding, 4th Battalion Welch Regiment, later Lord Lieutenant of Carmarthenshire, and a founder of TWW television. His wife was Lady Joan Wentworth-Fitzwilliam (1900–2001), daughter of Earl Fitzwilliam. In 1949 she married Lieutenant-Colonel Wallace Cuninghame, DSO, 16th of Caprington (1889–1959).

† They were the daughters of Military Knights: Louise Cockcraft (1930–2012), later Nickson, daughter of Lieutenant-Colonel Louis Cockcraft, DSO (1880–1963), and Dawn Simpson (1929–84), later Fahey, daughter of Major Edward Simpson, OBE, MC (1876–1954).

Guides troop. From May 1944, Group Captain Peter Townsend arrived as the new equerry, the King having chosen young men from the different services – Townsend from the RAF, Oliver Dawnay from the army and Toby Marten from the Royal Navy.

In the centre of this world were the two Princesses, such devoted companions to each other that they formed an impenetrable bond. There were the Elphinstone cousins, Margaret Elphinstone living with them from November 1943, and sometimes the Duke of Kent brought his children over from Coppins, though usually separately, because Prince Edward and his sister Alexandra proved too much of a handful when together.

The diaries of Alathea Fitzalan Howard give an idea of Princess Elizabeth's life during these years. Alathea took an almost obsessive interest in Princess Elizabeth. She disliked her own mother, found her father dull, and was living at Cumberland Lodge with her distinguished octogenarian grandfather, Viscount Fitzalan of Derwent. She relished any invitation from the ever-welcoming and inclusive Queen Elizabeth, finding in the castle 'with its gilded rooms and red corridors ... an atmosphere of happy family life'[17] that she had never known. She took part in Madame Vacani's dance classes and any outdoor activities to which she was summoned, these conducted under the ever-vigilant supervision of Crawfie. She took part in Girl Guide activities with the Princesses. They went skating and fishing together. They played charades; the royal Corgis were never far away. Alathea's diaries are filled with the predictable preoccupations of all teenage girls, one of them being the first time they were kissed by a young man.* As they grew older, wartime was alleviated by the occasional evening party that lasted till 4 a.m., with dancing in the Red Drawing Room and sitting out in the Green Drawing Room.

Alathea was three years older than Princess Elizabeth and had been better educated. She described the Princess as 'placid and unemotional ... she never suffers, therefore she never strongly desires'.[18] She regretted that her royal friend did not need the company of others, and could not be drawn out of her shell. In 1942 she

---

* By August 1943 Sonia Graham-Hodgkinson had been kissed by a man called Tim Barclay, in a car coming back from a party.

judged her 'unusually set in her ideas for fifteen, none of her friends could ever influence her'. She thought the Princess missed a lot by not being able to 'picture herself as the Princesses she reads of in past centuries – her own ancestors!'[19]

As Princess Elizabeth approached her sixteenth birthday, Alathea went further, finding her tastes childish, her nature simple and unsophisticated, her feet 'planted in less idealistic but infinitely firmer soil'. Therefore she could be happy as her thoughts never soared 'above the ordinary'.[20] In other words she lacked imagination. Throughout her life, she preferred straight facts to speculation. She was not given to whimsical philosophising.

★ ★ ★ ★ ★

In her April 2020 Covid broadcast from Windsor Castle, the Queen mentioned her wartime broadcast nearly eighty years before. On 13 October 1940 she spoke to children at home and overseas, inaugurating a series of broadcasts aimed at children evacuated abroad. She spoke of her shared love of the wireless's Children's Hour, and said: 'We know from experience what it means to be away from those we love most of all.' Her message was:

> We are trying to do all we can to help our gallant sailors, soldiers, and airmen and we are trying, too, to bear our own share of the danger and sadness of war. We know, every one of us, that in the end, all will be well; for God will care for us and give us victory and peace. And when peace comes, remember it will be for us, the children of to-day, to make the world of to-morrow a better and happier place.

Princess Margaret came on at the end to add, 'Goodnight, children.' The message was widely heard and generally well received. In Canada, children and grown-ups were impressed, some churches had wireless receiving sets installed so that it could be heard and, according to agency messages from New York, the broadcast was one of the most effective ever received from London. Alathea wrote: 'My heart went out to her.'[21] *The Times* judged: 'In these days the words are no mere convention; for what we are striving for is that our children should have good nights and good days when we have beaten down the evil that overshadows the nights and days of all civilized people.'[22] On 10 November the Archbishop of Canterbury was walking in the park at Windsor, when staying with May Ford, and he ran into the King and Queen with the young Princesses. He congratulated Princess Elizabeth on her 'quite admirably spoken broadcast to children – her first address, strange to think, to what may be her future subjects!'[23] Not everyone liked it. Jock Colville, her future Private Secretary thought her voice 'most impressive' but was embarrassed by 'the sloppy sentiment she was made to express'.[24] A record was sold in aid of the Princess Elizabeth of York Hospital for children in Shadwell.

Princess Elizabeth grew up a serious girl. In her character there was an element of the head girl of a smart girl's school. She expected people to listen to her and to take in what she said. She developed a retentive mind, with an excellent memory despite a slightly haphazard education.

From faraway Badminton, Queen Mary steered the children's education. She had long taken a dim view of Queen Elizabeth's 'all things bright and beautiful' approach to life. Queen Mary wanted more history in the children's syllabus and thought not enough time given to Bible studies. Knowing that the Archbishop of Canterbury saw the King and Queen, she prevailed on him. She kept in touch with Crawfie, who sent a long report on the Princesses' progress, which Queen Mary sent to the Archbishop. From this we learn that lessons began punctually at 9.15 a.m., and that Henry Marten covered the history of America, the discoveries and explorers from Columbus up to the then present day. He saw 'great stuff' in Princess Elizabeth and judged that she 'compared very well with Eton boys a year older than she'. He walked up and down, suddenly 'larking out': '"Is that quite clear to you, gentlemen?"' Both Princesses were playing the piano willingly, and entertaining the household with duets after Sunday lunch. Sir Owen Morshead 'such a delightful and learned person' met them in the library, talked over the history, then showed them round the castle. Canon Crawley did the same with St George's Chapel. Every hour of the day was filled:

Princess Margaret has developed wonderfully. She is much more of a companion now for Princess Elizabeth. I think Your Majesty will be delighted at the change in Princess Margaret. At lessons she is a joy to teach — always asking questions. Their French is perfectly delightful to listen to and what pleases me more than anything is, that at lunch which we have together and with Their Majesties they talk nothing but French to Mrs Smith (Mrs Smith is French).[25]

Hubert Tannar, headmaster of the Royal School in Windsor Great Park, put on a successful nativity play in St George's Hall, Princess Elizabeth leading the procession of three kings as they advanced the whole length of the hall carrying their gifts to Baby Jesus. The Princess looked like Edward V in her Coronation Crown and tunic of pink and gold. Princess Margaret played the small peasant child who had 'nothing to give' but herself and sang 'Gentle Jesus' in the last scene. The Dean of Windsor told Crawfie that it was 'the most peaceful half-hour he had spent since the outbreak of war'. Crawfie ended: 'Your Majesty I do not think there is much more to say. The children are happy and well; and are having knowledge poured in as fast as I can pour it in.'[26]

Mr Tannar loved amateur theatricals. The state portraits had been removed from the Waterloo Chamber. He painted cartoon characters where once they hung.* Princess Elizabeth helped weave in family jokes, with hidden allusions, references to the progress of the war, and in-jokes about members of the Royal Household. In *Aladdin* there was a dig at 'Sir Kerald Jelly', referring to the portrait painter, Sir Gerald Kelly, who had taken up permanent residence in the castle working away at large, stolidly conventional portraits of the King and Queen in their Coronation robes. Tommy Lascelles watched a performance of the *Sleeping Beauty* in 1942 and, having feared that he might drop off to sleep himself, was impressed: 'Some of the scenes would have done credit to Drury Lane, and the whole thing went with a slickness and confidence that amazed me.'[27] Lascelles also thought Princess Elizabeth made a 'charming' Aladdin the following year.

---

* These were exposed unexpectedly following the 1992 fire when again the portraits were removed.

THE WAR, 1939–45

In 1944, when Marten asked Tommy Lascelles how far he should go in instructing Princess Elizabeth about the constitutional position of the Crown, Lascelles said he should withhold nothing, even repeating Dunning's* celebrated 1780 resolution: 'That the influence of the Crown has increased, is increasing and ought to be diminished.'[28]

In 1941 Frances Towers† published *The Two Princesses*, written for the National Sunday School Union and advertised as containing 'twenty charming illustrations'. Her conclusion was:

> Princess Elizabeth, tall and self-possessed, is looking more like Queen Mary than ever, and one reads in the winningly serious little face that genius for duty that made a great king of the very ordinary man who was George the Fifth. There is merriment in her eyes, and friendliness and kindliness too. At her feet sit the inevitable Corgis ...[29]

Churchill sent Princess Elizabeth roses on her fifteenth birthday and she sent him a thoughtful and encouraging letter of thanks: 'I am afraid you have been having a very worrying time lately, but I am sure things will begin to look up again soon.'[30] She donated aluminium items from her little Welsh house to the war effort. She gained the Royal Life Saving Society's junior artificial-respiration award in 1941, and on 23 July, both Princesses performed a concert with songs, dances, piano pieces and even a duet in French – in aid of buying wool and comforts for the forces. They enjoyed digging for victory, producing vegetables. For four years running the Princesses performed in pantomimes, *Cinderella* in December 1941, *Sleeping Beauty* in December 1942, *Aladdin* in 1943 and *Old Mother Red Riding Boots* in 1944.

On 24 February 1942 Princess Elizabeth began her eighty-year association with the Grenadier Guards, when she succeeded her great-great-uncle, the Duke of Connaught, as Colonel. The old Duke had left more of an impression on her than some of her other elderly relations. She had seen him inspecting the Yeomen of the Guard and at other great occasions of state. He died aged ninety-one

---

* John Dunning (1731–83), 1st Lord Ashburton, a lawyer and politician.
† Frances Towers (1885–1948) was a teacher at Southlands School, Harrow. She wrote articles and short stories. Her only novel, *Tea with Mr Rochester*, was published posthumously. She loved Gothic architecture, Old Masters and mountains.

on 16 January. This appointment forged an extraordinary link with the past. The Duke was her godfather. He was a godson of the great Duke of Wellington, immortalised in the famous Winterhalter picture, *The 1st May*. Furthermore the Duke of Wellington had been Colonel of the Grenadier Guards from 1827 until his death in 1852.*

She was confirmed on 28 March by Cosmo Gordon Lang in the 'ugly private chapel' at the castle in his last duty as Archbishop before he retired. He had a long talk with her the night before, finding her 'not naturally very communicative' but showing 'real intelligence and understanding'. He was acutely aware of 'the responsibilities which may be awaiting her in the future – this future more than ever unknown ...'[31]

On her sixteenth birthday Princess Elizabeth signed on at the Labour Exchange, dressed in her Girl Guides uniform. She inspected some five hundred guardsmen as they marched past and gave an impressive party for them in the evening, before a private dance.

On 4 August she attended the christening of Prince Michael of Kent, which gave Queen Mary the chance to examine her on a rare visit from Badminton: 'Lilibet much grown, very pretty eyes and complexion, pretty figure.'[32] The Royal Family were at Sandringham when they heard that the Duke of Kent had been killed in a flying accident on his way to Iceland on 25 August. Meanwhile other relations were in danger: her cousin George Lascelles was imprisoned at Colditz Castle in Germany and her maternal cousin, John Elphinstone, was another of the '*prominente*' incarcerated there. Both survived.

It was a pleasant diversion for the wartime Prime Minister, Winston Churchill, to consider how best to prepare Princess Elizabeth for her eventual role as Queen. In June 1943 he recommended to Lord Simon, the Lord Chancellor, that since she was soon to be eighteen, she should be appointed a member of the Council of State, so that she 'should have every opportunity of acquiring experience in affairs'.[33] He asked the King to amend the Regency Act of 1937. She became first a Counsellor of State in July 1944, when the King

---

* Prince Albert was Colonel, 1852–61, then Prince George, Duke of Cambridge, 1861–1904. The Duke was Colonel, 1904–42. The first Colonel was appointed in 1656.

visited the Italian battlefields, soon after her eighteenth birthday. But an idea mooted by the Cabinet in January 1944 that she should be created Princess of Wales, which appealed to Churchill, was vetoed by the King who understood these things better than his ministers.

Horace Smith had trained his young protégée so well that she won the private driving class at the Royal Windsor Horse Show in 1944. He taught her to ride side-saddle, a skill she would presently need.* She often went out with a governess cart, two pet Corgis and Princess Margaret. Occasionally photographs were released showing Queen Elizabeth in the cart with her daughters riding bicycles behind her. These images represented a world of peace in strong contrast to the unpleasant images of Nazis stomping about in boots and black uniforms. When General Sir Alan Brooke spent a weekend at the castle, he came away describing the King, Queen and their two daughters as 'a thoroughly close-knit and happy family all wrapped up in each other'.[34]

The first of their friends got married, Winifred Hardinge to Anthony Murray, both Princesses attending the wedding on 10 July. Princess Elizabeth had attended her first ball at the castle in July 1941. She went out to dinner for the first time, sitting next to old Lord Fitzalan at Cumberland Lodge, on 25 November 1943, dressed in pale yellow chiffon. In March 1944 she lunched for the first time in a hotel, with her aunt Marina, Duchess of Kent, at Claridge's. On 1 May that year she attended her first official dinner – for the Dominion Prime Ministers at Buckingham Palace, sitting between Field Marshal Smuts of South Africa and William Mackenzie-King of Canada.

★ ★ ★ ★ ★

On 23 October 1942 the Princesses paid a rare visit to Buckingham Palace, heavily shuttered in wartime. Mrs Roosevelt had been invited by Queen Elizabeth over from the USA to see wartime conditions in Britain, more specifically to inspect US troops stationed here and

---

* Horace Smith was always concerned lest the Princess should have a bad riding accident. The worst experience was when she was badly bruised at Balmoral, being thrown from her horse against a tree.

to see the role women were playing in wartime. Princess Elizabeth impressed the President's wife as 'quite serious and a child with a great deal of character and personality. She asked me a great number of questions about life in the United States and they were serious questions.'[35]

For some time Audrey Withers, editor of *Vogue*, had wanted Cecil Beaton to photograph Queen Elizabeth in the simple, often re-worn outfits she favoured during the war. She also wanted photographs of the Princesses – 'the children who stayed in England' – having 'a happy, normal life'. She thought this would be 'excellent propaganda'.[36] It did not happen until Queen Elizabeth summoned Cecil Beaton to photograph the Royal Family with Mrs Roosevelt in the Bow Room, giving Beaton his first opportunity to observe Princess Elizabeth at first hand. For the next thirty years or more his forensic eyes would be observing her. That day he wrote:

> I was enthusiastic to see how very much more charming Princess Elizabeth has become than any of the photographs I have seen of her. She has her mother's smile – is extremely well brought up – and has a great knowledge of history.[37]

A further sitting followed a week later, when the Princesses wore their pink taffeta dresses, and then in 1943 Sir Eric Miéville, the Queen's Private Secretary, summoned Beaton to photograph them at Windsor Castle:

> The Princesses appeared on the Gothic landing I had elected for the pictures. They looked quite pretty in nondescript dresses – but there had been no time to plan anything specially nice for them and they did not seem to have had their hair freshly washed ... Princess Elizabeth has grown ... When her face lights into a smile she is delightful. She has the same hesitance of speech as her mother – though when the Queen is present her daughter is most silent.[38]

When he photographed the Princesses again in 1945, he noted what so many of the photographers who took portrait photographs of Princess Elizabeth also said:

Princess Elizabeth's easy charm, like her mother's, does not carry across in her photographs, and each time one sees her one is delighted to find how much more serene, magnetic, and at the same time meltingly sympathetic, she is than one imagined. In the photographs there is a certain heaviness which is not there in real life, and one misses, even in colour photographs, the effect of her dazzlingly fresh complexion, the clear regard from the glass-blue eyes, and the gentle, all-pervading sweetness of her smile.[39]

In other words, unlike Princess Margaret, she was not photogenic. Anthony Buckley said the same thing years later: 'You look through the lens and gasp – and then you see the result when it is printed ...'[40]

★ ★ ★ ★ ★

In January 1944 Lady Violet Bonham Carter told Winston Churchill that her son Mark, who had lately escaped from a prisoner-of-war camp in Italy, had been summoned to Windsor by Princess Elizabeth, Colonel of his regiment, the Grenadier Guards, to tell her of his experiences. This morphed into a dinner and dance with champagne and music.

On 21 April that year she reached her eighteenth birthday and Churchill celebrated this milestone event in a characteristically Churchillian way. He sent her his biography of the great Duke of Marlborough. Politely she thanked him: 'There is nothing I would rather have than your *Life of Marlborough*, and I thank you most warmly for giving it to me.' She then revealed what she had really enjoyed: 'I spent a very busy but very pleasant birthday among relatives and a great many Grenadiers, which made it a very happy day for me.'[41] A few days later she danced with Mark Bonham Carter and contemplated her future in public life: 'I feel it's *started*,'[42] she told him.

In November, consistent with his wish to prepare her as a future constitutional monarch, Churchill sent her a copy of the King's Speech that he was to deliver in Parliament the next day. He told her that this was a tradition that had been established in the reign of Queen Victoria. It was probably more successful than Peter Pears singing *La Bohème* to the Queen and Princesses as an introduction to opera that May. Even the tenor thought it 'most unsuitable'.[43]

* * * * *

In March 1945 Princess Elizabeth joined the ATS. She might have preferred to join the WRNS, but the ATS had headquarters in Windsor. This was a popular move in the country but not with Alathea, who thought she looked awful in her military trousers, was shocked that she was seen about wearing them and that she was allowed to drive all over the place – even halfway to London. Princess Elizabeth learned to map read and began a course at Camberley.

She did not serve for long. On 8 May peace was declared in Europe, the King and Queen and both Princesses appearing with Winston Churchill on the balcony of Buckingham Palace. That evening they went out into the crowd with a group of male escorts to join in the celebrations with the joyous Londoners. Years later she told Godfrey Talbot: 'I remember lines of unknown people linking arms and walking down Whitehall and we were all swept along by tides of happiness and relief.'[44] The war over. The King told Lady Cranborne that his greatest fear had been lest a parachutist landed in the Palace forecourt and kidnapped him. It never happened.[45]

The world was not the same. The princesses had known friends who had served and who had died; 145 Piccadilly, where they lived until 1937, had been destroyed by bombs. The Bath Club, where they had learned to swim, had gone the same way. But there was peace.

7
ENTER PRINCE PHILIP, 1941–6

'Whither the storm carries, I go a willing guest'
Prince Philip in Australia, 1945

For Christmas 1944 Prince Philip sent Princess Elizabeth a photograph of himself. According to Princess Margaret she 'danced round the room with it for joy!'[1]

His name was mentioned in conversation with Alathea in April 1941. She asked who he was. 'Prince Philip of Greece,' they said, and started to giggle. Princess Elizabeth then let Alathea into her secret. He was 'her boy'. The sisters asked Alathea if she had a 'boy'. Alathea mentioned her affection for Robert Cecil. 'We part today the wiser for two secrets,'[2] said Princess Elizabeth.

The now celebrated Dartmouth meeting in 1939 had taken place when Prince Philip was eighteen and Princess Elizabeth was thirteen. His life had not been easy, though he chose to believe that he had had a perfectly happy childhood. He had great respect for his father, Prince Andrew of Greece. When I was writing about his mother, he convinced me that he *thought* his father was a good father, but he failed to convince me that Prince Andrew *was in fact a good father.* He bridled at any criticism of him. When I wrote that in 1930 Prince Andrew had surrendered the role of husband and father, his comment was: 'Nonsense. I had a three-day holiday with him every summer.' The Queen told me: 'Philip never talks about his father.'[3] The sad truth is that he saw little of him.

Prince Philip was a member of the Greek Royal Family, though not a drop of Greek blood flowed in his veins. Seventeen-year-old Prince William of Denmark had been imported into Greece in 1863, and converted into King George I of Greece. They were basically German – Schleswig-Holstein-Sonderburg-Glücksburgs. Prince Philip was a quarter Danish, and a quarter Russian on his father's side, but mainly German on his mother's.

There was never a good time to be a Greek king. They went into exile so often that King George II of Greece said that the essential requisite was to have a suitcase permanently packed. Prince Andrew was the first of the family to speak Greek and joined the Greek Army. He met Princess Alice of Battenberg at the Coronation of Edward VII and they married in Darmstadt in 1903. She was the first great-granddaughter of Queen Victoria, born in Windsor Castle in 1885. Her mother, Princess Victoria of Hesse, was the daughter of Queen Victoria's daughter, Princess Alice, who had died young in 1878.

They settled in Athens, and had two daughters in quick succession, Margarita, born in 1905, Theodora in 1906, then later Cécile in 1911, and Sophie ('Tiny') in 1914. Prince Philip arrived on 10 June 1921 while his father was serving in the ill-fated Asia Minor Campaign.

The family fled from their home, Mon Repos, on Corfu, at the end of 1922, when Prince Andrew narrowly escaped execution by the Greek Government. They settled in Paris, relying on the munificence of Prince Andrew's rich sister-in-law, Princess George of Greece (Marie Bonaparte), whose grandfather had owned the casino in Monte Carlo. Like Edwina Mountbatten, she paid for part of Prince Philip's education, first in Paris, then at Cheam and later at Gordonstoun.

Prince Andrew hated being in exile (as all members of royal families do) and passed his time as a boulevardier. He would saunter to the Ritz to share drinks and jokes with his cronies, a shallow life. Princess Alice was more severe and more troubled. The First World War overthrew everything she held sacred. Her uncle, the Grand Duke of Hesse, was forced to step down and retreated from Darmstadt to Wolfsgarten. Worse still, her aunt, Tsarina Alexandra of Russia, was murdered at Ekaterinburg, with the Tsar and all of their children; the aunt (and godmother) she most admired, Grand Duchess Elisabeth, was thrown down a mineshaft.

She and Prince Andrew coped until their Silver Wedding in October 1928, after which everything went wrong. Alice suffered a serious religious-crisis breakdown, following which her behaviour became strange. Her mother sent her to a clinic in Berlin for a time, and then in 1930 took Prince Philip out for a picnic. When he came back, his mother had been removed to Dr Ludwig Binswanger's clinic at Kreuzlingen. He heard more or less nothing from or of her for the next seven years.

His father closed down their house outside Paris. The four sisters were married with undue haste, and from then on Prince Philip was itinerant with no home of his own. The key figure in his life was his stalwart grandmother, Lady Milford Haven, of whom he was somewhat in awe. She organised his school clothes, visited him at school and took him out for lunch on Sundays, which hopefully he enjoyed. When his father failed to organise the promised summer holiday, she took him to stay at her sister's North German Schloss, Hemmelmark.*

He was a good-looking blond Adonis. When his family fell apart, his attitude was: 'My mother was ill, my father was away. I just had to get on with it.'[4] And get on with it he did. He was not well treated. The Mountbattens thought nothing of inviting him to Adsdean then packing him off elsewhere when they needed his room for Goodwood week. He flourished at Gordonstoun, responding well to the outward-bound philosophy of its inspired German headmaster, Kurt Hahn. He told one author: 'Day began with a 400-yard jog trot round the garden followed by a cold shower and a wash.'[5]

He was at Gordonstoun in November 1937 when Hahn called him into his study to tell him that his sister, Cécile, her husband, her two sons, her mother-in-law and their entourage had been killed when their aeroplane hit a factory chimney at Ostend in heavy fog. This incident (which was shockingly traduced in the Netflix series of *The Crown*) was said to be the worst thing that had ever happened in Prince Philip's life. He minded all the more because his sister was pregnant. Her third little boy was born and died in the accident. Prince Andrew travelled with Prince Philip from England to Darmstadt for the funeral.†

---

* Hemmelmark was the home of the Kaiser's brother, Prince Heinrich of Prussia from 1894. He married Princess Irene of Hesse, younger sister of Victoria Milford Haven, Grand Duchess Elisabeth and the Tsarina.
† There is a row of their graves in the Rosenhöhe, near Darmstadt.

By then Princess Alice had extricated herself from Dr Binswanger's clinic and was living with a German family at Breibach, not far from Cologne. She returned to Darmstadt for the funeral of her uncle Ernst Ludwig, Grand Duke of Hesse, in October 1937. The death of her daughter finally shook her from her travails and she saw it as her duty to return to her family. She hoped that she and Prince Andrew might be reunited but he had no intention of returning to her. In 1939 she went back to Athens and took Prince Philip with her, wanting him to get to know the land of his birth. At that time he was in line to become King of Greece, the only people between him and the throne being his uncle Prince George ('Big George') and his father. He was spared that fate when on 2 June 1940, Prince Paul's wife, Princess Frederika, gave birth to a son.*

Prince Philip wrote later that, despite wishing to return to Dartmouth, he would have stayed in Greece had George II wanted him to: 'I could hardly speak Greek anyway and, as I was only eighteen at the time, I could hardly be expected to be of much use to the King without further education or service training. I strongly suspect that he could see the storm clouds gathering over the Mediterranean.'[6] Princess Alice wanted him to stay in Greece, but Mountbatten and others did not want him living under her influence. Therefore King George VI, King George II and Mountbatten decided that he should enter the British Royal Navy. His grandmother, Victoria Milford Haven, was the only one against this idea, believing, as well she might,† that there was no place for foreign princes in the British Royal Navy. Prince Philip was enrolled as a 'Special Entry Cadet' at the Royal Naval College, Dartmouth.‡

---

* King Constantine II of Greece (1940-2023). He became King in 1964. Married Princess Anne-Marie of Denmark. In those days, girls could not succeed to the throne, while Prince Peter (son of 'Big George') had been dropped from the succession to an unsatisfactory marriage. Had Prince Philip become King of Greece, he would not have been able to marry the Queen.

† Prince Louis of Battenberg, her husband, had been forced to resign as First Sea Lord in 1914, because it was unfairly thought (in the press) that he had pro-German sympathies, despite having served in Queen Victoria's Navy since 1868.

‡ He was meant to go straight to a Training Cruiser, but when war came, the cruiser had to be refitted.

A fiercely independent young man emerged from his dysfunctional family. He lived on his wits. He worked hard. He kept his emotions in check. There was a tough exterior, with an increasingly thoughtful person concealed inside. In later life, he inspired enormous loyalty since he knew his mind. Saying thank you or sorry did not come easily to him. Like the Queen, he did not care a jot what people thought of him. He got on with the job. He had a military (he would have said naval) approach to problems. He considered all the possibilities. He liked to argue, because by arguing a decision can be reached. He took nothing at face value. There was a considerable element of impatience in him, since he was aware of how little time there is to get everything done.

At the time of the Dartmouth meeting, Prince Philip was taking his naval career seriously, but discovering girls. He was fascinated by an American called Cobina Wright Jr.* He had spent part of the previous summer in Venice with Princess Aspasia, the unfortunate widow of King Alexander I of Greece, who had died from a monkey bite in 1920. In a ghosted biography written by his cousin, Queen Alexandra of Yugoslavia,† the story was told of how he took a girl

---

* Cobina Wright Jr (1921–2011), daughter of a New York stockbroker: 'Miss Manhattan' in 1939, a front-cover girl on *Life* in 1941, later a singer and film actress with 20th Century Fox. Later she became an alcoholic, though recovered.

† Queen Alexandra of Yugoslavia's biography was ghosted by Harold Albert, who wrote royal books under the name of Helen Cathcart. Some of it was based on the Queen's recollections, but much was cooked up from press cuttings. It was published in 1960, and attracted considerable attention. It was even reviewed by some serious writers. John Gore described it as 'lively, informative and interesting ... a "Laszlo-like" picture but (bar the subject) most readers will feel it deserves Laszlo's treatment and, within the confines of her memories, the author is not uncritical' (*Sphere*, 2 September 1960). John Connell: 'It gives the impression of having slithered tomboyishly into print. What on earth induced the Queen to publish it I cannot imagine' (*Books of the Month*, August 1960). The TLS even noticed it, considering it 'directed, one would say, chiefly to the readers of women's magazines' (*Times Literary Supplement*, 29 July 1960). Towards the end, Queen Alexandra mentioned him having read the draft: 'He had a stringent eye for errors and yet the task was distasteful, I know, for Philip does not yet feel that he merits a biography and considers that such studies would be better left

(Cobina) out in a motor launch, having persuaded his aunt that it was a fine night. She agreed so long as he kept moving. She would be listening for the sound of the engine. This worked for a while, but then there was silence. He was evidently rather sheepish when he told her: 'We had trouble with the sparking plugs.'[7] Though Prince Philip objected to much that Queen Alexandra wrote, he did not object to that story. But when she told a story of how she had primed a girlfriend to lure him away – and succeeded – he wrote: 'Do I see a tiny bit of jealousy creeping in?'[8]

Maury Paul,* the famous gossip columnist (Cholly Knickerbocker), revealed that Prince Philip 'fell so madly in love that same summer with Cobina Wright, Jr' and 'not only yearned to make the beautiful Cobina his Princess – but pleaded with her to elope in the good old American fashion'.[9] Cobina let slip later on that they had two dates together before she realised he was a Prince of Greece.[10]

In July 1939 Cobina was asked if Prince Philip would be coming to America to win her over. In Chicago she said: 'That's exaggerated. I'm not in love, and Philip is just a good friend. I heard from him last week and he's not coming. Conditions in Europe are so uncertain he cannot get away right now.'[11] This interview was given a few days before he met Princess Elizabeth.

His interest in Cobina did not abate. In January 1940 Nancy Randolph of the *Daily News* reported that he was stuck in Greece on naval duties and had been writing to Cobina's mother to ask why she was not writing back.[12] By then Cobina had taken up with

---

judiciously unwritten until he is dead' (draft, p. 357). To that, Prince Philip riposted: 'Either leave this out or put in the truth that I think it is dreadful & that I would much rather that it was not published. I can't help feeling that it is not particularly pleasant for a relation to cash in in this way.' Those lines were edited out. Queen Alexandra's lawyer, Austin T. Smith wrote that it was not a success: 'and indeed raised the wrath of the Palace. Needless to say it was done much against my advice and the advice of others but she was in urgent need of funds, the carrot was dangled and she took it.' (Smith to Ali Forbes, 12 May 1981).

* Maury Paul (1890–1942), American gossip columnist, who invented the term 'Café Society'. He was on to Prince Philip earlier than most journalists. Sadly he died of a heart condition in New York before seeing Prince Philip make good.

Robert Stack, the deep-voiced society movie hero famed for having given Deanna Durbin her first screen kiss in *First Love* (1939). Despite being a handsome member of the Greek Royal Family, Prince Philip was at a disadvantage when in pursuit of society heiresses. He was penniless.*

★ ★ ★ ★ ★

In January 1941 Prince Philip was on leave in Athens. The inveterate diarist and speculator Chips Channon met him at a party. That afternoon Princess Nicholas (mother of Princess Marina) had been telling Channon that it had been decided he was to be Britain's 'prince consort' and that was why he was in the Royal Navy. Channon was disappointed:

> He is a *charmeur*, but I should deplore such a marriage: he and Princess Elizabeth are too inter-related and the Mountbatten-Hesse family are famous for their ill-luck and madness. Disaster pursues them. Like Princess Nicholas I should prefer Alexander who is more manly.[13]

Prince Alexander of Yugoslavia (Princess Nicholas's grandson)† would have been a hopeless choice as consort. He possessed none of Prince Philip's qualities. Channon had concerns about the family disasters, of which there were many – the deaths of the Imperial family in Russia, the Tsarina and Grand Duchess Elisabeth being Hesse Princesses, and the tragic death of the Grand Ducal family in the air crash in 1937. Presumably he knew something of the illness of Prince Philip's mother.

---

* Presently Cobina was being chased across America by Palmer Beaudette, a motor millionaire from Michigan, in chartered planes and on 3 November 1941 they married at the Riverside Church in New York.

† Prince Alexander of Yugoslavia (1924–2016), son of Prince Paul, the ill-fated Regent of Yugoslavia, and Princess Olga (sister of Princess Marina). When in exile in South Africa, he caused a rumpus by helping himself to petrol. He was later dubbed a 'petrol pilferer'. The incident was covered up by General Smuts. In later life he lived in Paris and was a popular figure in Palm Beach.

Years later, when confronted by Basil Boothroyd, Prince Philip rather downplayed the suggestion that he had been chosen as a candidate: 'Inevitably I must have been on the list, so to speak. But people only had to say that, for somebody like Chips Channon to go one step further, and say it's already decided.'[14]

Prince Philip maintained an intermittent correspondence with Princess Elizabeth throughout the war. Journalists occasionally took an interest in him as a Greek prince. In 1940 he was described as personifying 'the popular conception of a Greek Apollo'.[15] He gained the respect of King George VI, who praised him in 1941: 'What a charming boy he is, & I am glad he is remaining on in my Navy.'[16] He served with the Mediterranean Fleet, in Home Waters, and with the British Pacific Fleet, in South East Asia and the Pacific. In February 1942 he was mentioned in despatches at the Battle of Matapan, in the south of Greece. He was promoted to lieutenant.

★ ★ ★ ★ ★

There were rivals, principally the Earl of Euston.* He was at Windsor until October 1941, but back by April 1942. Alathea was taken with him and worried that he was being singled out for Princess Elizabeth. She noted that they had both started to like him at about the same time, and was resentful when she saw him sitting out with the Princess at a ball. In May 1941 Sonia Graham-Hodgson told Alathea that she 'adored Hugh Euston',[17] so the parties of Jackie Philipps were stirring young female hearts.

What none of them knew was that since 1937 Euston had been in pursuit of Lady Brigid Guinness,† daughter of the Earl of Iveagh, proposing to her numerous times over a period of five years and being turned down every time. In August 1941 Chips Channon

---

* Hugh, Earl of Euston, later 11th Duke of Grafton (1919-2011), succeeded to the dukedom in 1970. Appointed a Knight of the Garter, 1976. Married 1946, Fortune Smith (1920-2021), Lady of the Bedchamber from 1953-66, & Mistress of the Robes to Queen Elizabeth II from 1967.

† Lady Brigid Guinness (1920-95), married, 1945, Prince Frederick of Prussia. Chips Channon was married to her sister, Honor.

tried to persuade his sister-in-law to marry him. By April Brigid was telling him that Euston was sending her 'passionate and poetic love letters', but she thought he would marry Princess Elizabeth 'who likes him'.[18] However, in August 1943, Myra Wernher, whose parents, Sir Harold and Lady Zia Wernher kept an eye on Prince Philip, told Alathea that he was the likely choice, 'though as yet he is not in love with her'.[19]

In May 1943 Channon believed that Euston was 'reserved for a higher destiny – the very throne itself'.[20] Some said Mountbatten arranged for Lord Euston to be sent out as ADC to Lord Wavell to clear the way for Prince Philip. According to Channon, however, Lady Iveagh asked him to fix this as she was fed up with the Brigid situation.[21]

By October 1943 Channon was writing that the Royal Family had encouraged the Euston romance but dropped him as 'too inert and *énervé*'.*[22] He wondered if the Marquess of Douro† might now be a suitable alternative. In February 1944 Billy Whitaker, another of the Grenadiers at Windsor, told him that Euston had never been seriously considered, while he thought Prince Philip was. At the end of October 1944, when staying with the Duchess of Kent at Coppins, Channon spotted the name 'Philip' frequently in the guest book. That, he suggested, was where Princess Elizabeth saw him.

Mountbatten was in South East Asia from August 1943, which meant Prince Philip had nowhere to go when on leave, so he stayed at Windsor instead. He saw Princess Elizabeth in *Cinderella* in 1941. Curiously, since presumably he hardly knew him, he attended the Duke of Connaught's funeral in St George's Chapel in January 1942. He was again at Windsor that August, Princess Elizabeth believing that he quite enjoyed himself, and back at the end of 1943. By this time Princess Elizabeth was pronouncing him to be 'charming' and 'great fun' though 'hardly ever serious', but when he was, 'he talked good sense'.[23] They had waltzed together, his arms round her waist, and she with hers round his neck.

She was still not wholly committed. She told another cousin, Diana Bowes-Lyon, that she wished her first cousin, Andrew

---

* In October 1946 Lord Euston married Fortune Smith.
† The Marquess of Douro, later 8th Duke of Wellington (1915–2014).

Elphinstone, was not so closely related as he was just the kind of husband any girl would love to have.²⁴ Prince Philip came to the showing of Noël Coward's film *This Happy Breed* in July 1944, laughing happily throughout the film. When they parted, he told her they would probably not see each other for two years. Soon afterwards he had a car accident in the Great West Road.

During that month, the Duchess of Kent took him to Wilton for dinner with the Herberts.* Sir Michael Duff, the effete owner of Vaynol, in Wales, was there for a night. He thought him 'charming' and just right to be consort:

> He has everything in his favour, he is good looking, intelligent, a good sailor, and he speaks ONLY English, the latter quality most admirable and necessary, when one considers the point of view of the man in the street who has an innate prejudice against any language but his own (even if it is only BAD language). I gather he goes to Windsor quite a lot. He is 24 [in fact twenty-three], and ripe for the job. But whether he likes P.E. or she him I can't say.²⁵

Prince Philip became an occasional visitor to Vaynol. In 1946 he and Sir Michael were driving to London together when the car broke down. Prince Philip was immediately under it, sorting it out. Duff quizzed him as to who might marry Princess Elizabeth. He must have enjoyed telling the old gossip he had no idea.

Princess Elizabeth visited her ailing grandfather at Glamis in October 1944. The Earl of Strathmore died there aged eighty-nine on 7 November. Lord Oliver Fitzroy, Hugh Euston's brother, had been killed.† From Scotland Princess Elizabeth wrote to Euston in India. It was symptomatic of the attitude of the young in wartime to write of war deaths as a normal hazard in their lives. She regretted

---

* Sidney, Lord Herbert (later 16th Earl of Pembroke and Montgomery) (1906–69), then Private Secretary to Princess Marina, and his wife, Lady Mary Hope (1903–95), her lady in waiting.

† Lord Oliver Fitzroy (1923–44) joined the Grenadier Guards on 13 March 1943, went overseas with the 4th Battalion on 10 July 1944 and was killed in action in Normandy on 6 August 1944.

that all the particularly charming people seemed to get killed. She despaired of getting to know officers who then went to war, and became war casualties. In the peace of Glamis it was hard to contemplate returning to an atmosphere of bombs and sirens and blackouts.

By February 1945 she had the photograph of Prince Philip, with a beard, glowering at her (her words) in a frame on the mantelpiece. She was much teased when it arrived, though Queen Elizabeth conceded that he was a good-looking boy. At Sandringham Princess Elizabeth wondered if the housemaids would guess who he was. When Gerrit van der Woude got engaged to Lady Penelope Herbert, her attitude was 'Not that I wish to get engaged myself! Oh! No!'[26]

Soon after the war the hearts of both Princesses were caused to flutter by a six-foot-four-inch captain who was part of the Royal Guard at Balmoral, Captain Roddy MacLeod,* 'a devastatingly attractive young giant (with fair hair and blue eyes, of course) from Skye'.[27] He taught them Highland dancing.

* * * * *

As the war ended, speculation about Prince Philip hit the American newspapers. Winifred van Duzer, a writer on the *New York Times*, wrote in May 1945 that his meetings with the Princess had become 'as nearly twosomes as a young man could hope for with a royal princess involved'. She made the valid point that Queen Elizabeth was determined that her daughter should have as wide a choice as possible of future husband. In fact that choice was not so wide, since Queen Elizabeth looked no further than the Grenadier Guards. Her choices did not extend to American officers currently in Britain. It was as if, by making her Colonel of Grenadiers, the King had given his daughter her own army from which to pluck a husband.

The writer hit on the Earl of Euston and mentioned the young Duke of Rutland, another Grenadier. If the latter was ever a

---

* Later Colonel Roderick Robertson-Macleod, DSO, MC, TD (1919–89).

candidate, he upset the Princess by ignoring her at a dance.* She cited the scarcity of foreign royal princes.[28]

★ ★ ★ ★ ★

On his visits to Australia Prince Philip was vulnerable to persistent journalists who extracted quotes from him. In 1940 he had been on leave from HMS *Ramillies*, spending some time in the outback: 'Best holiday I've ever spent was on a sheep station in Victoria, perfectly natural life, no frills or fads.'[29] He attracted attention as 'Mystery Man in Sydney'. A columnist calling herself 'Miss Midnight' spotted him dancing with a 'sub-deb' in Romano's. On one such occasion he threw the journalist off the scent: 'My dear fellow, I am afraid it is a case of mistaken identity.'[30] Soon afterwards the mystery man attended a service in the Greek Cathedral of St Sophia in Paddington, where he was welcomed by Archbishop Timotheos on behalf of the Greek community.[31] Later that year he was in Sydney. An eighteen-footer overturned. The crew were rescued and given plentiful whisky in the boardroom. 'It may have been a coincidence,' he said, 'but within the next half-hour six boats overturned.'[32]

Soon afterwards, in June 1945 he was spotted in Melbourne, while his ship, *Whelp* was being refitted. In the ship's ward room as 'Number One', he was hi-jacked into an interview by a lady reporter, who found him simple, natural and easy to talk to. He told her he was a sailor first and a prince by birth second. The only time he used the princely title was to get a table in a restaurant for a date. He liked Australians for their freshness and unaffected manners. He liked their womenkind. He had enjoyed a week spent in Tasmania. He was buying cosmetics for Princess Marina as they were hard to get in Britain. He also brought back sugar, cheese and chocolate. For himself he bought only a digger's hat.[33]

---

* In 1982 I was present when Lady Diana Cooper attempted to press her nephew, Lord Charteris, to have the Duke of Rutland appointed a Knight of the Garter. Charteris made it clear that this was not going to happen, citing 'a certain antipathy on behalf of the Sovereign'. Another version is that he tried to kiss her and was rejected.

ENTER PRINCE PHILIP, 1941-6

His particular friends at this time were Jo and Judy Fallon,* who lived at Vaucluse, a suburb on Sydney's Eastern Shore. Jo was a raffish society photographer, while his wife wrote for the *Sydney Morning Herald*. She recalled that when his warship came in, he would run down the gangplank, hail a taxi and head to wherever he was staying. She noted the 'extraordinary mixture of diffidence and dignity, seriousness and uproarious good humour' in his nature:

> We quickly found that he dislikes muddled thinking and careless judgments, and is trenchantly sarcastic if he detects these in an argument. His own opinions are crystal-clear, and he sees everything rather sharply as black or white, with no shades of grey in between. A thing is either right – in which case you can do it. Or it is wrong – in which case you don't do it ...[34]

At one time the Duke of Gloucester, then Governor-General, loaned him a shooting brake with royal insignia instead of number plates. Prince Philip did not like the special treatment this attracted, so returned it and rented an inconspicuous car.

On his arrival in 1945 he was still sporting a beard. Presently he shaved it off. At a race meeting in Melbourne, to which he went with his new friend, Michael Parker, the press were in hot pursuit. But they were after a bearded prince. As it happened, Parker was then bearded. Prince Philip was amused to be asked if his friend was the Prince and happy to confirm this. As a result Parker was pursued all afternoon and he was left in peace.

He was cautious never to be linked romantically with any girl. One evening he came to the Fallon house after a ball with a well-known debutante in tow. They had left the ball together and it had not gone unnoticed. The debutante was anxious to get home as her mother would be waiting. Prince Philip fell asleep in a chair and nothing would rouse him. Jo Fallon drove the girl home. Prince Philip's eyes promptly opened. He explained this had been a ruse to quell rumours. After a farewell party they gave for him, he wrote

---

* Joseph James Fallon (1911–71) and his wife Judy (née Molesworth) (1916–67). She moved to London and they divorced in 1954. She was the author of *Pacific Pantomime* (1952). He remarried.

in her visitors' book: 'Whither the storm carries, I go a willing guest.'[35]

Over the years there were two special girlfriends. Robin Dalton was the girlfriend of Prince Philip's cousin, David, Marquess of Milford Haven (also out in Australia with the Navy), and recalled them as 'a society beauty called Sue Other-Gee from Melbourne and Sandra Jacques, who was beautiful and modelled and sang in nightclubs. That was a very full love affair.'[36]

The two girls were somewhat different. Born in 1916, Sue* had spent time in London in 1936 and had been presented at court to George VI in May 1937. She had become engaged to Lord Adam Gordon† in 1939. That engagement had continued until April 1945, and then petered out in the way of wartime engagements. She had been one of the first of the Red Cross (VAD) to serve in the Middle East. She was later with the Australian Army Women's Medical Service (AAWMS), and served in New Guinea.

Prince Philip befriended Sue in 1940 and she was said to have seen him again in Britain in January 1942. She returned to Melbourne in 1945 and presently he was behind the bar at a party serving her drinks, and dancing with her in nightclubs. Everything about Sue was admirable.

In contrast, Sandra Jacques‡ was 'a classic beauty with red-gold hair, and a talent for wearing elegant clothes'.[37] The Ranee of Sarawak saw her photograph in an exhibition and judged her beauty 'stormy'.[38] She had appeared in *Seven Little Australians* (1939), one review praising: 'A voice soft yet clear, a dignified poise, a face expressive as well as pretty, and a personality full of delicate femininity.'[39] She was a nightclub singer and a model, made famous by the David Jones store,

---

* Naomi Priscilla (Sue) Other-Gee (1916–80), married, 1950, Lieutenant-Colonel Ewan Murray Robson, DSO, MBE (1906–74).

† Lord Adam Gordon (1909–84), great-nephew of the 11th Marquess of Huntly. Given his courtesy title in 1937 when his brother became the 12th Marquess. Comptroller of the Queen Mother's Household at Clarence House, 1953–74.

‡ Sandra Jacques (1922–2004), nightclub singer and model, married (1) 1943, Peter Gibbes (1917–2003) (divorced 1946); (2) 1950, Lieutenant-Commander David Teare (1923–2000); (3), Gordon Campbell-Ross (1921–unknown); and (4) Russell King. They were all airmen.

competing well with French models imported from Paris. She appeared in a biopic (released as *Smithy* in 1946), where she was one of 'an assortment of eye-filling talent' in small parts enjoying 'a pleasant change from advocating a special brand of toothpaste, bathing suits and even toilet soap'.[40]

Prince Philip's time in Britain in 1945 provoked a Greek newspaper, *Hellenicon Aema*, to suggest that Archbishop Damaskinos, Regent in Athens, had come to London to fix his engagement. In September the Palace denied this – not for the last time. Prince Philip had to settle his future. Clearly he had his doubts. In Australia he told Elizabeth Baillieu that he had to go back to England to marry Princess Elizabeth, but he didn't want to.[41] He was serving in the Far East when the war ended.

He returned to Britain from Tokyo in January 1946 to face his future.

8
SOUTH AFRICA AND ENGAGEMENT

'I notice that some English newspapers are always picking on him in a niggling way. What do they want? Whom do they think the Queen should have married? Some chinless wonder?'
Ex-Queen Helen of Romania to Olga Franklin, 1960[1]

On returning to Britain, Prince Philip trained cadets at the Petty Officers' Training School, HMS *Royal Arthur*, in Westwells Road, Corsham. It was Spartan and uncomfortable. He slept in an iron bed, his principal decoration some folding frames with a photograph of his father and one of Princess Elizabeth. He was second-in-command, supervising training in lectures, public speaking, religion and ethics, as well as physical training and parading. He was tough, believing in old-fashioned naval discipline. He spent his time mugging up on naval history, growing impressive potatoes, and played darts and skittles with the locals at the Methuen Arms. He had an MG car, which enabled him to bound up to London to take Princess Elizabeth dancing at Ciro's or Quaglino's or to join her at private parties. She confirmed that it was at this time that they began to see each other regularly.

★ ★ ★ ★ ★

Since 1944 Lord Mountbatten had been ramping up his plans for Philip, having spotted his potential at Dartmouth. He addressed a number of obstacles. The first was to make him a British national, ostensibly so that he could continue to serve in the Royal Navy.*
He was subtly converted from Greek Prince to British naval officer.

---

* Prince Philip was descended from Electress Sophia of Hanover. Thus, according to Lord Dilhorne, a later Lord Chancellor, he could claim British nationality automatically.

SOUTH AFRICA AND ENGAGEMENT

All this helped the marriage plans, but his family realised that the Prince would have to make up his own mind.

Victoria Milford Haven discussed the possibility of his marriage with him, without pressing him. She found him 'fully aware that he must give it careful consideration'.[2] His mother, Princess Alice, wrote to him that she had heard he 'paid an interesting visit, as well as lunching with a certain young lady & her parents'[3] before he left Britain in 1944. By February 1945 the family were busy discussing among themselves, if not with him, 'the future plans'[4] they had in store for him. The naturalisation issue was resolved on 28 February 1947 when, by his own wish, he ceased to be Prince Philip of Greece and Denmark and became Lieutenant Philip Mountbatten, RN.

Besides the Australian girlfriends, there were others in England. There was Georgina (Gina) Wernher, daughter of Sir Harold and Lady Zia. Lady Kennard (as she became) recalled that Victoria Milford Haven wanted her to marry her grandson, 'but she could understand that there were other plans ... Dickie certainly wanted him to marry the Queen ... He was a lost person.' He once said to her: 'You are so lucky to have a home to come back to.'[5] In 1944 Gina married Harold (Bunny) Phillips, a former lover of Edwina Mountbatten, and so was out of the equation.

Another girlfriend was the Canadian Osla Benning,* a debutante in 1939, the last pre-war season, nicknamed 'Oslo' in Lady Milford Haven's family, and living in Acacia Road, Regent's Park. As a debutante, 'she had a habit of seizing the microphone and belting out the hit song of the hour'.[6] She played the piano at parties. She worked in a munitions plant during the war and later in the Foreign Office. It was good news when she got engaged to the young diplomat, Guy Millard, in May 1944, though by the end of June that marriage was off, and in December 1946 she married John Henniker-Major, then private secretary to Ernest Bevin, at St Margaret's, Westminster.†

---

* Osla Benning (1921–74), Lady Henniker-Major.

† The story was that she kissed neither Prince Philip nor Guy Millard. But in later life, Mountbatten used to say to Osla that he wondered if Prince Philip would not have been happier with her. Prince Philip was particularly kind to her when she was dying.

In April 1946 Prince Philip made his way to Salem for the wedding of his widowed sister, Sophie, to Prince George William of Hanover. From there he went to Monte Carlo to meet the Comtesse de la Bigne, a friend of his father, Prince Andrew, who had died there in 1944. She handed over his few remaining personal effects.

In May Prince Philip took Princess Elizabeth to the Bagatelle Club in Mayfair and they danced to 'People Will Say We're In Love'. In June Lord Euston was a guest in a house party at Windsor Castle. A month later he was engaged to Fortune Smith, and they were married at Slaugham, Sussex, on 12 October. Princess Elizabeth did not attend. Some years later James Pope-Hennessy interviewed Lady Buxton, the groom's grandmother. She told him that 'The Queen [as by then she had become] was in love with Hugh Euston before the D. of Edinburgh & wilted after his marriage.'[7]

Prince Philip spent some of his summer with the Royal Family at Balmoral. Marriage was discussed but the King would not let them announce this formally. Princess Elizabeth confirmed to a trusted writer, Betty Spencer Shew,* that 'We had thought about getting married, but couldn't, and didn't do anything about it till after the South African visit.'[8] She was not yet twenty-one and the King wanted her on the trip, which had been planned since March 1946. The rumours circulated, provoking Tommy Lascelles to issue a curt denial: 'Princess Elizabeth is not engaged to be married. The report published is incorrect.'[9]

The King was concerned at the break-up of his happy family, 'Us Four'. Queen Mary believed the couple had been in love for some time, but that the King and Queen felt she was too young, needed to meet more men and was 'only nineteen and one is very impressionable at that age'.[10]

Queen Elizabeth needed to be won over. After the Scottish holiday Prince Philip wrote to her that he had been rather fed up 'and grudgingly accepting the idea of going on in the peacetime navy',

---

* Betty Spencer Shew (1915–71), court correspondent and author. Married 1940 Edward Spencer Shew, CBE (1908–71), a political journalist and author of books on murder. In 1947 Princess Elizabeth wrote to her in her own hand, giving her the timeline of her relationship with Prince Philip for a Royal Wedding souvenir book.

SOUTH AFRICA AND ENGAGEMENT

but those few weeks had made all the difference. He professed himself 'in love, completely and unreservedly'.[11] His cause was not helped by the antipathy of Queen Elizabeth's more reactionary friends, such as the Earl of Eldon, partly based on post-war antipathy to his German ancestry and connections. One courtier said to him disdainfully: 'We think you'll like Windsor Castle when you get to know it.' To which Prince Philip replied: 'Thank you very much. My mother was born there.'[12]

Choosing Prince Philip was possibly the one time that Princess Elizabeth acted absolutely out of character. When the engagement was announced, Queen Elizabeth remained cautious. To Tommy Lascelles she drafted a letter: 'One can only hope that she has made the right decision. I think she has – but he is untried as yet.'[13] She told Arthur Penn that her daughter 'had made up her mind some time ago'.[14] She also wrote: 'I say, Arthur, how annoyed the Grenadiers will be!'[15] They were. They refused to have Prince Philip as their Colonel in 1952.

He never fully won her over. In the 1990s she was entertaining friends to lunch in the garden at Clarence House. He emerged from a meeting in St James's Palace. They chatted but he turned down an invitation to join them. When he had gone, she said to her neighbour: 'Quite nice my son-in-law ... sometimes.'[16]

Inevitably there were tensions. 'I remember all the arguments,'[17] recalled Prince Michel de Bourbon, a guest at the wedding. He did not elaborate. As for Prince Philip, his career in the Navy was going to be different – peacetime engagements less appealing than the challenges of war. Lady Butter concluded that Prince Philip was 'a very feeling person who went to great lengths to hide it. He was also his own man and therefore no one could force him to do anything he didn't want to.'[18] Her sister Lady Kennard said: 'He thought it all over and believed he could make something of the job. And they have been very happy. He's been very supportive. Yes, he likes to flirt. He's a man.'[19]

All his family were praying he would take the great step. Lord Mountbatten was pushing him to the point at which he had to warn him off. Presently Prince Philip wrote to his sister in Germany to say that she might think him 'a mutt' but that it was what he had decided to do.[20] He would marry Princess Elizabeth. Prince Philip made no objection to the line in my book on his mother: 'They loaded the gun for Philip, but left him to pull the trigger.'[21]

In June 1947 Alathea heard from Sonia Graham-Hodgson that the engagement was imminent with a wedding date fixed for the autumn. Sonia told her: 'He has kissed her and the ring is already bought.'[22] He pulled that trigger.

In 1945 he had been a naval officer in tropical uniform, tripping down the gangplank in Sydney, surrounded by glamorous Australian debutantes. Now he was in the kilted world of Balmoral, playing charades with the King and Queen. No wonder he was sometimes fed up.

★ ★ ★ ★ ★

In the meantime Princess Elizabeth emerged from the sanctity of Windsor Castle into full public life. She was busy almost from the day the war ended. When she was eighteen, instead of being presented at court, she accompanied her father to a tin-plate mill near Newport in Wales. With her parents she visited mining valleys, the docks of Swansea and the Treforest Trading Estate, the first visit to Wales of a princess for eighteen years. She made her first speech in public, accepting the presidency of the Court of Governors of the Queen Elizabeth Hospital for Children at Hackney. There were eight public appearances in 1944; this rose to thirty in 1945, and even more in 1946. Queen Mary took her on numerous visits to factories, this being deemed a good way for her to meet a wide cross-section of workers.

On 19 August 1945 Princess Elizabeth joined the King and the Royal Family at the Thanksgiving Service in St Paul's Cathedral. She attended a Girl Guides rally in Glasgow. On 5 November there was a Royal Variety Show and a few days later she laid a wreath at the Cenotaph for the first time. Christmas was spent at Sandringham, where Mabell, Countess of Airlie, noted that life was more informal than in the days of George V. Princess Elizabeth's wireless blared incessantly. Lady Airlie observed her:

> In that family setting she seemed to me one of the most unselfish girls I had ever met, always the first to give way in any of the small issues that arise in every home. I thought that no two sisters

SOUTH AFRICA AND ENGAGEMENT

could have been less alike than the Princesses, the elder with her quiet simplicity, the younger with her puckish expression and irrepressible high spirits – often liberated in mimicry. Queen Mary described her as '*espiègle*' – which was precisely the right word, although it has no complete equivalent in English – adding 'All the same she is so outrageously amusing that one can't help encouraging her.'[23]

Princess Elizabeth made a two-hundred-mile tour of Ulster, and so it continued – the launching of ships, the taking of salutes, attendance at race meetings – and on 8 June 1946 the great Victory Parade, attended by the Royal Family, Winston Churchill, the Cabinet and the Dominions leaders. Before the summer holiday at Balmoral she went to Wales and was invested as a Bard. She became Chief Ranger of the Girl Guides of the British Empire.

Prince Philip attracted no media attention when he attended the wedding of Andrew Elphinstone to Princess Elizabeth's lady in waiting, Mrs Vicary Gibbs, on 29 May. He was one of many royal guests at the first post-war garden party at Buckingham Palace on 9 July. On 8 September he attended matins at Crathie Church when staying at Balmoral, though Princess Elizabeth stayed indoors with a slight cold.

His presence was noticed at the wedding of Lord Mountbatten's daughter Patricia to Captain Lord Brabourne, Coldstream Guards, on 26 October, due to his assisting Princess Elizabeth with her mink jacket. The King and Queen were there; the bridesmaids were Princess Elizabeth, Princess Margaret, Princess Alexandra and Pamela Mountbatten.* There was further interest in him in December when a question was asked in the House of Commons about his application for British citizenship.

---

* The Archbishop of Canterbury performed the service. Prince Philip's mother and grandmother were there, as were his aunt, Nada, Marchioness of Milford Haven, and her son David Milford Haven. The groom's mother, Doreen, Lady Brabourne, was there. In 1979 she was on the boat when Lord Mountbatten was blown up, and died of her injuries.

South Africa

There were a number of contradictory reasons for the South African trip. The King wanted to thank the South African people for their help during the war. He was exhausted by those years and it was hoped the visit would be something of a rest. However, Field Marshal Smuts, the Prime Minister of South Africa, was facing an election in 1948. He turned the visit into an exhausting tour, with political advantage to himself.

The King nearly came home because Britain was facing one of the worst winters on record, with deep snow, gales, floods and power cuts. For Princess Elizabeth it was difficult. She wanted to get engaged, but had to face a three-month separation. Instead of being with Prince Philip, she would be on show, attending civic receptions and sitting next to distinguished, gnarled old figures at lunches and dinners. She would get to know one of the most important countries in the Commonwealth, something she had been unable to do earlier due to the war. She was, as *The Times* pointed out, the 'born representative of the youth and future of the Commonwealth'.[24]

Off they went in style, sailing from Portsmouth on HMS *Vanguard*, at 7.25 a.m. on 1 February. It was a tough voyage. As *Vanguard* entered the Bay of Biscay, a south-easterly gale got up, and the ship showed what it could do by rolling. Lady Harlech's porthole leaked, staff cabins were flooded, heavy seas smashed the gratings, some china came to grief, and a young officer broke his wrist. The lights in Princess Elizabeth's cabin fused and she did not appear at dinner. Tommy Lascelles, the Private Secretary travelling with them, stayed in bed from Saturday night until Tuesday. Presently the ship entered warmer waters and the Princesses were able to watch rifle shooting on deck. When the ship crossed the line, their faces were heavily powdered. Lascelles wrote: 'The only members of our party to be involved were the two Peters [Townsend and Ashmore], who were well ducked, and the ladies' maids who unfortunately were not.'[25] Eventually the proceedings descended into chaos. Lascelles was pleased that they had two ladies in waiting 'of mature judgment who are not in the least afraid to speak their minds'. He thought Townsend was trying hard 'and is doing quite well'. One night the

Princesses played duets on the piano and sang to entertain the crew. On board, the temperature soared. Lascelles described it as a Turkish bath.

Vanguard sailed into Cape Town at 9.40 a.m. on 17 February. There was predictable excitement – huge crowds, gun salutes, a guard of honour, greetings from the Governor-General (Major the Hon Gideon Brand van Zyl, MC) and Field Marshal Smuts, a procession to Government House, and in the evening a state dinner. The next day addresses were delivered on the Grand Parade, and later there was a garden party and a civic ball. The King opened Parliament on 21 February. They set off on an exhausting tour of the various provinces. If the programme was overwhelming, there was free time for picnics and bathing. When they got to the Natal hills, it rained steadily so they were all forced to sit still. It was a much-needed rest.

Princess Elizabeth followed in her parents' wake until 3 March when she took centre stage, opening a new graving dock – Princess Elizabeth Dock – at East London, delivering a confident speech, cited in a *Times* leader as expressing 'the courage and confidence of a new generation, facing the challenge of a perilous world'.[26] This leader was undoubtedly written by Morrah,* who was travelling in

---

* Dermot Morrah (1896–1974): educated at Winchester and New College, Oxford, he had shared rooms with T. E. Lawrence. He was an academic, short of stature, with curling eyebrows, a lover of fine wines with a voice that suffered from a paralysed vocal cord causing him to speak with a croak. He loved crossword puzzles, solving them so fast that he did not bother to fill them in. He was in Queen Elizabeth's confidence and sometimes wrote speeches for her and the King. He once said to her: 'How can the Australians feel equal to the British, if they only see you passing by on one visit?' She replied: 'Well, they aren't quite, are they?' When his daughter was going to an event at which Queen Elizabeth was to be present, he said, 'Give her my love.' He was horrified that she did just that, but it gave him the chance to send a stylish letter, apologising for the informality, and adding, 'but not for the sentiment, which, as Your Majesty knows, is held by all your subjects, none more so than your obedient servant ...' He was appointed Arundel Herald Extraordinary to enable him to report on Queen Elizabeth II's Coronation from a front-row vantage point. At his memorial service in Westminster Cathedral, his friend, Dr C.R.S. Harris,

the royal party. He had come to the attention of Tommy Lascelles when he wrote an erudite introduction to a book, *The Royal Family in Wartime* (1943). He had also written *Princess Elizabeth* (Odhams Press, 1947), for her twenty-first birthday. This book investigated the true significance of the monarchy and wove many historical precedents into her young life. He commended Queen Elizabeth for creating a fine family atmosphere, with praise for Crawfie, who exemplified 'the admirable Scottish precept of plain living and high thinking'.[27] Morrah omitted no constitutional detail, or book the Princess might have read. On the long train journeys, Lascelles and Morrah played chess. There were times when Lascelles became exasperated and welcomed outside visitors to relieve the burden of family party conversation, which became intolerable as the weeks wore on.[28]

Princess Elizabeth relished the natural beauty of South Africa, visiting national parks. On 7 April they flew to Rhodesia for nine days. She inspected a company of Girl Guides there, and in Bechuanaland the Princesses were presented with gifts of diamonds and gold nuggets.

The big excitement was the celebration of Princess Elizabeth's twenty-first birthday in South Africa on 21 April, which was declared a national holiday. The Royal Family returned to Cape Town on the morning of Sunday, 20 April. A planned cableway trip up to Table Mountain was cancelled due to heavy rain-clouds (though possible the next day). At 3 p.m. she reviewed a march-past of seven thousand troops, ex-servicemen and others at Youngsfield, Wynberg, accompanied by Field Marshal Smuts. She attended a youth rally of all races at Rosebank showgrounds. The Royal Family dined with the Governor-General and his wife at Westbrooke and later saw a fireworks display. There was a ball at Government House, Princess Elizabeth dipping out briefly to appear at a Civic Ball in the City Hall. She was presented with twenty-one perfectly matched diamonds from the state diggings at Alexander Bay, polished for assembly as a necklace.

Editor of *The Economist*, delivered the line: 'Now that Chateau Dermot has been drained to the faggots...'

Princess Elizabeth making her famous 1947 broadcast

The most significant event was her speech to the youth of the Empire (broadcast in the UK on the BBC Home Service at 6.55 p.m.). This was generally thought to have been the work of Lascelles, who claimed to have 'lavished much care' on it,[29] but Graham Viney has established that it was primarily the work of Dermot Morrah, whose style was easily recognised from his leaders in *The Times* on subjects such as the effect of the visit and the coming-of-age of Princess Elizabeth.

Morrah drafted the first version, which Lascelles liked, telling him he could not recall one 'that has so completely satisfied me and left me feeling that not a single word should be altered. Moreover, dusty cynic though I am it moved me greatly.'[30] But the King and Queen and Princess Elizabeth thought otherwise. They invited Frank Gillard, of the BBC, to join them at the Victoria Falls Hotel and after church they sat down together in deckchairs on a quiet lawn. The King said: 'This will probably be the most important broadcast of my daughter's life and it is up to all of us, and especially you, to make it perfect.' They read Morrah's version, the King commenting: 'Can you imagine a young person of my daughter's age uttering such pompous platitudes?' Two hours later they had crafted something 'simple, unpretentious, sincere, genuine'.[31] Princess Elizabeth made a pre-recording of the broadcast and high-quality discs were sent to London, in case the connections were poor on the day. As it happened, the beam worked well. Princess Elizabeth proved a confident speaker.

The final speech contained memorable lines. She said: 'As I speak to you today from Capetown I am six thousand miles from the country where I was born, but I am certainly not six thousand miles from home.' Though she wanted to address everyone, she was 'thinking especially today of all the young men and women who were born about the same time as myself and have grown up like me in the terrible and glorious years of the Second World War'. After quoting William Pitt, she said: 'The British Empire has saved the world first, and has now to save itself after the battle is won.'

> If we all go forward together with an unwavering faith, a high courage, and a quiet heart, we shall be able to make of this ancient Commonwealth, which we all love so dearly, an even grander thing – more free, more prosperous, more happy, and a more powerful influence on the world – than it has been in the greatest days of our forefathers. To accomplish that we must give nothing less than the whole of ourselves.
>
> There is a motto which has been borne by many of my ancestors – a noble motto, 'I serve.' These words were an inspiration to many bygone heirs to the throne when they made their knightly dedication as they came to manhood. I cannot do quite as they did, but through the inventions of science I can do what was not possible for any of them. I can make my solemn act of dedication with a whole Empire listening. I should like to make that dedication now. It is very simple.
>
> I declare before you all that my whole life, whether it be long or short, shall be devoted to your service and the service of our great imperial family to which we all belong, but I shall not have strength to carry out this resolution alone unless you join it with me, as I now invite you to do. I know that your support will be unfailingly given.

God help me to make good my vow, and God bless all of you who are willing to share in it.[32]

Princess Elizabeth had made the promise to serve. She kept that promise faithfully for a remarkable seventy-five years.

At 4 p.m. on 24 April *Vanguard* sailed from Cape Town. During the voyage home, Tommy Lascelles assessed how Princess Elizabeth had done:

> She has come on in the most surprising way, and all in the right direction. She has got all P'cess Mary's solid and endearing qualities plus a perfectly natural power of enjoying herself without any trace of shyness. Not a great sense of humour, but a good healthy sense of fun. Moreover, when necessary, she can take on the old bores with much of her mother's skill, and never spares herself in that exhausting part of royal duty. For a child of her years, she has got an astonishing solicitude for other people's comfort; such unselfishness is not a normal characteristic of that family. But what delights me especially is that she has become extremely businesslike, and understands what a burden it is to the Staff if some regard is not paid to the clock. She has developed an admirable technique of going up behind her mother and prodding her in the Achilles tendon with the point of her umbrella when time is being wasted in unnecessary conversation. And, when necessary – not infrequently – she tells her father off to rights. My impression, by the way, is that we shall be subscribing to a w-p [wedding present] before the year is out.
>
> Her sister, too, has come on a lot and is much more agreeable in character, besides being very good company. There must have been many moments in this tour that seemed intolerably dreary to both of them, but on the whole they have been as good as gold.[33]

They disembarked in Britain on 12 May, ten years to the day since the Coronation in 1937. They were welcomed ashore at Portsmouth by a cheering crowd of half a million and given a civic welcome before taking the train to London. In a procession of four carriages they went to the Palace and made a balcony appearance. Crawfie was shocked by what she saw – the King and Queen 'positively worn out', Princess Elizabeth, thin, 'pale and drawn', and

Princess Margaret 'ill and tired out', and this after days at sea.³⁴

On 15 May there was another carriage procession to the Guildhall, still bearing the scars of wartime damage, for a celebratory luncheon, as was traditional at the end of royal visits in those days (and well into the Queen's reign). The verdict of *The Times*, again no doubt Dermot Morrah, was: 'Anticipation of its success was high: they have been eclipsed by the reality.'³⁵

On 26 May, soon after the Guildhall luncheon, the King gave a large family lunch party for Queen Mary on her eightieth birthday. The Duke of Windsor was in London, but he was not invited. On 11 June Princess Elizabeth was admitted to the Freedom of the City of London, saying in her speech that the newly invented British Commonwealth was not so much a single act of statecraft but a miracle of faith. She allied herself to the concept of the Commonwealth, something she would support wholeheartedly throughout her reign.

Freedom of the Borough of Windsor followed on 5 July, given to her in a ceremony in the Home Park. To a crowd of thousands Princess Elizabeth made clear how important Windsor had been to her: 'Indeed, I regard it as a home in a way that no other place can be.'³⁶

And then it happened. On 9 July the engagement was announced. The King agreed and, as naval regulations demanded, Prince Philip asked the permission of his commanding officer: 'Request permission to get engaged, Sir, and my fiancée says that if you refuse it won't be very good for your career!'³⁷

The following day the young couple were greeted enthusiastically at a Palace garden party and appeared on the balcony to be cheered by a massive crowd. That weekend they visited the Duchess of Kent at Coppins. The ever-observant Sir Michael Duff was there:

> Princess E looked radiant, & he not quite so much – I have known him for years & think him charming in a rather dull way. I don't think he has very endearing qualities but they may grow, he's a bit 'Naval' if you know what I mean & none of the gaiety of 'Dickie' Mountbatten (or what we all thought gay) and his manners are a trifle rough. She really looked very pretty, & they are <u>both</u> going to be called the Duke & Duchess of Something or other, which I think <u>quite right</u>. Philip of Greece gives me the impression of taking all the wrong & trivial things to heart, & not the things that <u>really</u>

matter – which is just lack of a sense of proportion. However, time will tell. He <u>scowls</u> a bit as though a fly were a permanent guest on his nose! I think all Royalty scowl, the male members especially. I suppose it's done in self defence! ... I wonder if the newly engaged couple will be forced to have an austerity honeymoon in keeping with the austerity wedding.[38]

When the news was official, Princess Alice, the groom's mother, wrote to Queen Mary: 'Lilibet has a wonderful character & I think Philip is very lucky to have won her love.'[39] The King presented the marriage to the Privy Council on 31 July, the meeting attended by the Duke of Gloucester, the Archbishop of Canterbury, the Lord Chancellor, Prime Minister Clement Attlee, Winston Churchill and senior Dominions representatives. After the Council one of its members, quite possibly Churchill, told her: 'You can now get married with our hearty approval.'[40]

9
THE WEDDING, 1947

The wedding at Westminster Abbey on 20 November was one of the first major royal occasions since the war, giving some hope for the future to a nation just emerging from years of deprivation. There was a carriage procession through the streets of London. Guests came from Europe and the Commonwealth, and there was a flash of colour to be enjoyed, though service dress (rather than full ceremonial dress) was the order of the day. Among the few guests Prince Philip invited he did not forget his friends from Australia, including the Fallons and Sue Other-Gee. Queen Mary's verdict was that the festivities had gone off well: 'a ray of light in a world which is very dreary at present'.[1]

Other guests had their say. Field Marshal Smuts excelled himself by telling Queen Mary: 'You are the big potato. The other Queens are all small potatoes.'[2] Princess Marie Louise asked him if he did not think the bride beautiful. 'Are we not blessed to have such a Princess?' Smuts was more restrained. He thought for a moment: 'She makes me very sad ... Yes, sad, because she is serious and wise beyond her years.' This was always the key to her character.

Sir Michael Duff was there. His account was designed to amuse Cecil Beaton (who, as Clarissa Avon once put it, 'always brought the worst out of everyone'):[3]

> The Royal Wedding was as pretty as an ice cream ... The real thing was enchanting. Queen Mary in ice blue, shimmering in the iciest of ice blue, nodding away like a contented potentate so ancient that she scarce held together. You felt that Pussy, Lady Cynthia, and Bertha Dawkins* were supporting her with unseen

---

* Queen Mary's Women of the Bedchamber: Pussy – Lady Constance Milnes-Gaskell (1885–1964), Lady Cynthia Colville (1884–1968), and Lady Bertha Dawkins (1866–1943).

hands. Occasionally this ageing mammal whirled her hand about as though a plague of flies had been let loose. Edwina Mount B[atten] had one too many paradise plumes while Juliana* positively crawled in what looked like seafood, which clung to her dyke-like hat. Grinners herself [Queen Elizabeth] looked like an inflated tangerine, her hat resembling a Don's, perked up with ill-gotten plumage. She looked IMMENSE and even her grin damped to the minimum by the gigantic contours of her face, it was like the sun trying to shine through the clouds. The King looked unbelievably beautiful, like an early French King, and HRH the Bride like a dream, and like a fairy tale Princess ... Our beloved Duchess,† sweet and pretty as ever, but I thought her clothes messy, which is unlike her.

Queen Mary gave the largest stomacher to the bride, and a tiara of vast diamonds, and bracelets to match, all from her own collection, so that she is now left with only 48 tiaras ... The King said to Juliet [Duff]: 'I think people have sent all their belongings they don't know what to do with.' Queen Mary refused to stand next to the King of Iraq, in the group, so finally Ena [the Queen of Spain] had to. There were colossal crowds, which made Attlee and co quite cross. Clemmy [Churchill] looked like a demented turtle, as she escorted Winston from the Abbey ...[4]

For Prince Philip there were family difficulties. His three surviving sisters were not invited because they were married to Germans. This upset them greatly – the more so because Queen Helen of Romania and the Duchess of Aosta were guests in the Abbey, and the sisters thought this unfair. But, for their brother's sake, they stayed away. Soon afterwards they came to Britain and stayed in Scotland. Prince Philip's youngest sister, Sophie, made a point of telling her children not to be heard speaking German if they were in public and likely to be overheard.

---

* Queen Juliana of the Netherlands (1909–2004). She abdicated in 1980.
† Princess Marina, Duchess of Kent.

**BUCKINGHAM PALACE
THURSDAY, 20TH NOVEMBER, 1947
WEDDING BREAKFAST**

Filet de Sole Mountbatten

Perdreau en Casserole
Haricots Verts   Pommes Noisette
Salade Royale

Bombe Glacée Princesse Elizabeth
Friandises

Déssert

Café

The wedding menu

At the reception the bridesmaids were egged on by the Mountbattens to chase the going-away carriage out across the forecourt. 'I wonder what *la Reine Victoria* would have said,' commented Princess Marina's friend, Zoia Poklewska.

Alathea noted 'the sublime happiness of the Princess'. She was impressed by the enthusiasm and affectionate excitement of the crowds. As the day ended, she concluded: 'My thoughts are still very much with PE, her wish of so many years ago at last fulfilled.'[5]

Charles Johnston[*] and his wife, Princess Natasha Bagration, knew Prince Philip well in his bachelor days, meeting him often at Coppins with Princess Marina, Natasha being an intimate cousin of hers and a second cousin of the groom. Prince Philip sometimes came to their London flat. Johnston was a Russian scholar and poet, deeply immersed in Russian literature. In 1950 he and Natasha would translate Turgenev's *A Sportsman's Notebook*. All of this made him an acute observer of the changing nuances in society. They were invited to the pre-wedding ball at Buckingham Palace:

> We'd been warned that it would be freezing inside, in the state rooms opened up for the first time since the war. But this turned out to be wrong. Altogether it was a very well-organised and happy party, with a genuine atmosphere of everybody being able to see each other, of real liking between the R. Family and the rest – in fact a more spontaneous feeling than would have been possible *en plus petit comité*.
>
> With it all, a strong impression of make-believe, as if everybody was tacitly agreed that it was a jolly gallant attempt to look like the late thirties, but not one that could take you in for a moment. Consciousness of borrowed dresses, hired tiaras, tails by Moss Bros,

---

[*] (Sir) Charles Johnston (1912–86), later Ambassador in Jordan, Governor of Aden, and High Commissioner to Australia (between 1965 and 1971). Educated at Winchester, he translated Pushkin's *Eugene Onegin* into English verse, preserving its stanza form, and published his own poetry. In 1944 he married Princess Natasha Bagration (1914–84), granddaughter of Grand Duke Constantine of Russia. She was frequently at Coppins. All this made him an interesting 'walking contradiction'. He was on the inside track but not enough for his liking. Natasha was treated as a member of the family; he was not. When the Queen Mother wrote to the Johnstons the letters began: 'Dearest Natasha and Sir Charles'.

chauffeurs in the Mall by Godfrey Davis and Daimler Hire. In fact just a bit like Vienna between the wars – none of the nagging nostalgia, not of the depressing shabby gentility – but all the same, compared with the thirties, a marked step in that direction ... Today, however, one has an uneasy feeling that it's Washington all the time ...'[6]

Johnston examined what Prince Philip's arrival meant to the British Royal Family. He thought 'the deer-stalking, grouse-shooting, ultra-autochthonous, Anglo-British, Picto-Scotch side, which is dominant and determines the surface impression' was now confronted by 'something which couldn't be less English: the international side, the unmentionable Russian and German connexions, the awkward Greek ones, the acutely embarrassing Jugoslav ones, the whole European Royal trade union with its special language of schoolroom nicknames and enthusiastic gutturals'. He concluded that Prince Philip was more Mountbatten than Greek with the naval wardroom predominant: 'Result: a shot of wardroom heartiness into the existence of a Scotch house-party.'[7]

The Johnstons were seated with Prince Philip's friends in the Abbey, where he was impressed by the groom's 'serious face and the care he took not to go faster than the two little pages could keep up. A moment going up the altar steps when the train got tight, and he saw it at once and waited. Same conscientiousness as in seeing that his old Russian and naval chums got good seats.'[8]

Shortly afterwards Prince Philip received sound advice from his Dutch counterpart, Prince Bernhard of the Netherlands: 'You are new at this thing, Philip, and you probably don't realize what you are up against. Practically everything you do will be a subject of criticism. You can't ignore it because some of it may be justified, and even if it isn't it may be politic to heed it. But don't let it get you down. In this job you need a skin like an elephant.'[9]

In the letter in which the King described his family as 'Us Four', he told his daughter that when they made the long walk in the Abbey he had been 'thrilled' at having her 'so close' to him and that when he gave her hand to the Archbishop of Canterbury he had 'lost something very special'. He hoped he had not been 'hard hearted' making her wait so long before getting married, and was so pleased that she had been able to come to South Africa with them. It was a touching letter written by a proud father, with a heavy heart.[10]

10
MARRIED LIFE, 1948

Princess Elizabeth's relationship with Prince Philip was different from that between her parents. George VI needed support and had been persistent enough to persuade Elizabeth Bowes-Lyon to marry him and thus obtain it. He needed her more than she needed him. As a strong and dutiful wife, she helped him be the one thing he craved to be – a good constitutional king. She never wanted to be described as the power behind the throne, but that was what she was. She was clever enough to stay behind the throne and give him the credit.

The King adored his elder daughter. She was close to him and only ever wanted to do her best for him. Princess Elizabeth was sure of her father's love. It has been said that a girl who has such a close and devoted relationship with her father will transfer it to the man she marries and that is for life. This man was not at all like her father. He was supportive and dutiful. But she was less sure of his affections than she had been of her father's. He would never fundamentally let her down. He was not cosy.

Princess Elizabeth found herself managing the 1940s equivalent of an 'angry young man', in his case argumentative, contradictory, easily bored, sometimes frustrated by the stultifying domesticity around him. Time would prove them to be like two well-planted, mutually supportive oak trees, but it was not the gentle Sunday lunch, walk in the park, afternoon-tea marriage of her parents. She came to handle him well. When he wanted something, she joked: 'I tell Philip he can have it, and then make certain he doesn't get it.' A childhood friend of the Queen said: 'She really wanted him, but the first six or seven years were difficult, him being the kind of man he was.'[1] Another said: 'He made her suffer.'[2]

King George VI was not easy. Sir Edward Ford, one of his secretaries, recalled that he had 'gnashes'. The veins on his neck would stick out when he was angry and he would rage for about three minutes. There were lighter moments. As they were leaving a garden party in Scotland the King suddenly said: 'I forgot to thank the band.'

Ford volunteered: 'Don't worry, Sir, I thanked them.'

The King said: 'With respect, Edward, it's not quite the same.'[3]

Duff and Diana Cooper lunched with the Royal Family when Duff received his GCMG in 1948. She found the King rather whining, complaining about the cost of heating, that he could not see Big Ben from the Palace because of the trees in the Mall, or that someone always took his book away before he could finish it. Diana Cooper's line about his family was: 'They don't listen to him much. It's *her* family and household. "All right, Daddy", then a quick turn away and "What did you say, Mummy darling?"'[4]

Before the wedding the King had appointed Princess Elizabeth to the Order of the Garter. He bestowed it on Prince Philip a few days later to give her seniority. He created him Duke of Edinburgh, the title he would hold for the rest of his life, but forgot to make him a Prince of the United Kingdom. The newly created Duke and Duchess honeymooned at Broadlands, the Hampshire home of Lord (in fact of Lady) Mountbatten, and then at Birkhall in Scotland.

Soon afterwards, on 24 January 1948, Charles and Natasha Johnston had the chance to see how the newlyweds were adjusting, when Princess Marina brought them over to Royal Lodge from Coppins for a drink, the King and Queen being away at Sandringham:

> He and Pss. E. seemed very well, happy and already settled into married life. Each has changed: his tough, wardroom manner had gone and he turned out to be an excellent and attentive host; and she showed no sign of pomposity and stiffness but was positively easy to talk to. We stood round the fire in the big green-painted Regency Gothic drawing room, then we sat down and I found myself at the other end of the sofa from her and she told me about her visit to Parliament during the Foreign Affairs debate...*

---

* This was her first visit to the House of Commons. She heard a Labour MP speak, and Winston Churchill. At the same time the Duke of Edinburgh was in the House of Lords, rehearsing taking his seat the following week.

Pss. E. ... seemed very easily amused at the stories I told. She hasn't yet got the incredibly accomplished charm of her mother, but the basis of it is certainly there: the power to establish a *sympathie*.[5]

Sir Charles predicted that Princess Elizabeth would preside over a new Elizabethan age and declared: 'I'm going to be one of the new Elizabethans.'[6]

The couple were about to move into Windlesham Moor and into Clock House, Kensington Palace, loaned by the Athlones, who were away in Canada. They were delighted to be leaving Buckingham Palace. Princess Elizabeth now had her own household. Since January General Sir Frederick 'Boy' Browning was in charge as her Comptroller Treasurer. He had married Daphne du Maurier, the famous novelist, in 1932 and would stay until just after the Accession in 1952. The Private Secretary was John 'Jock' Colville, son of Lady Cynthia, a Woman of the Bedchamber to Queen Mary. He had been private secretary to Neville Chamberlain, Winston Churchill and briefly to Clement Attlee. He served Princess Elizabeth from 1947 to 1949. Prince Philip's friend Michael Parker served as his Private Secretary and equerry to both of them. She had two ladies in waiting, Lady Margaret Egerton (who married Colville in 1948), and Lady Margaret Seymour (who married Philip Hay, Princess Marina's Private Secretary, also in 1948). There were two other ladies in waiting, by 1949 'Extra Ladies' – Lady Mary Strachey and Mrs Andrew Elphinstone.

On 3 March the Brownings went with the Edinburghs to Shadwell Basin to inspect the New Zealand sailing ship *Pamir*. Daphne du Maurier found Princess Elizabeth 'sweet, very gracious and charming, with a lovely smile and laugh, and yet shy in a nice sort of way'. But Prince Philip was 'a menace, older in manner than he looks, and I suspect could be very tricky if his will was crossed'.[7]

Windlesham Moor was a Victorian house set in fifty-eight acres between Ascot and Bagshot. Daphne du Maurier visited it when they were not there, finding it impersonal and bare, but loved the bathroom, which was stacked with glass bottles full of lotions and powders. She was impressed by a chromium-plated lavatory roll dispenser, which issued a tissue-like sheet at the press of a button.[8] As it happened, they did not spend much time there, because Prince Philip 'clinging to his naval career with the tenacity of a barnacle to a ship's keel',[9] as Dermot Morrah put it, moved into naval accommodation at Greenwich to undertake a six-month course of instruction.

In London they moved into Clarence House, the home of the Duke of Connaught until 1942, and then a wartime office for the Red Cross and other organisations. It needed considerable modernisation, which Prince Philip enjoyed tackling. They hoped to stay there for many years to come.

George VI loved the Order of the Garter. One of the first things he had done within three days of the Abdication, was to bestow it on Queen Elizabeth and to command that a Garter ceremony should be held in the summer of his Coronation. In 1946 the King had managed to prise from the government the right to appoint Knights of the Garter and Thistle in his personal gift. On St George's Day 1948, the six hundredth anniversary of the creation of the Order, the King revived the Garter procession and the full Installation service. He invested Princess Elizabeth and the Duke of Edinburgh in the Throne Room, then five new Knights, and installed them. The war had prevented any Garter ceremonies so thirteen new Knights created since 1937 were installed in pairs, among them some of the great heroes of the war: Alanbrooke, Alexander of Tunis, Montgomery of Alamein and Portal of Hungerford. The ceremony was broadcast on the Home Service and a series of gramophone records released.*

On Monday, 26 April, the King and Queen celebrated their Silver Wedding with a carriage procession and thanksgiving service at St Paul's Cathedral. Princess Elizabeth had not realised that this was one of those occasions when ladies wore day dresses to the floor, but with Orders and decorations.† She did not have a suitable dress

---

* A recording of the Queen's Installation was played to her in the last summer of her life. The commentators were not yet in their stride, men such as Wynford Vaughan-Thomas and Richard Dimbleby finding it all trivial, having been war correspondents. In due course they became admirable, culminating with Dimbleby's moving commentary for Sir Winston Churchill's funeral in 1965 (his own voice thick with cancer).

† The sartorial custom of the day dress to the floor continued into the Queen's reign, and was last most noticeable at Princess Margaret's wedding in 1960.

so wore an evening dress with a fur stole, and hoped Queen Mary would not catch her out.

Paris Visit

A visit to Paris by the Edinburghs was suggested by the Labour Foreign Secretary, Ernest Bevin, prompted by Jock Colville. The French had relished every moment of the Royal Wedding, and wanted her first ever visit to the Continent to be to their capital, sealing 'the bonds of Anglo-French friendship'. When Sir Oliver Harvey put this to Georges Bidault, the Foreign Minister, he welcomed it, only hoping that the attention of the French people would not prove 'too embarrassing'.[10] The King agreed that his daughter could go so long as she had a specific purpose – the opening of the exhibition *Eight Centuries of British Life in Paris*. It could only be a short visit between 14 and 18 May as Prince Philip had to be back at work.

Six weeks of preparation and attendant worries followed for the French protocol department: Princess Elizabeth could not host a party at the British Embassy, only the Sovereign could, and though technically the Ambassador had precedence over the Duke of Edinburgh, it was hoped he would not press that. For the French Head of Protocol, these matters somewhat overshadowed 'the allegory of youth, which is what the people of Paris want to see in this visit. The little Princess with her dazzling complexion brings them hope and the illusion of a world where happiness could exist.'[11]

The couple's accommodation at the British Embassy left much to be desired. Prince Philip complained that the huge and heavy print of Queen Victoria and Prince Albert above the hotel-like twin beds could easily fall on their heads. To reach the bathroom and lavatory, with its Heath Robinson-like plumbing, they had to go out into the passage, past the lift and along another passage. 'And to think that this is the British Embassy,' said the Princess to her cousin, Diana Bowes-Lyon, who was working in the city at that time.[12]

The formal parts went well – the opening of the exhibition and the laying of a wreath at the Arc de Triomphe. Madame de Bellaigue, who had taught the Princesses French, came on the trip to hear

Princess Elizabeth make a speech of seven minutes in French, 'with hardly any trace of an accent'. She was undeterred by the clicking of cameras or the loud ringing of church bells. The couple enjoyed the sections devoted to the British influence on the French music hall and the visits to Paris of Edward VII, his top hat displayed in a vitrine. The 'youth and freshness' of the young couple so gripped the French people that crowds flocked to see them wherever they went, turning the most informal occasions such as sightseeing into 'a Royal Progress'.*

President Auriol gave Princess Elizabeth the Grand Croix of the Légion d'Honneur, and the Duke the Croix de Guerre with palms (though the President was so shy that he bestowed the honours in the wrong order). A man of humble origins from near Toulouse, Auriol had retained something of his regional accent. He told the Princess she spoke better French than he did.

Grey skies on the first day broke into magnificent sunshine presenting Paris at its best – the hottest Whitsun weekend on record. At a dinner for sixty-four at the Embassy, Princess Elizabeth wore the Nizam of Hyderabad's diamond tiara and necklace. A cocktail party was given for young French naval officers by Captain Howard-Johnston and his wife Lady Alexandra (Haig), and one by Viscount Duncannon, the Ambassador's private secretary, for French people of their age. The boat ride on the Seine attracted crowds from the Pont d'Iéna to the Île St Louis. The race meeting at Longchamp mustered a quarter of a million people, twenty thousand more than usual, but held on a Sunday, it provoked complaints from the Methodist Church Union, the World Evangelical Alliance and the Lord's Day Observance Council. They made a private evening call on Prince and Princess George of Greece.† The couple had a small

---

* The French Head of Protocol had to foil the attempts of an impresario to appear with a young girl of ten, who would sing the '*Élégie des Nymphs de Vaux*'. He was forbidden to reappear but materialised ten minutes before the visit, with a little girl in tow, hoping to force their hand. Detectives sent him packing.

† Prince George of Greece (1869–1957), Prince Philip's uncle, sometimes known as 'Big George', and his wife, Princess Marie Bonaparte (1882–1962), who had paid for some of Prince Philip's education, and was a noted psychiatrist and friend of Freud. She had advised on the illness of his mother, Princess Alice, in the 1930s.

private dinner at the Tour d'Argent and then went to a nightclub where attendance was strictly vetted.[13] They paid a spectacular visit to the Opéra with the President, for a performance of three ballets, directed by Georges Hirsch, a noted Resistance figure. A roaring crowd of fifty thousand outside surprised Prince Philip. Old Prince George joined them. He spotted that Prince Philip was enjoying congratulating the ballerinas. He grinned and muttered: 'I think my nephew likes talking to the dancers. I'll go and join in myself to keep an eye on the young dog.'[14]

Princess Elizabeth and her husband both asked: 'How could the French people ever bring themselves to guillotine their king?' When she addressed that to Pierre-Henri Teitgen, considered the most eloquent minister, he was lost for words. When Prince Philip tried it on Jules Moch, Minister of the Interior, Moch replied: '*Parce qu'ils étaient les nôtres!*'*[15] The Ambassador mused on this point: 'It was an unusual experience to see the townsfolk of Paris cheer an English Princess from the Place de la Bastille.'[16]

Jacques Dumaine, the erudite Head of Protocol, considered the success of the visit was partly due to a sense of solidarity shown by a strong, surviving throne, the 'royal-mindedness' of the people of Paris, but finally 'this vision of youth and hope': 'For four days a little blue flower of sentiment took the place of worry in the garden of our minds and that is why Princess Elizabeth was so warmly welcomed.'[17]

That was the official version. Princess Elizabeth was already pregnant though this had not been announced. Prince Philip suffered from gastric problems. Seething in the background at everything 'the horrible Harveys' had done to the Embassy, Lady Diana Cooper was bitter about most aspects of the visit. She objected to the closed car, which prevented the crowds from seeing the Princess, was horrified to hear that an embassy official had scratched a number of guests from the party at the Hôtel de Lauzun as former collaborators, while Eric Duncannon's party was 'memorable for its horror'. It was the hottest day of the year, three hundred people were jammed in. Princess Elizabeth looked 'cucumber cool', the Duke, 'who had been poisoned at the Embassy, was like a rag'. They had lunched

---

* 'Because they were ours!'

with Madame Auriol at Fontainebleau: 'Her feet must have hurt. He spent his party in the loo.'[18]

Jock Colville recalled that the Tour d'Argent was empty the night they dined there, though Prince Philip spotted an alien camera observing them through a hole, and the visit to the nightclub he judged 'one of the most appalling evenings' he had ever spent.[19] Racing and dancing on a Sunday, the Lord's Day, greatly offended the Assembly of the Free Church of Scotland, who sent a copy of their resolution, expressing 'grief and concern'.[20]

Colville saw the magic that Princess Elizabeth could inspire: 'a visit by a young princess with beautiful blue eyes and a superb natural complexion brought gleams of radiant sunshine into the dingiest streets of the dreariest cities.' He noted: 'Princes who do their duty are respected; beautiful princesses have an in-built advantage over their male counterparts,'[21] and when his secondment was over in 1949, he was left with the lasting impression of 'the dedication and total honesty'[22] of Princess Elizabeth and her husband.*

★ ★ ★ ★ ★

On 5 June 1948 Princess Elizabeth joined her family at the Derby. On the same day it was announced that she would soon undertake no more public engagements. There was naturally excitement, anticipating a direct heir in the House of Windsor. She carried on her engagements throughout July, including attending the opening of the Olympic Games at the end of that month, before a Balmoral summer.

King George V had made no provision for titles for the children of daughters of the Sovereign. For that reason Princess Mary's children

---

* Not everyone approved of Colville's late-life revelations. He did not suffer like Crawfie, but Lord Bessborough (the erstwhile Eric Duncannon) warned him that he could publish certain things that he might not like, told him by his father and others – indiscretions about Churchill or Princess Elizabeth, which Lord Salisbury had also considered to have broken the trust essential between Private Secretary and Prime Minister. (Bessborough to Colville, 24 June 1986, draft in the Countess of Avon papers, Birmingham University.)

only received titles from their father, the Earl of Harewood.* In the case of Princess Elizabeth, the firstborn son would use the courtesy title Earl of Merioneth, his father's second title. Subsequent children would have been born Lord or Lady Mountbatten, their father's surname.† Just in time, on 22 October, George VI took the matter to Council and ensured they would be HRH Prince or Princess. This was formalised in the *London Gazette* of 9 November.

Queen Elizabeth was angered that Tommy Lascelles was dispensing with the time-honoured tradition of having the Home Secretary present (at least in the building) when the royal baby was born. With classic Lascelles logic, he pointed out that all the Dominions would wish to be represented, which could involve seven ministers on the premises.[23] The tradition was dropped. At 9.14 p.m. on 14 November Princess Elizabeth was 'safely delivered of a Prince', as the Court Circular put it. Prince Charles arrived. 'I had no idea that one could be kept so busy in bed – there seems to be something happening all the time!' wrote the young mother to her cousin, Mary Cambridge. 'The baby is very sweet, and Philip and I are enormously proud of him. I still find it hard to believe that I really have a baby of my own!'[24]

In the House of Commons Clement Attlee moved an address. Winston Churchill's voice trembled with emotion as he welcomed the new Prince, born 'into this world of strife and storm'. He continued: 'I hope that amongst those principles that will be instilled into him will be the truth that the Sovereign is never so great as when the people are free. There we meet on common ground.' Predictably Willie Gallacher, the Communist MP, made his traditional hostile intervention, but on this occasion he recalled that there had been 'bell ringing and joyful sounds in abundance' on the day of his own birth. He had been born on Christmas Day. The House laughed and the motion was passed.[25]

---

* The Princess Royal's husband had died on 24 May 1947, so George was now the 7th Earl. Gerald remained as the Hon. Gerald Lascelles.

† It was often asserted that Mountbatten was the surname of Prince Philip's mother. It was not. She was a Battenberg, but married in 1903. The Mountbatten name was not invented until 1917.

11
ANXIOUS YEARS, 1949–51

The birth of Prince Charles was overshadowed by grave concerns for the King's health. He had been experiencing cramp in his legs since January 1948. His equerry, Peter Townsend, noticed that at Holyroodhouse in the summer, the King complained about his legs: 'They won't work properly.'[1] During his holiday it eased a bit, but he still experienced discomfort. By October his left foot was permanently numb and his right foot in some pain. He called in his doctors. With Princess Elizabeth in the last days of her pregnancy, he was determined that she should be spared any anxiety, so nothing was said until Prince Charles was safely born.

The onset of arteriosclerosis was diagnosed and there was genuine fear that he might lose his leg. The King and Queen and Princess Margaret were scheduled to visit New Zealand and Australia, meaning that Princess Elizabeth would have to bear the burden of royal engagements in Britain, while coping with a new baby. Prince Philip's naval career was now in jeopardy. He went onto half-pay for some months so that he could be more supportive.

The King's tour never happened. On 23 November he cancelled all his engagements and prepared to rest for the foreseeable future. This caused considerable concern not only in Britain but across the world. Dermot Morrah was aware that the King's condition was more worrying than was being admitted. Neither he nor Tommy Lascelles trusted Sir John Weir, the King's homeopathic doctor. It was surely Morrah who wrote in a *Times* leader: 'On King George VI the physical has always been more than matched by the nervous strain.'[2] Meanwhile the King was confined to bed with his legs in an occlude for eight hours a day, a device designed to improve circulation.

By mid-December the King was attending quietly to affairs of state, though, as Lascelles wrote to Alec Hardinge: 'He won't be out of the medical wood for many weeks yet.'[3] The fact that everything went quiet at Buckingham Palace made people wonder if there was something wrong with the royal baby. Cecil Beaton waited anxiously for the call to come to photograph him. This finally happened on 14 December. Beaton did not see the King, but he captured touching images of mother and child, the baby opening his eyes and staring into the camera: 'the beginning of a lifetime in the glare of public duty'.[4] The King was well enough to attend the christening the next day, and to receive Lester Pearson (then Canada's Secretary of State for External Affairs) the day after.

Princess Elizabeth, Prince Philip and Princess Margaret joined the King and Queen for Christmas at Buckingham Palace. The King then left London for Sandringham on 8 January 1949 to convalesce further. Princess Elizabeth was there and promptly went down with a bad case of measles. The newly knighted Sir Gladwyn Jebb and his wife came to stay in February, Cynthia Jebb noting that the King was 'naturally alert, highly strung, simple and downright'. She commented on the obvious devotion between Princess Elizabeth and her father, and how well she and Prince Philip got on.[5] The King came back to London in time for a right lumbar sympathectomy operation (to remove an obstruction in his leg), performed at the Palace on 12 March. He was advised by his doctors that he must lead a more placid life from now on or thrombosis could occur.

In the meantime Princess Elizabeth threw herself into public engagements. That year there were events in Edinburgh, Liverpool, Wales, Birmingham, Northern Ireland, Colchester, the Channel Islands (a Tuesday till Friday), Yorkshire and Canterbury. On 14 April, accompanied by Princess Marie Louise, she was present in Westminster Abbey, when the Lord High Almoner, Bishop of Lichfield, distributed the Royal Maundy money on behalf of the King. Princess Elizabeth did so much that summer that the *Sunday Express* asked if she was doing too much: 'She frequently looks tired and occasionally strained.'[6]

In May 1949 the King was at Royal Lodge, enjoying his rhododendrons and making plans for more planting, and by July there was a hint of cautious optimism in Queen Elizabeth's letter to Mrs

Roosevelt. The King was 'really better, and with care should be quite well in a year or so'.[7]

Crawfie

In the midst of these worries, Queen Elizabeth had to tackle the issue of the articles Crawfie proposed to write about her former charges. There was a battle of wills between Queen Elizabeth and the former governess. Princess Elizabeth was not involved, though she felt betrayed because she and Princess Margaret had been so close to Crawfie for so many years.

Queen Elizabeth had assisted several authors in telling her daughters' story. Lady Cynthia Asquith had received considerable help, though not as much as she would have liked. Dermot Morrah and Betty Spencer Shew were given access and assistance with their books. Morrah was on good terms with Tommy Lascelles and had got to know Queen Elizabeth on the South African tour. Mrs Spencer Shew even received handwritten notes from Princess Elizabeth for her royal wedding book. She produced titles such as *Mid Pleasures and Palaces* and *Our Royal Children*.

There rose up an ambitious pair of editors in America, Bruce and Beatrice Gould of the *Ladies Home Journal*. They had failed to secure an article from Queen Elizabeth during the war but, undeterred, in 1948 they homed in on Princess Elizabeth. They wanted to commission Rebecca West to write about her, but were told that the only man likely to get approval was Morrah. They commissioned him for the vast sum of $2,500, despite his over-formal *Times*-leader style. Nevertheless he proved a good source of royal information. Everyone told him that the person he needed to talk to was Crawfie, but Crawfie would not talk.

By this time Crawfie had retired and married a divorced major called George Buthlay, who was a pernicious influence, a philanderer and a manipulator. His unit, the UNNRA (United Nations Relief and Rehabilitation Administration), had been involved in some dodgy business in the Middle East during the war. He stirred anger in his new wife, persuading her that she should have been made a Dame (DCVO) rather than CVO, and he played on Queen Elizabeth having failed to send her a wedding present. At one time Crawfie had written to Queen Elizabeth suggesting she might become a lady in waiting.

Crawfie had never had the remotest wish to sell her story, or to assist Morrah. But in 1949 she conceived the idea of writing her own story and put this to Queen Elizabeth, who told her categorically 'to put all the American temptations aside'.[8]

The Goulds then came to London and flattered Crawfie. The outcome was that she agreed to talk to the romantic novelist, Dorothy Black, who would craft the story. Crawfie got tied up in a contract, genuinely believing that if Queen Elizabeth did not like what she produced, the whole plan would be dropped. The Goulds rewrote much of the text in a style to suit their readers. They tweaked her text, their approach being 'they may be excellent for English readers who take royalty and a reverence for granted, this is not likely to be the best treatment for Americans'.[9] Much was romanticised and some of it relates closely to stories that had appeared in the popular press over the years and so was clearly inserted to beef up the story.*

The completed text was was shown to Queen Elizabeth who did not like it one bit, but Crawfie was tied into her contract so articles came out and the book followed. Crawfie was condemned for a serious breach of trust, and ostracised. In due course she left Nottingham Cottage and moved to Scotland.

Crawfie never wrote a word of those articles or the subsequent book. Nor did she write any of the articles that later went out under her name, but she was paid – at one time, £8,000, tax free. Even Tom Harvey, Queen Elizabeth's Private Secretary, had to concede that some good came from *The Little Princesses* because it informed

---

* This and later books were based on Crawfie's verbal memories given to Dorothy Black in a hotel. Crawfie herself was not especially literate. There is disparity between the letters written in her name by her less than admirable husband, George Buthlay, and the rather naive words of Crawfie when she wrote the letters herself. For the full horror of what the Goulds did to Crawfie, see Hugo Vickers, *Elizabeth The Queen Mother* (Hutchinson, 2005), pp. 279-291. In the early newspaper serialisations, letters from the Princesses were reproduced.

the Americans that the monarchy embodied all that is best in democracy.[10]

Crawfie fell on her face when a syrupy description of the 1955 Royal Ascot appeared in *Woman's Own* under her name, but Royal Ascot was cancelled, due to the National Rail Strike, between filing and publication. Princess Margaret's later-life verdict on Crawfie was: 'She snaked.'[11] Crawfie led a miserable old age, and died aged seventy-eight in 1986.

★ ★ ★ ★ ★

At the end of April 1949 Princess Elizabeth's office moved to Clarence House. The new Private Secretary was Colonel Martin Charteris, who took up his post in January 1950 and would stay with her until 1977, and proved without question the most inspirational of all the men who served her. In later life he was able to say, 'I love the Queen,' without fear that this would be misinterpreted. But he quickly learned that there was a line that must never be crossed.

On 4 July the Edinburghs finally moved into Clarence House, the Princess's personal standard flying from the flagpole. Parliament voted £50,000 to convert the place from its dilapidated state amid some controversy. It had no central heating, domestic hot water or wiring for electricity. The work took a year and a half and at least fifty-five craftsmen worked on it. The young couple spent as much time as possible restoring it, decorating it and organising it as a long-term home, enjoyably side-stepping the Household and others who wanted to mastermind it. A nursery was installed for Prince Charles.

Princess Elizabeth was one of many family guests at the wedding of her cousin, Lord Harewood to Marion Stein, a concert pianist, whom he had met through Benjamin Britten. The Princess Royal had to plead with her brother to obtain permission for George and Marion to marry, with Queen Mary, in particular, objecting to the union. There was nothing against Marion personally but her Viennese Jewish background was considered unconventional. She left Austria with her family for fear of Hitler in 1938. She had been intimate with the composer Benjamin Britten since 1944, but he was more interested in Peter Pears. The Harewoods were married in St Mark's, Mayfair, in North Audley Street, on 29 September. The King and Queen, the Edinburghs, Princess Margaret and the Gloucesters came from Scotland especially to attend the wedding.

Malta

On 15 October Prince Philip left for Malta to take up a post as First Lieutenant on HMS *Chequers*, leader of the First Destroyer Flotilla, Mediterranean Fleet.* After laying a wreath at the Cenotaph with her father on Remembrance Sunday, Princess Elizabeth joined him between 19 November and 28 December. She flew out with Lady Mountbatten, accompanied by Mike Parker and Lady Alice Egerton, arriving in time to celebrate her second wedding anniversary. It was essentially a private visit. They lived at the Villa Guardamangia, just outside Valletta, then the home of the Mountbattens. This was the first of several stays, the Duke serving there until July 1951. She was able to drive her own car, go shopping and attend polo matches or films as a naval officer's wife rather than a member of the Royal Family. While there she had some engagements, the re-hallowing of St Paul's Anglican Cathedral, the unveiling of new panels of the Malta war memorial in the cathedral, attending balls at the Governor's Palace and at the Phoenicia Hotel. For this reason she described Malta as the only place in the Commonwealth that she could truly describe as home.

She left one-year-old Prince Charles behind and, not for the last time, he spent Christmas without her – at Sandringham with his grandparents. Princess Elizabeth joined the family at Sandringham on New Year's Eve, by which time she was pregnant again. Tommy Lascelles quizzed Princess Elizabeth for her views on Lord Mountbatten, whom she had had ample time to observe in Malta. Lascelles wrote to his wife: 'I was amused last night by P.E.'s shrewd & penetrating analysis of "the simple sailor" ... It didn't look as if the S.S. or his wife have any influence at all in that quarter.'[12]

Queen Mary was at Sandringham, and though the Countess of

---

* From May 1950 the Duke commanded HMS *Magpie*.

Euston found her 'rather forbidding', she enjoyed her saying to Prince Charles: 'Don't forget your little bow.' The Countess also remembered the King insisted that as the ladies left the dining room they should turn and curtsey. One night Olivia Mulholland curtseyed before the Duchess of Beaufort. 'You curtseyed before Her Grace,' he shouted.[13]

Princess Elizabeth was in England that spring, a highlight of which was the state visit of President and Madame Auriol of France in March. Jacques Dumaine came with the President. He interpreted for the Duke of Gloucester on the train, noting 'he remains shy and incurious, although the hearty laugh which follows his short remarks' made his job easier. He observed Queen Elizabeth 'who is losing her battle against plumpness' and thought that motherhood had made Princess Elizabeth 'more beautiful and her complexion retains the texture of pink porcelain'. She greeted the Auriols as old friends and eased them into conversation with her aunts, the Princess Royal, the Duchess of Gloucester and Princess Marina.[14]

Despite the precarious state of the King's health, Princess Elizabeth was back in Malta between 28 March and 10 April, returning via Nice, where she had to spend a night. The King took the train up to Balmoral on 13 August but Queen Elizabeth stayed in London, awaiting the birth of the new baby. Prince Philip arrived from Malta.

Princess Anne was born at Clarence House on 15 August. Cecil Beaton asked if he could photograph her, and this was granted. By this time Prince Charles was running about and talking. Beaton observed: 'a most sturdy little chap ... with rather heavy pink cheeks, his eyes starlike, his pale gold hair as silken as only a child's can be'. The Prince enquired: 'Baby here?' Princess Anne was brought in, described by Beaton as 'a small baby with quite a definite nose for one so young, large sleepy grey-green eyes, and a particularly pretty mouth, with the upper lip curving to an almost exaggerated rosebud'.[15] Very often the Palace forbade Beaton to publish the best photographs, though they tended to slip out in subsequent years. On this occasion he caught a sweet one of Prince Charles kissing his sister, and some lovely images of mother and son showing them in close harmony. Princess Elizabeth declared the results 'most fortunate in every way'.[16]

Princess Elizabeth took her children to Balmoral on 18 September, bringing them back on 16 October in time for the christening, Prince Philip again returning for six days. She left her young children for ten weeks in Malta from 25 November 1950 until 12 February 1951, and again from 19 March until 24 April. In April she and Prince Philip paid their first visit to Rome, lunching at the Quirinale with the President, visiting the Pope and attending a horse race on the Appian Way. She celebrated her twenty-fifth birthday with a party at Hadrian's Villa in Tivoli. For the visit they were loaned a Rolls-Royce by the film star Massimo Serato (who had fathered a child with Anna Magnani in 1942). They visited Florence.

The Royal Family were out in force to celebrate the Festival of Britain with a service at St Paul's Cathedral on 3 May 1951, and a visit to the South Bank site the following day, Queen Mary consenting to travel around it in a wheelchair. Another of the King's much-loved Garter ceremonies took place on 9 May, when he installed King Frederik IX of Denmark, the Duke of Wellington, Earl Fortescue and the York family's neighbour from 145 Piccadilly days, Lord Allendale.

Then it all went wrong. The King looked 'obviously ill and in such pain that the procession had to be considerably curtailed'[17] when he installed his brother, the Duke of Gloucester, as Great Master of the Order of the Bath in Westminster Abbey on 24 May. The next day he was said to have gone down with influenza. In his place Princess Elizabeth presented new colours to the 3rd Battalion, Grenadier Guards, in the garden of Buckingham Palace, a spectacular ceremony attended by many members of the Royal Family, which required a formal and stirring speech: 'You march on to parade with one set of Colours and off with another ... Your old Colours were already emblazoned with honours from Tangier to Flanders. In the last fifteen years the devotion of many loyal Grenadiers has added new lustre to them ...'[18]

Princess Elizabeth helped her mother when King Haakon of Norway came on his state visit, her father staying quietly in his room. She read the speech at the state banquet, and she deputised for the King at the Birthday Parade, riding side-saddle in the scarlet uniform of Colonel of the Grenadier Guards, for which she had had fewer than a dozen lessons. *The Times* described her as 'a woman alone as the central figure of this almost overwhelmingly massive military occasion'.[19]

The King spent most of the rest of 1951 convalescing, his health the subject of numerous rumours. He was able to go up to Balmoral on 5 August, where Princess Margaret celebrated her coming of age on 21 August. The historian Hugh Trevor-Roper heard that Sir John Weir, who was with the King, had ignored the symptoms of his illness, and was trying to cure him with herbs. Only when Weir went out to shoot with Scottish dukes did the Household get the local doctor in, as a result of which other doctors were summoned to Scotland, and the King went twice to London. Finally, he was rushed to London for a belated operation.[20]

Queen Elizabeth, wearing a sprig of white heather, flew from Balmoral with Princess Elizabeth and Prince Philip, arriving at 9.45 p.m. A crowd of 250 people waited outside Buckingham Palace. Queen Mary spent ninety minutes at the Palace during the afternoon. Princess Margaret arrived. The night before the operation Queen Elizabeth and her daughters went to Lambeth Palace to receive the Sacrament in the Archbishop's chapel. The medical correspondent of the *Daily Telegraph* wrote: 'All will be disturbed by the carefully worded bulletin.'[21]

Lord Moran told Winston Churchill that 'There was a possibility of cancer of the lung.' Churchill asked why they talked of 'structural changes' and Moran told him that in those days the Royal Family were not supposed to suffer from cancer. Moran thought Lord Beaverbrook had been tipped off with some inside information, which inspired John Gordon, editor of the *Sunday Express*, to ask for 'an adequate explanatory bulletin' to 'relieve the national anxiety'.[22]

Tommy Lascelles wrote privately to Churchill, without the King's knowledge, informing him that the King had a growth on his lung. The lung was removed at Buckingham Palace on Sunday, 23 September. Four days later the Cabinet met and the Prime Minister, Clement Attlee, reported that the King was making progress, there were no complications, but 'there would be cause for some anxiety during a further period of about ten days'.[23] Counsellors of State were appointed, Queen Elizabeth and Princess Elizabeth acting in tandem. As such they authorised the prorogation of Parliament on

4 October. The next day the King was well enough to hold a Privy Council meeting at his bedside.

The King and Queen were meant to be leaving for their postponed visit to Australia and New Zealand on 22 January 1952 and to return in the summer. As it seemed unlikely the King would be well enough, the Prime Ministers of those countries were keen that Princess Elizabeth should come instead. On 9 October 1951 it was announced that she and the Duke of Edinburgh would indeed represent him.

12

DEMISE OF THE CROWN, 1951–2

Canada had not had a royal visit since before the war. Princess Elizabeth had been due to leave on 26 September 1951, but with the King so ill, the Prime Minister of Canada proposed that the visit should be postponed for some days. It became clear that if the tour did take place, the Princess would have to travel to Canada by air rather than sea. Churchill, as Leader of the Opposition, thought it wrong that the Princess should 'fly the Atlantic', running additional risk at an already difficult time. The King's operation had been successful but, he pointed out: 'a period of grave anxiety evidently lies before us'.[1] In Cabinet it was mentioned that she would be undertaking other flights during the trip. They chose not to veto her flight in the BOAC Stratocruiser.

The King was keen that Princess Elizabeth should undertake her visit. Because of his operation, she and Prince Philip did not fly out until midnight on 7 October. Travelling with her were black clothes and Accession documents lest the King should die. The royal couple visited Newfoundland, Prince Edward Island, Nova Scotia, Ontario, Saskatchewan, British Columbia and Alberta.

They arrived in Montreal in a drizzle of rain and were greeted by the Governor-General, Viscount Alexander of Tunis, and the Prime Minister, Mr St Laurent. The Royal Canadian Mounted Police (the 'Mounties') were in charge of security arrangements and risked blocking the press's view until they were finally moved aside.

As ever the media were in quest of human-interest stories to balance the official duties but were invariably disappointed. When the Governor-General arranged a square dance at Government House, the press had to be happy with one pooled photo and a press release. In those days, it was hard to find a balance between the sensibilities of the guests, and the needs of the press. John Hartley, covering the tour for *The Times*, commented that 'the very large press corps of over a hundred correspondents, broadcasters, photographers and cameramen' found this 'a most unusual tour, that it was unfamiliar and frenetic, and that everyone had to live very much for the moment'.[2]

The Canadian press, accustomed to the glitz of film stars, had to accept that Princess Elizabeth was not a creation of Hollywood. She was the genuine article and refused to behave as a star. Those who met her were impressed by her firm handshake, and the beautiful eyes that looked directly at them. She talked to hospital patients 'quietly and sincerely', gave them her undivided attention, and at times her sympathy.[3] Yet to many she was a remote figure seen only in the distance. There were other problems, not least the flashbulbs of the pressmen, which sometimes exploded, splinters of glass later being found in the Princess's fur coat. During the tour Martin Charteris urged her to smile more. 'I'm smiling till my face aches,' she told him.[4] When she did smile and laugh, it was often at times when the cameras were not there.

The tour was arduous. A formal visit to Quebec ended with a state banquet, a day of fourteen hours. As the royal party headed from Windsor, Ontario, to Kapuskasing in northern Ontario, the atmosphere became less formal. Some of the locals got close enough to Prince Philip to slap him on the back, and a tailor caressed the lapel of his jacket and announced it was a well-fitting suit. There was a waiter whose bowtie lit up when serving the royal party. The Duke asked where he could get one. On a train journey a radio journalist, Cort Thompson, dangled a microphone in front of the Duke in quest of an interview. Reluctant to be interviewed, the Duke said nothing. He sidestepped the man with a series of gestures.

Princess Elizabeth was unfazed when greeted at McGill University by cheerleaders calling: 'Yea, Betty, yea, Windsor, yea yea, Betty Windsor! Rah! Rah! Rah!'[5] And she was moved when an entire stadium of children sang the National Anthem and 'O Canada', both in French. John Hartley thought that she found it hard to switch from the formal (which demanded quite intense concentration) to the relaxed (which was unusual for her on such a visit). At times she appeared too restrained. She had not yet learned how to respond to the enthusiasm of the crowds and yet, Hartley noted: 'It was fascinating to watch as her qualities of inner self were gradually drawn to the surface.'[6]

In the middle of the trip, the royal party moved on to the United States for a visit to President Truman in Washington. The American press, which had had to endure the Canadians claiming the Princess as their representative of the Empire, were now countered by American journalists pointing out the Princess's close relationship to George Washington through her mother's family. An American correspondent observed how lucky the British were to have 'a Princess who is so capably being the symbol of British lustre, dignity and strength'.[7] The *Washington Star* declared that 'Our oldest inhabitants ... are hard put to recall the name of any past visitor quite comparable to her in terms of good looks and sweetness of personality.'

The Princess and the Duke then resumed their tour via the Maritimes of Eastern Canada to St John's, Newfoundland. Unlike past royal tours, there was a lot of air travel and not much leisure time. Not all went smoothly, but it gave the Princess the confidence she would need, all too soon, to be a good constitutional monarch. She exuded self-control and self-discipline. The Canadians felt that they got to know her. Before flying home, she stressed the words used by Lord Alexander when they arrived: 'He said then that the link with the Crown was a real and tangible strength, and one of the most important factors in uniting the people of the Commonwealth into one great brotherhood. You have shown me the reality of this, and I thank you for it.'[8] They returned by ship to Liverpool, where she visited the cathedral (rebuilt after the war) and the bells were rung for the first time.

After the visit, a Mr Vernon wrote from Canada, decrying the vulgarity of the Canadian and American press with headlines such as 'Princess Hits the Highspots'. He wondered if the Archbishop of Canterbury (Geoffrey Fisher who had succeeded Cosmo Gordon Lang in 1945) could prevail on her not to visit nightclubs (which she had not done). Lascelles replied curtly that the only way to prevent hostile comment on her 'innocent activities' was to discourage her from going to 'places where people dance'. The Archbishop replied to Vernon that there was nothing disagreeable about any of this and 'The Royal House in all ways is giving an excellent and good example of home life at its best.'⁹ Winston Churchill's verdict was: 'Why, Canada is quite touchy about being called a Dominion, but look what happened when the Princess went there.'¹⁰

Princess Elizabeth and the Duke of Edinburgh had not intended to miss Prince Charles's third birthday on 14 November, but the postponement of their trip meant they were not back until three days later. The child spent the day with his grandparents, and was presented with a magnificent cake by 'Boy' Browning. For various reasons his mother had missed three Christmases with him by 1954 – so many special days in his early life, unfortunate when her own parents had treated her with such all-encompassing love.

It has become an accusation that she hardly greeted him on her return at the station. Film shows him arriving, his hand held by his grandmother, full of expectation at seeing his parents. Princess Elizabeth alighted from the train, embraced her mother and greeted her son, touching his nose, and kissing the top of his head, but the camera was behind her. She embraced Princess Margaret. Prince Philip patted Prince Charles on the head and some attention was paid to him. It was not an exuberant greeting, but it has been twisted against her. She had many formal farewells to make – to the Mounties, for example. It is true that she did not take her son's hand as they left the station.*

★ ★ ★ ★ ★

While the Edinburghs were away, Clement Attlee asked for a dissolution of Parliament and Britain went to the polls. The Labour Government lost the election and on 26 October Attlee tendered his resignation to the King at Buckingham Palace. Winston Churchill formed a Conservative administration. The King stayed indoors at the Palace. The Duke of Gloucester laid his wreath at the Cenotaph. There was no State Opening of Parliament but in a message the King announced that in his stead Princess Elizabeth would be undertaking the Commonwealth tour in January.

---

* It must be conceded, however, that when the Queen Mother returned from the United States in 1954, she stooped to embrace both grandchildren and Prince Charles threw his arms around her neck.

Shortly after Princess Elizabeth returned to Britain, Richard Casey, then Australian Minister for External Affairs, lunched with her. He told Churchill he found her so serious that he felt she had been warned or had some instinctive knowledge that she would soon be called upon to serve. Churchill replied: 'Yes, there is too much care on that young brow.'[11]

On 30 November the King went to Windsor and on 21 December he went to Sandringham for Christmas with Queen Elizabeth, Queen Mary, Princess Elizabeth and her children and Princess Margaret. The Duke of Edinburgh arrived later, as did the Gloucesters, the Duchess of Kent and their children. The King's Christmas broadcast was pre-recorded in a series of sections. He spoke of his thankfulness to God, his doctors, surgeons and nurses, through whose faithful skill he had come through his illness. By the New Year he was able to go shooting again with a light gun. His doctors allowed him to smoke as this gave him pleasure. He was able to walk back from church on 30 December.

On 28 January 1952 the King and Queen and Princess Margaret came down to London, bringing Prince Charles and Princess Anne with them. The King had some consultations with his doctors and in the evening the Royal Family attended a performance of *South Pacific* at the Theatre Royal, Drury Lane, being cheered for a full two minutes as they entered the theatre. Three days later, on 31 January, the King was at London Airport to wave Princess Elizabeth goodbye. He looked gaunt and drawn, but made the wry comment: 'This is a magnificent airliner. A modern aircraft is certainly a lot different from the stick and canvas ones I used to fly.'[12]

Winston Churchill was at the airport as Prime Minister to bid the couple farewell. So was Oliver Lyttelton (later Lord Chandos) as Secretary of State for the Colonies. He had a 'feeling of doom' when he saw the King: 'I felt with deep foreboding that this would be the last time he was to see his daughter, and that he thought so himself.'[13]

Although the King had been gravely ill, Princess Elizabeth would not have gone on that tour if imminent death was expected. Yet, as father and daughter waved to each other on that cold January day, both must have wondered if they would ever meet again.

The King and Queen, Princess Margaret, Prince Charles and

Princess Anne went back to Sandringham on 1 February. The King was able to walk from church on Sunday, 3 February. Prince Charles and Princess Anne played in the garden with their nurses. The scene echoed the days at Sandringham in January 1936 as another King's life drew to its close. George VI was looking forward to taking a recuperative holiday in South Africa as the guest of Dr D. F. Malan at the end of January, the plan being that they would stay at Botha House, Dr Malan's official residence on the coast, south of Durban. Concerns about the trip were raised in Cabinet on 5 February.*

Meanwhile 280 hares were bagged on the last day of his life. Nine fell to the King's gun. Impishly the King told his shooting neighbour that he would get the hares before they reached him. Aubrey Buxton wrote:

> The first was bowled over by His Majesty on the crest of the bank. His friend looked across and was greeted with a gleeful grin. The second was far out in front when it made the hedge, but the King got it none the less. The third, and the last, was at full speed, for the drivers were close in, but His Majesty killed it cleanly against the hedge.
>
> It was his last shot.[14]

On that day Sandringham basked in the depths of winter, the atmosphere was relaxed, with the King shooting, and Queen

---

* Malan, a champion of Afrikaner nationalism, is best remembered for implementing his programme of Apartheid. Michael Stewart, a Labour MP (and future Foreign Secretary) and other MPs tabled a motion inviting the King 'to take into consideration the distress caused to many of His Majesty's subjects' that his stay in the official residence would cause. On 5 February the matter was raised in Cabinet, Churchill and others agreeing that it would be constitutionally improper for the United Kingdom Government to offer any advice to the King since it was a matter for the Union Government, the King being King of South Africa. Stewart would not be allowed to table his motion. An amendment tabled by Government supporters had redressed any effect on public opinion in Britain. Nor would the Government reply to a letter written by Fenner Brockway and other Labour MPs, addressed to Lord Ismay, the Secretary of State for Commonwealth Relations (CAB 128/24 – CC 52 10 – 5 February 1952, National Archives).

Elizabeth visiting neighbours. Sir Harold Campbell, who had been with the King since he was Duke of York, and Marion, Lady Hyde, were in attendance. Before retiring, the King discussed plans for the next day's shoot with Sir William Fellowes, his agent at Sandringham, telling him they would meet at Red Barn at 9 a.m. The following morning the King did not wake.

Lady Hyde wrote laconically in the notebook for ladies in waiting: 'The King went to bed early and died in the night.'[15]

13
ACCESSION, 1952

'There she goes, poor lonely girl. She will be lonely all her life.'
King George VI[1]

Tree Tops

Princess Elizabeth and Prince Philip flew into Nairobi via Libya, arriving on 1 February. They were greeted by the Governor of Kenya, Sir Philip Mitchell, and driven to Government House. There was a garden party and the next day a civic luncheon and a visit to Nairobi National Park. They went to the Sagana hunting lodge, a wedding gift from South Africa, for a short rest. Princess Elizabeth looked happy and carefree, while the Duke was in full voice. There was a scrum when they arrived. Prince Philip looked straight at one photographer and said: 'I will be taking my own bloody picture next!' Princess Elizabeth wrote in her diary that she 'did not want to miss a moment of Kenya's extraordinary landscapes'.[2]

Security was tight at Sagana Lodge due to threats from the Mau Mau (Kenya's Freedom Army). On hand was Colonel Jim Corbett, the great Anglo-Indian hunter, who had disposed of a great many man-eating lions, tigers and leopards in his long career. While the Duke played polo near Nyeri, Corbett and his sister sat in their car, keeping a beady eye focused across a ravine for potential trouble-makers. After a press call, the couple were left in peace to make their way to Tree Tops to spend the night watching game at the salt lick. They arrived there to the sound of angry elephants rampaging. Jim Corbett commended their courage:

In single file, and through dense bush where visibility in places was limited to a yard or two, they went towards those sounds, which grew more awe-inspiring the nearer they approached them. And then, when they came to the bend in the path and within sight of the elephants, they found that they would have to approach within ten yards of them to reach the safety of the ladder. A minute after climbing the ladder the Princess was sitting on the balcony and, with steady hands, was filming the elephants.[3]

To be safe John Hayward, the Warden at Aberdare, and Colonel Mervyn Cowie, Executive Officer of the Nairobi National Parks, had their rifles to the ready.

The royal party watched the passing show throughout the night and in the morning Mike Parker persuaded Princess Elizabeth to watch the sun rise over the jungle. An eagle hovered overhead and he was frightened it might dive onto them. Only later did he wonder if that was not roughly the moment when the King died. Elizabeth I had learned that she was Queen while sitting beside a tree at Hatfield. Elizabeth II went up the mugumo tree as a Princess, and descended it (unknowingly) as a Queen.

★ ★ ★ ★ ★

Back at Sandringham, Lascelles relayed news of the King's death to Edward Ford in London with the coded message: 'Hyde Park Corner'. It was Ford's mission to inform Queen Mary and the Prime Minister. When Jock Colville looked in on Churchill soon afterwards, he found him despondent, with tears in his eyes: 'I had not realised how much the King meant to him. I tried to cheer him up by saying how well he would get on with the new Queen, but all he could say was that he did not know her and that she was only a child.'[4]

In London the news was spreading. Charles Johnston, in his office at Whitehall, was told officially. He noted: 'The eeriness of looking out and seeing everything going on as usual; the Admiralty flag at the top of its mast, the King's guard of Household Cavalry riding gravely over the parade and in under Horse Guards Arch as the clock struck eleven. Then the flags started coming down ... The news was out.'⁵ Sir Arthur Penn, Queen Elizabeth's Treasurer, was told by a shopkeeper in Bond Street. Having lately been at Sandringham, he had not expected it. Making his way to the Palace, he saw posters with the news scrawled on them, flags being taken to half-mast and the faces of passers-by 'taut with a great distress',[6] Daphne du Maurier, reflected: 'It was queer the kind of feeling of sickness one had all next day – like starting a baby – and that sight of flags everywhere at half-mast, and the haggard faces, I suppose psychologists would call it mass emotion.'[7]

Sir Arthur Penn went by train to Norfolk, with Ruby Macdonald, Princess Margaret's dresser, on board with a suitcase of black clothes. At Sandringham he found the table piled high with telegrams, all needing an answer. Queen Elizabeth came in, talked of the past and of what lay ahead. For the next day or so, she and Princess Margaret had their meals alone together. Penn did not see the King's bereaved daughter for a while, but when he did, he wrote of Princess Margaret:

> Poor dear, she looked like a small ghost, & I felt very grieved for her – she & the King were such tremendous friends, & she hadn't of course the Queen's incomparable strength of character, nor, like Princess Elizabeth, a husband & children & an immense adventure before her.[8]

★ ★ ★ ★ ★

The pressing issue was to get the news to the new Queen. Lascelles sent coded telegrams but no one could in Kenya decipher them. He telephoned Government House but the Governor had left for Mombasa to see Princess Elizabeth off on the next stage of her journey. Prince Philip was asleep after the all-night vigil. Major Norman Jarman, Manager of Kenya Hotels, was having a glass of sherry with Martin Charteris at the Outspan Hotel before lunch. The editor of the *Nairobi Standard* newspaper called him to say there was a message on the teleprinter saying the King was dead. They needed confirmation. Jarman called Buckingham Palace, and the man who answered was shocked that the new Queen did not know. He urged that she be told as quickly as possible.

Charteris telephoned Mike Parker, then hurried back to Sagana Lodge. Meanwhile Parker turned on his wireless and heard the BBC announcement. He attracted Prince Philip's attention, and watched as he took the Queen up the garden, then saw them walking up and down deep in conversation. By the time Charteris arrived, the new Queen was back in the Lodge, sitting up straight, accepting her destiny. When asked what name she would take, she replied: 'My own, of course.'

The Queen was told at 2.45 p.m. (African time). By 5 p.m. the party were flying home from Mombasa. Sir Frederick Browning had flown straight to Mombasa. Forty-eight hours later he was on the plane back. He and Kathini Graham, who worked for Sir Philip Mitchell, managed to extract a black coat and black hat from the Queen's trunk on the ship at Mombasa, from which the royal party had been due to sail. The press were asked not to photograph the Queen as she left. They put their cameras on the ground and watched in silence as the young Queen drove away, briefly raising her hand in a parting wave. Daphne du Maurier quoted her husband: 'He said she was quite amazing on the aircraft, calm, collected, there was no gloom.'*[9]

* * * * *

In the meantime the Cabinet met for a second time on the day of the King's death and discussed how to recognise 'the present constitutional conditions in the Commonwealth' in the Proclamation. For the first time in history, the new monarch was to be formally described as 'Head of the Commonwealth'. Where appropriate, 'Imperial Crown' (first used by Henry VIII in 1553 or so and ratified in 1543–4) would become 'Crown', since the word 'Imperial' was deemed too closely linked to the Indian Empire and could offend the representative of India, since the Indians no longer owed allegiance to the Crown. 'Ireland' became 'Northern Ireland' and

---

* This is confirmed by a cine film, taken by Prince Philip on board the plane. The Queen is smiling. I was surprised by this, and checked with his archivist that it was really filmed then. It was. Prince Philip was no doubt doing a valiant job at keeping spirits up.

references to 'British Dominions' were dropped. The key wording was agreed as follows:

> ... Queen Elizabeth the Second, by the Grace of God Queen of this Realm and of all Her other Realms and Territories, Head of the Commonwealth, Defender of the Faith, to whom Her Lieges do acknowledge all Faith and constant Obedience ...[10]

The issue arose of the Queen's title in Scotland. The Scottish Nationalists wanted to know if she was to be styled Elizabeth I or Elizabeth II in Scotland, there having been no previous Queen Elizabeth in that country. In a curious compromise, it was decided that the higher number would be used. A future King James would be James VIII rather than James III. Meanwhile resentful Scottish Nationalist vandals were known to attack postboxes bearing the symbol EIIR.

★ ★ ★ ★ ★

The scene of the Queen coming down the steps of the plane, as if to claim her kingdom, was memorable. Harold Macmillan wrote that the Cabinet had been concerned about the new Queen's safe return – 'Many felt that the dangers of an air journey were by no means negligible'[11] but the Cabinet conceded she would wish to return home as quickly as possible. She touched down at London Airport at 4.20 p.m., on the day after the King's death, after a flight of more than nineteen hours. Her uncle, the Duke of Gloucester, and members of the Government were there to meet her. Sir Evelyn Shuckburgh wrote: 'One could just see the backs of their poor old heads: Winston, Attlee, A. E. [Eden], Woolton and so on. The twentieth-century version of Melbourne galloping to Kensington Palace, falling on his knees before Victoria in her nightdress.'[12] They were driven to Clarence House, where Queen Mary came from Marlborough House next door. 'Her old Grannie and subject must be the first to kiss her hand,'[13] she said, recognising the change in status.

The night after the King died, Winston Churchill made his broadcast, speaking of how the King's death had 'struck a deep and solemn note' in the life of the nation, stilling 'the clatter and traffic of twentieth-century life in many lands'. He commended the many qualities of the King, his simple dignity, his manly virtues and his sense of duty, how he had faced the last months of his life and addressed the recent months 'all the time cheerful and undaunted, stricken in body, but quite undisturbed and even unaffected in spirit'. He deployed the memorable words: 'During these last months the King walked with death as if death were a companion and acquaintance whom he recognised and did not fear ...'* And then he hailed the new Queen, saying that some of the greatest periods in British history had been under the reigns of queens. He ended stirringly: 'I, whose youth was passed in the august, unchallenged, and tranquil glories of the Victorian era, may well feel a thrill in invoking once more the prayer and the anthem: "God Save The Queen"!'†14

This was the first time a new monarch had succeeded to the throne overseas since the death of Queen Anne in 1714, so there were two Accession Councils, the first on the evening of 6 February in the absence of the Queen. The Queen's first duty was to attend the second Accession Council at St James's Palace on the Friday morning. Oliver Lyttelton was again present: 'There must have been nearly two hundred Privy Counsellors present in the large room next to the Picture Gallery. The door opened, and the Queen in black came in. Suddenly the members of the Privy Council looked

---

* Evidently Churchill had been rehearsing these lines for some time. When he stayed with Viscount and Viscountess Ridley at Blagdon, Northumberland, during the General Election of October 1951, it was known that the King was gravely ill, and he mused on the death of Lady Ridley's father, Sir Edwin Lutyens (in 1944). He used the very same words that he would later use in relation to the King. As Churchill spoke, so Ursula Ridley intervened to say that though her father had cancer, his had been rather a gradual loss of strength with no pain or discomfort, that he had had a persistent cough, but had not known that he was dying. 'No, no,' Churchill swept on, 'he walked with death, as if death were a companion' etc. Sir Arthur Penn was astonished that, 'with so much crowding upon him' the Prime Minister could find time to compose such a splendid broadcast. This was the explanation. (Kenneth Rose to Viscount Ridley, 15 May 1997).
† Harold Macmillan judged this 'the best piece of prose I have heard or read from him.' (Diary, 7 February 1952.)

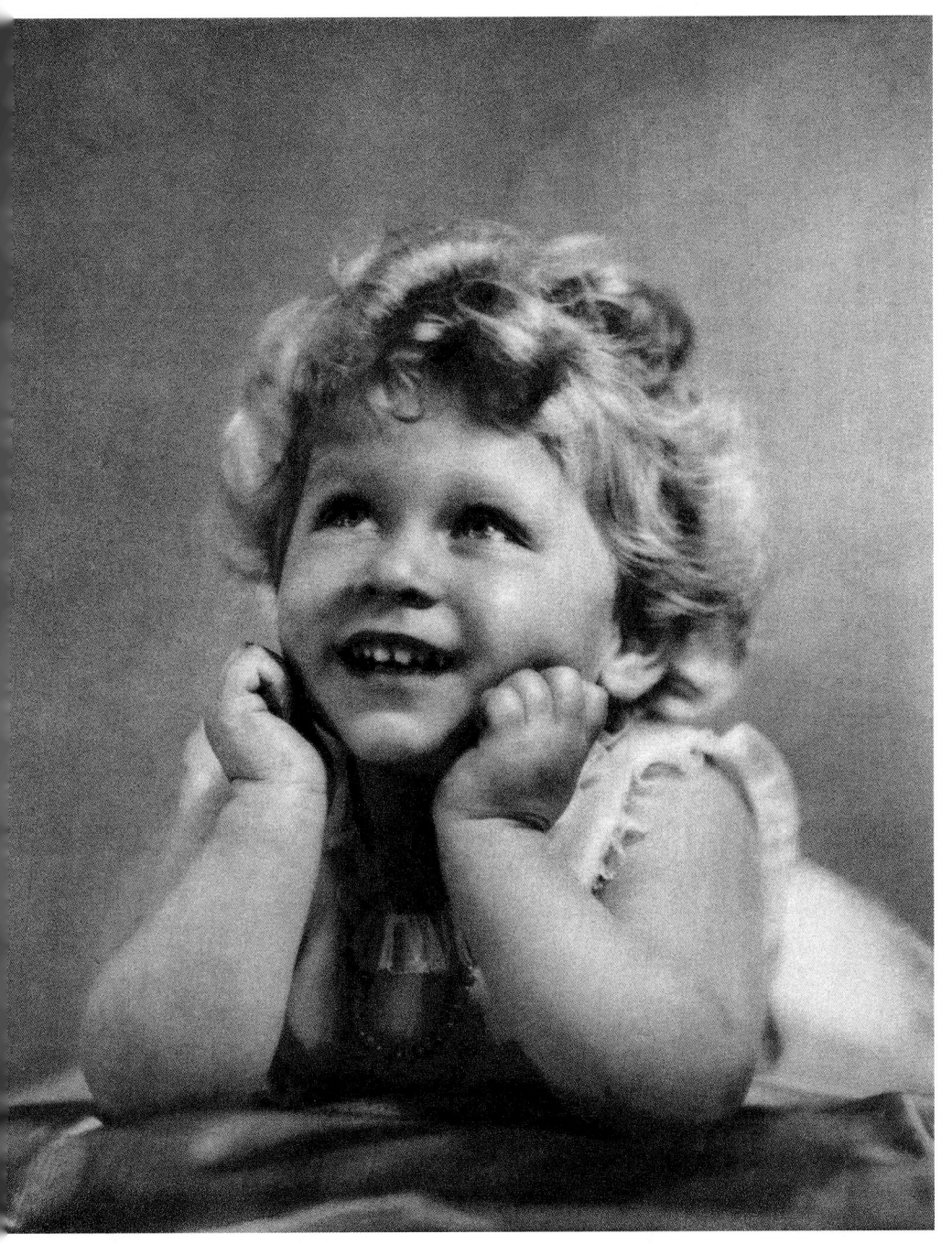
Young Princess Elizabeth by Marcus Adams, 1928

Princess Elizabeth with the Duchess of York and the Dean of Westminster (Dr William Foxley-Norris) after the Royal Maundy Service at Westminster Abbey, 18 April 1935

Princess Elizabeth as a toddler, waving to admirers

Princess Elizabeth greeting a disabled soldier

Princess Elizabeth on her way to Crathie Church
with King George V and Queen Mary

Princess Elizabeth making sandcastles
at Craigweil House, Bognor, 1929

George V and Queen Mary taking the
Princess to Westminster Abbey, 1 July 1934

Princess Elizabeth and Princess Margaret processing out of Westminster Abbey in front of their grandmother at the 1937 Coronation

The young princess riding in Windsor Great Park on the eve of her 14th birthday, April 1940

Princess Elizabeth as Aladdin and Princess Margaret at Princess Roxana, in a Windsor pantomime in 1943

The famous 1940 broadcast to the children of Britain

The Royal Wedding, 20 November 1947

Princess Elizabeth opening the exhibition – *Eight Centuries of British Life* – in Paris, 18 May 1948

Princess Elizabeth arriving at a gala ballet at Covent Garden, during the State Visit of the President of France, 9 March 1950

Princess Elizabeth admiring a teddy bear given to the infant Princess Anne at the Flower Ball, 22 May 1951

The Queen and Princess Margaret following the Queen Mother out of a BOAC aircraft just before her mother and sister left to tour Rhodesia in June 1953

immeasurably old and gnarled and grey. The Queen made one of the most touching speeches to which I have ever listened, and I, like many others, could hardly control my emotions.'[15] Harold Macmillan recorded: 'The Queen's entrance; the low bows of her counsellors; the firm, yet charming voice in which she pronounced her allocution and went through the various ceremonious forms of the ritual (including the oath to maintain the Scottish Church) produced a profound impression on us all.'[16] Vincent Massey, about to be Governor General of Canada, observed:

> It was a very moving occasion – the Queen, a slight figure dressed in deep mourning, entered the great room alone and, with strong but perfectly controlled emotion, went through the exacting tasks the Constitution prescribes. Her speeches were perfectly delivered. After this Prince Philip, who was in the room as a Privy Counsellor, stepped forward quietly and went out of the door with her.[17]

After that the Queen's styles and titles were proclaimed by Garter King of Arms. Queen Mary watched the Proclamation at St James's Palace with the Duchess of Kent and her sister. The Duchess reported that Queen Mary 'had been composed, and when the Heralds' procession moved off with the mace-heads sticking awkwardly out through the windows of the leading coach she said it was like something out of *Alice in Wonderland*, and they all laughed'.[18]

The Queen and Prince Philip were driven to Sandringham. They arrived in the afternoon and at 4.30 p.m. the King's homemade coffin was taken to Sandringham Church in an informal procession, the coffin borne on the shoulders of retired estate men, joiners and gardeners – 'browned elderly men ... in unaccustomed dark suits & bowler hats' – under the direction of James Emmerson, Clerk of Works there for thirty years. A few early snowdrops were peeping through the carpet of dead leaves 'as though to remind the mourners of the sure promise awaiting within beckoning'. A distant cock pheasant 'threw up a challenging cry', perhaps disturbed by the piper leading his late master to the church.[19]

When the royal party returned to the Big House, they resumed having meals together, with the Royal Household at the table. One day Sir Arthur Penn took the young Prince Charles (with Princess

Anne in her pram) to see some Grenadiers who had arrived. On the Sunday the new Queen and her family went to West Newton Church, and on Monday there was another service at the church before the procession from Sandringham to Wolferton Station, the train journey to London and the procession through the streets of London to Westminster Hall for the Lying-in-State.

Sir Arthur Penn stayed on at Sandringham to help the widowed Queen Elizabeth. Fifteen thousand replies to letters and telegrams were sent out in the next month. He described the grief in that Norfolk house. The 'familiar & sure' had become uncertain and there were 'overwhelming' problems in winding up what had ended and 'setting up a new routine'.[20]

The King's coffin was conveyed from Norfolk to London by train. The Lying-in-State took place in Westminster Hall. There was the haunting photograph of the three Queens awaiting its arrival – the new young Queen and her distressed mother, both heavily veiled and Queen Mary in full Tudor mourning, surely the last time this has been worn in public.* She looked like a figure from the Middle Ages. When the coffin arrived in Westminster Hall the only witnesses were the Royal Family, the Household and the members of both Parliaments. Daphne du Maurier was there:

> Most moving thing I have ever witnessed. I did not cry. Because I was moved historically not emotionally. That great Westminster Hall that has seen so many centuries, and then the heralds in their wonderful uniform, the Duke of Norfolk, Earl Marshal, in his scarlet coat with the Garter ribbon. Oh, God, I did not want to be me in a veil and a silly woman, I wanted to have a sword and be wearing armour. That's the way these things take me. The great door opened and we heard the horses of the gun-carriage, and then the coffin with the state crown and the royal standard came in, borne by Grenadier King's Company, and the Queen and Queen Mother walking behind ... I kept saying to myself 'This is history. I'm watching history.[21]

---

* The Cecils of Hatfield go in for full funerals and no memorial service. The Marchioness of Salisbury wore a Tudor cap of mourning when the Marquess's Garter banner was presented in St George's Chapel in April 1972.

ACCESSION, 1952

After the Lying-in-State, there was a full procession to Paddington, the train to Windsor, another procession up the Long Walk. Eton boys lined the route inside the Castle. They were meant to keep their eyes down, but one took a surreptitious look. He caught the eye of Field Marshal Lord Montgomery and quaked with fear that he might be reported.[22] The funeral took place at St George's Chapel.

A few days later, Monsignor John Heenan,* Roman Catholic Bishop of Leeds, praised the King in his cathedral, but added somewhat dismally: 'I hope I shall not be misunderstood if I say that this sorrow has not seemed to be a particularly Christian sorrow. For it has been almost unrelieved by any sign of hope.' He went on to say that the King's death was in no way 'a great tragedy'. He judged that the King had led a good life, had overcome his illness, had been prepared for death and would now appear 'before the judgment seat of God'. He had been given time to prepare.

Nor did he care for the way the BBC had handled the King's death, wrapping the nation in gloom for more than a week. He thought that the sick and old who depended on the wireless for 'relief from pain or monotony' had been ill served. He ended more optimistically, hoping that 'the guidance of the Holy Spirit be granted to our young Queen'. He hoped she would set such an example 'as wife and mother that her subjects will be compelled to yield her their admiration as they have already offered her their love and loyalty'.[23] In that wish he was not to be disappointed.

Some years later, in October 1955, when the new Queen unveiled King George's statue in the Mall, she gave her considered view of her father, and though delivered formally, the essential truths came across. She told the guests that, like his father, he had expected 'to support the Throne rather than to fill it'. She spoke of his resilience during the war: 'He was the living symbol of our steadfastness. He never wavered in his faith that, with God's help, the cause of freedom would prevail.' Touchingly, she concluded:

---

* John Heenan (1905–75), later Archbishop of Westminster, 1963–75, and Cardinal from 1965.

Much was asked of my father in personal sacrifice and endeavour, often in the face of illness; his courage in overcoming it endeared him to everybody. He shirked no task, however difficult, and to the end he never faltered in his duty to his peoples. Throughout all the strains of his public life he remained a man of warm and friendly sympathies – a man who by the simple qualities of loyalty, resolution and service won for himself such a place in the affection of all of us that when he died millions mourned for him as for a true and trusted friend.[24]

14

THE NEW REIGN, 1952–3

At Sandringham in the days after the King's death, Sir Arthur Penn observed excitement amid the grief:

> The Queen, & even more, Prince Philip are bursting with new ideas, & so they should be. Every generation shd exhale a brisk breeze to dispel old cobwebs, many proposals will be very good, others less so: some quite impracticable.
>
> The vital thing is to welcome them all with an open mind, to criticize nothing only because it is new, & to regard nothing as impossible merely on the ground that it is very difficult.
>
> I hope though that they won't be in too much of a <u>hurry</u>, & that they will be patient. Much tact will be needed on both sides.[1]

After the King's coffin had been conveyed to Westminster Hall, the Queen returned to Clarence House. The Brownings – 'Boy' or 'Tommy', as Daphne du Maurier called him – went back there too:

> No sooner were we in Tommy's office than his buzzer went, and it was the Queen asking for him, and he went off to his rooms, and when he came back I said: 'What did she want?' imagining her prostrate, and he said 'She wanted to approve the Court Circular before it was sent up to press' ... She was sitting in her black dress at her desk, perfectly calm, perfectly composed and if it's not going to be another Elizabeth like the first I shall turn Republican ... It's going to be terrific. I am so inspired, and so is everybody else, now that the really deep grief for the King has had its outlet; a new sort of patriotism will get everyone by the throat.[2]

Tommy Lascelles stayed on with the Queen until after the Coronation. He had come to admire her for quiet wisdom and perceptive views. Lascelles was not a man easily impressed. He had been present when the Queen came before her Privy Counsellors:

> In all my life I can recall no more moving incident than her entry into the crowded Throne Room at St James's Palace for the Accession Privy Council. There were, I suppose, over 100 of us Privy Counsellors assembled; there was not one who was not stirred by the sight of that slim figure in black moving quietly to the throne, and by the sound of her unfaltering musical voice as she read the message to us.

During the next twenty-two months as her Private Secretary, Lascelles saw the Queen almost daily:

> Her immediate grasp of the routine business of kingship was remarkable. She never seemed to need an explanation on any point. Time after time I would submit to her papers on which several decisions were possible. She would look out of the window for half a minute and then say: 'The second or third suggestion is the right decision' – and she was invariably right. She had an intuitive grasp of the problems of government and indeed of life generally, that I suppose had descended to her from Queen Victoria.[3]

Winston Churchill gave the new Queen a robust welcome in the House of Commons:

> A fair and youthful figure, Princess, wife and mother is the heir to all our traditions and glories never greater than in her father's days, and to all our perplexities and dangers never greater in peacetime than now. She is also heir to all our united strength and loyalty.
> She comes to the Throne at a time when a tormented mankind stands uncertainly poised between world catastrophe and a golden age. That it should be a golden age of art and letters, we can only hope – science and machinery have their other tales to tell – but it is certain that if a true and lasting peace can be achieved, and if the nations will only let each other alone, an immense and undreamed of prosperity with culture and leisure ever more widely spread can

come, perhaps even easily and swiftly, to the masses of the people in every land.[4]

The Queen was aware that in some ways she had an easier role than her mother and sister, as she described in a letter to Lady Salisbury. It began and ended formally, but in the middle she wrote: 'Oh, Betty, this is so awful for Mummy and Margaret. I have Philip and the children and the future but what are they to do?'[5]

★ ★ ★ ★ ★

Not everything was made easy for the young Queen and her consort. His position was less defined than hers. His mother, Princess Alice, warned him: 'I think much of the change in your life this means. It means much personal self-sacrifice for you, as I am fully aware, but every sacrifice brings its reward in a manner we cannot foresee.'[6] She was not wrong.

With the Queen's accession, Prince Philip's naval career came to an abrupt end, something he minded deeply. He could have reached the top of the Navy on his own merit, matching the achievements of his grandfather, Prince Louis of Battenberg, and his uncle, Earl Mountbatten of Burma, who would become First Sea Lord in 1955 and Chief of the Defence Staff in 1959. Three weeks after the King's death, Prince Philip's sister Princess Margarita of Hohenlohe told Chips Channon that Prince Philip had had a fit of sulks, was pacing 'the quarterdeck', was 'bored, frustrated and biding his time'.[7] There were times when he found it hard to adjust. In May Lady Rachel Davidson told Channon that he was 'desperately bored with his three womenfolk' and longing for 'male company',[8] his life dominated by his wife, mother-in-law and sister-in-law. Inertia at Clarence House must have been a stark contrast to the potential challenges of the cancelled Commonwealth tour.

Amid Privy Council meetings, a visit from the Mexican Ambassador, and the Lord Privy Seal lunching at Clarence House, recorded in Martin Charteris's Season Calendar for 1952, the Field Officer in Brigade Waiting, Colonel 'Geordie' Gordon-Lennox, visited on 9 April at 2.30 p.m. The Queen had automatically become Colonel-in-Chief of all the Guards regiments, vacating her post as

Colonel of Grenadier Guards (held since 1942). A new Colonel was needed. The Queen proposed Prince Philip.

Gordon-Lennox told her that Prince Philip had no experience and that the regiment wanted General Sir George (later Lord) Jeffreys (1878–1960), known as 'Ma' Jeffreys, who had served in the regiment since 1897 and seen action at Omdurman in 1898, in the Second Boer War, and at Mons, Loos, Ypres and in the German spring offensive in the First World War. He had been severely wounded and mentioned in despatches no less than nine times. From 1941 to 1951 he had served as an MP. Clearly his appointment had considerable merit but the Queen was disappointed. Prince Philip was given the Welsh Guards instead. This cost Gordon-Lennox the KCVO* that would normally have come his way.†

A further blow concerned the name of the Royal House, again to Prince Philip's disadvantage. It had been stated in 1948 that if George VI had not bestowed royal titles on Princess Elizabeth's children (as yet unborn) they would have held the surname Mountbatten. The name Windsor had been adopted by King George V for the Royal House in 1917.

Soon after the King's funeral, Lord Mountbatten boasted at dinner at Broadlands that the House of Mountbatten now reigned over the land. He had a valid point. When a reigning Queen marries, the Royal House takes the name of the husband. Thus Queen Victoria was the last of the House of Hanover, which became Saxe-Coburg-Gotha. When George V removed the German titles on 17 July 1917, his Proclamation stated that those who would bear the name of Windsor were to be 'all the descendants in the male line of Queen Victoria who are subjects of these Realms, other than female descendants who may marry or who may have married'. Therefore, the

---

* Lieutenant-General Sir George (Geordie) Gordon-Lennox (1908–88), received a CVO. He was given a KBE for having served as Commandant, the Royal Military Academy, Sandhurst.

† When 'Ma' Jeffreys died in December 1960, the Queen appointed Major-General Sir Allan Adair as the next Colonel. Prince Philip finally became their Colonel in 1975 and proved popular with the regiment. He stepped down in 2017. At that point the Queen made sure that the Duke of York was appointed. Though the Grenadiers did not initially want him, he proved a good Colonel until his other problems assailed him.

Queen, Prince Charles and Princess Anne did not have the name Windsor before her accession.

Prince Ernst August of Hanover was at Mountbatten's table. He went to see Queen Mary and she had a sleepless night over the name. She summoned Jock Colville and he passed on her concern to Winston Churchill. The Cabinet discussed the issue on 20 February, a mere two weeks into the new reign. No one liked the idea of the House of Mountbatten, more on account of the growing influence of Lord Mountbatten than hostility to Prince Philip.

Harold Macmillan had been irritated by a long speech Prince Philip had made to the British Association at the McEwan Hall in Edinburgh on 8 August 1951 about science in industry, patents and price rings. It had been heard by 3,851 people and widely seen on television. He had said: 'The instrument of scientific knowledge in our hands is growing more powerful every day. Indeed it has reached a point when we can either set the world free from drudgery, fear, hunger and pestilence, or obliterate life itself ... It is clearly our duty as citizens to see that science is used for the benefit of mankind. For of what use is science if man does not survive?'[9]

Macmillan wrote: 'I fear this young man is going to be as big a bore as Prince Albert, and as great a trouble.' He detected the malign influence of the Mountbattens: 'What does the Duke of Edinburgh know about patent law? It was significant that the passage accusing industrialists of buying up patents in order to suppress them was itself "suppressed" by the wish of the advisers (in the 2nd press release) but of course copied with approval in the *D. Herald.*'[10]

When the matter of the family name was again raised in Cabinet, on 6 March 1952, Churchill was caught in the cross-fire. He was keen to 'adopt a paternal and fatherly attitude to the Queen', thought the Queen Mother was pressing for the Windsor name, but that 'the Duke of Edinburgh has the normal attitude of many men towards a mother-in-law of strong character, accentuated by the peculiar circumstances of his position'.[11] With logic on his side, Prince Philip wrote 'a strongly, but ably, worded memorandum'*[12] advancing the notion

---

* During Prince Philip's lifetime I asked his office if I could see this message from Prince Philip. I was told that it could not be found. Nor could I find it in the National Archives.

that the Royal House should be called 'the House of Edinburgh'. Both the Cabinet and Opposition leaders were annoyed by this and more so by Mountbatten's 'tactless assertion'.[13]

The Prime Minister vetoed the idea on 12 March. On 7 April Lord Simonds agreed with Churchill: 'When [the King] conferred a dukedom upon HRH The Duke of Edinburgh he did not intend that the name of Edinburgh should supersede that of Windsor as the name of the Royal House.'[14] Prince Philip is said to have declared: 'I'm an amoeba, a bloody amoeba.' In the end, neither the Cabinet nor the Opposition would contemplate anything other than the House of Windsor.

Lord Simonds decided that George V and George VI had wanted the House of Windsor to continue, but conceded that the draughtsman who prepared the 1917 Proclamation had failed to ensure this. If nothing was done now, descendants in the male line would not be Windsors, they would be Mountbattens. The Cabinet therefore took the line that the Queen would want to respect her grandfather's wishes. A line was crafted to the effect that of course the Queen commanded personal loyalty and devotion from her people, but 'beyond it lies their grateful memory of Her father and grandfather who immeasurably strengthened the institution of monarchy and have given to the name of Windsor a significance that should not be lost'.[15]

A Proclamation was prepared to cover 'all the descendants who are subjects of these Realms, not just those in the male line'.[16] In the end Churchill gave the Queen formal advice simply to declare to the Privy Council that she and her children would bear the name of Windsor, and no Proclamation was required.[17] Reluctantly, the Queen accepted this formal advice as she was bound to do. On 9 April 1952 the Queen held a Council at Clarence House in the presence of Lord Woolton, Harold Macmillan, David Eccles and Sir Thomas Dugdale and it was 'declared in Council' that Windsor would stay as the name of the Royal House. There was no adverse comment in the press.

Prince Philip was enraged and Mountbatten was livid. Harold Macmillan, no fan of Prince Philip's or of the Mountbattens, was quietly satisfied: 'It is a very good thing that the influence of the Consort and his family shd have had an early rebuff.'[18]

★ ★ ★ ★ ★

In the summer of 1952 the Civil List came before Parliament, introduced by R. A. Butler as Chancellor of the Exchequer. The Queen was to get £475,000 a year. Clement Attlee, then Leader of the Opposition, made the point that the relationship with the Commonwealth made extra demands on the Queen's time. He did not want sweeping economies. He said: 'Public opinion today likes a certain amount of pageantry. It is a great mistake to make government too dull. We must not let the Devil get all the best tunes.'[19]

The proviso included £40,000 for life for Prince Philip. Even this did not pass unchallenged. Ernest Fernyhough, Labour MP for Jarrow, asked about the life provision, questioning what might happen 'if the domestic felicity of the Queen and Duke' went wrong. Despite murmurs of dissent from all sides of the House, he pressed on: 'It is no good pretending that Kings and Queens and Dukes and Princesses are all angels. They are ordinary human beings ... I hope the occasion will not arise where I may have to say: I told you so.'[20] The motion was carried and Prince Philip got his £40,000.

There were further family problems. One was the Queen's uncle, the Duke of Windsor. Although he had sent her birthday presents from his self-imposed exile, such as the cine-camera she had enjoyed before the war, she never saw him. But he still existed. In the intervening years, he had served as Governor of the Bahamas from 1940 to 1945. Now he and the Duchess of Windsor were dividing their time between Paris, the South of France and the United States, most particularly New York and Palm Beach.

The Queen Mother took the line that the Abdication had landed her husband on the throne, and that the consequent stress was largely responsible the King's early death. The Queen cannot fail to have been influenced by the idea that her uncle had let the side down. After the war the Duke came several times to England. He was not invited to Queen Mary's eightieth-birthday lunch at Buckingham Palace in 1947, although he was in London at the time. Neither was he invited to Princess Elizabeth's wedding. It is unlikely that the Queen saw him until he materialised in London for the King's funeral in 1952 at which time the Duchess stayed away. The Duke walked in his brother's funeral procession.

Queen Mary was keen that 'the feud' with the Duke should be ended. Four days after the King's death she wrote to Queen Elizabeth hoping that she, the Queen and Princess Margaret would see him '& bury the hatchet after 15 whole years'.²¹ They did see him, though Queen Elizabeth was 'not enthusiastic'. Queen Mary wrote, rather over-optimistically, to the Athlones: 'So that feud is over I hope, a great relief to me.'²² As ever, the Duke was keenly interested in how the new reign would affect him. During his stay he was informed that he would no longer receive the £10,000 allowance his brother had granted him as this had been an informal arrangement. Before he returned to Paris, he lunched with his niece and Prince Philip. He noted: 'Clarence House was informal & friendly. Brave New World. Full of self-confidence & seem to take job in their stride.'²³

He came over again from Paris towards the end of February and again lunched with the Queen at Clarence House to discuss financial issues. Chips Channon picked up that he made 'a poor impression on his niece'.²⁴ When the Duke came over for Queen Mary's eighty-fifth birthday in May, he had tea with the Queen Mother at Buckingham Palace. The Queen and Prince Philip were at Balmoral. The Duke visited his mother in October and November. The Queen and Prince Philip invited him to lunch at Buckingham Palace on 20 November, coincidentally their fifth wedding anniversary.

It would have been easier to handle the Duke of Windsor had the Queen Mother not been in the background. The Queen did as much as she could to smooth relations between herself and her uncle, but there was an additional problem – if you gave him an inch, he took a mile.

There was no hint that the Duke wished to return to live in England. The question of the Coronation arose. Winston Churchill understood that his attendance at royal funerals was one thing, at the Coronation another. When the Queen raised this with the Archbishop of Canterbury at lunch in November, he told her it would 'create a very difficult situation for everybody'. Tommy Lascelles at once wrote to Sir Godfrey Morley, the Duke's lawyer at Allen & Overy, making clear that no invitation would be forthcoming.*²⁵

---

* In the end the Duke and Duchess watched the ceremony on television in Paris.

THE NEW REIGN, 1952-3

Winston Churchill

On her accession, the Queen inherited Winston Churchill as her first Prime Minister. He had been the first person to greet her in his dark topcoat and top hat when she stepped off the plane. Churchill had been born in 1874. He had served in Queen Victoria's army. The young Queen shook the hand of a man who had wielded a sword at the Battle of Omdurman in 1898. He had gone on to serve in the governments of Edward VII under Campbell-Bannerman and Asquith, and George V as First Lord of the Admiralty and Chancellor of the Exchequer. Controversially he had urged Edward VIII to stand his ground at the time of the Abdication crisis, but to no avail. He made a strong comeback in George VI's reign, and at the outbreak of the Second World War in 1939, he was appointed First Lord of the Admiralty. In 1940 he succeeded Neville Chamberlain as Prime Minister, dominating the political scene throughout the war. Elected out in 1945, he had returned as Prime Minister in October 1951, in the last months of the King's reign.

Churchill enjoyed being Prime Minister in the new Elizabethan age. His relationship with the Queen developed from apprehension at her youth and inexperience to genuine and deep love on his part. The Queen respected him for his wisdom and guidance. He went for his first official audience of the new Queen at Clarence House on 12 February. Gradually the audiences became longer and longer. He was 'dazzled', as Jock Colville put it, and secretly impressed when she caught him out for not having read a Foreign Office telegram from Baghdad. He often said: 'She is a truly remarkable person.'[26]

His doctor, Lord Moran, wrote that for Winston the history of England was embedded in the Royal House. Moran quoted several comments by his famous patient. Looking at a photograph of the Queen in white with long white gloves and a radiant smile in February 1953, he said: 'Lovely ... She's a pet. I fear they may ask her to do too much. She's doing so well.'[27] A month later, he added: 'Lovely, inspiring. All the film people in the world, if they had scoured the globe, could not have found anyone so suited to the part.'[28] And in October 1954, he looked at photographs of the Queen meeting Italian film stars: 'She knocks 'em all endways.'[29] Churchill enjoyed his weekly audiences and they were soon talking about many things, not least about a shared interest in racing.

Churchill was involved in all the crucial issues that involved the Queen. One of these was where she and her family would live. The Queen and Prince Philip would have preferred to stay in Clarence House, but Churchill insisted that she had to live in the Sovereign's official residence. And so it came about that the young Queen took up residence in Buckingham Palace on 5 May, that great palace, much of which was taken up by state rooms and offices. An additional issue was that the Queen Mother and Princess Margaret were still living there. The Queen Mother was meant to be moving into Clarence House. Some cynics suggested that she was delaying her move in the hope that Marlborough House would become available with the death of Queen Mary.

The Queen and Prince Philip had no country home when the King died, so they opened some rooms in Windsor Castle to see if they liked it. They did and it soon became their favoured weekend retreat when the court was in London, remaining so for the rest of their lives.

* * * * *

As she adopted her new role, so the Queen developed her approach. In some ways she was two people – the Queen and the person inside the Queen. Most things she did on advice. Sometimes she would say to the Private Secretary: 'What should the Queen do?' not 'What should I do?' Trained in the constitution, she understood her role. Jock Colville found her 'at ease and self-possessed'[30] when he dined with her in April.

During these months the Queen assumed her responsibilities – meetings of the Privy Council, meetings with government ministers, High Commissioners and Ambassadors. When out in public, she wore the deep black of mourning as she went about her public engagements.

David Maxwell Fyfe, the Home Secretary, was present at many of the receptions for the Privileged Bodies and found 'There was something breath-taking in seeing the young figure of Her Majesty greet the successive waves of mostly aged men.' One day when he arrived

THE NEW REIGN, 1952–3

at the Palace, the Lord Chamberlain (Lord Clarendon) beckoned him to a window overlooking the garden: 'There was the Queen in a yellow shirt and jodhpurs, kneeling on the grass and calling to a dog to come to her. Within a quarter of an hour she had changed and was a Sovereign receiving her subjects.'[31] The Queen herself told a friend that she was gaining in confidence: 'Extraordinary thing, I no longer feel anxious or worried. I don't know what it is – but I have lost all my timidity, somehow becoming the Sovereign and having to receive the Prime Minister, for instance.'[32]

The Duke of Edinburgh was given a number of appointments he did not want such as Admiral of the Fleet, Field Marshal and Marshal of the RAF. He became President of a committee to advise on the design of seals, coins and medals. What he did like was to obtain his pilot's wings on 4 May 1953 because he had earned them on merit.

The Queen was able to spend time at Windsor Castle in April, where Lord Soulbury and Winston Churchill visited her. At the end of May she spent some days at Balmoral, before returning to London to lead her guards to Whitehall at Trooping the Colour. In June she was at Holyroodhouse. She would have installed Prince Philip as a Knight of the Thistle, but he had jaundice. (He was installed in 1953.) July was packed with engagements and then, after a weekend with the Duke of Norfolk at Arundel, she retreated to Balmoral between 7 August and 13 October. Churchill came to stay at Balmoral that summer, a prospect that somewhat alarmed the Queen, though it passed off well enough.

The autumn was equally busy, Prince Philip escaping to Rambouillet in France with Queen Juliana and Prince Bernhard, as a guest of President Vincent Auriol. Of 465 pheasants disposed of, he notched up 103. He took part in a stag hunt. There was a West Country tour – Devon, Cornwall and Somerset – and then the Queen's first State Opening of Parliament on 4 November. On that occasion the Imperial State Crown was carried in the procession by Lord Salisbury and not worn as she had not yet been crowned. She made the Declaration of Faith, a step towards her Coronation the following June.

The Royal Family gathered at Sandringham as usual for Christmas.

★ ★ ★ ★ ★

Queen Mary

During her life, Queen Mary had lost three sons. The death of George VI was a heavy blow. James Pope-Hennessy wrote: 'From this, the last great emotional shock of her life, Queen Mary did not recover. Her Household noticed that from now on the old Queen aged rapidly.'[33] She continued to visit exhibitions and the galleries of the dealers she favoured. In April 1952 she was ill for five weeks. Marlborough House was a port of call for distinguished visitors such as the General and Mrs Eisenhower from America, Robert Menzies and his wife from Australia, King Faisal and the Regent of Iraq. She watched the Trooping procession from her balcony, and she went to the Admiralty to watch Beating the Retreat from their window. Otherwise there were few appearances. Chips Channon, who loved nothing more than to monitor an impending royal death, noted that her health and memory were declining and she was aware of it.[34]

She went to Sandringham on 31 July, came back on 17 September, and went again for Christmas, but only got up in the late afternoon and seldom left her room. Towards the end of the year she developed a chill. Back in London on 29 January, she enjoyed a drive out to see the stands being erected for the Coronation in June. Her last such expedition was on a cold and icy day, 7 February 1953.

On 21 February she received Field Marshal Sir William and Lady Slim, who were being much fêted before heading to Australia where he was to be Governor-General. She then fell victim to gastric trouble and was confined to bed. Sir Horace Evans, her doctor, wrote to the Duke of Windsor, warning him that she had abdominal pains, but he could not operate due to the state of her heart. He told the Duke that he had the idea she would like to see him.

After 3 March regular bulletins were issued mentioning comfortable days, fair nights and sometimes slight improvement, but the gravity of the situation became clear when the Princess Royal curtailed her holiday in Trinidad. She joined the Duke of Windsor, similarly concerned, in New York and they sailed together, arriving in Southampton on 11 March. The Duke told newsmen he was delighted that Queen Mary had made 'such good improvement'.[35] Brother and sister visited their mother, then went to see the Queen.

THE NEW REIGN, 1952–3

Queen Mary's health being relatively stable, the Duke went to Paris for a few days, then to stay with his old friend Lord Dudley, shooting and attending a race meeting in Hertfordshire.*

Michael Duff told Cecil Beaton that when the Duke of Gloucester visited his mother, she said to her page: 'Oh, do get rid of him, will you? He does bore me so.' The Duke hovered a while at the bedside until the page appeared again: 'A whisky and soda in the library, Your Royal Highness.' Off went the Duke of Gloucester. On 16 March Queen Mary was less comfortable and less restful. The Duke of Windsor visited more frequently, aware that his mother would not get better. The doctors ceased their daily bulletins as of 23 March, but the next day there was a sharp decline and she died peacefully in her sleep at 10.15 p.m.

Queen Mary lay in state in Westminster Hall, and there was a procession through the streets of London. The funeral took place in St George's Chapel, and her coffin descended into the Royal Vault. The Queen gave a dinner party for twenty-eight at Windsor Castle, including Queen Frederika, Prince and Princess Paul of Yugoslavia (now back in the fold after his wartime exile in Kenya), but pointedly not the Duke of Windsor, who had again walked in the procession.[36]

The Queen lost a stalwart grandmother. She told Tommy Lascelles that it was hard to think of a world without Queen Mary in it.

---

* Letters between the Duke and Duchess at this time make disturbing reading and do neither of them any credit. The Duke must have suffered from conflicting emotions – concern for his mother in her pain and discomfort, yet residual bitterness at her continued refusal to receive his wife. Nor did he like how he had been treated. They would not, of course, have wished these exchanges published, but in that, as in more serious ways, they were ill-served by their evil lawyer Maître Blum.

15
THE CORONATION, 1953

'I remember the spectacle, and how glamorous The Queen was. She was stunning, and the whole thing was overwhelming. There was an element of magic.'
Prince Michael of Kent

Cecil Beaton's iconic photograph of the Queen against the backdrop of the Henry VII Chapel at Westminster Abbey captures her to perfection. There sat a beautiful young woman, with the trappings of monarchy – the Imperial Crown, the orb, the sceptre and the flowing purple train. None of this daunted her. She was assured and confident, on the brink of one of the most remarkable reigns in British history.

The Coronation* was the final step in confirming the Queen as monarch, after the accession, Accession Council, Proclamation and Declaration of Faith. The most important part of it was the anointing. The Cabinet settled on 2 June as the most appropriate day for the Coronation, that being a Tuesday, so that people did not have to travel on a Sunday. This was unfortunate: 2 June turned out to be a distinctly wet day.

The court came out of mourning on 1 June 1952 and shortly after her return from a brief holiday at Balmoral, the Queen presided over the Coronation Council and signed the Proclamation. The next day Garter King of Arms read it from a balcony at St James's Palace, flanked by the Officers of Arms and with the Earl Marshal, the Duke of Norfolk, at his side. During the next months, the Queen never failed to study the plans as they were submitted to her, and as the day approached, she rehearsed her own role with the help of a specially printed book of instructions of six tightly typed pages.

---

* I have written two books on this – Hugo Vickers, *The Coronation* (The Dovecote Press, 2013 and 2023) – in which the full story is told.

THE CORONATION, 1953

The Queen being greeted by the Duke of Norfolk at a Coronation rehearsal dinner on 28 May 1953

Prince Philip was appointed Chairman of the Coronation Commission but only attended two meetings, leaving the arrangements in the well-trained hands of the Duke of Norfolk, whose family had been the highest authority on matters of royal ceremonial since 1674. Duke Bernard had already presided over the 1937 Coronation. He was a rotund figure, looking considerably older than his forty-four years (in 1952). He was a masterly impresario, no detail being too small for him, down to the seasoning of the wood on the platform so that it did not creak and what shoes the pages should wear. He sent out the invitations. One peer feared his divorce might preclude him from being summoned. 'Of course you will,' said the Duke. 'This is a Coronation, not Royal Ascot.'[1]

The Queen hoped there would be widespread celebrations but did not want unnecessary expenditure. She gave the Dean and Canons of Westminster some striking blue copes with a lion and unicorn on the back. 'We're the Dean's beasts,' joked one.[2]

Crowned heads were not invited to the ceremony, which infuriated Queen Frederika of Greece and Queen Louise of Sweden, they being so closely related to Prince Philip. His three surviving sisters, Princess Margarita of Hohenlohe-Langenburg, Margravine Theodora of Baden and Princess George of Hanover, none of whom had been invited to his wedding, were determined to be there. Processing with them was his mother, Princess Andrew of Greece, who was singled out by Cecil Beaton as 'a contrast to the grandeur, in the ash-grey draperies of a nun'.[3] Her brother, Earl Mountbatten of Burma, was weighed down with Orders and decorations. As his late mother's elderly maid put it: 'Prince Dickie was simply magnificent. Absolutely a Coronation in himself!'[4]

One of the most memorable overseas guests was Queen Salote of Tonga, of the Friendly Islands in the Pacific. She was there because Tonga was a British colony. She proved a huge success with the crowds by sitting in an open carriage in the rain, the Sultan of Kelantan getting soaked opposite her.

The service was reassuringly traditional. If the Queen and the Duke wanted it modernised, they were too young to stand up to the Earl Marshal. The only conflict the Queen addressed was her wish to bring in Prince Philip and the Archbishop of Canterbury's attempts to push him out. One such issue concerned whether he would do homage before or after the Archbishop. When Fisher came to lunch at the Palace on 6 November 1952, Prince Philip told him to do as he wished. So, on the day, it was the Archbishop who did his fealty first. Prince Philip asked the Archbishop if he would be kissing the Queen's cheek. Fisher replied that, no, he wouldn't: 'I said that I regarded it as a very self-sacrificing act on my part, which tickled them both!'[5]

The Queen told the Archbishop that she wanted Prince Philip included in the service. It was agreed that he would take Communion beside her and indeed a prayer was added for him in that part of the service. Pleased as he was to do this, the Archbishop made it clear in his notes: 'There must be no association of him in any way with the process & rite of Coronation.'[6] Prince Philip did not care. Looking back years later, his comment was: 'Much of that day remains rather a blur in my memory, although I have the most vivid memories of individual incidents.'[7]

The Archbishop was pleased when Prince Philip suggested making an offering at the time of the Communion. In an almost Trollopian situation, Fisher was nervous that anything given at an Abbey service would have to remain part of their collection even though they were 'wealthy in plate of all kinds'[8] and nor was he wrong. He had hoped that the Duke's gift might go to Lambeth Palace chapel, which was being restored after wartime bombing and possessed nothing. The Duke solved the problem by offering a silver-gilt wafer box to the Abbey, and a chalice and paten for Lambeth, in case, he said, the Dean got hold of the box.

By March 1953 the Queen had approved the service. The Archbishop devised special readings for her to help her understand the different aspects of the Coronation; he preached sermons on consecration, majesty and dedication. He made the key point: 'The Queen has not chosen this office for herself. She comes to it because it is laid upon her. She is called to it by God: and she accepts it at his hands.'[9]

* * * * *

The most controversial issue was the question of television coverage. The Queen and her advisers were originally against it on the grounds that it would put undue strain on the Queen because 'any mistakes, unintentional incidents or undignified behaviour by the spectators would be seen by millions of people without any possibility of cutting or censorship'. In prolonged discussions, the strongest plea came from the Venerable Francis House, Head of Religious Broadcasting at the BBC, whose argument was that he wanted millions of the Queen's subjects to have the chance to join in fully with the service – and not just the processions.[10] The Archbishop worried about close-ups, noting that the Queen had a habit of licking her lips, but the Dean of Westminster was won over and approached the Earl Marshal. As late as August, the Duke's line was that 'religious services should not be made the means of providing Television Programmes', and he rammed home the final point – that he could edit things out, but 'Live Television goes straight to the World and any mistakes can never be rectified, and to my mind this is very important'.[11] So it continued, but eventually good sense prevailed. The whole Coronation was filmed for television, except for sacred moments such as the anointing and the Communion. When Cabinet papers were released in 1983 exposing the Queen's initial reluctance, figures such as Sir John Colville and Sir Edward

Ford were quick to point out that she saved the day. Colville claimed that the Queen had told Churchill that 'all her subjects should have an opportunity of seeing it'.[12] On 8 December the Earl Marshal announced that most of the Coronation would be televised.

On the day the Home Service started wireless broadcasting at 5.30 a.m., featuring numerous interviews with Commonwealth Prime Ministers before covering the procession and service. Television tuned in at 9.15 a.m. and was live until 5.20 p.m. Some 27 million people settled down to watch. To this day survivors remember their first experience of television as watching the flickering black-and-white images moving about small screens in their own homes on that memorable day.

* * * * *

Norman Hartnell was by now well established as the royal couturier. He had designed Princess Elizabeth's wedding dress in 1947 and outfits for the 1951 tour of Canada. For the Coronation dress he studied the precedents and produced eight different designs veering from the simple to the elaborate. The eighth sketch contained the heraldic emblems of Great Britain, including the Tudor Rose, the Thistle, the Shamrock and a Daffodil (which Hartnell then believed to be the national emblem of Wales).

This inspired the Queen to ask for emblems of the Dominions of which she was also Queen and led to a ninth and final design. Meanwhile Hartnell ran up against Garter King of Arms, who objected strongly to the Daffodil, telling him firmly: 'No, Hartnell. You must have the Leek.'[13] Hartnell retreated home, pulled up a leek from his vegetable garden. He was suitably disheartened by its appearance. Luckily he then remembered that the leek was the emblem of the Welsh Guards and 'in the end, by using lovely silks and sprinkling it with a dew of diamonds, we were able to transform the earthy Leek into a vision of Cinderella charm*'.[14]

Hartnell then worked on the other emblems – the Maple Leaf of Canada, the Wattle flower of Australia, the Fern of New Zealand,

---

* On her later Commonwealth tour, the Queen confused someone she was talking to when she mentioned that Hartnell had put a leek (leak?) on her dress.

the Protea of South Africa, the Lotus flower of India, Wheat, Cotton and Jute for Pakistan, and a different Lotus flower for Ceylon. When the Queen saw the finished dress, her comment was 'Glorious.'[15] Hartnell's première fitter, Isabelle Fowler, always known as Madame Isabelle, watched the Queen's face reflected in a mirror: 'Never have I seen such happiness.'[16]

All kinds of issues arose during the rehearsals. The Archbishop found the Regalia peers especially tiresome. Lord Hastings told the Archbishop it was 'utterly wrong' for them to be moving towards the altar while the Queen was kneeling at her faldstool in private devotion. The Archbishop said: 'Well, the Queen must decide.' To this they said: 'We hope that you will represent that this is the wish of the Regalia peers.' But Lord Portal disagreed. At the first rehearsal, the Archbishop asked the Queen and without hesitation she took his side. 'So that is that,' wrote Fisher. 'And I shall have great pleasure in telling the peers concerned at the next rehearsal.'[17]

The Duchess of Norfolk stood in for the Queen at most of the rehearsals, quietly instructing him about the placing of the crown. The Queen told him that she was prepared to risk the microphones and say, 'All right,' if and when it was indeed all right.[18]

The Queen attended several rehearsals, sometimes as a spectator and sometimes taking part. One day she sat contentedly in St Edward's Chair. She told the Archbishop she was happily reading the little book of devotions he had prepared for her. When she rehearsed, she appeared to the Archbishop 'sincere, gay, happy, intensely interested asking all the right questions about her movements and carrying them out very naturally and impressively'.[19]

A question arose about her curtseying to the congregation. Garter King of Arms was against it, but Lord Salisbury judged that a curtsey was a courtesy. Fisher told Garter that he would put it to the Queen personally. 'You must advise her rightly,' said Garter. Fisher noted privately: 'I shall certainly advise her in the sense that Garter would call wrong.'[20] When she came to the Abbey on 27 May they discussed it, the Queen keen to curtsey, Prince Philip against her curtseying to her subjects. She pointed out that she did so at the opening of Parliament (where in fact she inclined her head). Prince Philip accepted that reluctantly. Fisher informed Garter, and a half-curtsey was accepted (albeit reluctantly by Garter).[21]

On Sunday, 31 May, large crowds saw the Queen and the Duke driven the short journey to the Queen's Chapel, Marlborough House, for matins. Later that evening the Archbishop said prayers with them and gave them his blessing. He recorded 'a feeling of complete mutual trust free of all kind of constraint and I felt that the Queen and I were entirely in step for the Coronation itself'.[22]

Coronation Day

All the elements came together on the day. Richard Dimbleby took his place in the Abbey at 5.30 a.m., for a broadcasting stint of seventeen hours. Eight thousand troops moved into action, and the ticket holders arrived at the Abbey between 6 a.m. and 8.30. The Archbishop said matins in the chapel at Lambeth Palace, including a prayer for the Queen. Three carriages conveyed the principal members of the Royal Family – the Princes and Princesses of the Blood Royal. At 10 a.m. the Queen Mother's Procession left Clarence House, she and Princess Margaret travelling in the Glass Coach. In due course some 260 people took part in processions within the Abbey.

Lady Diana Cooper was disappointed by Princess Margaret – 'Wings clipped by the King's death, not all glorious within, rather dusky and heavy featured'[23] – while Chips Channon assessed the arrivals against his memories of 1937: 'Queen Mum was OK, but compared badly with Queen Mary's entry last time.'[24] In due course the Archbishops and Bishops Assistant (in their copes and mitres) joined the procession to await the Queen's arrival.

The State Procession included more than a thousand guardsmen, and the senior officers of the armed forces. The Queen and Prince Philip left Buckingham Palace in the Gold State Coach, pulled by eight Greys at 10.26 a.m., with the Duke of Beaufort (Master of the Horse), Lord Alanbrooke and others riding beside the coach. The Duke of Gloucester and Lord Mountbatten rode behind as Personal ADCs. Mountbatten had made an enormous fuss wishing to ride alongside the carriage, but the Queen had put him firmly in his place. Before her death Queen Mary had been shocked that Prince Philip was to be inside the coach. She thought his place was on a horse as a Personal ADC.[25]

THE CORONATION, 1953

At exactly 11 a.m. the coach arrived at the Annexe, and the Queen got out, wearing the crimson velvet Parliamentary train and the King George IV diadem. A piece of red thread had been stitched into the blue carpet to mark where she should stop for a fanfare. Audrey Russell, one of the BBC commentators, was horrified to see a young Gold Staff Officer kneel down and snip the red ribbon away. She need not have worried. The Queen stopped on the very spot. As Hubert Parry's anthem, 'I Was Glad', was sung by the massed choirs, the Queen processed up the full length of the main aisle. Cecil Beaton watched her:

And then the Queen, her demeanour of childish simplicity & humility, with pink hands folded in front, in contrast to the grandeur of her heavily encrusted dress, her hair tightly curled, the Victorian crown perched straighter on her head than usual, & the effect thus even better, her cheeks very pink.[26]

For the next two hours everything passed off smoothly, the Queen doing her part with simplicity and showing no outward trace of nervousness.[27] The television cameras were diverted for the anointing, which had to happen before the Queen received 'the royal ornaments'.[28] For that, the Queen wore a simple white dress over her Coronation dress, and the four Garter Knights held a canopy over her, somewhat clumsily as was observed.

The Mistress of the Robes robed the Queen in the Colobium Sindonis and the Supertunica – or cloth of gold – and she was handed the various items of regalia. At 11.37 the entire congregation rose. The Archbishop blessed St Edward's Crown on the High Altar. He advanced to the Queen, stretched his arms to the full length and held the crown above her so that all could see. He then lowered it slowly onto her head. He raised his hands on high and the Queen gave him a reassuring smile.[29]

The congregation cried, 'God Save The Queen,' and the Princes and Princesses, peers and peeresses and the Kings of Arms put on their coronets. It was a glorious moment, the white-gloved arms of the peeresses resembling the long necks of swans as they rose in unison. The Abbey resounded with fanfares and loud shouts of acclaim. Outside salutes were fired by artillery at the Tower of London and in Hyde Park to let the crowds know that their Queen was crowned.

This moment was shared by wireless in most corners of the globe. Through television it was widely seen. Young Prince Charles had been brought to the Abbey to witness that moment. The Queen was then escorted to the throne and symbolically 'lifted' into it. The Regalia peers gathered behind her. Next the Archbishop, and the Royal Dukes – Prince Philip as Duke of Edinburgh, her uncle the Duke of Gloucester and her cousin the Duke of Kent did their homage. And then the senior acceptable representative of each rank of the peerage followed suit, all the peers of the same rank kneeling in unison. The senior Baron, Lord Mowbray, Segrave and Stourton, was 'the comic piece in the whole procedure':*

> He came down from his homage all over the place, bunching up his robe and tripping over it and, as the Queen said, with mothballs and pieces of ermine flying in all directions.[30]

And as the Barons knelt, Lord Hastings who had caused the Archbishop such irritation, tripped and fell forwards rather noticeably, being with those peers on the Queen's left.

After the homage, the Queen was joined by Prince Philip for the Communion, which they took side by side. The service over, the Queen withdrew and put on the purple velvet train and the Imperial State Crown. Until now, by strict agreement, there had been no close-ups of her on television. A BBC censor, Ben Shaw, was waiting in the wings with a button that he could press to halt filming if the rules were broken. But as the Queen began to process into the aisle, the camera moved closer in, breaking all the rules. To his eternal credit Shaw saw this but did not have the heart to press the button. He served the nation well. The resulting moving

---

* The 25th Lord Mowbray, Segrave and Stourton (1895–1965). His barony dated back to 1283. Lord Mowbray was given a front-row seat in front of the Dukes so that he could emerge easily. His son was a Gold Staff Officer and, before the service, came over to tell him how lucky he was. 'Lucky? Lucky? My dear boy, these upstart Dukes were still tilling the fields when we were Barons!' This had an electric effect on the Dukes, and the Duke of Rutland hid Mowbray's coronet with his sandwiches in it. When the Queen was told this story years later she commented that Mowbray's behaviour was 'very Grenadierish'.

pictures of the Queen were stunning, something that modern TV viewers would take for granted but were exceptional in 1953.*

When the great service was over, Prince Philip suggested that the Archbishop should go in and see the Queen while she had a quick break before the long procession home. They traded the mistakes. The Queen had failed to genuflect as she reached the Amphitheatre. The Queen told the Archbishop that she had been willing him hard not to come out with the Armills, when he did. They decided they were 'all square'.[31] The Queen told him that he had put the crown on much better than she did when she had placed it herself after the Glorias.

Lawrence Tanner, at work as a Gold Staff Officer, commended the Queen's 'mixture of grace, charm, dignity and humility' as she curtseyed to the congregation when presented to all four sides of the Abbey.[32]

The only downside was the appalling weather, but nothing could counter the enthusiasm of the crowd. Media coverage was predictably positive. The *Guardian* was not known to be pro-monarchy, but Harry Boardman, their political correspondent, wrote:

> Others of our Queens, Elizabeth I and Victoria, for example, have swayed the hearts of their people after a time, but Elizabeth II captured them from the start. She has done it not merely in virtue of her youth and grace, but because she joins to these qualities the high seriousness we have come to associate with the House of Windsor. That gravity was hers today, and perfectly attuned to the occasion. It made its subtle appeal to all hearts. It stirred the sense of a young woman set apart and dedicated and even a little lonely and greatly deserving a nation's affection and support.[33]

On that wet day in June, Britain had acquired a newly anointed and crowned Queen. It is said that the monarch goes into the Abbey as one person and comes out as another. The ceremony was intensely moving for the Queen, and after the long procession back through London and the balcony appearances, she could be sure that she had the affirmation and support of the British people and those in the wider Commonwealth, and that she was truly Queen of England and the United Kingdom and all her other realms and territories.

---

* This can be seen on YouTube.

16
THE CORONATION SUMMER

Just before the Coronation, on 20 May, Lady Ward and her daughter-in-law Susan gave a glittering ball for Elizabeth Ward* at Hutchinson House to which the Queen, the Queen Mother, Princess Margaret, the Athlones, the Gloucesters and Princess Marina came. Chips Channon noted that twelve hundred people danced until dawn. The Queen was 'gay and laughing', the Queen Mother 'plump and resplendent', the Duchess of Buccleuch wore her fifth tiara, and Princess Marina left hers on the grand piano, entrusting it to the band leader. The next day it was impossible to buy an Alka-Seltzer in Belgravia.[1] The ball heralded a glittering Coronation summer.

Four days after the Coronation, on 6 June, the Derby was run at Epsom. There was enormous excitement that the Queen's colt, Aureole,† might win, rounding off the week with triumph on the turf. The sun shone brightly. An exceptional crowd of half a million were longing

---

* Jean, the Hon. Lady Ward (1884–1962), philanthropist and society hostess, was the daughter of Whitelaw Reid, one time US Ambassador to Britain. Susan (1915–81) was married to Lieutenant-Colonel John (Jackie) Ward, Silver Stick. Elizabeth (1935–88) married three times. Susan had a long affair with Primo de Rivera, the Spanish Ambassador, causing the Spanish Embassy to be known as 'The Casualty Ward'.

† Aureole (1950–74). Hotspur in the *Daily Telegraph* gave Aureole, sired by Hyperion, equal position as favourite with Sir Victor Sassoon's Pinza the day before. The Queen inherited him from her father. He was trained by Sir Cecil Boyd-Rochfort. He ran fourteen times between August 1952 and July 1954, reaching his peak that year when he won the Coronation Cup by five lengths at Epsom, the Hardwicke Stakes at Royal Ascot, and the King George VI and Queen Elizabeth Stakes, described as one of the most popular wins in racing history. His winnings made the Queen the leading owner in Britain in 1954. He then went out to stud.

for the Queen to win. The Queen and the Duke were driven down the course in a huge Rolls-Royce, with the hood open at the back. The Earl of Rosebery greeted them and there was the Duke of Norfolk once again. The atmosphere on the course was electric.

Aureole was frisky and played up in the parade. It was an exciting race, with the Aga Khan's Shikampur taking the lead until past Tattenham Corner, at which point Gordon Richards made a strong challenge on Pinza and overtook. Harry Carr also made a strong challenge on Aureole, overtaking Shikampur. But Pinza was a decisive four to five lengths ahead, giving Gordon Richards his first Derby win after twenty-nine attempts. Aureole finished second, the closest the Queen ever came to winning the Derby.

Despite her disappointment, the Queen welcomed Richards in the Royal Box to congratulate him with a winning smile. Tommy Lascelles was greatly amused by the astonishment expressed by the Russian Minister, that the Queen's horse could be beaten by a French horse* a mere four days after the Coronation.

That very social MP Chips Channon, perhaps feeling rejected, was disparaging about the new reign. He noted that the Queen 'did not smile as she drove down the course [at Ascot] to the accompaniment of cheers' and was told that she was bored with her house party and left them to their own devices, rather than exhausting them with activities as happened in the previous reign.[2] By the end of June, Colin Tennant, close friend of Princess Margaret, was decrying the social season as disappointing: 'It's because everything is revolving so much around the Queen that it all seems to be arranged for her & there's nothing for us. Our role is to give foreigners the impression that we are dazzled by the Queen & her activities, and I suppose they think all these functions very brilliant.'[3]

Gloriana

Amid state banquets, drives through London and a Service of Thanksgiving at St Paul's Cathedral, the Gala Performance took place at the Royal Opera House, on 8 June. It was Lord Harewood,

---

* Pinza was sired by Chanteur.

by then a Director of the Royal Opera House, who, as Benjamin Britten put it, 'bullied'[4] the Queen into having an operatic gala.

The Earl of Harewood by Cecil Beaton

Gloriana was an attempt to create an opera that provided an expression of national pride in the way that *Manon* had for the French and *Aida* for the Italians. The libretto was written by William Plomer, with music by Benjamin Britten. Harewood had lately read Lytton Strachey's *Elizabeth and Essex* (1928), and he and Britten thought this would be a good basis for the performance.

Gloriana underwent numerous teething problems,* yet by March 1953 it was more or less ready, and on 18 May the Queen and Prince

---

* See *The Tongs and the Bones – the Memoirs of Lord Harewood*, pp. 135–8; and Peter F. Alexander, *William Plomer – A Biography* (Oxford University Press, 1989), pp. 270–79.

Philip dined with the Harewoods, the Princess Royal and William Plomer to hear some extracts performed by Britten, Joan Cross (the soprano singing Elizabeth I) and Peter Pears (the tenor singing Essex). After the evening Prince Philip took the trouble to read the libretto.

The Royal Family enjoyed being told that the Lord Chamberlain's Office had objected to a scene in which a housewife emptied a 'receptacle' onto the crowd from her window. Employing their right of censorship (which continued until 1968), they obliged them to change this to a basin.

Life Guards, Grenadier Guards and Yeomen of the Guard were on duty in the Royal Opera House on the night. A crowd of two thousand craned behind policemen to view the arrivals.* The Royal Box was transformed into a cloth-of-gold tent by Oliver Messel and garlanded with flowers by Constance Spry. The sets and costumes were by John Piper and the dancing choreographed by John Cranko. Antique furniture was loaned from the Victoria and Albert Museum and elsewhere. John Colville judged the Messel decor 'superb' and thought the audience well dressed 'for a change', but found 'Elizabeth's squalid romance with Essex totally unsuited to the occasion'.[5]

The Queen sat between Prince Philip and Crown Prince Olav of Norway, with the Queen Mother, almost the entire British Royal Family (including the aged Princess Marie Louise) and many foreign guests, such as Dominion and Commonwealth Prime Ministers. Society figures were out in force, the lady guests simmering and shimmering in tiaras and fine jewels, the men with white ties, Orders and decorations, Garter Knights in knee breeches, wearing their Garters in public for the first time since 1939. Harold Macmillan was cynically entertained by the thought of all the tiaras being put away the next day as their owners did the washing-up.

Harewood had hoped that the audience would consist of artistically minded people gathered to honour the Queen (naively, he conceded), but instead it was 'Cabinet, Diplomatic Corps and official London first and foremost, and the rest apparently nowhere'.[6] Despite eight minutes of applause, and ten curtain calls, he conceded that it was 'one of the great disasters of operatic history'.[7] Press comment was 'guarded', and there were complaints at taxpayers'

---

* All this can be seen on YouTube, a fascinating fourteen minutes or so.

money being spent on the production, evidently £20,000 in a grant from the Arts Council.

Many acerbic views were expressed by society figures. Lady Pamela Berry described it as 'Hell – so dull and bad – actual physical agony to listen to at some points'.[8] Ann Fleming declared it 'high treason on the part of the Harewoods', explaining: 'Far from toning it down, each act revealed Elizabeth I in an increasingly undignified role, until finally discovered without her wig, and then a finale of lugubrious remorse. The scenes that were supposed to depict Merry England were the gloomiest, but I doubt if Elizabethan England is a good subject for homosexual talent.'[9] Lady Juliet Duff wrote: 'It doesn't seem to me quite the thing to portray the first Queen Elizabeth as an old, bald, lecherous woman at a Gala for a beautiful young Queen.'[10]

The only person who appeared to have loved it was Edwina Mountbatten. As she left, she told Lady Salisbury: 'Wasn't it wonderful? I could have listened three hours more.' Later the Duchess of Devonshire, who had sat next to her in the Royal Box, revealed that Edwina had slept – and snored – throughout the whole performance.[11]

Controversy raged for days in the correspondence columns of *The Times,* prompting the distinguished composer, Ralph Vaughan Williams to praise the Queen for having 'commanded' an opera from a composer 'from these islands', a gesture that added greatly to the prestige of British music.[12]

In retrospect Lord Harewood felt it had had the potential to be a great opera, which was confirmed by later stagings, but 'The audience had in fact proved unworthy of an event they should have felt it a privilege to attend ... a seductive evening in the theatre.'*[13]

The Queen herself bore Britten no grudge. Though not an opera lover, she gave the performance her full attention. She continued to be supportive, writing him many letters. She opened the Snape Maltings Concert Hall on 2 June 1967, on which occasion Prince Philip succeeded in upsetting Britten with an overheard comment:

---

* Benjamin Britten was greatly upset by the experience, not helped by a broadside from Peter Pears, suggesting that they should stick to their loyal Aldeburgh audiences and not venture into such national territory.

'Well, I hope the old man has written something we can understand this time.'[14] She was especially affected by Britten's arrangement of the National Anthem, commenting wryly that she had heard the Anthem once or twice before.[15] When the Snape Maltings Hall was burned down, she reopened it in 1970. In 1975 she invited him to be Master of the Queen's Music in succession to Sir Arthur Bliss, but he was not well enough to accept.

Prince Philip went on to commission a *Jubilate in C* from Benjamin Britten for St George's Chapel, in July 1961, to further St George's Chapel's centuries-old tradition of being at the forefront of commissioning church music. Britten received high honours. He was made a Companion of Honour in 1953 and given the Order of Merit in 1965. When he died in 1976, the Queen sent a message of sympathy to his stablemate Peter Pears. James Lees-Milne thought: 'What an advance this was, that the Queen should tacitly but publicly recognize a homosexual relationship.'[16]

★ ★ ★ ★ ★

Princess Margaret

The Queen Mother and Princess Margaret eventually moved into Clarence House in May 1953.* They lived there together, though not entirely in harmony. They kept different hours and the Queen Mother launched herself into a new role as the first ever working Queen Mother, persuaded by Churchill in the late summer of 1952 that she could play a strong part in public life. She was then fifty-two, and became ambassadorial, diplomatic and social. Having bolstered the King during his reign, she left the Queen and Prince Philip to do things their way, any interference being subtle and hard to pinpoint, albeit there. She was now essentially a somewhat unmerry widow. That she did not help Princess Margaret turned

---

* When MPs complained about the cost of the refurbishment, the Queen Mother wrote: 'Perhaps they would like me to retire decently to Kew and run a needlework guild.' (Letter to Sir Arthur Penn, in William Shawcross, *Queen Elizabeth The Queen Mother*, p. 677.)

into resentment from the younger daughter, who was already annoyed that she had not been given an education to match her natural talents and intelligence.

Princess Margaret had been cast adrift, no longer a resident of Buckingham Palace, Windsor, Sandringham and Balmoral, but a guest of her sister. They remained close, though the relationship with Prince Philip was never relaxed. Small wonder that she grew closer to Group Captain Peter Townsend, her father's popular equerry, who had been treated almost as a son of the family.

After the Coronation, unrecognised by the crowds, the Princess and Group Captain Townsend had slipped out of a side gate of the Palace. They bumped into Princess Alexandra, who asked what they were doing. 'Just looking, the same as you. After all, we're the Queen's subjects, too,'[17] replied Princess Margaret.

No sooner had the intelligentsia's furore over *Gloriana* died down than the newspapers were full of her romance with Townsend. The press had spotted that in the Coronation Annexe she had been chatting to the Group Captain and picked a piece of fluff from the shoulder of his jacket. The incident was not captured in any photographs but it was reported in the foreign press as evidence of intimacy.

Eileen Ascroft set off the story in Britain with a piece in the *Evening Standard*, called 'My Kind of Man', in which she cited Townsend 'a frequent riding and dancing companion to Princess Margaret'.[18] The *People* took this up on Sunday, 14 June, a mere twelve days after the Coronation, under the headline: 'Princess Margaret – Scandalous Stories of her "romance" – They must deny it <u>now</u>':

> It is high time for the British public to be made aware of the fact that scandalous rumours about Princess Margaret are racing around the world. Newspapers in Europe and America are openly asserting that the princess is in love with a divorced man and that she wishes to marry him. Every newspaper which has printed the story names the man as Group Captain Peter Townsend ... The story is of course utterly untrue. It is quite unthinkable that a Royal princess, third in line of succession to the Throne, should even contemplate a marriage with a man who has been through the divorce courts.

Rumours had been circulating in the American press for years. On 30 August 1951 a photograph snapped at Balmoral of the Group Captain with Queen Elizabeth and her daughters had appeared in the *Sydney Morning Herald*. In August 1952, William H. Stoneman speculated in the *Miami Herald* that Princess Margaret might marry Townsend even before his divorce came through in November that year. By December Patrick Nicholson was on to it, reporting in the *Vancouver-News Herald*: 'A possible royal romance is being whispered about in Ottawa's inner circles ...'[19] After the *People* article, it became a national crisis.

Peter Townsend was born in 1914 and raised in a conventionally loving family with strong religious beliefs, which he inherited. He joined the RAF in 1933 and became one of the most capable squadron leaders in the Battle of Britain. He won a DSO, a DFC and bar, was shot down and wounded, and was credited with having destroyed nine enemy aircraft. He loved flying but was aware of the ever-present threat of dying: 'It meant a falling down and down out of the boundless heavens and a horrible, shattering collision with the earth, with the crushing and mutilation of some frail body.' After a series of narrow escapes, his line on death was: 'Don't forget, I'm always here but I won't be unkind to you.'[20]

Townsend was appointed as a temporary equerry to the King in 1944 – an 'Equerry of Honour' – a new concept at court. He lived at Adelaide Cottage in Windsor Home Park with his wife, Rosemary Pawle, whom he had married in 1941 and with whom he had two young sons. Rosemary was rather a favourite of the King. In due course Townsend's three-month secondment was extended. His marriage failed after the South African trip of 1947, some say because he purposely neglected his wife. Due to her adultery (which led to her subsequent marriage) with John de László, son of the well-known society portrait painter, she was the so-called guilty party. By 1950 Townsend was Assistant Master of the Household. After the King's death, the Queen Mother invited him to run Clarence House, though this never came about. The Townsend divorce was finalised in November 1952.

The timeline of the romance with Princess Margaret was muddled by Townsend in his memoirs. There was a connection before the King died: a scene in the heather at Balmoral when Princess Margaret covered Townsend with a coat as he dozed, a time when the lady in waiting, Lady Jean Rankin, suggested he was falling in love with the Princess. He denied it. They became more closely involved after the King's death, drawn together by her grief for her father, and he by increased loneliness after the collapse of his marriage.

At some point in 1952 he confessed the affair to Tommy Lascelles, who told him fiercely that he had betrayed his position, that he was not a young man, he was a married man of mature years, and a father, and that he had played on the affection of a young and impressionable girl. 'You must be mad or bad,' said Lascelles. To others Lascelles declared: 'He has Theudas trouble.'*

Lascelles did not hesitate to discuss the issue with the Queen, who liked Townsend, and wanted her sister to be happy. But she was in an impossible situation, constrained by her position as Head of the Church of England, which did not condone the remarriage of divorced people. Furthermore there was the Royal Marriages Act of 1772, which obliged her to grant or withhold permission for members of her family to marry.

The affair was one of those tragic circumstances of its time. However admirable the pair were, their respective circumstances made marriage impossible. According to Townsend, he and the Princess dined with the Queen and Prince Philip and were better received by them than by Lascelles. In later life Princess Margaret took the line that Lascelles had never discussed the issue with her, but there is a letter from her to Lascelles, written at the time, thanking him for explaining the dilemma.†

Next Lascelles went down to Chartwell to discuss the matter with Churchill.[21] The Prime Minister told him that this would go down badly in the Commonwealth. It could only be allowed if Princess Margaret renounced her right to the throne. A plan was devised, approved by the Queen, that Townsend would be sent overseas so that matters could calm down. All this took place at an exceptionally busy time. The Queen made a ceremonial entry into Windsor and took part in the Coronation naval review at Spithead. Her horse, Choir Boy, won the Royal Hunt Cup at Royal Ascot, and on 23 June, she made a state entry to Edinburgh. The next day she drove in state to

---

* Theudas is a figure from the Acts of the Apostles: 'For before those days rose up Theudas, boasting himself to be somebody.'

† This letter was shown to me by Caroline Erskine, Lascelles's daughter.

St Giles' Cathedral, preceded by the Honours of Scotland, to take part in an act of Dedication, the Scottish equivalent of the Coronation.*

The Queen was back in London in time to see the Queen Mother and Princess Margaret off to Rhodesia on 30 June. Literally the next day, she and Prince Philip flew to Hillsborough, in Northern Ireland, taking Townsend with them. Their visit was slightly overshadowed by the press being as interested in the Group Captain as in the Queen. By then Princess Margaret knew that he was to be sent as Air Attaché in Brussels, but had every expectation of seeing him before he left. This was not to be. On 3 July the Queen and her party flew back from Ulster. Townsend recorded that she shook his hand on the tarmac in full view of the press and wished him well. So did Prince Philip. Later Townsend wrote: 'I never admired her more, above all for publicly defying the cries of scandal which were resounding about her sister and me. She was truly Elizabethan.'[22]

On the same day, Townsend was gazetted an Extra Equerry to the Queen, effectively a retired position.

The fallout from this crisis was a change in the Regency Act of 1937. When Lascelles had seen Churchill his plaintive cry was: 'One motor accident and this young lady might be our queen.' Lascelles hailed this as Churchill's 'unerring power of seizing a point'.[23] Sir David Maxwell Fyfe, then Home Secretary, wanted the Regency Act addressed. Thus R. A. Butler, Chancellor of the Exchequer, introduced a new Bill to Parliament on 22 July. Inevitably people assumed this was a ruse to oust Princess Margaret from becoming Regent should anything happen to the Queen. There was a fair amount of dissent, but it was logical that the Duke of Edinburgh would be more appropriate as the father of an under-age king. The Bill became an Act of Parliament on 19 November 1953, with Prince Philip as Regent-Designate.

Lascelles's plan was that by keeping Townsend out of the way until 1955, the passage of time would ease matters. In 1955 Princess Margaret would turn twenty-five. At that point her case would be slightly different, though she would not be entirely free of the Royal Marriages Act. He instructed Townsend to leave for Belgium on 15 July, two days before the Queen Mother and Princess Margaret

---

* This ceremony is cited as an instance of Lascelles getting it wrong. The Queen wore day clothes while the other participants were fully robed.

returned from overseas. At daybreak, on 15 July, Group Captain Townsend drove out of London, effectively into exile.

I knew Peter Townsend in the 1980s, having met him in the South of France with his family – a kind, gentle man, very friendly, easy to talk to. He lived near Paris with his second wife, son and two daughters. He had been a famous flying ace, but by this time there was passivity in his character. He was seventy and no longer the dashing pilot of his youth. I remember thinking he would never have been able to stand up to Princess Margaret.

17
THE COMMONWEALTH TOUR, 1953–4

'Thus formed, the Commonwealth bears no resemblance to the Empires of the past. It is an entirely new conception, built on the highest qualities of the spirit of man: friendship, loyalty and the desire for freedom and peace.
To that new conception of an equal partnership of nations and races I shall give myself heart and soul every day of my life.'
The Queen's Christmas broadcast from Auckland, 1953

The Queen was the first monarch to be proclaimed Head of the Commonwealth, a style ratified in Cabinet on the day that George VI died. As such she was Queen of thirty-two nations, then known as Commonwealth Realms. The Commonwealth had been formed in December 1931, with its founder members as the United Kingdom, Australia, New Zealand, Canada and South Africa. In 1947 India became independent and a republic with its own President, but wished to remain within the Commonwealth. Two years later, on 26 April 1949, the London Declaration confirmed India's acceptance of George VI as 'the symbol of the free association of the independent Member Nations and as such Head of the Commonwealth'.[1] This effectively created the modern Commonwealth, allowing republics to be members accepting the monarch as Head of the Commonwealth while retaining their own Head of State.

By the end of her reign she was Sovereign of only fifteen countries (including the United Kingdom). But there were fifty-six independent member states of the Commonwealth.* Many countries

---

* During the Queen's reign, some countries left and came back: for example South Africa dropped out in 1961 and rejoined in 1994 when Nelson Mandela was President. Fiji was temporarily suspended. Gabon and Togo joined in 2022.

sought and achieved independence. She never minded that as long as they remained in the Commonwealth. She worked tirelessly to retain the link with the other countries on an equal footing.

The Queen was particularly keen to undertake the Commonwealth tour of 1953–4 because she had been forced to cut short the previous one due to her father's death. Neither had she had a chance to see the world due to wartime restrictions. This tour had been planned for 1952/3, but the government wanted her to have been crowned. The Queen wanted to go in January 1954, so she could have Christmas with the children, but the oncoming elections in Australia and the decision to visit New Zealand first meant they had to leave earlier.

There were arguments between the British government and Australia and New Zealand about cost. The Cabinet wanted the Queen to travel in a certain style and turned down her offer to travel more modestly. SS *Gothic* was to have been used by the late King and had been refitted for Princess Elizabeth's interrupted Commonwealth tour of 1952. Robert Menzies, Prime Minister of Australia, was happy to contribute towards costs. Sidney Holland in New Zealand thought his country should pay only when she was in New Zealand.

★ ★ ★ ★ ★

The Queen and Prince Philip flew from London Airport on 23 November, seen off by the Queen Mother, Princess Margaret, Sir Winston Churchill and others. They arrived in Bermuda on 24 November, where the most memorable aspect of a short stopover was being driven in a 14-horsepower convertible, since cars had been allowed on the island only since 1946. Jamaica provided another stopover. On 25 November they arrived at Montego Bay and drove to Kingston. Ann Fleming, wife of Ian Fleming, hailed the visit as a great success, noting that the locals now stood for the National Anthem: 'It was apparently a rapidly declining custom here.'[2]

On 27 November the royal party embarked in SS *Gothic* and sailed through the Panama Canal, disembarking at Cristobal. Three days later they left Balboa for the Pacific crossing. On 16 December *Gothic* arrived off Fiji, where they witnessed the dance of the warriors, toured local schools and had the chance to see what one commentator called the effects of less than a century of benevolent administration.

An overnight stay in Tonga from 19 to 20 December seized the popular imagination since Queen Salote had made such a hit in England at the Coronation. She and her equally large son welcomed the Queen and the Duke, who arrived by flying boat. There was a traditional feast of tropical fruit and raw fish. The Queen and Prince Philip left the Friendly Isles suitably garlanded.

New Zealand: 23 December 1953 – 30 January 1954

By the time the Queen arrived in Auckland on 23 December, the first British monarch ever to visit New Zealand, the New Zealanders were 'on the tiptoe of expectation', as the High Commissioner, Sir Geoffry Scoones, described it.[3]

On all parts of the Commonwealth tour, there was massive excitement in seeing the Queen. Her Christmas Broadcast referred to the Commonwealth's 'equal partnership of nations and races'[4], which was well received. She said it was the first time she had spoken to New Zealanders in their own country.

A potentially embarrassing aspect concerned the Maoris. This was not helped by jibes in the British press to the effect that their greetings were artificial and synthetic, statements widely reported in New Zealand. There was some wrangling between the two races. The Waikato, home of the 'King' movement, were on the decline, a shadow of their nineteenth-century power. More go ahead were the Arawa, who were considered more influential and representative. To them was granted the honour of receiving the Queen.

At first, Sidney Holland, Prime Minister of New Zealand, refused to allow the Queen to visit the Waikato chiefs, which caused great offence, but suddenly he reversed the decision. This gave great pleasure to the Maori people as a whole, and helped soothe ruffled feelings and intertribal jealousy.[5]

On Christmas morning news broke that the 3 p.m. express train from Wellington to Auckland had plunged into the Whangaehu river late the previous evening due to a torrent of mud and water from the volcanic Mount Ruapehu, killing 136 people. Sidney Holland asked Prince Philip to join him at the mass funeral of twenty-one unidentified victims in Wellington. Prince Philip agreed readily and this made a 'deep impression in the country'.[6]

The Queen stayed with Sir Willoughby Norrie, the Governor General. There was carol singing on the lawn of Government House, Father Christmas arriving by sleigh and Christmas morning service at St Mary's Cathedral. And they could swim. The arduous visit to Wellington included the first opening of Parliament of the tour, the Queen in her Coronation gown, Prince Philip in dark naval uniform with Garter collar.

It was thought that two out of three New Zealanders managed to see the Queen. At her own request the tour was relatively informal and as many children as possible were positioned to see her. There were criticisms. The Mayors of the places the Queen did not visit were disappointed. She missed seeing much beautiful country scenery since inevitably she went to the more populated areas. Cavalcades passed too quickly through some of the less-populated areas. (In Blenheim people waited hours and caught but a momentary glimpse of her.) Roads were closed for too long. Mr Holland was much criticised for unduly monopolising her as 'Minister in Attendance', which went down badly with the essentially egalitarian New Zealanders. At the end of the visit, the High Commissioner reported: 'It ... has knitted people together, and they now know what their Queen looks like and is like. They have fallen in a big way for both.'[7]

Australia: 3 February – 1 April

In advance of their visit to Australia, the Queen and the Duke were given a copy of Ian Bevan's book, *The Sunburnt Country*, which contained seventeen essays by prominent Australians, aimed to give them an overview of the country and its people. One reviewer suggested: 'It has probably proved of greater value to her [the Queen] than all the advice of officials and pundits.'[8] Another reviewer volunteered: 'A depressingly large number of those who shake the royal hand will be politicians, fat and thin, bald and hairy, clad in blue suits and grey, some with cultured accents and some with grating tones.'⁹ The royalties accruing to the book were given to the Duke's British Playing Fields Association in London, and while in Sydney, he chose the Legacy Clubs and presented Legacy House with a first cheque for fifteen hundred pounds.

The Queen was greeted by the Governor-General, Field Marshal Sir William Slim. In December 1952, when a new governor-general was required, the Queen had said to Robert Menzies, the Australian Prime Minister: 'I understand that the Constitutional Rule is that you will nominate somebody and that I have no choice in the matter.' Menzies did not like that idea much so they each chose three names and Slim was top of both lists. 'So now, Ma'am,' said Menzies, 'I nominate Slim and you are bound to approve!'

When Slim was approached, he said he needed to consult his wife. 'You must understand that I have a considerable faculty for dropping bricks,' he said, 'but she has a genius for catching them before they hit the floor.' Slim was appointed.[10]

The Slims had the Queen and Prince Philip to stay for five days, necessitating considerable entertainment at Yarralumla, their official residence in a suburb of Canberra. They took on nineteen extra staff, never entertained less than twenty-four for lunch, frequently at least fifty for dinner, and had a garden party for 3,800. There were lighter moments. The Queen sat convulsed with laughter as Slim marched Prince Philip up and down the long drawing-room, practising his baton-drill as a new field marshal.[11]

The tour lasted nearly two months, beginning in Sydney and ending in Perth. At each capital city there was the same formula – an Opening of Parliament, Parliamentary luncheon or dinner, Lord Mayor's Ball and receptions involving children and ex-servicemen. Again there was criticism that the Queen and the Duke were not able to see 'the pastoral industry on which the wealth and prosperity of the country' depended.[12] But everywhere they went there were huge decorations. Famous sporting figures such as the cricketer, Sir Donald Bradman, and the veteran tennis champion, Sir Norman Brookes, were presented.

One of the contributors to *The Sunburnt Country* was Judy Fallon, Prince Philip's wartime hostess in Sydney. In November 1949 she had left Jo and gone to live in London. In 1954 she published some reminiscences of Prince Philip's visits to Australia, accompanied by some previously unseen photographs from his albums, which suggests he authorised these (as he sometimes did). Sydney newspapers related that Prince Philip slipped away twice to see Jo at his 'sumptuous' new home at Loch Maree, Coolong Avenue, as well he should have done. The Fallons had been kind to him when he was on leave in the 1940s, still a penniless naval officer.

The first time Prince Philip arrived on Jo's doorstep, he caught him in his swimming trunks and a dressing-gown and stayed two and a half hours, his only concern being to get back in time to change for a state banquet. Another visit was to an evening swimming party at which he stayed from 8 until 10 p.m. There were fifty guests, Hawaiian music on a gramophone and the pool was floodlit. Reports of these visits were denied.[13]

In Melbourne, Victoria, after an evening reception, Lady Brooks, wife of the Governor, Sir Dallas Brooks, saw the Queen sitting on the double stairway, exhausted, her tiara in her hand. Meanwhile Prince Philip and Mike Parker slipped out to a party in Hawthorn.[14]

These diversions were a welcome contrast to 'the interminable round of official introductions and hand-shakings',[15] prompting the Prime Minister to defend the right of long-serving public figures to meet their Queen. The Mayor of the Blue Mountains found favour with her when he refused to introduce his aldermen on the grounds that her time would be better engaged admiring the view. Menzies was nothing if not a devoted royalist but some thought 'his broadcasts and speeches about the Royal Visit could not fail to win him votes in the Election'.*[16]

An outbreak of poliomyelitis in Perth threatened cancellation of the visit to Western Australia. It went ahead but with no indoor ceremonies, the Queen sleeping aboard SS *Gothic* and eating only food prepared on board.[17] At the end of a universally acclaimed tour, in which 80 per cent of the population saw her, the Queen and the Duke sailed towards the Cocos-Keeling Islands, where they stayed for just ninety minutes on 5 April, then sailed on to Ceylon.

Noel Adams, a distinguished Tasmanian-born journalist and editor,

---

* Menzies won in 1954 and again in 1955 and continued to dominate Australian politics until 1966.

detected 'a rare sign of excitement' in the Queen's face on the day of departure. He attributed this to 'a feeling that she had accomplished the greatest and most exacting task of her life'.[18]

Sir Stephen Holmes, the UK High Commissioner, decried some of the arrangements and thought, 'The behaviour of the crowds at some of the race meetings was somewhat embarrassing.' Much attention was paid to including post-war immigrant Australians to make them feel that Australia was genuinely their new home. He concluded that 'A good deal was being asked both of the body and of the mind and it has been a source of great admiration to all in this country that the Queen should have been able to support so long and arduous and at times monotonous a programme.'[19]

Ceylon: 10–21 April

The Queen's visit to Ceylon, one of the countries of which she was Queen, nearly did not happen due to prophecies of mismanagement by the Ceylon authorities, the pronouncements of local astrologers and a petition from the left wing, with ninety thousand signatures protesting against it.[20]

Ceylon had been under British rule since 1815. The Governor-General was Lord Soulbury, a former Conservative minister. He was a classical scholar, who had appreciated a message in Latin inviting him to the press gallery of the House of Commons to test the acoustics: '*Quare non venis nos videre aliquando ut ait Maia Occidentalis?*'* He accepted in Latin. Within a month of arriving in Ceylon, he had made a speech in Sinhalese.

In September 1953 Sir Cecil Syers, the High Commissioner, wanted to cancel the visit due to recent political riots. Lord Salisbury, Secretary of State for Commonwealth Relations, was not keen. His line was 'that a visit by The Queen produces such an emotional upsurge of enthusiasm and warmth of feeling that any would-be demonstrator would be shouted down and might be roughly handled by the numbers of loyal citizens'.[21] Churchill agreed. Fortunately the Prime Minister, Dudley Senanayake, was ousted by the more

---

* 'Why don't you come up and see us sometime, as Mae West would say?'

flamboyant General Sir John Kotelawala, who immediately told Soulbury that the visit should go ahead.

Then there was a religious crisis over the proposed visit by the Queen to the Temple of the Tooth at Kandy, the famous Buddhist shrine, which contained a tooth of Buddha. Churchill was concerned that if the Queen visited the shrine, it would involve her removing her shoes and making a gift of gold: 'I am sure you will be the first to see that such an act by the Queen would not be possible because of misunderstanding among her Christian subjects in other countries.'[22] There was to be a magnificent royal procession (the Raja Perahera) with elephants, torchbearers and dancers, the first time it had been staged since 1815. Then the Temple authorities requested that the Queen should be shown the controversial tooth. They pointed out that it was a practice that had been carried out by all royalty who had visited Ceylon since 1815, that the Duke of Windsor had visited it as Prince of Wales in 1922 and the Duke of Gloucester in 1947, and that 'non-acceptance would be construed by the great majority of Buddhists, who number about 5,000,000 out of 8,000,000 inhabitants of Ceylon, as an insult to their religion, and that, in that event, it would be impossible for the Perahera to be held'.[23]

The new Prime Minister then weighed in, pointing out that if the Queen declined the invitation 'the repercussions would be most serious', the Royal Perahera would not take place, which would 'seriously affect all the functions arranged at Kandy' and be 'considered a great insult'.[24] In the end Lord Salisbury settled the 'tiresome business' by pointing out that removing shoes was 'an ordinary act of courtesy on entering a shrine of another religion'.[25]

In December 1953 the Sri Lankan Freedom Party decided unanimously to boycott all ceremonies involving the Queen. They held eight of the 101 Parliamentary seats and were led by S. W. R. D. Bandaranaike. Just before the visit the Ceylonese High Commissioner in London admitted the Communist element in Ceylon would not be welcoming the Queen, but plenty of others would. Fourteen thousand university students and high-school children were brought in as police cadets for added protection and Scotland Yard officers were sent out to Ceylon six weeks before the Queen arrived.[26]

The Queen spent eleven days in Ceylon, mostly in Colombo, but also at the ruined city of Polonnaruwa, Sigiriya and Nurawa Eliya.

She made a state drive round Kandy, attended a garden party at the King's Pavilion and viewed the Royal Perahera from the Octagon of the Dalada Maligawa, a parade of 125 lavishly caparisoned elephants, a thousand torchbearers and more than six hundred Kandyan dancers and drummers. She took off her shoes in private when viewing the Relic. To this day there is a photograph of the Queen at the Temple, viewed by tourists, blithely unaware of the hassle preceding the few moments she was there.

The visit to Ceylon, like the others, was pronounced 'an unqualified success',[27] though the High Commissioner warned that 'It would be a mistake to infer from the undoubted success of the Visit that the feeling of loyalty to the Crown is as deep, as personal, as emotional or as widespread in Ceylon as in the old Dominions.'*[28]

Aden: 27–8 April

They sailed to Aden in *Gothic*, her last port of call. Aden had been a British Crown Colony since 1839 and remained so until 1963. The Queen announced that the British would be giving the Government over £2 million in revenue from ships refuelling there.

Until this point the royal party had had well-planned departures at a civilised time of the morning. Years later the Queen recalled: 'It all went very well until we were to fly to Uganda. At that point Martin Charteris left the old world and went into the new and got it all wrong. We were due to fly and to arrive at 10 a.m. So we had to leave the yacht at 4 a.m., which was not enjoyable, as we'd had it rather easy. He got that all wrong.'[29]

---

* Soon after the Queen's visit, Ceylon veered to the left politically and headed towards becoming a republic. In 1956 Mr Bandaranaike became Prime Minister but was assassinated in his third year of office by an extreme Buddhist monk. His widow, Sirimavo, took over as Prime Minister and served three periods of office between 1960 and 2000. In 1972 Ceylon became fully independent and took back its earlier name of Sri Lanka ('Resplendent Island'). William Gopallawa (1897–1981), who served as the last Governor-General from 1962 to 1972 (the only Buddhist to serve in such a role), became the first President. Sri Lanka is now a Democratic Socialist Republic with a President and still part of the Commonwealth.

They flew to Entebbe in the Argonaut airliner, *Aeolus*, on 28 April.

Uganda: 28–30 April

The main purpose of the Queen's visit to Uganda was to inaugurate the Owen Falls Dam. Once again problems preceded the visit.

Uganda had been discovered by British explorers in quest of the source of the Nile in the 1860s. It was placed under the charter of the British East Africa Company in 1888, became a British Protectorate in 1894 and took its present form in 1914. The British Government wanted to create a Federation consisting of Uganda, Kenya and Tanganyika. Africans were afraid that these countries would fall into the power of the white settlers of Kenya, as had happened in Rhodesia. Buganda (a self-governing part of Uganda) was especially opposed to this. Buganda's charismatic Kabaka, Edward Mutesa II (often known as King Freddie), sought independence from Uganda, afraid that Buganda would lose the autonomy it presently enjoyed under British rule. He wanted it put under the protection of Great Britain.

Sir Andrew Cohen had been Governor since 1952. Oliver Lyttelton, the Colonial Secretary, described him as having 'more enthusiasm than judgement to the swift advancement of Africans'.[30] The Governor promptly exiled the Kabaka to London. In exile, the Kabaka became a martyr in the eyes of the Bugandans and the Lukiko (the Parliament of Buganda) passed the resolution asking that the Queen's proposed visit to Buganda be postponed. The Cabinet agreed that the Colonial Secretary should advise the Queen to drop her visit to Mengo, the headquarters of the Buganda Government.

Cohen consulted the Governor of Kenya, Sir Evelyn Baring, and the Commander-in-Chief, East Africa, about the possible danger of Mau Mau terrorists coming across the frontier into certain areas of Uganda scheduled for the Queen's visit. Cohen reckoned that by cancelling the visit to Kampala 'the security risk would be reduced to negligible proportions'.[31] He was concerned to avoid the 'unfortunate political consequences which would follow here from a cancellation of the visit at this stage and in the present situation'.[32]

THE COMMONWEALTH TOUR, 1953-4

The Queen approved the new programme and the visit went ahead. Most of the time she remained in the grounds of Government House, only flying to Jinja to visit the King's African Rifles, and making a short excursion to the Owen Falls Dam, which controlled the source of the Nile. She pressed a button, which caused the sluices of the Dam to open to considerable dramatic effect. Later she flew back to Entebbe.

Oliver Lyttelton came out for the visit. At the garden party the Queen had worn the pink diamond that the Canadian geologist Dr John Williamson had mined in Tanganyika and given her as a wedding present. Lyttelton mentioned at dinner that he had missed his chance of seeing it. The Queen summoned it from the safe and put it on especially for him.[33] On 30 April she spent the whole day in the Queen Elizabeth National Park to the extreme west of the Protectorate, inspecting a sleepy hippopotamus, and getting within fifty yards of a cow elephant and her calf to the slight concern of the vigilant hunters. In the course of the day they saw hundreds of elephants and hippopotamuses in the wild along with buffaloes, pigs and antelopes.[34] The Queen then flew back to Entebbe, having experienced no trouble from Buganda or the Mau Mau.*

Libya: 1 May

On arrival in Tobruk, the Queen and the Duke were received by King Idris I, who had been King only since December 1951 and was destined to be Libya's only Sovereign.† Gifts were exchanged. She appointed him a GBE. The Queen and the Duke left the King's palace and skimmed across five hundred yards of water in a royal barge. There they were reunited with Prince Charles and Princess Anne, who had been flown in from London for this last part of the

---

* The subsequent fate of Uganda was to be a tortured one. Achieving independence in 1962, the country was then dominated by Milton Obote and Idi Amin, two tyrannical leaders. It was estimated that 10 per cent of the population was slaughtered in the ensuing years.

† King Idris I of Libya (1890–83) reigned from 1951 until deposed by a group of army officers under Gaddafi in 1969. He died in exile in Cairo, aged ninety-four.

tour, not having seen their parents since the previous November. The parents stooped to kiss them. The new royal yacht, *Britannia*, was ready to be their floating home and to convey the reunited family back to London. They sailed thirty minutes later.

Accompanying them as equerry throughout the Commonwealth tour had been thirty-year old Viscount Althorp, son of Earl Spencer. He was allowed to fly home from Tobruk to prepare for his wedding to eighteen-year-old Frances Roche. In 1961 they would become the parents of (Lady) Diana Spencer.

Malta: 3–7 May

Britannia sailed to Malta, flags flying and floodlit, stem to stern, and escorted by fifteen ships of the Mediterranean, similarly lit up. The Mountbattens were stationed there and much to the fore. Mountbatten evidently 'thrilled the travellers *en route* with high speed manoeuvres as the great ships passed within half a cable's length of the royal yacht'.[35] He was jack-stayed aboard.

Gibraltar: 10–11 May

Their last port of call was Gibraltar, one of the Queen's Overseas Territories. This two-day visit exercised the Foreign Office more than any of the previous parts of the tour. British possession of Gibraltar had long caused considerable friction between Britain and Spain. The Rock had been captured by Britain following the Spanish Wars of Succession in 1704 and handed over in perpetuity under the Treaty of Utrecht of 1713.

However, the Spanish claimed that the Rock was rightfully theirs. General Franco based his insistence on the will of Isabella the Catholic who had 'enjoined the Spaniards never to alienate Gibraltar from the Spanish crown'.[36] As early as November 1951 Franco had asked the British to hand back Gibraltar to improve Anglo-Spanish relations. Relations between the countries deteriorated when the newspapers announced, in May 1953, that the Queen would visit twenty thousand of her loyal British subjects there.

This was interpreted in Madrid as the British Government reasserting sovereignty over Gibraltar – a 'red rag to the Spanish bull' and an act of 'calculated discourtesy'.[37] The Spanish Ambassador in London protested to Lord Salisbury in immoderate terms; Spanish newspapers pursued a vigorous campaign against the visit; Falange student syndicates staged demonstrations in various Spanish towns; two thousand hooligans congregated in front of the Vice-Consulate in Granada, and smashed the windows of William Davenhill, the elderly Vice-Consul, who had been living 'a *Cranford*-like existence' there since the turn of the century.

Franco encouraged attacks on the British Institute and the British Embassy in Madrid. A truckload of stones was brought in on official orders, the right size for throwing.[38] On 25 January 1954 fifteen thousand students (who had been given a special holiday for the purpose) marched through Madrid shouting abuse about the Queen, Churchill* and the British Government. The British Embassy was protected by police with sabres and batons.[39]

The British Government made it clear that there was no question of the Queen's visit being cancelled.[40] But death threats were issued against her and considerable discussion ensued as to how best she could be protected. Though an organised attempt was considered unlikely, a lone, crazed, would-be killer was always a possibility. Sir John Balfour, British Ambassador to Spain, recalled: 'Lighter relief was provided in March 1954 by a widely believed rumour that Her Majesty was pregnant and would therefore be returning home without making the call.'[41]

Matters were further fuelled in February 1954 when General Sir Gordon MacMillan of MacMillan, Governor of Gibraltar, made a speech urging the people of Gibraltar not to crowd the Queen's car 'since the British Royal Family does not have to be driven in bullet-proof cars surrounded by squadrons of armed police!' He said he only mentioned this due to 'unfortunate articles', which had appeared in the Spanish press, 'deprecating Her Majesty's visit'. Then he went too far, saying he could not invite any of Britain's 'Spanish friends' but that he would not be closing the frontier during the visit.[42]

---

* Winston Churchill had conceived the romantic idea of joining the Queen in Gibraltar, but was dissuaded when advised this could further endanger her life.

Oliver Lyttelton summoned the Governor to London to see the Prime Minister, pointing out that security arrangements were a matter for the Palace and the Cabinet and any pronouncements on those matters needed to be authorised by the Cabinet.[43] Churchill was annoyed. 'Bravado at the Queen's expense,' was his comment in Cabinet.[44]

Special agents were set to work in Gibraltar and Professor Bernard Malley, known at the British Embassy as 'Don Bernardo', a man with covert links to the Franco world, assured them that the Queen's visit was not a prime target.[45] In March British newspapers received reports that Lady Churchill was to be killed. In April the editors of three national newspapers were told: 'The Queen will be killed if she sets foot in Gibraltar.' Scotland Yard warned editors of the dangers of publishing such things for fear that it might swell the flood. Concerted efforts were made to guide the correspondents covering the trip.[46]

A few days before the visit Bernard Malley reported that his sources informed him that there would be 'no acts of violence encouraged or permitted during the Queen's visit to the Rock', due to the large influx of tourists expected.[47] At the beginning of May the Spanish closed down the Consulate-General at Gibraltar. They hoped to create discomfort for the inhabitants by restricting the entry of Spanish citizens, despite the Spanish Consul-General in London informing the Colonial Secretary that 'The Spanish Government had no objection to paying tribute to the Queen by hoisting the Spanish flag anywhere except in Gibraltar; and they wished to avoid any discourtesy to Her Majesty, for whom they had the greatest respect, during the forthcoming Royal visit to the Rock.'[48]

The visit passed off perfectly well. The Queen stepped off *Britannia* and was presented with the historic keys of Gibraltar, the original keys to the four gates of the great fortress. She reviewed the combined forces on the airport runway, a mere five hundred yards from the Spanish border. She urged the Gibraltarians to 'go forward in the future, in partnership and in amity, for the good government and sure safe keeping of the colony and fortress of Gibraltar'.[49] A highlight was Prince Charles and Princess Anne being introduced to the cheeky apes (Barbary macaques) that are such a feature of the Rock.

But relations between the Spanish and the Gibraltarians were not improved. Years later the Queen said going there 'was a mistake really, as the Spanish have wanted it back ever since'.[50]

The Governor was sufficiently forgiven for his speech to receive the traditional KCVO for attendance on the Queen.* After Gibraltar the Queen and her family sailed for Britain, dropping anchor at St Austell Bay, Cornwall.

London: 14 May

The Royal Family stayed on board *Britannia* and disembarked the following day, 15 May. The Queen Mother and Princess Margaret came on board. Churchill joined them and they sailed to Embankment Pier where other members of the Royal Family greeted them. There was a carriage procession to Buckingham Palace with crowds lining the route in their thousands. That evening the Queen and Prince Philip appeared on the balcony. At the 'welcome home' luncheon given by the City of London at Mansion House, the Queen's message was that Britain would never lack the friendly cooperation of the Commonwealth.

On 20 May the Queen and her children took the train to Balmoral for a short holiday, the Duke flying up later to join them. She told Anthony Eden that she was 'out of reach' but added: 'Sometimes it is rather nice just to think about catching a fish!! I don't expect we shall succeed as there are very few fish to catch.'[51]

---

* This was the same honour that was given to men of the standing of the Governor of Bermuda and the Governor of New South Wales, as the Queen left at the end of each stage of the trip. GCVOs were given to the Governors-General of New Zealand (Sir Willoughby Norrie), Australia (Sir William Slim) and Ceylon (Lord Soulbury).

18
CHURCHILL AND EDEN, 1952–7

The Queen had been schooled by Sir Henry Marten to support her prime ministers. Those who have spoken of her in public (invariably informing us of how much she liked them) stressed that she was the only person they could talk to who would be completely discreet, not in competition with them, and saw herself as a sounding board. James Callaghan, Prime Minister from 1976 to 1979, said that the premier could expect 'friendliness' if not perhaps 'friendship'.

In the midst of the Princess Margaret drama in the summer of 1953, the Queen found herself faced with an ongoing political dilemma that would dominate the next two years and more – the question as to when Sir Winston Churchill would finally step down as her Prime Minister. As early as 20 February 1952 he suffered a small arterial spasm, at which point his doctor, Lord Moran, discussed his future with Tommy Lascelles. Lord Salisbury wondered if Churchill could be persuaded to go to the Lords, remaining as Prime Minister with Eden leading the Commons. Lascelles did not want the Queen to have to suggest this.

Churchill and the Queen had established a good working relationship. When he spoke of her in public or in Parliament it was in almost Shakespearian tones. He was fond of her, and they enjoyed talking about racing. She had been alarmed at having to entertain him at Balmoral in the summer of 1952, though the visit passed off well. He was only a bit miffed at not being invited to shoot.

On 23 June 1953 Churchill entertained the Italian Prime Minister, Alcide de Gasperi, to dinner at 10 Downing Street (the same day as the Queen's state entry into Edinburgh). On leaving the dining room, his legs gave way. Somehow he got through a Cabinet meeting the next day, though his left arm was paralysed, his mouth drooping and his speech slurred, but he missed Prime Minister's Questions due, it was said, to pressure of work. He was moved to Chartwell, the story being that he was preparing for talks with President Eisenhower and the French Prime Minister at the Bermuda Conference, aimed to lessen world tension by getting the great powers round the table. Churchill was meant to leave by ship on 30 June. But Lord Moran was convinced he was near death. By 28 June he had cancelled his trip,* said to be exhausted by pressure of work. He would be out of action for some time, though the gravity of the illness was withheld.

The situation was made more complicated because Anthony Eden, the Foreign Secretary and Churchill's chosen and expected successor, was recuperating from a series of botched gall-bladder operations. There was some discussion (in which Tommy Lascelles was involved) about Churchill stepping down and Lord Salisbury forming a caretaker government, which Eden thought was a Lascelles plot against him. Churchill rallied and persistently refused to go.

On Sunday, 2 August, somewhat recovered, he went to see the Queen at Royal Lodge, Windsor. He told her he would decide his future depending on his ability to make his Conservative Party Conference speech in October. He asked her if he could invite President Eisenhower on a state visit to Britain in September or October. This did not happen. On 18 August he presided over the Cabinet for the first time since 24 June. His speech to the conference went exceptionally well so he stayed. His next excuse for staying was that the Queen was on her Commonwealth tour. That saw him through until May 1954.

In June the Queen installed him as a Knight of the Garter. He walked alone down the hill at the head of the procession. 'I haven't looked so dignified for a long time,' he told his doctor. It was a long day, starting at 8 a.m. and finishing at midnight.[1]

On 6 July Churchill told the Cabinet that he needed to bring about a summit meeting between the leaders of Britain, the United States and the Soviet Union (then the only three nuclear powers) to open the way to agreements about strategic arms reductions and thus avoid nuclear war. This provoked Lord Salisbury, the Lord Privy Seal, to threaten to resign (a threat he made with enormous

---

* The conference was postponed until December.

regularity). Harry Crookshank, Leader of the House of Commons, also threatened to go. Most of the Cabinet supported the American policy and most thought it was time for Churchill to retire. Churchill felt strongly enough about his initiative that there was some fear he might resign if blocked by his Cabinet, knowing that this would force a General Election. He failed to see that the Russians would never enter into such talks until the succession to Stalin had been settled, which remained years away, while in the United States, the Eisenhower administration expressed no interest.

In this impasse, Lord Swinton, the Commonwealth Secretary, and Lord Simonds, the Lord Chancellor, both asked Jock Colville independently to explain what was going on to Sir Michael Adeane, with the idea that the Queen might intervene. They maintained it was her prerogative to caution her Prime Minister against precipitate action. As it happened, the Russians unexpectedly resolved the problem by calling for multi-lateral meetings, which made Churchill's original proposal redundant.[2]

During these years Anthony Eden waited in the wings with increasing impatience. After a garden party at Buckingham Palace in the summer of 1954, the Queen told him that 'Winston seemed less truculent about going.' But Churchill did not go. As late as 30 March 1955 Churchill asked the Queen if she minded him putting off his resignation. She was constitutionally obliged to say no. Finally the Cabinet threatened to resign *en masse*, and the next day Churchill sent a private message to the Queen to say that he would step down on 5 April, thus ending a long and tedious game of cat-and-mouse.

The evening before his retirement, the Queen and Prince Philip dined at 10 Downing Street. There were about fifty guests, including senior cabinet ministers, the Duke and Duchess of Norfolk and some family friends of the Churchills. Prince Philip saw Loelia, Duchess of Westminster, put her substantial foot through Clarissa Eden's train. 'That's torn it, in more than one sense,' he commented.[3]

Sir Winston proposed a toast thanking the Queen and Prince Philip for 'all the help and inspiration we receive in our daily lives and which spreads with ever-growing strength throughout the British Realm and the Commonwealth and Empire. Never have we needed it more than in the anxious and darkling age through which we are passing.'[4]

The next day Churchill made his way to Buckingham Palace for his farewell audience. Jock Colville suggested to Sir Michael Adeane that the Queen might offer to create Churchill a duke, but only after ascertaining that Churchill would not accept. Colville then panicked lest he change his mind as he had done so often concerning his resignation. Colville recalled:

> I was greatly disturbed because as I saw the Prime Minister going off in his frock coat and his top hat and knowing as I did that he was madly in love with the Queen ... I was rather alarmed that sentimental feelings might indeed make him accept at the last moment.[5]

Fortunately Churchill told the Queen he would prefer to spend the rest of his days in the House of Commons. He thought a dukedom might ruin the political careers of his son Randolph and his grandson Winston (something they achieved on their own initiative). On his return Churchill told Colville that he thought the Queen 'looked almost relieved'.[6] At the audience, the Queen asked him if he recommend a successor. He replied that he would prefer to leave it to her. She immediately said that the case 'was not a difficult one' and that she would summon Sir Anthony Eden.[7]

Churchill left for a holiday in Sicily, and as he boarded the plane, he was handed a letter written in the Queen's own hand: 'My confidence in Anthony Eden is complete and I know he will lead the Country on to great achievements, but it would be useless to pretend that either he or any of those successors who may one day follow him in office will ever, for me, be able to hold the place of my first Prime Minister, to whom both my husband and I owe so much and for whose wide guidance during the early years of my reign I shall always be so profoundly grateful.'[8]

In response Sir Winston wrote that he had always tried to keep her 'squarely confronted with the grave and complex problems of our time'. He had quickly become aware of 'the comprehension' with which she faced her duties, the store of knowledge she had acquired, and her understanding of 'the relationships and the balances' of the constitution. He ended: 'I became conscious of the Royal resolve to serve as well as rule, and indeed to rule by serving.'[9]

Furthermore he praised the Duke of Edinburgh's 'remarkable qualities' that were already 'making an ever-deepening impression upon the minds of people of all classes and Parties'.[10] Thus ended the formal relationship between the Queen and her first Prime Minister, though he remained a feature of her life until well into his old age.

Sir Anthony Eden

The Queen had appointed Anthony Eden a Knight of the Garter in October 1954, telling him that she had wanted that for a long time. When he went to see her to 'kiss hands', they were chatting until he said: 'Well, Ma'am ...' at which point the Queen said: 'I suppose I ought to be asking you to form a government.'[11] She told him: 'I thought I wouldn't have any fun again after Winston left. But now I know I will.'[12]

Eden was only Prime Minister from April 1955 until January 1957. He, too, had been born in the Victorian age. He had served with great distinction in the First World War, had been awarded the Military Cross. He knew Persian and Arabic and had collected important nineteenth- and twentieth-century pictures. He had a well-rounded personality, was supremely elegant and had been a successful Foreign Secretary, known for his consummate negotiating skills.

The Queen had got to know Eden when he was Foreign Secretary. She commiserated about the trials he had endured at the Geneva Conference, where issues to do with the Korean War and and the First Indochina War were being discussed. Writing in her own hand, she continued:

> Since coming back [from the Commonwealth tour] I have been reading all the telegrams with increasing dismay that so many difficulties are appearing. Thank goodness for us that you have been there to keep a firm hand on not only people whom one imagined might be impossible anyway, but also on other people as well!
>
> How exhausting it must be to try and keep the peace between a lot of grown men behaving like spoilt children who want their own way or else ...![13]

Following the successful conclusion of the London Conference in October, a Nine-Power Conference addressing the failure of the EDC (European Defence Community), she congratulated him on his hard work and success: 'Now that Trieste seems fairly amicably settled, perhaps we can hope for a more peaceful time and not so many crises.' Eden had caught a cold from Mendès France, the Prime Minister of France. 'I must say it seems a poor way of expressing gratitude,' mused the Queen.[14]

The Queen found Eden easy to get on with, though she found his wife, Clarissa, more difficult. 'Terse' was her description. Clarissa's friend, Valentine Lawford, went so far as to say that the Queen was 'terrified' of her. She was advised to make a particular effort. At a wedding in the 1950s, Clarissa was surprised when she was tapped on the shoulder. She looked round. There was the Queen: 'It's me.'[15] Years later Clarissa made the point that Anthony Eden never advised the Queen on anything, unless she specifically asked for his advice.[16]

The Queen invited the Edens to Windsor Castle for the weekend in April. Soon after that Eden called a General Election on 26 May, which won him an increased majority of sixty seats. His premiership encompassed the Townsend saga in 1955 and the visit of Bulganin and Khrushchev* in 1956. Eden alerted the Queen about this visit on a commemorative regimental visit to Winchester. She was rather taken aback, but Prince Philip was relieved that, unlike the Tito visit of 1953, the Russians would not be their personal guests.

On 7 June 1955 Carozza, the Queen's horse, won the Oaks. In July she entertained the Commonwealth leaders at Windsor, at her own suggestion, and paid her first (probably reluctant) visit to Wimbledon to watch the tennis.

The Edens stayed at Balmoral with the Queen in the summer of 1955. Eden was livid that the staff cleaned their sitting room at 6 a.m., waking him up. Prince Philip cooked some kind of 'fish finger' dish.

Endless were the issues with which the Queen had to be involved. One such was the appointment of the Lord Clerk Register Keeper

---

* Nikolai Bulganin (1895–1975), Premier after Stalin, and Nikita Khrushchev (1894–1971), then First Secretary, were to visit Britain on a charm offensive seeking recognition by the West.

of the Signet, effectively the senior Officer of State in Scotland, a post dating back to the thirteenth century. In 1956 the question arose as to who would succeed Lord Elphinstone, who had died on 28 November 1955. The Duke of Buccleuch was a candidate, but many in Scotland were opposed to him, preferring the Earl of Crawford. The Queen made it clear to James Stuart, then Secretary of State for Scotland, that she would not appoint the Duke if there was any fear of him contemplating anything 'drastic'.[17] By this she meant separation from the Duchess, something that Duke Walter contemplated virtually every January.* The Duke was appointed.

Malcolm Muggeridge

On 22 October 1955 Malcolm Muggeridge published his controversial essay, 'The Royal Soap Opera', in the *New Statesman*. This did not evince much controversy in the United Kingdom but 'the floodgates of fury' opened when it was published in an expanded version in America, coinciding with the Queen's 1956 visit. Kingsley Martin, editor of the *New Statesman*, was excited to read it, especially since no one had criticised the Royal Family in print for many years.

The gist of the article was that Muggeridge could not bear to see another photograph of the Royal Family in the newspapers. He decried the fact that even Princess Anne waved limply to the photographers. He thought 'the whole show [was] utterly out of hand, and there is much graver danger than might superficially appear that a strong reaction against it might be produced'. He contrasted the 'adulatory curiosity towards the royal family' against the satirical material in *Punch* in the nineteenth century, and even the caricatures of Max Beerbohm. He thought that 'in adulating the incumbents, in insulating them from the normal hazards of public life the institution was in danger of being jeopardised'. He accepted that the present Royal Family was more respectable than their Hanoverian ancestors, but to put them above criticism was, 'ultimately, to dehumanise them and risk the monarchy dying of acute anaemia'.

---

* The Duke had a surprising mistress for a tweedy Duke in the form of the glamorous Brazilian socialite, Aimée de Heeren (1903–2006).

Muggeridge realised that the public enjoyed colour photographs of the Queen and Princess Margaret, that they seemed to relish 'the unspeakable Crawfie, and all the other dredgers up of unconsidered trifles in the lives of members of the royal family, down to and including Godfrey Winn'. His recommendation was an experienced public relations set-up 'in place of the rather ludicrous courtiers who now function as such'. He thought the Townsend saga should have been explained before the speculation took over. 'After all,' he wrote, 'if we are to accept that the Crown is useful constitutionally even though deprived of all real power, it must be maintained with some dignity.' He made a point that remains valid today, that they ought to be 'properly advised on how to prevent themselves and their lives from becoming a sort of royal soap opera'. He took a swipe at the photographers Cecil Beaton and Baron.

He considered that popularity was fatal to monarchy. He quoted Cromwell telling Fairfax that the same crowds that cheered him as they rode through the streets would have come as eagerly to see him hanged. He thought the monarchy had become 'a kind of ersatz religion', citing Chesterton's remark that 'When people cease to believe in God, they do not then believe in nothing, but in anything.' He wrote that film stars soon passed into oblivion, but that the Royal Family were in a different situation: 'Their role is to symbolise the unity of a nation; to provide an element of continuity in a necessarily changing society. This is history, not *The Archers*, and their affairs ought to be treated as such.' His conclusion was lame:

> The royal family and their advisers have really got to make up their minds – do they want to be part of the mystique of the century of the common man or to be an institutional monarchy; to ride, as it were, in a glass coach or on bicycles; to provide the tabloids with a running serial or to live simply and unaffectedly among their subjects like the Dutch and Scandinavian royal families. What they cannot do is to have it both ways.[18]

Muggeridge himself was shaken by the virulence of the attacks against him. When it looked likely that his membership of the Garrick Club would be reconsidered, he thought it wise to resign.

More impact was made in August 1957 when Lord Altrincham (who later dropped his title to be known as John Grigg) wrote an article in the *National and Evening Review*, which caused an enormous furore. Altrincham was not anti-monarchy but he was concerned that some drastic changes were needed. He criticised the Queen's way of life from childhood onwards: 'Crawfie, Sir Henry Marten, the London season, the racecourse, the grouse moor, the occasional royal tour.' He attacked presentation parties at which debutantes dressed in white and, bedecked with plumage, queued to curtsey to the Queen. His line was that the monarchy lacked political power but could set an example: 'the power to win hearts and fire the imagination'.[19] Sir Winston Churchill was predictably indignant about this attack on the Queen.

Altrincham and Muggeridge, whose earlier article was immediately reprinted, were sent hate mail, anathematised by the Archbishop of Canterbury, menaced with the threat of hideous deaths by over-ardent monarchists and even challenged to a duel. Enough manure was tipped through their letterboxes to feed their window boxes for the season. But Prince Philip took the words to heart. Presentation parties were abolished and informal Buckingham Palace lunches introduced so that a wide spectrum of people could be entertained relatively informally. Appointments to the Royal Household began to include figures from Commonwealth countries and veered away from the traditional Eton and the Guards image of earlier times. Sir Martin Charteris said later that the Altrincham article in particular had had a salutary effect, giving the Royal Household the impetus to make needed changes.

On the downside, the switch from more or less hereditary appointments, where families served for generations, meant there was a loss of vital historical continuity. A meritocratic system sometimes produced inadequate appointments – people who thought they understood the system, were keen to implement changes, were not always constructive and, at times, were self-seeking in a way that those raised within the system were not.

★ ★ ★ ★ ★

Before the Suez crisis erupted, the Queen gave the Duchess of Norfolk permission to hold a dinner and a ball for her daughter,

Lady Anne Fitzalan-Howard, at St James's Palace on 11 July. This was an occasion of unbelievable grandeur, with fifteen hundred guests, bidden to wear orders and decorations, with tiaras for the ladies. There was huge royal attendance - the Queen and Prince Philip, the Queen Mother, the Princess Royal, Princess Marina, the Duke of Kent and Princess Alexandra dined there privately first. The Duchess of Gloucester gave her own dinner party.

With his habitual attention to detail, the Duke checked that the floors were safe for so many dancers and he checked the lighting. The three main reception rooms were banked with flowers from Arundel. The Duke, with Garter riband over white tie, led off the dancing with the Queen, and Princess Margaret quick-stepped to 'Mack The Knife' under the floodlit trees.*

The Queen was staying with the Norfolks at Arundel Castle on 30 July, when she was forced to hold a Privy Council meeting to pass Orders in Council, mobilising troops, following President Nasser of Egypt's nationalisation of the Suez Canal four days before. After that the Queen retreated to Balmoral where she was visited by Dr Kwame Nkrumah, President of Ghana, and later by President Eisenhower.[20]

It has been suggested that the Queen's personal views about the Suez crisis were not in sympathy with those of her Prime Minister. Whatever she may have thought, she felt bound to remain impartial. Many years later Lord Mountbatten (believed by Eden to be a 'congenital liar')[21] told the author Robert Lacey that she had been anti-Suez. In 1976 Eden, by then retired as Lord Avon, remonstrated with Mountbatten, warning him that if this appeared in print, he would take legal action.

The crisis ended in ceasefire in November 1956 and coincided with a serious collapse in Eden's health. The Edens went to Jamaica in the hope that he would recover. On their return it was clear that his health was irreparably damaged and that he had lost the confidence of the House of Commons.

In the new year Eden asked if he could visit the Queen at Sandringham. The Edens took the train to Wolferton on 8 January

---

* Splendid though the occasion was, it did not find Lady Anne a husband. She became a successful racehorse trainer and finally married the cricketer, Colin Cowdrey, as his second wife, in 1985.

and stayed the night. He announced his intention to resign. The result was that the Queen would consult Lord Salisbury, Lord Kilmuir and Sir Winston Churchill as to Eden's successor.

The following day the Queen came to London, ostensibly to do some shopping, but in fact to accept Eden's formal resignation. At that last meeting the Queen told him that when she became Queen people told her how lucky she was to have Winston as her Prime Minister. By then she did not think that advice was true. Eden refused an earldom, though he told Adeane he would like the Order of Merit, which was not followed up.*[22]

The soundings took place and the outcome was that Harold Macmillan became Prime Minister. Because Lord Kilmuir and others left misleading accounts of the events of that time, Eden made a private record of what happened when he saw the Queen. She had consulted him about his successor:

> When I went to Sandringham and it was first realised what I intended, Michael Adeane quite rightly broached the topic at once. What are we to do, was the theme, there being no enthusiasm for either of the more obvious candidates, Rab or Harold. This led M. A. to speak of Menzies & the possibility of getting him over. I should have liked this above all things, but I had to point out that it was not practicable, which was accepted by M. A., but only reluctantly. Years later I told Bob.
>
> When I went for my final audience the Queen asked me formally & said what I repeated afterwards to M. A. Rab had deputised for me when I had been away & I had no fault to find with the way he had done so. This, I thought, should be in the scales in his favour. On the other hand, this was a situation when the unity of the Cabinet was essential to the survival of the Govt & I thought that there should be informal consultations through an intermediary with at least the senior members of the Cabinet & in reply to a question I said that Bobbety [Lord Salisbury] was the obvious choice for intermediary

---

* The Order of Merit was given to Arthur Balfour in 1916, David Lloyd George in 1919, to Winston Churchill in 1946, and to Earl Attlee in 1951. Macmillan received it in 1976 and Margaret Thatcher in 1990. The Order is in the personal gift of the monarch.

since he could not succeed himself but was a most influential member of the Cabinet & respected by the party.²³

The Queen summoned Macmillan to the Palace and his appointment was announced at 2.27 p.m. on 10 January. The Queen then returned to Sandringham, arriving there at 6.30 p.m. On 13 January the Queen had to come to London again for Harold Macmillan to tell her of his Cabinet changes and the following day to receive the retiring (sacked) ministers and swear in the new ones. She had to come down yet again for the funeral of her great-uncle, the Earl of Athlone, at St George's Chapel on 19 June.

The Queen sent a letter to Anthony Eden, telling him how deeply she felt his resignation. She concluded:

There is no doubt that you took the only possible course after the doctors had given you their verdict, but one can only guess at what it must have cost you to do it.

I want to thank you, not only for the loyal and distinguished service you have given to me, first as Foreign Secretary and then as Prime Minister, but for the many years' work, both in and out of office, which you have devoted to the greatness and prosperity of our country.

Much has been said and written during the last week about your record in the House of Commons and as a statesman; I am only anxious that you should realize that that record, which has indeed been written in tempestuous times, is highly valued and will never be forgotten by your Sovereign.²⁴

Eden replied, giving her a rundown of how he saw the plans of the Russians, the actions of the USA and the ominous situation in Syria. He continued:

But it is not of all this, with which Your Majesty is only too familiar, that I want to write. It is rather to try to express what my Sovereign's understanding and encouragement meant at a time of exceptional ordeal. It is the bare truth to say that I looked forward to my weekly audiences, knowing that I should receive from Your Majesty a wise and impartial reaction to events, which was quite simply the voice of our land. Years ago Baldwin told me that the post of Prime Minister was the most lonely in the world. That may be true in respect of colleagues. That I have not found it so is due to Your Majesty's unfailing sympathy & understanding.[25]

19

THE FAMILY IN THE 1950s

Throughout the 1950s the Queen was a young woman at the head of a large and extended Royal Family, something of a gerontocracy since many of them had been born in the reign of Queen Victoria. Gradually the older members died, the Queen dutifully attending their funerals or memorial services. Queen Mary had disappeared in March 1953, just before the Coronation.

Princess Marie Louise, a spinsterish cousin of the Queen, had been present at many royal events, including knocking back a large glass of gin before the Coronation procession from the Abbey. 'She was inclined to do that,' the Queen remembered. Shortly before she died, Princess Marie Louise published her memoirs, *My Memories of Six Reigns*, a book which was informative without being unduly revelatory. She died on 8 December 1956.

Less than five weeks later, on 16 January 1957, the Earl of Athlone, the Queen's great-uncle, died at Kensington Palace aged eighty-two. He was granted a military funeral at St George's Chapel. On 26 February 1959 Princess Arthur of Connaught died at her home in Avenue Road, north of Regent's Park, aged sixty-seven. She could have been a prominent member of the British Royal Family but suffered from severe rheumatoid arthritis and asthma. The Duke of Windsor used to visit her and recommended various American drugs. The Queen attended her memorial service in the Chapel Royal, St James's. Then on the night of 20/21 February 1960 Edwina Mountbatten died in North Borneo, not long after the snowy wedding of her daughter Pamela to David Hicks. She was buried at sea off Portsmouth, prompting the Queen Mother to say: 'So like Edwina. She always did everything with a splash.' Her death affected Lord Mountbatten financially and left him without a restraining influence. 'After she died he went off the rails,' said the Countess of Avon.[1]

More peripherally, the Marchioness of Carisbrooke died on 16 July 1956, in the middle of the state visit of King Faisal, and her effete husband, the Marquess (last grandson of Queen Victoria), died on 23 February 1960, liberating an apartment at Kensington Palace for Princess Margaret in the early days of her marriage.

★ ★ ★ ★ ★

The Queen was conscious of the sacrifice that Prince Philip had made for her. There is no question that he regretted surrendering his naval career. But he was a pragmatist and quickly set about using his new position constructively. He was fortunate to have able advisers: Kurt Hahn, his former headmaster at Gordonstoun, Sir John Hunt (the Everest explorer), Brigadier-General Sir Harold Hartley, a physical chemist, and men such as the naturalist, Aubrey Buxton, and the environmentalist, Max Nicholson.

In a later-life interview with Fiammetta Rocco, he snapped: 'It was not my ambition to be President of the Mint Advisory Committee. I didn't want to be President of WWF. I was asked to do it. I'd much rather have stayed in the Navy, frankly.'[2] He took on many things – running the royal estates to ease the Queen's burden, and setting up the Study Conference of the Human Problems of Industrial Communities within the Commonwealth and Empire. He realised that, when travelling with the Queen, he had seen 'quite a number of industries in this country [the UK]' and during their tours 'something of industry in almost every part of the Commonwealth'. He observed 'different atmospheres, the different attitudes of management and workpeople, the different community background, and so on'. One factory was much like another, but the living environments were often very different, and these he sought to discuss – the human problems within industrial communities and how they could be guided and improved.[3]

There was the Duke of Edinburgh's Award Scheme, based on the belief that the future of civilisation depended on 'the ability and willingness of the young people of today to give their best service to the community and to grow up as balanced individuals'. He liked to be informed; he hated pomposity. Sir James Robertson, Governor-General of Nigeria at the time of the Queen's 1956 visit (and coincidentally the great-uncle of the political interviewer Laura Kuenssberg), said of Prince Philip: 'He dislikes the top chap, who shows him round and doesn't know the answers.'[4]

It is frequently suggested that he found it hard to walk two steps behind the Queen. But was it? He had been raised as a minor member of the Greek Royal Family. He knew the system. In this respect he fared better than Prince Claus of the Netherlands (who suffered a nervous breakdown) or Prince Henrik of Denmark (who was less than supportive of his Queen). Prince Philip worked within the system and he worked around it. He had no defined role, but he made one for himself.

He was a man of striking contrasts. He championed British industry abroad while giving it constructive criticism at home. He was a supportive Chancellor of several universities while quick to pounce on what he perceived as 'self-satisfied intellectuality'. He did not like people to rest on their laurels. He was robust in expression. When, in February 1953, he accepted the Freedom of the Mercers' Company (founded in 1394), he told them that 'there is only one older profession than a Mercer', urged them not to forget their responsibility to the present and think only of 'their glorious past'. He continued: 'If I may say so, you would be like baboons – all behind and no forehead.'[5] This may not have been received with universal enjoyment at the Mercers' livery dinner.

The courtiers were suspicious of him, especially the Queen Mother's friends, such as Lord Eldon. As we have seen, Harold Macmillan and the Archbishop of Canterbury were dismissive of him. From early in the marriage, he was often away, be it serving in Malta or the odd visit to France or Germany (for troop purposes). The Duke made a ten-thousand-mile tour of Canada at the end of July 1954, visiting the British Empire Games in Vancouver.

In 1956 the Queen took the civilised view that he should be allowed to go on a long Commonwealth tour in *Britannia*. Though ostensibly to open the Olympic Games in Melbourne, an event that was attracting representatives from many royal houses,* it would seem that she

---

* Prince Jean and Princess Josephine Charlotte of Luxembourg, Prince Bertil of Sweden, Prince and Princess Axel of Denmark and the future Queen Margrethe

understood he was frustrated and should be allowed 'time and space'. A retired courtier, possibly Martin Charteris, told Fiammetta Rocco: 'I think Philip just got bored with the whole Royal business. All those stuffy engagements, all that handshaking. It wasn't his thing at all. He just got fed up with it.'[6] So off he went.

The Duke's Tour

The trip developed into a journey of 35,530 miles – 23,000 miles at sea in the Royal Yacht *Britannia* and 15,000 by air. He was away for four months from 15 October 1956 until he returned to Portugal on 6 February 1957. It gave him the excuse to visit remote parts of the Commonwealth never previously visited by a member of the Royal Family.

He met gold, tin and uranium miners, planters, shepherds, farmers, fishermen, whalers, scientists and industrialists. He found areas where children were taught by radio and medical help came by air, where people shopped by radio, sometimes ordering provisions that would last six months at a time.

He travelled via Gibraltar, Kano (Nigeria), the Seychelles, Ceylon, Malaya, New Guinea and arrived in Darwin, Australia, on 14 November. He was in Australia until 10 December. While there he visited his old friend, Hunter Patterson, at Hartwood Station, in New South Wales, who had entertained him in 1940. He stayed for the weekend of 25 November.

He was in New Zealand from 11 to 19 December. He visited Antarctica, the Falkland Islands, South Georgia, Gough Island, Tristan de Cunha, St Helena, Ascension Island, and returned to Gibraltar via Gambia. There were entertaining incidents, such as Michael Parker being chased by sharks in the Seychelles, a lion-dancer spotted wearing a wrist-watch in Kuala Lumpur, and the Governor of the Falklands being lowered onto the deck of *Britannia* in a basket.

Just before Christmas, as it got colder, Prince Philip gave permission

---

of Denmark (then aged sixteen) were among the royal visitors to the Olympics in Melbourne.

for beards to be worn and proceeded to grow one himself. He still sported one when visiting Gambia in February 1957.

By the time he returned, he had entertained fourteen hundred people at twenty-six lunches, dinners and receptions, had seen Ceylon 'enjoying the first enthusiastic rapture of full independence', explored New Guinea 'in a stone age world' after which he commented: 'Not unnaturally there are occasional fights between villagers using spears and bows and arrows, and sometimes people even get killed. Quite rightly, the Administration try and prevent this unseemly behaviour. I could not help thinking that it was perhaps, a little bit odd of us to object to these primitive weapons while we, on the other hand, are tinkering about with weapons capable of mass destruction of whole nations.'[7] In Antarctica he wondered if it could be used as 'a gigantic germ-free cold store where the periodic world food surpluses might be stored against lean years of famine'.[8]

Prince Philip arrived in Lisbon on 6 February 1957, the fifth anniversary of the Queen's accession. Due to his long absence there was press speculation that all was not well with the royal marriage. Joan Graham, London Correspondent of the *Baltimore Sun*, wrote that the British were not allowed to read any of the rumours. On 8 February her report declared that café society in Britain were gossiping, that this was percolating down to the masses, that there had been rumours of 'more than a passing interest in an unnamed woman' and that the reason for the trip was to get him out of the way and that '*Britannia* took devious routes at extremely leisurely speeds'.[9] She was roundly castigated for scandal-mongering and the next day reported that when she telephoned Buckingham Palace, the spokesman, presumably the press secretary, Richard Colville, growled an angry 'What do you want?' followed by a furious 'Goodnight,' and slammed the telephone down on her.[10]

The Palace denied the rumour in a statement. This was made worse by the announcement, two days before, that Michael Parker had resigned. Parker's marriage had collapsed and he felt this to be the only honourable course. Combined with the Duke's own long absence from wife and family and the fact that he did not immediately fly home to join them, the press had something of a field day.

Perhaps significantly, on the following day the Queen granted the

Duke of Edinburgh the style and title of Prince of the United Kingdom. A statement read: 'The Prime Minister and his senior colleagues felt that the services which the Duke of Edinburgh has rendered to the life of the Commonwealth, culminating in the long tour which he has just completed, should receive some significant mark of recognition.'[11]

Prince Philip was given a luncheon at Mansion House where he was warmly received. He spoke of his adventures, and he justified it as follows:

> For most of my life to be away four months from home meant nothing at all. In fact, it would have been surprising if I had spent four months consecutively at home. This time, for obvious reasons, it meant much more to me. But I believe there are some things for which it is worthwhile making some personal sacrifice, and I believe that the British Commonwealth is one of those things, and I am prepared to sacrifice a good deal if by so doing I can advance its well-being by even a small degree.[12]

That was the official version, but it was surely considerate of the Queen to let Prince Philip have those weeks of freedom. He was still a young man, only thirty-five. It may well be that some residual anxiety stretched into the summer of 1957. When James Pope-Hennessy lunched at Balmoral (reluctantly) in August, he wrote of the Queen as 'not shy, but she is clearly living at great tension, and does not give an impression of happiness ... One feels the spring is wound up very tight.'[13] To his brother he described her as a 'tiny, fidgeting Presence. I wanted to say: "Now, listen, I've got a new idea: Why don't you try standing still?" It's like someone warming up in a cold changing room before Gym.'[14]

In the wake of Mike Parker's departure, Prince Philip sought a new Private Secretary. His eye fell on an old friend from Gordonstoun days – Jim Orr, then serving with the Kenya Police.* Prince Philip wrote to him on 4 March, explaining that Mike 'had left to tidy up his matrimonial affairs' and would not be able to come back to him for at least two years, if at all. He thought it might be 'just up

---

* As they had been at school together, Orr always wrote: 'Dear Philip'.

your street. All you need is a sense of humour and you can't go wrong. From my point of view, I am sure you realize that I need someone who is prepared to think for himself and also tell me when I'm being a B.F.' He outlined the difference between his Household and the Queen's, stressing: 'The people who matter in the organisation are perfectly normal decent human beings with whom you would have not the slightest difficulty. Naturally there are one or two stiffs but you get them in every racket, as you well know.' He ended significantly: 'It's a small party but they are busy and therefore happy.'[15] Orr accepted and served until 1970.

Following the controversial voyage, there were many solo excursions by Prince Philip. He was always with the Queen when required, but his work for the Fédération Équestre Internationale and the World Wildlife Fund gave him the chance to travel the world. On 20 January 1959 the Duke again left Britain for a long period, going to New Delhi for an Indian Science Congress and to Agra. He visited Singapore, Sarawak, British North Borneo, Hong Kong, Gilbert and Ellice Islands, the Panama Canal, the Bahamas, Bermuda and finally returned home on 30 April. It was not conventional, but the Queen could be certain of Prince Philip's fundamental loyalty.

The Queen deferred to Prince Philip when it came to her children's education. Prince Charles attended Hill House School in Knightsbridge, run by an outward-bound headmaster, Colonel Stuart Townend (who could have been Colonel Nicholson in the 1957 David Lean film, *The Bridge over the River Kwai*). He went on to Cheam and to Gordonstoun. In later life he complained about the lack of sympathy of his parents, yet he also maintained that he liked being at home with his family. In January 1958 the Queen wrote to Anthony Eden: 'My son Charles is beginning to dread the return to school next week – so much worse for the second term!'[16]

Having detected shyness in his son, Prince Philip was keen to instil self-confidence in him. The intention was well meant, but the methods used were wrong. Where Prince Charles craved encouragement, he was berated. Cecil Beaton, photographing the family in 1960, noted that the boy seemed somewhat overawed by the proceedings, 'as if awaiting a clout from behind, or for his father to tweak his ear or pull the tuft of hair at the crown of his head'.[17]

Princess Anne took a more pragmatic stance from the start. Always worth listening to for her sound common sense, her line was: 'She was my mother and she was my Queen.' She was fearless. Where her brother was aware of every mischief a horse could employ, she leaped on and rode off. When she was young, she was deemed to be stroppy, but she was intelligent and observant. Generally considered her father's favourite, she had the best qualities of both her parents.

The Queen Mother

The Queen handled the Duke well. Her mother was another issue. She respected her and kept many traditions going as they had been in her father's day out of deference to her and respect for his memory, probably not thinking that her mother would be a presence for the next half a century. Mother and daughter were close. The Queen Mother could get her way without explicitly declaring her hand. She was a visible presence in her daughter's life, taking part in most state occasions, living close by at Clarence House, and Royal Lodge at Windsor, attending church on Sundays with the Queen and hosting drinks after matins. She stayed regularly at Birkhall near Balmoral, and at Sandringham, while also pursuing an independent social life. She plucked talented figures from the world of the arts, literature and museums and entertained them. She had her extensive racing interests.

Alongside this she travelled to many far corners of the Commonwealth, but despite her 1954 visit to the USA being a resounding success, she would never go there again. In 1957 she visited Rhodesia and Nyasaland; there was a long tour of New Zealand and Australia in 1958; and a three-week tour of Kenya and Uganda in 1959.

Princess Margaret

Princess Margaret became twenty-five on 21 August 1955, at which point she believed she had freedom to marry without the Queen's permission. Under the Royal Marriages Act she still had to give notice to the Privy Council, and she could marry so long as no objection was raised in the two Houses of Parliament within a year. So she was not entirely free. Group Captain Peter Townsend was expected back in Britain after his two-year exile in Brussels. Officially she had seen him only once, briefly, in England in 1954, though the well-informed Norman Barrymaine* assured his readers that there were other secret encounters during those years.

The marriage issue exercised Sir Anthony Eden when he and his wife went to Balmoral for the annual Prime Ministerial stay with the Queen. By then the Archbishop of Canterbury had asked the Princess not to do anything until she had spoken to him. The hope at Buckingham Palace and at Downing Street was that Princess Margaret would not marry Townsend. Eden's main concern was the effect the speculation was having on the Crown. Eden spoke to Princess Margaret and, according to his wife, Clarissa, when it was made clear to her that the Civil List allowance would cease, that was effectively the end of the matter.†

Townsend returned from Brussels on 12 October. Earlier that year he had given a series of interviews, 'yielding either to an uncontrollable impulse or perhaps because he had been advised to test popular opinion',[18] as the *Daily Telegraph* suggested. Evidently he had kept news agencies aware of his movements.

There were five meetings at Clarence House, four private dinner parties with friends, and two weekends with friends in the country. In the midst of this, on 14 October, the Queen Mother greatly exacerbated the situation by authorising a statement to be released:

> In view of the varied reports which have been published, the Press Secretary to the Queen is authorised to say that no announcement concerning Princess Margaret's personal future is at present contemplated.
>
> The Princess Margaret has asked the Press Secretary to express

---

* Norman Barrymaine (1900–91), journalist described as 'one of Fleet Street's most resilient survivors'; he worked for Lord Beaverbrook and later the *Daily Telegraph*; he was arrested as a spy by the Chinese in Shanghai in 1968 and detained for twenty months. In 1969 he became a double agent, as a way of investigating the workings of the Soviet Union.

† Whenever there was a serious issue to discuss at Balmoral, Prince Philip simply went out for a walk (the Countess of Avon to author).

the hope that the Press and public will extend to Her Royal Highness their customary courtesy and cooperation in respecting her privacy.*[19]

Princess Margaret went to see the Archbishop of Canterbury on Thursday, 27 October. Finally, she and Townsend had bowed to the external pressures and decided not to marry. On 31 October this was announced to the world. Aware of the great interest the public had taken in the romance, Princess Margaret issued her famous statement:

> I have been aware that subject to my renouncing my rights of succession it might have been possible for me to contract a civil marriage, but mindful of the Church's teaching that Christian marriage is indissoluble and conscious of my duty to the Commonwealth, I have resolved to put these considerations before any others.[20]

The BBC interrupted its programmes to give the news as did at least two New York radio stations. Princess Margaret was cheered as she arrived at Clarence House at midday. The Group Captain was doorstepped at Lowndes Square, looking 'pale and unsmiling'. He sent the butler out to tell the press that he would be making no statements: 'He is very distressed and will not be leaving the house.'[21] Princess Margaret was treated with sympathy in the press and generally commended for the nobility of her action. The Archbishop of Canterbury was meant to have said: 'What a wonderful person the Holy Spirit is!'[22] In fact, Lascelles's original ploy had worked. The love had run its course.

Townsend's woes were not over. His ambassador in Brussels, Sir Christopher Warner, introduced him to Norman Barrymaine, to help him record the round-the-world trip he would now undertake. Barrymaine did so, but horrified everyone by writing his biography – *The Story of Peter Townsend* (Peter Davies, 1958). Since Townsend

---

* Malcolm Muggeridge cited this in his onslaught on the monarchy: 'Has even the Foreign Office ever devised a more inept communiqué than the one about no statement of Princess Margaret's future being contemplated at present? If the intention had been to give the story another shot in the arm no more effective device could have been adopted.' (*New Statesman*, 22 October 1955).

was allowed to check the text (though not a contentious epilogue), we must assume that much of what it contains is true. The final 'relatively harmless' version was achieved after 'three days of haggling'.[23] Barrymaine took the line that the Princess did want to marry him, and that it took a long time before that wish subsided.

There was a further flurry of interest when Townsend returned to Britain after a trip at the end of 1958. He had seen Princess Margaret in March that year, but by then they had gone their separate ways. The publication of the Barrymaine book in September led to further onslaughts in the media. On 21 December 1959 he married Marie-Luce Jamagne, whom he had first met in Brussels in 1953. Townsend's conclusion on the saga was that Princess Margaret's decision had been right, but the example set was ultimately in vain. The 1960s led to a drop in standards of morality. In the long term, Princess Margaret, an unmarried princess who had been unable to marry a divorced equerry, lived to see Princess Anne, a divorced princess, marry an unmarried equerry in 1992 with scarcely a word of public criticism.

As for Princess Margaret, she undertook a Caribbean tour in 1955, a visit to Mauritius, Zanzibar, Tanganyika and Kenya in 1956 and she inaugurated the legislature of the new West Indies Federation on behalf of the Queen in Trinidad in 1958. This sowed the seeds of her long involvement with the Caribbean. They loved her and she understood them. To this day there are many Princess Margaret Hospitals on those islands. Later that year she toured Canada.

But between 1955 and 1960 she drifted. Her friend and lady in waiting Lady Elizabeth Cavendish introduced her to Antony Armstrong-Jones thinking she would find him lively company. He was a fashionable and talented photographer, the son of Ronald Armstrong-Jones QC and his former wife Anne Messel, by then Countess of Rosse. His uncle was Oliver Messel, the well-known stage designer and decorator, who presently designed a house for Princess Margaret on Mustique, and his maternal grandfather was the *Punch* cartoonist Linley Sambourne. He had been educated at Eton and had taken the official portraits of the Queen and the Duke of Edinburgh prior to their 1957 Canada tour.

When she and Armstrong-Jones married, society was shocked. Lord Pembroke declared he would go and live in Tibet. Lord Dudley said Armstrong-Jones should be given the title of Viscount Focus. Cecil Beaton, a long-time rival of Oliver Messel in public and private life, was appalled. But as a photographer, he thought this cleared him of Armstrong-Jones, who had been photographing the Duke of Kent and the Queen. 'Thank you for ridding me of a rival!' he told Princess Margaret. He was horrified when she told him that Armstrong-Jones had no intention of giving up.[24]

★ ★ ★ ★ ★

The other working members of the Royal Family were the Duke and Duchess of Gloucester, the Duchess of Kent (Princess Marina), and the Princess Royal. The Queen's uncle, the Duke of Gloucester, had longed to command his regiment, but had been forced to give that up by the Abdication. He was a stoic figure, to whom fell many of the more ponderous royal engagements. The polish on his boots literally bristled in the boiling sun when he took the salute in Jordan in 1953. The Brigade of Guards nicknamed him 'Uncle Pineapple' as he fell asleep on his horse when taking the Colonels' Parade on Horse Guards. He represented the Queen overseas in the 1950s, visiting British troops and inspecting war cemeteries. The Gloucesters visited Ethiopia, the Somaliland Protectorate and Aden in 1958.

The Duchess of Kent was particularly in demand for royal visits overseas. There had been her successful Far East tour of 1952 (with her son, the Duke of Kent), a visit to Canada and the USA with Princess Alexandra in 1954, then Latin America in 1959, visiting Mexico and Peru. Ghana became the first sub-Saharan nation to achieve independence on 6 March 1957 under the leadership of Kwame Nkrumah. The Duchess inaugurated the new Parliament on the Queen's behalf, following lengthy discussions at the Commonwealth Office as to the exact way in which this should be done.

Philip Hay, Princess Marina's private secretary, corralled Princess Alexandra into royal duties from an early age. She began by accompanying her mother on her engagements and undertaking foreign tours with her. The others were too young for royal service. In August 1959, after the Latin America visit, she left for a solo tour of Australia, also visiting Thailand, Cambodia, India, Iran and Turkey, and effectively dedicated her life to royal duties from then on.

The Queen's aunt, the Princess Royal, enjoyed her overseas visits and any home engagements where she could be useful. In 1960 she set off on *Britannia* to tour the Caribbean, visiting Barbados, British Guiana, British Honduras, Trinidad, St Vincent, St Lucia, Dominica, Montserrat, Jamaica, Montego Bay and the Cayman Islands. She hosted lunch parties on board the Royal Yacht, inspected Girl Guides and joined campfire ceremonies. Her main recreation was horse-racing and she joined the Queen frequently at race meetings.

After an initial flurry of appearances, the Duke of Windsor was not much in evidence in Britain during these years, especially after the death of Queen Mary. He visited London several times, had tea with the Queen and Prince Philip in December 1957, invariably paid a courtesy call on the Prime Minister (in the days of Churchill and Eden), attended the memorial service for his old equerry and friend, Fruity Metcalfe, in the Chapel Royal, St James's Palace and one evening in 1957 dined with former officers of the Welsh Guards. During these years he was forced to deny accusations about involvement with Nazis, which were dismissed by Winston Churchill in the House of Commons as 'beneath contempt'. The Duchess published her memoirs in 1956, which did not appeal to the Royal Family* but were harmless enough even in those days.

---

* The Duke of Gloucester fulminated against them to James Pope-Hennessy: 'Mrs Simpson? Bloody bitch. I only saw her three times. We none of us ever thought he was going to marry the woman. ... No, I didn't read her book and I'm not going to read it. Why would I waste eighteen shillings?' (*The Quest for Queen Mary*, p. 200).

20
DIPLOMACY, 1954–9

After the Commonwealth tour the Queen remained in Britain for some time. There were regional visits to different areas of the country so that she could become better known to her subjects. She visited Wales several times at the beginning of her Western Isles cruise to Scotland for the summer holidays, sometimes attending an *eisteddfod*. There were tours of Lancashire and Yorkshire. And there were state visits, which followed a long tradition stretching back to the most celebrated – the Field of the Cloth of Gold, in 1520, when Henry VIII invited François I of France to meet him in some splendour to cement a new treaty of friendship.

There were two or three state visits to Britain each year. The overseas guest usually stayed at Buckingham Palace, but sometimes after 1969 at Windsor Castle, and occasionally even at Holyroodhouse in Edinburgh. The modern tradition is that kings and queens pay one visit to each other during their reigns. Thus the Queen went abroad to visit another monarch and that monarch came to Britain. This usually happened just once during each respective reign, but sometimes there was a second state visit if this was deemed propitious, as happened with Norway and Denmark.

There were certain accepted traditions – the exchange of honours (if appropriate – the Americans do not accept them). Normally the Queen gave a fellow monarch the Royal Victorian Chain on the first visit and the Garter on the second, though the King of Sweden and the Emperor of Ethiopia were given the Garter on the first. A wreath would be laid on the tomb of the Unknown Warrior at Westminster Abbey. There would be a state banquet at Buckingham Palace and a return banquet hosted elsewhere by the guest. Queen Elizabeth the Queen Mother would entertain the state visitor and spouse to tea on the day of their arrival. Though there was often a political motivation behind these visits, essentially they were diplomatic occasions.

Before each visit, the Queen's speech of about five hundred words would be drafted, approved by the Secretary of State and submitted to her Private Secretary for alteration 'to suit Her Majesty's personal style' three weeks before the visit.[1] Copious briefing notes were sent out and these were far from bland. There were two versions, a confidential one for the Queen and non-confidential for general use. These included personality reports on the Head of State and all the members of the suite, with family details and whether they spoke English: 'Any information about hobbies, idiosyncrasies and disabilities, if known, should be mentioned'; background on the country and British relations with the country; topics of conversation to be avoided; and details of forms of address with phonetic pronunciation of the names of members of the suite.[2]

When the Queen visited the Shah of Iran in 1961, good subjects were highlighted as his prowess as a sportsman, his keen interest in education and the eradication of illiteracy. She was advised not to mention the deposition, exile and closing years in South Africa of his father, Reza Shah, or to mention corruption, oil royalties or the Shah's attitude to Bahrain (which he considered historically a part of Persia, not approving of Britain's special relationship with that country).[3] The Queen was briefed about Farah Diba, this crystallising into her speech at the state banquet: 'Your Majesty is no stranger to us: we have the happiest memories of your state visit to our country in 1959. But when you came among us then you came alone. Now, it is with great joy that my husband and I have had the pleasure of meeting the gracious Empress who sits by your side and shares with you some of the heavy obligations of monarchy.'*[4]

If the Queen went to an Eastern country, the medical precautions intensified. Blood supplies were sent to refrigerators at airports, all cooks, waiters and food handlers were subjected to a

---

* My mother took me to the Mall to see the Shah of Iran travelling with the Queen in a carriage on 5 May 1959. The splendour of the procession fired my imagination (at the age of seven) to the extent that I asked to see President de Gaulle's the following year.

'stool examination at a reliable laboratory to minimise the likelihood of amoebic and worm infections'.[5]

Visits from Overseas

In the 1950s huge crowds would line the routes. When the Queen went abroad, she often arrived impressively in *Britannia*. The royal visitors were given a massive welcome. Appropriately, the first state visit was from King Gustaf VI Adolf of Sweden and his wife, Queen Louise, between 28 June and 1 July 1954. Queen Louise was Prince Philip's aunt. She had learned to swear like a trooper in the First World War. When the King got an electric shock from a fence at Broadlands, all he could muster was 'Bother.' The Queen was amused when, on a car journey, King Gustaf wanted the window wound up. 'I will if you say please,' said Queen Louise.[6] He was a studious man, enthusiastic about everything he did, whether amassing his important collection of china, visiting archaeological sites or inspecting a military review. Years later the author Richard Hough revealed that Queen Elizabeth II found the King a bore.

The next visitor was Emperor Haile Selassie of Ethiopia between 14 and 16 October 1954. Clarissa Eden was predictably negative. She found the state banquet at the Palace 'the dreariest possible affair' with 'flowers of fantastic ugliness in flame & yellow, ruining the silver gilt'.[7] The visit to the Guildhall library was enlivened by the huge elephant tusks the Emperor presented to the City of London falling 'with a resounding crash just as they are about to be borne in'. At Mansion House Churchill became fidgety and Attlee fell asleep when the Emperor spoke for ten minutes in Aramaic. There was a dinner at the Ethiopian Embassy with 'wonderful footmen in red plush knee breeches & emerald plush swallow tail coats'. The Emperor again spoke in Aramaic, to which the Queen replied 'Thank you.' Clarissa was amused that Lady Salisbury said to Lady Scarbrough: 'Didn't the Queen do that *wonderfully* & without anything written down.'[8]

When the Shah came to lunch at the Palace on 18 February 1955, he spoke only to the Queen and Prince Philip, ignoring Harold Nicolson and Peter Fleming, who had been produced by the Foreign

Office. Prince Charles and Princess Anne came in and ran around, the Queen Mother taking them over to talk to the guests.

Prince Philip had been relieved that the Russian leaders, Marshal Nikolai Bulganin and Nikita Khrushchev were not staying with them. They visited Windsor Castle on 22 April 1955. On their return to Claridge's the two leaders could be heard vying with each other: 'The Queen said to me ...'

'No, she said that to me ...'[9]

The Queen knew the boy King Faisal of Iraq when he came on his state visit between 16 and 19 July 1956, on the eve of the Suez crisis, accompanied by his uncle, the Crown Prince (and formerly Regent between 1939 and 1953). He was only twenty-one years old. During the Second World War he had lived at Winkfield Row with his mother and gone to school at Sandroyd and Harrow, where he was close to his second cousin, King Hussein of Jordan. He had walked in the funeral procession of George VI, who had taken an interest in him, and had stayed with the Queen and Prince Philip at Balmoral in September 1952.

The King's later fate was tragic. The following year he became engaged to Princess Fazile of Egypt, whom he met on a cruise on the Bosphorus. She was only sixteen and there was some family opposition on account of her extreme youth. She was sent to Heathfield School for two terms. The wedding was set for July 1958. King Faisal was coming to his home, Stanwell Manor, near London Airport to visit his bride-to-be. The butler had all the Georgian candelabra out and a five-course dinner for twelve was planned.

But the night before he left Iraq, Colonel Abdul-Karim Qasim, a military officer (who later became Prime Minister), mounted a *coup d'état*. The next morning King Faisal, his uncle and other members of his family, were ordered to assemble in the courtyard of the Rihab Palace. The King was shot in the head and neck. He died soon afterwards, as did other members of the Iraq Royal Family and the Prime Minister, Nuri al-Said. The King's body was hanged. The naked bodies of Nuri al-Said and the Crown Prince were dragged through the streets of Baghdad amid what Anthony Eden called 'scenes of unmentionable beastliness'.[10] The Queen was considerably upset by King Faisal's death. On 30 July she was represented by the Duke of Gloucester at a memorial service at the Savoy Chapel, the chapel of the Royal Victorian Order (the King having been a GCVO).

President Heuss of Germany

The most significant state visit in the 1950s was that of President Heuss of Germany between 20 and 23 October 1958. Diplomatic relations had been resumed with Germany in May 1954. The visit was inspired by a conversation the President had had with the banker S. G. Warburg in January 1955, and had been much promoted as early as 1947 by the British Ambassador in Berlin, Sir Frederick Hoyer Millar. Sir Frank Roberts, a later Ambassador, wondered if it was not premature.

There had been no state visit from Germany since 1907. Heuss, a widower, was the ideal man to give Germany back its respectability. He had been President since 1949, an avuncular, easy-going man, fond of cigars and wine, untainted by any association with Hitler, a democrat and humanist in the liberal tradition, and a former professor of political science in Berlin, who had been dismissed from his academic posts when Hitler came to power, one of his anti-Hitler books having been publicly burned. He had spent the war years in private life. He was keen to promote Federal Germany as non-partisan.

His visit evinced respect and sympathy from the crowds rather than enthusiasm. At the state banquet the Queen reminded the guests of the part Britain had played in the unification of the three Western zones of Germany after the war and in the formation of the new Federal Republic. She said: 'The tragic events of the past half-century in the relations between our two countries are a part of history. We must now look to the future and through our alliance and our association with each other and with other countries of the West we must forge anew the bonds of amity and peace.'

At the Guildhall the President told the Lord Mayor that war between Britain and Germany 'must never happen again, and never will – that is how I understand the meaning of my visit, and that is how I interpret the spirit of friendship shown to me here'.[11] He gave £5,000 to the Coventry Cathedral restoration fund. The Queen was praised in the German press for having 'shown the courage and greatness to take a step towards friendship'.[12]

The Family Visits

It was appropriate that the Queen's first state visits abroad were to relations. The Queen visited her 'Uncle Charles', eighty-two-year-old King Haakon of Norway, who stood six foot three, in June 1955. He was her great-uncle by his marriage to Edward VII's youngest daughter, Princess Maud. (She had died in 1938.) The King was also Prince Philip's cousin as they both descended from the kings of Denmark. He had spent the war in Britain, living at Winkfield, had been at the wedding in 1947, was a godfather to Prince Charles and had made a state visit to Britain in 1951. He was also the Queen's senior Knight of the Garter, appointed by Edward VII in 1906.

The King was thrilled to have the young Queen with him, and his enthusiasm was infectious, but he found the welcoming ceremonies tiring and at the state banquet retreated to a sofa, saying: 'The young ones can go on standing.'[13] When she was leaving, he changed his programme to sail with them as far as the outer lighthouse of Oslo harbour.[14] A few days later he fell in his bathroom, fractured his thigh and was never seen again in public, dying on 21 September 1957.

In June 1956 the Queen and Prince Philip sailed to Stockholm, returning the visit made by King Gustaf VI Adolf and Queen Louise in 1954. Before the Queen and Prince Philip arrived, the Swedish press covered their front pages with photographs, and leading articles 'expressing in the most moving terms admiration for Great Britain and the Royal Family'.[15] The Swedes came out in force to see the Queen and the Duke rowed in the Swedish Royal Barge, *Vasaörden*, to the very steps of the Palace of Stockholm. The crowds never left the Queen alone, even when the visit ended, Princess Margaret and the Duke and Duchess of Gloucester joining them to witness events of the Olympic Games in the stadium and cross-country.

The visit greatly helped the King and Queen of Sweden, the *Daily Sketch* asserting that the Queen's visit might have saved the

Swedish monarchy. Sir Robert Hankey, the British Ambassador, agreed, pointing out that 'the indiscretions of the late King Gustav V and his predecessor', and 'the peculiarities of the late King's private life' had lately received wide publicity.*¹⁶ In contrast King Gustaf and Queen Louise led exemplary lives. The Ambassador concluded that the Queen's visit had given the Swedish people 'a living illustration ... of the place of constitutional monarchy in the modern world'.¹⁷

In June 1957 the Queen paid the first visit of a British monarch to Denmark for fifty years. King Frederik and Queen Ingrid were closely related to the British Royal Family. The Queen was aware that her great-grandmother, Queen Alexandra, had been a Danish princess and that her father had spoken of her with conspicuous affection. King Frederik was a giant of a man, who loved the sea and loved to conduct orchestras. Queen Ingrid had spent a lot of time at Bagshot Park with her grandfather, the Duke of Connaught. (Her father, King Gustaf VI Adolf of Sweden had been married to Princess Margaret of Connaught.) Prince Philip knew the country well. After the formal visit, the Queen and the Duke spent a rare quiet weekend with the Danish Royal Family at Fredensborg Castle, out in the country north of Copenhagen. The Ambassador concluded that the visit 'brought the King into the public eye to a quite unusual degree, and although on the first day he was unfortunately afflicted with lumbago and looked rather tense, as the visit went on he became increasingly relaxed and gay'.¹⁸

In 1958 the Queen and Prince Philip visited Queen Juliana of the Netherlands, touring a diamond factory and meeting two thousand representatives of the British Commonwealth. She gave the Dutch Queen the Order of the Garter. Prince Philip worked with Prince Bernhard for many years on the World Wildlife Fund. The

---

* King Gustaf V had been too friendly towards Hitler for the liking of his wartime Prime Minister. He was also openly homosexual and the court had been blackmailed when Kurt Haijby, a restaurateur with a criminal record, claimed he had been seduced by the King and had been his lover between 1936 and 1947. The Swedish Court paid out large sums to suppress the story and in 1952 Haijby was sentenced to eight years' hard labour for blackmail. The King's predecessor, King Oscar II, was alleged to have had two illegitimate sons by the opera singer, Marie Friberg.

Queen paid a rare visit to Amsterdam in May 1962, along with an array of other royal figures for Queen Juliana's Silver Wedding celebrations. There was a boat trip along the canals and a banquet.

The Queen's State Visit to Paris

Without doubt the most spectacular of the state visits in the 1950s was the Queen's visit to President Coty in Paris in April 1957. France was still reeling from the 1940 collapse, aware that Britain's lone stand against the Nazis had been a prime factor in winning the war. The visit took place in the wake of the Suez crisis.

Sir Gladwyn Jebb, the British Ambassador, and his wife Cynthia both left accounts. Jebb was a formidable figure, dour, intelligent, but not without conceit. Sir Anthony Meyer, then at the Embassy, wrote: 'He could be alarming to those who showed any fear of him.'[19] Cynthia, on the other hand, resembled a porcelain doll. She appeared fey but was perceptive, with a wider social vision than Gladwyn. The Ambassador had been optimistic from the outset:

> Given the general sentiments of the French nation and the enormous popularity in all countries of the Western World of Her Majesty and the Prince, it was certain in advance that this visit would prove a success; what was extraordinary was the degree of enthusiasm which it evoked on the part of France generally and the astonishing scope, efficiency and expense of the arrangements made by the French Government and the Municipality of Paris.[20]

Rooms at the Élysée Palace were specially decorated for the Queen. Jebb thought that the Opéra gala, which lasted from 10 p.m. until 11.55, after the state banquet, misfired despite massive crowds outside: 'The baneful influence of Serge Lifar,* though he has mercifully

---

* Serge Lifar (1905–86), famous Russian dancer with Diaghilev's Ballets Russe. He was ballet master at the Paris Opéra, 1930–44, and again, 1947–58. He was unpopular as a known collaborator in the Second World War. In 1958, he was forced to resign.

retired from dancing, still surrounds the institution and the less said about his ballet, entitled *Le Chevalier et la Demoiselle* the better.'[21]

In contrast the *Promenade sur la Seine* was a huge success: 'one of the most astonishing things of its kind that I personally have ever seen and I have yet to hear of anyone who had a different impression'.[22] Later that evening there was a late-night reception at the British Embassy, from which the Queen was scheduled to retire at 12.15 a.m. The Ambassador summed up the visit, attributing the 'upsurge of emotion all over France' to 'the simplicity, charm and grace of The Queen herself' and the 'virile and democratic demeanour' of Prince Philip:

> France is in some respects a monarchy without a monarch, but the French, nevertheless, tend to be very critical of any royal personage who, in their opinion, appears to be proud, contemptuous or reserved. The grace and distinction of Her Majesty's manner therefore won all hearts and, as I have said, this was the principal reason for the great success she achieved.[23]

Chips Channon wrote: 'All Paris has gone mad about the Queen.'[24] Cynthia Jebb judged the visit as the highlight of their time at the Embassy. It gave her 'a glow of happiness; great pride that we have such a perfect Queen'. The weather was ideal, Spring having come early so that all the trees were green, the chestnut trees in flower and the tulips, lilac and lilies of the valley blooming. A marquise adorned the courtyard of the Embassy with a red carpet stretching to the road outside. Cynthia Jebb examined the Queen:

> To my mind she is (almost) perfect. She is small, well made, well proportioned; she has dark hair, blue eyes, a lovely English skin. Her features are not good, but she is much prettier in real life than in photographs. She has an exceptionally charming soft, clear voice, high-pitched and pitched just right, like a singer would do, and with almost a bell-like quality. Her French accent astonished everybody here. She has not got the Queen Mother's well-known charm & smile, but I think that is how it should be as she is not out to charm and attract all and sundry. She has better qualities than that. One feels the presence of a very fine character, simple, kind and good;

always anxious to do the right thing; a person who would never let anyone down. And yet quite shrewd and quick about all that is going on. She is more 'a chip off the old block' in that there is something much like Queen Mary or the Princess Royal about her, for she is definitely royal. She is rather serious in her manner (and does not smile much) but when she does it is a lovely radiant natural smile.

Cynthia Jebb regretted that 'Apart from horses & racing I could not discover anything that interested her such as the arts or gardens or books.' She detected a similar lack of interest from Prince Philip:

Prince Philip is handsome, gay, laughing, informal, creating the easy democratic atmosphere in the wake of the Queen. He likes himself to pick out people in the crowds at a party; to ask who they are, find out about them himself, crack jokes with them, get lost in the general mêlée, get well left behind, separate from the detectives, have everybody waiting & searching for him & finally catch up again with the Queen and the advance guard. This informality makes him most popular (I don't quite know how much the courtiers approve of it, but I feel it to be a distinctly clever move, attracting quite a lot of attention to himself in a completely different form to that of the Queen, showing himself to be not a nonentity, nor a solemn, dull pompous Prince Albert). He shines out as a breezy sailor who has known what it is not to be a royalty, and who does not like pomp & ceremony. (I believe that Selwyn [Lloyd] (who stayed in the Embassy) does not care for him very much. That he is supposed to over-do things, and plays too big a part in that he recently made some speech of a political nature, airing his views, & altogether behaving unconstitutionally) nevertheless I would say that he handles a difficult position in a remarkable successful way, and I cannot imagine what other person whom the Queen might have married could have done as well ...[25]

Cynthia had invited Cecil Beaton to sketch the visit, rather than photograph it. He was as sharp as ever: 'The Queen did very well except a bit too Queen Mary-ish for the first day, & no grins thrown away,'[26] he wrote to Clarissa Eden. Whereas Cynthia thought the Queen 'in her Hartnell dress stole the show', Beaton told her: 'The

Queen triumphed over Hartnell's bad taste.'²⁷ But he conceded: 'She scored a bulls-eye every time she smiled.'²⁸

The Queen's room at the Élysée Palace was not comfortable and it was far from Prince Philip's room, and the dressing-table had lamps with dim bulbs, making it impossible for her to do her make-up. The Queen asked for simple meals, which enabled them to 'emerge from the festivities' with livers 'in good order', though 'some of the French felt they had been done out of their rightful banquets'. Certain events turned into a bit of a scrum.*

Cynthia was disappointed when the Queen was shown into the Petits Appartements at Versailles and only nodded at the treasures she was shown, saying: 'Yes, I see.'† At the Embassy reception a Hungarian orchestra played, and the guests were decked out in uniforms and decorations or bouffant dresses and glittering jewellery, some with magnificent high tiaras. The arts were represented by the composers Francis Poulenc, Georges Auric, and the writers Jean Cocteau, François Mauriac and, to Cynthia's annoyance, André Maurois.‡

The Queen arrived by boat on the Seine, in a glittering sheath dress, and processed through the rooms to the state dining room. Supper was not to be too late because President Coty was deemed to be an old man (though only seventy-five) and keen to get home to bed. Scarlet-coated footmen stood behind the royal couple during dinner, said to be a custom left over from the nineteenth century. A detour from La Celle St Cloud enabled the Queen to see Marcel Boussac's racehorses, then on to the Renault works, where Prince Philip detected that two of the workers were wired with microphones. 'Take that damned thing off!' he ordered.

A highlight of the trip was dinner in the Salle des Caryatides at the Louvre. The Queen had never been to the Louvre, so she had never seen the *Mona Lisa*: 'About a quarter of an hour later two men came

---

* Cynthia had not forgotten that the distinguished literary figure, Edmée de la Rochefoucauld, whose '*mercredi*' salons continued into the 1980s, had pushed in behind the Queen Mother at the Inter-Alliée the year before.

† The Queen did not show much interest in the Embassy rooms but lit up when Cynthia's dog Jasper appeared.

‡ André Maurois had upset the British during the war, by first coming to the UK and appearing to be supportive, but then running to Canada for fear of invasion.

staggering in carrying this celebrated picture and leaving it very informally against a chair. Thus we were able to have a close and intimate quiz at it.' Unfortunately this dinner was followed by a reception, originally meant for two thousand guests, but augmented to three thousand. Pandemonium followed. Lady Margaret Hay, lady in waiting, said to the Queen: 'Are you all right, Ma'am?' and she replied, 'Just.'

On their return to Britain, the Queen and the Duke went straight to Windsor and the next day they rode in the Great Park. In the days that followed, there was nothing but praise in Paris. One woman wept because she would never see the Queen again; a hairdresser said that if they had a queen like that in France, the whole country would be monarchists.[29]

Commonwealth Visits

Besides the state visits the Queen and Prince Philip travelled extensively in the Commonwealth, both then and later. Nigeria was heading towards independence. They paid a long visit between 27 January and 17 February 1956, considered one of the most important of the reign. The purpose of the visit was to unite the three regional governments (the Northern, Western and Eastern governments and the Federal Government) to see if they could work together in a framework with the Queen as its head. The Northern Region, with half the population, wanted the British to continue to help them. The Ibos to the east and the Yorubas to the west were keen to take the reins themselves.

A 'multiplicity' of Rolls-Royces was sent out in advance of the tour, which the Crown Agent's staff thought would add 'much to our glamour-value'.[30] At the House of Representatives on 31 January, Chief Akintola,* Leader of the Opposition, welcomed the Queen and the Duke 'whatever may be the difference in the political views of Government and Opposition'.[31] When the Queen opened the new Court of Appeal building in Lagos she stressed the importance

---

* Chief Ládòkè Akintola (1910–66), murdered in the first Nigerian military coup at Ibadan on 15 January 1966. His youngest son, Tokunbo (1951–73), inspired a lot of publicity as the first Black boy at Eton College.

of the rule of law to the freedom and orderly progress of any society.³²

At Lighthouse Beach the Governor, Sir James Robertson, was congratulating himself that there were no gate-crashers. The Queen said: 'It's so quiet and peaceful. No one to be seen, except one of your policemen, Sir James, under every bush.' He spotted many a white robe under the bushes. One night the lights fused at dinner. 'Oh, well! We all know the way to our mouths!' said the Queen. On the point of leaving Lagos Prince Philip came out in shirt sleeves and red braces and told Robertson that the Queen needed him. She presented him with the GCVO.³³

The Queen and Prince Philip then travelled inland to Kaduna, capital of the Northern Region, where they witnessed a spectacular Durbar. Sixty thousand people came from all over the region. There was dancing, daring horse-riding and acrobatics, in which six and a half thousand men and two thousand horses took part. These included Hausa horsemen, camel drummers, snake charmers, musicians and masked dancers, all in a colourful and dramatic display. A hundred and fifty tribesmen charged, hurling their caparisoned mounts at the royal dais, and coming to 'a slithering standstill in a confusion of dust and riotous colour'.³⁴ The Duchess of Grafton (then Countess of Euston), accompanying the Queen, recalled this as one of the most spectacular sights she witnessed during her many years of service, though she had to share a room with her maid: there was no air-conditioning and from the maid came 'gentle snoring'.³⁵ The Queen went to a leper colony on the Oji river on 9 February, where they beat tom-toms to let others from miles away know she was there.

The Queen and the Duke made a circular tour back to the coast at Calabar and Port Harcourt. They went to Ibadan, capital of the Western Region and up to Kano, a walled city in the northernmost part of Nigeria where the temperature was 104 degrees in the shade, before returning to Lagos for the flight home. At London airport, as on their departure, Prince Charles and Princess Anne were waiting.

Sir James Robertson, who did a magnificent job in uniting feuding factions, stated that for those who saw the Queen and the Duke 'their loyalty and devotion have acquired a new strength and a personal meaning'.[36] To a friend he described the visit as a great success:

> I didn't think she was unduly tired at the end; she rather liked the warm climate, and was very cheerful and happy on the last evening. She is shrewd and had a lot of common sense, and an excellent retentive memory for what she reads and is told. He is charming and excellent in talking to all sorts of people; and is able. He floored a number of our experts on their own ground. We found them very easy and their household staff was charming and most helpful.[37]

This tour was followed in November 1957 by a twelve-day visit by the Princess Royal to open the new University College Hospital in Ibadan. The Queen's aunt attended self-government celebrations in Western Nigeria. (In Onitsha she switched on the lights of a new market and swarms of yam beetles collected in great numbers and got into clothes and hair, and down the back of ladies' dresses.) In 1959 the Duke of Gloucester represented the Queen at similar celebrations in Northern Nigeria. These visits heralded full independence for Ghana in October 1960 at which Princess Alexandra represented the Queen.

The Queen came away thinking Nigeria 'full of promise ... along the hard but rewarding path to progress'. Above all, she wanted it to remain in the Commonwealth, which it did.[38]

★ ★ ★ ★ ★

There were two visits to Canada, one in 1957 and another in 1959. In October 1957, the Canadians were delighted that she was visiting them as their own Queen and then visiting the United States as Queen of Canada. Her visit took place in perfect Canadian 'fall' weather. In the middle of it, she and the Duke flew to Williamsburg to celebrate the 350th anniversary of the founding of the colony of Virginia, and stayed for four days at the White House. The Queen addressed the United Nations in New York, reminding them that the Assembly had been created with 'the aim of the preservation of peace between nations, equality of justice for all before the law and the right of the peoples of the world to live their lives in freedom and security'.[39]

Sir Harold Caccia, the British Ambassador, described the tour as 'exacting' and reported that President Eisenhower had said he would have fired all his staff if they submitted such proposals to him.[40] All went well: 'The American public from the highest to the lowest were spellbound.'[41] Caccia believed that the visit successfully closed the book on Suez. He wrote to Harold Macmillan: 'The Queen's visit has made a tremendous effect here. She has buried George III for good and all.'[42]

In turn the Queen wrote to Anthony Eden, saying she couldn't have chosen four more different countries to visit in 1957 than France, Denmark, Canada and the United States. She was surprised that the United States needed someone to lean on:

> ... and we were able to provide them with the necessary trip in the scale to ensure that they leant on us – the United Kingdom. It is extraordinary how much the Americans need the feeling that they are liked (even the President spoke sadly about how much his country is disliked in the world) – an illusion which doesn't seem to bother us as much!
>
> One can but hope that this year we may see an advance in the state of the world, for which everyone longs so much.
>
> I can't help feeling, having once again seen the way the American administration works (or doesn't work) that the life of the President is quite impossible for a hale and hearty man, let alone an ill man. Ike leads a terrible life, and is under no illusions as to why he is still there – but I do wish he wouldn't talk so much![43]

The Queen and the Duke were back in Canada on 18 June 1959 to open the new St Lawrence Seaway, which enabled ocean-going vessels to sail from the Atlantic to the Great Lakes of Northern Canada, hailed as the greatest engineering feat of modern times. To this, as Queen of Canada, she welcomed Eisenhower in Montreal, describing it as a monument to the enduring friendship between Canada and the United States. It cost more than £350 million. At the Robert Moses Power Dam in Cornwall, Ontario, she met the famous 'Power Broker', with Richard Nixon and Nelson Rockefeller.

There followed a six-week tour of the Provinces, and a one-day visit to Chicago. The Acting High Commissioner judged that the visit helped Canada assert its identity in developing a different character from her American neighbour on account of her loyalty to the Crown and her place in the Commonwealth:

> A strong sense of attachment has now grown up in the minds of the great majority of Canadians, coloured by warm admiration and affection for the Queen. This has been combined with a clearer grasp of the political and moral values for which the Throne stands, a wider appreciation of the constitutional advantages of Monarchy and rising recognition of what the Crown means to Canada in her association with other Commonwealth countries. The roots of Monarchy in Canadian soil now stretch wider and wider.[44]

The tour was long and arduous, but it meant that the Queen now belonged to the Canadians in a way she had not before. Prince Philip made his own impact:

> An invigorating touch was imparted by him to the events, and Canadians have not failed to appreciate his outstanding contribution to the success of the tour in terms of sheer hard work. His forthright lecture to the Canadian Medical Association on the general unfitness of Canadians has been taken in good part, although not without a good measure of serious self-examination, while his reported enquiries of a member of the Ontario Legislature as to when the 'obsolete and old-fashioned' liquor laws of that Province would be changed has been received with lively approval in all but the most temperate circles.[45]

During these years, between 1954 and 1960, there was an attempt to appoint Vincent Massey a Knight of the Garter. He had been a popular wartime High Commissioner to the United Kingdom, and the first Canadian-born Governor-General of Canada. The Queen and the Duke held him in high esteem. Prince Philip raised the idea with him when he visited Canada in 1954. This had to be approved by the Canadian Government, but the Prime Minister, Louis St Laurent, told Massey it would be 'politically embarrassing to the Government'[46] if he accepted.

John Diefenbaker (subsequently Prime Minister) suggested that he wait until he retired as Governor-General. Massey raised it again with Diefenbaker when he was Prime Minister. Diefenbaker appeared to support the idea, considering that the Governor-General was a special case where honours were concerned. Then he wavered. Lord Slim was given the Garter as retiring Governor-General of Australia in 1959, but Diefenbaker told Massey: 'Slim's appointment left one vacancy. But this mustn't go into your diary or mine.' Massey believed it was in the bag. He left office, heaped with praise, on 15 September 1959. With an election looming, Massey felt he should not raise the matter just then.[47]

In 1960 Diefenbaker betrayed Massey by telling Sir Michael Adeane that honours for Canadians were not appropriate. Adeane wrote to Massey on 13 June 1960: 'The Queen has instructed me to let you know in confidence that much as she would like to make you a Knight of the Garter – the first in the Commonwealth overseas – it is not possible for her to do so because ... the Government in Canada ... advised her that this would be inappropriate ...'[48] On 22 July 1960 she gave Vincent Massey the Royal Victorian Chain instead.*[49]

Years later, when designing a Commonwealth Walkway panel for outside Canada House, I illustrated Vincent Massey on it. This the Queen unveiled on 19 July 2017. I mentioned the Garter issue to her. She smiled and said nothing. How could she? Behind her were the then Governor-General and the High Commissioner.

At the end of the July 1959 trip to Canada, it was suddenly announced that the Queen was suffering from fatigue. She and Prince Philip flew home from America rather than sailing in *Britannia*. It was not fatigue. The Queen was pregnant.

---

* The Queen had greater success with Commonwealth Garters when she able to appoint men such as Lord Casey, Sir Paul Hasluck and Sir Ninian Stephen in Australia, Sir Keith Holyoake and Sir Edmund Hillary in New Zealand.

21
HAROLD MACMILLAN, 1957–63

Harold Macmillan became Prime Minister on 10 January 1957. It has been suggested that if Churchill played Melbourne to her Queen Victoria, then Macmillan was Disraeli to the Queen. A walrus-moustached man, the son of a crofter, he had moved into aristocratic circles. Like Eden, he had been to Eton and Oxford, and served in the First World War, where he had been seriously wounded. He loved the grouse moor; he was a great reader. He was lampooned to his advantage in cartoons as 'Supermac'. He had married Lady Dorothy Cavendish, daughter of the 9th Duke of Devonshire. He was a consummate actor, delivering his speeches with practised panache and sharp, theatrical timing, and a devious politician, whom the Edens blamed for misleading information about the Americans and Suez. Eden fell and Macmillan took over. Suez gave Macmillan the last chance to seize the reins of power.

On the morning of his summons to Buckingham Palace, Macmillan read *Pride and Prejudice*: 'very soothing'.[1] At his audience he addressed the Queen: 'I could not disguise from her the gravity of the situation. Indeed, I remember warning her, half in joke, that I could not answer for the new Government lasting more than six weeks. She smilingly reminded me of this at an audience six years later.'[2] He was anxious to put on record how he had been chosen, most particularly that 'Lord Salisbury merely acted as a means of conveying to the Queen the general view inside the Party.'[3]

Macmillan loved his audiences, finding the Queen 'not only very charming, but incredibly well informed'.[4] But he never cared for Prince Philip: 'I don't altogether like the tone of his talk. It is too like that of a clever undergraduate, who has just discovered Socialism.'[5]

The author Andrew Duncan claimed that one of Macmillan's

colleagues (quite likely wanting to have a go at him) told him: 'Curiously, she had often felt uneasy with Harold Macmillan, patrician, urbanity, wrapped in nettles, who tended to act granddad at their weekly audiences, discussing affairs of state while looking directly over her head at pictures on the wall, or a clock. There was also the suspicion that he did not tell her anything.'[6] The description is supported by Lord Williams of Elvel, who gleaned that Macmillan tended to lecture the Queen:

> There was a certain Balliol-type inability to suppress a sense of intellectual superiority, which was no doubt justified but was none the less irritating for all that. The result, according to one courtier, was that when Macmillan visited Balmoral, a junior secretary was detailed to take him for very long walks to get him out of the Queen's way. She was, in short, bored at being lectured and not being listened to.[7]

Two years after taking office, Macmillan wanted to call a General Election. He had refrained from doing so in June 1959, partly on account of the Queen's long and strenuous tour of Canada, and her pregnancy.* On 22 August he wrote to the Queen on the subject of dissolution.

Macmillan arrived at Balmoral on 7 September 1959 for the Prime Minister's annual stay and was greeted in the hall by the Duke of Gloucester, in a state of some disturbance: 'Thank Heavens you've come, Prime Minister. The Queen's in a terrible state. There's a fellow called Jones in the billiard room who wants to marry her sister, and Prince Philip's in the library wanting to change the family name to Mountbatten.'†[8]

On the same day he asked for dissolution, explaining at tedious

---

* On account of her pregnancy, Prince Philip laid her wreath at the Cenotaph in November, and her Christmas broadcast was pre-recorded.

† This was a reference to Prince Philip wishing – or perhaps more correctly Lord Mountbatten pressing – to make Mountbatten-Windsor the name of those descendants of the Queen in the male line who required a surname. This was effected in February 1960. The other problem was Antony Armstrong-Jones, who became engaged to Princess Margaret in that same month.

length to the Queen that this was 'the last great prerogative of the Crown' and had to be preserved lest it was needed 'at a time of national crisis'.[9] The Queen knew the constitution perfectly well. She agreed to the dissolution. On 18 September she had to go south to London to issue a Proclamation dissolving Parliament. A month later she went down again for a Privy Council after Macmillan's party swept in for another term of office and new Ministers needed to be sworn in.

On 3 February 1960, Macmillan delivered his 'Wind of Change' speech in Cape Town. This indicated his government's wish to grant independence to many British territories, thus reversing the Conservative policy of 1951. In his speech he said: 'The wind of change is blowing through this continent. Whether we like it or not, this growth of national consciousness is a political fact.'

Macmillan hoped this would include South Africa, but he made it clear that there were aspects of the policies of Prime Minister Verwoerd (who took over in 1953) 'which make it impossible for us to do this without being false to our own deep convictions about the political destinies of free men to which in our own territories we are trying to give effect'. So South Africa formed a republic in 1961 and broke away from the Commonwealth, not returning until Nelson Mandela brought the country back in 1994, following the abandonment of Apartheid.

The Queen did not go abroad during 1960, due to the birth of Prince Andrew. She delegated all such visits to other members of her family.

The Queen's Visit to Ghana, 1961

The Queen had been due to pay Dr Kwame Nkrumah a visit in 1959, but had to postpone her visit due to the imminent birth of Prince Andrew. The visit was rescheduled for November 1961, not long after South Africa's withdrawal from the Commonwealth at the end of May. Ghana, formerly the Gold Coast, had been the first country in Africa to achieve independence on 6 March 1957 due to the persistence of Nkrumah, one-time leader of the youth movement and Prime Minister since 1952. As early as 1947 he had proclaimed that 'Complete and absolute independence for the peoples of West Africa is the only solution to the existing problems!'[10] Princess Marina presided over the independence ceremonies and Nkrumah became the first President.

In 1961 the political climate was turbulent. In October Nkrumah arrested fifty political opponents and threw them into gaol, and on 5 November there were explosions in Accra (thought to be an attempt by dissidents to have the Queen's visit cancelled). There were fears that Nkrumah might be shot and the British Cabinet discussed advising the Queen to cancel her visit. Special Branch men from the Metropolitan Police were sent out to work with the British Security Service. Macmillan conceded that the most dangerous points would be when the Queen was driving in remote areas of the countryside. He made the more general point that people did not realise how many risks there were wherever the Queen went.[11]

The Queen herself was consistently determined to go, concerned that Ghana might follow South Africa out of the Commonwealth. She told Macmillan: 'How silly I should look if I was scared to visit Ghana, and then Khrushchev went a few weeks later and had a good reception.'[12] Even so there were worries that Ghana might leave the Commonwealth immediately after the visit. Sir Winston Churchill was also concerned for the Queen's safety. Macmillan agreed but pointed out: 'I need hardly say that Her wish is to go. This is natural with so courageous a personality.'[13]

Duncan Sandys, the Commonwealth Secretary, was sent out to test the political temperature. He drove the ceremonial route in an open car with Nkrumah, facing no issues. Nkrumah confirmed to Macmillan on the telephone that he was not considering withdrawing Ghana from the Commonwealth.[14] On 8 November Lord Hailsham, the Lord President of the Council, told the Cabinet that 'It would be almost impossible for H.M. to remain Head of the Commonwealth if she withdrew from this.'[15] It was agreed that the Cabinet would not advise the Queen to cancel and on the same day the Prime Minister made his decision known in the House of Commons.

The Chief Whip warned Macmillan that there was a growing movement in the Conservative Party against the Queen going on grounds of her safety. The Labour Party might vote against it in a motion and be joined by at least eighty Conservatives, acting with the best intentions. Macmillan told the Queen there was a serious possibility that if he advised her to go but was defeated in a motion in the House of Commons he would have to offer his resignation. As he put it: 'She could refuse my resignation, and ask me to carry on. I could agree, but I could not alter my advice. So the Queen would leave, with a <u>hostile</u> vote from H of C, and <u>flouting</u> their advice.'[16]

The Queen flew out as planned on 9 November, leaving the Duke of Gloucester to lay her 1961 wreath on Remembrance Sunday. There were more rumours that Nkrumah might be shot, fears centring round a magnificent firework display in Accra. Audrey Russell, reporting for the BBC, recalled:

> The Royal and Presidential parties sat in a specially designed box, protected by bulletproof glass and illuminated with shaded lights making it look like a tropical fish tank ... The Queen sat beside Nkrumah looking astonishingly calm and relaxed. The President was voluble and flamboyant as usual.[17]

Nothing untoward happened. The Queen and the Duke attended more than one Durbar of Chiefs, visited the new port of Tema and the site of the dam for the Volta river project. At the President's state banquet there were empty places as some of the Ghanaian guests were languishing in gaol. The local press described the Queen as 'the greatest Socialist monarch in the world'.[18]

When the Queen was safely home, Macmillan tackled President John F. Kennedy over his financial backing of the Volta Dam Project. He told him: 'I have risked my Queen; you must risk your money!'[19] The USA duly invested. Macmillan later judged the Queen's visit to Ghana as the bravest thing she did:

> The Queen has been absolutely determined all through. She is grateful for MPs and Press concern about her safety, but she is impatient of the attitude towards her to treat her as a *woman*, and a film star or mascot. She has indeed 'the heart and stomach of a man'. She has great faith in the work she can do in the Commonwealth especially. If she were pressed too hard, and if Government and people here

are determined to restrict her activities (including taking reasonable risks) I think she might be tempted to throw in her hand. She does *not* enjoy 'society'. She likes her horses. But she loves her duty and means to be a Queen not a puppet.[20]

* * * * *

The Queen and the Duke paid a state visit to President Tubman of Liberia, and a popular visit to Sierra Leone, seeing the site of the new Guma Dam. After three days in Gambia, the Queen flew home and the Duke of Edinburgh piloted himself to Tanganyika to represent the Queen at the independence celebrations. Princess Margaret presided over celebrations in Jamaica in August 1962, the Princess Royal over celebrations in Trinidad in September and the Duke of Kent over celebrations in Uganda in October, a decision made personally by the Queen.[21] Uganda became a full member of the Commonwealth, though its later history proved tragic.

* * * * *

Macmillan sought to bring Britain into Europe. A key occasion was the state visit of President de Gaulle in April 1960. The President and his wife were in Britain between 5 and 8 April. As the President was travelling up the Mall in the open carriage with the Queen, he insisted on rising to his feet to salute his old wartime office at 4 Carlton Gardens. I saw this as a child, and in the Mall in 2003 I asked the Queen if my memory was correct. 'Yes,' she said, 'with me very much trying to persuade him not to.'[22]

The visit was the first public appearance of the Queen since Prince Andrew's birth. The Queen Mother summoned her circlet, with the Koh-I-Noor diamond inset, from the Tower of London to impress the President at the state banquet, and she wore all five strands of Mrs Ronald Greville's vast diamond necklace, bequeathed to her in 1942. Mindful of the splendid celebrations put on in Paris in 1957, the Queen arranged a magnificent fireworks display which the Royal Family and other guests watched from the balcony of the Palace after the state banquet.

De Gaulle had talks with Macmillan and others at Buckingham Palace on the subject of the Common Market, of which Britain was not then a member. Macmillan told him he was afraid 'the Six' might aggravate economic difficulties and split Europe. Nikita Khrushchev, the Russian leader, had been to a summit in Paris and was much discussed. De Gaulle gave his opinion of Khrushchev: 'a cunning, intelligent, self-made man. He knew the fundamentals of the matters under discussion very well, although he was not always meticulous as to detail ... He was not a Stalin ... the Soviet Union was now a powerful country in the world and ... Mr Khrushchev wished to play a big role in the world.'[23]

The General enjoyed his visit. On returning to Paris he drew the British Embassy representative, Michael Hadow, to him by the arm and told him: 'I should like you to know how grateful I am for the magnificent arrangements in England by your Government and for the wonderful reception I was given. Everybody from the Queen down – the Government, people in official positions, politicians to the people in the streets – showed marvellous friendship. It was, in truth, a very emotional experience.'[24]

★ ★ ★ ★ ★

1963 was a tumultuous year politically, famously highlighted in poetry by Philip Larkin in '*Annus Mirabilis*', about how sexual intercourse began in 1963, some time between the end of the ban on *Lady Chatterley's Lover* and the Beatles launching their first LP. The year opened with the death of Hugh Gaitskell, Leader of the Labour Party, then in opposition, on 18 January 1963. The new Leader was Harold Wilson.

This was a low point in the reign. When the Queen visited Birmingham University on 24 May to be received by Lord Avon as Chancellor, there were only small crowds and very little cheering. Sir Martin Charteris told Lady Avon: 'This happens now & they are quite resigned to it.' She noted: 'The Queen was of course as unsmiling as ever.'[25]

That summer the political arena was awash with scandal. John Profumo, the Secretary of State for War, had been having an affair with a call girl, Christine Keeler, who had also been peripherally involved with the Russian military attaché, Yevgeny Ivanov. It was not long before he was being doorstepped outside his house in Chester Terrace, denying that he was on the point of resignation. On 22 March he made a statement in the House of Commons: 'Miss Keeler and I were on friendly terms. There was no impropriety whatsoever in my acquaintanceship with Miss Keeler ... I shall not hesitate to issue writs for libel and slander if scandalous allegations are made or repeated outside the House.' He sat down to 'a round of Ministerial cheers'.[26] He was supported on television by the osteopath Dr Stephen Ward: 'It is a dreadful thing that a man should be put in the position of having to do this as a result of entirely baseless rumours and insinuations that have been started by the press.'[27]

However, the matter did not end there. *The Times* declared that Profumo should have made the denial sooner. Presently he sued *Paris Match* and then an Italian paper, *Tempo Illustrato*. The allegations did not go away. On 30 May the Avons lunched with the Queen Mother at Clarence House, a party given for the former US Ambassador John Hay Whitney. Clarissa Avon wrote: 'After waiting for hours before lunch, in came the Queen & Profumo, who had been at a Privy Council together – this was the day before the balloon went up & Val* was in black with some prescience.'[28]

On 4 June Profumo applied for the Chiltern Hundreds, thus resigning his seat in Parliament. In a letter to Macmillan, who was shooting in Argyll, he confessed that he had misled him, his colleagues and the House, and was guilty of a 'grave misdemeanour'.† Macmillan replied that in the circumstances he had no alternative but to advise the Queen to accept his resignation.[29] On 11 June Profumo asked to be excused an audience with the Queen to hand back his seals of office. She agreed. On 26 June, at his own request, he was struck

---

* Valerie Hobson (1917–98), Profumo's wife, a well-known film actress.

† Later in the year, a performance in New York was recorded and a record released called 'Fool Britannia', in which Peter Sellers, Anthony Newley and Joan Collins lampooned many aspects of the Profumo affair. Peter Sellers impersonated a speech by Macmillan in the House of Commons, in which he said that it had been a matter of great concern 'to learn that a minister in my cabinet had committed a grave Miss Keeler with misdemeanour'.

off the Privy Council. Harold Wilson arrived back from Canada and pressed for Macmillan to follow suit and resign.

As early as 1960 Macmillan had hinted that he might have to resign due to the pain in his leg. He was disappointed that the Queen did not react 'with the consternation he had expected'.[30] At Balmoral in September 1963 he told the Queen that he might step down before the next General Election. In October he suddenly suffered from what he was told was inflammation of the prostate gland, either malignant or benign. Though he realised that the swollen prostate was not cancerous, he viewed the situation as an act of God forcing his resignation. He underwent an operation on 10 October, following which he remained in the Edward VII Hospital.

On 17 October he dictated a memorandum for the Queen in case she asked for his advice about a successor. He was anxious that any advice given should be recorded to protect the later political reputations of the Queen and (naturally) himself. He then asked to see the Queen in the hospital and she arrived on the morning of 18 October. For the occasion he put on a white silk shirt and on top one of his old brown pullovers. He was wheeled into the downstairs boardroom, doctors and nurses hovering outside in case of emergencies.

The Queen arrived, accompanied by Sir Michael Adeane. Macmillan observed 'those brightly shining eyes which are her chief beauty' and that 'she seemed moved; so was I.' When he told her he could not go on, she asked: 'Have you any advice to give me?'[31] Macmillan handed over his memorandum, which recommended the Earl of Home as the man most likely to hold the Conservative Party together.[32] Here Macmillan pulled a fast one. In the car, on the way back to the Palace, Adeane pointed out that Macmillan was no longer her Prime Minister. But she was happy to accept Macmillan's advice – to send for Home immediately but to use the 'older formula and entrust him with the task of forming an administration. He could then take his soundings and report to her.'[33]

By this advice Rab Butler effectively lost his chance to be Prime Minister for the second and final time. Macmillan considered Butler indecisive and not good on television, though neither was Lord Home a natural television performer.* One who was not sorry to see Macmillan depart was the Countess of Avon, still smarting from his duplicitous advice over Suez. She wrote to Cecil Beaton: 'I must say I cdn't have wished a more squalid exit for a man I have always disliked & distrusted!'[34]

The Queen congratulated Macmillan on how he had worked so hard for Britain and the Commonwealth, citing the Nuclear Test Ban Treaty as a particular achievement, and referred to 'a number of problems' affecting her own family and thanked him for the 'unstinted care' he had taken in giving her advice 'and helping me to find solutions'.[35] She offered him the traditional Earldom and the Order of the Garter, but he declined both, only accepting an Earldom in extreme old age.

The Queen summoned Lord Home and gave him twenty-four hours to see if he could form an administration. There had been fears of a revolt but he soon mustered a new Cabinet. Under the Life Peerages Act of 1963 he renounced his hereditary title and entered the House of Commons as Sir Alec Douglas-Home. Ben Pimlott was told by courtiers that the Queen was entirely happy to have Home as her next Prime Minister. He was an old friend; they shared an interest in dogs and shooting. He had held the second sword – the Pointed Sword of Justice to the Spirituality – at her Coronation in 1953. Nevertheless, Home was something of an outsider, more so than Rab Butler, Lord Hailsham or Reginald Maudling.

He served as the Queen's fourth Prime Minister from October 1963 for all but a year. On 22 November, during his premiership, John F. Kennedy, 35th President of the United States, was assassinated in Dallas, Texas. Prince Philip represented the Queen at the state funeral in Washington. In December the Queen and the Queen Mother attended a memorial service for the late President at St George's Chapel, Windsor, held there because the Queen was pregnant with Prince Edward.†

---

* As a result Butler left politics and became Master of Trinity College, Cambridge. During his time there his wife Mollie never offered Macmillan hospitality at Master's Lodge.

† The Queen unveiled the John F. Kennedy memorial at Runnymede on 14 May

Sir Alec lost the General Election on 16 October 1964 by four seats. Like all her other prime ministers, he had found her 'always up to date and fully versed in the niceties of every national and international problem'.[36] Constitutionally Home could have stayed on until defeated in the Commons or he could have tried to form a coalition with another party, but being the man he was, he saw defeat as defeat and he resigned.

Harold Wilson then became the first Labour Prime Minister of the Queen's reign.

1965, on an acre of British land given to the United States in his memory. His little son John was there, his hands held by his mother Jackie on one side and by Prince Philip on the other.

22
THE FAMILY IN THE 1960s

Lord Mountbatten used to claim that the reason no children were born to the Queen and Prince Philip for ten years was because the House of Windsor had not become Mountbatten. This is not so. The Queen and Prince Philip longed for another child and were excited when their third son, Prince Andrew, was born at Buckingham Palace on 19 February 1960. He was the first child to be 'born in the purple' – born to a reigning monarch – since the birth of Queen Victoria's daughter Princess Beatrice in 1857. There was a wave of public excitement too at the birth of this next son, automatically second in line to the throne. To several people the Queen wrote that it was likely he would be very spoiled, as proved to be the case. His elder brother and sister were fascinated by the new arrival in the family.

A few days before his birth, the Queen announced, on 8 February, that those of her descendants who would normally have used the surname Windsor, would now be called Mountbatten-Windsor. Lord Mountbatten was the person keenly behind this and he hoped that in time the House of Windsor would be called the House of Mountbatten-Windsor. To this end he would hover over Princess Anne's wedding certificate when she married Captain Mark Phillips in 1973. He was gratified to find her named as 'Mountbatten-Windsor'. He noted: 'The great thing about this is that the ambiguity about the position of Charles, Andrew and Edward is now cleared up, for since Anne has been officially recognised as "Mountbatten-Windsor" in the Marriage Certificate, so will the three boys.'[1]

The matter was not resolved. There was no surname given in documents when Prince Charles married Lady Diana Spencer in 1981. By then Mountbatten was dead so he was not there to enforce it.*

---

* Mountbatten would have been pleased to find Lady Louise Mountbatten-Windsor,

THE FAMILY IN THE 1960S

Prince Edward completed the family when he appeared on 10 March 1964. The Queen was able to balance her role as monarch and mother better with the younger two arrivals. She was often to be seen at Windsor, with Prince Edward in his little blue coat, held by the hand.

Prince Charles endured Gordonstoun between 1962 and 1967, relishing the time he spent at Timbertops in Australia between February and July 1966, principally arranged by Prince Philip through the Australian Prime Minister, Robert Menzies. Sir Charles Johnston, who had been High Commissioner in Australia, met him at this time, 'now grown up into a well-mannered boy, modest but not shy, with his mother's sense of humour. I was telling him about the kookaburra or laughing jackass. "Oh, yes, I want to hear it. I'm told it laughs exactly like my Uncle Harry.*"'[2]

Prince Charles enjoyed Trinity College, Cambridge, sent there between October 1967 and June 1970, on the advice of Robin Woods, Dean of Windsor, Lord Mountbatten and others. He came down with a 2:2 degree. He studied Welsh and the history of the Principality at the University of Aberystwyth between April and July 1969. Having turned eighteen in November 1966, he was eligible to act as a Counsellor of State. On 17 June 1968, in the presence of a full complement of Knights of the Garter and many members of the Royal Family, the Queen invested and installed him as a Knight of the Garter, an honour he had held by right as Prince of Wales since 1958.

Princess Anne went to Benenden where, before she arrived, the headmistress was asked to lunch with the Queen and Prince Philip and the young princess. At the lunch the headmistress said: 'We don't encourage hippomania. To this Prince Philip pointed out that she was not talking about hippopotami.[3]

Prince Edward's daughter, so described when she was bridesmaid to Catherine Middleton in 2011. Prince Andrew took the surname of Mountbatten-Windsor when he lost his princely titles in 2025.

* His great-uncle, the Duke of Gloucester.

Princess Margaret

For some years the Armstrong-Jones marriage was a success forging a link between the Royal Family and the artistic and high Bohemian world bursting into life in the Swinging Sixties. When it went well, it was stimulating. They entertained artists and authors. Princess Margaret was good at being both formal and informal. If it was a dinner with distinguished guests, she would be served first. If a more Bohemian occasion, she joined in, with cigarette in long holder.

But Armstrong-Jones was reluctant to rise to the occasion and support her. As time went on and cracks appeared in the marriage, the situation deteriorated.

In 1961, just before the birth of their first child, the Queen conferred the Earldom of Snowdon on Armstrong-Jones, prompting Prince Philip to comment privately: 'After all, a man who has had fifteen months of Margaret, deserves absolutely everything he can get.'[4] David, Viscount Linley, was born at Clarence House on 3 November 1961, and their second child, Lady Sarah Armstrong-Jones at Kensington Palace, on 1 May 1964.

The general public and media were not critical, but society figures were. The Duchess of Buccleuch told Alan Pryce-Jones that the feeling against the Snowdons was strong, even among the Princess's allies. Her line was that she was behaving monstrously, taking endless holidays, and that he was useless. On one flight, they took over half of a Boeing and caused endless flight alterations to pick them up.[5] On the other hand, Lord Snowdon was creative and forever designing new things, from spectacles to wheelchairs, and in due course the aviary at the London Zoo.

As the marriage deteriorated, Snowdon's treatment of his wife was inconsiderate to the point of cruelty. They might leave a party together, get to the door in vision of the press cameras and he would turn on his heels and go back in, leaving her to face them alone. Frequently he humiliated her. There must have been times when she was very unhappy. Princess Margaret could be tiresome about trivial issues, but she was generous on the big ones. She was nicer than she thought she was.

★ ★ ★ ★ ★

Prince Philip saw the advantages of several generations in the Royal Family: 'It involves a whole family, which means that different age groups are part of it ... There are people who can look, for instance, at the Queen Mother and say they identify with that generation, or with us, or with the children.'6

His mother-in-law underwent an appendectomy on 4 February 1964. Ronald Bodley Scott* oversaw the operation, Lord Evans (the former Sir Horace Evans), having recommended him before dying in September 1963. More seriously, she survived an operation in December 1966, which kept her in hospital over Christmas and into January 1967.

The Queen's aunt, the Princess Royal, died at Harewood House, on 28 March 1965, aged sixty-seven. She had been a tireless support, both in Britain and overseas, though in increasingly poor health. She was last seen in public when she visited the Duke and Duchess of Windsor in the London Clinic ten days before her death. Her son wrote: 'Her death was enviable ... There was no apparent crisis and I had no idea that in the quarter of an hour, which intervened before the car came, she had died quite peacefully in my arms.'7 But this was not the version of events believed by the Queen. She believed that Lord Harewood had told her about his illegitimate son, perhaps also that his brother Gerald had also sired a boy out of wedlock,† and that the shock was too great.

---

* Sir Ronald Bodley Scott (1906–82) enjoyed literature, once writing an entertaining article for the *Lancet* on how doctors were portrayed in the novels he enjoyed. Martin Charteris judged him a sensitive, professionally competent and intelligent man with a good spice of humour. In 1964 he wrote: 'He made a rather sticky start with the Royals, who I suspect found it hard to forgive him for not being Horace [Lord Evans], but having managed Queen Elizabeth's appendix very well (by which I mean he handled Q.E. rather than her appendix) his stock has risen quite sharply.' (Martin Charteris to Countess of Avon, 17 March 1964, Clarissa Avon Papers, Birmingham University.) Lord Evans (1903–63) was one of London's great general physicians, a towering and impressive man, who stood slightly slouched and inspired considerable confidence in his patients; a first-class clinician, both affable and forthright.

† Lord Harewood claimed that his mother already knew about his son, and that her only reaction had been: 'What will people say?' It was clearly not something

Lord Harewood had produced an illegitimate son with Patricia Tuckwell, an Australian violinist, whom he had known since 1959. They had met at Milan Airport, begun to talk and, as Patricia said, they talked for the next fifty-two years. Marion, his first wife, refused to grant him a divorce so he and Patricia made the decision to have a baby. Mark Lascelles was born in 1964.

In 1967 the Harewoods divorced and he asked the Queen's permission to marry Patricia, which was given on 'formal advice' so that the Queen did not have to address the issue personally. Harewood was forced to step down as Director of the Edinburgh Festival, and it cost him the chance to be appointed Director of Covent Garden. He was then effectively banned from court for some years, not invited to the funeral of the Duke of Windsor in 1972, which he minded, or to Princess Anne's wedding in 1973, despite his generous gift to her of a diamond stock pin, which was displayed with the Royal Family's presents at St James's Palace.

The Queen led the Royal Family at the Princess Royal's funeral at Harewood House while the Duke and Duchess of Windsor attended the public memorial service held in Westminster Abbey on the same day, the first time they had appeared together at an official engagement in London.

Princess Marina was especially popular when travelling widely on behalf of the Queen in the 1950s and 1960s. In the summer of 1968 it was discovered that she was suffering from an inoperable brain tumour. She died peacefully at her home in Kensington Palace on 27 August 1968, the news causing shock waves across Britain. The Queen came down from Balmoral to attend her funeral at St George's Chapel with most of the British Royal Family, including the Duke of Windsor who flew over from Paris.

---

she had anticipated. Her younger son, the Hon. Gerald Lascelles (1924–98) had married a minor actress, Angela Dowding (1919–2007), in 1952. They lived at Fort Belvedere. In 1962 he had a son, Martin, with Elizabeth Colvin (1924–2006). After his divorce from Angela, he married Elizabeth in 1978. Martin kept up the family tradition by marrying and having a son, and producing a daughter out of wedlock. The Queen did not bother with Gerald after his divorce, but she housed Angela in a Virginia Water cottage and continued to invite her to the Royal Box at Ascot. She visited her new home and attended her funeral.

In the same summer the Duke of Gloucester's health collapsed. He lost the power of speech and was confined to Barnwell Manor, his Northamptonshire home where he died in 1974. In the early 1960s he had suffered several small strokes, not helped by the amount of alcohol he consumed. The Duchess worried when he was at the wheel of the car, ready to grab it if he fell asleep, a concerning prospect. She thought she had dozed off when, in 1965, he was driving her back to Barnwell after Churchill's funeral. The car overturned, somersaulted three times and ended upside down in a field of cabbages. As the Duchess wrote: 'Prince Henry had luckily been thrown through the open door into nettles and brambles as the car went over the ditch.'[8] The Duchess was badly injured, regaining consciousness to find two miners replacing her nose and saving her from choking on the blood pouring down her throat. While unconscious, she saw the Queen in black, carrying a baby.* When the Duke dropped out of public life, the Duchess balanced staying with him and undertaking her engagements as well as some of his commitments.

The Queen attended the Duke of Kent's wedding to Katharine Worsley, daughter of Sir William Worsley, Lord Lieutenant of the North Riding of Yorkshire, in York Minster on 8 June 1961. Though primarily a serving Army officer, the Duke was often needed for royal engagements. He was frequently overseas with his regiment, where the Duchess sometimes joined him.

Princess Alexandra had been undertaking royal engagements since the 1950s. On 24 April 1963 she married the Hon. Angus Ogilvy, younger son of the 12th Earl of Airlie and his wife Lady Bridget Coke. He was a businessman involved with the Drayton Group of Companies and came from a family of courtiers. His father was Lord Chamberlain to the Queen Mother, his uncle had been an equerry to the Duke of Windsor (as Prince of Wales) and his grandmother, Mabell, Countess of Airlie, had been a Lady of the Bedchamber to Queen Mary. He joked that as he could not get away from the Royal Family he had decided to join them.[9]

Her wedding was celebrated with a magnificent ball at Windsor Castle, the Long Walk was floodlit and the guests bidden to wear

---

* After the funeral lunch, the Queen had carried in the infant Prince Edward, born the previous March, to show him to the guests.

white tie and tiaras. The Duchess of Buccleuch's tiara was so magnificent that many of the foreign royalties curtseyed to her. The next day the Queen organised two large green charabancs to convey fifty-five royal guests to Syon House for tea with the Duke and Duchess of Northumberland. On arrival Prince Philip disappeared with the Syon guide book, assimilated it in half an hour and proceeded to catch the hosts out on many points of history. The Queen's much-repeated comment on the day was: 'We look like a Women's Institute excursion, don't we?'

A raft of diplomatic problems also surrounded the wedding, Harold Macmillan wanting it in Scotland, mainly for political reasons. Princess Alexandra had travelled widely, and wanted to invite every Head of State she had met. including the Emperor and Empress of Japan, who luckily declined. Harold Wilson, who had lately taken over as Leader of the Labour Party after Hugh Gaitskell's death, was not invited, on the grounds that she did not know him. saying she did not know him. She did invite the Attlees, the Morrisons of Lambeth and the widowed Mrs Gaitskell. Her Private Secretary, Sir Philip Hay, had to explain: 'Although he had tried to persuade his employers to change their minds about this, he felt in retrospect that he had not pressed the point sufficiently strongly.' After the wedding Sir Philip called on Mr Wilson 'to express regret that any embarrassment had been caused'.[10]

Princess Alexandra had two children, James Ogilvy in 1964 and Marina Ogilvy in 1966. James was one of the four royal babies born in quick succession in 1964 – James on 29 February, Prince Edward on 10 March, Lady Helen Windsor on 28 April and Lady Sarah Armstrong-Jones on 1 May.

The Duke and Duchess of Windsor did not greatly impinge on the Queen's life until he began to fail in health. Since the Abdication they had lived in Paris, spending part of the year in the United States. Relations with the Royal Family were not easy, though never as bad as portrayed in the press.

The Duke underwent a serious operation in Texas in the winter of 1964 for an aortic aneurysm. In February 1965 he suffered a detached retina and was flown to London for two operations in the London Clinic, performed by the Queen's doctor, Sir Stewart Duke-Elder. The Duchess visited the clinic every day. Harold Macmillan, by then in retirement, spoke to Lady Monckton, a close friend of the Windsors. He noted: 'The Royal Family have sent enquiries, but no more. Public opinion, without knowing the various difficulties, is becoming rather critical of the Queen. People feel that after 30 years there ought to be a "family reconciliation" and that she should visit her uncle – who is now 70 and might not live long.'[11] He spoke to Sir Michael Adeane and soon afterwards the Queen visited the Duke in the London Clinic.

Then, and on a subsequent visit to him at Claridge's, the Queen met the Duchess for the first time since before the Abdication (when she was only a little girl). She invited the Duke to take recuperative strolls in the gardens of Buckingham Palace, accompanied by his wife, so that they could get some fresh air without being bothered by photographers. When he was better, she flew them back to Paris in an aircraft of the Queen's Flight.

Thus there was an element of reconciliation. The Duke had asked for two things to happen when he went into voluntary exile. He wanted the title of HRH extended to his wife, and he wanted a formal meeting with the Royal Family (originally the King and Queen), which would be recorded in the Court Circular. The former was not granted but when the Queen was to unveil a memorial to Queen Mary in the wall of Marlborough House on her centenary in 1967, she postponed the ceremony until a date could be found that tied in with the Duke and Duchess's travel plans. The ceremony took place on 7 June. Thus the Windsors were publicly lined up with the Queen and the Royal Family and this was a further step towards easing any residual tensions. However, they were not mentioned in the Court Circular and the Queen did not entertain them privately. That was left to the Gloucesters one day and Princess Marina the next.

When the Queen wrote to him, she addressed him as 'Dear Uncle David' and signed off 'I hope you are both keeping well and with love and affectionate thoughts' or 'with love from your affectionate Lilibet'.[12] Sometimes they discussed money. She told him that if 'Wallis' (addressing the Duchess by her name) survived him, she would pay her a voluntary allowance of £5,000 a year.

A preoccupation of the Duke's was where they would be buried. As early as 1961 the funeral plans were settled. The Duke and the

Duchess were to have services in St George's Chapel. Among other matters, it was agreed that flags would fly at half-mast on government buildings on the day of the Duchess's death and on the day of her funeral.*

In 1964 they had chosen a 'charming isolated location' in a rhododendron glade in the grounds of Frogmore, based on an agreement with George VI that they could build a suitable monument there. The Duke stressed that he had spent many happy years at Frogmore as a boy. After Princess Marina's funeral, the Duke was struck by 'the charm and seclusion' of the family burial ground – 'that tranquil and peaceful corner of the Windsor estate'.[13] He discussed it with the Duchess and negotiated burial there through his lawyer, Sir Godfrey Morley, and Lord Tryon, Keeper of the Privy Purse. The Queen agreed and the Duke wrote to her to say: 'This has naturally pleased and comforted us very much.'[14] The Queen confirmed her ready agreement to the new plan.[15]

★ ★ ★ ★ ★

There was another figure to be reckoned with during the 1960s and the 1970s. Lord Mountbatten became an increasingly interfering presence in the life of the Queen and Prince Philip after his retirement from the Royal Navy. His diaries give ample evidence to his self-appointment as a kind of shop steward on behalf of the Queen in various negotiations. On his retirement in July 1965, to his intense delight she gave him the Order of Merit, which was in her personal gift.† Later that month he arranged that she should install him as Governor of the Isle of Wight, giving her the chance to see Osborne House (he thought for the first time) and causing the gate to Carisbrooke Castle to be removed so that her car could get in. He was often in *Britannia* with the Queen and the Duke, the Queen finding it easier to give in and let him come than stave him off.

---

* This caused no surprise in any quarter, which is interesting, considering the fuss blown up in the media over the flag at Buckingham Palace when Diana, Princess of Wales, died a decade later.

† There was some fear that he hoped to be made a Field Marshal and Marshal of the RAF.

He was frequently at Sandringham and the other royal residences and he took a considerable interest in Prince Charles. If the young Prince believed he failed to gain any approbation from his parents, he got plenty of caring attention from the Queen Mother (with whom he enjoyed a lifelong bond) and more robust advice from Mountbatten (not all of it constructive).

Lord Mountbatten used to visit his sister, Princess Andrew of Greece, who had been living at Buckingham Palace since 1967. She would say that he only came in order to write letters on Buckingham Palace writing paper. After a difficult and peripatetic life, she had been based in Athens since 1938. She was still there in the 1960s, when the political situation became serious, and there was justified fear that King Constantine might have to leave the country in a hurry. Princess Andrew was profoundly deaf so it would not be possible to warn her on the telephone, or have room for her in the plane. Therefore her daughter Sophie visited her and issued an invitation from the Queen to come and live at Buckingham Palace. 'Lilibet said that? We go this afternoon.' Next time King Constantine's plane was being refitted, she was flown to London.

She occupied rooms overlooking the Mall, and bonded in her later years with Princess Anne. The Queen was good to her and often dined with her when she was alone at the Palace. It was harder for Prince Philip whose relationship with his mother had been less than close. He had lost her for so many crucial years in his youth, since she had been out of his life from 1930 to 1937, when he was between the ages of nine and sixteen. She died at the Palace on 5 December 1969.

Princess Andrew was laid to rest in the Royal Vault of St George's Chapel, Windsor, where her body remained until 1988. It was then conveyed to Jerusalem and placed in a crypt under the Russian Orthodox Church on the Mount of Olives, near where her aunt Ella's coffin rests. In 1994 she was awarded a posthumous Yad Vashem for saving members of the Cohen family in 1943 at considerable danger to herself.

When Princess Alice announced that she wanted to be buried there, Prince Philip said it would be difficult to visit her. She replied: 'Nonsense. There's a perfectly good bus service.'[16] But it was difficult for political reasons. Prince Philip and his sister Sophie were able to visit the crypt where Princess Alice's coffin lay at the time of Yad Vashem in 1994. Prince William visited in June 2018 and Prince Charles saw it in January 2020.

23
DIPLOMACY, 1960–9

In January 1961 the Queen and the Duke of Edinburgh flew to India, Pakistan, Nepal and Iran, visiting Archbishop Makarios in Cyprus on the way. They spent twelve days in India, sixteen in Pakistan, then a further eleven in India. Then came the state visit to King Mahendra in Nepal, after which there was the state visit to the Shah of Iran. Vijaya Lakshmi Pandit, the High Commissioner, said that the Queen did not come as 'an Imperial ruler but as the honoured guest of two independent nations – India and Pakistan'.

It was fifty years since the Delhi Durbar of George V, yet the days of Imperial splendour were never far away. When the Queen visited Benares (now Vaaranasi), she was seated in a splendid chair on top of an elephant in a procession to the River Ganges. Prince Philip caused controversy by shooting a medium-size man-eating male tiger in Jaipur. Diplomatically he claimed a whitlow (painful infection) on his trigger finger, so that he was unable to take part in a further tiger hunt in Nepal.

In Pakistan a million people thronged newly laid roads along the eleven-mile route from the airport to the President's House. The Queen stood in an open car next to President Ayub Khan. She drove herself in an open pony-trap to a picnic by the lake in the grounds of Government House. There was a reception for a thousand guests in a specially roofed forecourt in Lahore, at which she appeared on a balcony under an illuminated EIIR 'overlooking a sea of upturned faces, and was greeted with thunderous applause'.[1] During the visit, Tenzing Norgay, conqueror of Everest, was presented to the Queen.

Soon after her arrival, the Queen left for Peshawar and Karachi, Ayub Khan having vetoed the visit to Quetta, near the Afghanistan border, due to extreme bad weather. The High Commissioner wrote:

Her Majesty was very distressed at the prospect of having to disappoint the people who had been expecting Her in Quetta. Immediately after arrival in Peshawar therefore we sat down with the Private Secretaries at The Queen's request, to see if it were possible to enable Her to pay a brief visit on the following day, Sunday. This was done by postponing the visit to the Warsak Dam until this afternoon and sacrificing Sunday as a day of rest so far as The Queen and Her Party were concerned.

It was very striking how much the prospect of being able after all to discharge Her obligations to Quetta cheered The Queen. She has been so obviously happy since Her arrival here that it has been a real tonic to everyone.

When they got there every male in the area was lining the route clutching Union flags in frozen fingers. That story had a nice conclusion:

The Captain of the Queen's flight had decided that we had time in hand for the flight to Dacca. He therefore arranged at short notice that we should fly eastward along the white wintry wastes of the Himalayan mountains, among many others, the lofty peaks of Annapurna, Everest and Kanchenjunga at an intimate distance. We were flown three times round Everest's majestic summit where it stood resplendent above the clouds and we lunched on sole meunière within nodding distance of the spot from which Hillary and Tenzing began their final assault on that lonely promontory of bare rock. It was an unforgettable experience. And so to Dacca.[2]

Presently they returned to India for the second part of their visit. The High Commissioner concluded that 'The whole thing has been an unforgettable experience and there is a great deal of scratching of heads – Indian, British and third party – in the attempt to discover why it should all be so.'[3]

They flew to Nepal and on to Iran for the first ever state visit by a British monarch. The Queen visited Isfahan, Shiraz and the ruins at Persepolis, accompanied throughout by Lord Home, the Foreign Secretary. The Government wanted him there to temper the Shah's anxiety about the attitude of the Americans to his regime, essentially to 'steady the Shah in the face of Soviet pressure'.[4]

In May the Queen paid the first visit to Italy of a British monarch since 1923. They arrived in Naples in *Britannia*. They were received by President and Signora Gronchi and attended a gala performance of Verdi's *Falstaff*. More enjoyable for the Queen was a visit to the Italian Derby. They were received in the Vatican by Pope John XXIII. When, in 1962, Geoffrey Fisher was about to become the first Archbishop of Canterbury to visit the Pope since the sixteenth century, the Queen wrote to him: 'There seems to be a strongly deep-rooted distrust of the Roman Church in this country and I hope you won't get as many angry, pleading, hurt, or merely how *could* you do such a thing letters as I got last year before I went to the Vatican! It was quite a worry at the time.'[5]

They spent a day sightseeing in Venice, which Prince Philip knew well from earlier visits to his aunt, Princess Aspasia, on the Giudecca. They also visited Florence, Milan and Turin.

★ ★ ★ ★ ★

On 5 June 1961 the Queen entertained President and Mrs John F. Kennedy to dinner at Buckingham Palace.* This came about because they were attending the christening of a child of Jackie's sister, Princess Lee Radziwill. The Duchess of Gloucester was horrified: 'The poor Queen was terribly annoyed at having to invite some dreadful people called ... What is their name ... Oh, RADZIWILL.'[6] She had never heard of the family.

At the end of January 1963 the Queen and the Duke visited New Zealand and Tasmania and undertook a five-week, six-thousand-mile tour of Australia, their first return since 1954. Robert Menzies expressed his devotion in a speech for which he is remembered (not always charitably):

> You today begin your journey around Australia ... You will be seen in the next few weeks by hundreds of thousands and, I hope, by millions of your Australian subjects. Mothers will hold their children up to have a look at you as you go by, and they themselves, and

---

* When in 2011 the Queen hosted a state visit from President Obama, it is interesting to note that he was born in August 1961, some weeks after the Kennedy dinner.

their husbands will have a look at you as you go by. This must be to you now something that is almost a task. All I ask you to remember, in this country of yours, is that every man, woman and child who even sees you with a passing glimpse as you go by, will remember it with joy, remember it in the words of the old seventeenth-century poet who wrote those famous words: 'I did but see her passing by. And yet I love her till I die.'[7]

On 1 July the Queen installed Menzies as a Knight of the Thistle, the honour he chose in preference to the Garter.*

The state visit of King Paul of Greece and Queen Frederika in July 1963 was particularly controversial. The King and Prince Philip were first cousins, so a Greek state visit had been planned as long ago as 1953, but the Cyprus question intervened. In 1955 there was a falling-out between Anthony Eden and Alexandros Papagos, the Greek Prime Minister so no visit took place. By 1963 Greece was Britain's ally in NATO and a signatory to the Cyprus agreement.

The visit was overshadowed by the Ambatielos saga. A number of political prisoners had been detained in Greece for some years, which was judged a grave infringement of civil liberties. Antonis (Tony) Ambatielos, a prominent Greek Communist and seafarer, had been imprisoned during the Greek Civil War in 1945 and was still locked up. His wife, Betty, a Yorkshire-born Communist, was particularly hostile to Queen Frederika because she was the Kaiser's granddaughter and had briefly belonged to Hitler Youth.

When Queen Frederika was in London for Princess Alexandra's wedding in April 1963, protesters gathered outside Claridge's. She and her younger daughter, Princess Irene, slipped out through the Davies Street door, where Mrs Ambatielos tried to press a petition on her. There was a scuffle, during which the Queen and the Princess took sanctuary in the mews house of Marti Stevens,† the American nightclub singer, who revived them with Scotch whisky.

---

* 'I loved seeing old Bob being so honoured,' wrote the Duchess of Buccleuch (6 July 1963). Menzies remained in office until 1966 and in retirement succeeded Sir Winston Churchill as Lord Warden of the Cinque Ports.

† Marti Stevens (b. 1933), actress, singer and one-time close friend of Marlene Dietrich.

The Greek Government advised Queen Frederika to go home. She made the Queen laugh by saying she would only do so if the Queen threw a tomato at her! But Queen Frederika did object to the House of Commons being told that Mrs Ambatielos had not actually touched her. The King agreed that no state visit could take place until this was corrected.⁸

However, the King and Queen arrived in London as planned on 9 July 1963. For three days the city was a mass of marauding demonstrators waving placards, hissing and booing. There were ninety-four arrests on the first day. Mrs Ambatielos was detained when she stepped into the roadway near the Victoria Palace Theatre crying: 'Release my husband.'⁹ Five thousand extra police were drafted in. Bertrand Russell, ever contentious, led demonstrators outside Buckingham Palace while the state banquet was in progress and there were ugly scenes outside the Aldwych Theatre when the Queen took her royal guests to a performance of *A Midsummer Night's Dream*. The crowd chanted, '*Sieg Heil!*' and booed not only the Greek King and Queen but the British Royal Family too.

Harold Wilson, then Leader of the Labour Party, boycotted both banquets, but at a luncheon at the Guildhall the King of Greece politely thanked the British people for 'the most impressive display, which brushed aside every minor attempt by irresponsible people to cause misunderstanding between our two peoples'.¹⁰

Queen Frederika's view was that the media should have concentrated on the hundred thousand happy people, not the five hundred protesting.¹¹ In her memoirs she recalled the King's speech in the Guildhall: 'I could see by their faces that the audience was moved as there were tears running down several cheeks.'¹² Our Queen sent a message to the King of Greece: 'It is my heartfelt prayer that our countries may draw ever closer together in the years ahead and that the longstanding friendship between our peoples may continue to flourish.*'¹³

Soon after this visit, King Paul of Greece fell ill with stomach cancer and died on 6 March 1964. His death virtually coincided with the

---

* Panagiotis (Takis) Pipinelis, incoming Greek Prime Minister (between June and September 1963), agreed to see Mrs Ambatielos as a result of which seventeen prisoners were freed (though not her husband). He was released the following year.

birth of Prince Edward on 10 March, but the Duke of Edinburgh was able to fly out for the funeral, as did Princess Marina, the King's first cousin.*

The new King was Paul's son, Constantine, born in 1940. He had won a gold medal sailing in the Rome Olympic Games of 1960. On 18 September he had married Princess Anne-Marie of Denmark, second daughter of King Frederik IX and Queen Ingrid of Denmark. Prince Philip, Prince Charles and Princess Anne flew out to Athens for the celebrations. Despite his good looks and athletic prowess, the new King did not hold his throne for long. Following the Colonels' Coup in 1967 he was driven out of Athens remaining as *de jure* Head of State until a republic was declared in June 1973. For many years King Constantine and Queen Anne-Marie lived in London.

★ ★ ★ ★ ★

More countries became independent. The Duke of Edinburgh represented the Queen at independence celebrations in Zanzibar and Kenya. Arriving in Nairobi he asked President Jomo Kenyatta: 'Are you sure you don't want to change your mind?'[14] In 1964 he presided over the independence celebrations of Malawi and Malta, which became a republic in 1974. In 1966, the Duke of Kent represented the Queen at independence ceremonies in Gambia, Guyana and Barbados and Princess Marina represented the Queen at similar celebrations when Bechuanaland became Botswana on 30 September 1966.

In October 1964 the Queen and the Duke of Edinburgh visited Canada. This visit was controversial from the moment it was announced, malcontents in Quebec stirring up resentment and Dr Marcel Chaput, leader of the Quebec Republican Party, declaring that some of his people would let the Queen know 'and brutally – that she is no longer welcome in French Canada'.[15] Security was tightened when an eighteen-year-old, fresh out of gaol, announced

---

* Princess Marina and Princess Olga (in particular) complained that their wreaths were not visible and had cost an outrageous £53 each. When King Paul fell ill, a percipient Greek bought up all the laurel in Athens, selling it at exaggerated prices and making a quick turn.

that the Front de Libération Québécois was planning an attempt on the Queen's life. The British press fanned the flames with 'outpourings of gratuitous advice and sensational forebodings, which were deeply resented by responsible Canadians'.[16]

The Queen arrived in an atmosphere of 'threats and tension', and presently gave a speech that showed 'inspiration and perspective', saying in French that a 'dynamic State should not fear to reassess its political philosophy'. She conceded that it was not surprising that 'an agreement worked out 100 years ago does not necessarily meet all the needs of the present'.[17]

The speech was well received but the populace in Quebec City were less welcoming. Though only a small minority caused the problems, boos were heard over the cheers, and the police were rough in handling demonstrators. The weather was dismal. In conclusion, the tour had 'undoubtedly given rise to more controversy and anxiety, in Canada and Britain, than any before it'. There was a sense of relief that the Queen returned home safely and the Canadians were 'deeply affected by the way she bore herself'.[18] On her return, the Queen wrote to her Prime Minister, Sir Alec Douglas-Home: 'I only hope the visit may have done more good than harm.'[19]

★ ★ ★ ★ ★

On 1 February 1965 the Queen and the Duke of Edinburgh flew to Addis Ababa for their state visit to Emperor Haile Selassie of Ethiopia, returning his visit of 1954. By this time the Emperor had pulled Ethiopia out of the Middle Ages but it was still centuries behind the developed world. Physically small, he radiated magnetism and power. The journalist Michela Wrong described him as looking like a stunted teenager: 'With his predilection for sweeping military capes and oversized pith helmets, the effect could be downright comic – from a distance, it looked as though a wilful child had been let loose on his father's wardrobe.'[20]

When the Duke and Duchess of Gloucester visited him in 1958, the Duke was surprised to find something large sniffing at his heels while inspecting a Guard of Honour – a lion, but fortunately a well-fed pet of the Emperor. The Gloucesters' maid and valet went shopping in the bazaar, but as the Duchess put it, in her laconic style: 'They met two corpses hanging from gibbets, which rather put them off, and they returned hurriedly.'[21]

It took Sir John Russell, the British Ambassador, six months to arrange the visit. On the reconnoitre, Lees Mayall, on the Ambassador's staff, selected a particularly frisky horse 'not quite right in the head' for the Crown Equerry, John Miller. After a few bucks, Miller soon had it under control. It was not a candidate for the Queen.[22]

The biggest problem was the Queen's return state banquet. The Ambassador could only seat twenty-eight people, which meant nineteen Ethiopians. The Minister of Court sent him a list of fifty-eight. He contemplated inviting forty for coffee before the after-dinner reception, but realised that this would include figures such as the Minister for Foreign Affairs, the Lord Mayor and six or eight members of the Imperial Family. He brought in more tables and seated sixty guests.

The Ethiopian Court announced they wanted decorations given to fourteen members of the Imperial Family, twenty-three Cabinet Ministers and twenty members of the Palace staff. The Ambassador made clear that decorations would be given only to 'people who have some visible connexion with the visit and we cannot possibly cater for the entire Imperial Family and the entire Cabinet'.[23] There was discussion about the seating at banquets, the court wanting thrones for the principal royal guests. Sir John stated: 'We are trying to devise a compromise between the democratic habits of Buckingham Palace and the Imperial Judaic survivals which obtain here.'[24]

The visit was colourful and a success, despite a Volkswagen hurtling over the edge of a precipice, the driver being killed by the steering wheel crushing his chest. The Queen was happy because the Ambassador made sure that she could ride every morning before the official engagements began.* And the Emperor

---

* The later fate of the Emperor was less happy. He continued to be a world presence for some years. He came to Windsor to attend the 1972 Garter Ceremony, walking with the Queen Mother. But two years later he was thrown from power. Suffering from approaching Alzheimer's, he lost his grip. Famine was rife in Ethiopia and presently the Army mutinied.

On 12 September 1974 he was seized and taken from his Palace. He was held staged a war game in Addis Ababa with Galla horsemen.

Sudan had been a dictatorship under President Ferik Ibrahim Abboud, and though he had resigned in 1964, many were against the Queen visiting, including the Labour Foreign Secretary, Michael Stewart. Two new points emerged – Britain should not desert the Sudanese when they were in trouble, and the Ambassador thought the Queen was likely to get a better welcome than she might have done under the military regime.[25] The Palace did not want to go back on their word. The visit passed off well.

Germany

The state visit to President Heinrich Lübke in May 1965 was an important act of reconciliation – 'A Fairy Tale in our Sombre Times'.[26] Sir Frank Roberts, the British Ambassador in Berlin since 1963, had long been concerned that the Queen had paid state visits almost everywhere but not to the German Federal Republic. Rab Butler agreed, but the visit did not take place until 1965.

Sir Michael Adeane was anxious that a public statement should be made 'to counter possible suggestions' that the Royal Family were going to Germany because of private family ties and relationships.[27] When the King of Greece had visited, many of Queen Frederika's German relations had been invited to dinners but placed below minor politicians. Prince Philip told the Ambassador to tell the President that the Queen would not mind if her relatives were not invited to such occasions.

President Lübke said it was traditional that if a girl of the country came back after even many years her relatives should be invited to meet her. Sir Frank found himself 'between the hammer of Prince Philip and the anvil of President Lübke'.[28] The matter was resolved

---

prisoner for nearly a year and murdered by his captors on 27 August 1975. An attendant saw his body lying on his bed, almost certainly strangled: 'There was a smell of ether in the air and His Majesty was not lying in his usual position ... The shawl that he wrapped himself in when he went to sleep was lying in another part of the room. His face was ghastly and there was a bandage around his neck.' (Michela Wrong, *I Didn't Do It For You* (Fourth Estate, 2005), p. 245).

by the wise suggestion of Prince Ludwig of Hesse that members of German Royal Houses should only be invited when the Queen visited their part of Germany – the Hohenzollerns in Berlin, the Hanovers in Hanover. The Queen was able to dine at Wolfsgarten with the Hessens and at Langenburg with Prince Philip's sister, Princess Margarita, and to stay for a weekend at Salem with his other sister, Theodora, Margravine of Baden.

It was a long visit. The Germans produced a special train to convey the Queen about the country. She arrived in Bonn and attended a state banquet at the Palace of Brühl. She sailed up the Rhine, visited Darmstadt and Munich, Stuttgart and Marbach, saw the bombed, but now restored cathedral in Cologne, drove beside the Berlin Wall and entertained President Lübke and Dr Ludwig Erhard, the German Chancellor, in *Britannia*. The Queen made a great many speeches. The Embassy tripped up at Koblenz, introducing a passing reference to Marshal Blücher having crossed the Rhine to join Wellington, which upset the French.

Sir Frank Roberts was determined that the state visit should be reported properly on British television at a time when there was a diet of films showing British prisoners escaping from the Nazis. He was keen to show 'that the new German democracy had nothing in common with Hitler's Third Reich'.[29]

The press reception was excellent, especially in Germany, where there was talk of 'The State Visit of the Century', 'Munich Jubilant – it shook the Alps', 'Have we got Queen-mania?' and even 'Let's bury our Blasted Past'. For eleven days the visit was the only topic of conversation. As ever the Queen was conciliatory: 'In the last twenty years the problems facing our two peoples in Europe have brought us together again after two world wars in which your country and mine stood on opposite sides. This tragic period in our relations is happily over.'[30]

Sir Frank Roberts judged that the state visit had established 'a sure foundation for Anglo-German bilateral relations'.[31] Prince Philip's mother, Princess Andrew of Greece, was delighted. She congratulated him on his informal visits to Germany to shoot and for yachting: 'Every visit of yours here strengthens the ties between two countries...'[32]

Rhodesia

Like many African countries, Rhodesia was heading to independence, but since the collapse of the Rhodesian Federation, it had become somewhat isolated. The British felt it should be a slow process since the situation was still too segregated. When Ian Smith took over as Prime Minister, he wanted to rush matters forward with a Unilateral Declaration of Independence, which the British made clear would be illegal.

Harold Wilson went to Balmoral to ask the Queen if he could send Lord Mountbatten, lately Chief of the Defence Staff, out there as Governor. For once Mountbatten did not accept. Wilson persuaded the Queen to write a personal letter to Ian Smith, so that he could deliver it in person:

Dear Mr Smith,

I have followed the recent discussions between the British Government and your Government with the closest concern and I am very glad to know that Mr Wilson will be paying you a visit.

I earnestly hope that your discussions will succeed in finding a solution to the current difficulties.

I cherish happy memories of my own visit to Rhodesia.

I should be glad if you would accept my good wishes and convey them to all my peoples in your country whose welfare and happiness I have very closely at heart.

    Yours sincerely

        Elizabeth R[33]

Later the Queen told the Rhodesian people that she was confident they would continue to demonstrate their loyalty by acting in a constitutional manner. Some of the Queen's advisers thought this intervention undermined the monarch's essentially passive and symbolic role, and that the failure of such a direct appeal could result in serious loss of face for the Queen.

Rhodesia declared UDI on 11 November. In December the Queen appointed the Governor, Sir Humphrey Gibbs, KCVO, an honour in her personal gift. The Rhodesian situation remained a problem until independence was finally granted under Margaret Thatcher's government in 1980, after which it became Zimbabwe.

The Queen's Caribbean Tour

It was only *Britannia* that made possible a five-week voyage round the Caribbean. The Queen and the Duke started in British Guiana, visiting Trinidad, Tobago, Grenada, St Vincent, Barbados, St Lucia, Dominica, Montserrat, Antigua, St Kitts and Nevis, Tortola, Turks and Caicos Isles, the Bahamas and finally Jamaica. The Queen saw parts of the Commonwealth where poverty was rife but gaiety and spirits were high. On a one-day visit to Dominica she was able to discuss the Tranby Croft saga with the writer Elma Napier, daughter of Sir William Gordon-Cumming.

Tortola was hot. Dr Robin Tattersall* had the only air-conditioned room on the island, at his hospital. It was thought the Queen might welcome twenty minutes in that room. Unfortunately, the night before, Dr Tattersall had operated on a hopeless case, and the man had died. The only place to put the body was in a cupboard in that air-conditioned room. The Queen was kept in ignorance of this at the time, but in 1973 the doctor met Prince Charles on the British Virgin Islands and he could not wait to tell his mother on his return home.[34] The visit took place in broiling sun under the relentless gaze of journalists. When Prince Philip called the perpetual press retinue a bunch of mosquitoes, he was forced to issue an apology.

In Jamaica the Queen and the Duke were welcomed to the University of the West Indies by its Chancellor, Princess Alice, Countess of Athlone,† the Queen's eighty-three-year old great-aunt, who habitually wintered there. In Barbados they lunched with the Earl and Countess of Avon at Villa Nova.

In Barbados they lunched with the Earl and Countess of Avon at Villa Nova, and the Queen caught up with her cousin, Gerald Lascelles, on 15 February, when she visited the Belle Plantation

---

* Dr Robin Tattersall, OBE (b. 1930), a distinguished plastic surgeon and Olympic yachtsman. He posed with Suzy Parker for Richard Avedon. He settled in the British Virgin Islands in 1965.

† Princess Alice was Chancellor of the University of the West Indies, and the author Phyllis Shand Allfrey (1908–86) represented Dominica in the Federal Parliament of the Federation of the West Indies. Between them they controlled the education of much of the Caribbean. Neither had been to school.

Factory House to see sugar being processed. The Lascelles family owned it between 1780 and 1970.

The tour was not without reminders of the difficulties of these countries and islands. The Leeward and Windward Islands were keenly debating their future status with Britain. British Guiana was in a state of emergency with thirteen thousand British troops keeping order. In Barbados demonstrators waved red Communist flags with black swastikas. Many resented the Commonwealth Immigrants' Act, and some wanted independence but were not rich enough. The British Government offered some the status of 'non-colonials' with full British aid and protection. Roger Elliot, covering the tour, noted:

> Twenty years ago, when the Queen made her first overseas trip with her father King George to the Union of South Africa, the British Dominions and Empire included a quarter of the world's population, who were mostly ruled by Westminster. Today, the Commonwealth of Nations is only a trifle smaller ... but only a handful of territories like the small Caribbean islands are not yet independent, and they soon will be. Tensions have arisen between members like India and Pakistan; other independent states in Africa have suffered devastating coups; republicanism is abroad. The monarchy, in other words, is no longer held in such awe, partly because Britain no longer holds the same international role.[35]

Afterwards the Duke of Edinburgh went on an eleven-day tour of the United States. Elliot commented: '[This] is frankly a salesman's visit, organised by British industry and presented by an American public-relations firm.'[36] Prince Philip bridled. In New York he told his audiences that he had not come to sell socks. His approach worked well. Sales went up by about 35 per cent everywhere he went, and he raised more than a million dollars for the Variety Club of Great Britain's charities.[37]

★ ★ ★ ★ ★

The rest of the 1960s were likewise filled with state visits. Among these, King Hussein of Jordan and his then wife, Princess Muna, came to London in July 1966. Watching the Lord Steward and the

Lord Chamberlain walking in backwards, Sir Charles Johnston, who had been Ambassador in Jordan, found the banquet 'strangely impressive – and at this difficult and humiliating time in our affairs, soothingly evocative of the days when London was the centre of client monarchies'. The Queen wanted to talk to him:

> The Queen told me of a misunderstanding between her and Pss. M. [Muna] at dinner. Talking of political murders in the Middle East, the Q. had said they were so pointless. Pss. M. had said, that on the contrary, her husband's murder would have a great deal of point as then the whole regime would collapse. So the Q. had to explain that she didn't mean that it didn't <u>matter</u> ... The story told in the Q's distinctive style, like a frightfully grand Jane Austen – the irony, the piercing perception, the overstatement, not all that far removed from heartlessness.[38]

Earlier that month the Queen and Prince Philip had been to Northern Ireland. The two-day visit was marred by ugly incidents caused by Protestant factions in Ulster. While she got a tumultuous welcome in Belfast, a woman threw a beer bottle, which narrowly missed her Rolls-Royce, and a concrete slab, thrown from a fourth-floor window, crashed onto the bonnet of the car. A man and a woman were arrested in connection with the incidents.

In 1969 Windsor Castle hosted a state visit for the first time in the reign. President Giuseppe Saragat of Italy and his wife processed through the streets of Windsor in April. This was a popular development. Whereas Londoners resented state visits due to traffic jams, Windsorians loved them. It meant something exciting was happening.

24
HOME POLITICS, 1965–6

The death of Sir Winston Churchill on 24 January 1965 had been expected for ten days, yet people remembered where they were when they heard the news.* The Queen had stayed in touch with her first Prime Minister and was always solicitous of him. In 1957, when he was in indifferent health, Sir Michael Adeane wrote to him to excuse him from appearing at the Cenotaph on Remembrance Sunday, saying that the Queen did not wish him 'to take the smallest risk' to his health 'by prolonged exposure to November weather'.[1] He felt able to attend.

He had reached his ninetieth birthday on 30 November 1964 and appeared briefly at the window of his London home. During his last days following a massive stroke, the Queen attended Sunday matins at St Lawrence's Church, Castle Rising, in Norfolk where prayers were said for him. He died a week later.

Operation Hope-not had long been planned. The Queen commanded a state funeral. Sir Winston's coffin lay in state in Westminster Hall. His body was conveyed from Westminster to St Paul's Cathedral on a gun-carriage on Saturday, 30 January. It was a break with tradition that the Queen attended the funeral with most of the Royal Family, including the young Prince of Wales. Distinguished pall-bearers included former war leaders such as Lord Portal of

---

* For me it was a Sunday morning and I was waiting by a telephone box at Eton to ring home. The sermon in Lower Chapel was delivered by the Rev. R. D. F. Wild, who had been a prisoner of war. I was taken out of school by my parents, and my aunt, a Member of Parliament, slipped us into Westminster Hall, without queuing. There was an impressive stillness as mourners filed by the catafalque, the coffin covered with a Union flag, Sir Winston's Garter resting on a dark-blue velvet cushion.

Hungerford and Lord Montgomery of Alamein and politicians such as Lord Avon, Lord Attlee and Harold Macmillan. Trumpeters sounded the Last Post and Reveille and the coffin was borne uneasily down the aisle (one of the bearers had a twisted ankle). The former US President Dwight Eisenhower and the Australian Prime Minister, Robert Menzies, spoke on the BBC commentary.

After the service Sir Winston's coffin was taken to Tower Pier for the river journey upstream in *Havengore* to Festival Pier for the train journey to Oxfordshire.* He was laid to rest next to his father in Bladon churchyard, with his birthplace, Blenheim Palace, in distant view. The words on the Queen's wreath were written in her own hand: 'From the Nation and the Commonwealth. In grateful remembrance. Elizabeth R.'†2

The image of the Queen on the steps of St Paul's was a pivotal moment in the nation's history. Behind her were the Queen Mother, almost the entire British Royal Family, plus the Kings of Norway, Denmark and Greece, Queen Juliana of the Netherlands, representing countries that had suffered in the travails of the Second World War. President de Gaulle's head was held high among them. The heralds in their tabards lined the steps. The Queen was only thirty-eight, but she was confident in her role, an assured and respected Head of State in her own right. She was bidding farewell to her first Prime Minister and to the man who had served her father during the dark days of the war. Had he lived, the King would have been sixty-nine. He could have lived to stand there. This was one of many occasions when his daughter proved herself his worthy successor.

---

* The Duke of Norfolk, in charge as Earl Marshal, later revealed that the river procession would not have been possible a week earlier, due to the tidal conditions in the Thames. To this day *Havengore* bears a plaque stating: 'Not even *Golden Hind* had borne so great a man.' In September the Queen attended the twenty-fifth anniversary service for the Battle of Britain in Westminster Abbey and unveiled a large memorial stone to Sir Winston in the nave.

† In 2005 the Queen gave the Order of the Garter to Churchill's daughter, Lady Soames. She told her that she was giving her the same Garter collar as worn by her father. Mary Soames said that that could not be so as the collar was displayed at Chartwell. The Queen had known that and had arranged to have it exchanged, an example of her thoughtful attention to detail.

The following year the Queen turned forty – time for the journalists to assess her first fourteen years at the helm. Douglas Brown left a memorably perceptive description of her 'level gaze, so calm in its consciousness of duty fulfilled'.³

★ ★ ★ ★ ★

On 31 March 1966 there was a General Election. Harold Wilson had held power since October 1964. Sir Alec Douglas-Home had been replaced as Tory leader by Edward Heath. Wilson had a majority of just four seats, which made government almost unworkable. By going to the electorate in 1966 he succeeded in gaining a ninety-six-seat overall majority. The Queen opened the new Parliament on her fortieth birthday, 21 April. In those days, unlike now, the hereditary peers sat in the House of Lords and many of their wives were present in evening dresses, jewels and tiaras. It was enormously glamorous. There was a procession of members of the Royal Family into the Chamber – the royal ladies like stars in their evening dresses with Orders and tiaras – Princess Margaret with the Earl of Snowdon, the Duchess of Gloucester with her Duke, Princess Marina with the Duke and Duchess of Kent. Earl Mountbatten of Burma was there as Gold Stick in Waiting. Field Marshal Viscount Montgomery of Alamein bore the Sword of State.*

Harold Wilson frequently told the world how well he and the Queen had got on. He addressed this in the farewell speech he made on stepping down in March 1976. He was aware of the Queen's capacity for catching ministers out. He advised his successor 'to do his homework before his audience, and to read all his telegrams and Cabinet committee papers in time and not to leave them to the weekend'. He hoped James Callaghan would enjoy, as he had, the Queen's 'manifold kindness, understanding and trust'.⁴ Wilson would not have cared for the revelations of Andrew Duncan, vouchsafed to him by one of Wilson's Cabinet colleagues: 'The Queen thinks Harold is a prosy old bore, a *petit bourgeois*.'†⁵

---

* I feel so lucky to have been there. It left an indelible impression. A world long gone.
† It is worth conceding that this choice information came from a Cabinet colleague

In his memoirs, Wilson expanded on this. He thought that coming from such different backgrounds was a help, putting them on 'easy conversational terms from the start'. The Queen liked to ask him about growing up in those back-to-back houses in Leeds. In turn she told him what she had seen on her tours – enjoying more than anything else the visits to Commonwealth countries. 'I do not wish for one moment to lessen the dignity of the occasion,' wrote Wilson, 'but we just used to sit and chat.'[6] At Balmoral she drove him to Birkhall, saying, 'Shall we go and see my mother?' At a barbecue, she rustled up a steak for him.

The weekly audiences took place on Thursday afternoons at six thirty. Sometimes the Private Secretary flagged up relevant topics in advance with the Cabinet Secretary. His arrival often coincided with the final edition of the *Evening Standard* appearing, which the Queen had read, giving her the advantage. On one occasion in May 1974 Wilson won. He had spotted a scurrilous story by Sam White about President Giscard d'Estaing. Entitled 'President with a taste for freedom', it alleged that he enjoyed 'his leisure', that a man of forty-eight was likely to 'feel a little restless at that critical age', that he worked late in his getaway apartment in the rue de Rivoli. Beneath it, in a classic journalistic sequitur, was an account of the death of Félix Faure, a former President of France, 'in gallant company'.*[7] He told the Queen he was going to Paris to see the President. 'Ho-ho,' said the Queen. When Wilson came back, she asked: 'And what about ho-ho?' She was disappointed to hear there had been none.

In December 1967 Harold Holt, the Australian Prime Minister, drowned in Sydney Harbour. The Queen asked Wilson if Prince Charles should represent her at the funeral. He thought it an excellent idea. The Queen called him in and said: 'Charles, the Prime Minister has very generously said he will take you to Australia. Now you will do exactly what he tells you. If he says go to bed, you just go to bed even if you have to break off in the middle of a sentence.'

---

who may have wished to do Wilson down. The Queen would not have wanted to be thus quoted. Nor does it quite fit, unlike the Macmillan suggestion.

* President Faure was rumoured to have died while having sex with Marguerite Steinheil at the Élysée Palace in 1899.

The expedition gave Wilson the chance to get to know the heir to the throne.⁸

Richard Crossman

Not all politicians appreciated the State Opening of Parliament or the meetings of the Privy Council. Among the most recalcitrant was Richard Crossman, who served as Lord President of the Council between 1966 and 1968 in Wilson's Labour Government. Privy Council meetings sometimes involved travelling long distances, even to Balmoral, to effect constitutional business, almost as a cipher.

Crossman was a Wykehamist, with a first from Oxford. He had mixed in the homosexual world of W. H. Auden and Christopher Isherwood, and had an affair with the poet, Stephen Spender. His first wife, Erika Glück, who left him after nine months, was a German prostitute. He married twice more. Isaiah Berlin thought he liked stirring things up, but had no wish for a better society, just liked the excitement: 'Rather like Bakunin,* he wanted revolution, but didn't mind very much if it did not come.'⁹

Such was the man who was sworn into the Privy Council in 1964, bitterly put out to have to rehearse the process from 11.10 until 12.15 p.m. with its arcane ritual, and then go to the Palace to 'kiss hands'. There he found the Queen, a tiny woman with a beautiful waist, standing with her hand on the table for forty minutes as they went through 'this rigmarole'. Everyone was uneasy until it was over: 'Then at the end informality broke out and she said: "You all moved backwards very nicely," and we all laughed.'¹⁰

In September 1966, he wrote that if he waited for the Queen to begin a conversation, nothing happened. He was conscious that both sides bored each other. But he noted: 'She has a lovely laugh. She laughs with her whole face and she just can't assume a mere smile because she's really a very spontaneous person.' Godfrey Agnew, Clerk to the Privy Council, told him that she found it hard to suppress her emotion: 'When she is deeply moved and tries to control it she looks like an angry thundercloud. So, very often when

---

* Mikhail Bakunin (1814–76), influential Russian revolutionary anarchist.

she's been deeply touched by the plaudits of the crowd she merely looks terribly bad-tempered.'[11]

When Crossman went to see the Queen at Sandringham in January 1967, he found her deftly fitting pieces into an enormous jigsaw puzzle, without looking round. He gleaned that it was a help when the Queen got to know her ministers. Godfrey Agnew said he did not think the Queen discriminated between politicians of different parties: 'They all roughly belong to the same social category in her view.'[12] In 1968 Crossman managed to shorten the formal side of Privy Council meetings, leaving more time for social engagement with the Queen. Drinks were served, and the Queen gave the Privy Counsellors a vivid description of an all-in wrestling match she had seen on the television. She had thought it great fun and described it 'writhing herself, twisting and turning, completely relaxed. It was an eye-opener to see how she enjoyed it.'[13]

The most telling conflict between Crossman and the Royal Household concerned the State Opening of Parliament, set for 31 October 1967. Crossman was fed up when the College of Arms informed him of what was expected of the Lord President on the day – processing in morning dress. He decided he could escape the whole thing with a 'diplomatic illness'. The Duke of Norfolk complained to Harold Wilson that the Lord President was refusing to attend owing to his 'anti-monarchical sentiments'. Wilson wrote back saying that Crossman had a phobia about public occasions of that kind. The Duke wrote direct to Crossman saying that only the Queen could give him leave not to attend.

A week before the State Opening, Crossman rang Sir Michael Adeane, who asked him to come to Buckingham Palace to see him in his office. Adeane told him that Wilson had just been in to discuss the Queen's Speech with her, and that Crossman should not have written to the heralds or the Duke but come to him. 'I could have cleared it with the Queen,' said Sir Michael, 'and I can clear it now if you really don't want to go. Indeed, all you need to do is to write a letter to her asking to be excused without stating any reason why.' Then Adeane added: 'Of course, the Queen has as strong a dislike of public ceremonies as you do. I don't disguise from you the fact that it will certainly occur to her to ask herself why you should be excused when she has to go, since you're both officials.' Crossman wrote that evening to Adeane to say he would be there. He concluded: 'His handling of the affair had been as masterly as that of the Duke of Norfolk had been clumsy.'[14]

As for the day itself, he judged it 'like the *Prisoner of Zenda* but not nearly as smart or well done as it would be in Hollywood'. He felt ashamed of the 'appalling speech' he had written, which the Queen had to read, and he noticed that 'When she read the sentence about curbing the power of the Lords* she made a little pause and read it with just a *frisson* and the whole House had a *frisson* too.'[15]

In June 1970 Edward Heath won an unexpected majority in the General Election, and there was a change of government. Harold Wilson left Downing Street, and the Ministers went in turn to see the Queen and return their seals of office. Crossman went along on 22 June for a 'perfectly decent and formal meeting'. In the course of it, he asked her if she minded elections. The Queen replied: 'Yes, it means meeting a lot of new people.'

Crossman thought: 'All this simply means that, just when she has begun to know us, she has to meet another terrible lot of politicians.'[16]

Wilson was displeased when Crossman published his diaries, revealing private conversations with the Queen: 'Any unauthorised disclosures of what had passed when Ministers had had audiences of The Queen or when she had entertained them at Windsor or Balmoral would serve to destroy the present relaxed and informal nature of her contact with her Ministers,'[17] he wrote. A later minister, William Whitelaw was more circumspect in his memoirs, reflecting on the Queen's qualities:

> I suppose the Queen's remarkable and detailed knowledge of any subject should not be surprising, in view of her experience over the years, but her understanding of places, people and their problems has never ceased to amaze me. Personally, I soon learned that it is extremely unwise to attempt a bluff of any sort with Her Majesty.

---

* 'Legislation will be introduced to reduce the powers of the House of Lords and to eliminate its present hereditary basis, thereby enabling it to develop within the framework of a modern Parliamentary system. My Government are prepared to enter into consultations appropriate to a constitutional change of such importance.'

The wise course of action is never to pretend that you know an answer unless you are totally sure of it. If you do not know, admit quickly, otherwise you will certainly be caught out in the most charming manner.[18]

Aberfan

On 21 October 1966 a colliery spoil tip collapsed in the Welsh village of Aberfan, killing 28 adults and 116 children. Spoil had been deposited on a site above the village and, following heavy rain, some 150,000 cubic metres of saturated debris was dislodged and flowed towards the village at considerable speed in a landslide. Pupils at Pantglas Junior School had just made their way from assembly to their classrooms and they were prime among the victims.

The Duke of Edinburgh and Lord Snowdon visited the bereaved on 23 October, but the Queen did not go until 30 October, believing that her presence might hinder the rescue operation. When she arrived with Prince Philip she was given a posy by a child bearing the message: 'From the remaining children of Aberfan'. Her decision to delay was somewhat criticised and at later tragedies, at Lockerbie and Dunblane, the Queen was quick to visit the scene of the accident. This is often cited as a rare example of the Queen putting a foot wrong, but her decision makes perfect sense. The priority was the rescue work.

On 9 March 1973 the Queen paid a second visit to Aberfan to open a new community centre and laid a wreath near the graves of the many dead. She revisited it during her Diamond Jubilee tour of Wales in 2012.

A few days after the tragedy, the Queen opened St George's House behind St George's Chapel. This was an initiative of the Duke of Edinburgh and Robin Woods, the Dean of Windsor and was set up not exactly as a conference centre but as a place to foster discussion on a great many matters of importance. It was converted from some canons' residences, these proving too big. While the work was taking place, the Queen telephoned Robin Woods and said she wanted to come and have a look round.

'When, Ma'am?'

'Now.'

Down she came and they walked round together. One door was closed. 'You don't want to see in there,' said the Dean, warning her that it was where the builders had their tea and kept their pots and paints.

'Oh yes I do,' said the Queen. When they went in she found the walls covered with page-three girls. 'Most unusual wallpaper,' she said.[19]

25
CHANGING TIMES

Those who surrounded the Queen in the early years of her reign, were men and women of an era now long past. They looked different. They lived in a different way. Their values and traditions would be alien to the present generation.

Every year the Queen and a large contingent of the Royal Family stayed at Badminton with the Duke and Duchess of Beaufort for the Horse Trials.* 'Master', the 10th Duke, had been born in 1900. He was a splendid figure in his own right. A descendant of the Plantagenets, he was a man of inflexible habit, his life revolving around the sporting seasons. When James Pope-Hennessy visited him and enthused about a pair of Canalettos of Badminton, declaring them 'perfectly lovely', the Duke muttered: 'I don't know about their being lovely, but they're very like the house.'[1]

In 1981 he produced a book of memoirs, which he neither wrote himself nor bothered to read (it not being his sort of book), though he signed some copies. The book contained the memorable line: 'Obviously the hunting of the fox has been my chief concern.'[2] His *modus operandi* was that if a creature moved he ran after it. If on

---

* The Queen stayed for one last Badminton in 1984, the Duke having died in February. She was less in sympathy with his successor, the dapper David Somerset, a more international playboy with his private plane. Master's death could have been a scene from Max Beerbohm's *Zuleika Dobson* (1911). Hounds bayed in the parish churchyard the night before he died. There was then one of the best runs at the next meet after his death. Caroline, Duchess of Beaufort, commented: 'Master has inhabited the fox.' At Christmas 1984, anti-hunt demonstrators attempted to dig up the late Duke and planned to post his head to Princess Anne at Gatcombe Park. His coffin now lies under a substantial sarcophagus, topped with a ducal coronet. He will rest in peace.

four legs, he hunted it. If on two and female, he seduced it. He had many mistresses. He had been corralled into marrying Queen Mary's niece, Lady Mary Cambridge, though no one had told him that she could not have children, and she became increasingly eccentric as old age approached. The Queen saw a lot of him on ceremonial occasions, since he served as Master of the Horse, riding in state processions and in her Birthday Parade on Horse Guards.

When the Duke died in 1984, fulsome tributes were paid to him in magazines written for the faithful, such as the *Field*, 'The noblest Master of them all',[3] and *Horse & Hound*. 'Thank you, Master,'[4] ran one headline, for many fine days in the field.

The Duke of Norfolk, who had arranged the Coronation, was much around as he was HM Representative at Ascot, and Steward of the Jockey Club. He built a modern house in the grounds of Arundel Castle, and loved cricket, taking the English team to Australia as their manager in 1962–3. It was said of him: 'His often unmoving face concealed a considerable sense of humour and power of anecdote.'[5] The author, Andrew Duncan, was more brutal:

> He is a man of consummate antiquity, too obvious a target for mockery, too obviously competent to deserve it. To watch him puffing through ceremonies, red round cheeks blowing in and out like bellows, skin hooded and wrinkled like a turtle, is to watch a vision of the past. Probably one of the few men left in England who demonstrably believed every word he said, he had committed his life to his heritage, with an intensity that found opposition difficult to understand.[6]

The Duke had an innate sense of ceremony. I watched him in the paddock at Royal Ascot in 1974, in the last year of his life. Although only sixty-four, he was sitting under a tree, like an octogenarian. When the Queen came into the paddock, he rose and advanced slowly towards her. Clearly she had seen him, but she gave no sign of it. As he approached, he moved his cane from the right hand to the left, took off his top hat and transferred it to his left hand. He arrived in front of her at the exact moment to bow and shake her hand. (And he won the Gold Cup with Ragstone that afternoon.)

Like the Duke of Beaufort, he had no sons. He had four daughters. He and the Duke of Beaufort walked side by side in the Garter procession each year, rising with aristocratic indifference above the painful fact that the Duke of Norfolk's wife, Lavinia, had been one of Beaufort's conquests, moving for a time in the 1950s into a caravan on the Badminton estate.

The Earl of Scarbrough was appointed Lord Chamberlain at the beginning of the reign. In a varied career, he had been a distinguished colonial administrator, and Governor of Bombay between 1937 and 1943. As such he was head of the Queen's Household until 1963. Now the Household was changing. Lord Cobbold, the new Lord Chamberlain and a former Governor of the Bank of England, was keener on a meritocratic team than on the traditional almost hereditary element, which invariably included education at Eton, and service in the Guards – courtiers often denounced as 'tweedy' despite their inherent good sense and understanding.

The Queen's first Private Secretary, Sir Alan (Tommy) Lascelles, an erudite and forceful man, stayed until the Coronation. He remained something of an adviser for some years afterwards, and had considerable influence in persuading the Queen of the merits of James Pope-Hennessy's biography of Queen Mary. His successor was the more conventional Sir Michael Adeane, who served from 1953 until 1972. As so often in those days, his was almost an hereditary appointment. He was the grandson of Lord Stamfordham, the former Arthur Bigge, who had been Private Secretary to George V from 1910 to 1931. Bigge first attracted the attention of Queen Victoria when she summoned him to Balmoral to tell her about the brutal death of the Prince Imperial (son of Emperor Napoleon III) in the Anglo-Zulu war in which both had served in the British Army. She took a shine to him and in 1881 scooped him into her household. In 1895 he succeeded Sir Henry Ponsonby as her Private Secretary. Michael Adeane was Assistant Private Secretary to the Queen's father from 1945, serving alongside Edward Ford and Martin Charteris, who were roughly the same age.

Edward Ford was the son of the Dean of York. He had been a tutor to the young Prince Farouk of Egypt and one of George VI's private secretaries. He had been an Assistant Private Secretary to the King from 1946 and to the Queen from 1952. Adeane tried to move Ford out of the way by suggesting he become Private Secretary to the young Prince of Wales, but as Ford said: 'What was I to do? Tie his shoelaces?'[7] He thought that Prince Charles, then aged twenty-three, needed a younger man. So he took voluntary retirement at fifty-seven and was not paid until he got his pension at sixty. Later he was brought back into the fold as Secretary of the Order of Merit, serving from 1975 until 2003.

In 1972 Adeane retired. He and the Lord Chamberlain, Lord Cobbold, tried to ditch Martin Charteris, but he appealed to the Queen and told her he should be her next Private Secretary. She agreed and he served until 1977. From 1966 Philip Moore was part of the team. He had been High Commissioner in Singapore, and went on to be the dullest Private Secretary on record between 1977 and 1986. Charteris had served the Queen since 1950 and in his short tenure as Private Secretary (until 1977) wrote the best speeches for her and presented her publicly as near as possible to the person she was. He had the capricious qualities enjoyed by many members of the Charteris family and carried out his duties with a light touch, which disguised a firmer determination. He could sometimes be observed in the background of a royal engagement laughing heartily and slapping his knee as the Queen delivered a joke he had written.

The first Mistress of the Robes was the Dowager Duchess of Devonshire, born Lady Mary Cecil and known as 'Moucher'. The ladies in waiting tended to be aristocrats, including the Countess of Leicester, whose abiding memory was of the Queen musing about names for her horses. Early on, the Queen appointed the Countess of Euston (Fortune Smith, later Duchess of Grafton), wife of one of her early suitors, Hugh Euston. Fortune succeeded the Duchess of Devonshire as Mistress of the Robes in 1967. She continued in the role until her death at the age of 101, though in later years she did not appear at royal events.

The Household was greatly enriched by the presence of Patrick Plunket. He was the nearest thing to a brother that the Queen had. His parents had been close friends of the Yorks. They were killed in an air accident when their plane crashed on William Randolph Hearst's estate, San Simeon, in California in 1938. The King and Queen kept an eye on Patrick and his siblings, appointing him an equerry in 1948. He often stayed with the Royal Family, and went shooting with them. In the Queen's reign, in 1954, he was appointed Deputy Master of the Household. He had served in the Irish Guards, and was a man of taste. He rescued Cecil Beaton when he was looking for a good venue to photograph the royal babies and, in 1972, did not hesitate to cut down a cherry tree and place it in a state room at Windsor Castle for Queen Juliana's state visit. Had a bomb fallen on the Guards Chapel at his memorial service in 1975, it would have wiped out more or less the entire Royal Family, the more interesting elements of the aristocracy and many of England's most creative figures.

Sir John Miller, the Crown Equerry, presided over the Royal Mews between 1961 and 1987. He was involved in all aspects of the Queen's equestrian life, both private and formal, and rode in sixty-four birthday parades. He was an expert equestrian. His obituary in the *Daily Telegraph* stated: 'He blew the hunting horn at Balmoral to welcome the Waleses home from their honeymoon, and was responsible for mounting members of the family when they expressed an interest in riding.'*[8]

Not known for hanging back on royal occasions, Miller showed different faces to the world. To the Queen he was simperingly polite, but he could growl at lesser men, especially if they got in the way of the horses. He was not of the modern world. He once walked into a glass panel at Ascot. Another time he turned his carriage over on Horse Guards Parade. He went to the Palace, blood all over his face, his bowler hat squashed, and told William Heseltine, the Queen's Press Secretary: 'I'm just going to see the Queen to tell her the horses are all right.'[9] The Queen told him to go to hospital at once.[10]

* * * * *

It is generally thought that the press was deferential until recently, but besides the attacks by Muggeridge and Altrincham, there were plenty of digs at the Queen. They attacked her figure, her voice

---

* This is a perfectly correct use of equestrian language, but it was picked up by *Private Eye* and the television programme, *Have I Got News For You?* I wrote that obituary.

was criticised as piping or fluting, and there was a suggestion that she was priggish. The intelligentsia resented that she did not like opera, preferring her horses and dogs. She was a knowledgeable equestrian, an expert on breeding and bloodlines, one of the interests that kept her grounded.

The line 'My husband and I ...' was frequently employed in take-offs, due to the Queen's frequent use of the expression. In the record *Fool Britannia* (1963), made in the wake of the Profumo affair, there was a skit taking off the Queen, with in-jokes such as 'And it's the last time we shall give a knighthood to an American actor',[*] references to Prince Philip going to a ten-week polo tournament rather than a trade conference, and him struggling with the crossword. The Queen: 'According to some of the papers, you're very good at four-letter words', along with jokes such as 'Charles, finish your cherry brandy and go to bed'[†] and 'Anne! How many times have we told you not to ride your pony at the tea table?'[11]

The first Press Secretary was Commander Sir Richard Colville, a stern naval commander, who treated the press with contempt, earning the nickname 'The Abominable No-Man'. Martin Charteris called him 'Sunshine' for his never-smiling face.

From 1958 until 1981 Anne Hawkins, a niece of Princess Alice, Duchess of Gloucester, was Assistant Press Secretary, described by one Royal Household official as 'a walking directory and frightfully good at her job'. In those days the Press Office would rebuke an errant journalist with a choice phrase such as: 'Nobody was particularly pleased by your article.' Tim Heald had written facetiously in the *Toronto Star*. He got a message that they had read his piece.

Anne Hawkins particular disliked Helen Cathcart, who wrote what would now be considered a succession of anodyne books about the Royal Family. The books were not as annoying as the articles

---

[*] Douglas Fairbanks Junior (honorary KBE) was alleged to have had an affair with Margaret, Duchess of Argyll, and was allegedly the man in the celebrated photograph.

[†] In June 1963, on an expedition to Stornoway from Gordonstoun, Prince Charles had found himself in a bar and, not knowing what to do, ordered himself a cherry brandy as was sometimes served out shooting. The world exploded around his ears.

in women's magazines, in which Cathcart would maintain that the Queen had had tea with Lady Rupert Nevill and discussed the latest antics of Princess Anne. When confronted by Anne Hawkins, the feeble justification was: 'That's what they would have talked about.'

Helen Cathcart was never seen. She was represented by her agent, Harold Albert, who lived at Liphook and made persistent enquiries on her behalf. Many suspected that he was Helen Cathcart, but when they visited him, they invariably came away less certain. After his death, it was confirmed (by the present author in his obituary) that he was indeed Helen Cathcart.

When William Heseltine became Press Secretary in 1968, there began a gradual thawing of relations between the Palace Press Office and the media. Heseltine had served as Private Secretary to Sir Robert Menzies, and later as official secretary to the Governor-General of Australia, Viscount De L'Isle. He had done a short spell at the Palace in the early 1960s.

Under the new regime considerable access was given to Andrew Duncan, who followed the Queen around between October 1968 and July 1969 when researching his book, *The Reality of Monarchy*. He observed her on her chaotic South American state visits that autumn,* at various home engagements, on her state visit to Austria in 1969, his year culminating with the Investiture of the Prince of Wales at Caernarfon Castle.

Andrew Duncan was described by Tim Heald as 'a myopic, frizzy-haired twenty-nine-year-old with a sardonic style and an eye for detail'. Heald observed him in Norway, not watching the main events but 'engrossed in conversation with an obviously anonymous detective or official'.[12] Evidently he paid £18 10s to insure the Queen's life for £10,000 in case she died before he finished his book.

He was allowed 'on the record' conversations with various members of the Royal Family – Prince Philip, Prince Charles, Princess Margaret and Lord Snowdon, as well as Lord Harewood and Angus Ogilvy. His research sometimes led him into unexpected

---

* The Queen flew to Brazil on 1 November 1968 where she was joined by the Duke of Edinburgh, who had visited Mexico for the Olympic Games. Together they paid a state visit to President Artur da Costa e Silva (who died the following year) and afterwards to President Eduardo Frei Montalva of Chile.

situations. On a visit to the Fleet at Plymouth, he was climbing a rope ladder to the *Eagle*, when a flood of bilge water showered over him. He was due for an interview with Lord Cobbold, the Lord Chamberlain, who sniffed at 'the smelly apparition' and commented: 'I hear you've had a bit of rough weather', before continuing as though nothing had happened. The resulting book, *The Reality of Monarchy*, was in a different vein from the saccharine emanations of Helen Cathcart or Graham and Heather Fisher. The book was serialised in the United States and had the good fortune (for sales) to be denounced by a former editor of *Burke's Peerage* as a 'contemptuous smear'.[13] Anne Hawkins commented later that Duncan had 'stitched us up'.*[14]

Duncan gave a vivid portrait of the Queen's daily life, captured a number of Prince Philip's controversial asides, and however much he mocked the system, as usual there emerged a dutiful Head of State, going about her sometimes tedious business with good humour and dedication. One of her friends told the author that the Queen threw her affection to her dogs as she couldn't with humans 'because of her upbringing' and praised the 'slightly unfeminine abilities she's mastered'.[15]

Prince Philip was frequently attacked in articles throughout the 1950s, especially in the Beaverbrook press, Lord Beaverbrook hating Mountbatten. Andrew Duncan took the traditional line – that he was frustrated at not being able to make more of a contribution to public life due to the constraints of his position.

★ ★ ★ ★ ★

The Queen and Prince Philip settled into middle age in the last years of the 1960s and the early years of the 1970s. Attention was more directed to Prince Charles and Princess Anne as they emerged

---

* Reviews of the book varied considerably. Alf McCreary wrote in the *Belfast Telegraph*: 'His prose has the power of a sledgehammer and he writes candidly, sometimes mercilessly ... Mr Duncan may have influential friends. I suspect he may have one or two influential enemies as well' (14 May 1970). Hugh Massingham slammed it in the *Sunday Telegraph* (10 May 1970), while Dermot Morrah thought him 'cynical' though 'well informed' in the *Daily Telegraph* (14 May 1970).

into adulthood. Prince Philip told Andrew Duncan that the general public found a young Queen with a young family 'more newsworthy and amusing'. He thought this phase of their lives was 'the least interesting period of the kind of glamorous existence'. As people got more accustomed to them, he thought, 'Either they can't stand us, or they think we're all right.' He wondered if when they became really ancient 'there might be a bit more reverence again'.[16]

The *Royal Family* Film

The *Royal Family* film developed from Lord Mountbatten's lengthy series on his life and times, produced by his son-in-law, Lord Brabourne, which was launched at the Imperial War Museum in December 1968. At first there was an idea for a film biography of Prince Charles, following Dermot Morrah's published life, *To Be a King*, but instead it was decided to show the work of the Queen, helping people understand what she did and who she was, and presenting an idea of what eventually lay in store for Prince Charles.

William Heseltine proposed the idea in a note to the Queen, asking for 'some indication of your views before I get into too deep waters with the BBC'. He was to be at Windsor in connection with the forthcoming Italian state visit,* and wondered if the Queen 'could spare a little time' to see him.[17] The Queen replied (laconically): '2.15 p.m. tomorrow Tuesday would do.' Heseltine was given the go-ahead to explore the idea, though this was followed with 'long and anxious consideration by the Queen and Prince Philip'.

Richard Cawston directed it and Lord Brabourne was involved. As Heseltine put it later: 'The documentary *Royal Family* was made by the foremost exponent of the genre, only after the constitutional and all other consequences were considered, and very carefully.' In those days the activities of the Royal Family were either recorded formally in the Court Circular or in gossip columns, or occasional newspaper reports. The Queen and Prince Philip had made a point of protecting their children from the

---

* President Saragat was due to come to Windsor Castle in April 1969, the first state visit in Windsor since that of King Manoel of Portugal in 1909.

media. This had led to speculation in some quarters that Prince Charles and Princess Anne were 'backward if not positively retarded'. There was already speculation forming as to whom they might marry.

Television had to be addressed because, in an increasingly powerful media age, the Royal Family risked looking remote. Richard Cawston, the director, wanted to balance the official life with some off-duty moments to present the family as bright and attractive. It was possible to direct the narrative from within, rather than 'calmly sit back and let Television devour them on its terms'. It was the first time many viewers had heard the Queen talk, other than when giving speeches. It was decided that this would be a one-off exercise, and the film would not be shown again for many decades.

The stills photographer, Joan Williams, was recording various scenes and needed some re-enacted at the end of a long day. Prince Philip, whose patience with photographers was limited at the best of times, was especially irked by this. As Heseltine put it:

> Indeed a feature of his participation throughout was his ready acquiescence with Cawston's requests when discussed in the Committee which he chaired, and his fuming impatience with Cawston and his team when they came to take some actual film involving him.

This came to a head at Holyroodhouse in the summer of 1968. Anne Hawkins was there as acting Press Secretary when Prince Philip blew up over some minor crisis. Anne stood up to him and explained 'in words of one syllable that this was how they worked, that he had agreed to it in principle, and that he had better not make such a fuss over it when they actually appeared to do their job. He was never quite so bloody about it thereafter!'[18]

The film was shown on 21 June 1969. It was viewed by almost as large an audience as those who watched the moon landings a month later. By October 1979 it had been seen by more people than any other documentary ever made, had been bought by 125 countries, shown eleven times in the UK, and twice from coast to coast in the United States. In retrospect many believed it was a mistake to make it, opening the floodgates, fuelling an insatiable appetite in journalists for more intimate revelations about the Royal

Family. Prince Philip hoped that 'If people see whoever it happens to be, whatever head of state, as individuals, as people, I think it makes it much easier for them to accept the system or to feel part of the system.'[19] An unexpected downside was that some of the younger members of the family began to enjoy seeing themselves on the television in this way, and even thought they were 'potential stars'.[20]

The Investiture of the Prince of Wales

Prince Charles entered public life in 1969 with a series of interviews in advance of his Investiture at Caernarfon Castle on 1 July. His interview with Jack de Manio changed his reputation overnight. He came across as articulate, self-deprecating and entertaining. That was broadcast on St David's Day, 1 March. In one of his interviews he expressed his wish to serve: 'I have this feeling of duty towards England, towards the United Kingdom, the Commonwealth: and I feel there is a great deal I can do, if I am given the chance to do it.'[21]

The Investiture was a major state ceremony, first devised in 1912 by Lloyd George for the Prince of Wales (later the Duke of Windsor), who had been nothing short of reluctant to take part. Lord Snowdon had been appointed Constable of Caernarfon Castle in 1963 and worked, not always in harmony, with the Duke of Norfolk.

Unlike the Duke, Snowdon was media savvy and wanted the proceedings well covered by television. There were enjoyable clashes between the old world and the new. When the heralds were processing, Snowdon put on a Sandie Shaw record. When Sir Anthony Wagner was being particularly resistant to his plans, Snowdon asked: 'Oh, Garter, can't you be more elastic?' The appointment of Lord Heycock to carry the Golden Rod was the kind of mischievous humour enjoyed by the heraldic mind. The Duke of Norfolk was asked what would happen if it rained. Without a jot of irony, he replied: 'We all get wet.' Snowdon designed himself a bottle-green uniform. The Duke muttered about him adding a hat and calling himself Robin Hood.

On the great day, the thrones for the Queen, Prince Philip and Prince Charles were placed in the centre of the castle, underneath a huge Perspex cover, designed by Carl Toms, so that the TV cameras could see through it. Some of the Royal Family sat on the right and the Regalia peers to the left.

The Queen and most of the Royal Family travelled to Wales in the Royal Train. The Duke of Norfolk prevailed on Sir Michael Duff to entertain them all for breakfast before the Investiture ceremony. Duff had enjoyed entertaining Princess Marina and her family at Vaynol, his estate in Wales, over many years. One of his celebrated turns was to dress up as Queen Mary. Sir Charles Johnston recorded that it must have been a Firbankian fantasy for him:

> With his marmalade-coloured hair he is certainly something new in Lord Lieutenants. He is reported to have said to the Duke of Norfolk: 'Wh... wh... It's all over I suppose I might g-g-get the G-G-Garter?' To which Norfolk replied sternly: 'Michael, unless you stop dyeing your hair, you won't get anything.' So much in character for both of them, it must be true.★[22]

There had been fears of bombs on the day, so security was intense. Nevertheless there were two open carriage processions, one for the Queen and another for the Prince of Wales. Once the Queen and the Duke of Edinburgh had arrived at the dais, the Prince was summoned from the tower where he had been waiting (endlessly catching glimpses of himself on television) and he was invested in royal robes and a specially designed coronet. He promised to be the Queen's liege man of life and limb.

The Queen presented him to the people of Wales at various points of view from the castle. There were striking antiphonal fanfares arranged by Sir Arthur Bliss from different battlements. There was a mixture of Welsh singing and English pronouncements; Prince Charles spoke in Welsh and even referenced 'a very memorable Goon' (Sir Harry Secombe). For a few hours the often neglected Principality of Wales was the focus of the world's attention. After the magnificent ceremony, the Prince undertook a four-day tour of Wales.

★ Lord Snowdon was given a GCVO in the Investiture Honours List. Duff received nothing.

Sir Charles Johnston watched the ceremony on that rare novelty, colour television, at his club:

> A splendid and moving performance – but how professional our monarchy is getting in its public relations aspect. And what a high standard the Prince of Wales is setting himself. Groans from all the members of White's whenever *le Tony* (Ld. Snowdon) appeared on the screen and various suggestions about what he should do with the key of the Castle when he produced it.[23]

26
THE EARLY 1970s

'Our year has been very hectic with travels to Australia, New Zealand and Canada,' the Queen wrote to the Duke of Windsor.¹ Prince Charles and Princess Anne joined the Queen and Prince Philip on their Antipodean trip in 1970, confirming Prince Philip's thought that their presence would capture the imagination of the public. For the outward journey the Queen was glad to have a book of racing anecdotes, sent by Jim Orr, to 'pass away the many hours cooped up in the VC 10'. She told Orr she was sorry to be going away for so long, though aware that she would be busy: 'I hate the idea of missing the spring, though, and the early part of the flat season!'²

The visit celebrated the two hundredth anniversary of Captain Cook's voyages and was one of the most physically difficult tours for the Queen. After brief visits to Fiji and Tonga, she was in New Zealand from 12 to 30 March, and opened Parliament. She covered a large part of both North and South Island, but in Australia she largely followed Captain Cook's footsteps along the east coast, Sydney, Canberra, Melbourne and Brisbane and the coast of north Queensland. She arrived in *Britannia* with Princess Anne, while Prince Charles flew to Wellington separately. Prince Philip (who had been visiting the space launching centre at Cape Kennedy, USA), was also on board *Britannia*.

The last time the Queen had been in Australia, in 1963, there had been complaints about too many red carpets and too many town halls for formal gatherings. William Heseltine was the prime mover in the idea that the Queen should do walkabouts. It was not an entirely new concept. William IV had walked in St James's Street so much that fears were expressed for his safety, and the Queen had walked along Valletta's main road and Kingsway (now Republic Street) in Malta in 1967. For months Sir Patrick O'Dea, the Queen's

Secretary in New Zealand, and Lieutenant-General Sir Reginald Pollard, her Australian Secretary, discussed the plan.

The first of the new walkabouts took place in Wellington on 12 March, the Queen, Prince Philip and Princess Anne mingling with a crowd of eight thousand for twenty minutes, despite security concerns over demonstrators protesting about New Zealand's involvement in the Vietnam War. As ever Prince Philip added spice to the day by asking a group of youngsters if they were 'bumming around'. They said they were – they were working at a wharf.[3]

So keen were the Royal Family on walkabouts that they got roundly soaked in Christchurch. Inevitably conversations were superficial – the Queen's 'Have you come far?' remark began to be quoted. Her safety was a factor, but she would have been no safer in an open car. It was recalled that massive American security had not saved the life of President Kennedy in 1963. The walkabouts were a resounding PR success, providing informality without detracting from dignity.[4] There was a demonstration when the Queen opened Parliament, an old lady beating a demonstrator over the head and proclaiming: 'We've come to see the Queen, not you.'[5]

The emphasis throughout the tour was on youth. The Queen was seen by about a quarter of a million children. Later she told the Duke of Windsor that it was rewarding seeing Charles and Anne welcomed on these tours.[6] However, when reporters interrupted the Prince's morning swim, he told them to 'piss off'. Nor did Princess Anne conceal her boredom. When asked if she had used the word 'bloody', she replied: 'Quite likely, quite likely.'[7] On the other hand she acquitted herself so well when confronted with demonstrating students that she was cheered by them for her calm handling of the incident.

She was amused when a group of noisy students pushed themselves out of the crowd and presented the Queen with a glove on the end of a stick – for waving. The Queen non-plussed them: 'Thank you so much. That's just what I always wanted.'[8] The press tried to drum up a romance with an old Timbertop friend of Prince Charles – Stuart McGregor. Talking to Michael Parkinson years later, Princess Anne said she realised that the press thought she did 'not fit the image that they thought I ought to have'. One night she had a vivid nightmare in which she was lying down in the middle of a crowd when she was meant to be talking and shaking hands. She was relieved to wake up.⁹

At the state banquet in Canberra, John Gorton, the Prime Minister, assured the Queen of Australia's loyalty to the Crown: 'We are growing apace, but nevertheless the old values remain. Our allegiance to the throne, our loyalty to you, our Queen, are enduring.'¹⁰ Because the visit celebrated Captain Cook's landing, the Aboriginals declared a national day of mourning on 29 April, and wore black with red headbands – to denote the blood spilled by their ancestors at the hands of the invaders. They objected to issues of land ownership. In 1970 there was a less than sympathetic understanding of those sensitivities.

At the end of the five-week tour, the Queen was optimistic: 'It is impossible to escape the conclusion that things are looking very bright for Australia's future.'¹¹ The more informal approach had worked. The monarchy had entered a new era.

The Royal Family returned to Britain on 4 May. In the meantime, Malcolm Muggeridge mocked the Royal Family as 'a nice respectable mother, a rather idiosyncratic dad, and a problem sister ...' The Labour MP Willie Hamilton had taken against the Royal Family when a royal car swept past his school: he had longed to throw a bomb.¹² He received a lot of publicity in the 1970s for his anti-monarchical views, ever ready with a disobliging soundbite. Eventually he capitalised by writing a book called *My Queen and I* in 1975. That too garnered publicity, but thereafter he was taken less seriously since his outpourings were deemed to be publicity gambits for personal financial gain. As stated in his *Times* obituary, his book 'proved in the long run rather an embarrassment to Hamilton's cause: his view of the monarchy, when presented in full in one place, was very obviously one-dimensional'.*¹³

Edward Heath

The General Election on 18 June 1970 resulted in a surprising win for Edward Heath's Conservative Party. He secured a majority of thirty-one seats and the Liberal Party lost half of theirs. Harold Wilson conceded

---

* Hamilton was ousted as Labour MP in 1986, and died in 2000.

defeat at 3.30 p.m. the following day, but could not see the Queen until 6.30 p.m. as she was enjoying her Friday visit to Royal Ascot. Heath was summoned at 7 p.m. He found a smiling Queen. That night there was a party at Windsor Castle to celebrate the seventieth birthdays of the Queen Mother, the Duke of Gloucester (who was not well enough to attend), the Duchess of Gloucester (born in fact in 1901), Lord Mountbatten and the Duke of Beaufort. Heath asked if he might arrive a bit late for the party as he had to discuss Cabinet appointments. The Queen threw back her head and laughed. She told him that the family had been wondering whether he would still be able to come and that his late arrival would be understood.[14] So Heath attended the party and Harold Wilson stayed at home.

Thus the Queen acquired a curmudgeonly bachelor as her sixth Prime Minister. Hugo Young was to write that 'by common repute' the only prime minister with whom the monarch never succeeded in developing an easy relationship was not Mrs Thatcher but Edward Heath, 'a failing which gave Her Majesty something in common with much of the human race.'[15] Heath was never good with women; he was shy and reserved. In common with all her Prime Ministers, he enjoyed his audiences with the Queen.[16]

The Queen did not like his disdain for the Commonwealth, which led to a conflict as early as January 1971, when he prevented her from attending the Commonwealth Conference in Singapore. This was at a time when Rhodesian independence and the selling of arms to South Africa were burning questions. Nor did the Queen find his visits to Balmoral easy. She liked to walk with her Prime Minister, and he was often out of breath.

★ ★ ★ ★ ★

The Queen Mother's seventieth birthday on 4 August attracted enormous publicity. From that year onwards her birthday at Clarence House became an annual feature. The Prince of Wales took his seat in the House of Lords, on 11 February 1970, and went on to address the House twice, speaking on recreation in June 1974 and on youth service in 1975. In 1971 he trained at RAF Cranwell, then joined the Royal Navy, being frequently at sea until 1976. Princess Anne achieved fine results as an equestrian in her own right.

In 1971 the Queen summoned back from Tokyo, where he had been serving at the Embassy, Prince William, the elder son of the Duke of Gloucester, to help run the Barnwell estate. His younger brother, Prince Richard, was a full-time architect. Princess Alice, Countess of Athlone, celebrated her ninetieth birthday in February 1973 with a party at the Turf Club attended by the Queen, most of the Royal Family and Queen Juliana of the Netherlands.

The Queen had made a six-day 4,500-mile tour of Canada's North West Territories and the Province of Manitoba in July 1970. When the Queen and the Duke flew home, Prince Charles and Princess Anne went to Washington to stay at the White House with President and Mrs Nixon for four days, an occasion on which Princess Anne was observed to be particularly bored.

There was a further Canadian tour in May 1971. The Queen, the Duke and Princess Anne flew to British Columbia to celebrate the centennial of the province's entry into the Confederation. Pierre Trudeau, the bachelor Prime Minister since 1968, had married Margaret Bernard on 4 March. Ron Allison, the then Press Secretary, recalled that Trudeau 'rather wanted to go presidential, but when the Queen came over, he soon realised that she had an amazing capacity for pulling crowds that he could never match and he became a monarchist'. He noted her 'amazing skill' and furthermore that while everybody else flailed about in the sun bathed in sweat, the Queen had developed a knack for moving about as little as possible. He never saw her perspire.[17]

Emperor Hirohito

In February 1971 Emperor Hirohito of Japan accepted the Queen's invitation to come on a state visit. He addressed the letter 'Madam My Sister' and signed it 'Your Majesty's Good Brother'. In it he said: 'I once visited your country when I was the Crown Prince and have always cherished the pleasant memories of it.'[18] This was the first ever state visit by a Japanese Emperor to Britain.

The Second World War had left deep scars due to the atrocities meted out in Japan to British prisoners of war. There was still considerable resentment against the Japanese in Britain, but there had been progress towards reconciliation. Official diplomatic relations had been restored in 1952, the new British Ambassador, Sir Esler Dening, presenting his credentials to Emperor Hirohito. A further important step was Princess Alexandra's 1961 visit. She was the first member of the Royal Family to visit Tokyo since the Duke of Gloucester's Garter mission in 1929. She was received by Emperor Hirohito and presented him with a 'bottom scraper' – a device used to clean the undersides of ships.[19] The Emperor was given permission to wear his Garter star.* She was accompanied by her mother's Private Secretary, Sir Philip Hay, somewhat reluctantly as he had been a prisoner of war.† The press were fascinated by Princess Alexandra for her youth, charm and informality, which was in such contrast to the more aloof aura around the Japanese Imperial Family. Back in England she received many letters from relatives of those who had suffered in the war, complaining that she had gone.[20]

Princess Chichibu, the Emperor's sister-in-law, worked tirelessly to improve Anglo-Japanese relations, making an official visit to London in July 1962. She became Patron of the Japan-British Society in Tokyo and was prominent during Princess Margaret's visit for British Week in 1969. As mentioned earlier, Prince William of Gloucester was serving at the British Embassy, and after the 1970 Australia trip, Prince Charles visited Japan in connection with EXPO70.

The Emperor's state visit was mooted for years, but happened when it emerged that he was keen to revisit Europe. He arrived in Britain in October 1971, following a state visit to Paris during which he called on the Duke and Duchess of Windsor at their home in the Bois de Boulogne. Shortly before his visit to London, the Emperor was quietly reinstated in the Order of the Garter, and a new banner raised over his stall.

Sir John Pilcher, the British Ambassador in Tokyo, accompanied the Emperor. He was convinced that the Japanese wanted to

---

* The Emperor had been appointed a Knight of the Garter in 1929 but demoted from the Order in 1941.

† Hay suffered from malaria for the rest of his life. He reconnoitred the visit with Group Captain Neville Stack, Deputy Captain of The Queen's Flight. Inevitably this exercise was dubbed the 'Haystack' visit.

modernise their monarchy and find out how another Royal Family 'tackled the problems of the contemporary age'. He described the Emperor's temperament as that of a mild, dedicated professor:

> No extrovert he: knowledge must be prised out of him. Words come hardly to him, though his delivery is emphatic. Timid reserve characterises him; the ambiguity of silence would be more his forte than the withering rebuke. He is essentially a man of peace, diffident and almost humble about his own role, sceptical probably about its holy attributes.[21]

The only demonstrations against the Emperor came when a man threw his coat into the Mall, and someone dug up the tree he planted in Kew Gardens, both of which were quickly brushed aside. There was negative comment in newspapers and a number of letters of objection from former prisoners of war. *Private Eye* produced a front cover: 'NASTY NIP IN THE AIR'.[22] Prince Philip realised the bland words drafted for the Queen's speech did not go far enough. He added:

> We cannot pretend that the problems of the past did not exist. We cannot pretend that our two peoples have always been peaceful and friendly. However, it is precisely this experience which should make us all the more determined never to let it happen again.[23]

Lord Mountbatten refused to attend the banquet, supposedly preferring to attend a Burma Star reunion, then annoyed the Queen by insisting on a private audience with the Emperor at Buckingham Palace, 'getting in on the act', as Lady Pilcher put it.

The Emperor was taken to the London Zoo. He was shown Chi-Chi, the famous old panda, who had been fed on bamboo and chocolate to put her in a good mood. He could speak perfect English, but preferred to use an interpreter. He asked why Chi-Chi and An-An had never produced any offspring. 'They mistook the orifices' was duly translated into Imperial Japanese. Prince Philip, accompanying the Emperor, felt an urgent need to inspect something in the reptile house before he doubled up laughing.

Many column inches were devoted to the visit in the Japanese press. Some referred to 'the silent reception accorded the Emperor, stony-looking crowds, the Mountbatten "snub", etc.',[24] but the Japanese reading the copious newspaper accounts were impressed by the enormous trouble the Queen, Prince Philip and the Royal Household took to make 'flawless preparations'.[25] Princess Anne remembered the Emperor as a sweet old man.

This led to the important return state visit to Tokyo by the Queen and Prince Philip between 7 and 12 May 1975. The Imperial Household Agency was nervous that the Queen's open approach to her visit would reflect badly on the Emperor's 'cloistered life'.[26] She insisted on driving through Tokyo in an open convertible Cadillac rather than in a car with dark bulletproof glass. Sir Fred Warner, the Ambassador, was aware that there was 'a tradition in Japan of political assassination' and that the Japanese police had a 'proper fear' for the Queen's safety. President Gerald Ford had visited shortly before and had been guarded by an astonishing 160,000 Japanese police and, as Warner put it, 'might as well have been wearing a cloak of invisibility'.[27] The Emperor was against the idea of what became known as 'the Open Car Drive', but the Queen was determined. Since it passed off well, the Japanese police emerged as heroes of the plan and the exercise went down in Japanese history.

Prince Philip was frequently asked: 'Your first visit to Japan?' 'Yes,' he said. In truth he had been present, on board HMS *Whelp* in September 1945 at the time of the Japanese surrender.* When relating the story, he said: 'I'm not always as tactless as people make out.'[28]

A benefit of the Queen's visit to Tokyo was that the Emperor was impressed by the openness of the British Royal Family. The Imperial Family 'felt that a window had been thrown open and a gust of fresh air let into their lives'. On both sides the overwhelming view was that the Queen's visit, with its innovations, 'marked a significant step towards reconciliation and renewal of old friendships'.

---

* When Emperor Hirohito died in 1989, Prince Philip volunteered to represent the Queen, feeling he was the right person, since he had served in the Second World War and did not mind any criticism that might come.

Finance

The issue of the Royal Family's finances arose regularly. The Civil List had been set in 1952 and was meant to last the reign. In 1969 the Duke of Edinburgh had appeared on British television, announcing: 'We may have to move into smaller premises, who knows?' The family had sold their small yacht and he thought he might have to give up polo. 'We go into the red next year,' he said memorably, qualifying that by saying: 'Which is not bad house-keeping if you come to think of it. We've in fact kept the thing going on a budget which was based on costs eighteen years ago. So there have been considerable corners that have had to be cut, and it's beginning to have its effect.' He was aware that asking for money was never popular: 'I don't think anybody likes seeing money – anybody getting any more money frankly, except the people who are getting it themselves.'[29]

Anthony Barber, Chairman of the Conservative Party, announced that the situation should be reviewed. Willie Hamilton jumped up to object.

The Select Committee on the Civil List recommended in 1971 that the Queen's income from public funds to cover the running of her office, which had been set at £475,000 a year in 1952, should be increased to £980,000. The Commons debated this. An Opposition amendment was defeated 300 to 263.

The question of the Civil List arose again in 1975, there being a need for an increase, three-quarters of which was due to increases in wages and salaries within the Royal Household. The new recommendation was that provision would be made only for children of the Sovereign and that the Queen would contribute £1.5 million out of her own resources. Margaret Thatcher, in her first speech as Leader of the Opposition, broadly supported the Government. Jeremy Thorpe, Leader of the Liberal Party, pointed out 'the cost of discharging the functions of the Head of State' was 'significantly less than the cost of running the Embassy in Paris'.[30]

Uganda

A curious diplomatic issue arose over the Queen sending her annual Christmas card to the President of Uganda, by this time the controversial Idi Amin. She normally sent a card to the Heads of State of Commonwealth countries. Her 1971 card did not arrive in Uganda until 5 January 1972. Amin was 'delighted, but he would have been even more delighted if it had arrived before Christmas'.[31] He used the card in radio and press stories to suggest that it was 'a message of encouragement endorsing the regime'.[32]

In 1971 the full evil of Amin was not widely known. Briefing notes described him as 'popular, and a natural leader of men, but simple and practically illiterate; a man of the people ... once a good heavyweight boxer and rugby player ... well-disposed to Britain ... God fearing and deeply religious',[33] opinions that have not passed the test of time. He had been well treated when he suddenly decided to visit Britain in July 1971, evidently 'to discuss "military matters"'.[34] He and his wife, Mama Malyam, lunched with the Queen at Buckingham Palace on 13 July and he had talks with Edward Heath and Sir Alec Douglas-Home, by then Foreign Secretary, the latter not hesitating, privately, to pronounce Amin mad. Amin was flown in an aircraft of the Queen's Flight to Scotland, where the Duke of Hamilton gave him a tour of Holyroodhouse. On leaving Britain Amin told a reporter:

> The reason for my visit was to thank Her Majesty The Queen for the assistance that has been given to Uganda by the British Government in the fields of education, military training, health and the like, and also to thank her for allowing the body of Uganda's first President* to be returned home. I decided that before I went anywhere else in the world I must come to Britain first to thank the Queen personally.[35]

Amin wrote to the Queen to acknowledge her Christmas card and thanked her for 'the good work that your Subjects have been

---

* The Kabaka – Sir Edward Mutesa II, who had died in suspicious circumstances in London in November 1969.

doing in Uganda over the years and for assistance that your Government has rendered to Uganda'. He invited her to join him at the tenth anniversary celebrations of independence.

Sir Martin Charteris was adamant that there was 'no possibility of the invitation being accepted'. The Palace asked the Foreign Office to compose a suitable reply. The Queen changed 'I fear that my commitments at that time will prevent my accepting' to 'I am most disappointed that my commitments at that time will prevent my accepting your invitation.' As the anniversary approached, the Foreign Office sent a draft message for the Queen to consider. It read:

> On the occasion of Independence Day I send to you and to the people of Uganda my good wishes for the peace of your country.

The Queen asked for 'positive advice' from Sir Alec Douglas-Home as clearly a message had to be sent.[36] The East African Department was worried that if the Queen did not send a message, Amin might 'vent his displeasure on the British community'.[37] Sir Alec duly sent off a telegram in the Queen's name, subtly different from the earlier draft:

> I SHOULD LIKE *THROUGH YOU** TO SEND MY GOOD WISHES TO THE PEOPLE OF UGANDA ON THE OCCASION OF THE TENTH ANNIVERSARY CELEBRATIONS OF UGANDA'S INDEPENDENCE.

In 1972 the Foreign Office suggested that the Queen should not send Amin a Christmas card, or to his Acting High Commissioner in London (though he would be invited to the annual Diplomatic Reception at Buckingham Palace and to the Queen's Silver Wedding Service). This entirely accorded with the Queen's wishes.[38]

Only later did the world discover that Amin relished killing and frequently visited the corpses in the morgue to taste the blood of the deceased, an ancient tradition of the Kakwa tribe from which he came. He not only killed but he tortured. 'I like you very much,

---

* Author's italics.

my friend,' he would say, to a hapless victim, then turn to a henchman to instruct: 'Give him the VIP treatment.' In eight years Amin was responsible for the deaths of at least 300,000 Ugandans and he removed the South Asian minority from the country.

★ ★ ★ ★ ★

The death of King Frederik IX of Denmark in January 1972 led to the succession of his elder daughter, Queen Margrethe II, a brilliant Queen, who reigned until 2024. She was a designer of sets and costumes, writer of children's books, an archaeologist, like her grandfather, King Gustaf VI Adolf of Sweden, and more besides. When the Queen installed her as a Lady of the Garter in 1980 she wore a white gown with a ruff collar under her robes and looked like a medieval queen. Her husband, Prince Henrik, the former Henri de Monpezat,* was a less than supportive consort.

Then the Queen and the Duke of Edinburgh, with Princess Anne, undertook a seven-week tour of South East Asia and the Indian Ocean, again using *Britannia*. They visited Chiang Mai and Bangkok in Thailand, sailed to Singapore, visited Kuala Lumpur in Malaysia, and paid a flying visit to Kelantan State on the east coast of the Malay Peninsula. They visited Brunei and paid a one-day visit to Kuching before returning to Singapore. Lord Mountbatten got himself on board for part of the trip. Sir Martin Charteris reported from Kuala Lumpur: 'All goes well with us. Singapore was a most interesting experience: now we are rather more fenced in by Protocol but it is all v. friendly.'[39]

---

* Prince Henrik (1934–2018) came to resent not being made King of Denmark. He liked to voyage in the Danish royal yacht, *Dannebrog*, enjoying the convivial company on board. In 2017, towards the end of his life, he began to issue unpleasant statements, on one occasion announcing that he did not wish to be buried next to the Queen. It was swiftly announced that he was suffering from dementia. The present author once lunched with him in Paris. I told him how magnificent the Queen of Denmark had looked at her Garter installation. Did he thank me for the compliment? No, he looked sickened at the news, an indication of his ungracious attitude.

THE EARLY 1970S

In April 1972 Queen Juliana of the Netherlands paid a state visit to Windsor Castle. Cecil Beaton was an after dinner guest at the castle. Sometimes critical of the Queen's appearance over the years, this night he was ecstatic:

> She was positively dazzling, the light so soft gave her an incandescent look. Her eyes flashed like crystal, her teeth dazzling, her smile radiant. Something has happened to her that has made her a great star. Her dress was not particularly becoming, her hair as dowdy and stiff as ever, but none of these things mattered. She was at the peak of her looks, and they are looks that work. One would not wish to change any detail, the neck straight and long, the poise, the healthiness ... a work of art. It was good to be thrown into such a good mood by the encounter with perfection that one went on to enjoy the other interests of the evening with great relish.[40]

27
THE STATE VISIT TO PARIS, 1972

The Queen's second state visit to France was 'a flattering departure from precedent', according to the British Ambassador, Sir Christopher Soames. Britain had been hoping to join the Common Market at the time of her 1957 visit, but de Gaulle had twice declared: '*Non!*', first in 1962 and again in 1967. Though Britain did not formally join until 1 January 1973, this visit was the precursor. She and Prince Philip came as guests of President Georges Pompidou. It took place between 15 and 19 May. Soames compared the two visits:

> That of 1957 had mainly commemorated the comradeship of the war; it also came just after the ill-fated adventure together at Suez and just before the return of General de Gaulle to the scene and the subsequent parting of the ways. The visit of 1972 only took place because that period of estrangement was over, and its function was to herald a new and positive relationship as partners in the European Community. Where 1957 looked back, 1972 looked forward.[1]

The Common Market legislation was still before Parliament, so the visit was taking place at a delicate moment. But the new *entente* with France was in a euphoric phase. As Sir Christopher put it: 'If the visit had been left until later our new relationship might already have been subject to the strains and abrasions which are inevitable in doing business with a people with so highly developed a sense of self-interest as the French.'[2]

Numerous political and diplomatic problems had to be resolved before the Queen arrived in the French capital. These included how to involve the twenty-four Commonwealth missions accredited to France,[3] and whether the Queen would arrive in a French Caravelle or a British plane, Sir Martin Charteris being determined that she travelled only in British, Canadian, Australian or New Zealand aircraft because otherwise 'the standard of maintenance' could not 'be checked with any certainty'.* This issue moved from 'a point of detail' into a 'point of substance', and very nearly involved the President himself. In the end the Queen arrived in a VC10, but took internal flights in aircraft of the Presidential Flight (it being recalled that she had travelled in a US presidential aircraft in 1957).

The Lord Chamberlain's Office squashed a plan by a French firm to print the Queen's portrait on a yoghurt carton. The French wanted a special portrait photo taken, but the Queen opposed that because it created a bad precedent.[4] By 4 February 1972 the programme was more or less settled, including how to get the insignia of the Order of the Bath to the Élysée Palace in time for the Queen to present it to the President, along with a slight worry that the GCB was being described as *Ordre du Bain* in French.[5]

On 27 March Sir Christopher Soames mulled over the four speeches (three by the Queen and one by Prince Philip), which he hoped would be delivered in French.[6] The first speech by the Queen included the words: 'We may drive on different sides of the road, but we are going the same way.'[7] As late as 28 April Sir Martin Charteris sent the Foreign Secretary's office 'a boiled-down version of that submitted by the Foreign and Commonwealth Office' for his comments, warning, 'The Queen may, of course, make massive alterations to the text, but it will be useful to know whether Sir Alec thinks it is on the right lines.'[8] The Foreign Office was still picking over the speeches three days before the visit. Prince Philip was to address a Chamber of Commerce lunch. His speech was deemed worryingly controversial. He proposed to begin:

---

* In the past Sir Martin had found himself in an embarrassing position with the Turks, Brazilians and Chileans and, as he put it, 'perhaps more to the point, looking to the future, with the Thais, with whom we have had a good deal of difficulty on this point'. On the visit to Thailand in the spring the King had suggested that the Queen should fly from Bangkok to Chiang Mai in a Thai aircraft and she had refused, at which point Thai pride had been deeply hurt. (Charteris to Soames, 24 January 1972, FCO 57/404 – NA).

From time to time, a State Visit may steal the limelight and focus popular attention on the sentimental relationships between two nations, but it is the day to day trade and commerce which really sets the scene.

Prince Philip planned to talk of 'heated exchanges on economic, political and strategic issues', to address the case of a man involved in trade, commerce and industry being eager to 'find and exploit ways in which he can increase his activities and profits', ambitions only restricted by the rules of the game. He wanted to urge Europe to help less fortunate nations, to speak of the need to protect the natural environment, keeping Europe's major rivers and the inland seas of the Mediterranean, Baltic and North Sea clean and healthy. He would conclude: 'My only hope is that we do not become so obsessed with the expectations of success or failure of our immediate plans that we forget the need to solve equally important long-term problems which affect us all.'[9]

The proposed speech was attacked by James Adams, of the European Integration Department of the Foreign Office, who wanted 'drastic amendment', one paragraph being 'a gift to anti-marketeers', another 'a policy statement about Europe's attitude to the Third World', and a further one implying that 'the enlargement of the Community is a rather unimportant development', giving the impression that 'assistance to the Third World in environmental policies will somehow be pursued outside the Community framework'. Adams wrote:

> It will be recalled that at least two speeches by the Duke of Edinburgh on our membership of the Community have excited comment. The first, made in late 1966 or early 1967 in Paris, appeared to indicate enthusiasm in the venture and was warmly (and correctly) received in the Community as evidence that Britain was again preparing itself for membership. Another speech, however, made, I think, last year, appeared to show a marked distaste for the Community and was very much criticised. I think it would be a pity if this impression were reinforced during the state visit to France, and I think the draft speech unamended could be interpreted by the press in that sense.[10]

THE STATE VISIT TO PARIS, 1972

The Foreign Office decided that only Adams's first point should be pressed.

A graver issue was the failing health of the Duke of Windsor. Normally he and the Duchess absented themselves from Paris when formal visits of this nature took place, but he had been seriously ill since the autumn of 1971 with cancer of the throat, which had required several stays in the American Hospital. By the early summer he was back at the house in the Bois de Boulogne under the care of nurses. The Queen had been kept informed of his condition, but only on 28 March did William Heseltine inform Soames that she wished to pay him a private visit at his home in Paris on the afternoon of 18 May. From then on the Duke's ever-worsening condition was a matter of increasing worry.

On 10 May Sir Christopher Soames cabled Sir Alec Douglas-Home to inform him that if the Duke of Windsor died on 12, 13, 14 or on the morning of 15 May, the state visit would have to be cancelled. On 10 May Jacques Sénard, the Chief of Protocol, called on Soames to say, 'The President very much hoped that it would not be necessary to cancel the visit.' Sénard expressed the hope that, should the Duke die on one of those days, the funeral could be arranged to take place after the Queen's visit. Soames suggested that at least the first two days of the visit could still go ahead: 'The programme could of course be modified to enable the Queen to call on the Duchess of Windsor soon after her arrival.' The Ambassador's message was clear:

> Though I realise the difficulties at home I must emphasise that Pompidou clearly attaches the greatest importance to at least this part of the visit taking place and I fear that a total cancellation though rationally understood would be taken amiss and could rankle with him. We should not forget that his visit to Chequers had to be cancelled.[11]

The Ambassador summoned the Duke's French doctor to the Embassy and impressed on him the importance of the Duke not dying during the state visit.[12]

★ ★ ★ ★ ★

As usual the Queen was well briefed. General de Gaulle had died two years earlier. He had tried to be the leader of Western Europe and a friend to the developing countries: 'Although this grandiose vision ultimately showed itself to be an illusion it had a real and deep appeal to the French people, and its afterglow lingers on.' As for the President:

> President Pompidou's eye is not focused on the far horizon. His primary aim is to ensure a leading position for France in Western Europe. To counterbalance the growing strength of Germany, it was necessary to bring in Britain. This was certainly one factor which led the President to the historic decision to lift the Gaullist veto and allow Britain into the EEC on reasonable terms ... President Pompidou hopes to wield influence on the world stage by developing European policies in the French mould ...[13]

Character studies were produced of the principal figures the Queen would meet (including Madame Liliane Bettencourt, later famously involved in disputes over her L'Oréal fortune). One report revealed that Madame Pompidou was the daughter of a country doctor and that her aunt had died in Ravensbrück concentration camp: 'She met and married her husband in 1935 when she was a student in Paris and he a teacher in Marseille. By nature a Bohemian, she has little taste for public life and is said to have had misgivings when General de Gaulle appointed M. Pompidou Prime Minister in 1962.'[14] As the visit approached, Soames noticed that while the French had started off unimaginatively, in the end they 'spared no effort or expense to make the aesthetics of the visit altogether exquisite, and, being the French, they succeeded'.[15] The President was hoping 'that some of the supra-political magic of monarchy might rub off upon himself'.[16]

Finally the last draft for the visit was approved. All was set, the Duke of Windsor did not die so, on the morning of Monday, 15 May, the Queen and the Duke of Edinburgh set off from Windsor Castle to Heathrow and flew into Orly airport in a British VC10. With her were Sir Alec Douglas-Home and his wife, her suite, including the Duchess of Grafton (Mistress of the Robes), Sir Martin Charteris, William Heseltine, Robin Ludlow (Press Secretary), Lord Plunket (Deputy Master of the Household), and others.

THE STATE VISIT TO PARIS, 1972

During the procession in a new open Citroën SM Maserati (especially built for the President) to the Élysée Palace, Robin Ludlow was amused to see the car stop and the President decant the interpreter since the Queen spoke perfectly good French.

The Queen and the Duke were staying at the Grand Trianon at Versailles, part of which is traditionally used to house Presidential guests. When they arrived, a man ran up the Union flag and was told at once to change it for the Royal Standard. There were various receptions and in the evening they walked over to the President's side of the Grand Trianon for dinner in the Galerie des Cotelle and an hour-long performance of the second act of *Giselle* in the Théâtre Louis XV at Versailles. Gérald van der Kemp, the Curator, took them on a short tour of the Petits Appartements (which they had seen in 1957). The cream of French political and social life was present, including the artist Marc Chagall. The French press enjoyed identifying which ladies were dressed by which of the great couturiers – Christian Dior, Pierre Cardin, Givenchy, Balmain or Jean Patou. Sir Christopher Soames regretted the cloudy weather on the first day:

> In Paris the emphasis was on sovereign splendour, on ceremony and spectacle. At the Élysée on the Queen's arrival, M. Pompidou welcomed the entry of Britain into Europe in the same room as that in which the General had twice pronounced his veto on it. Versailles that evening seemed restored to the purposes for which it had been built: it looked like a dream of vanished royal splendour – only the television lights and the crush of prominent French men and women using their elbows to get near the Queen and the Duke of Edinburgh marred the great reception in the Galerie des Glaces. In the streets of Paris the cold and a preference for seeing it all in comfort on the television thinned the crowds a little in the first two days.[17]

Soames wore his GCMG from the wrong shoulder (he corrected it on the second night).

On the second day, the Queen laid a wreath at the tomb of the Unknown Soldier underneath the Arc de Triomphe. Prince Philip made his speech to the Joint Chambers of Commerce, on which Soames commented in classic diplomatic language:

As everyone had come to expect, the Duke of Edinburgh provided an effective element of counterbalance to the visit. His speech to the Chamber of Commerce was very much his own ...[18]

Meanwhile the Queen lunched at the British Embassy with 'eight or nine leading French personalities', including the couturier Pierre Balmain, the writer Jean d'Ormesson and Maurice Druon of the Académie Française. The highlight of the day was the dinner at the British Embassy,* after which the guests were driven to the Champ de Mars for a spectacular equestrian performance. The Ambassador was again disappointed by the weather, but reported: 'Nevertheless some 15,000 Parisians were ready to get happily drenched to the skin on the Champ de Mars where the Queen watched the famous "Cadre Noir" from Saumur (they are for French horsemanship what the Academy is for French literature).'[19] The Garde Républicaine also performed.

On the Wednesday, 'the psychology of the visit changed'. The weather perked up, and the French were impressed to find that 'The British monarchy majesty can subsist with human warmth and simplicity, as it has never done in France whether under the flummery of the Bourbons or the Olympian austerity of General de Gaulle.'[20] The Queen and the Duke flew south and visited Arles. There, Prince Charles joined them from his ship, and Prince Philip visited bulls on the property of Francis Fabre, the airline magnate, then toured a bird observatory and later the flamingo colony. A keen ornithologist, he astonished his hosts by being able to identify a Little Stint, the smallest of the British waders.

After the Pont d'Avignon, St Rémy and the Roman ruins at Glanum, the royal party settled for the night at the famous Oustau de Baumanière at Les-Baux-en-Provence. The Provençal people clapped and cheered in the squares and narrow village streets in numbers 'which made the Préfets happy and the politicians envious, especially the Communist mayor of Arles'.[21]

---

* I was in Paris at that time, visiting the Duke of Windsor's Private Secretary, and recall standing in the crowd to witness their arrival and that of the President and his wife. I was amazed how that narrow street suddenly filled with a cavalcade of police motorcycles.

The press coverage was positive:

> On the day, the Queen's simple elegance and charm, Prince Philip's masculine vigour and the Prince of Wales's youthful glamour captivated the photographers and feature writers rendering further official prompting unnecessary or irrelevant. Britain's Queen drove even local politics from the front pages and television screens. For once the local rag took on the vestments of *Point de Vue*.[22]

An hour after arriving back in Paris the royal party was at Longchamp where the Queen presented the Queen Elizabeth II Cup. At 4.45 p.m., after the sixth race, they were driven to the Duke and Duchess of Windsor's house in the Bois de Boulogne. Every day during the state visit, the Ambassador had telephoned the Duke's doctor with the coded question: 'How is our friend today?' The Duke had been determined to keep going until his niece's visit.

This meeting was important for all concerned. In November 1971 Edward Heath had pointed out that he was worried about the perception of the Duke of Windsor in 'the evening of his life'. He thought that if Emperor Hirohito could visit him, it seemed a shame that the Queen did not.[23] The state visit provided that opportunity and the Queen, Prince Philip and Prince Charles had tea with the Duchess in the library. Sir Martin Charteris, also present, said they talked about 'anything and everything except the one thing on everyone's mind – the poor man dying upstairs'.[24] The Duchess of Grafton recalled that the Queen did not like the pugs jumping up.[25]

After tea the Duchess of Windsor took the Queen upstairs. The Duke had insisted on dressing and was seated in a chair in the upstairs salon, attached to various medical tubes. But he rose to give his niece the statutory Coburg bow, somehow not dislodging the tubes. Some photographers were allowed into the garden to witness the Duchess waving farewell to her royal visitors. It was a gesture of reconciliation, achieved just in time.

That evening there was a small dinner party at the Embassy at which President and Madame Pompidou were present. This was followed by a reception for twelve hundred guests, after which there was an informal dance. The Ambassador enjoyed his party:

Back in Paris on the last evening the two aspects of the visit seemed to come together. The secret formula of style without pomp will long be remembered of the Queen by the 1200 people who came to the British Embassy; the scene in the decorated pavilion as she opened the dancing was enough to widen the most blasé eyes in Paris.[26]

And so the spectacular visit drew to its close. *Britannia* sailed from Rouen with fifty thousand people waving goodbye. 'There is no one else in the world they would do that for,' commented Soames.[27]

Back in Britain, there were some sour notes. Peter Shore, the Labour Opposition spokesman on the European Economic Community (EEC), complained that Heath had used the Queen as a political tool. He condemned the state visit as 'ill-advised and mistimed'. He disapproved of the Crown being used 'as it has been used this week, to give authority to a particular treaty'.[28] Sir Christopher Soames thought otherwise:

> If success is the fulfilment of expectation and intention, this visit more than succeeded. Though it conformed to the traditional pattern of protocol it was far more than just another of those state visits at which the Parisians shrug their shoulders and grumble about the traffic. It was an event in French life. It seized the imagination of the French people and enhanced their view of Britain. The Queen provided for them the magic they expected. They saw her as a figure of royal mystique yet with human warmth. It was this that enabled the visit to accomplish, as nothing else could have done, its essential political purpose. For it was more than merely a glittering and successful international ritual. It was an act of state. It was intended to make its mark on the history of our two countries, and it did so ... I hope you will agree with me that the Queen had a very real and useful job to do in France and, if I may say so without impertinence, she did it to perfection.[29]

28
POLITICS AND FAMILY, 1972–6

Hardly was the Queen back in Britain than the Duke of Windsor died. Had he remained King and if his brother had predeceased his daughter, then on 28 May 1972 Princess Elizabeth would have become Queen that day (and lived to celebrate her Golden Jubilee rather than her Platinum).

Later in the week the Duke's coffin was flown to Britain and he lay in state in the Nave of St George's Chapel, Windsor. The Duchess was not well enough to accompany it, but she flew over on the Friday to be met by Lord Mountbatten and stayed at Buckingham Palace. John Utter, the Duke's Private Secretary, who came with her, recalled that the Queen could not have been kinder to the Duchess, said she could stay at the Palace or come to Windsor, and stay as long as she liked.[1] They lunched together in the Chinese Dining Room. But it would be wrong to suppose this was easy for either side. The Duchess was already unwell, losing her train of thought, and the Queen hardly knew her.

A special lament was played at the beginning of Trooping the Colour on Horse Guards Parade on the Queen's official birthday. As the procession returned, a poignant photograph was taken of the Duchess watching from a window of the Palace. That evening she went down to St George's Chapel, when the doors were closed after the Lying-in-State, to be met by Prince Charles and Lord Mountbatten. The funeral took place in the chapel on Monday, 5 June. The Countess of Avon told Cecil Beaton how solicitous the Queen was, helping the Duchess follow the service: 'The Queen showed a motherly and nanny-like tenderness and kept putting her hand on the Duchess's arm and glove.'[2]

At lunch the Duke of Edinburgh and Lord Mountbatten, sitting either side of the Duchess, raised the question of the Duke's papers.

She was anxious to do what was best and agreed they should come to Windsor. The Queen Mother decided at the last moment to accompany the family when the Duke was buried in the Royal Family's Private Burial Ground at Frogmore.

At the graveside the Queen asked the Duchess which side of him she would wish to be buried. The Duchess loved plain trees, often collecting the leaves and putting them on her dressing-table in Paris. She thought she had lived in his shadow and that no one would put flowers on her grave. She indicated the side under the plain tree, so that the leaves could fall on her grave. The Duchess flew back to Paris in an aircraft of the Queen's Flight.

Her later fate as she fell into the clutches of her sinister lawyer, Maître Suzanne Blum, was of a horror almost beyond belief.*

Within days the Queen and Prince Philip received a state visit from the Grand Duke and Grand Duchess of Luxembourg, part of the process of getting the European heads of state together. The Queen created Grand Duke Jean a Knight of the Garter. In 1984 she appointed him Colonel of the Irish Guards and he regularly rode in the Birthday Parade.

In December the Queen gave John Utter an honorary CVO at Buckingham Palace. She told him that there was now another sad grave in the Frogmore burial ground.† On bank holiday Monday, 28 August, Prince William of Gloucester had competed in the Goodyear International Trophy Air Race near Wolverhampton. He took off with his co-pilot, Vyrell B. Mitchell, but turned too sharply, lost height and the port wing struck some trees, plunging to the ground. The plane burst into flames and both men were killed. The Queen had been due to accompany Prince Philip and Princess Anne to the Munich Olympics, but she cancelled her visit.

In her memoirs, the Duchess of Gloucester wrote the haunting line: 'I was completely stunned and have never been quite the same

---

* For the full saga, see Hugo Vickers, *Behind Closed Doors* (Hutchinson, 2011). There is also a film, *The Duchess and I*, starring Joan Collins and Isabella Rossellini, due in 2026.

† In fact there were two new graves. Admiral the Hon. Sir Alexander Ramsay, husband of the former Princess Patricia of Connaught, died on 8 October, aged ninety-one. He was buried at Frogmore. His widow died in 1974.

since, though I have tried to persuade myself that it was better to have known and lost him than never to have had him at all.'³ Prince William's death impacted the life of his younger brother, Prince Richard, who had married Birgitte van Deurs earlier that summer. Within days he had moved into Kensington Palace* and taken on his brother's duties. Prince Richard had hoped to pursue a career as an architect. He became a working member of the Royal Family, a role he accepted without question and performed for more than fifty years.

★ ★ ★ ★ ★

On 20 November the Queen and the Duke of Edinburgh celebrated their Silver Wedding at Westminster Abbey, after which there was a luncheon at the Guildhall. The Queen began her speech with some disarming words devised for her by Martin Charteris: 'I think everybody will concede that on this of all days I should begin my speech with the words, "My husband and I ..."' After great applause, which effectively silenced that old joke, she continued: 'We – and by that I mean both of us – are most grateful to you for your generous welcome ...'⁴ Thanking the Earl and Countess of Avon for their gift, the Queen wrote: 'It seems incredible to me that we could have been married for as long as twenty-five years – but then one realises that today is Charles's twenty-fourth birthday and he flies the red helicopter like his father now! Thank goodness Edward is only eight and a half still!'⁵

★ ★ ★ ★ ★

Britain entered the Common Market in January 1973 and the Queen and the Duke joined Edward Heath at a gala at the Royal Opera House – *A Fanfare for Europe*. There were more state visits – the President of Mexico in April and General Gowon of Nigeria in June, and a twelve-day tour of Canada, to Ontario, Saskatchewan, Prince Edward Island and Alberta. That visit was marked at a time

---

* The Queen had offered the Duchess Princess Marina's apartment in 1970. She moved there from York House, St James's Palace.

when Canadians were considering whether or not they wanted the Queen to be Queen of Canada or just a friendly visitor from an increasingly detached Britain. In a forthright speech in Toronto the Queen said she had come as Queen of Canada by which she meant of all Canadians. She wanted the Crown to be a link, not only between Commonwealth nations but also between Canadian citizens 'of every national origin and ancestry'.[6] Pierre Trudeau, the Prime Minister, supported the speech, some said for politically opportunist reasons.

The engagement of Princess Anne in the summer of 1973 ended the brief appointment of Robin Ludlow as Press Secretary. He had been recommended by William Heseltine as a complete outsider, but was only there between 1972 and 1973. In his short time at the Palace he ensured that journalists and photographers were assigned better positions for royal occasions. When the Duke of Windsor died, he invited Duggie Dumbrell, the Press Association's Court Correspondent, to sit with him from 8.30 a.m. till 6 p.m. each day to see how he handled press enquiries. He came to grief partly because he told the press that Princess Anne would not be marrying Lieutenant Mark Phillips, and then she did. More than that, however, Anne Hawkins did not think he fitted in. One night he was suddenly called over to the house of Sir Martin Charteris, who told him: 'I want you out. You can leave tonight.' Ludlow offered to stay on until a successor was selected and that was agreed.[7]

He was replaced by the more successful Ronald Allison, who had been BBC Court Correspondent, the first time a reporter had been appointed – a kind of poacher turned gamekeeper. His arrival at the Palace caused some anxiety to one member of staff. Like so many journalists, Allison had had 'a mole' within the Palace. The poor man approached him nervously, but Allison told him they should just forget about it.

Princess Anne

Princess Anne's engagement to Lieutenant Mark Phillips, was announced on 29 May. Born in September 1948, Phillips was an officer in the 1st The Queen's Dragoon Guards, and one of the world's leading three-day eventers. His father, also an officer, was a farmer and the director of a sausage company, and his mother came from the Tiarks banking family. They lived in Gloucestershire. No one suggested that Mark Phillips was in any way academic, and in everyday life he was so paralysed by shyness and indecision that it was hard for him to order his breakfast without stammering in agony. He was widely nicknamed 'Fog'. Lady Diana Cooper, never lost for a sharp analogy, described him as 'a perfect disciple of Krishnamurti – cleansed of all thought',[8] but when in the saddle or conducting a voice over as someone rode round a course, he became brilliantly articulate.

Phillips was champion four times at Badminton – in 1971 and 1972 on his horse Great Ovation, in 1974 on Columbus and in 1981 on Lincoln. He was a reserve member of the British equestrian team for the 1968 Summer Olympics in Mexico. In 1970 he was part of the British three-day-event team that won a world title in 1970, a European title in 1971, and Olympic gold medals in 1972. He was placed thirty-fifth individually in those Olympics.

Not everyone welcomed the union. Jonathan Dimbleby revealed that Prince Charles greeted the news with 'a spasm of shock and amazement'.[9] He resented the break-up of the family unit. *Private Eye* had a field day, sending it up in episodes of *Love in the Saddle*.* The engagement interview was stilted as they tended to be. Princess Anne was bored by the inanity of the questions, and her inarticulate fiancé paralysed into monosyllabic answers.

The wedding on 14 November 1973 was as splendid as anything seen in London for decades. There were full carriage processions to and from Westminster Abbey, the Royal Family out in force, foreign royalty there, including Princess Grace of Monaco, the bride glamorous in a stylish gown, her father in uniform (though his Thistle star fell off in the carriage) and Mark Phillips in a substantial scarlet uniform. The sonorous tones of Michael Ramsey, the Archbishop

---

* It was full of spoof equestrian terms such as spoggling sticks, stog-hooks and saddle-cranks. And when it all comes together, 'A man, a woman, together for a life-time ...' the mood is broken: 'As if sensing her mood, the proud Gaddafi deposited a heap of fresh steaming manure on the dew-spangled turf.' (The penultimate episode.)

of Canterbury, in his golden cope, added thespian dignity to the occasion, which seemed to have come from an age long past.*

1973 was a time of threats from the IRA, and it is possible that both bride and groom were wearing bulletproof vests to protect them from random snipers. Back at the Palace, Lord Mountbatten enjoyed Prince Philip's speech: 'Unaccustomed as I am to speaking ... at breakfast ...' Mountbatten was as charitable in his diary about the groom's speech: 'Mark made a very modest and nice little reply in such a low voice that not everybody heard what he said.'[10] Fortunately Idi Amin did not materialise in London. He had once proposed that he should marry Princess Anne to patch up British-Ugandan relations and had threatened to attend.

Mountbatten was impressed that Prince Charles insisted on having a twenty-fifth birthday party that night because he did not want his mother to feel alone and unhappy after her daughter had gone. 'What a sweet and thoughtful person Charles is,' noted Mountbatten.[11]

A year later, on 22 March 1974, Princess Anne was nearly kidnapped in the Mall. In an interview with Michael Parkinson in Australia in 1983, she related how the car had been stopped at about 8 p.m., and a man with a gun tried to make her get out. In the fracas four shots were fired in which three men were badly wounded. With impressive sangfroid, Princess Anne refused to get out: 'He said I had to go with him ... I wasn't going to go with him.' He was not expecting that and did not have a plan B. There ensued what she called 'a tedious discussion'. She was dragged partly out of the car, but got in again. 'The back of my dress split – all the shoulders went and that was his most dangerous moment. I lost my rag at that stage.'[12] She ended up on the floor of the car with Mark Phillips on top of her. Eventually rescue came and the fleeing assailant was floored in St James's Park.

Prince Charles managed to call his sister from San Diego. He was

---

* Michael Ramsey had been the first Bishop to do homage to the Queen in 1952. He was eccentric. He once stopped in a procession and changed his trousers in the middle of the aisle. So the civil servants warned the Queen that he might do something eccentric. The next day Tommy Lascelles reported that 'fortunately or unfortunately' he had shown nothing but perfect decorum (Owen Chadwick, *Michael Ramsey*, pp. 77–8).

immensely impressed by her 'bravery and superb obstinacy ... My admiration for such an incredible sister knows no bounds.'[13] The Queen and Prince Philip were abroad at the time. Lord Mountbatten, travelling with them, praised Princess Anne as 'plucky'. Prince Philip said: 'Yes! They tried it on the wrong girl, didn't they?' adding presently, 'If the man had succeeded in abducting Anne she would have given him a hell of a time in captivity!'[14]

A ransom letter demanding £1 million was found near the car. On 15 August, her twenty-fourth birthday, Princess Anne was appointed GCVO for her 'calm and brave behaviour' and Mark Phillips was appointed CVO. Inspector James Beaton, her protection officer, who was badly wounded, was awarded the George Cross. Following this incident there was a discreet but definite increase in royal security, with always a back-up vehicle to accompany a royal car on official engagements.

Zaïre State Visit

One of the most disagreeable state visits the Queen was obliged to host was that of President Mobutu of Zaïre between 11 and 14 December.

Mobutu Sese Seko had been President since 1965. Born in the Belgian Congo in 1930, he had risen above a difficult early life, learned to read and write fluently, become a good sportsman and eventually a stowaway. He was caught and forced into the Belgian Congolese Army. He studied the works of Churchill, de Gaulle and Machiavelli and became a journalist. He was wedded to the idea of challenging colonial rule. He served as secretary to Patrice Lumumba (Leader of the Mouvement Nationale Congolais (MNC), considered by many to be an old-style Communist) and made his name. In 1960 he arrested Lumumba, causing Harold Macmillan to write in language which jars uncomfortably in today's climate, 'that they will kill him (and perhaps eat him!) wh[ich] will bring discredit on the Congo Govt'.[15] They killed him in January 1961. Mobutu, by then a general, seized power in a bloodless coup in 1965. He resorted to torture to hold power. Four Cabinet ministers were executed in public, the Education Minister Pierre Mulele had his eyes pulled from their sockets, his genitals ripped off, his arms and legs amputated while still alive. In 1971 the country was renamed Zaïre and the next year Mobutu renamed himself 'Mobutu Sese Seko Nkuku Ngbendu Wa Za Banga' (the all-powerful warrior who, because of his endurance and inflexible will to win, goes from conquest to conquest, leaving fire in his wake). Such was the man who was invited to Britain in 1973.

The state visit was the result of pressure from successive British Ambassadors to Zaïre. Mobutu was due to visit London in June 1971, but cancelled the visit when he discovered the Queen would not be meeting him personally at the airport.

The problem with this visit was that the President made all the decisions. The Zaïrians tested everyone's patience by continually altering the plans; they were inefficient, arrogant and boorish. The President did not help by attacking Britain in a speech to the United Nations on 4 October, which was published in a special supplement of *The Times*, the day of his arrival.

Mobutu was told that his official suite must contain no more than twelve people. In August, without asking the Queen, he announced he would be bringing his three-year-old son. The names of the suite were given only on 21 November and it consisted of sixty-seven people. On 4 December the Zaïre Ambassador told the Lord Chamberlain's Office that he was giving a reception at Claridge's for the President on 14 December and wished to invite all of the Royal Family: 'This he did, but not surprisingly none were able to attend at such short notice.'[16]

On the day, when the Duke of Kent mounted the steps of the plane to welcome the President, he was almost knocked over by a dozen Zaïre cameramen and police pouring down them. The President himself was nearly knocked down and his arrival on the tarmac was 'an undignified muddle'. To the horror of officials, they spotted a figure carrying a Yorkshire terrier down the steps in contravention of quarantine laws. It was taken to Buckingham Palace and a steak ordered. The Queen was furious. She sent her Corgis to Windsor and ordered the dog to be sent away. It was flown that day to the Zaïre Embassy in Brussels.

There was further chaos. There was no wreath for the President to lay on the tomb of the Unknown Warrior, and he made the wrong speech to the Lord Mayor of Westminster. When he addressed the London Chamber of Commerce, he was meant to speak briefly but ended up talking in French for forty minutes. At the Guildhall his reply to the Lord Mayor's address was 'a mumbled thank-you'.

When the visit was over, Sir Martin Charteris asked the Foreign Office what precisely the positive dividends of this visit had been. With its habitual denial, the Foreign Office concluded:

> There was no positive dividend from this visit, but that, however awkward President Mobutu showed himself to be as a guest (and clearly he and his party lived up to the Zaïrians' reputation for boorishness), there would certainly have been a very substantial negative reaction had the invitation not been extended. Mobutu personally appears to have enjoyed his visit and to have appreciated the attention paid to him, particularly by HM The Queen. We can reasonably hope that the visit has gained for us some goodwill, on which we may hope to draw in our future dealings with Zaïre. We have quite considerable investments in Zaïre and, although this matter is in no way related, we hope that the State Visit may ease our path in dealing with the effects of a wave of nationalisation aimed at foreign countries which the President announced on 30 November.*[17]

---

* In later years Mobutu was twice re-elected in single-candidate elections. He amassed a considerable personal fortune with palaces and cars for himself while many Zaïrians starved. He thought nothing of chartering Concorde to take his family shopping in Paris. He indulged in kleptocracy and nepotism. He capitalised on Cold War tensions. He maintained largely good relations with the United States. With Belgium he was either intimate or hostile. With Soviet Russia he was cautious and suspicious. He visited China and met Chairman Mao, China being anxious to halt Soviet gains in Central Africa. In May 1990, when the Cold War ended, Mobutu lifted the ban on other political parties. He grew physically frailer and during an absence in Europe for medical treatment for prostate cancer, the Tutsis captured much of eastern Zaïre. Then rebels helped by the Ugandans and Rwandans marched towards Kinshasa. Mobutu was unable to resist and, following failed peace talks, on 16 May 1997 he was overthrown and fled. Laurent Kabila took over as President. Marie-Antoinette Mobutu, who had accompanied him to London, died of heart failure in Switzerland in 1977, after which he married his mistress, Bobi Ladawa. Mobutu died in Rabat on 7 September 1997.

Edward Heath

The Queen undertook a two-month tour of Pacific Island Territories, New Zealand, Australia and Indonesia from January to March. Princess Anne and Captain Mark Phillips flew out with her, and they were joined by the Duke of Edinburgh and the Prince of Wales in Christchurch for the Commonwealth Games. In the midst of it, her dual role as Queen of Australia and of the United Kingdom clashed. Edward Heath had been warned about the Queen's overseas tour, but nevertheless he went to the polls. On 6 February he requested the Queen to grant him dissolution of Parliament,* sending her a telegram, which reached her on board *Britannia*.

The Queen was meant to return for Polling Day, set for 28 February, but on that day she was opening the Australian Parliament in Canberra. She flew back to preside over the creation of a new government on 1 March. Following the General Election, Edward Heath failed to win a majority. In a House of Commons of 635, Labour had 301, the Conservatives 297 and the minor parties 37, which included the Liberals with fourteen. Heath reported to the Queen, then attempted to create a coalition with Jeremy Thorpe, Leader of the Liberal Party, which would have secured an overall majority. He failed. On 4 March he tendered his resignation. As he left the Palace his protection officer said goodbye to him: 'You are no longer Prime Minister and therefore no longer entitled to special protection.'[18]

The Queen sent for Harold Wilson and requested him to form an administration. On the following two days the Conservative ministers were received in audience, some delivering up the seals of office and others on relinquishing their appointments. New Labour ministers were received and new Privy Counsellors sworn in. Wilson maintained that his March 1974 Cabinet was the most experienced of the century, even more so than Campbell-Bannerman's in 1905. Some thirteen of its members had sat in Cabinet before.

On 12 March the Queen opened the new Parliament, arriving in day clothes, and there was no state procession. She was escorted

---

* A dissolution could not be granted by the Counsellors of State, though on that day the Queen Mother and Princess Margaret held several Councils, acting as 'Counsellors of State under Her Majesty's Commission'.

into the Palace of Westminster by the Marquess of Cholmondeley, Lord Great Chamberlain, in morning dress and carrying his wand. The following day she resumed her Pacific tour. She and the Duke of Edinburgh returned home with Lord Mountbatten on 23 March.

During the following months the Tories could have engineered the defeat of the Government because of its precarious position in the House of Commons. They refrained from so doing. Theoretically the Queen could have refused to grant another dissolution though in practice she would have been unlikely to do so. In October Harold Wilson called a further election at which he secured 319 seats, an overall majority of three. This time the State Opening was conducted as usual with carriage processions and the Queen wearing the Imperial State Crown.

From October 1974 until March 1976 the Queen found herself with Harold Wilson as Prime Minister once again. He was a familiar face.

★ ★ ★ ★ ★

The Queen with her filly, Highclere, in 1974

The Queen hardly ever travelled for pleasure. In 1967 she visited Guy de Rothschild at Ferrières. In June 1974 she made another rare private visit to France to see Highclere win the 1,000 Guineas at Newmarket, and then won the Prix de Diane at Chantilly. On 30 April Queen Margrethe of Denmark and Prince Henrik came on a state visit to Windsor, arriving at Greenwich in the royal yacht, *Dannebrog*. They were followed in July by the King and Queen of Malaysia.

The prime events of 1975 were the Queen's visit to Mexico and the important state visit to Emperor Hirohito in Japan. In September 1975 she assumed the role of Queen of Papua New Guinea. Here she was colloquially known in the local pidgin language as 'Missis Kwin' and 'Mama belong big family'. General Franco died in Spain. As was appropriate, the Ambassador represented the Queen at the funeral, and then Prince Philip attended the inauguration of King Juan Carlos as King, thus marking the restoration of the Spanish monarchy. The young King of Sweden came on a state visit, to Edinburgh in July.

Patrick Plunket

On 28 May 1975 Patrick Plunket died. He and Lady Margaret Hay (a former lady-in-waiting) died within days of each other in the summer of 1975. To a letter of sympathy from Jim Orr, the Queen replied: 'Patrick especially will be very much missed for his great talents which seemed to have blossomed in this atmosphere. It is tragic to see his lovely little house at St James's which he never managed to live in ...'[19] He was a considerable loss.

Princess Margaret

In March 1976 Princess Margaret's marriage to Lord Snowdon came to an end when the *News of the World* printed a photograph of the Princess on holiday in Mustique with her young friend, Roddy Llewellyn, subtly editing out the other people sitting opposite. This gave Snowdon the opportunity to take umbrage. He was in Japan and issued a statement saying how sorry he was at the collapse of the marriage. Because his friends were more loyal to him than some of Princess Margaret's were to her, he was more sympathetically respected in the press. He succeeded in painting himself as the victim, to the surprise of many of their mutual friends.

Christopher Balfour, a friend to both, wrote: 'To say their marriage wasn't going well would be an understatement. They were getting on incredibly badly, something I had the misfortune to witness first-hand.' He related how Snowdon invited six dancers back for dinner at Kensington Palace after a performance at Covent Garden, knowing perfectly well that this would cause a crisis. The evening became so unpleasant that Balfour and Pamela, Lady Harlech, threatened to leave so as not to witness more rudeness or disrespect to Princess Margaret.[20]

The Queen had been so concerned that she drove alone to Nymans Cottage in Sussex on his mother's estate, to talk to Snowdon. When she got there, she found him entertaining a group of friends in an atmosphere of drugs. Her mission was doomed. She had no option but to leave.[21]

Lord Harewood had been the first member of the Royal Family to divorce and this had caused a sensation in 1967. Princess Margaret's separation was more serious, as she was closer to the throne. There was a hail of publicity. Princess Margaret was religious. She did not want to divorce. They left it for two years and she finally accepted the divorce in 1978 so that her husband could marry his pregnant girlfriend. She herself did not remarry. Snowdon married Lucy Lindsay-Hogg on 15 December 1978. Their daughter, Frances, was born on 17 July 1979.

Harold Wilson

From the point of view of publicity, it was fortuitous that Harold Wilson chose 16 March to resign as Prime Minister. It pushed the Snowdon separation off the front pages.

The resignation fulfilled a plan Wilson had discussed with the Queen the previous September at Balmoral. At that point his wife Mary pencilled 16 March 1976 as the hoped-for date. There was none of the will-he-won't-he shenanigans of Churchill between 1952 and 1955. Nevertheless his biographer, Philip Ziegler, wrote: 'It is still a matter of wonder that Wilson did not change his mind as the chosen date approached.'[22]

There was much speculation about the resignation. Ziegler suggested that the fight had gone out of him. He had enjoyed defeating Heath; he was pleased to break Asquith's record for time in office. But he began to feel ill before confrontations or sackings. Prime Minister's Questions in the House preyed on his nerves. Administrative matters became tiring. He started drinking brandy before difficult meetings and developed elements of paranoia, believing there were threats against him. On the other hand he was not yet sixty. Ziegler was an establishment biographer. He advanced various elaborate theories about possible scandals that might have caused the resignation, but concluded: 'Material so melodramatic would be a delight for any biographer.'[23] He found no supporting evidence. His conclusion was that Wilson had aged considerably since 1964; there may have been mild confabulation of the brain, and there were serious worries about political issues, such as inflation, which he did not want to face.

Wilson was pleased that the Queen and Prince Philip came to dinner at Number 10 on 23 March 1976 and stayed until 11.45 p.m. But apart from that, his departure from Downing Street on 5 April aroused little emotion.

Field Marshal Lord Montgomery died on 24 March,* leaving a vacancy in the Order of the Garter. These Orders of Chivalry create unlikely bedfellows. Wilson was delighted to be given the Garter on St George's Day, while the Duke of Grafton (the former Lord Euston), the other appointee, was irritated to have to walk beside him in the procession. At the Garter lunch, the Queen Mother looked across the table and saw the Queen sitting next to Wilson, laughing her head off. She said to Lord Avon: 'Isn't it wonderful how she's tamed him?'[24]

Wilson's health declined quite quickly after his resignation.

---

* For reasons of protocol the Queen was represented by Prince Philip at the military funeral at St George's Chapel, but she went out, unrecognised, in a headscarf, to watch the procession in Windsor.

Eventually he would have to have a policeman walk beside him in the Garter procession and would forget his waistcoat or to wear his plumed hat. Mary Wilson would steer him about when she could. Alzheimer's and colon cancer took over. He died on 25 May 1995.

A ballot was held for the new leader, and James Callaghan emerged as the next Prime Minister, winning comfortably over Michael Foot in the last round.

James Callaghan

James Callaghan, who served from March 1976 until May 1979, was the first Prime Minister landed on the Queen without her having any say in the matter – not even a tenuous one. Since leaders were elected within the party, she lost one of the key residual powers of the monarch (the remaining one being to dissolve Parliament). She knew Callaghan well enough as he had held all the great offices of state, including Home Secretary at the time of the Prince of Wales's Investiture. Like Wilson, he was a monarchist, albeit a bit more formal in his relations with her.

Callaghan offered no unusual insights into the Queen's character in his memoirs, *Time & Chance*. Elsewhere he made the same points as all prime ministers – the enjoyment of audiences, the knowledge that the conversations were confidential, and he made the additional point of the Queen offering 'friendliness' rather than 'friendship'.[25] He was in many ways a traditionalist, patriotic, loving the Royal Navy and respecting the Boy Scouts. The Tory politician Kenneth Baker described him as 'the Prime Minister of Dock Green'.[26]

★ ★ ★ ★ ★

On 21 April 1976 the Queen celebrated her fiftieth birthday with a ball for five hundred friends at Windsor Castle. There were state visits from President Geisel of Brazil in May and President Giscard d'Estaing of France in June. This visit included a reception at the Royal Scottish Academy in Edinburgh and a luncheon at Holyroodhouse. Princess Margaret was sent to meet him, possibly as a way of restoring her public image. The Queen looked quietly amused when the officer of the guard addressed the French President in French with embarrassingly schoolboy English emphasis: *'Monsieur le Président – La Garde d'honneur du Garde Écossaise est prêt à votre inspection.'*[27] Giscard himself made his speeches in an enjoyable Maurice Chevalier accent.

In May the Queen and Prince Philip paid a state visit to Finland and in July they attended bicentennial celebrations in the United States before going on to Canada to open the Olympic Games in Montreal. In advance of the Canadian visit, Pierre Trudeau, the Prime Minister, launched an attack in which he stated: 'We don't need the Queen or Harold Wilson to run Canada.' These Games inspired more courage from the Queen. Fears were expressed that there might be terrorism, as had happened in Munich in 1972. The Queen opened the Games and stood for an hour, an immobile target, as the athletes paraded past, and all was well. Princess Anne rode Goodwill, the Queen's horse, in these Olympics, later describing this as 'a rare, possibly unique case, of the same person breeding both horse and rider'.[28] At the end of 1976 Prince Charles left the Royal Navy.

The Queen by Baron – a photo to mark her 27th birthday in April 1953

The Queen on the way to the Accession Council at St James's Palace, February 1952

Queen Mary at the premiere of the film *The Woman in the Hall*, at the Leicester Square Theatre, 31 October 1947. She died on 24 March 1953

The Queen and Prince Philip with Anthony and Clarissa Eden just before they left Balmoral after their visit in October 1955

The Queen and Prince Philip on the balcony of Buckingham Palace, with their children, after the Coronation, 2 June 1953

The Queen with her children on holiday at Balmoral in the summer of 1952

Trooping the Colour as Colonel-in-Chief, Grenadier Guards, 11 June 1960. The 3rd Battalion, Grenadier Guards trooped for the last time before being disbanded

The Queen and Prince Philip after she opened the 5th session of the 30th Parliament in Hobart, Tasmania, 25 February 1954

The Queen attending a session at the Federal House of Representatives in Lagos, Nigeria, February 1956

The Queen decorating a man at Rideau Hall, Ottawa, July 1959, during her 45-day visit

The Queen, Queen Mother and Prince Charles at Princess Margaret's wedding, 6 May 1960

The Queen with the Duke of Norfolk at the Derby, 3 June 1960

The Royal Family leaving St George's Chapel after the dedication of the King George VI Memorial Chapel, 31 March 1969

The Queen speaking at a State Banquet in Malaysia in 1971. The wife of the Malaysian Prime Minister and Princess Anne are on her right

The Queen and Prince Philip with the Duchess of Windsor after the Duke's funeral, 5 June 1972

The Queen with her cousin Gerald Lascelles, about to tour his Belle Plantation sugar factory in Barbados on her Caribbean tour, 15 February 1966

The Queen with the newly engaged Prince of Wales and Lady Diana Spencer, 1981

29
AUSTRALIA, 1975

The biggest political crisis in Australia's history occurred in 1975 when the Governor-General, Sir John Kerr, dismissed the Prime Minister, Gough Whitlam. As a constitutional monarch, the Queen's role was to support, not to interfere. Sir John Kerr was appointed Governor-General on 11 July 1974 on the advice of Gough Whitlam. The only control she exercised over him was that he had to ask her permission to leave Australia to go overseas.*

Kerr would write frequently to Sir Martin Charteris, who would show his letters to the Queen, then reply, often consulting William Heseltine, because he was Australian. Charteris's letters back contained phrases such as 'I gave this to the Queen this morning and I know she will read and absorb it in the next day or two.'[1] Kerr wrote to her about the illness of his first wife (who died on 9 September 1974), whether the Prince of Wales should buy a property in Australia, even that he was overweight, and had lost twenty-two pounds in two weeks. Clearly, he took comfort in passing on this news, and from time to time Sir Martin boosted him. 'You are certainly having a brisk time as Governor-General,'[2] he wrote. Another time he described Kerr's role as no bed of roses.

By July 1975 the Labor Government was falling apart. When the Liberal Leader, Malcolm Fraser, blocked supply in the Senate,† Whitlam should have gone to the country but was determined to

---

* Kerr had to ask permission to attend the Coronation of the King of Nepal in 1975.

† When, controversially, Albert Patrick Field (1910–90), an unknown figure, was appointed to the Senate by the premier of Queensland in June 1975, as an anti-Whitlam member, Gough Whitlam described him as 'an individual of the utmost obscurity, from which he rose and to which he sank with equal speed'.

serve out his three years. The Governor-General was left in a quandary. Was he a mere figurehead, or should he take action? He attempted to break the impasse.

A leader in the *Canberra Times* advanced the idea that he 'could, for good and sufficient reasons, revoke the commissions of a Prime Minister, or of other ministers. It is within his power to take steps that could lead to dissolution of the Parliament and to a general election.'[3] Sir John assured Charteris: 'I have no intention of course of acting in the way suggested. There is ample room for the democratic processes to unfold.'[4]

The situation worsened and Kerr was afraid that Whitlam might advise the Queen to terminate his commission as Governor-General and replace him with someone more amenable. On 2 October 1975, Charteris wrote:

> If such an approach was made you may be sure that The Queen would take most unkindly to it ... but I think it is right that I should make the point that at the end of the road The Queen, as a Constitutional Sovereign, would have no option but to follow the advice of her Prime Minister.[5]

Kerr told the Palace that at a dinner Whitlam had jested: 'It could be a question of whether I get to the Queen first for your recall or you get in first with my dismissal.'[6] By 22 October he believed that the crisis was still political rather than constitutional. On 4 November Charteris told him he believed the reserve powers still existed, even if they had not been used for many years: 'The fact that you have powers is recognised, but it is also clear that you will only use them in the last resort and then only for constitutional and not for political reasons.'[7] Sir Martin quoted to Kerr what Arthur Meighen,* a Canadian, had written about the role of their Governor-General:

> The plain duty of the Governor-General ... is to make sure that responsible government is maintained, that the rights of parliament are respected, that the still higher rights of the people are held sacred.

---

* Arthur Meighen (1874–1960), Canadian politician and lawyer, who twice served as Prime Minister of Canada in the 1920s.

It is his duty to make sure that parliament is not stifled by government, but that every government is held responsible to parliament, and every parliament held responsible to the people.[8]

On 10 November, the Chief Justice of Australia, Sir Garfield Barwick, advised the Governor-General that in the present circumstances, the Prime Minister ceased to retain his commission and that, as Governor-General, it was his 'constitutional authority and duty' to invite the Leader of the Opposition to secure supply, and form a caretaker government pending a general election.

The following day Sir John Kerr did just that. He terminated the commission of Whitlam's administration and invited Malcolm Fraser to form an interim government. In a long memorandum, he explained that his reason was to find a democratic and constitutional solution to the present crisis and to break the deadlock.[9] Whitlam made his famous outburst: 'Well may we say God Save the Queen – because nothing will save the Governor-General.' A few days later the Governor-General called this: 'a foolish unrestrained attack on me ... which did him much harm'.[10]

Kerr had not told the Palace of his intended action. Sir David Smith, his official secretary, telephoned London in the small hours of the night and was put through to William Heseltine. He thought better of calling the Queen at 2.30 a.m. but went to the Palace early to be sure to reach her before she heard the news at 8 a.m. There he found an irate Martin Charteris, who had been called at 4.15 a.m. by Gough Whitlam, speaking 'as a private citizen'.

On 12 November Gordon Scholes, Speaker of the House of Representatives, wrote to Buckingham Palace asking the Queen to restore Whitlam as Prime Minister. Sir Martin repeated politely that it would not be proper for the Queen to get involved. Under the Constitutional Act, these matters were within the jurisdiction of the Governor-General.

On 17 November, Kerr sent the Palace a long account of the business, in which he mentioned that should Whitlam win the general election, 'as he may well do', then he was considering it might be necessary for him to step down as Governor-General. On the same day Sir Martin wrote:

If I may say so with the greatest respect, I believe that in NOT informing The Queen what you intended to do before doing it, you acted not only with perfect constitutional propriety but also with admirable consideration for Her Majesty's position.[11]

Sir John had been within his rights to break the political deadlock, creating a situation where the Australian people had their say in a general election. Sir Robert Menzies, Australia's longest serving Prime Minister, wrote privately to Kerr to say his action was 'beyond reproach'. He commended his right under constitutional law and his 'remarkable moral courage'.[12]

Gough Whitlam remained bitter about Kerr, and produced a massive defence of his government in *The Whitlam Government 1972–1975*. His main gripe concerned Kerr's actions after the dismissal:

> Every reader and viewer knows how Kerr deceived me and failed to act on my advice during the dispute between the House of Representatives and the Senate in November 1975. It is not so universally realised how he showed repeated contempt for the House of Representatives. He dismissed me and appointed Fraser while an Opposition motion of no confidence in my Government was still being debated. After the Senate had passed the Budget and the House of Representatives had carried a motion of no confidence in Fraser, Kerr maintained Fraser in office. He thus did not wait for the result of the vote of no confidence in me and disregarded the result of the vote of no confidence in Fraser. Moreover he had his proclamation dissolving both Houses of Parliament before he agreed to see the Speaker who was formally conveying to him the House's resolution of no confidence in Fraser and of confidence in me.[13]

Whatever Whitlam thought, he disregarded the Governor-General's important stipulation in appointing Fraser that there should be a general election, so that ultimately the democratic process could get underway and the people could decide who they wanted to govern them. When this happened in December, Fraser won a landslide majority.

★ ★ ★ ★ ★

Sir David Smith, a considerable constitutional expert (who advised both the Palace and Sir John Kerr), dismissed Whitlam's claim that it had been a coup: 'The change of government was in accordance with the letter, the conventions and the spirit of the Australian Constitution, and no one knows that better than Whitlam himself.'[14]

Buckingham Palace would have preferred that a political solution be reached before the crisis was allowed to get to its final stage. The thought was that the Senate might have caved in.[15] The Queen received hundreds of letters complaining that the Governor-General had behaved in a way that destroyed democratic government. The Palace supported the Governor-General and pointed out that he caused recourse to the ultimate democratic jurisdiction – a general election.

For forty-five years, the Governor-General's correspondence with the Palace was kept secret. An academic and apparently a committed Republican, Jenny Hocking fought for four years to change this and in 2020 she succeeded. Jenny Hocking concluded the letters shattered the last illusion of 'royal neutrality and non-involvement'[16]. Paul Keating, pro-republican and later Prime Minister, dismissed her claims: 'The idea that the Queen may have wished or actively conspired in arrangements with Sir John Kerr to affect a party political outcome in Australia amounts to no more than tilting at shadows.'[17]

30
THE SILVER JUBILEE, 1977

As 1977 approached, the thoughts of the Royal Household turned to how to mark the Queen's Silver Jubilee, twenty-five years on the throne. James Callaghan did not want government money expended on a national celebration, and the Queen, with her innate modesty, did not want to put the nation to expense. However, Sir Martin Charteris was keen that she should be celebrated and conceived the idea of her visiting all the realms of which she was Head of State, and travelling extensively through the United Kingdom. As usual, he read the mood better than the detractors.

'Spontaneous' celebrations need to be planned and the Jubilee was no exception. Historically, Jubilees have been inspired by a lone voice coming up with the idea. In 1809 the Committee of Merchants and Bankers of London provided the spark for George III to celebrate his Golden Jubilee the following year. Lord Braye, a Liberal Unionist and Catholic peer, prompted Queen Victoria to mark her Golden Jubilee in 1887.

It took Illtyd Harrington, Deputy Leader of the Greater London Council, to launch a campaign in the *Evening Standard* in August 1975, advocating 'a Royal Jubilee Festival'. This prompted Roy Jenkins, the Labour Home Secretary, to announce in the House of Commons that the Silver Jubilee would be celebrated in the summer of 1977. The London Celebrations Committee for The Queen's Silver Jubilee was formed, chaired by the patrician Earl of Drogheda, Chairman of the Royal Opera House and the *Financial Times*.* He outlined what he had hoped to achieve:

---

* I worked for this Committee from February 1977, and wrote the authorised history of its work: *We Want The Queen* (Debrett, 1977). That book was somewhat controlled by the Committee. I said more in *A Walk for The Queen* (The Dovecote Press, 2012).

We are very lucky to have the Queen and the Royal Family and not a depressing figure like a Jimmy Carter or an even more depressing figure like a Gerald Ford. The Queen works very hard and she doesn't lose her mystique. Thank goodness they haven't taken to riding bicycles like the Scandinavians ... The Jubilee was a peculiar blend of official ceremony with our celebrations grafted on. Without our Committee there would have been no fireworks, many fewer concerts, nothing on the river. It has all been a great success.

Jeffrey Sterling (Chairman of Town and City Properties) was chosen as Deputy Chairman and Honorary Treasurer: 'One of the few property men in London, who hasn't gone bust,' said Lord Drogheda. 'So he must be good.'[1] He raised money from the City of London. He made sure that the Committee included someone from every aspect of London life, civic to sport, culture to the environment, so that he could call on them if something needed to be resolved.

Prince Charles summoned all the Lord Lieutenants to a meeting at St James's Palace and told them to make sure the young people enjoyed the Jubilee. The Duke of Beaufort commented: 'That's what we're trying to do, to make sure that they remember 1977 as a year of great celebration.'[2]

The British tend to be apathetic and suddenly wake up to realise there is fun to be had. Until the end of April, few people in Britain were interested but suddenly Jubilee fever spread throughout the United Kingdom, in a great wave that continued until the end of that year.

The actual anniversary of King George VI's death, Accession Day, 6 February, fell on a Sunday. The Royal Family simply went to church. A small crowd gathered at the gates to Royal Lodge to see the Queen arrive. The Sunday papers generally took the line that the Queen's reputation had gone from strength to strength, and that she had de-mythologised the monarchy without detracting from its mystique.

The major overseas tours were either in the first or last part of the year. On 9 February the Queen and Duke of Edinburgh departed for Western Samoa (a state visit to Chief Malietoa Tanumafili II), Tonga, Fiji, Australia, New Zealand and Papua New Guinea, the Queen returning to Britain on 31 March. In Tonga the Queen was served avocado and prawns. She stuck to the avocado. Some German photographers ate more adventurously and went green. The Queen was given a suckling pig to eat on board *Britannia*. As soon as the donors were safely out of sight, it went overboard.[3]

While in Australia, the retirement of Sir John Kerr was discussed. He had been widely denigrated since the 'dismissal' issue. More or less whenever he appeared in public, he was confronted with demonstrations and his reliance on alcohol landed him in embarrassing situations. At his farewell audience with the Queen, it was agreed that he should go, but the timing was not set. Thus Kerr was able to come to London for the Jubilee celebrations.*

On 4 May the Queen received addresses from the House of Commons and the House of Lords in Westminster Hall: 'In a meeting of Sovereign and Parliament, the essence of Constitutional Monarchy is reflected.' She reflected on the changes in Britain since 1952 and reaffirmed her position as Queen of the United Kingdom. Her key words were:

> The problems of progress, the complexities of modern administration, the feeling that Metropolitan Government is too remote from the lives of ordinary men and women, these among other things have helped to revive an awareness of historic national identities in these Islands. They provide the background for the continuing and keen discussion of proposals for devolution to Scotland and Wales within the United Kingdom. I number Kings and Queens of England and of Scotland, and Princes of Wales among my ancestors and so I can readily understand these aspirations.
>
> But I cannot forget that I was crowned Queen of the United Kingdom of Great Britain and Northern Ireland.

---

* In August Charteris and Sir Paul Hasluck, a former Governor-General, met to discuss their concerns that Kerr might be planning to write his memoirs. He was put on notice that he must not reveal his communications with the Queen. (He published *Matters for Judgment* [Aprolon, 1978].) Hasluck came away with the view that Charteris was not impressed by Kerr and was glad that he was going. Just before he stepped down, there was an unfortunate incident when he was visibly inebriated, presenting the Melbourne Cup in November 1977. Because of the hostility, he moved to London for a time where he presented a somewhat 'worse for wear' appearance in certain London clubs. I remember seeing him at Royal Victorian Order services. He died of a brain tumour in 1991.

THE SILVER JUBILEE, 1977

Perhaps this Jubilee is a time to remind ourselves of the benefits which union has conferred, at home and in our international dealings, on the inhabitants of all parts of this United Kingdom.[4]

In the same month the Queen entertained President Jimmy Carter and other world leaders to dinner at Buckingham Palace when they attended the economic summit meeting – the third G7 Summit, at which world leaders addressed issues such as creating jobs, reducing inflation and energy issues. On 17 May she undertook the Scottish part of the Jubilee celebrations, arriving in Glasgow for carriage rides, with Household Cavalry escort, and visiting Cumbernauld, Stirling, Perth, Dundee and Aberdeen. In Edinburgh, at St Giles' Cathedral, the Queen installed the Prince of Wales as a Knight of the Thistle.

The Queen as Sovereign of the Order of the Thistle, followed by her uncle, The Duke of Gloucester – 27 June 1952

Back in London, on 30 May the entire Royal Family (including Princess Alice, Countess of Athlone, who could remember Queen Victoria's 1887 Jubilee) attended the Silver Jubilee Gala of opera and ballet at Covent Garden. The audience were in white tie, with Orders and decorations, and tiaras abounded. Trumpeters from Kneller Hall opened the programme with a fanfare, Trojans marched down the aisles to an extract from Berlioz's *The Trojans*, and in the second half, there were some choral dances from the ill-fated Coronation *Gloriana*, and Dame Margot Fonteyn and Rudolf Nureyev spun across the stage in a *pas de deux* from Liszt.

The more public Jubilee celebrations began on 6 June when the Queen lit the first of 102 bonfires in Windsor Great Park. This was the work of another committee in Windsor, which put together an impressive array of events through the summer. The bonfire plan was created by Major Michael Parker (not Prince Philip's old friend), an imaginative impresario who put on the Royal Tournament every year for twenty-seven years. The Queen lit the fuse. As it fizzled along, the bonfire was ignited prematurely from within (electrically ignited incendiaries) by an over-enthusiastic Major in the Royal Signals. The Queen said: 'You really don't need me at all.' Bonfires were lit across Britain, Princess Alexandra lighting one in Hampshire, the Duke of Kent another at Sandringham. The Queen watched on a giant television screen as Sir Edmund Hillary lit one in New Zealand, and strummed on a guitar.[5]

The following morning the Gold State Coach came out of the Royal Mews to convey the Queen and Prince Philip to St Paul's Cathedral for the National Service of Thanksgiving. One observer noted that the Queen looked 'perfectly glorious' amid the spectacular crowds. The number of people in the Mall exceeded all expectations – there was just a sea of happy faces: 'a loving, adoring, frenetic, happy cross-section of people'. Royal pages in the garden of St James's Palace, almost somersaulted over each other, exclaiming: 'Oo – Margot's in pink.' Princess Margaret had chosen shocking pink while the Queen was in a lighter pink, her hat adorned with twenty-five pink bells. Princess Alice was among the Royal Family present in the cathedral. She entered by a side door and sat next to Lord Mountbatten, who noted: 'What a remarkable person she is. She is getting very bent but is very alert and bright.'[6]

THE SILVER JUBILEE, 1977

At the luncheon given by the Lord Mayor of London at the Guildhall the Queen delivered another inspired speech written by Sir Martin Charteris. She told the guests: 'When I was twenty-one, I pledged my life to the service of our people and I asked for God's help to make good that vow. Although that vow was made "in my salad days when I was green in judgement" I do not regret nor retract one word of it.' The Queen observed that a Silver Jubilee was 'not exactly a period of rest for us' but the chance to meet 'so many people in so many countries of the Commonwealth, to renew old friendships and to make new ones'.[7]

The next day the Queen gave a banquet for Commonwealth leaders attending the Commonwealth Conference in London, held at Lancaster House. There was fear that President Amin might insist on attending. He had tried to persuade the Queen to send him an aeroplane to get him to the Commonwealth Heads of Government Meeting in Ottawa in 1973, to which he was not invited. In February 1977 there was discussion as to whether Uganda should be suspended from the Commonwealth, the British Government having broken relations with Uganda the year before. Because of feared reprisals, Uganda was not suspended. On 23 February Amin cabled Sonny Ramphal, the Secretary-General of the Commonwealth, that he intended to be present in London, that he was following the debates in Parliament and the British press and that one reason he would be there would be to 'frankly put my views on the weakness of the British Government to all heads of Commonwealth Governments'. He informed him that he would bring 250 people with him, 'including dancers of the Heart Beat of Africa'.[8] This bluff threat he repeated on Radio Uganda.

One of the reports he had read was Lord Gladwyn's question in the House of Lords, phrased in somewhat unparliamentary language: 'Is it likely, if this creature does attend the Commonwealth conference, that any self-respecting person is going to attend any function or meeting at which he is present?'[9] The Cabinet did not want Amin to come but as late as May were dithering about 'both the strength of public opinion in the country against President Amin attending and also the possible damage to the Commonwealth, to the success of the Conference and to our relations with Afro-Asian countries if he were excluded'.[10]

James Callaghan did not want Amin to come, but he could not

forbid it. He sent Sir Sonny Ramphal to Kampala, to dissuade him. Ramphal was flown to a game farm by Amin in his helicopter for a ceremonial opening. When they got there, they found the German Ambassador looking furious. 'This is the sixth time this game farm has been opened! And you came by helicopter – we had to drive.'[11]

Amin did not come to London, but on the day of the St Paul's Cathedral service Lord Mountbatten asked the Queen why she had looked so cross during the service. She replied: 'I was just thinking how awful it would be if Amin were to gate-crash the party and arrive after all.' Mountbatten asked her what she would have done. She told him 'she had decided she would use the City's Pearl Sword, which the Lord Mayor had placed in front of her, to hit him hard over the head'.*[12]

On 9 June there was a river progress from Greenwich to Lambeth, and in the evening the Queen opened the Silver Jubilee Walkway by unveiling a plaque on the South Bank Lion on the south side of Westminster Bridge. This initiative was inspired by the environmentalist, Max Nicholson, as a permanent reminder of the celebrations. It was the first ever urban trail and designed to open up the South Bank of the Thames.† That night there was a magnificent fireworks display,

---

* In 1979 Amin was overthrown by Tanzanian forces and Ugandan exiles after which Milton Obote returned to power. On 11 April that year Amin went into exile, first to Libya as a guest of Colonel Gaddafi, who had long supported him, and later to Jeddah, where he eventually died at the age of seventy-eight on 16 August 2003. The journalist, Patrick Keatley, wrote of him: 'Amin brought bloody tragedy and economic ruin to his country, during a selfish life that had no redeeming qualities.' (*Guardian*, 18 August 2003.)

† In those days the South Bank was a mass of warehouses and cranes but these were becoming obsolete. Whenever a place such as Hay's Galleria was to be built, planning was granted so long as a riparian stretch was included. In 1994 the Queen opened the Queen's Walk. It is now possible to walk all the way from Westminster Bridge to Tower Bridge. The Jubilee Walkway Trust was formed and eventually the route linked up north of the Thames. For the Golden Jubilee it was run up the Mall; for the Diamond Jubilee a sixty-kilometre route was created, circling more widely and joining up the Olympic sites. From this the Commonwealth Walkways were developed, and in the UK, routes in Glasgow, Windsor and Birmingham (for the Platinum Jubilee). I have been Chairman since 2012.

still impressive despite classic British rain. Charles Wintour stood next to James Callaghan, the recalcitrant Prime Minister, as they watched the sky light up. 'Just what the people needed,' said Callaghan, whose government had paid not a penny towards it.[13] At the end of the week Sir Martin Charteris wrote to Sir Alan Lascelles: 'Last week was unforgettable. The Queen is in tremendous form in spite or because of everything.'[14]

The show went on. In Cardiff the Queen raced down the presentation line. She travelled to the special service in an open carriage. Afterwards she went over to speak to the Chapter Clerk when a voice in the crowd called out: 'Cor. Look at 'er.' This made her freeze momentarily and she quickly veered to the other side of the crowd, leaving the Duke to say a few words. The Chapter Clerk thought the Queen 'very shy' and not at all 'confident of her reception'.[15]

By 18 July the Queen was tired. According to her press secretary (privately), she was having 'a terrible week in the West Midlands', then had garden parties and investitures to do, which were again tiring. But she was due for a long holiday from 16 August until 10 October.[16] This was a time when the Queen could leave her smart clothes behind, wear tartans and no make-up.* At Balmoral, the Queen gave a fancy-dress party for her staff. She was amused to discover that a number of them intended to come as her. On the night she said: 'I'm having a lovely time having cast off my glass slipper.'[17]

On 27 July the Queen witnessed the Silver Jubilee Review of the Fleet at Spithead. In August she paid a tight security visit to Northern Ireland, without doubt the most dangerous of all her visits. The Government was not sure that she should go, but as with Ghana, she insisted. Sir Martin Charteris said later he could have vetoed the Government's plan. It was not the Queen's idea or the Private Secretary's. 'All the Queen said was "We said we'd do it, and it would be a pity if we don't." On the strength of this we went ahead. We met nobody out there, but the Queen was happy to be there.' He said: 'I hoped to get out with honour, but we got out with triumph.'[18]

In October the Queen and Prince Philip visited Canada, the Bahamas, the British Virgin Islands, Antigua and Barbados. They

---

* Princess Margaret, on the other hand, might arrive at Balmoral in a powder-blue siren suit, and always wore make-up.

returned home in Concorde in record-breaking time, the 3,686-mile journey taking three hours and forty-two minutes.

At the end of the year, Sir Martin Charteris retired as the Queen's Private Secretary and prepared to take up his post as Provost of Eton. On 1 November there was a post-Jubilee reception. He said the Jubilee had been 'a terrific success, and despite what we [the London Celebrations Committee] had done, it was "because the people wanted it".' I told him I was a terrific admirer of the Queen and he said: 'Oh! She's a terrific prole,* the Queen.' He then defined his theory of privilege, that it was all right if you accepted responsibility, which she did in full measure. I asked him if he was looking forward to going to Eton [as Provost]: 'Well, I'm miserable to be leaving the Queen ...'[19]

Sir Martin was succeeded by Sir Philip Moore who served from 1978 until 1986. He was generally considered a rather dry figure, and the Queen's speeches became accordingly dreary. 'Another suet pudding of a speech,'[20] she used to say.

On 15 November the Queen was a few minutes late arriving for an Investiture at Buckingham Palace. She came in saying: 'I apologise for being late but I have just had a message from the hospital. My daughter has just given birth to a son.'[21] The recipients all clapped. At the end of a momentous year she had become a grandmother for the first time. On 22 December Princess Anne's baby was christened Peter Mark Andrew by the Archbishop of Canterbury, at Buckingham Palace.

On New Year's Eve one of the television companies created a touching montage of the Queen receiving flowers throughout the Jubilee year – flowers from children, flowers placed behind her in the car, flowers everywhere. And to accompany it, they played the unusual 1977 hit from the Yorkshire-based Brighouse and Rastrick Band 'The Floral Dance', which stayed in the charts for six weeks. It was an entirely appropriate way to end a year that left a huge impression on anyone lucky enough to remember it.

---

* 'Proletarian' – in other words she related to the working man.

31
THE LATER 1970s, 1978–9

Jubilee euphoria revived interest in the Queen, only to be overtaken by speculation about the marital possibilities for Prince Charles, since he had unwisely stated that he thought thirty was a good age at which to marry. That milestone passed on 14 November 1978, with no bride in the offing.

Towards the end of 1977 the Queen was seen wearing glasses to read a speech, which caused a flutter in the media. They came out in church too. She was happier to acknowledge the passing years, unlike Princess Margaret, who continued to have her hair dyed auburn until the end.

The media hounded Princess Margaret due to her unconventional relationship with Roddy Llewellyn, seventeen years her junior. The consensus was that she would do precisely what she wanted, regardless of public opinion. The tabloid version of Llewellyn was that he was promoting a short-lived career as a pop singer, singing alongside Petula Clark, and enjoying holidays in Mustique. The truth was that he was very good with Princess Margaret, a tonic after Snowdon, and she was equally supportive of him, but it was a relationship easy to mock. Her travails were not helped by Peter Townsend publishing *Time and Chance*, his memoirs, covering their romance, something he had long promised not to do. His book attracted considerable publicity.

In May Princess Margaret was finally divorced from Lord Snowdon on the grounds of two years' separation. This coincided with Princess Margaret falling ill, it was said with hepatitis, and spending ten days in hospital. In fact she had a nervous breakdown, missed her daughter Sarah's confirmation,* but was well enough to

---

* The Queen invited Sarah Armstrong-Jones to the Windsor Horse Show, looking

attend a reception at Windsor Castle for all those who had helped with the Jubilee.* The divorce played into the hands of those who liked to castigate the monarchy. Peregrine Worsthorne put up a case for restraint, which, he wrote 'might be a far more welcome mark of the nation's gratitude to the Queen than all the tons of fulsome adulation'.[1]

As a devout Anglican, Princess Margaret did not like the idea of being divorced, and nor did she contemplate remarriage. Snowdon needed to remarry quickly – and did so on 15 December, to his long-standing girlfriend, Lucy Lindsay-Hogg.

Prince Michael

The next issue for the Queen was the marriage of Prince Michael of Kent. For some years he had been involved with Baroness Marie-Christine von Reibnitz, the estranged wife of the merchant banker, Thomas Troubridge. The Queen had always been fond of her cousin. He was in a uniquely complicated position within the Royal Family. His older siblings, the Duke of Kent and Princess Alexandra, had been performing royal duties from an early age. But Prince Michael was not required for such (although over the years he undertook many). He was told to make his own way in the world, but not to make use of his royal status.

Baroness Marie-Christine von Reibnitz was born in 1945, the only daughter of Baron Günther von Reibnitz and his wife. In 1971 she married Thomas Troubridge, a banker. They separated in 1973, divorced in 1977 and the marriage was annulled in 1978. She was lucky to be supported by Lord Mountbatten, who took it upon himself to square the marriage with the various elements of the Royal Family. The Queen gave her blessing, which was required under the Royal Marriages Act, and involved a meeting of the Privy

---

after her while her mother was ill. Queen Frederika of Greece was also there, dressed in a flowing sari-type dress, having adopted the style of an Anglicised Indian.

* 'To see her one would never have imagined that there had been all the fuss of the previous week.' (HV diary, 7 April 1978).

Council. When the bride announced that their children would be raised in the Church of England, the Pope forbade them to marry in church in England, so they were married in Vienna.

Mountbatten was delighted to learn that Prince Charles had spoken out against the Catholic Church at a Salvation Army Congress in London, on the eve of the wedding.[2] The crucial words were: 'It seems to be worse than folly that Christians are still arguing about doctrinal matters, which can only bring needless distress to a number of people.'[3] Only in 1983 were the couple permitted to have a Roman Catholic ceremony at the Archbishop's House in London. By marrying a Catholic, Prince Michael lost his place in the line of succession.*

The Romanian State Visit

Significantly, neither James Callaghan, the Prime Minister, nor David Owen, the Foreign Secretary, made even a passing reference to the state visit of President Ceauçescu of Romania, the first such visit by a Communist leader. Of all the tyrants the Queen was obliged to entertain during her reign, he was the worst. Even the Foreign Office conceded: 'President Ceauçescu is lacking in personal charisma.'[4] The verdict of Sir William Heseltine was: 'I would say without qualification that Ceauçescu was the most repellent guest she ever had to make do with.'[5] Nevertheless she received him with due courtesy, doing her duty as demanded by the government of the day.

It was the first such visit by a leader of a Communist Party. James Callaghan referred to President Ceauçescu as 'a world statesman with a profound knowledge and understanding of international issues'.[6] The Ceauçescus were forced on the Queen by Callaghan and David Owen.

It was well known in Britain that human-rights violations were

---

* The children born to Prince Michael retained their place in the succession: Lord Frederick Windsor, born in 1979, and Lady Gabriella Windsor, born in 1981. Prince Michael was reinstated in the line of succession in 2015, following the Succession of the Crown Act.

taking place in Romania. Men were being imprisoned, starved of food and drink before interrogation, beaten, drugged and sometimes injected with strong sedatives that induced apathy. No member of the Royal Family had been to Romania, though Prince William of Gloucester was to have visited in 1972, but his death prevented this. Before the visit Eric Deakins, a Labour MP, wrote to David Owen to complain. Lord Goronwy-Roberts, Minister of State for Foreign and Commonwealth Affairs, promoted the state visit by stating that 'contacts and exchanges of visits with Romania, and with other countries of Eastern Europe, are important in pursuing détente, in seeking to widen the areas of cooperation, and in creating an atmosphere in which trade can flourish and bilateral problems be discussed and solved'.[7] He made it clear that Romania was a signatory of the Final Act of the Conference on Security and Cooperation in Europe and that the Prime Minister would have the chance to review this with the President. An important factor was the creation of a new Romanian aviation industry and the manufacturing of the British airliner BAC 1-11 under licence from British Aerospace (only nine of the promised eighty-two eventually appearing).

The visit provoked intense criticism in the British press, most notably from the influential columnist Bernard Levin, who published three damning articles in *The Times*, concentrating on the numerous roles the President had assumed, the distribution of jobs to members of his family, the persecution of Romanian Christians, and oppression in his country. His last article backfired since the family he highlighted were suddenly granted passports to go to the United States, leaving the journalist 'puffing into a balloon with a hole in it.'[8]

The Queen was wary before the unwelcome President and his wife arrived in Britain on 13 June. She had been warned by President Giscard d'Estaing that they had ransacked their apartment at the Élysée Palace in Paris, so she commanded that all treasures from the Belgian suite, where the couple would stay, should be removed.

Among the annoying things the Ceauçescus did was to dig up the floor of the Belgian Suite in search of electronic bugs. His Chief of Staff kept complaining about the 'manifesters' (protesters). Sir John Johnston had to explain that in Britain people were allowed to 'manifest'. On the night of the return banquet, Johnston arranged for a police van to 'break down' opposite the banquet entrance to Claridge's to block the 'manifesters'.[9] When the Queen spotted the Ceauçescus walking in the garden, she hid behind a bush.[10]

Ceauçescu was given the statutory Grand Cross of the Order of the Bath.* At the Queen's banquet, her guests wore white tie, the President wore a lounge suit, with the GCB star pinned to it, and the Romanians wore white suits and 'looked like gnomes'. The return banquet was 'black tie and national dress' – in other words 'lounge suits'.[11] When the President departed, the British Ambassador in Bucharest reported: 'On the faces of those left on the ground, there was a marked air of relief.'[12] The visit left a sour taste in Britain, with the blame squarely resting on the Labour Government, not the Queen.

★ ★ ★ ★ ★

If the Romanian visit was omitted from David Owen's memoirs, he was happy to write about the state visit to President Scheel of the Federal Republic of West Germany, soon afterwards, deeming it 'a resounding success', due 'above all' to 'the Queen's contribution'.[13] The Queen went to Bonn, Mainz, Berlin and Kiel. The royal party went aboard *Britannia*, voyaging through the Kiel canal to review the Federal Navy. Since a thick fog prevented them seeing beyond the bows of the Royal Yacht, they concentrated on lunch. The Queen was pleased that the two countries competed now on only the sports field and in the market place.

In July the Queen and the Duke took Princes Andrew and Edward with them when they visited Newfoundland, Saskatchewan and Alberta, and opened the XIth Commonwealth Games in Edmonton, a tour memorable for a row over the Queen's speech being seen as a call against separation by Quebec, and Pierre Trudeau appearing in the Royal Box at Edmonton in an open-necked shirt and sandals with no socks.

When the Queen opened Parliament in London on 1 November,

---

* This honour was removed from Ceauçescu 'by order of the Sovereign' just before he and his wife were captured and shot by the Romanian Army in December 1989. (Hugo Vickers, *Royal Orders* (Boxtree, 1994), p. 107.)

she looked up with an expression of controlled irritation. This was thought to be either because the shambolic herd of MPs was still shuffling in, or her only way to express annoyance at having to read the Government's words about devolution.* Reams of newspaper space were devoted to Prince Charles's significant thirtieth birthday.†

Between 12 February and 2 March 1979, there was a visit to eastern Arabia. The Queen observed local customs throughout, no alcohol was served and, as stated in the official programme: 'Coffee is served again, followed by rosewater and incense (the signal to depart).' The Queen wore dresses to the ground in the daytime and, in the presence of King Khalid of Saudi Arabia, a sapphire silk dress with long sleeves. All the bouquets were given by men, since very few ladies appeared during the visit.

The Queen arrived by Concorde in Kuwait, travelled to Bahrain in *Britannia*, where she was received by the Amir, Shaikh Isa bin Sulman Al Khalifa. No bets were placed at the race meeting in Bahrain, since betting was forbidden. Before their arrival in Saudi Arabia, the King released twenty-five Britons, who had been convicted on charges of drinking alchol, selling spirits and drunk-driving, a gesture that had not been accorded to the Americans, French and Germans, when Presidents Carter and Giscard d'Estaing, and Chancellor Schmidt visited. The Queen watched a camel race and attended a desert picnic given by the Governor of Riyadh, Prince Salman. The royal party sat on cushions and were served lobster, roast turkey, beef and fifty lambs. Orchids were flown in from Holland for the evening, mangoes and pineapples from Paris.

At Qatar the Queen was afforded an aquatic welcome, with masses of small craft and motorboats. Trees were specially planted, museum gardens filled with flowers, and a zoo built. The Queen then went

---

* The crucial line was: 'Draft orders will be laid early in the session to provide for the referenda on devolution to Scottish and Welsh Assemblies to be held when the new electoral registers are available' (*The Times*, 2 November 1978).

† I had been commissioned to write a book about Prince Charles by Debrett, being held over as a royal wedding book. Informing Anne Wall (the Queen's Assistant Press Secretary) about this, I said it was 'designed for when he gets married in five or six or ten years' time'.

'At least you're realistic,' she said. (HV diary, 27 April 1978.)

to Abu Dhabi, Dubai and Oman. Lavish gifts were presented to her, including a solid gold palm tree, eighteen inches high, a gold tray encrusted with amethysts, a knee-length gold necklace, a pinafore of gold chain mail and many diamond-studded watches. The Duke of Edinburgh was presented with several gold swords covered with diamonds, and two beautiful carpets. The value of these gifts was thought to exceed £1 million.

Margaret Thatcher

Margaret Thatcher had ousted Edward Heath as leader of the Conservative Party in 1975. By 1979 the United Kingdom was enmeshed in strikes and chaos. It was the Winter of Discontent. When Callaghan returned from Guadaloupe in January, he inspired the *Sun's* famous headline: 'Crisis, what crisis?' On 28 March Mrs Thatcher instigated a vote of no confidence in the Government, which lost by one vote. Callaghan went to the polls in April. On 4 May the Conservatives won a majority of forty-three seats.

The new Prime Minister had been born Margaret Roberts in 1925, qualified as a chemist and a barrister and married a successful businessman, Denis Thatcher, and swiftly produced twins before entering the House of Commons as MP for Finchley in 1959. Heath appointed her Secretary of State for Education and Science in 1970.

It was the first time that the Queen had had to deal with a female at the helm of government. Some felt there was no great rapport between the two, the Queen's style being 'matter-of-fact and domestic' while Mrs Thatcher's had the bearing of a queen.[14] Mrs Thatcher had risen to office by hard work and ambition; the Queen had arrived by hereditary right. Kenneth Harris pointed out that both worked hard and conscientiously, were aware that their children might have suffered from having 'busy, duty-bound, responsible public figures' as parents. Both depended on their husbands. Neither was 'intellectual, introspective or philosophical'. Both were 'direct, matter-of-fact, down-to-earth, practical and perceptive'. Neither was 'vain, narcissistic or pretentious'.[15] If it was never a warm relationship, the Queen respected her, and Mrs Thatcher was an exceptionally loyal monarchist. Princess Margaret told a friend that the only time she saw the Queen cry was over the suggestion that she and Margaret Thatcher did not get on.[16]

Mrs Thatcher was not an easy guest at Balmoral in the late summer, since she did not share the Queen's love of traditional outdoor Scottish life. Her office tried to ensure that she and the Queen did not appear at the same event in the same colour. The Palace was not having that. A message came back that the Queen seldom noticed what other women wore.

There was apparently a clash with Margaret Thatcher when Dr Graham Leonard was appointed Bishop of London in 1981.[17] When there were problems with the Thanksgiving service for the Falklands victory in 1982, the Queen told the Archbishop: 'I don't think you should ever leave a Christian service feeling sad.'[18] The Queen took a close interest in ecclesiastical matters. It was alleged that because Hugh Montefiore explored the question as to whether Jesus Christ (though celibate) might have been homosexual at the 1967 Modern Churchmen's Conference, the Queen blocked him becoming a diocesan Bishop.[19]

* * * * *

Differences arose with Mrs Thatcher over the Commonwealth. Lusaka was chosen as the host city for the fifth Commonwealth Heads of Government Meeting to which, at first, Margaret Thatcher did not want to go. The new Prime Minister upset the Africans by stating that she might not be able to push sanctions against Rhodesia through the Commons, and shortly before the scheduled Conference, the Rhodesian government bombed Lusaka. Robert ('Piggy') Muldoon, Prime Minister of New Zealand, announced that he might advise the Queen – as Queen of New Zealand – that Lusaka was a war zone and it was unsafe for her to visit it. The Secretary-General of the Commonwealth, Sir Sonny Ramphal, persuaded Joshua Nkomo to declare a ceasefire during the Queen's visit. The Palace announced that the Queen was determined to go, just as she had been with Ghana in 1961.

At the Conference the Queen worked her magic on President Kenneth Kaunda. Sonny Ramphal said she 'brought to Lusaka a healing touch of special significance'.[20] Kaunda surprised everyone by inviting Mrs Thatcher to dance. The Lusaka Accord was established, addressing issues of racism and racial prejudice. In particular the impending collapse of the Rhodesian Government prompted the Commonwealth to declare that Apartheid was an 'affront to humanity', which had to be totally eradicated.[21]

Bishop Abel Muzorewa, Prime Minister of Rhodesia, took part in the Lancaster House Conference between September and December the same year, leading to a new constitution being agreed, the ending of the war, and the launch of the new state of Zimbabwe, a mere eight months after the Lusaka meeting.

Lord Soames was sent out as Governor of Rhodesia to steer it to independence, with Andrew Parker Bowles as his ADC. This proved an inspired appointment, the Queen later commenting to his commanding officer: 'I know that "Comrade Parker" has done extremely well in Rhodesia in dealing with Mugabe and Co!'[22] In April 1980 the Prince of Wales represented the Queen at the independence celebrations, which ended a long saga in Anglo-Rhodesian politics.

In the summer of 1979 the Queen attended a concert at the Festival Hall to mark the hundredth birthday of Sir Robert Mayer, founder of the aptly named charity Youth and Music. It was a light joke that he was in love with Lady Diana Cooper, then aged eighty-six. The Queen talked to Lady Diana, who, myopically, failed to recognise her. 'I'm so sorry, Ma'am,' said Lady Diana, 'I didn't recognise you without your crown on!'

The Queen replied: 'Well, I thought it was Sir Robert's evening so I left it at home.'[23]

Both the Queen and Margaret Thatcher attended the Great Children's Party in aid of the International Year of the Child in Hyde Park on different days at the end of May. Here I had the chance to see two elements in the way the Queen operated. I was to show her the International Village,* where some Indian dancers were performing. Luckily I had been warned that she liked facts. She asked where they came from. 'They come from Southall, Ma'am,' I said,

---

* Following my Jubilee work, I was employed as administrator, helping with this event when 180,000 children were entertained in Hyde Park over two days.

'but originally from the Punjab'. She laughed. There was a young man from New Zealand. I gave her half the story: 'He's won a prize.' When she talked to him she immediately asked: 'I understand you've won a prize. What was it for?' Minutes later his mother was saying how amazed she was that the Queen knew he had won a prize.

★ ★ ★ ★ ★

There has often been a death in the Royal Family over the August bank holiday weekend. Prince George, Duke of Kent, was killed in August 1942, Princess Marina died in August 1968, and Prince William of Gloucester died in a flying accident in August 1972. The Queen was at Balmoral on her summer holiday when the shocking news came that Lord Mountbatten had been assassinated at Mullaghmore, County Sligo, the provisional IRA claiming responsibility.

During the last few years Lord Mountbatten had been an ever-present figure in royal circles, though Andrew Duncan pointed out perspicaciously that he had 'always had an influence on the Royal Family – although not, perhaps, so much influence as he would like to think'.[24] He took a not always constructive interest in the love life of the young Prince Charles. He tried to persuade his brother-in-law, King Gustaf VI Adolf, to abdicate (he failed), and more or less fixed the marriage of the new young King, Carl Gustaf, to his German wife, Silvia Sommerlath. He was less successful in persuading the Duchess of Windsor to put the Duke's money into a charitable foundation (rather overplaying his hand).

Honours had been heaped upon him. He was Governor of the Isle of Wight, and Colonel of the Life Guards, which meant he alternated with Field Marshal Sir Gerald Templer* as Gold Stick.[25]

There was decline. In June 1970 he all but collapsed holding the Sword of State at the Opening of Parliament. The Queen hurried

---

* Sir Gerald loathed him. He came up with the line: 'Dickie, you're so crooked. If you swallowed a nail, you'd shit a corkscrew.' General Sir Robert Ford was a pall-bearer at Mountbatten's funeral. Following the coffin up the aisle of Westminster Abbey, he observed the look of grim satisfaction on Sir Gerald's face. 'I never want to see a look like that again,' he said (Sir Robert Ford to author).

through her speech and Princess Anne was poised to catch the sword if it fell. The Queen told the Duke of Windsor that the doctors had 'put him to bed for a fortnight'.[26] By November 1978 he was looking decrepit at a later State Opening, when he was part of a rather slender royal procession, and at the Royal Victorian Order service a few weeks later, 'his eyes were pinched and his jaw dropped'.[27] In the summer of 1979 Prince Philip told Lady Alexandra Metcalfe: 'We're having a lot of trouble with Dickie.'[28]

Mountbatten should have heeded warnings about the possible dangers, if not for himself then for his family. In 1974 Lord and Lady Donoughmore had been kidnapped in Ireland.* In April 1978 his cousin, Prince Moritz of Hesse,† had been kidnapped at his home in Schleswig-Holstein, the kidnappers proudly stating that Mountbatten was their next target. In the wake of that, Mountbatten had a meeting with the Home Office, who offered him a permanent security officer, but he decided his personal security was adequate.

The Earl, by then seventy-nine, customarily holidayed with his family at Classiebawn Castle and was in the habit of going out in his boat to fish. On 27 August he took out *Shadow V*. With him were Lord and Lady Brabourne, their twin sons, Nicholas and Timothy Knatchbull, Doreen, Lady Brabourne (mother of Mountbatten's son-in-law), and a young boatman, Paul Maxwell.

The boat was blown up by remote control using fifty pounds of explosives. Mountbatten's body was found floating face down in the

---

* The 7th Earl (1902–81) and his wife Dorothy (1906–95) were kidnapped by three masked men (a breakaway group of the IRA) at their home in County Tipperary. Shots were fired. A week later they were released, dumped blindfolded in Phoenix Park, Dublin. It was thought that the kidnapping was in connection with the hunger strike of the Price sisters.

† Prince Moritz (1926–2013) asked his kidnappers if he could put on a pullover. Pointedly he chose one that he only wore in the evening. His housekeeper saw him leave wearing it, and instantly got the message. She called the police, road blocks were mounted and Prince Moritz was rescued within ninety minutes. Prince Moritz was a brave man. In old age he was told to stop deep sea diving. He refused. When he was dying, he called his housekeeper to the hospital to thank her for all she had done. He then pulled out all the tubes and an hour later he was dead (Prince Karl of Hesse to author).

sea. Nicholas Knatchbull and Paul Maxwell were killed and Lady Brabourne died the next day in hospital. John and Patricia Brabourne were gravely injured and in hospital for weeks afterwards, both making remarkable recoveries (though in wheelchairs with legs extended when they attended their son's wedding in November). Lord Mountbatten became the IRA's most prominent victim. Inevitably this impacted on the future security of the Queen and the Royal Family.

Prince Charles flew back from a holiday in Iceland and Prince Philip returned from France; they were at Eastleigh Airport when the coffin was flown back.* The Queen, many members of the Royal Family and foreign Heads of State attended the military funeral at Westminster Abbey with a procession down the Mall, every detail of which had been scrupulously planned by Lord Mountbatten. He had even attended to the menu to be served for those mourners who accompanied his body on the train to Romsey Abbey with a summer and a winter menu, since he did not know in which season of the year he would die. He told Mrs Pandit, one of the great ladies of India, that as she put down her cup of coffee, the train would arrive at Romsey Station. She forgot about this until the day, but as she put down her coffee, she remembered and looked out of the window: Romsey Station.

Throughout the funeral the Queen kept her composure. At Broadlands, after the burial, she was seen to be red-eyed.

The Queen invited the surviving Knatchbull twin, Timothy, and his sister for the weekend at Balmoral. Their flight was diverted to Glasgow so they arrived late at night, expecting to find everyone asleep, but the Queen and Prince Charles had waited up, plied them with soup and sandwiches, and only with difficulty was the Queen persuaded not to do all their unpacking. Over the next days she kept a motherly eye on Tim. His brother Philip and Prince Edward came over from Gordonstoun. Prince Philip gave Tim more robust support, including him in everything but without fuss. He appreciated both forms of care.[29]

Lord Mountbatten would have been eighty in July the following

---

* A poignant message was sent that Lord Mountbatten's dog would also be on board and needed to be taken back to Broadlands.

year. On that milestone anniversary he might have hoped to receive the Royal Victorian Chain, the only decoration that he could still have added when in full dress uniform.* Jim Orr wrote Prince Philip a letter of sympathy to which Prince Philip replied: 'Much as we all mourn Dickie, the real tragedy is the death and mutilation of members of the Brabourne family. Fortunately Patricia, John & Timothy are making remarkable recoveries but it is not certain yet whether Patricia will fully regain her sight.'†

On 20 October a large contingent of the Royal Family, led by the Queen, were present at the marriage of Lord Mountbatten's grandson, Lord Romsey, and Penelope Eastwood at Romsey Abbey. At the reception, the Queen asked Charles Smith, Lord Mountbatten's butler, how he was getting on. He said things could never be the same. 'It can never be the same again for any of us, Charles,' said the Queen.[30]

Princess Margaret got into trouble in Chicago when she was quoted (or possibly misquoted), describing the Irish as 'pigs'. At the St Paul's Cathedral memorial service, Prince Charles spoke of the 'vulnerability of civilised democracy ... the kind of sub-human extremism that blows people up when it feels like it', and asked: 'What on earth was the point of such mindless cruelty?'[31]

* * * * *

On 13 October 1979 President Suharto of Indonesia came on a long-deferred state visit to Britain. He had held power in his country since 1968, having ousted President Sukarno from office. Briefing notes described him as 'a tough and impressive leader' while his wife

---

* On a collar day, he would wear the Collar of the Garter, the riband of the Order of the Bath, stars of KG, GCB, GCSI and GCIE, neck badges of the Order of Merit, and the Grand Master's badge of the Star of India, aiguillettes and a great number of medals. The Royal Victorian Chain could have gone round his neck, over all that.

† She did. In the water she had been floundering until she somehow remembered her father's oft-related tales about sinking in the *Kelly*. He had said the mistake drowning people made was to flail about thus fending off rescuers. She put her arms down. John Brabourne pulled her head out of the water.

was 'a power behind the throne ... believed to have been responsible for stiffening Suharto's resolve at crucial moments during the political crisis at the conclusion of which he was appointed President'.[32]

Anthony Blunt

In November Margaret Thatcher named Sir Anthony Blunt, the former Surveyor of the Queen's Pictures, as a confessed spy for the Russians – the elusive 'Fourth Man'. This was prompted by Andrew Boyle's *Climate of Treason*, in which he disguised Blunt as 'Maurice', all of which was exposed in *Private Eye* on 8 November. Blunt had confessed in 1964 and been granted immunity. Every Prime Minister and Home Secretary had known this since 1967. The Queen's then Private Secretary, Sir Michael Adeane, had been informed and had been advised that if this became public, for example Blunt confessing, the Queen should take no action. When his treachery was discovered, it was thought propitious to leave him in peace, presumably because he was a double agent. As his protector Brian Sewell put it in a letter to *The Times*: 'The 1964 bargain must have brought benefits in counter-espionage.'[33]

Much discussed was whether the Queen herself knew. She did, certainly by 1973, because Edward Heath wanted her to be informed. Evidently she 'took it all very calmly and without surprise: she remembered that he had been under suspicion way back in the aftermath of the Burgess/Maclean case,' and wanted 'to keep a curtain of plausible deniability'.[34]

Shrewd readers of the honours system should have picked up an obscure clue. In 1972 Blunt retired from his unpaid position as Surveyor of the Queen's Pictures, a role that essentially involved 'rehanging or redecoration or some matter of policy in connection with restoration'.[35] On retirement he would normally have been advanced from KCVO to GCVO (progression in the Order jokingly said to be as certain as death), but this honour was not given. He was gazetted him as 'Surveyor Emeritus' by the Lord Chamberlain's Office, to the intense annoyance of Sir Martin Charteris (who was not consulted). Presently Blunt's successor, Oliver Millar, spotted no

GCVO, and arrived anxiously in Charteris's office to ask why his job had been demoted. Charteris told him to ask no questions. Millar knew nothing of Blunt's perfidy. When Millar retired in 1988 he was duly promoted to GCVO.[36]

Blunt gave a long interview to *The Times*, after a controversial lunch of smoked trout, fruit salad, wine and coffee, followed by a cigar. Having been publicly exposed, he was stripped of his knighthood. He was then spirited away and resigned from all public offices and clubs. He died at his Highgate home in 1983, aged seventy-five.*

★ ★ ★ ★ ★

The decade ended with Margaret Thatcher as Prime Minister, a new era about to arrive, and with an atmosphere of hope and positive change.

---

* Blunt had been at Marlborough with the Poet Laureate, Sir John Betjeman. *Private Eye* penned a spoof, written by Richard Ingrams and Barry Fantoni:

> Poor old Bluntie. So they've got him
> Mole revealed, they say 'at last',
> On a bleak November morning
> What an echo from the past!

32
ROYAL ENGAGEMENT AND WEDDING, 1980–1

Britain did not behave generously to the Shah of Iran, who had been deposed in January 1979 and fled his country. Since then he had been itinerant. The Government would not allow him to come to Britain, despite formal visits, attendance at Royal Ascot and his personal friendship with the Queen.* Already in frail health, he went to Aswan in Egypt, then to Marrakesh, to Paradise Island in the Bahamas, and Cuernavaca in Mexico. Henry Kissinger prevailed on Jimmy Carter to allow him into the USA for medical treatment, and in October, the President reluctantly agreed. He returned to Aswan in March 1980. There Michael DeBakey (who had attended the Duke of Windsor in 1964) performed a splenectomy. But the Shah did not recover. He died on 27 July 1980, aged sixty. Egypt gave him a state funeral and he was buried in the Al Rifa'i Mosque in Cairo. Among the mourners were two fallen men – ex-President Richard Nixon and King Constantine of Greece. Great Britain was only represented by the British Chargé d'Affaires.

The sudden abdication of Queen Juliana of the Netherlands on 30 April 1980 (her seventy-first birthday) prompted questions as to whether the Queen should abdicate. Prince Charles was then so popular that some wanted him to be King sooner than later. One poll suggested that sixty might be a good age for the Queen to step down. In hindsight it is amusing to see comments such as: 'By the time she celebrates her Golden Jubilee in 2002, Prince Charles will be fifty-three.'[1] Little did they know. Queen Juliana's abdication greatly irritated our Queen, who considered it a cop-out. 'Very hard on Beatrix,' she recalled.[2]

---

* The Shah used to send her caviar at Christmas.

ROYAL ENGAGEMENT AND WEDDING, 1980-1

In the early months of 1980, the royal finances were again discussed in Parliament. Buckingham Palace had announced that Household expenses were under review and that they were seeking a three per cent reduction in annual expenditure. In March the Chancellor of the Exchequer announced that the Civil List would rise from £2,778,400 to £3,317,300 (a 19 per cent increase).

At the end of April the Queen's state visit to Switzerland, the first ever by a reigning monarch, inspired some republicans with placards declaring: 'Queen, go home!'[3] This was a whistle-stop tour – fifteen minutes in Lucerne, a brisk visit to the castle at Chillon, forty-five minutes at the Headquarters of the British Red Cross. The Queen and Prince Philip spent a rare private weekend away staying with the Prince and Princess of Liechtenstein. Thanks to modern aeroplanes the Queen was able to fly to Australia for four days to open Canberra's new High Court building, though her visit costing £200,000 was deemed controversial due to the expense.

1980 was the year of the Queen Mother's eightieth birthday, leading to the now expected adulatory press. Birthday celebrations began at Holyroodhouse with a garden party and Beating the Retreat. The Queen Mother was not wholly pleased that the Service of Thanksgiving was held on 15 July, somewhat before the actual anniversary on 4 August. On the day itself, the Queen Mother did her traditional walkabout and in the evening the Royal Family attended a special gala staged by the Royal Ballet at the Royal Opera House.

Of the state visits later that year, those to President Pertini of Italy, to Pope John Paul II, to President Habib Bourguiba of Tunisia, and to President Chadli Bendjedid in Algeria passed off satisfactorily. But the one to King Hassan II of Morocco was awkward. The King changed the programme endlessly. He kept the Queen waiting on numerous occasions. When they arrived at the Palace in the car, no one would let her in. They did not dare wake the King from his siesta. So she sat in the black Rolls-Royce in the heat, until the gates were opened.[4] The banquet on the first night was late. Lunch next day was three hours late. The King tried to frustrate a visit to a Leonard Cheshire home. As soon as she was alone in the car, she tapped on the glass and told the chauffeur to drive her there. She was representing Britain so she held her ground, one of the many instances when the Queen did what a Queen had to do. The confidential report described the horrific few days as 'an object lesson in the dangers of absolute monarchy'.[5]

In September Prince Andrew enrolled at Britannia Royal Naval College, Dartmouth, to serve for two terms as a helicopter pilot. He trained for a gruelling fortnight with the Commandos at Lympstone in Devon, marching for thirty miles, hiking for twelve miles in full combat gear, undertaking a six-mile endurance test and a nine-mile speed march. He completed an aircrew survival training course at Lee-on-Solent and moved to RAF Leeming in North Yorkshire for a flying course.

★ ★ ★ ★ ★

From Jonathan Dimbleby's 1994 biography of the Prince of Wales, we learn of the distance between him and his parents and his increased reliance on Mountbatten in the 1970s. Broadlands became an open house where Mountbatten encouraged him to 'sow his wild oats'.[6] One girl entertained there frequently, particularly towards the end of 1972, was Camilla Shand. Dimbleby outlined their shared humour – the Goons, 'silly accents and daft looks', and concluded: 'She was affectionate, she was unassuming, and – with all the intensity of first love – he lost his heart to her almost at once.'[7] But he dithered and in December 1972 he went to sea in HMS *Minerva*.

Whatever Camilla had made of the dalliance with the Prince, there was now to be a separation of eight months. She did not wait long. On 15 March 1973 her engagement was announced to Major Andrew Parker Bowles, the dashing Cavalry officer with whom she had been involved before Prince Charles. On 4 July they were married at the Guards Chapel in London. The Queen Mother, a close friend of his parents, and Princess Anne (a former girlfriend of the Major's) attended the wedding and Princess Margaret went to the reception. Arguably, Prince Charles went into a sulk, which lasted until 2005.

After a constructive year promoting the Silver Jubilee Appeal, the Prince drifted. Even Dimbleby, his apologist, stated that his life revolved around flying, hunting, playing polo, skiing, driving his Aston Martin, or going to dinner parties and nightclubs. The Royal

Household had difficulty persuading him to undertake a trip to Canada. Gradually, however, he became dedicated to his duties.

Girlfriends such as Lady Sarah Spencer and Anna Wallace married. The Queen's rather overactive Press Secretary, Michael Shea, specifically denied that he was intending to marry Princess Marie-Astrid of Luxembourg, which was never a possibility since she was a Roman Catholic.* As his thirtieth birthday approached, so the pressure increased. The question was complicated by his renewed involvement with Camilla Parker Bowles. They had been together in 1972. They were again together in the years before he married in 1981. Presently the world would get excited about Lady Diana Spencer, presenting it as a great love story, but the truth is that the real love story was Charles and Camilla. They would each marry other people, there would be times when they were separated, but somehow, inevitably, they were drawn back to each other.

Jonathan Dimbleby assessed the relationship as it was in the early 1980s, before Diana came into the picture:

> Whatever the precise character of this intimacy, some of those closest to them began to suppose that they were having a clandestine affair, which they feared would become known and cause a public scandal. Their private consternation was shared by one or two members of his own family, to the point he was warned that an illicit liaison would be damaging to his own standing and to the institution in which he was so crucial a member.[8]

When Martin Charteris raised the matter of one officer having an affair with the wife of another officer, the Queen refused to address it. Camilla's life was complicated because her husband did not have, then or later, a reputation for monogamy. Alice Roosevelt, the stalwart daughter of President 'Teddy' Roosevelt, would not have approved. She said: 'I prefer a polyg who monogs, to a monog who polygs.'[9]

Mountbatten had pushed for a marriage with his granddaughter,

---

* Lady Sarah married Neil McCorquodale on 17 May 1980; Anna Wallace married John Fermor-Hesketh on 2 December 1980; and Princess Marie-Astrid married her second cousin, Archduke Carl Christian of Austria, on 6 February 1982.

Amanda Knatchbull. Prince Charles was not surprised when her reply was an instant refusal.[10] In the end he did not choose a bride from the world of high-achieving women, like Queen Silvia of Sweden. Geographically, he veered to the world of Sandringham, beloved by generations of his family. Lady Diana Spencer first met Prince Charles in 1977 when her sister Sarah was dating him.* There was a significant meeting in July 1980, when he spoke to her of the murder of Mountbatten, and she told him how sad she had been for him and how he needed someone to look after him. He began to contemplate her as a possible bride and was much encouraged by his friends, including the Parker Bowleses, who pressed her suitability.

On paper she was perfect. She was the scion of an aristocratic family, the Spencers of Althorp in Northamptonshire. Her father, Earl Spencer, was well known to the Queen, and had been her equerry on the Commonwealth tour. The Queen and Prince Philip, the Queen Mother, Princess Margaret, the Princess Royal, the Duchesses of Gloucester and Kent, the Duke of Kent, Princess Alexandra and the Earl of Athlone had been present at his wedding to Frances Roche. Both of Diana's grandmothers and four of her great-aunts were ladies-in-waiting to the Queen Mother.

Born on 1 July 1961, Diana Frances Spencer was raised at Park House, Sandringham. Her parents were divorced in 1969, her mother having bolted, and her father succeeded as 8th Earl Spencer in 1975. He took up with and later married Raine, Countess of Dartmouth (daughter of the romantic novelist, Barbara Cartland). Diana went to Riddlesworth School in Norfolk, where at that time her professed ambition was to marry Prince Andrew. When she became involved with Prince Charles, she presented herself as a fun-loving country girl. She would not be the first or last girl in history to give a hoped-for husband the impression she thought was expected of her. She was working as a primary-school teacher at the Young England Kindergarten in St George's Square, Pimlico. Things hotted up when she appeared at a party to celebrate Princess Margaret's fiftieth birthday, held at the Ritz in London in November 1980.

* They would, of course, have been familiar with each other, both living on the Sandringham estate.

ROYAL ENGAGEMENT AND WEDDING, 1980–1

During these months Diana Spencer was pursued mercilessly by the press every time she emerged from 60 Coleherne Court. Her mother wrote to *The Times* appealing that she be left in peace. There came a time when Prince Philip wrote to his son, saying that it was unfair to keep her hanging about. Either he should propose or let her go.* Prince Charles interpreted this as a command to marry.

The ultimately ill-fated saga of that marriage has been raked over endlessly with many contradictions. Dame Frances Campbell-Preston, one of the Queen Mother's staunchest ladies-in-waiting said: 'I could tell you something I had seen with my own eyes at Clarence House, but equally I could direct you to someone else who was in the same room at the same time and they would tell you the opposite.'[11] Diana called Prince Charles 'Sir' until the day of the engagement. They hardly knew each other. It has been claimed that Princess Margaret said that Camilla had no intention of giving Prince Charles up.

The engagement was announced on 24 February 1981, and the world went into raptures. The couple gave an interview in which, to the question were they in love, Prince Charles gave the now infamous answer: 'Whatever "in love" means.' Not one newspaper reported that at the time, but those words became retrospectively significant. At the time, it did not fit the media narrative, though perceptive observers were privately horrified.

Soon after the engagement Lady Diana accompanied Prince Charles to an evening at Goldsmiths' Hall attended by Princess Grace of Monaco. The world saw the primary-school teacher transformed. She wore a surprisingly deep-plunge black dress by the Emanuels, inspiring Lady Diana Cooper to comment: 'Wasn't that a mighty dish to set before a King?'[12]

During the long months leading to the marriage, Diana's state of nerves increased and she began to suffer from bulimia. She did not see much of Prince Charles. He continued with many solo engagements, including visits to New Zealand, Australia, Venezuela and the United States. She was convinced that he was still involved with and in love with Camilla. Not everyone was happy about his choice.

---

* The late Prince Karl of Hesse saw this letter and told the present author that it was a perfectly nice and sensible letter – not a command.

There were those who knew her in Norfolk who predicted trouble, aware of her fragile nature.

Both bride and groom had serious doubts. During Ascot week, Prince Charles looked over at Diana at dinner and said to his neighbour that he longed to see her in a tiara. He then asked: 'Do you think you can fall in love after you're married?' During that week, on 17 June, Diana suddenly burst into tears in the Royal Box. She claimed she had been stung by a wasp, which was untrue. She was taken back to Windsor Castle where she rested. Prince Charles was flying to New York for one night to attend a gala performance of *Sleeping Beauty* by the Royal Ballet at the Metropolitan Opera House. She put a note in his dinner jacket, saying she loved him. The next day, with tears in his eyes he told the same friend: 'I am not sure that I can handle this.' The friend said it was not too late to abandon the plan. To which he said: 'I am afraid it is.'[13]

A more distant observer, Sir Charles Johnston, was bewitched by Diana: 'I've never seen such a strong charge of innocently provocative sex. One prays for the happiness of the couple — and there are certain doubts in one's mind which makes the prayer very much more than a formality.'[14]

There was a second telling interview — shown the night before the wedding — when the couple sat in the summerhouse at Buckingham Palace, talking to Andrew Gardner and Angela Rippon. Prince Charles only mustered enthusiasm when he spoke of the role of the New Zealand opera singer, Kiri Te Kanawa, singing 'Let the Bright Seraphim'. There came a moment when Angela Rippon pointed out that, as from the day of the wedding, he would have a bride by his side. He muttered: 'It'll be marvellous to have some support.' Diana said: 'You'd better like it.' She wanted to be a supportive wife and was prepared to do all that was expected of her in respect of the royal duties. Her attitude was more positive.

On 27 July there was a dinner and dance at Buckingham Palace in advance of the wedding. The following night there was a supper party for European and Commonwealth Heads of State, Commonwealth Heads of Government, Governors-General and other foreign representatives, again at Buckingham Palace. There was a fireworks display in Hyde Park and the Prince of Wales lit a beacon, the first in a chain crossing the United Kingdom.

The wedding took place on 29 July at St Paul's Cathedral, attended by numerous European monarchs, though not the King and Queen of Spain, who objected to the couple flying to Gibraltar to start their honeymoon in *Britannia*. King Juan Carlos rang the Queen some days before the wedding to say the couple should leave from Algeciras. She would not budge, so they did not attend.[15]

Earl Spencer had wanted to wear uniform but his daughter vetoed that. They left from Clarence House, the London home of the Queen Mother. Lord Spencer was in poor health, following a stroke some years before and his chauffeur was at his side to assist him up the steps to St Paul's Cathedral. Sir John Johnston, Comptroller of the Lord Chamberlain's Office, was with them. Lord Spencer kept saying: 'Can we go now?' Johnston said: 'No, not yet. I will tell you when to go.' He wanted a gap between the ecclesiastical procession and the bride's procession, otherwise no one would see the bride to full advantage. He said to Diana: 'Don't move yet.'

Mindful of the many rehearsals, she said: 'You've told me this so many times, but you haven't told me how I look.'

The Colonel replied: 'I'm terribly sorry. You look wonderful.' And then, as he put it: 'I sent them off.' Johnston's view was that, whatever happened later, it was a 'very happy and exhilarating' day.[16]

The Archbishop of Canterbury conducted the service (during which the bride and, supportively, the groom fluffed some lines); Kiri Te Kanawa sang while the register was being signed. Years later, Diana claimed she could see Camilla Parker Bowles sitting in the congregation in the Cathedral. She might well have seen her in a photograph later, but it would have been impossible at the time.[17]

The events of the day were watched on television by 700 million people across the globe. The sun rose slowly in the sky over London. The police thanked the public. The public thanked the police. Diana went into St Paul's Cathedral with her head down. She came out with her head up. Surely she was now in with a chance. Back at the Palace, the Queen arrived at the garden door and kicked off her shoes. On the balcony the couple kissed, initiating a feature demanded by the ever-romantic crowd after future royal weddings.

The honeymoon was a Mediterranean cruise, in the course of which President Sadat of Egypt and his wife came on board (on 12

August).* There, the Prince wrote a telling letter. In it he said: 'All I can say is that marriage is very jolly and it's also exceedingly nice being together in *Britannia*. Diana dashes about chatting up all the sailors and the cooks in the galley etc. while I remain hermit-like on the verandah deck, sunk with pure joy into one of Laurens van der Post's books.'[18] On their return to Britain, the Prince and Princess of Wales took up residence in an apartment at Kensington Palace.

At first most people were delighted. The reaction to Diana was universally positive. The heir to the throne had fulfilled his duty by taking a wife and was paving the way for another generation in the Royal House. Only in time did the problems surface — the eating disorders, the obsession of the press, the suspicions of the bride about Camilla, the competition between wife and husband (she diverting attention from what he perceived as his vital work). Which came first — the illness or the unhappiness? The Queen came to find her tiresome. She thought things went wrong as the result of illness. It is possible that it was the other way round. One thing is sure: Prince Charles could not cope with her.

At Sandringham Diana had a tantrum. The walls are not thin, but what was heard that day was hard to forget. Prince Charles could not calm her, and neither could anyone else. Many years later, when the marriage had unfurled, he was in the corner of a room looking utterly forlorn. He was spotted there by a sympathetic friend, who said to him: 'Don't worry. It will go away.'

He replied: 'Oh, no, it won't.' He was right.[19]

Diana had many natural gifts. Like all of the great princesses in history, she was good with the young, the old and the sick. She had a subtle, slightly undermining sense of humour. She attracted unceasing press attention, which did not diminish with time. The media indulged in their customary pursuit — building someone up only to knock them down. They tried that with Diana. For a long time it failed.

---

* The President did not long survive. He was assassinated by fundamentalist army officers on 6 October, the Prince of Wales flying out to Cairo four days later to represent the Queen at his funeral.

33
ENTER WILLIAM AND HARRY, 1981–6

Harold Macmillan pronounced that the greatest danger to the Royal Family was hired assassins and random lunatics. Royal Families accept that assassination is an occupational hazard. They do not hide. Many were assassinated, even in the twentieth century.* There were several such incidents in 1981. On 9 May the Queen arrived in *Britannia* at Sullom Voe in Shetland with the King of Norway to inaugurate the largest BP oil terminal in Europe. There had been days of dense fog which had prevented the police from getting there from the Scottish mainland as a result of which only brief security checks had been made. Just as the Queen arrived there was a small explosion at the power station five hundred yards away. This was thought to have been an electrical fault and the Queen was 'characteristically unruffled'. It was in fact a bomb, planted by the Provisional IRA, who were deeply disappointed that the opening ceremony had not been disrupted.[1]

The Queen was potentially in further danger when, on 13 June, shortly before the Royal Wedding, she was riding to Horse Guards for the Birthday Parade as Colonel-in-Chief of the Welsh Guards, the colour being trooped that day. As she turned into Horse Guards Approach, a man in the crowd fired at her. She did not flinch. She dropped her reins, controlled her horse and rode on. She went right through the parade as if nothing untoward had happened. No one

---

* Apart from the Russian Imperial Family, there were two Kings of Yugoslavia, in 1903 and 1934, and King George I of Greece in 1913. There was an attempt on the life of the King and Queen of Spain in Madrid in 1906. The Queen knew the young King of Iraq (1958), and had met King Faisal of Saudi Arabia and Emperor Haile Selassie, both of whom were murdered in 1975. And there was Lord Mountbatten in 1979.

on the parade ground knew what had taken place. Even television viewers were told little until the lunchtime news. For a few moments the Queen could not have known that blanks were being fired. Her husband, son or cousin could have been shot dead behind her. An officer rode up to reassure her.

The following Monday, before the Garter lunch, Lady Longford congratulated the Queen on her horsemanship. The Queen brightened. She said: 'It was the Household Cavalry who upset my horse.' The officer who dashed forward caused it to buck and rear but she controlled it.[2] After that incident, whenever the Queen was in an open carriage, officers rode closely beside her, which made taking aim more difficult. Some officers had walkie-talkies in their helmets.

It was no doubt less alarming for the Queen to find that her car could not get through a blizzard on the A46 in Gloucestershire on the night of 13 December 1981, returning from a visit to Princess Anne at Gatcombe Park. Her detective, Commander Michael Trestrail, Head of the Royal Protection Department, who was with her in the car, went into the Cross Hands, Old Sodbury, and arranged for them to give the Queen sanctuary. She was ushered into the building, unseen by the drinkers and taken to room twelve by an outside stairway. She might have had to stay the night, but around midnight, seven hours later, it was possible for her to be driven home. Business at the pub soared when the news got out.

In 1982, a few days after the birth of Prince William, there was a shocking incident at Buckingham Palace. On 9 July Michael Fagan, an unemployed house painter, found his way into the Palace and gained access to the Queen's bedroom. This was his second impromptu appearance. On an earlier occasion he had scaled a drainpipe and come in through an unlocked window. He startled a housemaid, ate some cheese, tripped several alarms, which proved faulty, drank half a bottle of wine and left. He succeeded in getting past electronic alarms, police and palace guards.

On his second entry, he again set off an alarm, but security thought it was faulty and silenced it. He cut his hand on an ashtray and found his way into the Queen's bedroom, temporarily unguarded during a security change-over. The Queen was not nonplussed by the arrival of a total stranger in her bedroom. He sat on the end of her bed and she talked to him calmly for ten minutes. She tried to telephone for the police but no one came. He asked for cigarettes. The Queen called a maid, who summoned a footman and two policemen. Fagan was taken away, charged, then committed for psychiatric testing and spent six months in a mental institution. William Whitelaw, the Home Secretary, made a tentative offer to resign but the Queen did not accept it. Nevertheless a massive security review was undertaken.

Hardly had the dust settled when, on 17 July, Commander Trestrail resigned 'for personal reasons'. The Fagan incident inspired a male prostitute, Michael Raunch, with whom he had been in a relationship, to try to blackmail Trestrail but failed. Trestrail told him he would report that to the police at once. Raunch then offered his story to a newspaper for £20,000.* The paper passed the information to the Palace. In the eventual report Trestrail was cleared of any wrongdoing, confirmed as having conducted his duties with perfect loyalty, but it was noted that he had led a secret double life.† Colleagues described him as 'a very sound man in every way',[3] and William Whitelaw wrote that he was 'highly regarded by the Queen, and indeed by all at the Palace. I personally knew him and admired his work.'[4]

Three days later, on 20 July, four soldiers were killed in an IRA bomb in Hyde Park. Andrew Parker Bowles was in command at Knightsbridge barracks. Seven horses were wounded, and he witnessed many being destroyed. He was able to save the life of Sefton, later a famous racehorse. The Queen rang Parker Bowles that evening. He bemoaned the loss of the horses. She said: 'Horses can be replaced. Men can't be.'[5]

* * * * *

---

* Commander Trestrail was beaten up on the Metro in Rome during the Queen's 1981 state visit (HV diary, 18 December 2002).
† It was suggested that Margaret Thatcher wanted an in-depth investigation to establish if other homosexuals were working at the Palace. The belief was that the Queen resisted this, well aware that there were. On 13 February 1983 Trestrail gave a single interview to Simon Freeman of the *Sunday Times* in which he made clear that he had never been a security risk.

The Queen observed the excessive interest the media took in the new Princess of Wales, expecting that in time it would subside. It did not. Prince Charles found himself overshadowed by his wife's popularity. In the autumn the Waleses undertook a four-hundred-mile tour of the Principality where, not unnaturally, the crowd wanted to see the new Princess. Far from enjoying her success, Prince Charles joked that he was just a collector of flowers.* Nor was she well, because she was pregnant, causing the postponement of their proposed visits to Australia, New Zealand and Canada.

So intense did the media interest in Diana become that the Queen summoned newspaper editors to Buckingham Palace to ask them to give her some space. The editor of the *Sun* refused to attend. When the editor of the *News of the World* suggested that Diana could send a servant to the village shop to buy her wine gums, the Queen told him she had 'never heard of anything so pompous'.[6]

Birth of Prince William

On 21 June 1982 the Princess of Wales gave birth to Prince William, who weighed in at 7 pounds 1½ ounces at 9.03 p.m. This gave the Queen a direct male heir in the next generation. He was christened William Arthur Philip Louis on the Queen Mother's eighty-second birthday, 4 August, at Buckingham Palace. His godparents were King Constantine of Greece, Princess Alexandra, Lord Romsey (now Earl Mountbatten of Burma), the Duchess of Westminster, Lady Susan Hussey (lady in waiting to the Queen) and Sir Laurens van der Post (Prince Charles's much admired guru).

The early years of 1982 were dominated by the Falklands War when Argentina invaded the islands and Margaret Thatcher responded by sending a task force to regain possession of them. This was a bold move by the Prime Minister who, after consultations, took the risk, then cut through all the red tape to get the task force on its

---

* This situation got considerably worse later on – most notably when they spent six weeks in Australia and New Zealand in 1983. Again the crowds seemed keener to see the Princess of Wales than her husband to the point that they gave up separate walkabouts and walked together as a pair.

way. Prince Andrew was serving on board HMS *Invincible* and the Queen made it clear that there was no question of him not serving. So he went out and returned at the end of the successful operation, with something of the air of the conquering hero, a rose clutched between his teeth when he disembarked at Spithead on 17 September, his parents there to welcome him home.

Soon afterwards the tabloids discovered his relationship with the actress, Koo Stark. She would have been an intelligent and in many ways ideal bride, but suffered greatly at the hands of the tabloid media. When she and Prince Andrew asked the Press Secretary, Michael Shea, for advice, he remained seated rudely and suggested that Prince Andrew should be seen out and about with as many girls as possible, thus deflecting attention. As a result he acquired the nickname 'Randy Andy'. Shea also proposed some financial ideas in which he would have a stake.[7]

In September Prince Edward went to Wellington, New Zealand, to be a house tutor for two terms at Wanganui Collegiate.

On 12 October Margaret Thatcher offended some commentators by taking the salute at Mansion House at the Falklands victory parade, conveniently scheduled for when the Queen was away on a four-week tour of Australia and elsewhere. It was felt that she was usurping the Queen's role as Head of State.

★ ★ ★ ★ ★

Between 13 February and 11 March 1983 the Queen and the Duke of Edinburgh visited the Cayman Islands, Jamaica (where the Queen addressed Parliament), Mexico (a state visit to President Miguel de la Madrid), and the USA. This was the Queen's first visit to California but because of recent IRA activities there were no walkabouts. One night in Hollywood she witnessed a gala performance by old stars such as Frank Sinatra and George Burns, in the company of the First Lady, Mrs Reagan. The President and his wife celebrated their thirty-first wedding anniversary on board *Britannia* on 4 March and invited the Queen and Prince Philip to their ranch, a visit undertaken in torrential rain. The Queen and Prince Philip spent three days in Vancouver where twenty thousand people turned out to see them.

The Queen very rarely made a mistake. But after a state visit to President Daniel Arap Moi of Kenya, where she was able to see the new Treetops, she went on to Bangladesh. Her host was President Abu Sayeed Chowdhury. She rose to propose his health, addressing him as 'the President of Pakistan'. There was a deathly hush and she retrieved the situation: 'It used to be Pakistan. Now it's Bangladesh.'[8] The incident was not reported.

In March 1984 a five-day state visit to King Hussein of Jordan became controversial, when the Queen's speech at the state banquet upset President Herzog of Israel. A tight security net was put around the Queen and she was distressed to hear that a British diplomat had been shot in Athens by an Arab gunman on account of the tour. Some private remarks made by the Queen to Queen Noor of Jordan were picked up by a long-range microphone, adding to the tension. No sooner had she returned to London than she was invited to visit Israel.

In between these formal events there were occasional social ones. One such was the party given by Drue Heinz, wife of H.J. Heinz (of '57 Varieties') to mark her husband's seventy-fifth birthday, at Ascot Place, near Winkfield, at the end of July 1983. A stage coach took the guests to the edge of the lake. They were rowed across and came to the lawn for drinks and dinner. Many more arrived after dinner when there was dancing in a Big Top, and almost everywhere a guest looked, there was a bucket of ice with a magnum of pink champagne in it. Princess Margaret used this occasion as a vendetta against Princess Michael of Kent.* She told Mrs Heinz that she would not bring the Queen if the Michaels were invited. There were many memorable vignettes, including Mary Lee Fairbanks, wife of 'Young Doug' dancing close to the Queen and

---

* Princess Margaret and Princess Michael were never friends. Princess Margaret claimed never to have spoken to her. Princess Michael went to America with the Countess of Dudley (former starlet, Maureen Swanson) and there was a falling-out as a result of which Lord Dudley wrote a long, vicious poem about Princess Michael. This was read towards the end of a dinner given by Lord Weidenfeld in March 1983. When Princess Michael heard about it, she complained to the Queen and the Dudleys received a solicitor's letter. All copies of the poem were ordered to be destroyed. At least one survives.

sinking to the floor in an elaborate curtsey. Her dress concertinaed to her waist and stayed there, when she stood up, to the amusement of the not so generous society guests.⁹

Birth of Prince Henry of Wales

The birth of Prince Harry on 15 September after a nine-hour labour, marked a watershed moment in the marriage of the Prince and Princess of Wales. Prince Charles emerged from the hospital and told the waiting crowd that he would soon have enough boys for a polo team. He then headed off to play polo.

Diana suffered a severe bout of post-natal depression after Prince Harry's birth. Soon afterwards, the Waleses went up to Scotland to stay with Anne, Duchess of Westminster. During their stay, Prince Charles went out salmon fishing, while Diana read a book nearby. She put the book down and walked along the bank. Unaware of where she was, Prince Charles cast and caught Diana just above her eye with his fly. The fly was stuck and had to be cut off. Barry Mannakee,* the number three detective, was on duty and he took her back to the house. She did not need to go to hospital, but she needed sympathy and Mannakee gave it.

Back in London, her regular protection team soon noticed a change in her behaviour when in Mannakee's company and were jointly concerned about the implications. In due course more and more people started to notice this, and finally her regular protection officers felt they had no choice but to confront her with what they and others were seeing, a difficult conversation to have, but one they hoped could be resolved discreetly. They stressed the inevitable dangers to her and to her reputation and that Mannakee had a wife and two young daughters. After a period of denial, she admitted an inappropriate relationship with Mannakee.

Therefore when the Princess of Wales told Martin Bashir in her infamous Panorama interview that there were three people in the

---

* Barry Mannakee (1947–87), married since 1966. He was one of the PPOs for the young princes and was on duty to give the regular PPOs some time off and to be assessed as to his suitability for further duties.

marriage, there were indeed three people, but the third person was Mannakee, nor Mrs Parker Bowles.

In due course, the protection team tried to arrange for Mannakee to be transferred but faced resistance from the Prince of Wales who liked Mannakee and wanted to keep him on. An argument was put forward that the long hours would disrupt Mannakee's family life, given that he had small children. When told he was being moved Mannakee turned to Diana, calling her on her direct line. She was extremely upset. In due course, inevitably, Prince Charles noticed this and asked the protection team to explain why. They told him that it was because Mannakee was being removed. He suggested they keep him, but the protection team told him that Mannakee must go or they would resign. Mannakee was moved.

The Mannakee relationship continued for a while but soon became untenable due to the complications involved in keeping it going and so in due course it petered out and Diana moved on.

It was this affair that caused Charles to conclude that his marriage had 'irretrievably broken down', as he told Jonathan Dimbleby on camera in 1994. There being no future for the marriage, in due course he resumed his relationship with Camilla. But, as stated, she was not the first 'third persion in the marriage', as claimed to Bashir. Mannakee was.

The affair had a tragic postscript. On 15 May 1987 Barry Mannakee was killed when riding a pillion on a motorcycle driven by Steven Peet when his bicycle collided with a car, driven by a young female, as it emerged from a T-junction in Woodfort, East London. Prince Charles told Diana about the death when they were on their way to Monaco by plane. She took to believing that the death was a conspiracy by those around her – for her protection. This was grossly unfair.

★ ★ ★ ★ ★

In October 1984, the Queen was in Kentucky with Lord Carnarvon on a rare private visit to study bloodstock in Kentucky and Wyoming, after an official visit to Canada, when the call came through that the Provisional IRA had planted a bomb at the Grand Hotel in Brighton during the Conservative Party Conference. This exploded at 2.54 a.m. on the night of 12 October, killing Sir Anthony Berry, John Wakeham's wife and Lady Shattock, and seriously injuring Norman Tebbit and his wife Margaret, who spent the rest of her life in a wheelchair. The news that reached Kentucky at 5 a.m., local time, was that the entire Cabinet had been wiped out. Lord Carnarvon said that on no account was the Queen to be woken. He reached the Private Secretary eventually and his instructions were that the White House was not to be allowed to talk to the Queen until she had spoken to Mrs Thatcher. The White House kept ringing and they kept saying that the Queen could not be found. In due course Margaret Thatcher came on the line. Her opening words were: 'Are you all having a lovely time?' Evidence of her *sangfroid*.[11]

34
CRITICAL TIMES, 1986–8

Sarah Ferguson appeared on the royal scene in 1985. She was a friend of the Princess of Wales who introduced her to Prince Andrew. They were soon engaged, at a time when the Prince and Princess of Wales were worn down by cares. In contrast this couple gave the impression that their natural high spirits would see them through any troubles that might lie ahead. Some worried for Diana, none for 'Fergie'. She and Prince Andrew had a happy-go-lucky, gung-ho approach to life, in which jesting played its part.

Sarah Ferguson drew a short straw. The Princess of Wales had all the finest dress designers working for her. Her new sister-in-law would always be second best. Sarah was born on 15 October 1959, the daughter of Major Ronald Ferguson, who had been Prince Philip's polo manager and was now with Prince Charles. He was in many ways an absurd figure. He had failed exams to get into the family regiment, the Life Guards, but when Mountbatten had become Colonel, he had shoehorned him in. He was notoriously unfaithful and had destroyed other marriages. His wife Susan left him when Sarah was quite young, and after the divorce, she married another polo player, Hector Barrantes. They lived mainly in Argentina. Sarah was a cousin of Princess Alice, Duchess of Gloucester, and of Robert Fellowes, Diana's brother-in-law, who became the principal Private Secretary in 1990. She had been a chalet girl, had had a number of boyfriends, and worked in an art gallery. She was an easygoing likeable girl. The Queen preferred her to Diana. Prince Philip was less enamoured. His comment was: 'Well. He chose her.'[1]

Her first royal engagement was the Queen's sixtieth-birthday Service of Thanksgiving at St George's Chapel, Windsor, filmed by the BBC. To rewatch a recording is to glimpse a world now gone. The voice of the then Dean, Michael Mann, bristled with sanctimonious arrogance. People don't talk like him any more. Nor do they talk like the Dean of the Chapels Royal who read some prayers. In those days the Lord Chamberlain's Office could still intimidate with a stare. The BBC's commentator, Tom Fleming, was good. He could identify the congregation.

The Queen wore bright daffodil yellow, with *Dynasty*-style Joan Collins shoulder pads. Prince Charles read a Lesson. The Princess of Wales was there with Prince William in his little blue coat. The Earl and Countess of Harewood and Gerald Lascelles had been allowed back into the fold after their complicated divorces. In the Quire were seated the Knights of the Garter, and in the Nave the Queen's lesser relations, along with figures such as Harold Macmillan, James Callaghan (who arrived in a cashmere overcoat), and Margaret Thatcher (visiting the chapel for the first time). The former influential Dean, Robin Woods, stood head and shoulders above the others. Group Captain Peter Townsend (still an extra equerry) came with his second wife.

Sarah Ferguson joined the Queen in the Scottish Coach to travel through the town of Windsor in the rain. In the afternoon six thousand children advanced to Buckingham Palace in a glorious procession up the Mall, bearing daffodils for the Queen. The next day, 22 April, King Juan Carlos of Spain and his wife, Queen Sofia (formerly a Princess of Greece), came on a state visit to Windsor Castle. And two days later, the Duchess of Windsor died at her Paris home, aged eighty-nine.

★ ★ ★ ★ ★

The Duchess's years of widowhood were years of illness, suffering and intrigue. She was very rich. She had no immediate relations of her own; she was not on close terms with her husband's family; she had a dishonest lawyer, an avaricious Swiss banker, a sly butler, and a dodgy doctor, so she was in considerable danger. Maître Suzanne Blum ousted her lawyer and two secretaries, after which she was in sole control. By 1978 the Duchess was unable to speak and hardly moved. She was fed intravenously through tubes. The Royal Family were interested in the Duchess's plight, but powerless. Blum held the keys.

The Duchess's body was flown from Paris and the Queen, the Duke of Edinburgh, the Queen Mother and many members of the British Royal Family were present at her private funeral in St George's Chapel. As agreed by the Queen as far back as 1961, flags flew at half-mast on public buildings on that day. One of the Duchess's friends commented that the service was everything the Duke could have hoped for – the Royal Family there, beautiful singing by the choir, the scene seemingly lit by candlelight. The plan was that the Duchess had the identical service to the Duke. That happened, but they removed any mention of him, and the Dean failed to insert any mention of the Duchess at her service. The Queen was angered by that lapse.

After the funeral, the Queen and the Duchess's remaining staff accompanied the coffin to the private burial ground at Frogmore, where the Duchess was laid to rest beside the Duke. For the Queen it was the end of a long saga. Her uncle had abdicated, her father had become King, and he had died young. Coming in, she walked past the grave of her uncle the Duke of Gloucester, whose military career had been destroyed by the Abdication. The Queen was moved to tears. One of the nurses, a Hungarian, upset her by saying: '*Mais vous pleurez, Madame* ... Your tears show you are not the hard-hearted woman I had been led to believe.' Later the Queen confided: 'I could have struck her!'[2] This was a rare occasion when the Queen's emotions got the better of her. That evening she did not take calls from those who rang.*

The Michael Shea Affair

Just before Prince Andrew's wedding, there were rumours of a clash with the Queen over Margaret Thatcher's stance against South African sanctions. This became a crisis at the Palace on Saturday, 19 July, when the Press Secretary, Michael Shea, told Sir William Heseltine that Bernard Ingham had called from Number 10 to warn him that the *Sunday Times* were about to publish a sensational front-page story

---

* In April 1987 the Duchess's jewels were sold for record prices by Christie's in Geneva.

on the growing rift between the Queen and her Prime Minister. Andrew Neil, the editor, was claiming that this gave 'an unprecedented insight into a ruling [sic] monarch's political views'. The next day the *Sunday Times* produced an enormous spread by Simon Freeman and Michael Jones, the political editor, entitled 'Queen dismayed by "uncaring" Thatcher'.

The paper went further than a rift. The gist was that 'sources close to the Queen' had let it be known that she was 'dismayed' by many of Thatcher's policies and found Mrs Thatcher's approach 'uncaring, confrontational and socially divisive'.³ The specific points were:

1. The Thatcher Government must be more caring to the less privileged in Britain.
2. The Queen was concerned about the long-term damage to the social fabric of the country during the miners' strike of 1983-4.
3. She had misgivings about Mrs Thatcher allowing bombers to use British airbases for their raid on Libya in April 1975.
4. She thought the Government's policies undermined 'the consensus in British politics', which had served the country so well since the Second World War.

This was published at a time when many countries had boycotted the Commonwealth Games about to take place in Edinburgh. In the main article there was a subtle paragraph:

> The fact that most people, including many Tory loyalists, believe this version of the week's events is testimony to the wiliness of the Queen and the immense, though shadowy, power of the Palace lobby. Far from being a straightforward countrywoman, a late-middle-aged grandmother who is most at ease when she is talking about horses or dogs, the Queen is an astute political infighter who is quite prepared to take on Downing Street when provoked.⁴

In the days before the article was published, Shea ('an immensely vain man, in the grip of hubris') boasted about how clever he had been in getting an important piece of journalism slanted to give a picture of the Queen's views, which he thought would play well with the public. Privately he panicked. He denied that he had said anything that could remotely be construed as it was presented in the paper. He even gave William Heseltine a memo on the Monday, which denied having volunteered any information on the Queen's opinions about sanctions or anything else, and furthermore advised Heseltine not to contact Andrew Neil in case he made capital out of the call. In the midst of this Shea presided over a press conference about plans for Prince Andrew's wedding. He was asked about the Thatcher business, but refused to discuss it: 'I am simply not going to answer questions on this subject here today.'[5]

Having accepted Shea's original denial, it took Heseltine a while to pin Shea down as the villain. Mrs Thatcher was upset. Sir William went to Windsor where the Queen was entertaining various European visitors and suggested that before the article came out she should telephone the Prime Minister to say she had no prior knowledge of it and did not subscribe to its contents. This the Queen did.

Members of Parliament entered the fray, Enoch Powell making the point that he did not believe the Queen would ever play foul with her ministers: 'I do not believe all the hoo-ha which certain persons, no doubt for their own interests, have been putting around. You might, if you were a dirty dog, try to get your object by suggesting a difference between the sovereign and her ministers. But only a dirty dog would do that.'[6] A young journalist at the *News of the World*, Andrew Morton (later to be Diana's mouthpiece), revealed that *The Economist* claimed the article had been read to Shea. He asked Shea if he was the Palace mole. Shea replied: 'Ah. That might be your conclusion.'[7]

The Thatchers arrived at Holyroodhouse to stay with the Queen for the Commonwealth Games a week after publication. The article was not discussed. From Edinburgh Heseltine wrote a letter to *The Times* in which he explained the role of the Queen in respect of her Prime Minister and stressed: 'After thirty-four years of unvarying adherence to these constitutional principles, it is preposterous to suggest that Her Majesty might suddenly depart from them. No sensible person would give a moment's credence to such a proposition.'[8] He made it clear that no Press Secretary would be informed of the Queen's private opinions. Neither would he have the right to express them publicly.

In due course, Shea was exposed as the villain. Even when he owned up, he was sufficiently self-delusional to claim to have been grossly misrepresented. Margaret Thatcher wrote in her memoirs: 'Although the press could not resist the temptation to suggest disputes between the Palace and Downing Street, especially on Commonwealth affairs, I have always found the Queen's attitude towards the work of the government absolutely correct.'[9] In the second volume of his authorised biography of Thatcher, Charles Moore wrote: 'Over a rather longer period of time, the government's low opinion of Michael Shea's behaviour was borne in upon Buckingham Palace, and he was quietly edged out of his post ("not fast enough" in the view of Sir William Heseltine).'[10]

Buckingham Palace ousted Shea by securing him a job with Hanson plc – the polite way in which those things are done.* Years later, Noreen Taylor reviewed one of his novels, *Berlin Embassy*: 'He just can't help congratulating himself on a life of success, prosperity, personal happiness and even a little celebrity. His shoulders fairly bristle with epaulettes of triumph.'[11] Having met Shea a few times, I support this view. Shea asked for a knighthood (KCVO), which was not forthcoming. He wrote not a word about the *Sunday Times* saga in his self-serving autobiography, but he quoted Marcel Proust: 'As we journey into our own pasts, vast tracts of it are left best unvisited.'[12] One can well see why.†

★ ★ ★ ★ ★

On 23 July Prince Andrew married Sarah Ferguson. Foreign royalty poured in; Mrs Reagan flew over. It was a full blown Westminster Abbey wedding. There was a hint of what might come later when

---

* There is a pertinent line in Shea's autobiography: '...if you want rid of someone from your empire, you send them on their way with excellent window-dressed references' (Shea, *A View from the Sidelines*, p.101).

† Michael Shea tried to buy his grace-and-favour house in Pimlico at an advantageous price. He was rejected. He died aged seventy-one on 17 October 2009, not before he had influenced a few authors in his favour – Ben Pimlott and Sarah Bradford, to name but two. He is remembered, rightly or wrongly, for calling the Queen 'Miss Piggy' or referring to her 'Miss Piggy face'.

the Princess of Wales and the bride gate-crashed Prince Andrew's stag night at Annabel's, dressed as policewomen. The contrast between this wedding and the last was further exemplified by the Palace balcony kiss. Charles and Diana had kissed each other shyly, but this pair engaged with the crowd as if to say, 'We can't hear you, what do you want?' Then they went for it to an almighty cheer. They set off into what appeared to be a happy-go-lucky marriage.

The Princess of Wales looked wistful that day. She now had an ally at court, but at the same time her own marriage was unravelling, and it has been suggested that her closeness to Mannakee had been detected.

★ ★ ★ ★ ★

On 25 September the Queen came down to London to open the 32nd Commonwealth Parliamentary Conference in Westminster Hall, and on 11 October she set off to the People's Republic of China for a state visit to President Li Xiannian.

No English monarch had ever visited China before, so it was hailed as the greatest visit of the Queen's reign before she had even set out. Some of the Chinese had a hint of what to expect as Peter O'Toole was in Beijing filming the life of the last Emperor, Pu-Yi, the Forbidden City adorned as it would have been in the days of the Middle Kingdom. The Queen was housed in an exquisitely decorated guesthouse in suburbs of west Beijing. She was formally welcomed at the Gate of Heavenly Peace outside the Forbidden City, and went on to the Great Hall of the People, a Russian-built edifice, with marble steps down which Margaret Thatcher had stumbled briefly on her visit in 1982. The Queen proved adept with chopsticks. She walked on the Great Wall and visited Shanghai. As ever the visit was deemed a considerable success, though Alan Hamilton of *The Times* thought she had made an 'often glum progress through Asia' and only perked up on the way home at a race meeting in Hong Kong.[13]

Prince Philip was considered to have let the side down with a number of indiscretions, the most famous being his reference to 'slitty eyes' at Xian when they were visiting the Terracotta Warriors. By this time Michael Shea could do no right. His attempts to downplay the remark were clumsy, but the last word can be left to a perceptive student who was there at the time, and wrote to *The Times*: 'The real embarrassment should lie with the British press and their incessant search for hollow sensationalism.'[14]

The Queen was now sixty. Presently she announced that she would no longer be riding in the Birthday Parade. Her horse Burmese retired and she took the opportunity to give up before she needed to. Anne Wall, her Press Secretary, explained that this avoided press agitation if she suddenly had to stop. Nor did she have to train with a new horse. She had always ridden side-saddle, which meant lots of practice in the Royal Mews. From then on she attended the Parade in Queen Victoria's Ivory Phaeton (though in the year of the Diamond Jubilee in 2012, she and Prince Philip travelled in the Glass Coach).

The euphoria of the 1981 Royal Wedding had been so great, that perhaps a backlash was inevitable. From the mid-1980s there was one disaster or scandal after another. Princess Michael of Kent was frequently in the news, the worst time being when her father was posthumously exposed as a Nazi. Prince Edward dropped out of a year-long commando course with the Royal Marines, then set up 'The Grand Knockout', soon to be known as *It's a Royal Knockout*. This was a well-meant charitable endeavour that raised more than £1 million for charity. The Queen and Prince Philip were evidently nervous about the younger royals cavorting about, but the Queen was never good at saying no. When Prince Edward asked the press what they had made of it, he received a lukewarm response and stormed out, a scene frequently re-broadcast to his discredit.

In February 1988 he began work as a theatrical production assistant at the Palace Theatre, London. He started a project with Bryan Forbes and become Patron of the National Youth Theatre. He set up Ardent, a company that made documentaries, which he ran for some years. He wanted to make all kinds of films, but backers were only interested in royal documentaries such as *Edward on Edward*, about the Duke and Duchess of Windsor. Prince Edward was often to be seen striding about on the battlements of ancient castles.

The Murdoch press now treated the Royal Family as a soap opera. *Spitting Image* portrayed them as caricature puppets on television. Sarah Ferguson proved a rather lively friend for the Princess of Wales.

She seemed to have pressed Diana into antics such as prodding Major Hugh Lindsay with an umbrella at Ascot. They played up to the cameras while on the ski slopes. At a film premiere of the latest James Bond film, *The Living Daylights*, Diana broke a stunt bottle over Prince Charles's head. In Hollywood in 1988 Sarah broke a 'glass' bottle over the head of the Yorks' Private Secretary, Sean O'Dwyer. On the same trip, there was a glittering gala dinner. A voice called out, 'Love you,' and the Duchess responded, 'I'll see you later.' A visit to Canada by the Yorks turned into a romp. They prepared to live in a house near Sunningdale, dubbed 'South York' in tribute to *Dallas*, a house generally considered unnecessarily extravagant.

While this new informality was welcomed in some quarters, it was considered undignified in others. The Duchess enjoyed the perks of royalty and the glitz, failing to appreciate that the role of members of the Royal Family was to serve – to support the Queen in her duties. Her ultimate 'crime' was to point out to the Princess of Wales that if she hated her life so much, she did not have to stay. An unhappy child at school is never so unhappy as when another child points at the gate and suggests: 'Why don't you run away?'

Since October 1986 Diana had been involved in an affair with the young Life Guard James Hewitt, with whom she rode in Hyde Park. It was known that the Wales marriage was in trouble and there were plans to find things the Prince and Princess might enjoy doing together. Andrew Parker Bowles thought Hewitt would be a suitable riding instructor. When Diana first went to Windsor, Hazel West (wife of George West of the Lord Chamberlain's Office) used to go with her so there could be no hint of scandal. But, like Major Ferguson, Hewitt proved over-sexed. Diana used to have him smuggled into Kensington Palace in the boot of the car.[15] When that affair ended in 1991, as with Mannakee, Diana considered it had never happened.[16]

In public, Diana cut considerable new ground in her engagements. AIDS was a health scare that had begun to claim the lives of homosexuals in many lands, including prominent figures in the arts in London and New York. There was stigma about this illness: people treated sufferers almost as they had lepers. On 9 April 1987 the Princess shook hands with an AIDS victim when opening Britain's first purpose-built AIDS ward at the Middlesex Hospital in London. This changed perceptions. In May 1988 she visited the counselling centre of Relate: Marriage Guidance in London.

Rumours about the unhappiness of the marriage appeared in the press. Penny Junor promoted her biography of Prince Charles, by declaring on Radio 4 that he had married the wrong woman. Lynda Lee-Potter was quick to defend Diana: 'I think he was lucky to get her – and so were we. Prince Charles grew up in a royal cocoon. Princess Diana didn't.'[17] On 20 May 1987 the *Daily Mail* reported that Prince Charles was 'increasingly dismayed about the way he feels his marriage and his private life are being misrepresented by some sections of the Press'.[18]

Prince Charles courted controversy with his public interventions, in particular when he described city planners as doing 'a worse job than the Luftwaffe' on London.[19] He attacked Paternoster Square near St Paul's Cathedral, started his model village at Poundbury in Dorset, and published his book, *A Vision of Britain*. Much of what he did was constructive and unquestionably well meant. But it brought him into the political arena, and was frequently eclipsed by the rumours concerning his marriage.

Then came tragedy. The Waleses, the Duchess of York (pregnant with Princess Beatrice) and their friends the Palmer-Tomkinsons and Major Hugh Lindsay (the Queen's former equerry) were skiing in Klosters in the spring of 1988. On 10 March, partly to escape the ever-intrusive reporters, Prince Charles went off piste with the Palmer-Tomkinsons and Lindsay. There was a sudden avalanche. Prince Charles was within inches of death but the guide, Bruno Specher, shouted at him: 'Go, Sir, go.' Patti Palmer-Tomkinson and Hugh Lindsay were swept four hundred metres downhill. She was rescued, unconscious, with serious leg injuries. Hugh Lindsay was killed.*

The Queen and Prince Philip were at an engagement at Queen's Club, marking a tennis anniversary. Sir William Heseltine was concerned that they might think Prince Charles had been killed.

---

* Major Lindsay had married Sarah Brennan the previous July. She had worked in the Buckingham Palace press office. She was not with them as she was expecting a baby in May. The Duke of York was serving at the Portland Naval Air Station.

He established the facts and relayed them to Kenneth Scott, the Private Secretary on duty with the Queen. She was fond of her equerry and was upset to be told the news at a public engagement. Nevertheless she completed the engagement.

Prince Charles and his friends came home. He was haunted with guilt, blaming himself for subjecting his companions to danger. The media used it to highlight the growing rift between him and his father. On the other hand A. N. Wilson commented that the tragedy came at a time when 'He and his wife have been subjected to merciless and impertinent intrusion into their domestic life.'[20] Prince Charles and Diana became more distanced. They attended Major Lindsay's funeral at Sandhurst with eight other members of the Royal Family. Prevented by the rules of etiquette from attending in person, the Queen was represented by her then equerry, Lieutenant-Commander Timothy Laurence RN.

35
DARK DAYS, 1987–90

The one time I sat next to the Queen at dinner, the Iraq war was in progress. She said: 'I think we've finally found a use for the Parachute Regiment.' It occurred to me how many global issues she had to deal with, most of which would not concern the rest of us. One such was Fiji, where there was a military coup on 14 May 1987. Ten masked and armed soldiers entered the Fijian House of Representatives and stopped the proceedings at the instigation of Lieutenant-Colonel Sitiveni Rabuka, third in command of the Royal Fiji Military Forces. The Prime Minister, Dr Timoci Bavadra, was ousted. The Governor-General, Ratu Sir Penaia Ganilau, swore in Rabuka as the new Prime Minister, but would not recognise the legitimacy of the Council of Ministers. Rabuka then suspended the Governor-General and declared himself Head of State. The Queen put out a message that her Governor-General remained 'the sole legitimate source of executive authority'. She continued: 'Anyone who seeks to remove the Governor-General from office would in effect be repudiating his allegiance and loyalty to the Queen.'

A state of emergency was declared. The Foreign Secretary, Geoffrey Howe, announced that he wanted a swift return to parliamentary democracy and there were fears that the Queen would lose her position as Queen of Fiji. Later that month Dr Bavadra came to London, hoping to see the Queen and to persuade her not to approve the new government. Sir William Heseltine offered to meet him, but he said he would only meet the Queen. Instead he had two meetings with Sir Sonny Ramphal, Secretary-General to the Commonwealth.

Meanwhile the Fijian Supreme Court ruled the coup unconstitutional and the Governor-General tried to reassert executive power. On 25 September Rabuka staged a second coup. From London came another message: 'The Queen is saddened by news of the latest developments in Fiji coming so soon after the recent announcement about the formation of a caretaker government to work towards restoring democracy in Fiji.'[1]

The outcome was that Fiji declared itself a republic on 7 October while the Queen was in Vancouver for the Commonwealth Heads of Government Meeting. She was dropped as Head of State and Fiji was dropped from the Commonwealth. The Queen issued another statement: 'Her Majesty is sad to think that the ending of Fijian allegiance to the Crown should have been brought about without the people of Fiji being given an opportunity to express their opinion on the proposal.'

In 1990 a new constitution was ratified, reserving the office of President, Prime Minister and two-thirds of the Senate to indigenous Fijians. Rabuka was elected as Prime Minister in 1992 and a new constitution was established in 1997, at which point Fiji was re-admitted to the Commonwealth. However, in 2009, following further coups, Fiji was again suspended, because Commodore Frank Bainimarama, Commander of the Fiji Military Forces (who installed himself as Prime Minister in 2006), refused to hold democratic elections in 2010. In 2014 suspension from the Commonwealth was lifted.

★ ★ ★ ★ ★

On 13 June the Queen finally bestowed the title 'Princess Royal' on Princess Anne, the title traditionally given to the eldest daughter of the monarch, previous holders having been Queen Victoria's daughter the Empress Frederick, Edward VII's daughter, Princess Louise, Duchess of Fife, and the Queen's aunt, Princess Mary (daughter of George V), who had died in 1965.

In June Margaret Thatcher won a historic third victory at the polls, sweeping back into Number 10 with a majority of 102 seats. The Queen opened the new Parliament on 25 June, and Mrs Thatcher's political future looked set firm for some years to come.

There was the habitual official travel overseas, including a visit to West Berlin, while in May 1987 the Queen paid a rare private visit to France to visit stud farms and to see the new Training Establishment at Le Quesnay. There were two visits to Canada. On her first visit to Quebec for twenty-three years in 1987, the impression was that the Separatist movement, which had never had a direct quarrel with the Queen, had lost its impetus. When the Queen went again in July 1990, it appeared that Quebec was on the point of breaking away to be recognised as a distinct French-speaking province within Canada. The failed Meech Lake Accord, which had aimed to persuade the Quebec government to endorse a 1982 plan to decentralize the Canadian Federation, had increased tensions between Quebec and the rest of Canada.

Brian Mulroney, the Prime Minister, tried to involve the Queen by saying she had supported the Meech Lake Accord in the past. The Queen countermanded, stating that she had followed the 'threat of internal divisions' with 'anxiety and deep concern' and hoped that her 'presence during this difficult period of uncertainty might be seen as a reminder of times past and encouragement to look forward to a secure and happy future'.[2]

Either due to the political acrimony, or possibly jet lag, the Queen 'seemed to find it hard to project her usual radiance, even in the most congenial surroundings'. On a walkabout she relied on 'a fixed smile, an expression which stayed with her through most of the visit'.[3] In Quebec she strolled around a park despite protesters. She was as conciliatory as ever, saying: 'My fondest wish is that Canadians come together and remain together rather than dwell on the differences which may divide them.'[4]

* * * * *

On 20 November 1987 the Queen and Prince Philip celebrated their fortieth wedding anniversary quietly at Luton Hoo. They had gone there for their wedding anniversary invariably in the days of Sir Harold and Lady Zia Wernher, and this time were the guests of their grandson, Nicholas Phillips.*

While the press in Britain were generally favourable to the Queen, the opposite was the case towards the younger members of the

---

* Nicholas Phillips (1947–91) later committed suicide in the garage at Luton Hoo, said to have been deeply in debt.

family. Six years into the marriage there were hints that the media attention was driving the Princess of Wales to a nervous breakdown. She remained enormously popular with the general public. The view was expressed that the only man in England not in love with her was her husband.

As the Queen, male members of the Royal Family and Margaret Thatcher laid wreaths at the Cenotaph on Remembrance Sunday, 8 November, they were unaware that many innocent victims had died in an IRA bomb explosion causing carnage in Enniskillen. Eleven civilians died and sixty-four were injured. Nine days later the Prince and Princess of Wales paid their first visit to Northern Ireland to comfort the victims. From this emerged Mr Gordon Wilson, whose daughter had died. He urged forgiveness rather than retribution with the famous lines: 'I bear no ill will. I bear no grudge.' These words were hailed as the most inspiring heard in the twenty-five years during the Troubles in Northern Ireland.

The Queen was not pleased when the contents of her Christmas broadcast were leaked to the press. Michael Cole, the BBC's royal correspondent talked about it at a lunch with nine other correspondents, which was later leaked to the media. Cole was 'switched to other duties' and soon left the BBC to work for Mohamed Fayed, the controversial Egyptian businessman who had acquired Harrods and been assigned the lease on the Duke and Duchess of Windsor's house in the Bois de Boulogne. Cole was to be Fayed's mouthpiece.

In her Christmas message the Queen said she welcomed the many letters she received from members of the general public as they kept her in touch with people's views and opinions, some of which were 'full of frank advice for me and my family and some of them do not hesitate to be critical'. She highlighted a fine example of tolerance:

> Mr Gordon Wilson, whose daughter Marie lost her life in the horrifying explosion at Enniskillen on Remembrance Sunday, impressed the whole world by the depth of his forgiveness. His strength and that of his wife and the courage of their daughter, came from their Christian conviction.[5]

1988

In January the Queen invited the press to Sandringham and allowed them to photograph her grandchildren clambering over a fire engine. She made it clear that she then expected to be left in peace.

There were rumblings about replacing the Queen as Head of State in Australia when she and Prince Philip visited to celebrate the Bicentennial. However, there was no great impetus to change the system, and the Queen was held in great respect. In Britain a Gallup poll put the Queen at the top of the list of those whom people wanted to meet and four out of five Britons preferred to have her as Head of State than the concept of an elected President.

The Queen was on board *Britannia,* heading to Scotland from Liverpool, when she heard of the arrival of Princess Beatrice of York* on 8 August (at 8.18 on 8.8.88). The baby was flown to Balmoral with her parents for inspection during the Queen's Scottish holiday. A historic state visit was made to King Juan Carlos of Spain in October, the first since the death of Franco in 1975 and the first ever by a British monarch. MI5 officers worked closely with the Spanish over security, and even as the Queen arrived, Basque separatists killed two policemen and seriously injured ten others in two bomb attacks. Both the Queen and the King of Spain referred to the ongoing political tensions over Gibraltar. Her speech at the Cortes received a ninety-second standing ovation.

Prince Charles turned forty on 14 November. Tom Shebbeare, Director of the Prince's Trust, gave an interview to the *Observer* stressing his achievements, and not disguising his irritation that his work with the Trust and other endeavours were eclipsed by speculation about his deteriorating marriage. Anthony Holden, formerly his champion, cashed in with a book† declaring that the Wales marriage was in grave trouble. This deeply annoyed the Prince and reduced Diana to tears at breakfast. Shebbeare pointed out that Holden had not had a private conversation with the Prince for at least ten years. 'Holden will never starve,' was the Prince's restrained

---

* The Yorks' second daughter, Princess Eugenie, was born at the Portland Hospital, London on 23 March 1990.

† *Charles: A Biography* (Weidenfeld & Nicolson, 1988).

comment at the time.⁶ But the antagonism between Holden and the Prince now grew apace, Holden deeply resenting the planted attacks on him in various media outlets. Sir Peter Gillett, Governor of the Military Knights, summed up the establishment reaction: 'I must say that chap Holden is a first-class shit.'⁷

The book overshadowed the Prince's birthday celebrations, which included a party for fifteen hundred young people in Birmingham. Prince Charles did his best to undermine the canards invariably thrown at him, in *Private Eye's* long-running, irreverent spoof, *Heir of Sorrows*, in a light and entertaining speech:

> Only the other day I was enquiring of a bed of old-fashioned roses who were forced to listen to my demented ramblings on the meaning of the universe ... At this point a row of Welsh leeks – cocky little things – which were lurking in a nearby vegetable patch, chipped in to say they expected the shed would be filled with semi-naked Kalahari Bushmen performing a fertility dance together with several Tibetan Buddhist monks, who had proceeded from Saffron Walden by levitation with advance copies of the tabloid papers, which would be strewn in my path in an ancient Buddhist greeting. 'Don't be ridiculous, they wouldn't dare to,' I replied. 'Oh yes they would,' chorused half an acre of Brussels sprouts.⁸

That evening the Queen gave a party at Buckingham Palace with the Dark Blues and Phil Collins performing. It went on until 2.45 a.m.

On 21 December Pan Am Flight 103 on its way from Frankfurt to Detroit was destroyed by a bomb at Lockerbie in Scotland, in what was judged the worst terrorist attack in the United Kingdom's history. There were 270 fatalities – 243 passengers, 16 crew and 11 residents. It happened close to Christmas when it was hard to change plans. The Palace sent the Duke of York, who was stationed at Rosyth, to get him there before Mrs Thatcher, who invariably rushed to such scenes. The Duke got there just before her, but upset everybody by stating that he felt sorrier for the American passengers than the locals. 'We got our horse there first, but he let us down when he got there,' was the verdict of one member of the Royal Household.⁹

On 24 January the Palace sent a distraught-looking Prince Charles, a month after the incident. It did not pass unnoticed that the Princess of Wales was on holiday in the British Virgin Islands, Princess Anne skiing in the French Alps, and the Yorks likewise in Klosters. When soon afterwards thirty-four people died in a train crash at Clapham, the Duchess of York went more or less straight from her holiday to the memorial service at Winchester Cathedral – her visit described as a dash.

The Queen was criticised by George Gale in the *Daily Mail* for not going to the scene: 'She performs her routine duties well enough ... She could and should comfort people with her presence when a great disaster occurs, but she stays away.' Robert Fellowes, by then the Queen's Private Secretary, concluded that the Queen should have been the first to visit. In future the Royal Family moved quicker. Following the departure of Michael Shea as Press Secretary, the post was now held by Robin Janvrin, formerly in the Navy and the Foreign Office. He was hailed as 'adept at the diplomatic art of blowing polite smokescreens'.[10]

1989

The Royal Family had not spent Christmas at Windsor in 1988, the excuse being that the castle was being rewired, but equally the extended Royal Family was becoming too numerous. The Queen was happy to have only her immediate family at Sandringham.

When Emperor Hirohito of Japan died aged eighty-seven on 7 January, there was an internal Palace dilemma as to who should represent the Queen at his funeral, his death reviving memories of wartime atrocities. The *Sun* proclaimed: 'Hell is waiting for this truly vile emperor.' Right-wing fanatics in Tokyo sent a dustcart through the city with a slogan: 'Queen Elizabeth you must go to hell.' Insults were trumpeted by loudspeakers and Sir John Whitehead, the British Ambassador, lodged a strong protest.[11] The more responsible British media welcomed the new Emperor, Akihito, and his wife Michiko.

Leaders from 164 countries attended the funeral, including the new American President, George H. W. Bush. Prince Philip volunteered himself, because he was of a certain age and did not mind the adverse publicity, of which there was a certain amount (including a written protest from the artist, John Bratby). He was also prepared to be dropped as Patron of the Burma Star Association (which did not happen). In Japan he paid his respects at a Commonwealth War cemetery. The funeral itself looked like something from another age, as an enormous enclosed bamboo palanquin, draped with black curtains, was carried by fifty-one imperial guards, preceded by monks, and followed by mourners in black, some heavily veiled, sheltering under a sea of umbrellas. Prince Philip wore a black overcoat with medals.

★ ★ ★ ★ ★

April 1989 was packed with activity, some good, some bad. In March there had been an outcry when Lord Carnarvon, the Queen's close friend and racing manager, ousted Dick Hern* from his post as her trainer and wanted him evicted from his accommodation at West Isley. This caused a furore in the racing world. Brough Scott wrote: 'Since he lives for training, that was almost like asking him to sign his own death warrant and it was only after the most vehement of protests from some of his owners that Hern was after all allowed to continue to the end of this season.'[12]

The incident was made worse because Hern was confined to a wheelchair following a hunting accident in 1984, though perfectly capable of performing his duties, and was at that time undergoing heart surgery. He was replaced by William Hastings-Bass (later Earl of Huntingdon).† This matter did not go away. In 1992 Lord Carnarvon said: 'Geoffrey Wheatcroft has written a piece in the *Daily Telegraph* saying that I and I alone had made the Queen unpopular on the Turf.'[13] Wheatcroft wrote: 'Even the Queen against whose name there has never been a breath of scandal, finds friends among what my colleague Hugh Massingberd has called the less attractive fringes of the aristocracy. The treatment of Major

---

* Dick Hern, CVO, CBE (1921–2002), racehorse trainer responsible for sixteen classic wins between 1962 and 1995.
† In June at the Derby the Queen cheered when Lady Beaverbrook's Nashwan, won the Derby. Trained by Dick Hern, and with Willie Carson in the saddle.

Dick Hern by the Queen's racing manager, Lord Carnarvon, accomplished the difficult task of making the monarch unpopular on the Turf, the most slavishly loyal community in the country.'[14]

More positively, Monty Roberts came into the Queen's life. She had read about him and, aware that he visited friends in California, sent Sir John Miller (who had just retired as Crown Equerry) out to his ranch to see what he was doing. When this moustached figure arrived, Monty Roberts took one look at him and, not without justification, thought he came from Central Casting in Hollywood. He was convinced it was a joke and looked for hidden cameras in the trees. In his turn Miller was suspicious that Roberts was a charlatan, with a gadget in his pocket that gave electric shocks to the horses.

In due course these suspicions subsided. Miller gave the Queen a favourable report, so she invited Roberts to Windsor in April 1989. She watched him at work in the Royal Mews – as did the Queen Mother and Prince Philip. Roberts 'tamed' twenty-three horses in five days, getting a rider into the saddle within twenty-nine minutes. Even Princess Anne was impressed.

On one visit, Monty Roberts rode in the park with the Queen. A woman called out: 'Yoo-hoo. Do you work here?'

'Yes, I do,' replied the Queen, riding on, the kind of incident that occurred occasionally and she enjoyed.

Roberts was born on 14 May 1935 and had worked with horses since the age of three. He took part in rodeos for about twenty-two years, and frequently won. He was horrified by the abusive way his father tied up the hind legs of horses to break them in. He learned the language of the horse. Once he tamed a wild Mustang in the wild open spaces and within three days had a rider in the saddle. He had worked with the actor James Dean, turning him into an equestrian. His philosophy was to make horses do things because they wanted to, not because they were forced to. He called this process 'Equus'. His method was to chase the horse round the riding school until it grew tired. Once it lowered its head he changed tack and become its friend and protector, because by then it had begun to trust him.

The Queen had loved horses all her life. She had been disturbed by the harsh way in which they were trained in wartime, but could not interfere with the war effort. Monty Roberts's visit occurred during the Easter court and though she had guests to 'dine and sleep', she cancelled all her engagements to watch more. She told Monty Roberts: 'You have to take this to the world and I want a book. I've dreamed of horses being trained with no violence and I love what you're doing.' As he put it: 'There is no question that Her Majesty took my work to the world and with her influence the world is changing dramatically away from violence in training horses.' He went to forty-one countries in thirty-three years, and tamed 3,300 horses, only two receiving minor injuries. In the last years of the Queen's life, Roberts involved shell-shock soldiers, both male and female, in the process and by taming the horses they gained the confidence they had lost.*

He invented the Monty Roberts blanket which protected horses all over the world as they entered the starting gates at the races. Michael Clayton, editor of *House & Hound*, sent him touring all over Britain. 'He did more for the animal kingdom than anyone,' said Terry Pendry, the Queen's Stud Groom and manager, who soon learned to follow his methods and introduced them to the Household Cavalry.[15]

---

* Monty Roberts was appointed an honorary MVO in 2011. He was invited to the Queen's funeral in 2022.

36
THE EARLY 1990s, 1989–91

As the Royal Family headed into the 1990s, the assaults of the tabloid press had dented their popularity. An opinion poll in the *Sunday Times* found the Queen Mother marginally more popular than the Queen at 90 per cent. But 47 per cent thought the Queen should eventually abdicate. It was clear that the marriage of the Prince and Princess of Wales was coming adrift, but it seemed impossible that they would separate. They rarely performed joint public engagements.

Prince Charles confessed to Selina Scott on CBS Television in America that he felt trapped. He liked to squeeze in a game of polo between official engagements, one in the evening and another the next morning: 'It's the only way I can survive in the summer. Otherwise the summer would be a total nightmare – there are permanently things happening. If I didn't get the exercise – or have something to take my mind off other things – I'd go potty.'[1] At the end of June 1990 he broke his arm falling off his pony as he took a difficult shot at Cirencester Park.

Relations between the Prince and his mother were at such a low ebb that at Balmoral that summer when the Queen saw a guest cutting up his food for him, she was less than sympathetic. He missed the fiftieth anniversary service of the Battle of Britain amid rumours was that he was depressed. He retreated to France to stay with friends, the de Waldners, and was captured by a random photographer looking mournfully out of a window. Only by November was his right arm again fully operational.

Princess Anne's marriage also unravelled. In April 1989 Mark Phillips was accused of having at least a fling with Pamella Bordes, a former Miss India, who had worked in a brothel and had a House of Commons pass. She had been involved with several men, among whom were Andrew Neil, editor of the *Sunday Times*, Donald

Trelford, editor of the *Observer* and the international arms dealer Adnan Khashoggi.

She told her story to the world, accompanied by colour images of her, topless and in scanty knickers: 'We were being drawn to each other. So we spent the evening drinking and talking until very late, certainly after everyone else had left.' She had visited Gatcombe Park. Phillips denied any impropriety: 'It was a professional weekend. We were flat out doing the job we had to do.'[2] Since Miss Bordes's public profile was being steered by Max Clifford, the (later disgraced) publicist, her story was more likely aimed to promote her aspirations to stardom. Eventually she conceded that no sex had occurred. The story fizzled out.

Soon afterwards, however, intimate letters written by the Queen's equerry, Timothy Laurence, to Princess Anne were stolen. A Commander in the Royal Navy, who had served in *Britannia*, Laurence had been appointed equerry to the Queen in place of Major Hugh Lindsay. The *Daily Express* threatened to publish these letters but were warned that they would be prosecuted for being in possession of stolen property.[3] Laurence was dropped from one or two equerry duties and the tabloids predicted the end of the Anne-Mark marriage. She had Laurence escort her at Ascot, to which she also brought her eight-year-old daughter, Zara. On 23 August Laurence was invested as an MVO while a guest at Balmoral (a slightly lower rank than he might have expected),* when he stepped down as equerry to take up naval duties in Portsmouth.

On 30 August the press succeeded in getting on to Major Peter Phillips, Mark's father, who admitted 'with noises off from his Labradors'[4] that Anne and Mark were to separate.† The Palace had denied it strenuously for years, but the following day, without warning Mark Phillips, it announced that the couple had 'decided to separate on terms agreed between them'.[5]

---

* He was promoted to GCVO in 2025.

† In 1990 Major Peter Phillips was banned from driving for two years for being three times over the legal limit of alcohol when he hit a parked car. He was described as 'a sad and lonely man', who lived alone, watched television and drank tumblers of whisky. His wife had died in 1988 after several weeks in a coma. He died in 1998.

The Times noted that this was the third such separation in the Queen's reign, the others concerning Lord Harewood and Princess Margaret.* Their leader writer observed: 'The Queen's daughter has never been a fairy tale princess, however, and the monarchy is stronger for it. There was a time when she did not float on the same high flood of public affection as her mother and grandmother.'[6]

Mark Phillips owned land around Gatcombe Park and moved into Aston Farm, two miles away, with six hundred acres. He was granted total access to their children. Amicable relations were established between the separated parents despite Phillips's somewhat chequered former and later love life.†

* * * * *

One of the roles of members of the Royal Family was to visit disaster areas. The Prince and Princess of Wales were quick to visit Hillsborough at Sheffield after 766 people were injured and 96 died at the stadium on 15 April, when the crowd got out of control at the semi-final FA Cup between Liverpool and Nottingham Forest. The Duke and Duchess of Kent attended a memorial service for the 96 dead. The Princess of Wales attended a memorial service for the fifty-one people who had lost their lives in the *Marchioness* pleasure-cruiser on the Thames on 20 August. Likewise, in September, as Captain General Royal Marines Prince Philip visited the bandsmen injured by the IRA at the Royal Marines School of Music in Deal in an attack in which eleven bandsmen died. He condemned the action of the terrorists: 'Not very charitable, to put it mildly. It will not help the IRA win anything ... This sort of thing happened every night during the Blitz. It is amazing how tough and resilient the British people are.'[7] In November he and the Prime Minister

---

* *The Times* could have added Lord Harewood's brother, Gerald Lascelles, to this equation.

† Phillips had a daughter in 1985 with a New Zealand art teacher, Heather Tonkin. This was confirmed in a 1991 DNA test. In 1997 he married Sandy Pflueger, an American Olympic dressage competitor. They had a daughter, Stephanie, before separating in 2012, at which point Phillips entered into a relationship with another equestrian, Lauren Hough.

were present at the memorial service for the murdered Royal Marines bandsmen in Canterbury Cathedral.

* * * * *

Peripherally, there were other scandals. Major Ronald Ferguson had been exposed as a regular visitor to the Wigmore Club, an upmarket massage club, where the masseuses offered sex services to their clients. The Queen was obliged to meet him at the Royal Windsor Horse Show and at Smith's Lawn. He was indeed 'a modern-day Icarus, who burned his wings in orbit around the Royal Family'.[8] His nadir was yet to come. It could be thought that the Queen's very dutiful cousin, Princess Alexandra and her husband, Angus Ogilvy, might have been spared tabloid intrusion. They were hugely popular with the media and also with the general public and known to devote their lives to royal service. However, they were subjected to extensive and unwelcome tabloid publicity when their daughter became pregnant by a stubble-bearded photographer and married him just before the birth of their child.

* * * * *

On 4 August 1990 the Queen Mother attained her ninetieth birthday, prompting the traditional acres of adulatory newsprint she habitually inspired. Her longevity meant that she eclipsed the Queen. This was partly due to her well-honed thespian qualities, but had originally been earned by her support to the King and Britain during the war. Her style was another factor – the pale chiffons, the feathery hats, the Winterhalter evening dresses and the flowing white fur stoles, not to mention the quantity of sparkling jewels. Her philosophy was that if she met someone she wanted to send them away happier for the encounter. The self-effacing and more executive Queen was much in her shadow.

In August 1990 both Queens went round an exhibition at the Guildhall in Windsor – *90 Memorable Years* – on separate days. The Queen examined every photograph and took much in. She was followed by a cohort of photographers with cameras at the ready. Suddenly something amused her and she flashed her famous smile.

The cameras clicked furiously. When the Queen Mother went round, she turned willingly after each picture and smiled. They clicked politely. The Queen Mother was on auto-pilot.

Soon after this Princess Margaret turned sixty. The Queen gave her the Royal Victorian Chain, of which Princess Margaret was inordinately proud, prompting her to attend the State Opening of Parliament several times in order to wear it. Kenneth Rose was a bit snide: 'She thinks it's the Garter,' which the Queen never gave her.

★ ★ ★ ★ ★

Margaret Thatcher had been in power for eleven years. In December 1989 Sir Anthony Meyer had mustered 33 votes against her 314, in a feeble challenge to oust her. However, by November 1990 the Conservatives had been trailing behind Labour for eighteen months. Mrs Thatcher had become combative and was said to be out of touch with her party. It is axiomatic that what brings success is often the same as what brings ultimate failure. The first great leap of an athlete breaks a record; the last breaks their leg. And so it was with Margaret Thatcher. Back in 1979 she was applauded for not listening to the ministers. By 1989 she was criticised for being out of touch. The poll tax was a disaster. On 1 November Geoffrey Howe resigned as Deputy Prime Minister.

At the State Opening of Parliament on 7 November, the Queen read Mrs Thatcher's proposed policies, which included welcoming the unification of Germany and furthering good relations between the United Kingdom and the Soviet Union 'to buttress the new democracies in Eastern Europe'.[9] On 12 November Mrs Thatcher attended the Lord Mayor's Banquet at the Guildhall, wearing an enormous cape with a ruff collar. She looked as magnificent as Queen Elizabeth I. She made a robust speech:

> Since I first went in to bat eleven years ago, the score at your end has ticked over nicely. You are now the 663rd Lord Mayor. At the Prime Minister's end, we are stuck on 49. I am still at the crease, though the bowling has been pretty hostile of late. And in case anyone doubted it, can I assure you there will be no ducking the bouncers, no stonewalling, no playing for time. The bowling's going to get hit all round the ground. That is my style.[10]

The day after the banquet, Geoffrey Howe made his devastating resignation speech. He, too, made a cricketing allusion: 'It is rather like sending your opening batsmen to the crease only for them to find, the moment the first balls are bowled, that their bats have been broken before the game by the team captain.' Michael Heseltine threw his hat into the ring. Thatcher won the first round, but was four votes short of the required majority of 15 per cent. She was in Paris at this time, considering her role as an international stateswoman more important than this latest squabble. She declared she would 'fight on and fight to win' but was prevailed upon by certain colleagues and by Denis, her husband, to stand down.

The Queen was upset by the way that Mrs Thatcher was forced out of office. In the midst of the crisis, she told a friend: 'She may be tired, and maybe she does have to go.' The Queen hated the way that Heseltine had treated her outgoing Prime Minister." Hardly had Mrs Thatcher left office than the Queen appointed her to the Order of Merit. Denis Thatcher was made a baronet, a form of hereditary knighthood that had been allowed to lapse, and in 1995 the Queen further honoured Mrs Thatcher by making her a Lady of the Garter, only the second such appointment of a non-royal lady (the first having been Lavinia, Duchess of Norfolk). In 1992 Margaret Thatcher left the House of Commons and became a life peer as Baroness Thatcher.

This major political upheaval was another example of how important it was to have a constitutional monarch waiting in Buckingham Palace, ready to deal with whoever was sent to her as the new Prime Minister.

The Conservative Party selected John Major. He was born in 1943 and entered the House of Commons as MP for Huntingdon in 1979. He had enjoyed a meteoric rise. He was promoted by Margaret Thatcher to be Foreign Secretary and three months later Chancellor of the Exchequer when Nigel Lawson resigned. He won the fight against Michael Heseltine and Douglas Hurd. So John Major was the Queen's Prime Minister. As one commentator put it: 'Until recently John Major was virtually unknown in Britain. Now he is unknown all over the world.'

★ ★ ★ ★ ★

Hardly had 1991 begun than Britain entered the first Gulf War with Iraq. Princess Margaret had to cancel her visit to Mustique but her son, Viscount Linley, went. The Duchess of York went skiing. Unlike the Falklands, no member of the Royal Family was serving in this conflict. This inspired a hostile attack in the *Sunday Times*: 'Questioning the position of the monarchy in our constitution now goes well beyond the usual small minority of inveterate republicans. A growing number of young people, by no means all on the political left, are also beginning to question the purpose of the monarchy, perhaps encouraged to do so by the behaviour and lifestyles of too many of their royal contemporaries.'[12] On 24 February the Queen made a rare broadcast, such as her parents had done during the Second World War, expressing pride in the Armed Forces and praying for a swift and lasting peace, with minimal loss of life.

There was controversy when the Queen went to the Commonwealth Observance, being celebrated as a multi-faith service. This used to be held at St Clement Dane's Church, in London's Strand, but after protests, she suggested that it be held in Westminster Abbey, and this has been its location ever since.

President Lech Wałęsa of Poland* and his wife came to Windsor in April. The Queen tended to look particularly happy with those self-made presidents. Wałęsa beamed amicably from the carriage.[13] Extracts from the visit were shown in the Edward Mirzoeff documentary, *Elizabeth R*, the Queen telling Wałęsa that it was nice to bring the gold plate out every now and again but they did not live like that every day. The Queen welcomed him: 'When the flame of freedom finally burst through in Poland in 1989, its light soon spread to other countries in East and Central Europe. Our entire continent owes you its gratitude for the part you personally played in lighting that flame.' She stressed the need to consolidate the newfound liberty to create a democratic and prosperous Poland. 'You can count on us as reliable friends and partners in this endeavour.'[14] Later the President

---

* Lech Wałęsa (b. 1943), the son of a carpenter, had worked as a car mechanic and as an electrician in a shipyard before becoming a political activist and in due course one of the great figures of the Solidarity union. He became President in December 1990, so this was an early state visit in his time of office. In 1983 he had been awarded the Nobel Peace Prize.

said he could not find his wife in the huge bed at Windsor, but that he admired the British monarchy as 'a beautiful combination of tradition and modernity' and 'something permanent which must not be destroyed'.[15]

In May the Queen and Prince Philip paid a twelve-day state visit to President George Bush in the USA. She gave an honorary KCB to General Schwarzkopf (for his help with the Gulf War),* addressed a joint meeting of the United States Congress, the first British monarch ever to do so, and visited Kentucky. When she made her first speech, she disappeared behind the dais, evidently the fault of the protocol chief, Joe Reed. She got a standing ovation in Congress the next day with the opening line 'I hope you can see me today,'[16] devised for her by Robert Fellowes, and delivered with excellent theatrical timing. She thanked President Bush and the Americans for their support in the recent Iraq War, said the United Nations was an 'essential instrument' in maintaining peace and praised the British spirit. Quoting Ralph Waldo Emerson, she said: 'England sees a little better on a cloudy day, and that, in storm of battle and calamity, she has a secret vigour, and a pulse like a cannon.'[17]

The visit was further memorable for Irish-American demonstrations against British policies in Northern Ireland, which the Queen did not see, her attendance at her first ever baseball game and a visit to a dwelling for low- and moderate-income people, where the owner, Alice Frazier, startled her by hugging her. The Queen 'smiled weakly and quickly pulled away'.[18] At the end of the official visit she was able to make a private visit to William S. Farish and his wife in Lexington, Kentucky, to tour the local stud farms.

Prince Philip reached seventy. Perception of him would gradually change, but in 1991 he was still widely caricatured as a man making gaffes. My suspicion is that Prince Philip knew exactly what he was doing. A profile in the *Independent* was more on message, pointing out that he could have been 'a Palm Beach freeloader, using his name to decorate the letterhead of dubious companies and his face to enliven women's magazine features'. It observed correctly that he

---

* In the Mirzoeff film, when Robert Fellowes tells her this honour is to be bestowed, she imitates the knighting with a letter-opener. Both she and her Private Secretary were aware that that does not happen with an honorary knighthood.

was 'impatient of all sycophancy and incapable of hiding his boredom at routine and protocol' but concluded that he had 'in his own peculiar way, done a pretty good job ... found himself a role and fulfilled it with vigour.'[19]

When the Queen opened Parliament on 31 October, Prince Philip was away so she took the Prince and Princess of Wales in the carriage with her. As they seldom made joint appearances, this was an attempt to suggest a form of unity, but it did not happen again. The speech was difficult to read and dull.

Perhaps to identify with those of her age, the Queen had allowed her hair to go completely grey during the Balmoral summer. Before that there was just a streak of white at either side. She seemed determined to look middle-aged, even wearing her spectacles during the carriage drive to Westminster, not always well dressed and with frumpy hair. In the past the Queen had worn a wonderful, almost medieval coat, richly lined with white mink (first seen during the 1972 state visit to Paris). This time she wore an old-fashioned stole.

She was still supported in royal duties by her widowed aunt, Princess Alice, Duchess of Gloucester, who was ninety that Christmas. The red helicopter would arrive at Barnwell or Kensington Palace and whisk her away, though in London an occupational hazard was that invariably the grass had just been cut so was blown all over her. But she liked travelling by helicopter as she got to her engagements on time. 'Even the Queen was late for one recently,' she said wryly.[20]

37
ANNUS HORRIBILIS

On the brink of the fortieth anniversary of her reign, the Queen made clear that she had no plan to abdicate: 'I feel the same obligation to you that I felt in 1952. With your prayers and your help, and with the love and support of my family, I shall try to serve you in the years to come.'[1]

1992 should have been a year of some celebration, but it marked the climax to all the scandals and innuendo that had haunted the Royal Family since the mid-1980s. When the crunch came, it came in spades. The first casualty was the Duchess of York. Incriminating photographs of her with her arms around the Texan Steve Wyatt were found on top of a wardrobe in a London apartment. On the flight home from Palm Beach, the Duchess put a paper bag on her head and bombarded her father with bread rolls and sugar in full view of accompanying journalists. Charles Anson, the Queen's Press Secretary, took a strong line: 'The knives are out for Fergie.'

Robert Harris went on the attack: 'Being asked to call Fergie "Your Royal Highness" is like being asked by a remote tribe to join in its worship of a gnarled tree-stump.' He wrote that John Osborne had described the Royal Family as 'the gold filling in a mouth full of decay'. He concluded: 'Well, the decay is still there, and so is the filling – but it is looking looser and more tarnished than it has for years.'[2]

The separation of the Yorks was announced on 19 March (six years on from the day of their engagement). Andrew Morton dissected the York marriage as it crumbled. His conclusion was portentous: 'At the Palace the fears go deep. For this might not be just the end of a royal marriage, but the beginning of the end of a dynasty.'[3]

Presently John Bryan, another Texan, aged thirty-six, materialised, said to be advising both Duke and Duchess of York on their marital situation. He was soon holidaying with the Duchess, in a blaze of media attention, one going so far as to suggest: 'A picture, a mere glimpse of that near-legendary balding pate, now peeling from the Oriental sun, would have been enough to override an exclusive of Madonna in the nude as far as the tabloids were concerned.'[4] He was described as her 'financial adviser'. It proved to be a euphemism.

★ ★ ★ ★ ★

When the Queen went round her fortieth-anniversary exhibition at the Victoria and Albert Museum in April and heard her 1947 speech of dedication, she jumped from one foot to the other, mock-imitating it: 'Whether it be long ... whether it be short ...' When told that Queen Victoria had had eleven Prime Ministers, she announced with glee that she had had ten times as many – taking the Commonwealth into the equation.[5]

There was also one of the finest documentaries of her reign – *Elizabeth R*, directed by Edward Mirzoeff. This took the Queen through a year of her life (1990 to 1991), showing her dutifully at work, with occasional voiceovers in which she spoke of her approach to her life. She emerged as a serious executive Head of State, and it caught her character in several memorable vignettes.

She said she hoped she had been well trained, that she did not mind her diary being set months ahead, something the younger generation found hard. She demonstrated superb theatrical timing. When told that Jimmy Carter had sold the Presidential yacht, she paused and smiled. She posed for a portrait to Andrew Festing, and put Kenneth Scott, one of her Private Secretaries, on the spot with one of her favourite questions: 'Are you sure?' She brooked no nonsense. Lord Airlie, the Lord Chamberlain, informed her rather cautiously, before the diplomatic evening, that the Kuwaiti Ambassador would be there alone, due to a family tragedy – his wife's brother. 'Murdered,' said the Queen.

In another scene she talked of Edward Heath going out to tackle Saddam Hussein: 'You're expendable,' she said. Heath laughed but may not have been amused. Perhaps because of this public tease, the

Queen gave him the Garter that April. He was not on the list of five candidates put forward by the Marquess of Abergavenny.*[6]

Furthermore the documentary gave an insight into the Queen as a farmer, preferring animals to arable, her considerable equestrian knowledge, and the training of gun dogs. She took her grandchildren on pony rides at Balmoral. When faced with anything the least bit controversial, she took refuge behind the noncommittal 'interesting'. There was a screening for invited journalists, which inspired lots of laughter (as it did when the Queen saw it privately). The laughter was, by and large, very much with the Queen.

★ ★ ★ ★ ★

The Queen told a friend she was expecting 'a noisy time'[7] when she spent eight days in Australia for the 150th anniversary of Sydney City Council. She had a new Prime Minister, Paul Keating, who already had a complicated relationship with the Royal Household. He loved French clocks, owning a dozen or so. He had wanted to see the Queen's collection, persisted and was eventually given permission. That story changed from him pleading into the Queen inviting him.[8] At Sydney airport his wife failed to curtsey to the Queen, and he put his arm round the Queen's waist as he escorted her – a gesture that is widely remembered. More seriously, he insulted her by announcing in her presence that he wanted Australia to be independent by 2001.[9] He made much of how Great Britain had deserted Australia during the Second World War.† Back in London, the

---

* Edward Heath was delighted to be a Knight of the Garter. In June he beamed a broad smile in the procession. Ever anxious about his security, he wanted his detective to walk in the procession beside him. He was told that this was not going to happen.

† Keating came to the Adelaide Festival some days later, and everyone except me appeared to enjoy his joke: 'When I left Canberra my colleagues asked if it was wise to go among all those arty types. They urged me to put my arm round everybody.' I observed where his car was and that he would have to go through a small gate in the fence to get to it. I nobbled him: 'Prime Minister, you're making my life very difficult. I'm an English writer who's come here to give a lecture about the Royal Family. Don't you think it's good to maintain a link with

Queen Mother did not disagree when I volunteered that this was not the first time the Queen had had a Prime Minister behaving like a naughty boy. 'No, it isn't,' said the Queen Mother.[10]

On 27 March the Queen was represented by Lord Airlie at the Scottish memorial service for the ninety-eight-year-old Earl of Southesk, husband of Princess Maud, granddaughter of Edward VII, and therefore deemed to be the oldest member of the British Royal Family. This feudal service was in direct contrast to the kaleidoscope of scandals that came to roost in the Royal Family, a more staid version of which he had joined back in 1923.

The Wales marriage continued to crumble. Diana hated Highgrove and would come down to find that that Prince Charles had gone to see Camilla Parker Bowles.[11] While the Queen Mother took life easily, Prince Charles was the opposite. 'I sometimes feel that when the Prince of Wales is making a fuss about losing a comb, he should follow her example,' said the Queen's Librarian.[12] Diana's father, Lord Spencer, died in the Wellington Hospital aged sixty-eight on 29 March. There was some lack of unity at his funeral.

Princess Anne and Captain Mark Phillips were quietly divorced in a four-minute hearing at the Principal Registry of the Family Division in Somerset House on 23 April. By the time the family gathered for Easter at St George's Chapel, they were a depleted group – the unhappy Waleses, the lone Duke of York, the lone Princess Anne and the lone Princess Margaret. Prince Philip steered the Queen Mother about because, at ninety-one, she needed a hand with the steps.[13]

★ ★ ★ ★ ★

The distinguished political commentator Peter Hennessy thought that a general election would change things, but on 9 April 1992 Neil Kinnock plucked defeat from the jaws of victory. John Major was re-elected and the Conservatives were granted another five years in office.

When the Queen and Prince Philip paid a state visit to President

---

the Queen? She only comes here by invitation.' As he signed autographs for others, he said: 'They're living under a life sentence. They just come here anyway. They have a hard road to hoe.' (HV diary, Adelaide, 6 March 1992.)

Vincent Tabone in Malta in May, they found many upset by the antics of the Duchess of York and there was concern for the Queen as a mother. The Maltese came out in force to greet her, hailing her as 'part of our Maltese family. If you were welcoming back your mother after a long absence, you would be excited.'[14] Before she opened the European Parliament in Strasbourg, part of her speech was leaked. The contentious line was that the differences of parliamentary tradition were insignificant against a background of European commitment to reconciliation and democracy. John Major was quick to reassure Tory Euro-sceptics that the speech did not represent a surrender of British sovereignty. As ever the actual speech, delivered in perfect French, was not controversial. The wording had been 'made sinister only through some ham-fisted leaking by the Foreign Office and subsequent damage limitation'.[15] On a four-day state visit to France, the Queen stressed the importance of the European Community in healing wounds caused by the division of Europe into Communist East and free West.

★ ★ ★ ★ ★

The hammer blow to the Wales marriage came in June, with the publication of Andrew Morton's *Diana – Her True Story*. Even before it came out, there was speculation that the Princess had assisted its author, as evidenced by the Demarchelier portrait on the front cover and her private photos in the book. The publisher, Michael O'Mara, advertised the book as containing one story that would be front-page news all over the world. He was not wrong.

An official visit by the Princess of Wales to Egypt was overshadowed by speculation, especially when Andrew Morton's office was burgled, an attempt was made to bribe the printers in Norfolk for an advance copy, and the Queen asked close aides to ascertain the intended contents.

The devastating serialisation hit newsstands on 7 June.* Diana laid

---

* I was present at a dinner at Downside at which Andrew Knight (Chairman of News International) was a guest on the evening of Friday 5 June. He told us about the Morton book and that they were confident it was genuine. With a premonition of the horror of what was in store, I left the dining room and was sick.

every grievance she could muster against her hapless husband. There were accounts of suicide attempts, and Camilla Parker Bowles was publicly named as the other woman in his life. In retrospect it seems almost incredible that so many people took the charitable view that Diana had not been directly involved in the enterprise.* Many an article was written about the survival or otherwise of the House of Windsor. Michael Cole, confidant and spinner to Mohamed Fayed, asked Morton if he was frightened of killing the goose that laid his golden egg. Morton replied: 'I can make a good living from the ashes of the House of Windsor ... People are still writing about the Tsars.'[16] Most commentators sided with the Princess of Wales, because the Prince kept his silence. Anthony Holden, who had suffered from his wrath, wrote: 'To my mind, Morton's revelations about the friendship of Charles and Camilla Parker Bowles are more damaging than the misery to which he has reduced Diana.'[17]

Diana had known that trouble was coming – in particular the existence of the so-called 'Squidgygate' tape, recorded in 1989 – and needed to get her version out first. But what she did was unforgivable. There was a sticky meeting at Windsor, after the Garter ceremony, where the Waleses discussed the issue with the Queen and Prince Philip. Diana's line was that Charles had never wanted to marry her and that her position was intolerable vis-à-vis Camilla. There was talk of lovers being taken if the marriage did not work.

While the Queen maintained her neutrality, Prince Philip wrote to Diana after that meeting – there were six letters from him and five replies from her between 18 June and 4 October. He pointed out that he hoped she was aware that Prince Charles had made a great sacrifice for her, that he and the Queen had never been happy about his relationship with Camilla, and that he did not advocate anyone taking a lover. He hoped that a *modus vivendi* could be established.

Prince Philip wrote that he thought her too possessive of her sons and regretted that he and the Queen did not know their grandchildren better. He reminded her that he had been an outsider when he married. He was sad that they had had only four years

---

* Diana's stepmother, Raine, Countess Spencer, said she believed Diana was 'behind the Morton book'. (Countess Spencer to author, France, recorded 2 September 1992)

'before Mama succeeded' and that he had given up his naval career for what? The Head of State had a role. No one else did. He commented on the success of the marriages of two generations of Gloucesters, the Michaels of Kent and the Ogilvys. He hoped that as she and Charles both loved music, they could attend more such events together. He urged that Lord Charteris or Dean Michael Mann (of whom he had a higher regard than some) might act as mediator. He did not like her describing herself as 'a woman in her position' and made a sarcastic remark that he could not understand why anyone would prefer Camilla to her. In the last letter she told him it was clear that he 'really cared'. To which he replied: 'Phew.'

Prince Philip read the book on flights to and from Canada in July.* He was not impressed. He thought too much had been revealed. He worried that every time there was a private discussion between Charles and Diana, details appeared in the *Daily Mail*. He recognised one or two phrases from his correspondence with her popping up in the press. She continued to deny involvement with Morton, and while he appeared to give her the benefit of the doubt, he had clearly detected her hand.[18] Sadly that well-meant correspondence did not achieve its goal.†

★ ★ ★ ★ ★

---

* In July 1992, the Duke visited Canada as part of the celebration of the 125th anniversary of Confederation. He flew home, arriving back at Windsor on 18 July.
† Prince Philip's office invited me to read these letters on 20 November 2002 in order to refute a suggestion inspired by Paul Burrell's *Daily Mirror* serialisation of *A Royal Duty* following which Simone Simmons told the *Mail on Sunday* that Prince Philip had called her 'a harlot' or a 'trollop'. He had not – and Burrell confirmed that on page 161 of his book. Burrell had seen Prince Philip's letters in 1993. I advised the Palace to put out a press release, in which *inter alia*, they reminded the world that the letters were Prince Philip's copyright, a device invariably used by the Duke of Windsor. Part of the statement read: 'Prince Philip wishes to make it clear that at no point did he ever use the insulting terms described in the media reports, nor that he was curt or unfeeling in what he wrote. He regards the suggestion that he used such derogatory terms as a gross misrepresentation of his relations with his daughter-in-law and hurtful to his grandsons.' (Press release, 23 November 2002.)

On 18 July Lady Helen Windsor married Timothy Taylor at St George's Chapel. Most of the Royal Family were there, the Waleses seated either side of Prince Harry, neither addressing a word to or even looking at each other. Nevertheless, it was a beautiful wedding and it worked. The unsmiling Queen appeared to agree. She watched the young couple exchange their vows, and thought it 'extraordinary ... all her family in disarray around her'.*[19]

When the Queen Mother celebrated her ninety-second birthday on 4 August 'she wafted through the day' untouched by the foregoing horrors. The Waleses arrived for lunch separately. Only the gradually ageing Queen with her grey hair made her mother look old.[20]

★ ★ ★ ★ ★

An array of newspapers are laid out each morning in the breakfast room at Balmoral for the Royal Family to peruse over their coffee. On Thursday, 20 August, they were covered with photographs of a topless Duchess of York with her toes being chewed by her afore-mentioned 'financial adviser' John Bryan. The pair were on holiday with her two small daughters at La Mole, near St Tropez in the South of France. 'Fergie's Stolen Kisses', proclaimed the *Daily Mirror*. 'Fergie's final boob', proclaimed the *Sun*. Fergie went to see the Queen, who was, by the Duchess's own account, 'furious'.

The Duchess left Balmoral in shame, after which Prince Philip took a negative view of his estranged daughter-in-law. Like Diana, she received a number of letters from him over the years, in her case rather sterner. She put them in the bank.

The Duchess produced a book of memoirs in 1996, portraying herself as having lived in a claustrophobic world at Buckingham Palace, undermined by courtiers. She admitted she was not the right person to have been a member of the Royal Family, and maintained that her separation from the Duke was 'not because we'd stopped caring for one another, but because I had reached the end of my royal rope'.[21] Others suggested that she wanted to marry Steve Wyatt

---

* A courtier commented that day: 'We do our weddings well. It's our marriages that don't work.'

(though he lacked money), and took up with John Bryan after Wyatt returned to America.

Throughout these misadventures, the Duke of York was remarkably tolerant and, as has been amply proved, remained her loyal ally. In a perceptive profile of him by Maggie Alderson, she wrote that he had been portrayed as 'the most libidinous and glamorous male Royal for decades', but by 1992 he had turned into something of a bore. He was devoid of malice, fair-minded and generous, ever-forgiving of his errant wife. He had never developed from being a clumsy teenager and all too keen on his own rather blue jokes delivered at inappropriate moments. As he grew up he was sexually oriented but not willing to take on 'the emotional baggage' that came with a relationship.[22] A friend even said that he believed Fergie's head had been stuck on someone else's body in the photographs – quite possibly presaging his own fate many years later.

Hot on the tail of this came the 'Squidgygate' tape, published on a newspaper hotline. It was a twenty-three-minute flirtatious conversation between Diana and her friend James Gilbey, seemingly made by a boffin who had strayed on it and seen its financial merits. It contained such remarks as 'I can't stand the confines of this marriage' and 'Bloody hell, after all I've done for this fucking family.'[23] That Diana knew this was likely to be made public explains why she was so keen to get her book out first.

The Queen approached her state visit to President Richard von Weizsäcker in Germany in October in the role of peacemaker. Particularly concerning was the visit to Dresden. There was still residual bitterness over the bombing by Marshal of the RAF Sir Arthur 'Bomber' Harris. Ten demonstrators had been arrested when the Queen Mother unveiled his statue at St Clement Danes. Twice in October his statue had been attacked with paint, the word 'shame' daubed on the plinth. Maastricht was an issue, the Bundesbank was playing up, and there was a resurgence of right-wing German extremists. The Queen did her best to conciliate: 'Like all close friends, we do not always see eye to eye but, as friends, we should try not to let the sun go down on our quarrels.' There was booing in Dresden and eggs were thrown at her car, but the Queen strolled alongside crowd barriers and chatted to friendly children. She was able to enter what had been divided East Berlin.

The grim climax to all the year's horrors came on the Queen's forty-fifth wedding anniversary on 20 November, when a devastating fire broke out in Windsor Castle, destroying the roof of St George's Hall and damaging the Grand Reception Room and other rooms in Windsor Castle. The blaze could be seen from miles away. A mammoth rescue was mounted, valuable items being handed out in a human chain, and fortunately few items of furniture or pictures were lost. Prince Andrew rushed about, directing operations.

The fire seemed symbolic of a final collapse of the House of Windsor. Prince Philip was away in Argentina while the Queen wandered forlornly in raincoat and headscarf, inspecting the damage. This was followed by a public outcry when Peter Brooke, the Secretary for National Heritage, suggested the taxpayer should foot the bill for the restoration.

Four days later, on 24 November, the Queen attended a long-planned anniversary lunch at Guildhall. She had a bad cold and spoke with difficulty. She took inspiration for her speech from a letter written by her former Assistant Private Secretary, Sir Edward Ford. She thanked the Lord Mayor for his hospitality and then said:

> 1992 is not a year on which I shall look back with undiluted pleasure. In the words of one of my more sympathetic correspondents, it has turned out to be an 'Annus Horribilis'...
>
> There can be no doubt, of course, that criticism is good for people and institutions that are part of public life. No institution – City, Monarchy, whatever – should expect to be free from the scrutiny of those who give it their loyalty and support, not to mention those who don't ...[24]

On 26 November the Prime Minister advanced a long-planned announcement that the Queen had offered to pay income tax on her private income from April 1993 and to refund the Civil List payments for most of the Royal Family. The Prince of Wales announced that he would pay tax on his income from the Duchy of Cornwall. The only Civil List annuities that the Queen would not refund were those for the Queen Mother and the Duke of Edinburgh, whose annuities would die with them and not recur.

Just as the British public were absorbing this came the shocking announcement on 9 December that the Prince and Princess of Wales were to separate. Despite everything few believed that such a separation was possible. John Major announced this in the House of Commons, adding that there was no reason why, one day, the Princess should not be crowned Queen at her estranged husband's side. Lady Thatcher told Charles Moore: 'The best thing that can happen to this country is that [The Queen] should celebrate her diamond jubilee in 2012 ... It will add to our stability and our prestige in the world.'[25] Princess Margaret asked Prince Charles. 'Do you mind if I go on being friends with her?' and he said that was fine. The Royal Family did not want Fergie back.

Three days later, Princess Anne married Commander Timothy Laurence, the Queen's former equerry, at Crathie Church, near Balmoral. Hostility in the press obliged the Queen Mother to fly to Scotland for this ceremony, despite being ninety-two years old. It had been unacceptable for Princess Margaret, an unmarried princess, to marry Group Captain Peter Townsend, a divorced equerry. Now a divorced princess was able to marry an unmarried equerry with relatively little fuss. Princess Margaret was seated in the same row as Prince Charles and Prince Andrew, and commented: 'We've done well. We're all divorced.'[26]

Despite all this, in December, the Queen distributed the Christmas presents to the staff as if nothing had happened, though in a discussion at St George's House, the College of St George's consultation house in Windsor Castle, about happy families as the ideal, Prince Philip said: 'Not always so easy to achieve.'[27] The next reliable news I had of the Queen was in February 1993, from a general who described her as looking 'very tired',[28] which was hardly surprising.

38
THE MID 1990s, 1993–6

The Queen's skill was to press on regardless, despite good news or bad. Her sense of humour was still intact, which must have required a particular mindset.[1] Private jokes sustained the Royal Family in times of trouble. Another skill was her attention to detail. She told a later Lord Chancellor, Lord Irvine of Lairg, that she had a man coming to be knighted and the briefing notes were somewhat inadequate. 'Try him on modern art, Ma'am,' he said. Next time she saw him, she said: 'Just the ticket.'[2] One man being invested with an MVO was impressed by how the Queen controlled the Investiture. The more nervous the recipients were, the more solicitous she was, but if they began to recite their autobiography, she subtly moved them on.

★ ★ ★ ★ ★

The dynamics within the Royal Family were forever shifting. The Princess of Wales and the Duchess of York were considered troublemakers. Princess Anne was as executive as ever, Prince Andrew an amiable dullard, Prince Edward involved with Sophie Rhys-Jones, but still some years away from marrying her. The Queen Mother's health preoccupied the family, but from every setback she rose like a phoenix, and remained a strong force in the background. Princess Margaret was close to the Queen, and still in good health and voice. The general line, taken by people like Lord Carnarvon, was that the monarchy was fine, but let down by some of the younger members of the family.

Patrick Jephson was now Diana's Private Secretary and official adviser, keen to maintain her work within the bounds of Palace propriety. She was busy, though her Press Secretary admitted that every outing was 'a potential poo-patch'.³ She was increasingly paranoid, having her rooms 'swept' regularly for bugs. While she garnered good publicity, the inner royal circle, who had witnessed the marriage unfold, were aware of all that Prince Charles had suffered – uncontrollable tantrums and the children played against him, not to mention examples of infidelity.

More trouble came when Lord McGregor published his theory that both the Prince and the Princess of Wales had been feeding the press. Then Dulcie Boling, a Rupert Murdoch media executive, achieved a global scoop by publishing the Camillagate tapes in *New Idea* in Australia. Since it had appeared over there, it was soon available in the UK. This was a particularly damaging late-night conversation between Prince Charles and Camilla Parker Bowles, and left no doubt as to their relationship. The Tampax reference was especially unfortunate. As with the Squidgygate tapes, there was a far-fetched theory that a random surfer in a shed had stumbled across the conversation and recognised the Prince's voice. It is as good as certain that the Prince's telephones were bugged by security services until finally someone realised: 'We've got him.'*

The scandals were not over. A polo PR girl called Lesley Player, who had been sacked by Major Ronald Ferguson, produced a book about their love affair, all of which made him look yet more ridiculous. The Queen Mother's private secretary, Sir Alastair Aird, read it flying to his holiday, concealed behind a copy of *The Times*. He passed it to his friends, and once they had all read it, they buried it on a beach, ashamed to own it. So a piece of Major Ron lies deep in the sand.

* * * * *

After the fire at Windsor, the State Apartments were in a sorry state. The state portraits in the Waterloo Chamber were removed, exposing the pantomime cartoons from the war. The walls of St George's Hall were bared to the stone, the panelling largely gone, and the

---

* I advanced my theories on Radio 4's *Today* show with Brian Redhead on 13 January. I made the point that we had all said silly things on the telephone that we would not wish to see in print.

floor a mass of charred timbers. Some of the Garter shields were in place, others lay in the rubble. The roof had gone and the sky was visible, though concealed with a metallic cover. There was the smell of damp. The vase in the Grand Reception Room had been boxed in – the contrast between the surviving gilding and the destruction wrought by the fire was acute. Yet other state rooms had survived, undamaged, and looked as good as the newly restored rooms at Versailles had in 1980.[4]

To pay for the restoration, the Queen opened Buckingham Palace in the summer, when she was not there. This proved so great a success that the Palace has been opened to support the Royal Collection ever since. During the restoration, the Queen climbed the scaffold to inspect the work. Princess Margaret tried to join her, but could not face the height.[5]

There was interest in the fortieth anniversary of the Coronation in June, at which time Paul Johnson wrote that the Queen was 'becoming a matriarch, a pillar of our times, a person so durable, comforting and etched on our consciousness that we can't imagine the country without her – as Sherlock Holmes put it of Dr Watson "the one fixed point in a changing world".' He concluded:

> The original Elizabethan Age was so glorious that there can only be one. But the people of Britain have not done badly under the present monarch either. If not a golden age, it is certainly wrought in silver and I dare say, when it is long over, ancient men and women will tell their progeny that they were proud to have lived 'in good Queen Lilibet's time'.[6]

On Derby Day, the Queen saw her horse, Enharmonic, win the race before the classic Derby race. She tried to persuade the Queen Mother, then nearly ninety-three, to slow down. On the Sunday before the Garter ceremony, there was an argument, following which the Queen sped out of Royal Lodge in her car, only to find herself on the front page of the *Sun*, cited as having been driving at 60 m.p.h. The Queen persuaded her mother not to attend the Garter service. The Queen Mother did not want to disappoint her page, Lord Mornington, grandson of the Duke of Wellington. 'Don't worry,' said the Queen. 'I'll take Arthur.' So that year she had three pages, which was helpful as suddenly the rain came beating down as the procession wound its way down the hill. The Queen's train got wetter and consequently heavier to carry.[7] After the service, the Queen said that with all the old velvet steaming, it smelt like the saddling enclosure after a big race. At a later Garter ceremony, the pages got into a muddle with the Queen's train, folding it wrongly (as often happens when people fold sheets). The Queen could not move until they resolved it, work undertaken by two flustered youngsters under her stern gaze.

Prince Charles missed that 1993 Garter ceremony due to a polo accident, though the Princess of Wales attended. There was a photograph of him hurling his helmet to the ground – a petulant reaction. A few days later Lord Charteris said he hoped 'the present incumbent would go on for another fifteen years', and his wife remarked, 'Martin says everyone should just shut up now,' advice that should have been heeded.[8]

The old order was changing. The Queen Mother lost her two great stalwarts, Sir Martin Gilliat and Ruth, Lady Fermoy, in 1993. She underwent a phase of frailty, looking somewhat other-worldly when she unveiled a statue to General de Gaulle in Carlton Gardens, but by the time of her ninety-third birthday on 4 August, she was calm and serene again, restored to normal strength. On 31 July the Queen was at Sandringham. The King of Spain telephoned during dinner. 'I wonder what Juanito wants,' she said, as she left the room. King Baudouin of the Belgians had died. She was apparently close to him. It was the only time she attended a royal funeral in Europe.*[9]

In December the Princess of Wales made the dramatic announcement that she was stepping down from public life. In a public speech that greatly irritated the Prince of Wales, she said she needed 'time and space'. The so-called retirement did not last long. Sir Michael Peat, the Keeper of the Privy Purse, a man who did not hesitate to act ruthlessly when circumstances called for it, let it be known that Kensington Palace was for working members of the Royal Family. In fear of losing her home, she returned to work. Meanwhile the

---

* The royal men were in uniform. It was particularly unfortunate that Prince Philip's valet gave him the garish riband of the Leopard of the Congo to wear instead of the purple Leopold.

Duchess of York was happy to tell any number of journalists how and where she had gone wrong.

*****

Paul Keating won at the polls in Australia in March 1993 and decided this gave him a mandate to turn Australia into a republic. It was the duty and perquisite of Commonwealth Prime Ministers to visit the Queen when they came to British shores. He came over in September when the Queen was at Balmoral. Before his visit, he told the Australian press: 'I do count myself as one of her admirers. I find the Queen to be charming company to say the least and amusing when she chooses to be.'[10]

The Queen being in Scotland, he made his way to the Gothic spires of Balmoral. He was expecting a banquet but instead enjoyed – or endured – a picnic from Prince Philip's special barbecue, no doubt amid the midges. It was evidently 'decidedly nippy ... the Deeside forests ... turning to autumn gold'.[11] He had an audience of the Queen the next day – in other words a private chat with her. Robert Fellowes said later that he had been 'the perfect guest, a genuine expert on Renaissance clocks. He may be a Rottweiler in the Houses of Parliament but he is a very cultured man – a mixture of Norman Tebbit and Denis Healey. He did what he had to do – he removed the Queen from the question [of independence for Australia].' Fellowes thought he had 'behaved pretty well' over the public statement he subsequently made.[12]

Keating should not have made a statement. He revealed that he had told the Queen Australia should become a republic. Years later he clarified this: 'The Queen accepted this view with equanimity. Upon momentarily digesting what I had said, without hesitation the Queen said, "I will, of course, take the advice of Australian ministers and respect the wishes of the Australian people."'[13]

Sir Robert's account of the visit was diplomatic, the Queen's less so. According to a friend, she did not like him. He talked the whole time. But her punch line, which he did not quote, was: 'Don't use the monarchy as a football.'[14] Princess Margaret was even more astringent: 'Everyone had a terrible time with him at Balmoral. They loathed him. It doesn't matter about Australia. It can go. As

Prince Philip said. "If Australia goes, at least we won't have to go there any more ..."[15]

Keating may have been restrained in his post-Balmoral statement but he was back on form when he promoted Australia for the Olympics in Monte Carlo, stating that the choice of Sydney for the games meant he could make Australia a republic by 2000. The line taken by the British press at this time was: 'Hands off our Queen.' The matter rested until 1999.

* * * * *

A few days after the Australian visit, on 23 September, Margaret 'Bobo' MacDonald died at Buckingham Palace at the age of eighty-nine. She had been a stalwart in the Queen's life since she was six, first as nursemaid and later as dresser. She even accompanied the Queen on her honeymoon. She was sufficiently intimate to say to the Queen, 'You can't wear that,' to which the Queen deferred. When she came back to the Palace after an evening engagement, the Queen would look up to see if Bobo's light was on. The Queen rarely attended funerals, other than of close relations, but flew down from Balmoral with Prince Philip to attend Bobo's at the Queen's Chapel at St James's Palace. Back in London in the autumn, the Palace view was that matters had calmed down.

* * * * *

The Queen was accustomed to difficult overseas visits. One such was Cyprus for the Commonwealth Heads of Government. First, many countries dropped out – Australia, New Zealand, India, Pakistan and Canada – though Benazir Bhutto of Pakistan was there. The visit was further overshadowed by memories of the execution of nine Cypriot anti-Colonial fighters (Eoka heroes) in the 1950s. The Queen was asked to apologise because she had allegedly signed the death warrant. She was called a murderess – 'The Killer Queen'.

She arrived on 18 October, based on board *Britannia*. There was no red carpet greeting, and the National Anthem was not played. Abuse was hurled at her in Nicosia, and the window of her borrowed Rolls-Royce was smashed by a Greek-Cypriot protester while in a police garage. School teachers joined a protest group, leaving children free to throw stones at British soldiers. At a time when South Africa was about to rejoin the Commonwealth after thirty years, this surly behaviour from a Commonwealth island, along with the way Australia seemed to be heading, was not propitious. At the banquet, the Queen was sanguine: 'I will certainly not be betting on how many of you will have the Head of the Commonwealth as your Head of State.'[16]

The Cypriots were upset by how the British press reported what were passed off as a few isolated incidents. In turn the British objected to the Queen being insulted in a foreign country. As the Queen and Prince Philip flew home, forty of the 220 crew of *Britannia* were struck down with a mystery illness.

In December South Africa finally ended white minority rule after 350 years. President de Klerk passed through London and visited the Queen, the first such meeting with a South African leader since 1961. This paved the way for South Africa's return to the Commonwealth, which happened the following year to the Queen's enormous delight.

In the remaining month of 1993, questions were raised about the monarch's position as Head of the Church of England, and the possibility of Prince Charles not taking the role on his accession, due to his perceived distance from the established church. The Venerable George Austin, Archdeacon of York, described by Valerie Grove as 'a ringer for Gerald Campion playing Billy Bunter',[17] ignited the matter by stating the Prince was unsuitable to be King due to his association with Camilla Parker Bowles and described Diana as 'an aristocratic virgin'.[18] Dr John Habgood, Archbishop of York, then weighed in by saying that it was not a prerequisite that the monarch be popular (though the Queen was popular in her own right). He dismissed the Head of the Church of England matter as irrelevant tabloid nonsense.

At the end of 1993 there was a chance to get Princess Margaret's take on recent happenings. She spoke of the Princess of Wales: 'She came to Sandringham for a minute. The Queen, who can't say *no* to anyone ... The trouble was that he undermined her [Diana] consistently from the start, and gave her no support ... Then he began to get difficult over the children, which was the cause of all the trouble last year ... I don't know why she wanted to come back. I longed to tell her to go away. It was the same with me and Tony. He undermined me.'[19]

1994

That year the Royal Household formed the 'Way Ahead' Group, which met to suggest internal reforms in the monarchy. In March the Queen and Duke visited the Caribbean – Anguilla, Dominica, Guyana, Jamaica, the Bahamas and Bermuda.

Prince Charles was advised by his Private Secretary, Richard Aylard, to cooperate with the author and broadcaster Jonathan Dimbleby over a book and an interview. On 29 June this was shown on television. If it was designed to be favourable to the Prince, it failed abysmally. He was seen as reluctant to accept his public duties, even complaining about having to go to a film premiere, something that others might have considered a treat.

The only part now remembered is his admission that he had been unfaithful, albeit only after his marriage had 'irretrievably broken down'. Prince Charles had no idea that he was to be asked about Camilla in the film. Aylard was in the room when it was filmed. He looked in his direction, hoping to be rescued but no rescue came.[20] The camera moved in to make sure the viewers missed not the slightest twitch of his discomfort. Barbara Cartland's opinion proved more down to earth than might have been expected from such a romantic novelist. She declared that the Prince of Wales 'should learn not to tell the truth'. She was against his admission of adultery and worried that letters did not always get through. 'The trouble is that he has no one to advise him except the Queen Mother. If only Mountbatten was alive.' Did she think Mountbatten's advice was good? 'Well, of course, it was always very much *for* Mountbatten, but yes.'[21]

The documentary was followed by the published book. Robert Fellowes did his best to excise certain passages, but could only do so much. The Prince berated his parents, particularly his father, who was depicted as rebuking his son in public and in private, mocking him, reducing him to tears, while his mother was described as detached and failing to protect him against the brutish behaviour of Prince Philip. My verdict was: 'I wish the book had not been written.'[22] Publicity for the book clashed with the Queen's significant state visit to the Russian Federation in October 1994. In 1988 Margaret Thatcher had made clear that an invitation from Mikhail Gorbachev, General Secretary of the Central Committee of the Communist Party, to the Queen would be declined on the grounds that it would give him a propaganda coup that would weaken the West's efforts towards further political freedom in Russia. In April 1989 the Queen entertained Gorbachev to lunch at Windsor Castle.* There was some comment about her receiving him at the castle and not Buckingham Palace, but this was more convenient for Heathrow airport. A procession of twenty-three cars made its way up the Long Walk. Gorbachev came out with a firm invitation, to which the Queen replied that she hoped to accept 'in due course'. Mrs Thatcher confirmed this as 'a very definite yes.'[23] Prince Edward visited Moscow a few days later.

The Queen was particularly excited to be going to Russia because she had long believed that, like China, Russia was a country she would never see. There were obvious difficulties. George V had failed to rescue his cousin, Tsar Nicholas II, who had been assassinated with his family in 1918. The Queen and the Duke went first to Moscow, which included a walkabout in Red Square. The problem with that was that Boris Yeltsin, the Russian President, had forbidden any Russians to be in the square. The only people they met were overseas tourists.

They went to the Bolshoi Ballet and Prince Philip visited his great-aunt Ella's convent.† In St Petersburg they were occasionally confronted by British uniforms of the Tsar, which had been preserved for many decades. These they tended to ignore, focusing on today's Russia rather than on the past, although they visited the Fortress of St Peter and St Paul, where members of the Imperial Family were buried.

---

* The Queen included Sir Isaiah Berlin and Sir Peter Hall among the more traditional guests.
† There were nuns, but they were deemed to be troublesome and were kept away. The convent was occupied by craftsmen and -women making icons.

I was accredited to that visit and witnessed much of what took place.* I was in a hospital in St Petersburg where effective artificial limbs were made for disabled patients. It afforded me a chance to observe the British media at work. To hear them discoursing behind the scenes was an unpleasant eye-opener. 'I heard that so I checked it with my man at Balmoral ... I ran it past my guy at Sandringham' confirmed that there were moles lurking within the Royal Household. There was a classic incident in which a student was asked what the Queen had said to her. She told the Queen she had been in Manchester. It appeared, though this was not corroborated, that the Queen had said, 'Bad luck.' The press went crazy. Judy Wade, covering the trip for *Hello!*, (largely on CNN in her hotel room), screeched: 'The Queen has finally lost it!' Tabloids rang up *Coronation Street* stars for their views.

More fascinating to observe (as I did for ITN) was the formal arrival of the Queen and her suite in St George's Hall, inside the Kremlin, on the first night. Two nights later the Queen gave a banquet for President Yeltsin on board *Britannia*, in St Petersburg. By then he was so struck by her that he arranged a spontaneous march-past on the quayside, and as the Queen left, he kissed her hand. He had made a new friend he would never see again.

It was an unforgettable sight to watch *Britannia* sail away into the mist. The Queen and the Duke could be seen on an upper deck. Every time she looked to the left, he looked to the left; when she looked to the right, he looked to the right. They were in perfect harmony (and they did not do that so that I could write it here). It was touching.

★ ★ ★ ★ ★

Soon after this I had the chance to hear Robert Fellowes's assessment of the monarchy. He had been disappointed by the absence of crowds

---

* The Queen was pleased that I recognised her wearing the Empress Dagmar brooch on the second day. I was invited on board *Britannia* for the reception after the banquet on the last night. So I shook the good hand of President Yeltsin. His left hand had been damaged as a youngster, when he was playing with a grenade, which went off.

in Red Square. He said that the Queen's particular strength was that 'she was hard-working, conscientious and dutiful ... She steered a clever course, by not trying to be anything she wasn't.' He spoke of Prince Charles's 'many genuine qualities, for example, love of the arts (not shared by his mother). His big mistake was to believe that these days it was possible to have any kind of secret private life. The intrusion of the press et cetera.' I said I thought that the Queen was eclipsed by the continued existence of the Queen Mother. He thought she would become 'the Mother of the Nation'. He said: 'This might *not* help the Prince of Wales,' but the Prince was 'now aware that he was freer to operate as Prince of Wales than he would be as king.'[24]

The Queen had known Robert Fellowes since he was a baby. When he took the job, her comment was: 'That's the first Private Secretary I've cradled in my arms.' She very much liked him. He was a wholly honourable man, even if he tended to see the good in people, and did not like to look into what he called 'the dark recesses of the soul'.[25]

There is a trivial but telling example. At Royal Ascot, the ancient figure of the Dowager Marchioness of Winchester and her brother would plant themselves outside the Royal Box, knowing exactly where the Queen would emerge and waylaying her.* The Marchioness then put out a press release to say she had been graciously received by Her Majesty. She had not. She was a rather disliked figure on the social scene. She was Indian and had married the once bankrupt Marquess when he was ninety and then rather un-sportingly sued him for non-consummation of the marriage. She was a determined social warrior. When she wrote her name in the book at Clarence House, hoping to be invited by the Queen Mother, Sir Martin Gilliat would say: 'She'll be lucky.' He saw through her. Robert Fellowes thought her a sweet old thing.

If 1995 had not begun well, a highlight was the fiftieth anniversary of VE Day. The Queen, the Queen Mother and Princess Margaret appeared on the balcony of Buckingham Palace. Such appearances

---

* I can remember seeing the Marchioness and her brother at Ascot in the 1970s, resolutely in front of the Royal Box, looking up, their backs turned from the racing.

were effective. When the Royal Family took part in processions and other such formal events, the crowds came out in force. Nevertheless, I heard that the Queen looked out of a window, fearing that there would be no crowds, and that Field Marshal Lord Bramall buttonholed John Suchet at ITN and told him: 'It's your job to see that the crowds are there.' Any tabloids that suggested it would be a failure were soon eating their words. I noted:

> The Queen, the Queen Mother and Princess Margaret made a memorable image on the balcony, fifty years on (so wise to pack the Duke of Edinburgh off to Paris) — and there were memorable scenes — the Queen Mother at St Paul's, in the park, all the foreign Kings and Queens, the Queen alone in the park, standing as the symbolic head of the Nation. And is there not another reason why the three ladies on the balcony inspired such adoration? It is because *we do not know what they think*. A lesson to the younger ones ...[26]

In June the Queen installed two new Companions of the Order of the Garter, the slightly fragile Margaret Thatcher, walking next to the large, craggy figure of Sir Edmund Hillary, the man who conquered Everest (who was not pleased to have to walk with her).

1995 included the memorable state visit to President Nelson Mandela in South Africa in 1995. Mandela had been freed on 11 February 1990 and became President of the ANC Party the following year. At the Commonwealth Heads of Government Meeting held in Harare, the Queen had expressed the hope that the changes in South Africa would prove beneficial.[27] To her delight South Africa rejoined the Commonwealth in 1994. The Queen had not been back since 1947.*

On 20 November, the Queen's wedding anniversary, the monarchy received another devastating blow when the Princess of Wales gave her BBC *Panorama* interview. This was recorded surreptitiously on

---

* Mandela's return visit in the summer of 1996 found him walking out into St James's Park to plant a tree in the early morning, with a troop following him as their Pied Piper. He told the spectators that he would not be able to water it, and asked them to take care of it for him. Mandela called the Queen 'Elizabeth'. 'Yes, wasn't that funny', commented the Queen, when reminded of it years later.

5 November at Kensington Palace, overseen by Stephen Hewlett,* who was only one of seven BBC figures who knew about it. It was edited in secret at the Grand Hotel in Eastbourne. Tony Hall described it as 'the biggest story I've ever known'. The only stipulation Diana made was that she would forewarn the Queen.[28]

It has since been revealed that Diana was tricked into it by devious misinformation, but even so, she was not averse to letting her views be known. It was mean-spirited and proved a self-inflicted wound. She aimed to damage her husband and she succeeded. She also damaged herself. The Waleses had been separated for three years, but no divorce proceedings had been instituted, since neither wished to cast the first stone. Now, with a master-stroke, the Queen intervened. She told the couple that enough was enough and commanded them to get divorced. By so doing, she took the responsibility upon herself.

1996

Early in the new year, Prince Charles wrote to Diana about the divorce. The matter was handled as effectively as is possible in such a lawsuit, the grounds given as their long separation since 1992. The divorce became absolute on 28 August 1996, Diana continuing to occupy her apartment in Kensington Palace. After that the tensions between the Waleses subsided to some degree.

Looking back over these years, on his retirement as Press Secretary in 1997, Charles Anson conceded that there had been difficult times, but remembered in particular, the film, *Elizabeth R*, the state visits to Russia in 1994, to South Africa in 1995, and Nelson Mandela's return state visit to Britain in 1996. In particular he commended how good the Queen had been to him: 'A Sovereign who did not waver, and whose firmness of resolve had been a huge asset in his not always easy job.'[29] Robert Fellowes commended him for how he had handled 'the false testament of knaves and fools' and on his '*sangfroid*'.

---

* Stephen Hewlett (1958–2017), journalist with the *Guardian*, the *Observer*, and much on Radio 4. He died the following year of cancer.

39
A VERY BAD EXPERIENCE, 1997

Reasoned argument was impossible in a controversial and highly publicised monarchy debate on Central Television in January 1997, chaired by Trevor McDonald. It was conducted in a bear-pit atmosphere engendered to keep viewers watching. Most of the panellists regretted subjecting themselves to such a farrago of nonsense. Votes were taken on various issues. Sixty-six per cent of the 2.5 million voters favoured keeping the monarchy. Another clear message emerged, however: the nation did not want Camilla Parker Bowles as Queen.

Meanwhile, Diana, Princess of Wales, as she was now styled, went to Angola on a landmine expedition, hoping she might be given an envoy job. She upset ministers by calling for a world-wide ban on anti-personnel landmines. She protested that she was only trying to help. The so-called 'War of the Waleses' looked set to calm down with the appointment of Stephen Lamport as Private Secretary to the Prince, in place of the divisive Richard Aylard. The seeds were sown for Prince and Princess to rebuild their reputations.

On 9 March three grand chairs in Garter blue velvet were brought out for the confirmation of Prince William in St George's Chapel, an event attended by his parents, the Queen, Prince Philip and the Queen Mother, King Constantine and Queen Anne-Marie of Greece, Sir Angus Ogilvy, the Duke and Duchess of Westminster, Lady Romsey and Lady Susan Hussey. The small congregation sang 'Love Divine' and 'O Jesus I have promised.' In the preceding days, the Dean of Windsor had not been taken in by calls from the media, which invariably began: 'We just want to discuss the religious aspects of the service ...'[1]

A VERY BAD EXPERIENCE, 1997

Tony Blair

A General Election was called, which had the effect of a temporary media ceasefire on the Royal Family. After eighteen years, the Tories were defeated, and even before the results were declared, plans were in motion for John Major to leave Downing Street. 'Things can only get better' was the optimistic early-morning cry of the people on Friday, 2 May, as Tony Blair swept into victory and Major headed to the Oval to watch cricket.

Britain was suddenly 'New Britain' and a rising generation of politicians was singing from a different hymn sheet. Old values were cast aside. There was a cocky new leader. When he went to kiss hands, he wrote of how they talked 'general guff about the government programme' and how when his wife, Cherie, was introduced the Queen was 'clucking sympathetically'.[2] Though Blair professed strong support for the monarchy, he frequently undermined the Queen. He walked to the State Opening of Parliament, holding his wife's hand, in contrast to the Queen in the traditional state carriage procession. The BBC commentary was notable for David Dimbleby's relish of New Labour and disdain for what he called the 'flummery and flammery' of the ceremonial proceedings.[3]

A few days later the new Prime Minister watched the Birthday Parade from 10 Downing Street, wearing a blue tie. The Queen wore pale yellow and was accompanied on the dais by two gnarled old cavalry generals, Lord Michael Fitzalan-Howard (wearing his GCVO over his belt), and Sir Desmond Fitzpatrick (with his GCB likewise over the belt). The Queen smiled radiantly as the Scots Guards marched off to 'Black Bear' and the BBC commentator, Julian Tutt, offered a salutary reminder to Blair that he might think it irrelevant, but he was sure that he would respect 'the traditions of service, help to others, duty and discipline embodied in the uniform'.[4]

Britannia took part for the last time in a major historical event – when Hong Kong was handed over to China, becoming as it were 'a Chinese take-away'. The Prince of Wales attended the ceremony on 1 July and sailed off in the company of the last Governor of Hong Kong, Chris Patten, and the new Labour Foreign Secretary, Robin Cook. Thus 156 years of British rule came to an emotional end.

With the help of Mark Bolland, Prince Charles was busily promoting the emergence of Camilla Parker Bowles, whose role in his life he had declared as 'non-negotiable'. She was brought forward in a series of strategically planned moves. Until 1997 she could not stay in a royal house like Birkhall, though there were a number of other houses, such as Chatsworth, where the two could be together. The line at this time was that she was coping and keeping Prince Charles 'sane'. He was averse to taking advice and did not read newspapers. He complained that when his parents were at Sandringham they had 'all those awful tabloids'.[5] She became Patron of the National Osteoporosis Society and in July was featured in a television documentary. Prince Charles gave a fiftieth birthday party for her at Highgrove in July.

While the British public continued their love affair with the Princess of Wales, the establishment had little good to say. Roy Strong quoted Edward Adeane, former Private Secretary to Prince Charles, who said of the Waleses: 'He's opera and she's *Phantom of the Opera.*'[6] There were two verdicts on that marriage: she was ill so it went wrong; it went wrong so she became ill. The Queen subscribed to the first view. In June Diana showed her dresses at Christie's in London prior to their sale in New York. Meeting her for the last time, I felt 'it was such a waste that she would not be our Queen one day'.[7]

But then Diana threw in her lot with Mohamed Fayed, who was only too happy to use her as a pawn in his endeavours. He bought the yacht, *Jonikal*, and invited her to bring her boys on a Mediterranean holiday, with his son, Dodi, in close attendance. Diana had become used to star treatment. Seeing her conveyed about in Harrods helicopters that summer, however unattractive the association, it was hard not to conclude that at least the Fayeds would protect her. Mohamed Fayed was surrounded by bodyguards. At the 'Villa Windsor', as he inaptly renamed the Duke and Duchess of Windsor's house, there were huge dogs in cages, and smiling security guards with holsters. Visitors were in no doubt as to what would happen if the nod was given. They would be ripped to shreds.[8]

On 11 August the *Sunday Mirror* printed muzzy photographs of the Princess in the South of France. Coverage of this was confused, with speculation about Cleo and Mo, yet unborn

Egyptian half-brothers and -sisters alongside young William and Harry at a future Coronation, and Prince Charles saying, 'If she's happy, then I'm happy.'[9] The Princess, it seemed, was seizing happiness and sexual fulfilment in her lonely Hell.

Dodi Fayed was not then well known to the general public, though he soon became so. Out it all came – his jilted fiancée, his fondness for cocaine and other unattractive character traits. He had tried to lure a girl to the 'Villa Windsor' with hints of what might take place on the Duchess of Windsor's bed. It was also said that his father despised him but was using him to capture the divorced Princess. On the other hand Raine Spencer volunteered that he was 'very nice' and 'not at all like the father'.[10] Diana took her boys on one holiday, but they had no intention of coming on subsequent trips. They joined the Queen and the Royal Family on *Britannia*'s final Western Islands cruise where the newspapers were removed from view. They wanted nothing more to do with the Fayed family.

In August, apart from a visit to minefield victims in Sarajevo, Bosnia, on 10 August (speedily arranged to boost her failing popularity), Diana had further holidays with Dodi Fayed, leading her to Sardinia and finally on the ill-fated visit to Paris, all of which was played out in the full glare of the media.

'Yet each man kills the thing he loves'[11]

On the night of 30/31 August Diana and Dodi Fayed were at the Ritz in Paris. They left by car, were chased by paparazzi, and both died as a result of the car crashing in the Pont de l'Alma tunnel. The facts are straightforward. It was Fayed's son, Fayed's hotel, Fayed's apartment, Fayed's drunk driver, Fayed advising the couple, and Fayed alerting the press. Fayed believed he had captured the most famous young woman in the world. Instead he was responsible for her death. It was a sordid, muddled death, in chaos at the end of a weird phase of playboy life.[12]

Diana's death heralded a week of global public grief, flowers being laid in profusion between Kensington Palace and Kensington High Street, and at embassies and high commissions across the world.

Candles were lit, people wailed in the streets. There was an unleashing of grief – until then more often seen at roadside accident sites on the continent – or a frenzied scene from the film, *Zorba the Greek*.

A long and distressing week followed, between the death on the Sunday and the funeral the following Saturday. On the first day, it was the shock. Next it was horror at the way the paparazzi had chased the car, then that Henri Paul, the driver, had been drinking before being summoned to drive the couple home. When those issues were exhausted, the press turned on the Queen. Where was she? Why was she not sharing the nation's grief? Why was she still at Balmoral and not in London? The press had to divert guilt from themselves. As Lord Spencer made abundantly clear, he blamed the media squarely for his sister's death.

It was a global shock, the first time in history that such an event hit the world simultaneously everywhere. People in Australia knew it before the British woke up. The Queen was attacked in tabloid headlines: 'Show us you care.' She was comforting her bereaved grandsons. There was a strange mood in the air, with people in London, who had not known Diana, attacking the family at Balmoral, as they attempted to come to terms with the loss. Although brutally done, John Julius Norwich made the point that it would have been worse had the general public not turned to their Queen at this seismic moment. They needed her as they had at difficult moments in her reign.[13]

For years afterwards there were conspiracy theories, all too readily believed by many, the worst that Diana had been murdered, possibly on the orders of the Duke of Edinburgh.* Fayed's bouffant-haired PR man, Michael Cole, did an all-too-effective spinning job for Fayed, sending arrows into the air in the days following the tragedy. Years later all the arrows landed in Fayed, but by then the world had moved on. Cole did a better job for Fayed than the Queen's Press Secretary, Geoff Crawford, did for the Queen (not helped by him being on leave in Australia at the time and only getting the news on CNN).

The mood was set by Tony Blair. When he discovered that the

---

* In a far-ranging conversation with Prince Philip in Hampshire in the summer of 2000, he volunteered to me that he considered Fayed to be 'a creep'.

Royal Family were not planning to say anything, he arranged for a microphone to be ready outside church on that Sunday morning. He saw it as his duty to capture the way in which Diana had touched people's lives and hailed her as 'the People's Princess'. Blair had been an admirer of Diana: '... Just as we were changing the image of Britain, she was radicalising that of the monarchy,' he wrote.[14] On the same day Prince Charles flew to Paris with Diana's sisters to escort his ex-wife's coffin home.

In the television studios that week, republican journalists like Polly Toynbee thought they had finally nailed the monarchy. It was not easy standing up for the Queen.* It was obvious to the sensible-minded that she was staying in Scotland to give comfort and strength to her grandchildren so that they could face the world at the funeral. Princess Margaret said later that the Queen's family were all about to leave Balmoral – Prince Charles to go to France to paint; she was about to go to Italy. She asked the Queen if she could stay on for the next few days. 'You're the fourth person who's asked me this morning,' said the Queen. Princess Margaret also said: 'We tried to get Harry to break down but he just wouldn't.'[15]

Much was made of the flag not flying at half-mast on Buckingham Palace. The only flag ever flown at the Palace in those days was the Royal Standard and it was never flown at half-mast because the Sovereign never dies, only changes. In interviews I pointed out in vain that the Union Flag at Windsor Castle (a military fortress) was at half-mast, but it did not suit the media to show that.† The fuss over the flag was media-led.‡ Robin Janvrin was at Balmoral. He

---

* I was greatly touched when a few weeks later, the Constable of the Castle, Sir Patrick Palmer, made a point of saying to me: 'You played a straight bat on behalf of the Queen that week.' (HV diary, 28 September 1997.)

† During that week there were flowers all over the lawns in the Lower Ward of Windsor Castle and queues stretching down the hill to the Theatre Royal. One evening a Military Knight and his wife were sitting on their patio. It was dark and dead quiet. But when he looked over the wall, the whole area was packed with silent mourners.

‡ It is interesting to recall that no comment was made about flags flying at half-mast on the day of the Duchess of Windsor's funeral in 1986. Few noticed and no one cared. But in 1997 the mood was volatile.

obtained the Queen's permission that the Union Flag could be flown at half-mast on Buckingham Palace after the Queen left for Westminster Abbey, at which point her Royal Standard would be lowered at the Palace since she had gone out of residence.[16] He told Malcolm Ross: 'I'm covered in blood.'*[17]

Blair thought Diana's death must have been 'deeply troubling' for the Queen.[18] Having gone through the war, she had a different approach to this crisis than now prevailed in Blairite Britain. Had she been in London when the accident happened, she would have stayed there. But she was in Scotland. To some extent it was business as usual. She was criticised for taking the grandsons to church on the morning of their mother's death. Some thought that awful, others that it was correct.

She had horses due to race that week. Sir Michael Oswald rang her to say that he did not think it appropriate to run them. 'Oh, do you think so?' she said. He had already cancelled them, which the Queen rightly accepted.[19] Patrick Mitchell, Dean of Windsor, went up to Balmoral. He said: 'There were barbecues and long walks and Prince Harry particularly liked driving the Discovery.' He said, 'It was a haven, but when you came out of the gates, the paparazzi were hanging over the bridges.'[20] Also there was John Ovenden, about to be appointed a Canon of Windsor and Chaplain in the Great Park. Prince Philip had all the newspapers spread out in his study. 'What do we do about those?' he asked the Canon.[21]

At Birkhall the Queen Mother refused to allow the television to be on the whole week. Anyone who wanted to see the news had to sneak down to the servants' quarters. Princess Margaret was heard to comment: 'Well, that sorts it out, then.' Concerted efforts were made to ensure she did not go out and express that view more widely.[22]

The Queen had no moral or legal right to bury the divorced Princess of Wales. The sons were too young to contribute. Diana

---

* Until that point, when it was ordained that the Union Flag be flown on all public buildings, for example on the Queen's birthday, the one flagpole that did not fly it was the one on Buckingham Palace. The Queen did not like the new plan, but Malcolm Ross told her that she would never see the Union Flag on the Palace because she would not be there.

now belonged to the Spencer family and they had to be consulted. In the intense discussions it was agreed that the funeral would be at Westminster Abbey and that Diana would be accorded full royal honours, the coffin covered with the Royal Standard used by 'other' members of the Royal Family, that is to say with an ermine surround.*

Lieutenant-Colonel (later Sir) Malcolm Ross, Comptroller of the Lord Chamberlain's Office, was present at RAF Northolt when Diana's coffin was flown back from Paris. As the cortège drove into London, he saw the traffic at a standstill: 'Three lanes of traffic had stopped on the opposite side of the road, and two lanes on our side. People were standing all along the route.' There was no plan in place for Diana's funeral, but he realised that he must dispense with most of the military, extend the procession back to Kensington Palace, and he ordered a gun-carriage, so that people could see the coffin as it passed by.[23]

Robert Fellowes was under pressure from all sides. One day during that week he found a typed note from Prince Philip on his desk and thought: That is all I need. He wondered if he was to be fired. Prince Philip quoted Isaiah, along the lines of: 'Heed not those that speak with forked tongues.'[24]

The intense pressure on the Queen forced her to come down to London a day earlier than planned. In the past, for the funerals of Princess Marina, Prince William of Gloucester and Lord Mountbatten, there had been announcements in the press that she was breaking her holiday to attend their funerals. That was considered an appropriate mark of respect: she flew down in the morning and back again the same day. But for Diana, the media demanded more.

Blair saw how the mood of the nation was turning ugly. His advisers were sharply interested in how he was perceived to be handling the situation. His spin doctor Alastair Campbell's attitude was that he was surprised to be 'helping the royals work their way through a difficult public opinion situation' while judging it 'a genuinely interesting professional challenge'.[25] On the Wednesday Blair contacted Prince Charles. As a result, the Royal Family changed

---

* Princess Marina's coffin had been covered with such a standard. The Duchess of Windsor's coffin was covered only with flowers.

their plans and the Queen agreed to broadcast. They went to church on the Thursday for private prayers for Diana. Afterwards they looked at flowers, from which a crucial image emerged – Prince Harry reaching for his father's hand. They flew down on the Friday.* 'We were a day late,' conceded Lord Charteris.†[26]

As the plane touched down, Princess Margaret was in tears. 'I can't bear Lilibet having to go through this,' she said.[27]

When the Queen arrived at Buckingham Palace, she and Prince Philip got out of the car and looked at the flowers massed against the railings. One member of the public handed the Queen some flowers, telling her they were for her. A voice called from the crowd: 'Look after the boys.'

Prince Philip replied: 'That's what we've been doing.'

Following the live, measured broadcast the Queen gave later that afternoon from the Chinese Dining Room at Buckingham Palace, the unpleasant atmosphere softened. The broadcast took a lot out of her. The world listened to her in silence. The Queen paid tribute to Diana, speaking 'as your Queen and as a grandmother', and described Diana as 'an exceptional and gifted human being'. She said she 'admired and respected her'. As ever she appealed for unity:

> I hope that tomorrow we can all, wherever we are, join in expressing our grief at Diana's loss, and gratitude for her all-too-short life. It is a chance to show to the whole world the British nation united in grief and respect.

Prince William was not at all sure he wanted to walk behind his mother's coffin on account of the media's behaviour. Prince Philip took the long view and told the boys: 'I think, when you are older,

---

* Another problem was that the private rooms at the Palace were closed down for the summer and many covered in dust sheets. The Queen's rooms at Windsor Castle were prepared – in case she needed to stay there. As it happens, she stayed at Buckingham Palace.

† This conversation proved interesting. I said of the Princess of Wales: 'She had a good heart'. 'Really?' he replied. 'You surprise me.' His verdict was: 'She wanted to destroy the monarchy and she damn nearly succeeded.' He revised that to her wanting to destroy Prince Charles.

you would regret not having walked behind your mother's coffin.' He added: 'And I will walk with you.'* That clinched the matter.

That evening the coffin was conveyed by hearse from St James's Palace to Kensington Palace, a solemn motorcade passing through the darkness to the modern phenomenon of flickering camera flashes from the silent crowd. On Saturday, 6 September, the King's Troop drew the gun-carriage from Kensington Palace, to be greeted by a primeval wail from a mourner in the streets. Mercifully this was not repeated. The cortège passed through London, the only sound the hoofs of the horses and the roll of the gun-carriage wheels. As it passed Buckingham Palace the Queen and the Royal Family came out to watch and the Queen bowed her head. Prince Philip (head up and standing well), Prince Charles (in a blue suit as Diana had liked him in that), the two boys and their maternal uncle, Lord Spencer, joined the procession at the Mall approach by St James's Palace, despite police concerns for Prince Charles walking in public with his provocative former-brother-in-law. As they walked under Whitehall, when Prince Philip thought the cameras were off him, he could be seen patting Prince William reassuringly on the shoulder.

The funeral in Westminster Abbey had contributions from Elton John, and a well-crafted, though ultimately divisive address from Lord Spencer. The crowds had sung the National Anthem earlier. Now they clapped the speech. As one in the Abbey put it, it was like Robespierre riding up the aisle on his horse. A long procession took Diana's body to her family home, Althorp in Northamptonshire, flowers being thrown onto the hearse. She was apparently buried on an island in a lake.

Prince William was kept back from returning to school for a while. When he rejoined his house, he was mightily relieved. He just wanted to be back at school and away from all the frenzy.[28]

That week was the nadir of the Queen's reign. Grief for Diana overwhelmed the British and, indeed, the global public. For months afterwards it was picked over in the media. Anyone who had missed the death could see images of Diana moving about on their screens

---

* This says a great deal about the wisdom and forward thinking of Prince Philip. I think he was right, yet many years later both boys stated that they should not have been made to do this. They did it well and were enormously respected.

as if she were still alive. The way the Queen had been treated was shocking and unpleasant.

In September the Queen replied to those who wrote to her in a printed letter which described the death of Diana as 'indeed dreadfully sad' and as 'a huge loss to the country'. She thought the public reaction to the death and the Westminster Abbey service had 'united the people round the world in a rather inspiring way'. She was very proud of the bravery of William and Harry. To one whom she knew well, she added a personal note: 'emotions are still so mixed up but we have all been through a very bad experience.' [29]

Within a month of Diana's death, Andrew Morton exposed to the world the full extent of Diana's cooperation with his book.

40
REGROUPING, 1998–2000

As at the end of a war, nothing was quite the same after Diana's death. The Queen had said: 'I for one believe there are lessons to be drawn from her life and from the extraordinary and moving reaction to her death.'[1] On the evening after the funeral, Robert Fellowes told Alastair Campbell that he was 'clear the whole week would see the Royal Family change'. Her Deputy Private Secretary, Robin Janvrin, agreed. He too called Campbell, telling him that 'a relationship had been forged in days that would normally have taken years'. Now 'they could push on for change'.[2]

The Government sent a spin doctor into the Palace in the form of Simon Lewis. He was keen that the monarchy be not seen to modernise too abruptly and aware of the Royal Family's distrust of the Government. Blair was no more republican than Harold Wilson or James Callaghan, but ministers such as John Prescott and Clare Short were, and Alastair Campbell was deemed hostile.

New ideas were implemented, such as themed days on which the Queen and the Duke of Edinburgh went on visits connected with different industries, books, newspapers, and tourism, and held an evening reception. The Queen signed a football, which was perhaps the least successful stunt they cooked up for her. She went to a pub, the media thought for the first time, though she had visited one in Stevenage in 1959.

In October, not long after Diana's death, the Queen and Prince Philip went on state visits to Pakistan and India, to find the media primarily obsessed by Diana, and preoccupied with what the Queen might or might not say about her in her speeches. She was obliged to make brief references to her in speeches in Parliament in Islamabad and in Delhi.

The trip to Pakistan and India had elements of controversy (as

I saw for myself since I was accredited to this trip). If the Queen went to Pakistan first, as she did this time, India was annoyed. There was an inexperienced new Foreign Secretary, Robin Cook, who did not handle it well, even dashing home between the two visits to see his girlfriend. He pleased the Pakistanis but upset the Indians by telling journalists that the British Government would be happy to broker a peace deal with India over Kashmir. Headlines pronounced: 'Cook spoils the curry'.* The Queen said later that Robin Cook had been surprised by the hostility of the press in India. The Pakistan visit included a spectacular evening banquet at the Fort in Lahore (which the Queen loved), with impressive fireworks.

In between Pakistan and India the Queen and Prince Philip spent a quiet weekend in Murree, a mountain resort in the most northern region of the Punjab in Pakistan, popular in the days of the British Raj as a resort to escape the intense heat and where the Government had a summer retreat frequently used by Heads of State. The Queen recalled:

> Philip and I both came from different directions and the weather was very bad. The planes were only just able to fly. Then we drove up and up this windy road and it got colder and colder. It was a very odd thing to do, especially after it had been so hot.[3]

The Indian press were angered when, on Foreign Office advice, the Queen said she hoped the two countries would 'renew efforts to end historical disagreements'.[4] The Queen went to Amritsar, where Brigadier-General Dyer had killed 379 Indians and wounded a thousand more† in 1919. There were demands that she should

---

* Back in London I told Baroness Thatcher that I thought Robin Cook had been attempting to marginalise the Royal Family and make state visits seem a waste of time. She said: 'Robin Cook is just as foxy in his mind as he is in his looks.' (HV diary, 14 November 1997.)

† Entering the site, Prince Philip saw a sign stating that two thousand had been wounded. When he pointed out that this was wrong, it was interpreted as one of his gaffes. The *Daily Express* ran a column with a map: 'Around the world with the Duke in 80 blunders.'

make a public apology. It was made clear even before the visit that the Queen did not go round the world apologising: 'The fact of this visit indicates a concern about the event and recognition that it happened.'[5] When the Queen visited Jallianwala Bagh, the site of the massacre, and laid a wreath, the atmosphere lifted and the demands subsided.

However, the media stirred up dissent throughout the visit, particularly in India. A press conference announced that the Queen would not be making a speech in Madras. There was an implication that the Queen was not enjoying herself; Robin Cook had been carpeted by Blair but then praised for his efforts. An almighty drama unfolded. It seemed that the press had an agenda – the Government wishing to embarrass the Queen, Robin Cook treating state visits as a waste of his time, with the implication that the Queen was no longer useful as an ambassador for Britain.

The crowds did not equal those of 1961. The young journalists complained: 'It's not Diana.' Security issues removed the spontaneity; the crowds were held back. I wondered what the royal couple made of it all, with a hundred years on the road between them. I noted:

> And yet it all looks great. Cochin is a prime example. A radiant Queen arrived at the hotel, met by dancing girls & with flowers thrown at her feet ... She visited St Francis Church, India's oldest European church, in a blaze of heat and sunshine.* I saw her close to in 'Jew Town'. Nick Owen (ITN) was forced to ask her: 'Are you enjoying the tour, Ma'am?' and found himself withered by one of her most beatific smiles. He retreated to dread a wigging from Geoff Crawford. He was like a little boy, set up by the class, knowing that he was in for a caning, which by better sense he could have avoided.[6]

On returning to Britain, Prince Philip's apt comment was: 'The press was on one tour. We were on another.'[7]

★ ★ ★ ★ ★

---

* Outside the church the Queen was given an earthen jar by an 'untouchable' to show that an 'untouchable' could now meet a queen. 'Queen takes pot in India,' mused a tabloid journalist, playing with a potential headline.

Although it would be wrong to suggest that the effects of Diana's death soon dissolved, the Queen's personal popularity was not greatly dented. She and Prince Philip were greeted with considerable respect when they celebrated their Golden Wedding with a magnificent service at Westminster Abbey, and a luncheon at the Banqueting House. It was on that occasion that the Queen paid tribute to Prince Philip as her 'strength and stay'.

They were able to celebrate with an evening party at Windsor Castle. A few days before, there was a press conference at which the restored rooms were shown in their new splendour. The press were told that the restoration had been achieved within the time frame and within the budget. They were so disappointed – nothing negative to report. All they could say was that it could have been done differently. At the party, as it grew late, the Queen's main preoccupation was to persuade her ninety-seven-year-old mother to go to bed.

If the Royal Family had been reserved in showing their emotions at the time of Diana's death and funeral, the decommissioning of *Britannia* on 11 December brought tears of conspicuous emotion to their eyes. John Major had decided it should go, and Tony Blair had made electoral mileage out of stating that his government would not replace it. *Britannia* had been the one place where the Queen could truly relax between royal visits. It was where the family had enjoyed their honeymoons. It was where she could entertain Heads of State for a return banquet. As a maritime nation, it was an impressive asset for the United Kingdom. It was the end of an era.

The Queen and Prince Philip attended the farewell party for Robert Fellowes on 10 February 1999. He made his speech: 'Any rockets that I have received from the Duke of Edinburgh have been richly deserved,' while praising the Queen for having 'led by example from the top'. There were high hopes for the new Private Secretary, Robin Janvrin, whose line whenever anything happened was 'What have we learned from this?'[8] Likewise the Queen, when confronted with an idea, always asked him: 'What use is it?'

★ ★ ★ ★ ★

Prince William, then at Eton, had a good house master, Andrew Gailey, who helped him over that difficult time. Obviously William had loved his mother, but unquestionably he had suffered from the worry of what she might do next, or what would happen to her.[9] He achieved excellent exam results within the year. At Sandringham at Christmas 1997 the boys looked happy. Princess Margaret asked Prince Charles: 'Don't they miss their mother at all?' They were having a good time, which 'compensated' – the family's way of coping.[10]

The Queen was worried about the state visit of Emperor Akihito of Japan and with reason since the media whipped up considerable hostility, even more so than for his father's. She said privately that she was not sure it was right to give the Emperor the Garter, but the Government wanted it and all his recent predecessors had received it. Prince Philip expressed the same view, which was quoted in *The Times*. This caused a furore and a denial was swiftly issued: 'For very many years the Duke has worked for reconciliation and for a greater understanding between the two countries.'[11]

On the day the Emperor arrived, 26 May, ITN sent a car to the house of a former prisoner of war to film him looking at his wartime photos. They took him to the Mall to film him setting fire to a Japanese flag – directing the cameras at him while the state procession passed behind him, and then took him home. War veterans turned their backs on the Emperor, whistled, played mouth organs, held up signs, wore red gloves, booed and hissed. This was unfair since, unlike his father, Emperor Akihito had played no part in the Second World War.

For security reasons the Queen and the Emperor travelled to Buckingham Palace in the closed Irish State Coach, the Empress and Prince Philip in Queen Alexandra's coach. At Westminster Abbey to which the Imperial couple went to lay the traditional wreath on the tomb of the Unknown Soldier, there was a barrier, the police letting some people through.* There were a number of TV camera-hungry protesters. The veterans demanded that the

---

* I was stopped at the barrier. I asked if I could go through. 'That's for protesters,' said the policeman. 'Are you a protester?' I replied: 'No, I've come to see the Emperor. Do I have to be a protester?' He let me through.

Emperor apologise for the war but whatever he said would not satisfy them. In 1998 (arguably in 1971) it was time to move forward, to make friends and ensure good relations between the two countries.

Now that Diana was no longer occupying headlines, attention reverted to the quiet, continuing work of the Queen. She paid state visits to Brunei, Malaysia, France and Belgium. She opened Parliament on 24 November and announced the removal of most of the hereditary peers. The ceremonial procession was somewhat curtailed. The Duke and Duchess of Gloucester and the Duke of Kent attended for the last time.

Prince Charles celebrated his fiftieth birthday at Buckingham Palace, a milestone birthday to which Camilla Parker Bowles was not invited. She hosted an alternative event at Highgrove to which no members of the British Royal Family went, though some overseas ones did. A few months before, Lord Longford, then aged ninety-two, had sat next to the Queen at the Garter luncheon. She asked him what he thought about Camilla Parker Bowles. He said he hoped they would marry. The Queen said: 'It's a strange relationship – I don't think they will.'[12]

In the new year of 1999, a step forward was taken. Mark Bolland tipped off the press that Camilla would leave the Ritz in the company of Prince Charles after the fiftieth birthday party for her sister, Annabel Elliot. Banks of photographers waited for this moment. The world's media went into overdrive.

The Queen Mother

The decline in health of the Queen Mother and Princess Margaret caused the Queen considerable anxiety. In January 1998 the Queen Mother fell at the Sandringham Stud and broke her left hip. She was whisked into a Range Rover and taken first to King's Lynn and then to the London Clinic. Trevor McDonald had been in Washington, reporting on the unravelling of President Clinton's involvement with Monica Lewinsky. So seriously did ITN take the Queen Mother's fate that they flew him home and went on to 'Operation Alert' until further notice. The Queen Mother was made of sterner stuff than most ninety-eight-year-olds. She survived. I lunched with her at the Castle of Mey on 22 August by which time she was again in full health.

The general public loved the Queen Mother's brave appearances in public. But every time she came out, the Queen was petrified that she might fall. She was as tense as the public were enthralled.

Princess Margaret

I had seen Princess Margaret stumble twice in 1997. As the Duke and Duchess of Windsor's possessions came under the hammer at Sotheby's, New York, in February 1998 – the Queen preferring that this ten-day sale did not take place in London – so came news that she had suffered a stroke in Mustique. She was flown back to London. Never as robust as her mother, she succumbed to her illness. Her left side was weak, she fell quite often, and was afraid of having another stroke. She seldom smiled, and became forgetful of her private engagements (such as a lunch with her cousin Jean Wills or an evening at the ballet). The Queen was not sympathetic to malingering. On one occasion she went to Princess Margaret's room, threw open the window and insisted she got up.

In 1999 Princess Margaret was able to return to Mustique, though the great days of Mustique, orchestrated with such inspiration by Colin Tennant, were over. Having given Les Jolies Eaux, her house high above Gelliceaux Bay, to her son David, she was deeply upset when he put it on the market. In March she was having a shower after breakfast in bed, turned the wrong tap and scalded her feet. Due to her stroke the year before, her reactions were slow, she was dazed and could not move. Some days later Anne Glenconner telephoned the Queen, who had her sister flown home on Concorde.

The Queen had a discussion with Janie Stevens, one of Princess Margaret's close friends and a lady in waiting, after a dinner with the Carnarvons in April 1999. Janie said: 'When you get back tomorrow, Ma'am, you'll have to put your foot down.'

Princess Margaret was well enough to attend Prince Edward's wedding, but in a wheelchair, with a doctor close at hand. By the time of the Queen Mother's ninety-ninth birthday on 4 August, she was walking with a metal cane. On 26 November Princess Margaret fell ill again, though fears that she had suffered another stroke proved unfounded. She was well enough to attend a memorial service for Sir Hugh Casson three days later.

Prince Edward

On 19 June 1999 Prince Edward married Sophie Rhys-Jones in St George's Chapel, a lower key wedding than those of his older siblings. When they spoke after their engagement, the bride-to-be was at pains to point out that she had not lived with Prince Edward, but had been assigned rooms at the Palace. They had had plenty of time to get to know each other, were in their mid-thirties and maintained that the basis of their union was that they were 'the very best of friends'.[13]

The groom wanted to produce some surprises on the day. He arranged a special Royal Marines fanfare for Sophie as she came up the steps, the BBC agreed not to film Princess Margaret arriving in her wheelchair, the bride, Sophie, organised beautiful flowers – agapanthus, white lilies, Bianca roses and rosemary. The Queen commissioned some special kneelers for the young couple, made by Belinda, Lady Montagu. Princess Alexandra's previously wayward daughter, Marina Mowatt, now separated from her husband, made her first reappearance at a royal event since her wedding. The day itself went well, the Queen in pale lilac, lace and feathers. She looked majestic, like Queen Mary, and happy.[14]

Crown Prince Abdullah of Saudi Arabia paid a four-day visit to Britain and on 14 September he lunched with the Queen at Balmoral. She invested him as an honorary Knight Grand Cross of the Order of the Bath, and after lunch she asked him if he would like to take a tour of the estate. He was hesitant but encouraged by his Foreign Minister to accept. The Land Rover was outside so he got into the front and his interpreter into the seat behind. He was alarmed when the Queen got into the driver's seat and drove off. Women were not allowed to drive in Saudi Arabia and therefore the Crown Prince had never been driven by a woman, let alone a Queen. She chatted to him, but he asked her to slow down and concentrate on the road.[15]

On 19 October President Jiang Zemin of China came on a state visit. This was the first visit to the United Kingdom by a Chinese leader and was designed to improve relations between Britain and China following the handing back of Hong Kong in 1997. The President minded about protests. A man was arrested after running towards the carriage in which the President and the Queen were travelling. There were protests from Free Tibet campaigners. The biggest protest came from Prince Charles who refused to attend the state banquet. Here he entered difficult diplomatic and political territory. Had he become King shortly afterwards, and had the Government wanted him to go to China, the Chinese might have refused to have him or he might have refused to go. Thus he broke the unbreakable rule that the Royal Family must stay out of politics.

On 11 November 1999 the Blair Government succeeded in removing most of the hereditaries from the House of Lords. Of the 750 such peers, only ninety-two were allowed to continue sitting in the chamber, ninety of these elected – the Earl Marshal (the Duke of Norfolk) and the Lord Great Chamberlain (the Marquess of Cholmondeley in the Queen's reign) being *ex officio* members. That arrangement continued until beyond the Queen's reign. Despite what many have maintained, this inevitably threatened the hereditary monarchy.

The Government were up to mischief. The Queen and Prince Philip had been in South Africa and flew home from Mozambique on 16 November, with Robin Janvrin in attendance. The next day the Queen read the speech at the State Opening of Parliament. Where the speech should have informed the two Houses of the proposed legislation to be laid before them, it was filled with party propaganda about the Labour Government's aims for the future. There were phrases such as 'It aims to build on my Government's programme of reform as they seek to modernise the country and its institutions to meet the challenges of the new millennium. My Government's aim is to promote fairness and enterprise, providing people with real opportunities to liberate their potential ... My Government are helping people back into work. The New Deal has helped 145,000 young people into employment ...'[16] I complained to the *Daily Telegraph* that the purpose of the speech was to announce future Bills:

It was therefore more than shocking that [the Prime Minister] should use this occasion to oblige the Queen to comment on his recent achievements – more people in work, employment up by 700,000. Effectively the Prime Minister tricked the Queen into promoting his propaganda.[17]

The Palace accepted that they should have been more vigilant, but between the Queen's return and the delivery of the speech: 'There wasn't time to object.'[18]

Australia

As a result of the Scotland Act of 1998, the Scottish Parliament assumed full devolved powers on 1 July 1999. On 6 November a referendum was held in Australia 'to alter the Constitution to establish the Commonwealth of Australia as a republic with the Queen and Governor-General being replaced by a President appointed by a two-thirds majority of the members of the Commonwealth Parliament': 54.8 per cent of the population voted 'no' to 45.13 per cent 'yes'. John Howard had been the Liberal Prime Minister since 1996. He handled the campaign adroitly. He pointed out that the Australian Government was completely independent. The Queen did not control the Governor-General, and although she appointed him, she did so on the advice of the Australian Prime Minister. She was personally popular in Australia. As he put it, she had 'done her duty in a conscientious fashion over many decades'.[19] Furthermore the governmental system worked well, so there was no need to change it.

The way he framed the deal offered no appealing alternative. In the UK, the Queen monitored developments. Plans were in place to deal with a pro-Republican outcome. All was well, and since then Australia has remained a monarchy. When the Queen visited in 2000, she told them: 'Whatever the future may bring, my lasting respect and deep affection for Australia and Australians will remain as strong as ever.'

★ ★ ★ ★ ★

REGROUPING, 1998–2000

The occupational hazard of living a long life is to lose friends. The Queen became increasingly isolated as her contemporaries died, her cousin Jean Wills, her childhood companion and cousin Lady Mary Whitley, and her greatest Private Secretary, Lord Charteris, all died in the latter part of 1999. Although peripheral to the Queen's life by this time, her first cousin and childhood playmate at Windsor, Gerald Lascelles, had died in Bergerac, on 27 February 1998 at the age of seventy-three. The Queen did not attend his memorial service at the Grosvenor Chapel, in South Audley Street. She and Prince Philip were jointly represented by her former Private Secretary, Lord Moore of Wolvercote.

After a *Newsnight* debate, Derek Draper* predicted that when the Queen Mother died there would be a battle between the tabloid editors David Yelland and Piers Morgan, one saying she was the greatest, and the other that she was a gin-soaked racist. This he thought would be followed by a move for the Queen to abdicate and questions as to the suitability of Prince Charles as the next King. His final thrust was that once Prince William went to university and met 'real people' he would not want to do it.[20] When Sir Brian McGrath, Prince Philip's former Private Secretary heard this, he commented that 'the only solution was that the Prince of Wales should push off with Mrs Parker Bowles, and the Queen live for some years more, and that Prince William should succeed because he'll have the support of all those who, for all the wrong reasons, misguidedly admired his mother'.[21] It is indicative of the line then taken by established courtiers.

The Government had a final horror in store for the Queen before the year was out. Blair invited the Queen and Prince Philip to see in the new Millennium in London's Dome. Part of the festivities included flying acrobats performing extraordinary feats. Prince Philip noticed that they were doing it without safety harnesses. Blair went through agony dreading that one would fall and kill the Queen, and

---

* Derek Draper (1967–2024) had been involved in some major political scandals; he later left politics and became a psychotherapist. He married the *Good Morning Britain* presenter Kate Garraway, who nursed him in the long illness he developed from Covid-19.

it would be his fault (seemingly his main concern).* Fortunately that did not happen but there is an abiding image of the royal party holding hands with the Blairs as 'Auld Lang Syne' was sung. At midnight the Queen kissed Prince Philip, and he kissed Princess Anne on both cheeks. 'They went back to Sandringham pretty quickly after that,' said one of the Queen's team, though they were back for a Millennium service in St Paul's Cathedral on 2 January.[22]

As the Queen went into the new Millennium, the general feeling was that Blair was coming to appreciate her role, as tended to happen. The Royal Household remained nervous of the Labour Government and some felt that the Queen's advisers did not stand up for her adequately.

---

* In his memoirs, he toyed with various headlines: 'QUEEN KILLED BY TRAPEZE ARTIST AT DOME'; 'BRITAIN'S MILLENNIUM CELEBRATION MARRED'; 'BLAIR ADMITS NOT ALL HAS GONE TO PLAN'. (Tony Blair, *A Journey*, pp. 260–61.)

41
THE GOLDEN JUBILEE, 2002

In 2002 the Queen's Golden Jubilee was approaching. The years that preceded it were a time of great anxiety for the Queen. The Queen Mother reached 100, Prince Philip turned eighty, yet there was illness and then there were deaths. By 2002 the Queen was a lone, matriarchal figure at the head of a fractured family.

A General Election was called for 7 June 2001. Roy Hattersley declared: 'William Hague has not yet fulfilled his destiny, which is to lose the next election.' The Labour Party retained power. Hague resigned and was succeeded by Iain Duncan Smith. The State Opening was set for Wednesday, 20 June. Some said that Blair chose this date to annoy the Queen because it was in the middle of Royal Ascot, possibly suggesting she did not have to attend.[1] She was there and Ascot was not missed. On 4 July, in Edinburgh, the Queen installed Princess Anne as a Lady of the Thistle in St Giles' Cathedral.

The destruction of the World Trade Center in New York on 9/11 was a global shock, and coincided with personal tragedy for the Queen. At dinner at Balmoral she received a call telling her that Lord Carnarvon was gravely ill. By the time she left the table he was dead. Carnarvon was a close personal friend as well as a racing adviser. Private secretaries knew to leave the room if he rang up. It was the only time in her reign that for once she was distracted and did not attend immediately to her red-box papers. She flew down from Balmoral to attend his funeral, the Duke of Edinburgh with her. To respect the American tragedy, the Queen ordered the American National Anthem to be played at the Changing of the Guard at Buckingham Palace. She made her memorable statement: 'Grief is the price we pay for love.'

On 3 November Princess Sophie (Princess George of Hanover), Prince Philip's last surviving sister, died in Germany at the age of eighty-seven. A regular at the Windsor Horse Show each year and at all the major royal celebrations, the visits of Prince and Princess George were memorable, not least for Prince George's tendency to let his bath water run over, or to forget his comb when he left for London. On 14 January 2002 Prince Philip, Princess Anne, Prince Edward, the King and Queen of Greece and others flew to Germany (and back the same day) for her memorial service at Wolfsgarten and heard Prince Philip deliver a touching tribute to his sister. It was an almost Tolstoyan scene as the black-clad mourners made their way on foot to the little chapel in the grounds, picking their way through the winter snow.*

★ ★ ★ ★ ★

The Queen Mother had sailed through her centenary year in 2000, attending the Garter ceremony and every day at Royal Ascot, with an evening party in Windsor Castle on the Wednesday, at which she stayed up until 1 a.m. She lunched at the Guildhall, getting on famously with John Prescott, that most Old Labour of Ministers, and ticked off the Archbishop of Canterbury for stealing her wine. Dressed in peach, she popped up and down at appropriate moments at her St Paul's Cathedral service. There was a fine moment when rays of sunlight made the gold on the tunics of the State Trumpeters glimmer as they moved balletically round the Whispering Gallery.

'I haven't seen anyone I know at all so far,' said the Queen, as she came in. The nonagenarian Lord and Lady Longford slept unconcernedly throughout the service, at the end of which the Queen Mother glided down the aisle, on her two elegant sticks, her gaze surfing the congregation without resting on anyone in particular. While the entire congregation was 'lost in wonder, love and praise', to quote one of the hymns, the Queen was as concerned as ever that her mother might trip and fall.

Major Michael Parker staged a fantastic parade on Horse Guards. The Queen Mother stood through most of it. The march-past of charities was led by William Tallon, her page, with her Corgis in

---

* I was included in this trip, having made friends with Princess George when writing the authorised biography of her mother, Princess Andrew of Greece.

tow. Birthday crowds had been 160 in 1975 and 3,000 in 1988. On the day of her hundredth, there were about 40,000. The Queen's telegram was opened outside Clarence House with a sword by her equerry, William de Rouet. A full day followed, ending with the Kirov Ballet at Covent Garden, overshadowed by news that the Queen Mother's other page, Reg Wilcock, had collapsed. He died a week later.

The Queen Mother insisted on walking the full length of St George's Chapel at Prince Philip's eightieth-birthday service in June 2001. In May Graham Turner had written two long articles about him. At the reception, Prince Philip joked: 'I wish that fellow who writes about me in the *Daily Telegraph* could have seen how many girls I kissed today.'[2] Princess Margaret arranged a short performance by the Royal Ballet for her brother-in-law.

The Queen Mother spent a few days in the London Clinic before her hundred and first birthday and was boosted in time for her birthday appearance. There was a further health panic in Scotland in September, and she made a last public appearance in December.

Princess Margaret was more or less confined to Kensington Palace, seldom leaving her room. In December 2001 she was wheeled round the corner by her butler, Harold Brown, to help celebrate Princess Alice, Duchess of Gloucester's forthcoming hundredth birthday with a parade by her regiment, the King's Own Scottish Borderers. The Queen and Princess Margaret sat either side of their aunt. When the BA146 touched down bringing the Queen Mother and Princess Margaret to Sandringham for Christmas, decanting two wheelchairs, the Queen must have looked on with some misgivings. Prince Philip, himself 'a bit peaky' and doing too much,[3] coped by taking long walks.

After the Christmas holidays, Princess Margaret left by car for London. She attended the second birthday party of her grandson, Arthur Chatto, on 5 February, returning to Kensington Palace with balloons attached to her wheelchair. She suffered a massive stroke and died at the London Clinic on the morning of 9 February aged seventy-one. Prince Charles went to Sandringham to be with his grandmother, and as part of the process contrived since Diana's death, he broadcasted a slightly stilted tribute to his aunt.

Princess Margaret's coffin was brought back to Kensington Palace.

Her butler, Harold Brown, covered it with her Coronation robes for those who came to pay their private respects. The Queen was impressed by this, but said she did not want the Coronation robes used in public. David Linley arranged a touching send-off for his mother, with flickering lights in every window of Kensington Palace and candles carried by the royal mourners and residents who followed the hearse as it was piped along the approach road. Princess Alice, Duchess of Gloucester, sat under the magnificent porch of her house, dressed in black with a black felt hat, her nurse at her side.

There had been so much negative press about Princess Margaret in her later years that the ignorant TV presenters took the line: 'She was a boozer and smoker, wasn't she?' As the week went by, the more considered obituaries and the release of sensational photographs of the princess in her youth gradually influenced the public mood. Sir Edward Ford commented: 'No Prime Minister would have got such coverage – twenty eight-page supplements.'[4] By the time of the funeral she was once again the beautiful princess of the 1950s for whom the world had had such high hopes.

The funeral in St George's Chapel was essentially private. The Queen Mother was flown down from Sandringham the day before, and entered by a side door, to avoid being seen in a wheelchair. Lord Snowdon was there and the Royal Family was out in force. At the end of the service, the Queen Mother rose to her feet to respect her daughter. She left by the north quire aisle, her wheelchair only proceeding when she had established there would be no photographers outside. At the same time, the coffin, followed by Princess Margaret's children, the Queen and Prince Philip, went out via the Great West Door. When the organist finished playing, he thought the congregation had gone. When he looked down from the organ loft they were still there, so moved that a deep silence had fallen over the chapel. The Queen Mother was driven back to Royal Lodge, caught by one photographer, while in her vehicle on the Long Walk. She never left Royal Lodge again.

★ ★ ★ ★ ★

The Queen entered the year of her Golden Jubilee with some trepidation. The Royal Household were concerned about its potential

THE GOLDEN JUBILEE, 2002

success or failure.* The last twenty-five years had been fraught with problems and the media was considerably more hostile. To lose her sister was a dismal start to the Queen's year.

Three days after the funeral, the Queen set off on the first of her overseas Jubilee tours. She knew that her mother could not live long and was nervous if she saw a courtier on a mobile phone. 'I can see myself coming down those steps again,' said the Queen.[5] But the Queen Mother did not die.

The Queen visited Jamaica, New Zealand and Australia. The Jamaican visit was a particular success: 'Thousands – old and young – have turned out, cheering, waving, singing, dancing, blowing kisses ...' noted Gyles Brandreth.[6] On the last night the lights failed at King's House, just as the Queen was putting on her tiara. They failed again as the Queen and Prince Philip came downstairs into the banqueting hall. They were led in by candlelight. An hour later the electricity was switched on again. 'Memorable,' was the Queen's laconic verdict.[7] She returned home on 4 March.

Realistically there was only one day on which the Queen Mother could die during Jubilee year and somehow she succeeded in doing so. It may have suited her that the Prince of Wales and his boys were away in Klosters and thus her grandson was spared the agony of a death bed scene. She waited until the Queen was back at Windsor Castle with most of her family arriving to spend Easter with her. The Easter eggs were laid out, and on the evening of Good Friday, the Queen Mother gave gifts to her faithful staff, Leslie Chappell and Jacqui Meakin. On 30 March, the Saturday between Good Friday and Easter Day, the Queen was riding when she was alerted to a sudden decline in the Queen Mother's health. She was with her mother when she slipped into unconsciousness and died. Sarah Chatto and Margaret Rhodes were there too. The Queen took the Queen Mother's Corgis back with her to Windsor Castle, and presently took on her racing stable.

---

* Having worked for the London Celebrations Committee for the Silver Jubilee in 1977 I did not share these concerns, aware that there would come a moment when the public woke up and realised that they could have fun celebrating it. And that is exactly what happened.

The country entered a spell of national mourning. The Prince of Wales made a broadcast, which, to harsh critics, seemed to emphasise his own grief at his grandmother's death rather than her life and achievements. He had dreaded that moment and indeed had dreams in which she had died, waking with relief to find she was still alive. He would miss her because he believed she was the only person who understood him.

Members of the Royal Family mingled with those who queued for the Lying-in-State. The Queen and Prince Philip came to look at wreaths in the Lower Ward of Windsor Castle, and the night before the funeral the Queen addressed the nation. None of this happened by chance. Every day the press were fed something to satisfy their needs.

There was a procession down the Mall, witnessed in silence by people of all ages, nationalities and creeds. When they arrived at Westminster Hall, the Queen was waiting, a lone figure with the Archbishop of Canterbury. When her car emerged from Westminster Hall, there was discreet clapping. It was as if, at that moment, affection was transferred from one matriarch to another. The Queen was greatly touched.

Prince Andrew had the inspired idea of the grandchildren standing vigil at the Lying-in-State as the sons of George V had in 1936. They were given twenty minutes of training.

On the way to Windsor many people bowed or curtseyed to the passing cortège. Once the coffin had been placed on a dais in St George's Chapel, Prince Charles went over to Royal Lodge to grieve in private among the camellias and rhododendrons. He picked a white flower for his button-hole. At 6 p.m. he joined his family and watched his grandmother laid to rest next to George VI. He threw the white flower onto her coffin and the black slab was lowered. So often over the years he had sat next to Queen Elizabeth at Garter ceremonies. Now she was under a cold stone.[8]

Martin Charteris used to say: 'See what happens when her mother dies.' The Queen Mother was 101; she had led a full life. She was now at peace. The Queen minded the death of her sister more, as they had been close companions from childhood. Now she blossomed. Her clothes became brighter. I remember asking: 'Did we have to wait until the Queen Mother died before the Queen began to dress well?'

THE GOLDEN JUBILEE, 2002

The reply came: 'No, you had to wait until Hardy Amies died.'*

Angela Kelly had been the Queen's dresser since 1994. She came via Sir Christopher Mallaby, British Ambassador to West Germany from 1988 to 1992, who had presided over the Queen's visit in October 1992. She revolutionised the Queen's late-life style, creating coats with large buttons and Boy George hats. At the Palace party to thank supporters of the Golden Jubilee, the Queen looked flamboyant in bright red. Angela Kelly became a force to be reckoned with at the Palace, one of those who served the Queen personally and therefore had an intimacy that the courtiers did not enjoy. She did a good job for the Queen. It was said of her: 'She doesn't know how to dress herself, but she certainly knows how to dress the Queen.'[9]

The Queen Mother's death brought Old Britain back to its feet. The Blair Government did not know how to respond. They did not know whether to order shops to be closed on the day of the funeral. On 19 April there was a magnificent memorial service for Princess Margaret in Westminster Abbey. She had arranged beautiful music, three choirs (the Abbey choir, St George's Chapel and King's College, Cambridge), Dame Felicity Lott and Bryn Terfel singing – in a sense a concert in her memory for the benefit of her friends, charities and supporters. The Queen, returning by car to Windsor, asked, 'Who is this Mr Fauré?' She had loved the requiem performed.

Thus ended a draining period of mourning for the Royal Family, but the response to it had been stimulating. There was enormous sympathy for the Queen losing her mother and sister. By dying when she did, the Queen Mother had performed her last duty to the United Kingdom. The mood changed: the media reacted positively to the Queen. It seemed that everyone wanted the Jubilee to be a great success. It was like coming out of the dark ages.

Missing her mother and sister, the Queen came to rely on the Countess of Wessex. Sophie was a successful member of the Royal Family since she supported the Queen without competing with her – a mistake made by Diana, Princess of Wales, and others. Prince Edward was close to both parents. They enjoyed a cosier relationship than the other siblings, often sitting down together to watch television.

---

* Hardy Amies died on 5 March 2003.

2002 was something of a turning point in the lives of the Wessexes. Prince Edward closed Ardent. Sophie had continued to run her public relations company after marriage. In April 2001 she had been embarrassed by a heist in which a *News of the World* reporter posed as an Arab sheikh and extracted indiscretions from her about members of the Royal Family, Tony Blair and Gordon Brown.

These events and the recent deaths in the family provided an opportunity for the Wessexes to give up their business interests and assist the Queen during the Golden Jubilee year. Many patronages and presidencies had fallen vacant and needed royal support. In a quiet and understated way the Wessexes succeeded in becoming bulwarks to the monarchy.

There was sympathy for Sophie when she suffered an ectopic pregnancy in December 2001, and more so when she nearly lost her baby, Louise, born prematurely after a placental abruption. Sophie was in Frimley Park Hospital, the baby then taken to St George's Hospital, Tooting, as a precautionary measure, and Prince Edward, who had been on an overseas visit to Mauritius, rushing between the two. There was huge relief when mother and daughter were safely back at Bagshot Park, their home, on 23 November. Sensibly Prince Edward decided that Louise and her younger brother James (born on 17 December 2007) would not use princely titles, making their passage through school easier.

Prince Andrew took over Royal Lodge in Windsor Great Park. Prince Charles finally moved into Clarence House, retaining most of his grandmother's pictures, but employing Robert Kime to redecorate it. He hung her Garter banner in the hall. He also took over Birkhall, her Scottish home near Balmoral. Her coats were left on hooks in the hall. 'Well, I suppose it's all right,' said Prince Philip, 'as long as he doesn't start wearing them.'[10]

★ ★ ★ ★ ★

If the Silver Jubilee had been designed in such a way that the public thanked the Queen, the plan for the Golden Jubilee was that the Queen would thank the public. During the year she made many overseas visits as did members of the Royal Family. Once the black ties came off, the Queen headed to the West Country. After a bit of a glitch, Jeffrey Sterling took over the financing of the Jubilee. There was a spectacular 'All the Queen's Horses' at Windsor, a classical concert and a pop concert in the grounds of Buckingham Palace, with Brian May, of the rock band Queen, playing 'God Save The Queen' from the roof of the palace. Camilla Parker Bowles appeared in the royal box at the classical concert, seated in the second row, next to Sir Michael Peat and Princess Alexandra.

For the service of thanksgiving, the Gold State Coach rolled out of the Royal Mews to take the Queen and the Duke of Edinburgh to St Paul's Cathedral, its first appearance since 1977.

Among the Queen's regional visits she went to Yorkshire on 11 July. With Prince Philip she lunched with the Earl and Countess of Harewood for the Golden Jubilee Celebration, dubbed 'The great Yorkshire Golden Jubilee Jamboree', which had taken three years to plan. Originally it was to be a garden party at Harewood House, but the programme swelled to include a fifty-five-minute visit to the set of *Emmerdale*. Then, to the dismay of the Harewoods, the Palace decided to send her to Temple Newsam to receive the Commonwealth baton, which meant she might have to leave before the garden party. In order to match the publicity generated by *Emmerdale*, George Harewood invited Terry Venables, the new manager of Leeds United, to make a surprise appearance at the Garden Party.

The visit was significant due to the years of estrangement Lord Harewood had suffered following his divorce and remarriage in 1967. He had been banned from court for seven years. Since then Patricia, the new Lady Harewood, had handled a difficult situation with enormous dignity. She was never granted official precedence at court,* but she made George Harewood happy. As Alastair Forbes wrote in the *Spectator*, when reviewing his memoirs: 'The name Patricia is repeated at every opportunity, like a recurring Wagnerian love motif.'[11]

---

* A private document is circulated to the Royal Households. It used to emanate from the Duke of Edinburgh's office. Lord Harewood was included. Lady Harewood was not.

The Countess of Harewood by Cecil Beaton

The Queen had met Patricia publicly in Leeds during the Silver Jubilee celebration in 1977 and she had been given a Silver Jubilee medal. For this visit, aware of the Queen's eagle eye, Patricia removed the Sotheby's Duke and Duchess of Windsor sale catalogue and a scurrilous Kitty Kelley book from the shelves. She worried about the royal photos in frames in the Spanish Library, including one of Queen Alexandra signed 'Old Grannie'. As she wrote: 'With George, the Master of Parenthesis and Digression, and the Queen's keen interest in her own family, here was a real danger of upsetting the timetable!'[12]

The press missed the most interesting moment of the day because it happened privately. The Queen's glass-topped Bentley arrived on the dot of twelve fifteen. George bowed and kissed his cousin, then presented Patricia, Mark Lascelles (the erstwhile illegitimate son), his then wife Andrea, and Viscount Lascelles's two eldest children, Emily and Ben. It was Mark's daughter, Charlotte, dressed in lilac, with a cashmere cardigan and a pink rose, her hair crowned with a flower, who did a faultless curtsey and presented the Queen with her bouquet. It must have been a surreal moment for the Lascelles family that the girl, issue of the 1964 baby who had unwittingly caused the ostracism, was to the fore on that memorable day, a moment of reconciliation.

At lunch George gossiped and laughed with the Queen, while

THE GOLDEN JUBILEE, 2002

Patricia covered a multitude of subjects with Prince Philip. After lunch, as the Queen paused by a tapestry, Prince Philip hissed: 'You must get on – we're late.'

The Queen replied: 'Not by *my* watch.'

The pageant itself was spectacular and Terry Venables was such a hit that he had to be rescued from the fans by the police. Lady Harewood concluded:

> It is quite extraordinary the effect the Queen has on people. There is a tremendous amount of nervousness, even with G who has known her all her life, partly because of the fear of things going wrong, but even Ben, aged 23, said that he was suddenly overwhelmed with nerves when he was presented. She is the ultimate professional – after all, having been in the job for fifty years she should be – but what is not evident from a distance is her very real charm, the brilliant blue eyes and the dazzling smile which lights her whole face. She knows every detail of her programme and is quick to set right the slightest waver with muttered but explicit asides to her staff who know exactly what is required and do it.
>
> Prince Philip is in a way almost more remarkable – a very intelligent and effective man who has had to stay two paces behind his wife for most of his life and who, no matter how often his alleged 'gaffes' are quoted, has been an absolute rock of stability for her and for this country. They will be a hard act to follow.*[13]

The Golden Jubilee celebrations left the country happy, but not for long. Things moved so quickly in the media that they were soon obsessed by Paul Burrell, Diana's erstwhile butler, going to court and the Palace making an intervention during the trial.

---

* Lord Harewood last appeared at Windsor in June 2011, for Prince Philip's ninetieth birthday service. With Patricia at his side, he was wheeled into the nave, his eyes now a very pale blue. He died a month later on 11 July aged eighty-eight. The Queen was represented by Prince Michael of Kent at his funeral, and by Princess Alexandra at his memorial service. Patricia lived on at Harewood, loved by the Lascelles family, and died on 4 May 2018, aged ninety-one. I wrote a long obituary of her for the *Daily Telegraph*. The Queen was represented at her funeral by Dame Ingrid Roscoe, Lord Lieutenant of West Yorkshire.

Paul Burrell

Paul Burrell had joined the Waleses' staff in 1987. He considered himself Diana's 'rock' in life, and indeed Sir Christopher Airy, then Private Secretary, described him as consistently loyal. After Diana's death he was co-opted onto her Memorial Fund Committee. On 21 March 1998 he attended a glittering black-tie event in Hollywood with certain stars, which raised £2 million. This transformation from servant to star did not play well with the Establishment. While he hoped he was doing his best to uphold her posthumous interests, they thought the butler was getting above himself. Presently he was dropped.

He was then accused of having stolen over three hundred of her possessions possibly worth £6 million.[14] He had seen her mother destroying many of Diana's papers. He maintained that he had been given a number of the items and that he was holding others on trust. The Spencer family turned against him, and in January 2001 Scotland Yard sent a team to search his house. He went to trial at the Old Bailey on 14 October 2002. It attracted such global attention that *Vanity Fair* sent the legendary Dominick Dunne to cover it.

On the afternoon of 25 October, the Queen and Prince Philip were driven to St Paul's Cathedral for a service to commemorate the victims of terrorist attacks in Bali, the worst in Indonesia's history. Slightly unusually, the Prince of Wales accompanied them. On the way the Queen mentioned that Burrell had told her he had taken certain items into safe-keeping. Prince Charles reported this to the court and, after some deliberation, Burrell walked free.

The press went mad, accusing the Queen of conveniently recovering from amnesia just before Burrell went into the dock. It was suggested that she was perverting the course of justice. Neither the Queen nor anyone at the Palace had had the slightest idea that this would bring the trial to a close.[15] In conclusion the prosecution's case was proving weak, and this was the perfect excuse to wind it up.

Soon afterwards Burrell sold his story to the *Daily Mirror* for £300,000, revealing little of interest. The tabloids turned on him – and other papers speculated as to what he could have said, should have said, or might have said. The saga then moved on to an allegation of homosexual rape within the Prince of Wales's household.

Prince Charles's new Private Secretary, Sir Michael Peat, had been sent over from Buckingham Palace to pull that office into shape. He investigated and while the press screamed that this would be a whitewash, they underestimated his ruthlessness. The police had searched Burrell's house without a warrant. The Wales household loathed Michael Fawcett and there were rumours of financial misconduct though these were not ultimately proved. As the affair subsided, the Queen received seventeen hundred letters of support from members of the general public urging her to take no notice of the tabloids.

In 2003 Burrell further alienated the Royal Household by publishing *A Royal Duty*. In it he claimed that the Queen had been so moved at his departure that she could not say goodbye. In fact he complained about this and was sent a signed photograph about two weeks later. Prince Philip considered suing over the publication of extracts from his letters to Diana, but was advised not to. As his Private Secretary said: 'The ones who really suffer are William and Harry.'[16]

42
RESOLUTION, 2003–7

The British public had been accustomed to seeing pictures of the Queen Mother coming out of hospital. It seemed too soon to see the Queen leave the Edward VII Hospital in London in January 2003, in a grey trouser suit, her hair immaculately done, after an operation on her knee. On that occasion she walked with a stick.

In the summer the Queen went to Westminster Abbey for the fiftieth anniversary of the Coronation. Returning via the Mall, she unveiled a Jubilee Walkway panel, which marked the incorporation of the Mall into the Jubilee Walkway. I had lately taken on the role of Chairman and was excited that the Queen would be at the panel at exactly 11.40 a.m., the moment when the crown had been placed on her head fifty years before. I said so in my short speech, and she gave a slight nod of recognition.

In these later years I gleaned that the Queen did not watch the Stephen Poliakoff television film *The Lost Prince* because it fictionalised the life of her uncle, Prince John, who had died as a teenager in 1919, and that Lord Luce, the Lord Chamberlain, had longed to see Legoland. Having no grandchildren, he suggested a visit with the Queen. They both loved it. He described the Queen as 'the one person he worked for who grew in stature the more he knew her'. He found there was greater enthusiasm for the Queen on engagements in the country rather than London, where people were more restrained. In the wider country there was strength in the grass-roots reaction.[1]

At Trooping the Colour in 2003, the Duke of Edinburgh joined the Queen in her carriage since his horse had retired. He was eighty-two and the Queen was seventy-seven. Earlier that year the Queen told Princess Alexandra over dinner that she wished to give her the Garter, an exceptional honour for a female cousin, respecting her particular years of service. Princess Alexandra wanted to think the offer over, but the Queen said it would be gazetted next day. On the Monday after the Birthday Parade, she installed her. This would not have happened if Princess Margaret had been alive.*

Just before George Bush came on a state visit in November, a *Daily Mirror* journalist secured a job in the Palace by deceit. He published fifteen pages, revealing where the President would stay and the Queen's fondness for Tupperware at breakfast. Piers Morgan, the editor, justified the heist by saying it exposed a major lapse in security.

Since the death of the Queen Mother, the Queen had tended to go for drinks after church with Margaret Rhodes, her cousin, who had a house in the Great Park now that the Queen Mother was no longer at Royal Lodge. When she paid a particularly successful state visit to Paris in April 2004, it was curious to think that some of the ministers she met had not even been born when made her first state visit in 1957.[2] When she attended D-Day anniversary celebrations, it was noticeable that Presidents Chirac and Putin, the Kings of Norway and of the Belgians, and the Queen of the Netherlands arrived by bus, but the Queen came in a motorcade and received unquestionably the biggest cheer of the day.

In July the Queen unveiled the Diana Memorial Fountain in Hyde Park, a curious construction built out of 545 pieces of Cornish granite and aimed 'to reflect Diana's life', the water flowing in two directions and cascading, swirling and bubbling into a calm pool at the bottom. The Spencer family were well represented. The Queen, Prince Philip, Prince Charles, Prince William and Prince Harry arrived in a convoy. The ceremony was not dissimilar to the unveiling of the memorial to Queen Mary at Marlborough House, at which the Windsors had been present – a show of public unity between the Windsors and the Spencers. On leaving the Queen said to Lord Spencer: 'I hope you are satisfied.'

'Yes, Ma'am, very satisfied,' he replied, with a Coburg bow.[3]

The Royal Family lost two more popular members towards the

---

* When Sir Malcolm Ross had reminded her that St Andrew's Day was approaching and it was time to appoint new Knights of the Thistle, the note came back with the answer: 'Says who?'

end of 2004. The Queen occasionally visited Princess Alice, Duchess of Gloucester, as did Princess Alexandra. She was 102 on Christmas Day 2003. By the summer of 2004, she was no longer coming downstairs and in October she began to sink. She died at 10 p.m. on 29 October. The Queen came up from Windsor privately and was present when the coffin was transferred to the small private chapel at Kensington Palace.

Because the Queen was going on another state visit to Germany, court mourning was declared for Saturday and the day of the funeral, which was Friday, 5 November. As happened with Princess Margaret, the coffin was piped down the broad walk, with just a small group in the high street watching the lit hearse emerge. The funeral was at St George's Chapel, after which Princess Alice was buried at Frogmore next to her husband and to the son she lost when he was but thirty years old. She was remembered as the epitome of a perfect princess, who had quietly and diligently undertaken her royal duties, ever supportive of the Queen.

In Germany the Queen attended a concert to raise funds for the restoration of the Frauenkirche in Dresden amid demands in the German newspaper, *Bild*, that she should apologise for wartime bombing. Instead, at the banquet hosted by President Köhler, she spoke of the 'precious' peace that had existed since 1945: 'Stereotypes wither when human contacts flourish, and we should encourage our young people to know more about each other's countries.'[4]

At the time of Princess Alice's funeral, Sir Angus Ogilvy, was in intensive care in St Mary's, Paddington, suffering from cancer. He was occasionally allowed home to Richmond. Following a crisis he was put into Kingston Hospital where his chauffeur visited him, telling him how much he had enjoyed working for him for the past seventeen years. 'Well, I'm not going anywhere,' said Sir Angus. 'We'll have another seventeen years.' But at 3 a.m. the following morning he died. He was seventy-six.

Sir Angus's funeral was also at St George's Chapel. The Queen's wreath, which had been 'Lilibet' for Princess Alice was 'Elizabeth R' for him. James Ogilvy, his son, gave a fine address in which he said that in the forty years he had known his father, he had never heard him say an unkind word about anyone. Among the wreaths were some mauve tulips from Camilla Parker Bowles. The Royal

Family sat near the altar. She sat in the Garter stalls next to the empty Sovereign's stall between the Constable of the Castle and Lady Dunne.

Camilla's attendance at this service, albeit not next to Prince Charles, highlighted the anomaly of her situation. There had been the highly publicised wedding of Lady Tamara Grosvenor and Edward van Cutsem at Chester Cathedral on 6 November, attended by the Queen and many members of the Royal Family, which Prince Charles and Mrs Parker Bowles refused to attend because again they would not be sitting together. Prince Charles made the excuse that he needed to visit soldiers of the Black Watch back from Iraq.*

In the seven years since the death of Diana, Princess of Wales, Camilla Parker Bowles had made some well-managed public appearances, the occasional public meeting with a kiss on the cheek. There were holidays together, and it was known that when in London, she was living with the Prince at Clarence House. Three key figures needed to be convinced that the relationship was permanent: the Queen, the Archbishop of Canterbury and the Prime Minister. The Queen's liberal-minded Private Secretary, Robin Janvrin, felt that time had moved on and that they should marry. The Queen came to accept this. The Archbishop, Rowan Williams, accepted the concept of remarriage and Tony Blair was predictably positive (though he made no reference to it in his memoirs).

On 10 February the forthcoming marriage was announced. She would be styled HRH The Duchess of Cornwall and, as a softener, would not be Queen Consort but Princess Consort. The seemingly impossible was going to happen.

If the Establishment was happy, the media and the general public were divided. From the day of the announcement until the wedding, everything that could go wrong did go wrong. The couple wanted

---

* The van Cutsems had been particularly good to the young Princes when they were left at a loose end by their parents – Prince Charles busy with Camilla, and Diana on her excursions with Dodi Fayed. When they had nowhere to go, they went to the van Cutsems. There had been a falling-out between Camilla and Mrs van Cutsem. On one occasion Mrs van Cutsem had told Prince Charles something he did not wish to hear and he slammed the telephone down, though he later conceded she had been right.

to be married in a civil ceremony at Windsor Castle, but it transpired that meant anyone could get married there. It was moved to the Guildhall in Windsor. There was a media leak that the Queen would not be going to the civil ceremony, at which point the Palace Press Office put out an unhelpful statement that this was because it was 'low key'. There was much talk of 'own goals' being scored by the monarchy. TV programmes such as GMTV called it 'a fiasco'. Patrick Jephson, formerly Private Secretary to the Princess of Wales, said on *Larry King Live* (CNN) that he could detect Camilla 'actively briefing the press now' while Robert Lacey, a writer who moved with the flow, snapped back that Diana had done the same.[5]

Had I been a press secretary 'spinning' this union, I would have pointed out that the Prince of Wales had secured the Protestant succession by producing two sons. From this second marriage there would be no more children. What he sought was companionship for his later years, like so many British men in later-life marriages.

Clarence House wanted to control the service, but the Dean of Windsor took the initiative and told them it must not be a hole-in-the-corner affair. The wedding was set for 8 April. Tony Blair was about to call a General Election, but then, on 2 April, Pope John Paul II died after a long illness, so the election was not called until 5 April. In a frenetic week, it became clear that George Bush would be going to the Pope's funeral, which would clash with the Royal Wedding on 8 April. If that was the day, then the Archbishop of Canterbury would have to go to Rome as would Blair (there being more votes in going to the Pope's funeral than to the wedding).

Prince Charles and Mrs Parker Bowles looked positively forlorn when they attended a Requiem Mass at Westminster Cathedral on 4 April. Prince Rainier of Monaco did not help matters by dying on 6 April, or Prince Ernst of Hanover by going into a coma.

In the end Prince Charles postponed the wedding till the next day (the Saturday – the day of the Grand National). He represented the Queen at the Pope's funeral in Rome, alongside three US Presidents, and even President Mugabe of Zimbabwe, who contrived to shake his hand. Much spinning went on during the week, Deborah, Duchess of Devonshire, telling the world that Charles and Camilla had been steadfast to each other for thirty years, and Jilly Cooper extolling their virtues.

The day of the wedding dawned. The chapel was transformed into a bower of flowers, with blossom trees in Gothic boxes under the organ screen, spring flowers in the Cloisters, daffodils of many varieties and freesias. The Queen arrived, knowing little of the plans since Clarence House had not informed her of the strange guest list or the seating plan in which precedence was thrown out of the window – Garter Knights and Royal Household were seated behind generous sponsors of the Prince's Trust, Mrs Drue Heinz placed in the Prince of Wales's Garter stall ... The Queen came in with Prince Philip and the Dean of Windsor. Prince Philip had his 'crocodile face' on, the jaw set firm, unspeaking, his head looking around. The Queen told the Dean: 'The BBC [pronounced with emphasis - the Bee Bee See] told me I had to be here at two thirty ...'

At the reception, the Queen likened her son's second wedding to finally getting into the winning enclosure. Prince Charles said that he wished his beloved grandmother had been there to share the happy day, though insiders were certain that no such marriage could have happened in her lifetime. The Queen then went off to watch the Grand National.

The interesting aspect of this wedding is that virtually until the day on which it was held Camilla Parker Bowles was treated as the evil mistress. From the moment Prince Charles married her, she became the supportive wife. She was now a member of the Royal Family and the press treated her with respect. It was not long before they found that she had a good effect on Prince Charles. A previously tetchy figure, he was now relaxed. The long sulk was over. The press found the new Duchess of Cornwall pleasant, easygoing, informal, and not at all the villainous person they had created in myth around her. Neither was she vindictive. She could have taken revenge on those who had attacked her. She allowed it all to drift away. It is not possible to think of a single incident when she missed a step since the wedding day. From that day in April 2005, the Royal Family entered a calmer era.

★ ★ ★ ★ ★

Tony Blair won another general election on 5 May 2005. The Queen opened Parliament in state on 17 May. The same afternoon she flew to Canada, arriving in Saskatchewan, and immediately visited the First Nations University of Canada, meeting students from the Montreal Lake Cree Nation, then attended a media reception at the Radisson Plaza Hotel, and even received the Liberal Prime Minister, Paul Martin, in audience. Not many seventy-nine-year-olds undertook such a programme. On the brink of her ninth decade, the Queen's continued steadfastness garnered increasing respect. The inevitable but small band of Republicans, who thought they had nailed the monarchy in 1997, accepted that she was now in an unassailable position.

Relations between Buckingham Palace and Clarence House were still not ideal. Sir Michael Peat had been running that office since 2002 and stayed on until 2011. Sir Malcolm Ross moved there from the Palace in 2006. While he had only ever been called once out of hours while at Buckingham Palace (and that over the death of Diana), he was called endlessly in his new job and retired gratefully in 2008.

At the beginning of 2006 two television programmes were devoted to Rolf Harris painting the Queen. She resisted commenting on portrayals of herself, a wise decision since the results were so variable. 'Interesting' was her safe comment. With Harris's picture, she went further and said 'friendly'. What emerged was the breadth of her conversation as she posed. She spoke of how her Corgis bit the sentries when they stamped their feet, the heat of Sydney, and joked that Canada had had fourteen inches of rain, all in one day, landing on her and on the waiting crowds. When asked if she minded being painted as she got older, her reply was: 'Nah!'[6]

She had been painted by Lucian Freud in 2001, one of the lasting achievements of Robert Fellowes. Freud had been made a Companion of Honour in 1983 and given the Order of Merit in 1993. Negotiations were predictably complicated, but in due course the painter came to a studio set up in St James's Palace and the Queen sat for him. She soon became aware that if he talked, he stopped painting so she remained silent. The portrait came with him for the sittings in a shoe box. It was small and originally showed the Queen in a day dress. It was decided later to add the George IV diadem, which meant an extra panel, making the little portrait look elongated, and there was something uncomfortable about the Queen wearing a circlet with day clothes. She was aware of the significance of sitting to this great artist. 'I think it might be a little bit of history,' she said.[7]

When it was finished, she resisted commenting other than to say: 'Very nice of you to do this. I've very much enjoyed watching you mix your colours.'[8] When Andrew Parker Bowles asked her about it, she said: 'Interesting.' Prince Philip expressed himself more robustly,[9] as did the media. The *Sun's* art critic, Tim Spanton, declared: 'It's a travesty, Your Majesty.' Lord Hindlip superimposed a photograph of the Queen over half of the picture. The two merged perfectly. I have spent long minutes looking at it. Close to, the shading of the face is grim, but seen from a distance it is remarkable.

* * * * *

Between 12 and 16 March 2006 the Queen and the Duke were in Australia, for the Queen to open the XVIII Commonwealth Games. The Queen dazzled like a Christmas tree with her jewels at a dinner for six hundred, and was given a fabulous welcome at the opening ceremony with Dame Kiri Te Kanawa heralding her forthcoming eightieth birthday, singing 'Happy Birthday', leading into the National Anthem. John Howard spoke of the future. As ever her quiet dignity in dealing with the Australians served her well. Given the grim potential alternatives as Head of State, her position looked secure, the heir to the throne's less so.

On 21 April the Queen celebrated her eightieth birthday with a walkabout in Windsor. At first she spent time in a closed Windsor Castle, talking to the residents. Then the great gates opened and the Queen and the Duke came out, she in pink, he in a raincoat. As she did her walkabout, she handed Lady Susan Hussey a mass of cards and flowers, which were carried back to the castle in relays. She walked past the Guildhall and only got into her car near the entrance to the Royal Mews.

While Buckingham Palace was in a relatively good state, Clarence House was not. William Tallon maintained that there were three camps there – those of the Prince of Wales, the Duchess of Cornwall and Michael Fawcett (the last two being the most in tune with each other).[10] The Duchess of Cornwall made an effort with the press.

She would talk to Nicholas Witchell of the BBC, though the Prince of Wales could not bring himself to do so following the incident in 2005 when his remark that he could not stand Witchell had been picked up by a microphone in Klosters. The line in Prince Philip's office was that the heir was 'a loose cannon'.[11]

The other contrast was the Prince's extravagance compared to his mother's modest habits. He liked organic food. She did not, once commenting that she did not want her food eaten by several worms first. She breakfasted with the radio on. At lunch she ate meat or fish, followed by a pudding, cheese and fruit. She often dined off a tray. If alone, the food would be left on a hotplate. She would ring for coffee. If it was a dinner, she would take her dry martini (more or less neat gin) in with her. She never drank wine, and only rarely champagne. Her chef only travelled with her on long tours. She favoured simple food.[12]

On the Saturday evening before her birthday, the Queen gave a dinner party for 120 friends such as the Carringtons, the Wellingtons, Prue Penn and Sir John Johnston. Then on St George's Day, 23 April, she attended a big service at St George's Chapel. The Dean preached a sermon stressing how at times in her reign when she had been attacked she turned the other cheek. At the reception her line was 'It was rather like being at one's own funeral.' To mark the occasion of her eightieth birthday, she appointed the Duke of York and the Earl of Wessex to be Knights of the Garter, Prince Andrew number 997 and Prince Edward number 998.*

The eightieth-birthday souvenirs tended to show her as a little girl or a young woman, possibly because the eightieth-birthday portraits were unsatisfactory. On 15 June there was a huge service at St Paul's Cathedral in which the Archbishop of Canterbury defined the Queen as a force for good. It was clear that we were living in a golden age that would not last for ever. We should relish every minute of it.

After becoming an octogenarian, the Queen allowed herself a few privileges and luxuries. She chartered a yacht and took her

---

* On pointing this out to Prince Edward that day, I dropped the idea that maybe Prince William should be the thousandth Knight. This idea was taken 'right to the top'. And it happened. Prince Andrew's Garter was rescinded in 2025.

family on a Western Isles cruise that summer, one of her great joys being to have her family with her. When she went to America in May 2007, she achieved a lifetime ambition by attending the Kentucky Derby, with her friends the Farishes.* For a monarch who had virtually never gone abroad for her own pleasure, it was a treat to attach that to an official visit. The only other times she had done anything similar was to visit Guy de Rothschild at Ferrières in 1967 to see the stud, witnessing her horse, Highclere, win the Prix de Diane in 1974, and some stays in Kentucky to explore the studs.

★ ★ ★ ★ ★

The Queen retained her stalwart ladies in waiting such as Lady Susan Hussey and Mary Morrison. She did not like her favoured staff to retire. Inevitably death swept some away. Sir John Miller, the former Crown Equerry, died on 17 May 2006, aged eighty-seven. Sir John Johnston, former Comptroller at the Lord Chamberlain's Office, died on 10 September aged eighty-four. For many years the Johnstons had lived at Adelaide Cottage, and during the Christmas holidays when the Royal Family was at Windsor *en masse* they provided a home from home for those who found the Christmas atmosphere stifling. When he retired, the Johnstons moved to Studio Cottage behind Cumberland Lodge in the Great Park. The Queen frequently visited them, and continued to visit Sir John after his wife's death in 1995. Sir Edward Ford, formerly the Queen's Assistant Private Secretary, died aged ninety-four on 19 November. The Queen and the Duke attended all three memorial services in person, all at the Guards Chapel, a testament to the esteem in which the Queen held them.

In September 2007 Robin Janvrin retired as Private Secretary, giving way to Christopher Geidt. Now the Queen was being advised by a team of the same age or younger than her own children. Around the time of the takeover, Samantha Cohen, the Queen's Press Secretary, gave a party for journalists, serving them champagne and delicious canapés. The new Press Office policy of entertaining journalists, good and bad, to keep them on side was effective.

---

* William Stamps Farish III (b. 1939), and his wife, the former Sarah Sharp.

The main preoccupation of the Royal Family in the early part of 2007 was the apparent split in the relationship between Prince William and Catherine Middleton, his girlfriend from St Andrews, where they were both at the university, just as the world speculated (as usual) that they were about to get married. The split might have been genuine, or perhaps a ruse to get the press off their backs for a while. The press called Catherine Middleton 'Waity Katy' and was disparaging about her mother. Her existence was not much easier than Diana's had been. At times she had to crouch on the floor of taxis to avoid photographers.

Prince Harry's problem was that he wanted to serve in Iraq, but when his presence was detected there, he was withdrawn He was given a desk job in Alberta, Canada, about as far from Iraq as is conceivable.

Tony Blair was under considerable attack during the early months of 2007, especially following the Iraq war. In 2006 he had hung on as Prime Minister despite the worst council elections for Labour since 1968. The Conservatives had gained 131 seats and Labour lost 182, a serious kick in the teeth for the Prime Minister. He finally stepped down on 27 June, at which point Gordon Brown became Prime Minister.

Cherie Blair had displayed a reluctance to curtsey. The Queen had been known to say: 'I can see her knees stiffening when I come into the room,' and the Queen Mother had been overheard in the background: 'Stiff knees, stiff knees.' After the farewell audience Cherie Blair came down from the farewell audience saying: 'And I curtseyed to her.' The Queen had won in the end.[13]

43
CHALLENGING TIMES, 2007–11

Gordon Brown

In his own words, Gordon Brown's 'path to No. 10 ... had been anything other than smooth'.[1] Arriving at the Palace, he had 'a congenial and businesslike conversation about the work that lay ahead',[2] and told the Queen he was about to appoint a raft of new Privy Counsellors. He arrived in the Chancellor's Vauxhall. He left in the prime ministerial Jaguar.

Brown's private persona was different from that perceived by the public. He was thought to be surly and disagreeable, but those who knew him found him engaging. He inherited something of a poisoned chalice from Tony Blair, with bad results in council elections, but was set to lead his party into the next election. When he stayed with the Queen at Balmoral in August 2009, he had his traditional audience with her. She came out saying: 'I've been all over the world.' Guests were not impressed when an architect staying asked the Browns if they were likely to conceive a child during their visit, a reference to Cherie Blair having disclosed in her memoirs that on her 1999 visit she had left her 'contraceptive equipment' at home.[3]

★ ★ ★ ★ ★

On the tenth anniversary of Diana's death, 31 August 2007, Princes William and Harry arranged a memorial service in the Guards Chapel. Prince Charles wanted the Duchess of Cornwall to attend, but she did not wish to divert attention from Diana. The BBC had Michael Cole on BBC *Breakfast*, spinning for Mohamed Fayed, telling the world that Diana's name had been blackened so that Prince Charles could marry his mistress. Fayed was not invited to this service. The Prince of Wales was greeted in silence by the waiting crowds, though the Queen and Prince Philip, who came down by overnight train from Scotland, were greeted with a loud cheer. The Queen was described as 'majestic, old, small, beautifully dressed in sharp purple', Prince Philip as 'lean, gnarled and old' while Prince Charles looked 'grey and pained of feature'.[4] After the service the Queen and the Duke flew back to Scotland.

Prince Harry's eulogy was a welcome contrast to Lord Spencer's in the Abbey. He spoke of how he and William could separate life into two parts – having both parents and then the ten years with no mother. He commended his mother's love and laughter and included a benign reference to his father: 'She, like our father, was determined to provide us with a stable and secure childhood.' And he ended: 'Put simply, she made us and so many other people happy. May this be the way that she is remembered.'[5] The Bishop of London delivered a stern sermon stating it was time that those who used the Princess's name for their mischief to desist. 'Let it end here,' he said.[6]

The long-delayed inquest into the death of Diana lasted from October 2007 until April 2008 and saw Fayed launching outrageous accusations that Dodi and Diana had been 'murdered by the British Royal Family', that Prince Philip was related to Frankenstein and a Nazi. After six months, the expenditure of about £10 million and the calling of 252 witnesses (though not the Duke of Edinburgh in person), the verdict finally settled on 'unlawful killing' – the result of gross negligence by the drunken chauffeur, Henri Paul, exacerbated by the pursuit of paparazzi photographers. Prince William and Prince Harry thanked the jurors for their decision. Fayed was warned by Gordon Brown that enough was enough. Fayed stated: 'I'm sure the Princes are blessing in their deep heart what I am doing to discover the truth.'[7] The Princes thought no such thing.

★ ★ ★ ★ ★

The Queen and Prince Philip marked their sixtieth wedding anniversary with a service in Westminster Abbey, celebrated the day before, on 19 November. They were on their way to a Commonwealth

Heads of Government Meeting in Uganda. Prince Philip was consulted about where they might possibly break the journey. Anxious not to explain why, he suggested Malta, though he knew the effect this would have – he and the Queen would be in the place where they were happiest on such a significant anniversary.*

Some half-million Ugandans came out to welcome the Queen when she arrived for the conference – one of the largest crowds to gather in the country's history. She was hailed in local newspapers as 'one of the most glamorous women in the world'.[8] Don McKinnon pulled off a coup by getting Prince Charles invited. He had not been wanted in Malta in 2005. It was essential to involve him, especially since at that time it was by no means certain that he would succeed his mother as Head of the Commonwealth.

On 22 December the Queen became the longest-lived British monarch at eighty-one years and 243 days. A few days before, she had acquired another grandson, James, Viscount Severn, second child of the Wessexes, born on 17 December.

In March 2008 the Queen visited Northern Ireland, rather nervous at the prospect, and soon afterwards received President Nicolas Sarkozy of France on a state visit to Windsor. The First Lady, Carla Bruni,† was Sarkozy's third wife, and more glamorous than the wives of some earlier Presidents, such as Yvonne de Gaulle. Her interesting career included dating Eric Clapton and Mick Jagger.

Prince Philip's Health

Prince Philip drove out with his carriage every day when he was free to do so. He remained surprisingly fit for a man of eighty-six, but in April 2008 was packed off to hospital with a chest infection,

---

* Viewers of ITN will recall that visit as the occasion when a quizzical Prince Philip materialised behind the presenter, Romilly Weeks, as she was in mid-flow, telling the world that this was 'such a romantic gesture'. 'Is it?' he asked, with a broad smile.

† Carla Bruni (b. 1967), met the President in November 2007 and married him the following February. She gave birth to a daughter in 2011, said to be the only time a French President has 'publicly' fathered a child while in office.

missing the Edmund Hillary memorial service.* He came out saying: 'I think they just wanted me out of the castle.'⁹ He began to look a bit wizened. In October 2004 he had appeared at St James's Palace with a shiner, having fallen in his bath and landed his thumb in the eye. His friends conceded that he was slowing down, though he was still either helpful and positive or snappily dismissive. Having been cooperative in a film about Windsor Castle with Robert Hardman, he was 'in a particularly tiresome mood' when Trevor McDonald tried to interview him at Wood Farm, near Sandringham. Sir Trevor was more of an autocue man† and he was ill at ease with the Duke. An entertaining part of the film was a drive about the estate, with the Duke at the wheel. Sir Trevor looked nervous, with reason as the lanes round Wolverton were not easy. Prince Philip later claimed: 'I was as good as gold.'¹⁰

Prince Philip did as he pleased. When bidden to read the lesson in St George's Chapel on St George's Day 2008, he read only part of it. The Queen was devoted to Prince Philip, but some found her more relaxed when he was not around.

I liked his ways. I had published a book on St George's Chapel to which he had contributed the foreword. He asked how it was going. When I said it was early days and I didn't know, he barked: 'Well, either it is or it isn't.'¹¹ He asked again on 7 June. I said the reaction had been 100 per cent positive but it was not on the College of St George website. 'You should get on to Michael Hobbs,' he said. I told him I had been so on to Michael Hobbs that he no longer replied to my emails. A few days later it was up on the College website.

To mark the 660th anniversary of the founding of the Order of the Garter, the Queen appointed three new Knights, Lord Luce as 999, Sir Thomas Dunne as 1,001, and neatly sandwiched between

---

* It says much for their attention to detail that the Queen and the Duke discussed where the Military Knights would stand, which way round the Garter banner would be laid on the nave altar and if the Queen would be able to see it when the Dean gave the blessing. Prince Philip missed a touching moment: as the 'Karanga' was sung, a lark began to sing near the North Door.

† When fronting Prince Edward's wedding in 1999, he asked the production team: 'Could I have an autocue? I'm quite well paid for reading autocues.'

them, Prince William as the thousandth Knight of the Garter since its creation in 1348. The ceremony on 16 June 2008 produced Catherine Middleton, prominent at an official engagement for the first time. She arrived with Prince Harry and Helen Asprey, from the Prince of Wales's office, to watch the procession come down the hill. She was 'slim, well dressed and with porcelain features – discreet, modest, not shy'. Some who knew her described her as having great sex appeal, others as 'purposeful'. Prince William looked splendid in his Garter robes, tall and elegant, not overpowered by them as some are. He gave Catherine 'such a sweet smile'.[12]

St George's Chapel was where Peter Phillips, son of the Princess Royal, married Autumn Kelly on 17 May that year, a union that gave them two daughters, Savannah (born in 2010) and Isla (born in 2012), making the Queen a great-grandmother. The couple separated in 2019.

Prince Charles reached the age of sixty on 14 November. There was a party at Buckingham Palace, with many royal guests from Europe and the President of Afghanistan. One was Prince Karl of Hesse, Prince Philip's nephew. Next day he lunched with the Queen and Prince Philip, especially keen to see his uncle, since he was now eighty-seven, the age at which his mother, Princess George, had died. He found him 'very shrunk and his eyes deep'. Prince Karl regretted that the Charles and Diana marriage had not lasted. He and his family used to write to 'Char-Di' as he called them. He said of the Queen and Prince Philip: 'They too had their problems, but they persisted.'[13] The Queen included references to Prince Charles in her Christmas broadcast this year:

> I think we have a huge amount to learn from individuals such as these. And what I believe many of us share with them is a source of strength and peace of mind in our families and friends. Indeed, Prince Philip and I can reflect on the blessing, comfort and support we have gained from our own family in this special year for our son, The Prince of Wales.
>
> Sixty years ago, he was baptised here in the Music Room at Buckingham Palace. As parents and grandparents, we feel great pride in seeing our family make their own unique contributions to society.

Through his charities, The Prince of Wales has worked to support young people and other causes for the benefit of the wider community, and now his sons are following in his footsteps.

2009

In April 2009 US President and Mrs Obama arrived on a state visit to Britain, memorable for Michele Obama putting her arm round the Queen, which was considered controversial. Both ladies had been examining their high heels and therefore looking down. When they stood up it was an involuntary gesture of support.

There was a chance to observe and talk to the Queen at the Castle of Mey party at the Goring Hotel on 19 May. This was an annual get-together for members of the Royal Family, the Queen Mother's Household, staff and supporters of the trust that looked after her former home in the north of Scotland. On several occasions the Queen attended it:

> The Queen arrived, dressed in dark purple – and alone. There were plenty of ladies in waiting around, but she didn't have one in tow. Baroness Thatcher arrived in almost shocking pink. Liza Anson said that it was very sad that she didn't know what was going on. I said: 'But she curtseyed to the Queen, so she did know who she was.' Liza said: 'I said in a loud voice: The Queen.'
>
> I'm not quite sure how it happened – I didn't plant myself in a four-hander conversation with the Queen, Andrew Parker Bowles and Serena Balfour. She shook hands with all of us. The Brigadier began by asking the Queen about her horses – how many she had at Newmarket. The Queen answered him, hadn't huge news to impart, so I ventured: 'But you had success at the Windsor Horse Show, Ma'am,' and she spoke of that, the Brigadier saying: 'The Princess Royal had a very wet evening, but yours was fine …' The Queen said hers indeed was and affirmed that the King's Troop had done their bit well, how in one turn, the horses had to go down and the riders too. She had enjoyed seeing that in daylight the next day.
>
> Then she turned to me and asked: 'And how are your things in

the ground going?' So I was able to tell her about the new 60 km route – the Jubilee Greenway. 'And the Duke of Gloucester came the other day on a bicycle to see it.' This got the full grand piano smile. 'On a bicycle? How most unusual!' She said she had been to the Olympic site at the very beginning and someone had suggested that this would be a good time to see it again. I was able to say: 'It's like the last scene in a James Bond film – trucks whizzing about.' And that I thoroughly supported that idea. The Queen seemed convinced that a visit soon would be a good idea. [She went on 3 November.]

She looked wonderful – that neat helmet of white hair, the rich purple dress, the small hands, the haze of down on her cheeks, which I hadn't noticed before, which should make her more photogenic. She was so alert and bright – and she stayed for ages. Andrew Parker Bowles said that it was 'immensely flattering' that she asked about the Walkway discs.[14]

As 2009 drew to a close and the Royal Family retreated to Sandringham, the Queen's spokesman made it clear that paparazzi photographs would not be tolerated, and if need be there would be prosecutions if the press's own guidelines were broken.

The Queen's public standing was good. Matthew Parris assessed her, claiming not to be a monarchist, but an 'Elizabethist'. He defined her well-known qualities as being hard-working, conscientious, well-judged and steadfast, and to these he added her reserve, something unusual in an age when people emoted in public. 'No tears, no confessions, not even much public laughter – and no interviews.' He praised her ability to combine privacy with such a public role. And then he wondered if she enjoyed being a monarch: 'The Queen rules because she must: it is her duty, and sometimes a painful one. I admire this more than I can say.'[15]

★ ★ ★ ★ ★

A few days after Easter, in April 2010, the United Kingdom was in the throes of another General Election campaign. This time there were televised debates with the party leaders, Gordon Brown, David Cameron and Nick Clegg. Alastair Stewart hosted the first on 15

April, during which Brown looked 'dour and satanic', Cameron 'nervy and waxy-looking' and Clegg 'cocky'. 'I agree with Nick,' became the catchphrase of the night. Brown tried to present himself as 'the experienced old hand at politics, a safe pair of hands, et cetera, whereas of course we all know that he has completely ruined the economy and presided over the worst recession in modern times'. Clegg was generally thought to have acquitted himself best. Later in the evening, Peter Mandelson was filmed dancing with a lady of seventy-six in Huddersfield 'trying to look as though he was enjoying himself'.[16] In the run-up to the election a microphone still attached to Gordon Brown in his car caught him describing a Mrs Duffy as 'a bigoted woman'.*[17]

Election Day arrived on 6 May. It was soon clear that Gordon Brown had lost but that Cameron had not won an outright majority. The Conservatives won 306 seats, Labour 258, and the Liberals 57. In the ensuing days, Cameron formed a coalition with the Liberals, and on 11 May Gordon Brown was finally persuaded to concede defeat and resign. He went to the Palace with his wife and two sons. When the Queen gave him her signed photograph, four-year-old Fraser exclaimed: 'It's the Queen!' She was taken aback: 'But I'm the Queen. I'm the Queen.' They all laughed and the Browns left.[18]

David Cameron

The Queen, whose first Prime Minister had been born in 1874, was now served by a man born in 1964. Had she noticed him? He once played a rabbit in a school play at Heatherdown, alongside Prince Edward. He recalled reading the lesson in front of her, and swearing when he forgot to say: 'Thanks be to God.'[19] At his first meeting as Prime Minister, he said he would like to form a government but that he 'wasn't entirely sure what kind of government that would be'.[20]

On 25 May the Queen opened the new Parliament, memorable for a soldier in the Blues and Royals losing his helmet. The Queen

---

* *The Week* said that BIGOT now stood for 'Brown is going on Thursday'.

came to another Castle of Mey party the same evening and I could not resist asking her if she had noticed him. 'The Queen perked up at once and, of course, knew all about him. She told the story of how it had fallen off but been retrieved by "an idiotic policeman" ...'[21]

After many years, on 16 November Prince William and Catherine Middleton announced their engagement. He had finally proposed while they were on holiday in Kenya the previous month. The wedding had important constitutional implications because it could – and indeed soon did – produce another generation in the House of Windsor.

2011

Prince Philip was on form as he headed towards his ninetieth birthday. He hosted a lunch for Knights Grand Cross of the Order of the British Empire at St James's Palace on 23 February. The idea for this came from a businessman greatly promoted by Margaret Thatcher: Sir Cyril Taylor had been made a GBE. Taylor rose to make a speech, and it looked as though he was clutching seventeen pages of notes. It began 'Prince Philip is half Greek and half Danish.' Prince Philip was having none of it. 'Oh, sit down,' he said, not once but twice, and in the end Taylor gave up.[22]

The Royal Wedding took place at Westminster Abbey on 29 April. The world's media descended on London.* The last time that the man in the street somewhere distantly abroad had focused on Prince William would have been in September 1997 when he was a forlorn teenager following his mother's coffin. He did not go off the rails. He coped. He did well at school and at university. He was not entering a dynastic marriage. He had found Kate, now to be called Catherine. It was a love match. They had had nine years in which to get to know each other, there had been the short split,

---

* I was up against Graham Smith, of Republic, in one television programme. He said that he now had seven thousand members. I was cut off before I was able to point out that he was therefore matched man for man in the numbers of foreign journalists who came to England to cover the wedding.

and they had come back together again. This was a good story, however anyone looked at it. Fortunately, in 2010, there was a more restrained response to this wedding. It was not over-hyped as the Wales and York weddings had been.

The Queen and Prince Philip were both in good health and were in the Abbey. Prince William ran it all well. He fixed the guest list, nothing leaked from any of the brides' relations. The journalists realised that no scoops were coming, so they, too, relaxed and enjoyed it. On the day Carole Middleton, the bride's mother, stepped out of the car, gave a discreet wave to the media and went straight in. She judged that to perfection. She told the Dean of Westminster she had often heard that when you are really nervous your knees knock together. She had not realised it actually happened.

Catherine, the bride, looked stunning in her Catherine Walker bridal gown and was well and memorably supported by her sister Pippa Middleton, as head bridesmaid. Catherine's dyslexic brother learned the Lesson by heart and delivered it well. More people watched the ceremony than that of any previous wedding, due to the proliferation of the internet – Facebook, Twitter, YouTube, and the fact that there were many more televisions in China.

The following weekend Michael Middleton, father of the new Duchess of Cambridge, was photographed on his ride-on mower at his home, mowing the lawn as if nothing had happened. When it was all over, Dame Frances Campbell-Preston, who had been lady in waiting to the Queen Mother, wrote to Jamie Lowther-Pinkerton, Prince William's Private Secretary, to say how splendid the day had been. He wrote back to say that the transparent radiance of the young couple had permeated the whole occasion. The same, alas, could not have been said after the 1981 Royal Wedding.

It was said by insiders that the Queen had never looked happier. As she headed towards her Diamond Jubilee, she saw her young grandson marrying the girl of his choice.

★ ★ ★ ★ ★

Between 17 and 20 May the Queen paid her ground-breaking state visit to Ireland at the invitation of the President, Mary McAleese, the first such visit since George V's in 1911. The visit was only possible following the signing of the Good Friday Agreement, one of Tony Blair's great achievements. It was designed to recognise good relations between the United Kingdom and the Republic of Ireland. There were bomb threats in advance of the visit so security was tight – the largest operation in the history of the Republic.

David Cameron was immensely impressed by the Queen going to Ireland, though she told him: 'All I did was decide it was time for a visit.'[23] Lord Mountbatten had been assassinated by the IRA. The Queen took the same line as Mountbatten's daughter, Patricia. They put personal feelings aside. In an interview on *Woman's Hour* Countess Mountbatten had spoken of the release of the man who had murdered her father: 'I didn't feel that the twenty years he had been sentenced to was a day too long for the horror of killing old people and children, but I did feel that if letting him go a year early was going to advance the peace process, that was the thing that really mattered because it was so desperately important to try and get peace back into Ireland in a proper way.'[24]

The Queen stayed at Farmleigh, the state guest house in Phoenix Park. Among her engagements she visited the Garden of Remembrance, the National War Memorial Gardens, and met leaders of the Ulster Defence Association. She went to Croke Park sports stadium, where football spectators had been shot by the British Army in 1920. The highlight was the dinner at Dublin Castle, at which the Queen spoke some words in Gaelic. President McAleese responded by saying, 'Wow,' three times. On the third day, she was able to visit some racing studs and went to a party at the National Convention Centre in Dublin at which the Chieftains and others performed. The last day included a visit to the English Market in Cork at which she made an unscheduled walkabout along the Grand Parade.

Two important events followed. When the Queen went to Belfast in June 2012, she came face to face with Martin McGuinness, and shook his hand. It was a remarkable moment: a man formerly of the Provisional IRA, who had been in prison for six months in 1973 for possessing 110 kilos of explosives and five thousand rounds of ammunition, not forgetting the IRA's involvement in the murder of Lord Mountbatten.

The second event was the state visit of the President of Ireland, when Michael Higgins came to Windsor Castle in April 2014. That was far from a routine visit. The speech was particularly sensitive. It was not a run-of-the-mill Foreign Office speech about better trade relations. Words like 'reconciliation' could not be used as that implied union between the Republic and Northern Ireland, and there could not even be capital letters for certain words. What the Queen had said was that the British and Irish were 'neighbours and friends'. Crucially she said: 'There is a balance to be struck between what has happened and cannot be changed and looking forward to what could happen if we have the will and the determination to shape it ... We are walking together towards a brighter and more settled future. We shall remember our past but we shall no longer allow our past to ensnare our future. This is the greatest gift we can give to succeeding generations.'[25] With these words she took a step to moving things forward diplomatically. Martin McGuinness was again present.

The next day the Queen and the Duke came to St George's Chapel to celebrate the 150th anniversary of the Royal College of Organists. Edward Young, her Assistant Private Secretary, said they were very relaxed and in no hurry to go home. He explained that the speeches at the state banquet the night before had gone particularly well. By that time the Queen was nearly eighty-eight and the Duke nearly ninety-three. They were still doing their bit for Britain.[26]

★ ★ ★ ★ ★

Prince Philip reached the age of ninety on 10 June 2011. The day itself was business as usual, a meeting with an organisation for the deaf, and in the evening the Colonels' Conference, followed by the traditional dinner with the Colonels of the various Guards regiments. Reluctantly, Prince Philip took part in two documentaries. ITN showed contributions from Princess Anne, King Constantine of Greece, Countess Mountbatten and a few others (including me), and he was interviewed by Alan Titchmarsh (the Duke 'refusing to answer his questions and only becoming animated when he spoke of his annoyance at the decommissioning of the Royal Yacht Britannia').[27] The BBC interview was even worse, conducted by

The Queen and Prince Philip with their children at Buckingham Palace, after the Coronation, 2 June 1953. Their Christmas card for that year

The Queen and Prince Philip at a reception for Commonwealth guests in the Hague during the State Visit to Queen Juliana, 26 March 1958. Also in the photo: Begum Ra'ana Liaquat Ali Khan (who owned the photograph) (to the left), the author's aunt, Joan Vickers, MP (behind the Queen) and the British Ambassador, Sir Paul Mason (to the right)

The Queen with Margaret Thatcher and her lady in waiting Mary Morrison at Balmoral, photographed by Andrew Parker Bowles

The Queen at the polo with Colonel Richard Watt (left) and Sir John Miller, the Crown Equerry, May 1982. Taken by the author

Two photos of the Queen with one of her horses at Balmoral.
Taken by Andrew Parker Bowles

The Queen with the author at the Great Children's Party in Hyde Park, 30 May 1979

Arthur Vickers (aged 3) presenting flowers to the Queen after the unveiling of a Jubilee Walkway panel in the City of London, in Golden Jubilee year, 2002

The Queen in Cochin,
Southern India, October 1997.
Two photos by the author

The Queen in the Garter procession at Windsor in June 2009, taken by George Vickers, then aged 8

The Queen with the author, Arthur, Alice and George Vickers in Parliament Square after the Diamond Wedding Service, 19 November 2007

The Queen with the author in the garden of Buckingham Palace, before the unveiling of a Commonwealth Walkway panel to mark CHOGM in London, April 2018

The Queen waiting to meet Liz Truss as her newest and final Prime Minister at Balmoral, 6 September 2022

Terry Pendry with Emma, the Queen's pony, paying their respects as the cortège arrived in Windsor Castle for the funeral and committal, 19 September 2022

Fiona Bruce. He told her in no uncertain terms that, 'since you ask', he was cross at being interviewed and only did so because 'there was a certain inevitability about it'.[28]

Prince Philip's birthday was celebrated with a service of thanksgiving at St George's Chapel. His own relations made a huge effort to come, some from as far afield as Canada, because Prince Philip had been exceptionally generous to them over the years, invariably with no fuss. They particularly relished the occasion because he was there with them. So often those royal gatherings were for a funeral. This was a subtle chance to say thank you. The Queen gave a lunch party for 103, almost all of them relations.

On 30 July Zara Phillips, the Princess Royal's daughter, married Mike Tindall, the former rugby union player, who had seventy-five caps to his name and had played in the English squad that won the World Cup in 2003. That injected an interesting new element into the Queen's life. He was a very different figure to have at the table from men such as 'Master', the old Duke of Beaufort, or the Duke of Norfolk, who had peopled her world in the early days of her reign.

The Queen's last visit to Australia was in October 2011. She and Prince Philip made a number of visits to different cities, including Canberra, Brisbane, Melbourne and Perth. Where before there had been demands for a republic, on this trip Julia Gillard, the Prime Minister, hailed her as 'a vital constitutional part of Australian democracy'. The Queen always worried before such trips, and even the Royal Household was concerned as to how she would be received.[29] One of the reasons for the success was that the Queen and Prince Philip carried out a rigorous programme at an age when many elderly Australians were languishing in retirement homes.

The year ended on a concerning note. On 23 December Prince Philip was airlifted from Sandringham to Royal Papworth Hospital, Cambridge, with chest pains. He underwent a successful coronary angioplasty and the replacement of a stent. He spent four nights in hospital, during which time the Queen took a helicopter flight of seventy miles to see him. Normally the Royal Family were not great hospital visitors, so her visit indicated particular concern that she might lose him. Presently he was declared out of danger, but the Queen would not let him leave hospital in time for the Boxing Day shoot, telling him firmly: 'I need you for the Diamond Jubilee.'[30] He was discharged on 27 December. Within five days he was carriage-driving in the morning and shooting hares in the afternoon.[31]

Prince Philip's heart scare was a wake-up call. It was a warning that the glorious life-long show could not last for ever. On the other hand those who had known the Queen Mother at eighty-six said the Queen was better at the same age, and that it might be wise to look beyond the Diamond Jubilee and prepare for a seventieth anniversary – a Platinum Jubilee.

44

THE DIAMOND JUBILEE, 2012

There were fewer concerns about the Diamond Jubilee than there had been about the Golden. Life was calmer and it was appreciated that a sixty-year reign was a remarkable achievement. Princess Anne said that the main concern of the Royal Family was to alleviate the burden placed on the Queen and Prince Philip, she being eighty-six that year and he ninety-one, and not to over-tire them. The Queen and the Duke did not travel overseas, but the rest of them did. Princess Anne went to South Africa, Mozambique (a new member of the Commonwealth) and Zambia.

Accession Day arrived. The next day the Queen came down to London from Sandringham and the Duke the following Monday. One of the Queen's first engagements was to open the Jubilee Greenway outside Buckingham Palace on 29 February. When we at the Jubilee Walkway Trust realised that the Diamond Jubilee would coincide with the London Olympic Games, we devised a sixty-kilometre route round London. I had informed Buckingham Palace of this plan some two years before. They said it was too early to make decisions, but my letter would go 'into the file'. I decided to treat that as a 'yes' and we went ahead on the grounds that, once completed, it would be accepted.

I thought we had the necessary funds and wrote accordingly to the Palace. A letter came back saying that the Queen was pleased to hear that the necessary funding was in place. As it happens, it was not. But Jim Walker, Director of the Walkway Trust, showed that letter to Transport for London, and they produced £800,000 since they wished to encourage walking in London. The central disc was placed in front of the main gates of Buckingham Palace.

The Changing of the Guard was specially delayed for the ceremony. The Duke of Gloucester received the Queen and Prince Philip, as

Patron of the Trust. Prince Philip was in particularly combative mood, declaring in no uncertain terms that the horses would shy, and that we had made the marker square when it should have been round. I remembered Sir James Robertson's letter about how he hated Chairmen who delivered slick speeches without knowing what was going on. His parting thrust was: 'So – are you going to walk it?' I replied that I had walked every inch of it (twice as it happens) and at that point a wry grin crossed his face. He was satisfied.*

On 20 March the Queen delivered a speech to the Lords and Commons in Westminster. The assembled guests were amused when she said that 'at the last count' she had had 'the pleasurable duty of treating with twelve Prime Ministers'. Later, with a confident lilt in her voice, she said: 'The happy relationship I have enjoyed with Parliament has extended well beyond the more than three and a half thousand Bills I have signed into law.' She made it sound as if she had enjoyed every minute. She left her audience in no doubt that she intended to carry on:

> We are reminded here of our past, of the continuity of our national story and the virtues of resilience, ingenuity and tolerance which created it. I have been privileged to witness some of that history and, with the support of my family, rededicate myself to the service of our great country and its people now and in the years to come.[1]

The theme of service was stressed in St George's Chapel on 30 March at a service to mark the tenth anniversary of the deaths of the Queen Mother and Princess Margaret. The Queen was there with most of the Royal Family, relations from the Strathmore side, family, Household and staff, and some friends. The erstwhile swains of Princess Margaret were now white-haired old men in suits; Roddy Llewellyn was on crutches. The immediate family paid their respects at the King George VI Memorial Chapel.

---

* The other initiative of the Walkway Trust was to get Peter Beales to grow a special Platinum Jubilee rose, for the Chelsea Flower Show. It won a gold medal. Special Jubilee Walkway frames were made for the stand. As a further postscript, Edward Young, the Queen's Assistant Private Secretary, said later: 'The Queen being the Queen was taking a great interest in the disc.'

THE DIAMOND JUBILEE, 2012

A special feature of this Jubilee was the lunch for twenty other kings, queens and reigning princes at Windsor Castle on 17 May, among them former monarchs such as King Michael of Romania, who had first become king in July 1927. Not for the first time, Queen Sofia of Spain was advised not to come due to an ongoing row about Gibraltar. In the past, a visit to or from Japan would have involved weeks by sea, but Emperor Akihito and his wife were able to fly in for the lunch. The Queen sat between King Michael and King Simeon of the Bulgarians for the group photograph. King Michael reminded the Queen that he had given 'little Princess Elizabeth' some Romanian dolls when he came over for the 1937 Coronation. 'How nice to be called Little Princess Elizabeth,' said the Queen.[2]

The next day the Armed Forces Parade and Muster took place at Windsor: 2,500 armed forces marched past the Queen and the Duke of Edinburgh in the quadrangle of the castle and a great procession arrived in the arena where the Windsor Horse Show was staged. Members of the Royal Family, foreign monarchs, the troops and Royal Company of Archers, Gentlemen at Arms and Yeomen of the Guard were all on parade. Tears came into the Queen's eyes at the flypast with '60' and 'EIIR' in the sky. A few days later, Prince Philip complained that he had been unable to see the flypast due to a canopy. He said: 'They did a 60 – then an ER – they couldn't afford EIIR' (but they did – I checked). 'I asked them what they were going to do next. They said they were going to do a P!' He clearly thought that was highly entertaining.[3]

On 23 May the Queen and many members of the Royal Family attended a huge reception at the Royal Academy so that she could meet artists, musicians, actors and authors. Prince Philip was in combative mood again following the St George's House lecture. He walked like a man of forty, his suit was sharp, his shoes sparkled, his shirt well pressed. His face was bronzed but his eyes bloodshot and his voice a little falsetto. He was explaining that they had not wanted the *Gloriana* barge, given them by Lord Sterling. Nor did he want a new royal train or a new royal yacht. The River Pageant, arranged by Lord Salisbury, was looming. Prince Philip said he hoped for a gale on the day. He was not to be disappointed.

The River Pageant took place on the day after the Derby. The day dawned misty, with rain and soon turned into a bitterly cold and wet day, making it a trial for participants and spectators alike. Although a magnificent idea, which inspired great initiative in the many boat owners who took part, it was not an unqualified success. Besides the vile weather, the BBC relied on ill-informed commentators who played it as a light affair, ignoring the extraordinary work put in by so many for that day. However, it was a great sight, especially at first:

> The Queen and the Duke of Edinburgh embarked in the Royal Barge of *Britannia* to go downstream from Chelsea Harbour, the Queen in white, the Duke in full dress as Admiral of the Fleet. At 2.45 the great Pageant was underway. It was Canaletto twenty-first-century-style. Suddenly the great bells were ringing, beautiful *Gloriana* was being rowed by the likes of Matthew Pinsent and Steve Redgrave – the Heralds were aboard *Connaught*. There were any number of oarsmen and rowing boats and then the boats carrying the flags of the Commonwealth countries – a glorious sight.
>
> The Queen watched these come past – then *Spirit of Chartwell* moved centre river. It was vast and magnificent – very moving. But (wisely) neither the Queen nor the Duke sat in the grand thrones specially made for them.*⁴

Havengore (which had carried Churchill's body upstream after his funeral) came by, followed by a vast, if more disparate procession of motor boats. The pageant continued until six o'clock, by which time there was a downpour. A man tweeted a radio programme: 'Thank you for being our Queen for sixty years. Your reward is to stand in the rain for four hours.'⁵ Tower Bridge was opened and a choir of girls sang beautifully, drenched to the skin.

Prince Philip went back to Windsor and immediately out carriage-driving. The next morning he did the same, but felt ill and was admitted to the Edward VII Hospital in London for tests. He missed the remaining Jubilee celebrations. News that he was in hospital

---

* Apart from the bad optics – the pair enthroned so grandly – both the seats were soaking wet. The Queen managed two cups of tea down below, and the Duchess of Cornwall had hers laced with whisky as she used to when hunting.

reached the twelve thousand ballot winners who enjoyed a picnic of gazpacho, salmon mousse and Coronation chicken in the grounds of Buckingham Palace before the spectacular Diamond Jubilee concert performed at the Victoria Memorial.

Musicians such as Robbie Williams, Jessie J, Gary Barlow and Cheryl Cole performed. Cliff Richard said he could sing from every decade of the Queen's reign. There were classical performances from Lang Lang, Alfie Boe and Renée Fleming. Grace Jones and Annie Lennox took part, while the voice of Tom Jones was as strong as ever. The Queen joined the younger members of the family (several of the younger ones tie-less) in the latter part of the evening, wearing her Admiral's boat cloak. Her expression never changed. Gary Barlow performed the moving 'Sing' with the Commonwealth Band and the Military Wives, Shirley Bassey belted out 'Diamonds Are Forever' and Elton John's playing was as wild and energetic as ever, even if his voice was not what it had been.* There were Paul McCartney and Stevie Wonder, and the whole of the Palace was turned into a Camden street projection, fireworks bursting in a great crescendo, lighting the sky.

The Queen came onto the stage with the Prince of Wales and the Duchess of Cornwall. At that point many were unaware that the Duke of Edinburgh was ill. Prince Charles urged them to shout loudly as he might just hear them, and a cry went up: 'Philip, Philip, Philip.' The Queen lit the Diamond Jubilee beacon.[6]

The following day, the Queen attended the Thanksgiving Service at St Paul's Cathedral. She had been at her grandfather's service seventy-seven years before in 1935, at the age of nine. Arriving by car with her lady in waiting, Lady Farnham, she cut a lonely but assured central figure, dressed in white and pale green, with the Cullinan brooches. The hymns were boosted by trumpets, and the Archbishop of Canterbury gave a good address. After the service, Lord Airlie said how moving it had been and how different from Westminster Abbey in 1997.[7]

---

* I had promised my son Arthur that I would take him to an Elton John concert one day. I got him a ticket for the picnic and concert and said later that I was lucky to have fulfilled that promise, with the added benefit of Shirley Bassey and Cliff Richard as the warm-up act.

On the way back to Buckingham Palace after lunch at the Guildhall, the Duchess of Cornwall sat beside the Queen with the Prince of Wales opposite. It was clear, if it had not been so already, that the Queen was on excellent terms with her daughter-in-law. On the balcony for the flypast by the Red Arrows, only the immediate close family were present. The Queen stood with the Prince of Wales, the Duchess of Cornwall, the Duke and Duchess of Cambridge and Prince Harry. There was no Princess Anne, no Prince Andrew and no Wessexes (the latter visiting Prince Philip in hospital). This was a contrast to the large family gatherings after Trooping the Colour, with every unrecognisable distant cousin. It was something that Robin Janvrin had been trying to achieve for years. After a *feu de jour*, an informal and a formal National Anthem, and a wave from the Queen, the windows closed behind her and the crowds gradually dispersed.

What emerged from the Jubilee was total respect for the Queen, a constant in a fast-changing world. She looked composed, a little wistful, but when she smiled, her face radiated true beauty. It was impossible not to feel immensely drawn to her. Finally, after years of being eclipsed by the Queen Mother, then William and Catherine being predominant in 2011, this year was the Queen's.

The Queen went to Balmoral to rest. Prince Philip came out of hospital on Saturday, 9 June and spent his ninety-first birthday alone at Windsor. He wanted to be there as he never missed the Lords Taverners matches. For Trooping the Colour on 27 June the Queen and the Duke travelled in the Glass Coach, to prevent him catching another chill. The Prince of Wales was promoted Admiral of the Fleet, Field Marshal and Marshal of the RAF, and Prince William wore his new Thistle star, having been invested with George VI's Thistle insignia at the Palace the day before. Prince Philip drove his carriage four-in-hand every day the following week.

The main Jubilee celebrations were followed by the London Olympics. On 27 July the opening ceremony took place at Stratford, east London. It contained the unexpected sequence of just over six minutes when James Bond, played by Daniel Craig, was seen arriving at the Palace in a taxi and making his way to the Queen's private drawing room to be admitted by her long-serving page, Paul Whybrew. Viewers were astonished to see a figure looking like the

Queen, and even more so when she turned and it *was* the Queen. Bond escorted her to the Palace garden where a helicopter took off, with Bond and apparently Her Majesty inside it. In an imaginative sequence the statue of Sir Winston Churchill waved at the passing helicopter, which then flew down the Thames, through Tower Bridge and to the Olympic site. Models parachuted out.

The Queen entered the arena, dressed as in the film sequence, and took her place in the Royal Box. She had a brief, wry expression on her face, but she looked cross and did not smile when she declared the Games open. She had been entertaining Heads of State since four thirty and was tired. The Queen's approach to stunts of this kind was to treat them later as if they had never happened. I suspect that if anyone mentioned it to her, she would not have responded. It was her way of maintaining dignity.

The Royal Family went to Scotland. Prince Philip had been at Cowes, but on 15 August he was again hospitalised, this time in Aberdeen Royal Infirmary. Once more it was said to be a bladder infection and he was there for 'investigation and treatment'.[8] He came out after five nights. He was still convalescing when the Queen visited the Opening of the Paralympic Games.

Royal news was enlivened when Prince Harry found himself in a sting in Las Vegas, when one of the girls sold photographs of him cavorting naked in a hotel suite at the Encore Wynn Resort. Inevitably there was media frenzy, put into perspective by General Sir Mike Jackson's view that, after the hell of being in the front line in Iraq, he did not blame the young man for letting his hair down. Prince Harry's popularity soared. Less popular were paparazzi photographers catching the Duchess of Cambridge topless when she was staying with the Linleys in France. Her lawyers obtained an injunction, but it showed that the paparazzi were still prepared to be invasive.

2013

The Queen had a bad knee, which made walking slightly uncomfortable for the rest of her life, and in due course, subtle concessions were made. The Clerk of Works at St George's Chapel introduced an extra step on the way into the quire from the north quire aisle. A railing was introduced on the Great West Steps, ostensibly to help the elderly Garter Knights. That way the Queen accepted it. From 2016, at the Opening of Parliament, she went up in the lift, rather than by the stairs, and later, after Easter services, she came out through the Cloisters rather than up the steep steps of the Deanery garden.

On 8 April Baroness Thatcher died at the Ritz in London, at the age of eighty-seven after years of ill health and loneliness following Sir Denis's death in June 2003. To some she was the greatest Prime Minister, decisive and effective; to others she was anathema. She had been the first woman to hold that office. She was accorded what was almost a Ceremonial Funeral in St Paul's Cathedral, not quite as grand as Sir Winston Churchill's State Funeral. There was a gun-carriage and the coffin was covered with a Union Flag. With world leaders flying in from far corners of the globe, it was clear that the Queen and the Duke of Edinburgh would be there.

Gradually Prince Charles and the Duchess of Cornwall were brought forward. The Queen dropped out of long-haul flights, so they went to the Commonwealth Heads of Government Meeting in Sri Lanka in her place. At the next State Opening of Parliament on 8 May, they were present, seated to the left of the throne, a subtle reminder that one day he would be making the speech. Time had moved forward sufficiently for the Queen to be made to say: 'My government will work to prevent sexual violence in conflict worldwide.' As usual the most significant line was: 'I pray that the blessing of Almighty God may rest upon your counsels.'[9] With that she left the Chamber and the politicians could fight it out.

From time to time the Queen would visit an old friend. One such was her Mistress of the Robes, Fortune, Duchess of Grafton. The Duke, who had had both legs removed, had died in April 2011. Fortune had moved into Whitelands House, off King's Road in Chelsea, where she became a neighbour of Dame Frances Campbell-Preston, the Queen Mother's most forthright lady in waiting.* This led to an interesting encounter. Dame Frances's son, Colin, in his gardening

---

* They both lived to a great age: the Duchess of Grafton died aged 101, and Dame Frances aged 104.

clothes, was surprised to run into the Queen in the lift, especially as he was clutching a bottle of gin for his mother. He explained: 'It's always such a bore when you run out.' The Queen acquiesced.[10]

On 2 June the Queen and the Duke attended a service to commemorate the sixtieth anniversary of the Coronation, for which St Edward's Crown was brought from the Tower of London and placed on the High Altar.

On 6 June Prince Philip attended a Palace garden party and was then taken to the London Clinic for an abdominal operation. As his grandson Peter Phillips said: 'You have got to remember his age, both their ages ... They do a lot more than most pensioners of their equivalent age so ...'

The Queen sat in on the *Today* show. When John Humphrys asked her how the Duke was, she put him in his place. 'I've no idea. He's only just gone in.'

'Well, he was looking well yesterday,' volunteered Humphrys.

'That's because he's not ill,' replied the Queen.[11]

The Queen visited the Duke on his ninety-second birthday, and uncharacteristically, since the Royal Family were not known for hospital visiting, he received many visits from other members of his family. The doctors had detected a shadow on his pancreas, and they cut him right across his stomach. The verdict was inoperable pancreatic cancer. He had an autoscopy, which left him talking with little throat-clearing coughs. He convalesced for two months at Windsor Castle, having good days and bad days, sometimes just sitting in the sunshine. There was a view that he might not be seen in public again. But, as ever, the Duke outwitted the pessimists. On 12 July he went up to Wood Farm at Sandringham and resumed royal duties on 12 August by presenting medals to the Royal Society in Edinburgh. He joined the Queen at Balmoral.

In Prince Philip's absence, the Duke of Kent stood with the Queen at the Birthday Parade, and there was an iconic image of three generations at the Garter ceremony when the Queen walked between the Prince of Wales and the Duke of Cambridge, in their dark-blue velvet Garter robes.

If the Queen needed cheering up, she did not have to wait long. She had a runner, Estimate, in the Gold Cup at Royal Ascot. This was an exciting race, Estimate holding its place well, then suddenly spurting forward at the end to win the Gold Cup, the Queen's greatest win on the turf in six decades as an owner, and the first time a reigning monarch had won that race. The Queen did not emote during the race but was plainly delighted when the race was won, and her racing manager, John Warren, seated beside her, clutched her arm. The racegoers erupted with joy and cheered her enthusiastically.

Meanwhile a long media vigil began outside the Lindo Wing waiting for the Duchess of Cambridge to give birth. This turned into a subtle kind of revenge, the press having called Catherine 'Waity Katy' in the long years before her engagement. Hordes of media camped out for a fortnight, often in broiling sun, filling the airwaves with rambling monologues about everything imaginable – whether the Duchess might go to another hospital, how Londoners were looking forward to the birth, possible names and titles, the succession to the Crown, and even what the waiting journalists were up to outside the hospital.

On 22 July the House of Windsor acquired a new king-in-waiting when the Duchess gave birth to Prince George at 4.24 p.m. on 22 July.* Early that morning, the young Duchess had left Kensington Palace and been spirited into St Mary's, Paddington, by a back door. Prince George was a healthy baby boy of about eight pounds. The Post Office Tower lit up with a revolving sign, 'It's a boy', Niagara Falls was floodlit blue and white and out came all the long-prepared newspaper supplements.

Prince Charles had collected Diana and Prince William from the Lindo Wing, in a suit and tie, and went back to Kensington Palace in a chauffeur-driven car, but Prince William was a more hands-on father. He arrived in an open shirt, manipulated the baby seat himself and took the wheel of the car. This gave an indication of impending informality in the next generation. The Queen saw the infant before she headed up to Scotland. On 23 October he was christened George Alexander Louis at the Chapel Royal, St James's Palace.

At the end of the year, the Queen and the Duke could be seen

---

* The rules of succession had been changed. Had the baby been a girl, she would have held precedence over future princes. Thus, later, Princess Charlotte is in line before Prince Louis.

travelling to King's Lynn by train for the Christmas holidays. An inveterate reader, the Duke was clutching a book.

2014

The Queen's maternal cousin Lady Mary Clayton* died on 13 February aged ninety-six. She lived near Cumberland Lodge in Windsor Great Park. She had been a childhood companion of the Queen and Princess Margaret at Glamis Castle, and occasionally appeared in documentaries talking about their youthful antics. The Queen never missed attending her birthday party. She and Prince Philip, Princess Beatrice and the Countess of Wessex attended her funeral at the Royal Chapel on 7 March. Sent there to represent Prince Michael of Kent, I had the opportunity to observe the Queen and Prince Philip, then eighty-seven, and ninety-two. Prince Philip was bronzed, alert and fit. It was hard to believe that he had been so ill:

> [After the service] The Queen stood by the Chapel door, watching her cousin's hearse being piped away – she, a small, solitary figure in black, standing all by herself.
>
> A nice gathering at Cumberland Lodge ... Suddenly Rosie [Stancer] came in with the Queen. I saw Prince Philip & he me. He said they had a book by me, *The Kiss*, in a vitrine and so I told him that story, mentioning Major Clough, aged ninety-three – 'at a time when that was very old'. He will be ninety-three in June! I told him about the Duchess of Windsor and Maître Blum. He said he knew that Blum was 'an awful woman'. He didn't know that the Duchess had been for ten years on a life-support machine while they creamed off the estate...
>
> I stayed by the door & at a certain point the Queen turned round. 'Oh, hello,' she said and shook my hand. Somehow I managed to volunteer that I thought it curious that the Maori King would not

---

* Lady Mary Leveson-Gower (1917–2014), daughter of Rose, Countess Granville (1890–1967), elder sister of the Queen Mother. Lady Mary's daughter, Rosie Stancer, is a well-known Arctic explorer.

meet Prince William – when in 1954 Sidney Holland had not wanted her to meet his predecessor, only changing his mind at the last moment. The Queen said: 'Yes, isn't that odd? He's very grand but he's only a bus driver ...' I suggested that he probably wanted publicity – so that when he did meet the Prince there'd be lots of photos. She took that in.

Sir Simon Bowes-Lyon, of St Paul's, Waldenbury, loomed. The Queen said to him: 'I had a woman being invested this morning. She was huge, twice my size, and she said to me, "I'm a friend of Sir Simon Bowes-Lyon." So I said: "Well, I might be seeing him this afternoon."' He replied drily: 'We do have a number of large women in Hertfordshire.' She is amazing – the Queen – she is so alert and responds by random access to so many different things.

Prince Philip then said: 'Can you drag yourself away?' And so she did.[12]

On 3 April the Queen and Prince Philip visited Rome, lunching with the President, Giorgio Napolitano, and having a private audience of Pope Francis at the Vatican. Gone were the days when the Queen would wear black evening dress, tiara and Garter riband; this time she was in day clothes. It was the first time she had met the new Pope and the first time she had been abroad for three years. A few days later came the state visit of the President of Ireland, Michael Higgins to Windsor Castle.

In July the Queen was in Glasgow for the opening ceremony of the Commonwealth Games. Scotland was much on her mind as the Scottish Referendum was taken to the vote (on 18 September). This issue worried the Queen more than anything in her long reign.[13] At Crathie Church on 14 September, some well-wishers asked her about the impending vote. She said, 'People should think very carefully about the future,' before they voted. Buckingham Palace were quick to stress 'the Queen's constitutional impartiality' on that issue and that it was down to the people of Scotland to decide.[14] If you were standing on the edge of a cliff and the Queen made a remark like that, she would not have been advising you to jump.

The Referendum gave a 'No' vote – 55.3 per cent versus 44.7 per cent. David Cameron betrayed the Queen by revealing that she had 'purred' down the telephone at the result. His remarks were picked up by a stray microphone. I suggested to two of the Queen's key advisers that next time he saw her and spluttered his apology she would let him go down, down, down and then, after a suitable theatrical pause, say: 'Tell me about the trade figures, Prime Minister.' They both admitted that would be in character. Scotland remains part of the United Kingdom to this day. In his memoirs, Cameron said he made the Queen 'a heartfelt apology'.[15]

2015

On 6 February Tony Abbott, Prime Minister of Australia, made an insignificant yet tactical error that magnified into an issue of no confidence. He had become a Liberal Prime Minister in September 2013, and the following March he advised the Queen to reintroduce the honour of knights and dames in the Order of Australia, which had been dropped in 1986. He bestowed the Order on Quentin Bryce and Peter Cosgrove, two outgoing Governor-Generals, and on Australia Day 2015, he appointed Prince Philip. Such honours did not interest Prince Philip and he had to be persuaded that he had done enough for Australia to have earned it. The appointment caused a furore in Australia, and in February there was a leadership spill vote, which Abbott survived, only to be ousted from power in September. The new Prime Minister, Malcolm Turnbull, abolished knights and dames again (though the few existing ones were unaffected).

The Cambridges' second child, Princess Charlotte, arrived at 8.34 a.m. on 2 May, in the middle of a General Election campaign. Her very young elder brother arrived at St Mary's, Paddington, to the delight of the crowd, and presently the world had their first glimpse of the baby. It was considered prudent that this birth should in no way disrupt the election campaign so the Duchess and her infant daughter were whisked home from hospital on the very day of the birth.

Five days later the United Kingdom went to the polls. Since Gordon Brown's resignation there had been a coalition government jointly overseen by David Cameron (Conservative) and Nick Clegg (Liberal), a not entirely comfortable arrangement. To universal surprise Cameron won an overall majority and was therefore able to drop Clegg and form a government with the largest share of the popular vote since Lord Salisbury's victory in 1900. Ed Miliband, the Labour leader, had a victory speech all prepared. But he suffered the greatest Labour defeat for years, the party more or less wiped out in Scotland.

In the run-up to that election Edward Young and Chris Martin, Cameron's private secretary, had met at Windsor Castle and discussed every possible outcome except an overall majority. They went to evensong. The Queen had tipped off the Dean about these discussions and mischievously, he inserted a prayer: 'We pray for all those in positions of authority, including those public servants charged with the smooth oversight of the election process.' The outright majority meant that the Queen had to return to London earlier than planned by helicopter.

In May 2015 there was some discussion as to whether Cameron should say: 'I have just been to see Her Majesty The Queen who has *invited me to form* a majority Conservative Government' or 'I have just been to see Her Majesty The Queen to *inform her* that I will form a majority Conservative Government.' The confusion arose as to whether Cameron was simply continuing as Prime Minister or forming a new government. In the end they compromised by using a tactic employed by Agatha Christie in *The Murder of Roger Ackroyd* (1926). Cameron said: 'I have just been to see Her Majesty The Queen ... and I will now form a majority Conservative government.' The two Private Secretaries were pleased with the three unspoken dots.[16]

The Queen and Prince Philip staved off many of the normal effects of old age by maintaining a full work schedule, stimulated by intelligent and well-informed people. There were the odd slips, as when Prince Philip was being photographed with other members of the Royal Family and veterans at the RAF Club in Piccadilly on 10 July. He was caught on film swearing at the photographer to get a move on and take the picture.

Prince Philip was never known to be patient. His short-term memory was not as good as it had been and he looked liverish at a Buckingham Palace Garden Party, his eyes pale and glassy, and sometimes he missed the thread. Yet he had been on fine form at the Royal Yacht Squadron on the Isle of Wight. He was ninety-four that summer.

Milestones were a feature of the last years of the reign. On 9 September the Queen became Britain's longest reigning monarch, as she overtook the 63 years 216 days of Queen Victoria. When her friend Lady Penn congratulated her, she replied: 'It isn't a competition, you know.'[17] On the day, she was on a train with Nicola Sturgeon, then First Minister of Scotland. She made a speech that this was a milestone to which she did not 'aspire'.

The Queen went to Malta between 26 and 28 November to attend the Commonwealth Heads of Government Meeting in Valletta. Malta was the only place in the Commonwealth that the Queen could really call home since she had spent happy years there as a young wife between 1949 and 1951. She brought Prince Philip, Prince Charles and the Duchess of Cornwall with her, and sometimes she was paired with her son, while Prince Philip joined Camilla. At a banquet, Justin Trudeau, the young Prime Minister of Canada, then aged forty-three, and son of Pierre Trudeau, spoke of how she had visited Canada in the 1950s and 1960s, and on one forty-five-day tour in 1959, visiting ninety towns and cities. She replied: 'Thank you, Mr Prime Minister of Canada, for making me feel so old.'[18]

The next day, she was conveyed across the Grand Harbour, retracing her father's 1943 crossing and unveiled a disc by the terminal to open Malta's Commonwealth Walkway.* She went on to a rather soggy polo match before flying home. At Christmas, it was reassuring to see the Queen on the screen, 'bright as ever, conciliatory and optimistic'.[19]

---

* Commonwealth Walkways were springing up all over the world. The Princess Royal unveiled one in the Falkland Islands and in Edmonton, Canada, the Prince of Wales another on the Gold Coast in Australia, and yet another in Wellington, New Zealand. There was one in Samoa, and another in the Cook Islands. Regrettably Prince Harry's office vetoed him unveiling a Walkway marker in Nelson's Dockyard in Antigua, even though he was out there on behalf of the Queen and was to walk right past it. In the end, the Governor-General, Sir Rodney Williams, gave up his Sunday morning to perform the short ceremony. Malta was the only time the Queen unveiled a Commonwealth Walkway abroad. When the Foreign Minister tried to present me, she said: 'He turns up all over the place.' I may have made the last of many speeches to her on foreign soil.

45
FICTIONAL REPRESENTATIONS

An occupational hazard for the Royal Family was to be portrayed on stage or screen. Giles, the *Daily Express* cartoonist, often lampooned royal happenings with light humour. When Prince Philip declared it 'a bloody awful newspaper', he portrayed Lord Beaverbrook being taken to the Tower of London, with the caption: 'At least he takes it or he wouldn't know it was a bloody awful newspaper.'[1] In 1963 there were skits in performances in *Fool Britannia*, with Peter Sellers, Joan Collins and Anthony Newley. *Crown Matrimonial* portrayed the Queen Mother and the Duchess of Gloucester on stage in 1972, when they were both alive. Somewhat tastelessly, Sue Townsend fictionalised the Queen Mother's death in her 1992 novel, *The Queen and I*, with the Royal Family living on a housing estate. The Royal Family were not always as lucky as they were with Alan Bennett's *A Question of Attribution,* a subtle take on the Anthony Blunt saga, starring Prunella Scales* as the Queen, in 1989.

The 2006 film, *The Queen*, starred Helen Mirren. It was a powerful fictional re-creation, with the effect of making people more sympathetic to the plight of the Queen during the Diana week of 1997. It was judged a great film, despite the caricature portrayals of Prince Philip and the Queen Mother, and it was not generous to Prince Charles. Mercifully there was no Mohamed Fayed; Blair was well played. Some liked the imagery of the stag. There were times when Helen Mirren almost turned into the Queen. The film was shown at Balmoral towards the end of the

---

* Prunella Scales had stayed at Windsor for a 'dine and sleep', so had the chance to examine the Queen's mannerisms. Some time after the play, she was in a line-up and the Queen said to her, as she passed by: 'I expect you think you should be doing this ...' (Prunella Scales to author, 20 September 2001).

Queen's stay, and she watched it. Of that film, Robin Janvrin said: 'It was all wrong, and all right.'[2]

Peter Morgan produced *The Audience* in 2013, a fictional take on the Queen's relationship with various Prime Ministers. Helen Mirren was again excellent, veering from a young Queen to an older one. It contained a smart opening line from John Major: 'I only ever wanted to be ordinary.' The Queen: 'And in which way do you consider you've failed in that ambition?'[3]

The 2014 play, *King Charles III*, with Tim Pigott-Smith as Charles opened with greyness and mauve as the funeral of the Queen was enacted. The new King was soon embroiled in a constitutional crisis when he refused to sign a Bill curbing the powers of the press. Camilla, William, Kate and Harry were all played on stage. It ended with the King forced to abdicate and the young couple taking over – a proactive Kate portrayed as the saviour of the monarchy.

Then came *The Crown*, running in six series with sixty episodes between November 2016 and December 2023. This was particularly unpleasant because it twisted the truth. Sometimes the writers took two events that had happened and clashed them together to create something that had not. Peter Morgan had been perceptive over the Queen's relations with her Prime Ministers in *The Audience*. He deserted that in *The Crown*. He claimed that he had adhered closely to the truth, but he had done no such thing.* The problem was that it was a lavish production with a well-written script, good actors, fine costumes and sets, so people believed it to be true. It was not.

Prince Philip consulted his lawyer about the episode in which he was unjustly accused of causing the death of his sister in the plane crash in November 1937. Fortunately he heard me put the record straight on Radio 4's *Today* and so let the matter rest. The nonagenarian former tabloid editor, Clive Irving, pointed out:

> The Crown has now won 123 awards and it has now effectively supplanted any other source, dramatic or documentary, as the most trusted picture of recent Windsor history. All the biases and personal preferences for who's good and who's bad baked into that script are

---

* I have analysed all sixty episodes in *The Crown Dissected*.

now also those of millions of viewers – the cumulative effect over years is quite unlike that of a single book or drama and ineluctable.[4]

★ ★ ★ ★ ★

At Sandringham in January 2016, some geese frightened the ponies and they shied when Prince Philip was driving his carriage. He was not strong enough to control the reins. The girl grooms with him seized them, but he needed four stitches in his hand.[5]

Celebrations for the Queen's ninetieth birthday in April 2016 extended over two days. On the first day she was at the post office in Windsor and then in Alexandra Gardens, by the Thames, opening the new bandstand. Aged ninety-four, Prince Philip sang along with 'When I'm 64'.[6] The next day, a large crowd, including royalty watchers festooned with Union Flags, assembled near the castle to see the Queen on her walkabout. She unveiled the latest panel opening the Queen's Walkway (a route with sixty-three markers around Windsor, one for each year of Queen Victoria's reign, which she had just overtaken). State trumpeters sounded a fanfare to mark a ceremonial moment in an otherwise informal walk to the Guildhall. In the evening she tried to light a beacon by the advance gates of the Long Walk. It only lit after she left.

President Obama and his wife, Michele, arrived by helicopter at the castle to have lunch with the Queen the next day, the occasion when ninety-five-year old Prince Philip took the wheel of the Range Rover and drove the Presidential couple, to the consternation of the Secret Service.

In a documentary to celebrate the Queen's milestone birthday, Prince Charles talked of her great achievement at being ninety, while he was sixty-seven. Prince William was twice quoted in the idiom of his generation: 'She's been there, done that, got the T-shirt.' Catherine was the star, and Sophie Wessex was perceptive. The two York Princesses spoke sweetly of their grandmother.[7] When no new Knights of the Garter were appointed on St George's Day to fill three vacancies, Robert Hardman asked if I thought the Queen was treating the Garter Knights like her Corgis and letting them die off.[8] On 16 May Lord Shuttleworth and Sir David Brewer were named. On 15 May there was an equestrian celebration, a host of German relations, and the TV cameras picked up Princess Beatrice texting behind the Queen.

The Queen knew that her presence had considerable effect. When Terry Pendry put on a fund-raising Race Night to benefit the College of St George at the Royal Mews, she put in an appearance after a long day at the Derby. All thirty-six tables were sold and there were eight televised races, the horses with fun names such as 'Donald Trump'.

Not all the news that night was good. Sir Brian McGrath, Prince Philip's stalwart Private Secretary (from 1984 to 1992) was dying. He had retired several times, but simply left through the Privy Purse Door and returned through the French windows (as he put it) to resume his place at his desk. He was still there aged ninety. He had not been paid since 2001, but as he said: 'I have an office and four very pretty girls to look after me and I get a free lunch.'[9]

Sir Brian was an ebullient man, not easily contained in a small space. He looked after Prince Philip's German relations, which could involve rescuing a wayward German relation from prison in the sub-continent, or advising Princess Alexandra about some slippers Prince Philip might like for Christmas. He said he was really 'just a nanny'. He accompanied Prince Philip on carriage-driving weekends, and would mix his boss a dry martini, stir it with his finger, give it a quick taste and hand it to the Duke.

In his last days, there were concerns about him hurtling down the M4 in his Jaguar. His health gave way. 'Tell the Queen to send me her doctor. He'll kill me,' he said, with bravado. Hearing he was ill, the Queen said: 'I hope it won't be too long.'[10] He died that night. Greatly 'regretting' his loss, Prince Philip attended his funeral. All the Royal Family were represented, though, significantly, not the Prince of Wales.

Sir Brian's successor, Brigadier Sir Miles Hunt-Davis, retired in 2010. He was much liked, totally straightforward and with none of the guile of some courtiers. He was never a personal friend of Prince Philip and during his seventeen years, he had an intimate conversation with him on only two occasions. Having Sir Brian around might have been difficult but, though different in character, Sir Brian and he worked well together.

Prince Philip was further isolated when his stalwart archivist, Anne Griffiths, fell ill with cancer. She had originally come to the Palace in 1952 as a clerk to help with correspondence before the Coronation. She had been on board *Britannia* on Prince Philip's long voyage in 1955 to 1956. She oversaw his archives and he trusted her implicitly. So discreet was she that her sister-in-law never knew if Prince Philip called her Anne. He did. She came into the office early in 2017 to tidy her papers and died on 3 March 2017, aged eighty-four. Prince Philip attended her memorial service. Sir Miles died in retirement on 23 May 2018. From 2010 until the end, the Private Secretary was Brigadier Archie Miller-Bakewell, latterly a part-time job.

★ ★ ★ ★ ★

The Queen's more formal birthday celebrations took place in June. There was a service of thanksgiving at St Paul's Cathedral on Prince Philip's ninety-fifth birthday. The next day the crowds came out in force to cheer the Queen in her Kermit-the-Frog green coat at Trooping the Colour. On Sunday there was the Patrons' Lunch in the Mall. The Royal Family, including Lady Louise Windsor, the Wessexes' daughter, went up and down the Mall talking to stall-holders. The Queen only smiled on these occasions if genuinely amused.

On the Monday, the Queen was furious that a decision had been taken quite early in the morning that the outside Garter procession should be cancelled. This was done so as not to tire her. Fortunately for the Household there was a bit of a shower, since the waiting crowds were inevitably disappointed. The procession had not been cancelled since 1971. The participants arrived by car, the Queen looking pale.[11]

★ ★ ★ ★ ★

David Cameron had promised to hold a referendum on the issue of the United Kingdom remaining in the European Union. This he honoured. In March the *Sun* disclosed: 'Queen backs Brexit', a suggested leak via either Nick Clegg or Michael Gove from a 2011 conversation. Stephen Hewlett said on Radio 4 that whatever the Queen might have said did not justify that headline.*

The referendum was held on 23 June 2016, and 51.89 per cent voted out, with 48.11 per cent voting remain. Since Cameron had backed remain, he announced that he would step down, hoping to stay until the leadership contest on 9 September. He had hoped to tour Europe saying goodbye. He might even have been given some farewell banquets, and gone to Balmoral for the traditional Prime Ministerial weekend. However, Andrea Leadsom dropped out, leaving Theresa May uncontested. Cameron therefore submitted his resigna-tion to the Queen on 13 July. 'I was the future once,' he said, in his last appearance at Prime Minister's Questions. He left his successor with an insuperable European problem – how to deliver Brexit.

It did not take long for Theresa May to form her new cabinet – the 'Cameroons' were out (George Osborne and Michael Gove). Boris Johnson was appointed Foreign Secretary. Her next years were spent trying to deliver the poisoned chalice of Brexit and ultimately failing.

* * * * *

In the latter months of 2016, the Queen lost her cousin, Margaret Rhodes. The Queen had been good to her, giving her a house in the Great Park, allowing her to publish a successful (if not wholly accurate) book of memoirs. The Queen and her cousin were close. I saw Margaret Rhodes greet the Queen after church in the Royal Chapel in October. 'And how are you getting on?' The Queen did not answer. Margaret Rhodes died soon afterwards, on 25 November, aged ninety-one.

Towards the end of that year, the Queen handed over a number of her patronages to other members of the family, which indicated a degree of withdrawal. There followed a crisis more serious than was admitted at the time. On 22 December the Queen and Prince Philip were meant to be taking the train to Norfolk for Christmas. All of a sudden it was announced that they had heavy colds. They

---

* Since then Valentine Low has suggested she was a remainer, but more likely she did not want to upset existing arrangements.

went by helicopter, something the Queen did not like, especially in winter fog.

An employee had arrived for work with a heavy cold and infected the Duke, who had in turn infected the Queen. This was dangerous for nonagenarians, even those with their strong resistance. They drank milk straight from the cow, and ate unpasteurised cheese.

The Queen walked into Sandringham House, went straight to her room and remained there for the ensuing days, unseen by the guests. She missed the Christmas service for the first time in thirty years. She had pneumonia.[12] Westminster Abbey panicked sufficiently to make sure they had enough black copes for a funeral.[13] Prince Charles was worried at the imminent prospect of suddenly finding himself King. It was always said that he longed to take over but, not surprisingly, the reality daunted him.

The Queen was still at Sandringham when she entered the year of what a handful of people called her 'Sapphire Jubilee' – sixty-five years on the throne, not an event being publicly celebrated. They were sighted at church at Windsor on 19 February, the Queen very 'beautiful' and the Duke 'bounding past, fit as a fiddle'.[14] In March he flew to Germany for the eightieth birthday of his nephew, Prince Ludwig of Baden. In his speech he wished him well 'so long as he was enjoying life', by which it can be deduced that he, Prince Philip, was still enjoying life in his ninety-sixth year. He was still undertaking a full round of royal duties, despite having said at ninety that he just wanted to enjoy himself.

On 4 May 2017, Buckingham Palace alerted the media that an important announcement was to be made. Fearing the worst, journalists leaped onto planes from places as far away as Australia, thinking there was a royal death. Sir Christopher Geidt, the Queen's Private Secretary, told the assembled Royal Households of Buckingham Palace, Windsor, Balmoral, Sandringham and the other Royal Households that Prince Philip would be retiring from royal duties.*

Besides the obvious factor of age, the reasoning behind the retirement remains unclear. Geidt may have been preparing a strategy for the next generation to take over, in particular the Prince of Wales.

---

* Journalists then had to find interviews, stock obituaries, et cetera, to record in the United Kingdom in order to justify the expenditure of their panic visits.

FICTIONAL REPRESENTATIONS

Geidt had been doing sterling work in the Commonwealth, travelling to the key countries such as Australia, New Zealand and Canada, to pave the way for Prince Charles to be the next Head of the Commonwealth, which the Queen fixed adroitly when the Commonwealth Heads of Government met in London in April 2018. It would not have been put to the vote, had the outcome been in any doubt.

When Geidt addressed the Royal Households he asked that they should now work together to support the Queen. This was considered a clarion call to Clarence House, since it was no secret that the Prince of Wales's Household and the Queen's had not always seen eye to eye. This was ill received by Prince Charles and Prince Andrew. It was said that they joined forces (a rare collaboration) at a time when the Queen was worried about Prince Philip. They effected a coup to get rid of Geidt as Private Secretary, unquestionably a bad ploy. In October Geidt stepped down and was succeeded by Sir Edward Young.

★ ★ ★ ★ ★

The new Prime Minister, Theresa May, called a General Election, hoping to shore up her position. When the country went to the polls on 9 June, she threw away a respectable majority and had to rely on an arrangement with the Democratic Unionist Party (DUP) to carry on. Theresa May wanted the State Opening on Monday, 19 June, so Garter Day was cancelled. That proved premature since she could not get her act together with the DUP, so the State Opening was postponed till the Wednesday. This meant the Queen opening Parliament in the morning and returning post-haste to Windsor for her Ascot lunch and an afternoon of racing.

The conflagration at Grenfell Tower, a high-rise building in London, occurred on 14 June. Seventy people died at the scene, and two more in hospital. Seventy were injured. When Theresa May visited the site without meeting victims, she was unfairly criticised as doing so for political advantage. When the Queen visited for forty-five minutes, the atmosphere was emotional. She brought calm and respect. She was not seeking public approval: she was there to comfort her people, the more impressive as she had visited a portfolio of other tragedies – from Aberfan to Dunblane. Prince William came with her. The BBC journalist, Peter Hunt, described it as 'a masterclass in how you respond to a moment of national tragedy'.[15]

On the day of the Birthday Parade, the Queen issued an inspirational message about Grenfell Tower and commended the work of the emergency services. She commanded a minute's silence. The Queen had also visited Manchester after the terrorist attack in the stadium in May. When she came to a state room to be photographed with the Lay Stewards of St George's Chapel that Sunday, she told me: 'They're sending me all over the place at the moment.'[16]

The State Opening took place on 20 June, once again in the middle of Ascot week. The Queen flew to London and back in a three-seater helicopter. She wore day clothes, and eagle-eyed commentators decided that it was significant that she wore a blue hat with yellow flowers in it, the colours of Europe. She was accompanied by a decidedly grumpy-looking Prince of Wales, cajoled into it at the last moment because his father had been sent to the Edward VII Hospital in London with an infection, possibly caused by the heatwave. The Duke went home on Thursday 22 June, and was well enough to inspect the Little Ships on the Thames at Windsor with Prince Michael of Kent on Monday 26 June. The next day, the Queen, Prince Philip and a large contingent of the Royal Family attended the funeral in Knightsbridge of Countess Mountbatten of Burma, who had died on 13 June at the age of ninety-three. Prince Charles gave an entertaining address, largely involving anecdotes about himself,* while the surviving twin, Timothy, told the congregation how, when his parents were so wounded after Mullaghmore in 1979 and unable to speak, their hospital beds were moved together so that they could hold hands.

The last time Prince Philip performed publicly with the Queen was on 19 July when she visited Canada House and unveiled a Commonwealth Walkway panel marking the 150th anniversary of Canada as a Confederation. As so often I was present at milestone occasions such as this, and it was the last time I ever spoke to Prince Philip. On 2 August he undertook the last of some 22,219 public

---

* 'Very good,' commented the old Grenadier Guard sitting next to me. The Prince would have had to express pro-Corbyn loyalties for it to have been otherwise.

engagements in the forecourt of Buckingham Palace. He had been Captain-General of Royal Marines for sixty-four years, and he took the salute marking the end of the 1664 Global Challenge. It was a wet day. He wore a raincoat and bowler hat. He strode through the parade without a stick and chatted to the young men and the veterans. He watched the cadets march past, and when the parade gave him three cheers, he responded with a valedictory wave of his bowler hat. The role of Captain-General was given to Prince Harry.

After that final engagement, the Queen let the Duke do exactly as he pleased. He was at his happiest at Wood Farm and he more or less settled there. In the course of the next two and a half years, that was his home. He enjoyed his carriage-driving, read voraciously and painted a little. From time to time she went up by train to Norfolk to stay the weekend. Once again she gave him a loose rein. In a sense they separated. Penny Romsey, the new Countess Mountbatten, often stayed with him there.

Prince Philip joined the family Christmas at Sandringham and for Easter at Windsor Castle, though he did not attend the traditional service. In 2017 he presided over a regimental dinner, went to the Festival of Remembrance at the Royal Albert Hall and joined the Queen on the balcony of the old Home Office building at Whitehall for Remembrance Day, wearing his Admiral of the Fleet greatcoat, and looking decidedly ill. He did not appear there again.

The press decided that the Prince of Wales laying the wreath for the Queen was the 'most significant transfer' of duties. Had his parents not been there too that might have been the case. It was just sensible to let a ninety-six-year-old and a ninety-one-year-old take a less prominent role.

There was a private party to celebrate their seventieth wedding anniversary, but no public celebration. The Queen made a speech with tears in her eyes, speaking of the sacrifices Prince Philip had made for her.[17]

46

PRINCE HARRY AND PRINCE ANDREW

Prince Harry

On 27 November 2017 Prince Harry and Meghan Markle announced their engagement on Twitter. The appeal of this engagement was that the bride's multiracial origins introduced a modern element into the Royal Family. Unlike any other royal bride, she had addressed the United Nations – on International Women's Day in 2015. She had lived in Los Angeles and Toronto. She was a television actress, best known for her appearance in *Suits*. She had been married before.

In 2004 Meghan Markle had entered into a relationship with Trevor Engelson, an actor and producer, and they were married on the beach at Ocho Rios, Jamaica, on 10 September 2011, followed by a four-day extravaganza. Not long afterwards, she headed into *Suits* in Toronto and their relationship came to an end. They were divorced in 2013. She cohabited with the Canadian restaurateur Cory Vitiello, who owned the famous Harbord Room restaurant in Toronto, between 2014 and 2016.

Soon after meeting, Harry and Markle spent a clinching five days in a tent 'under their stars' in Botswana. They snatched time together in Canada and London. At the end of October 2016 the media latched on. Prince Harry was soon complaining that the press focused on Markle's ethnic background. On 6 November his office issued a statement: 'Prince Harry is worried about Ms Markle's safety and is deeply disappointed that he has not been able to protect her ... He knows commentators will say this is "The price she has to pay" and that "This is all part of the game." He strongly disagrees. This is not a game – this is her life and his.'[1]

The clandestine meetings continued. The relationship was sanctioned by Markle in the September 2017 edition of *Vanity Fair*. 'We're two people who are really happy and in love.'² Soon afterwards they held hands at the Invictus Games in Toronto.

In their interview on the day of the engagement, the couple gave evidence of a modern relationship, the holiday in Botswana, their cohabiting in Nottingham Cottage. The bride spoke with confidence though stretched credulity by suggesting that on their first date she had not known much about who Prince Harry was. More pointedly, they appeared to share a strong interest in Commonwealth countries and a commitment to work positively.

Unlike previous royal brides, Markle was invited to join the Queen and the Royal Family at Sandringham for Christmas 2017, attending church with the family. At the end of April 2018 she took her place on the platform with Prince Harry and the Duke and Duchess of Cambridge at a forum at the offices of Aviva plc to announce how they would advance the work of the Royal Foundation, of which they were Joint Patrons. Markle said: 'There is no better time than to really continue to shine a light on women feeling empowered and people really helping to support them, men included in that.' She wanted to 'hit the ground running'.³ One commentator described her as 'whip-smart'.

Prince Harry would never have been allowed to marry such a girl at an earlier time in the reign for obvious reasons, but the union was welcomed by a younger, more tolerant generation. Staff at Windsor Castle surrounded the young couple at the Christmas party in 2017, nicknaming the bride 'Sparkle'. Prince Philip was not taken in. He referred to her as 'the American'. Nor were the Royal Family entirely happy, Prince Charles taking a Mountbatten line – have fun with her, but don't marry her. The Queen suggested that Harry should wait a year.

Difficulties were soon evident as some staff left. Her half-brother, Thomas Markle, wrote to a US newspaper publicly urging Prince Harry to get out while he could, as he had not seen how awful she was. Shortly before the wedding, her father fell into a trap and was filmed preparing to come to the United Kingdom. A row ensued. He had a heart attack and did not come. Prince Harry never met him. For this, in my view, there can be only one of three reasons. First, Meghan was ashamed of him. Second, he may have done something. (In an interview he said that when Harry rang to ask permission to marry Meghan, he replied that he could 'so long as he never raised his hand against her'. So presumably he lived in a world where that kind of thing happened). The third and most likely reason is that she was afraid he would say something that might ruin the relationship.

The wedding took place at St George's Chapel on Saturday, 18 May, in an atmosphere of enormous goodwill. It was almost impossible to move in Windsor as the world's media descended and the public slept out in the streets to see the carriage procession. But there were tensions behind the scenes, the bride proving demanding. In the absence of her father, she wanted her mother, Doria Ragland, to escort her down the aisle. After much dissension, the solution was that she left Cliveden in a royal car with her mother, travelled to the Great West Steps alone with her host of bridesmaids and pages, and entered the chapel, making a Julie Andrews lone walk to the organ loft. Prince Charles then escorted her through the Quire.

On the day the customary cushions were brought in for the Prince of Wales and the Duchess of Cornwall, both of whom had bad backs. Genuine stars were filmed walking down the hill to the chapel. It was not certain if Prince Philip would come, but at the last moment he felt up to it. He and the Queen arrived by car at the Galilee Porch.

A particular feature of the service was Bishop Michael Curry from Chicago, who milked his moment, exhorting the congregation on the power of sacrificial, redemptive love, and the importance of fire. The decibels rose, the Bishop talked on, the television cameras picked up the bemused expression on the groom's face, the well-trained thespian gaze of rapture on the bride's, the studied, noncommittal look of the Queen, and amused horror on the faces of the younger members of the Royal Family, who should have been more careful. The poor conductor of the Gospel Choir was poised on high heels for an agonising eight minutes until the Bishop finally ran out of steam.

Given how quickly the new Duchess of Sussex turned popularity to media hostility, it is worth noting contemporary views. Many were alarmed that the bride had no family members to support her other than her mother. It was said that the Queen did not like the dress — too white and with ungainly shoulders. Someone close to the Queen said her attitude to the actual wedding was: 'You get on with it. It's nothing to do with me.' My conclusion was:

> It will either be a huge success or a monumental failure. Meghan said: 'It's a new chapter.' How many chapters are there? Will she tire of nice, vulnerable, non-cerebral Prince Harry and head back to the States to become President of the USA? It's not impossible. She's an actress, so you can't tell what she's thinking. I wonder how it will pan out?[4]

On 6 May 2019 Prince Harry came into the Royal Mews at Windsor to give the media the news that a boy had been born. Then the world was told that Duchess of Sussex had gone into labour. She was the first woman to give birth and subsequently go into labour, according to the timeline. A photo showing the child's feet was released on Instagram on 12 May. The child (wrapped and not seen) was photographed with the Queen, Prince Philip and Doria Ragland looking down on it and that image was released (setting a pattern of publishing the backs of the children's heads that would later become familiar). For the christening on 7 July the new parents refused to announce who the godparents were. At that point, if not before, it was obvious that things were going to be tricky. I for one did not care who the godparents were but I resented not being told.

There was soon a split between the Cambridges and the Sussexes, the latter setting up their own Household independently. The Duchess of Sussex refused to have cars on the sports ground because she could see them from nearby Frogmore Cottage. Observers noted that Prince Harry's speeches already had a Californian ring to them. In October 2018 they had visited Australia, deemed a successful tour, but every speech that Harry made was vetted by Meghan. At Commonwealth Observance in 2018, before the wedding, the couple had been totally in tune. The following year, 2019, he appeared uncomfortable and the rapport between them looked nil. He seemed unhappy on Easter Day, and in a general sense a man who had 'bitten off more than he could chew'.[5]

In October 2019 the Duchess of Sussex used an overseas visit to Africa to tell Tom Bradby of ITN that she was miserable. The Royal Family became concerned as to what was going on in the Sussex Household, more so than for Prince Andrew whose troubles were mounting.

The pair left for Canada, but Prince Harry returned, keen to discuss a way forward with the Queen. He wanted a half-in, half-out arrangement, whereby he would be self-financing but could still work for the Royal Family. In the new year of 2020, the three Private Secretaries, Sir Edward Young, Sir Clive Alderton and Simon Case, went into summit mode on the Sandringham estate and drafted their proposal.

Prince Harry went to Sandringham for the meeting and was told it was either all in or all out. He returned to Canada – reluctantly out.

★ ★ ★ ★ ★

On 12 October 2018 Princess Eugenie married Jack Brooksbank in St George's Chapel. This was a happier wedding. It did not attract as much publicity, and the Duke of York was annoyed that it would not be filmed for the major networks, though he persuaded a company to record it. The groom was alarmed that Prince Andrew insisted on a carriage procession through Windsor, afraid that no one would be there to cheer them. But Windsor loves a procession and there was a good crowd.

The press were universally horrible before the day. The Duchess of York sent the groom's mother gifts such as black silk pyjamas, embroidered 'MOG' (mother of the groom). Andrea Bocelli performed during the service. Guests included the Crown Prince of Bahrain, Robbie Williams, Naomi Williams and Cressida Bonas. Many of the younger members of the Royal Family, who had been excluded from the Sussex wedding, attended this one. Prince Philip again accompanied the Queen, as upright as ever. After the reception the Queen went back to her room saying: 'What a lovely day. What a lovely couple.'[6]

Prince Andrew

Throughout 2019 the Duke of York was as busy as any in the Royal Family with engagements at home and abroad. That year he undertook 190 engagements, with eighty-four overseas. That made him the sixth hardest-working member of the family. In November he was in Thailand, and on Remembrance Sunday he laid his wreath at the Cenotaph. On 11 November he held a regimental council meeting of Grenadier Guards, but that proved the last of his official solo engagements.* Three days later he recorded his ill-fated interview with Emily Maitlis, which was aired on Saturday, 16 November.

Prince Andrew had been under attack concerning the financier and convicted paedophile Jeffrey Epstein since 2011, when it became public that Epstein had helped him pay off £15,000 of the Duchess of York's debts. His role as Britain's trade envoy was terminated. In 2014 there were allegations that Epstein had arranged for him to have sex with Virginia Roberts Giuffre. A raft of further allegations followed. Pressure intensified after Epstein was found dead in his cell in New York on 10 August 2019. There were calls for Prince Andrew to be extradited to the United States. The NSPCC, of which he had been Patron until 2009, distanced itself from him.

The Emily Maitlis interview was a disaster. To do it in Buckingham Palace was a mistake, with wine glasses on the table, even if they contained water. It would seem that he thought he could talk about Pitch@Palace, and that he could clear his name. He did himself no favours. Maitlis was clever to knock each point home by repetition: 'You went for a walk with a registered sex offender?' Yes.

The Sunday after it aired, Prince Andrew deluded himself into thinking the interview had gone well. Within the week he was asked to step down from public life, and from that day onwards the only events he took part in publicly were family funerals, and he sometimes joined the Royal Family for Christmas and Easter services.

---

* The Duke was allowed to be represented at the memorial service for Sir Donald Gosling in Westminster Abbey on 11 December, an occasion attended by many members of the Royal Family. On 18 December he was present at the annual pre-Christmas lunch at Buckingham Palace, which the Queen gave to thank her family for their support during the year.

That December he hoped to be allowed to join the family at Christmas matins in 2019, telling his brother that at this time the Royal Family must show solidarity. Prince Charles did not agree. He ended up having to go to an early service, Prince Charles walking with him. He continued to live at Royal Lodge and spent his time riding or playing golf in the park. In due course he surrendered all his public positions including the colonelcy of Grenadier Guards.

When Cecil Beaton had photographed the Royal Family at the time of Prince Edward's birth in 1964, he had been particularly impressed by Prince Andrew, then aged four, finding him 'cheerful and polite and willing to please'. He described him:

> He is a boy with quality that shines out with his niceness, and goodness and good spirits. He is trained to behave well, to be polite and amenable, but he has the right instinct. Whatever tests one puts him through he comes out well. 'May I take some more? Or would you be bored?' – 'I'd like some more.'[7]

While others did not share this impression, certainly in later life, it is almost certainly that polite little boy who was fixed in the Queen's head. His problems caused her considerable distress in the last years of her life. She was deeply concerned about his future, one idea, developed in the last year of her life, being to set up a foundation that he could administer. She did not believe he had behaved improperly. Following the interview he could do no right. There was even criticism when he escorted his mother into Westminster Abbey for Prince Philip's memorial service in March 2022, both having travelled from Windsor in the same car. It is fortunate that she did not live to witness the dénouement.

47

THE ROAD TO COVID

'In the event that I am reincarnated, I would like to return as a deadly virus to contribute something to solving over-population.'
Prince Philip, 1988

There were two years before the Covid pandemic closed down the world and the Queen was driven into isolation at Windsor Castle. During that time she faced the Prince Andrew and Prince Harry issues, but by and large life continued its normal flow. She distributed the Royal Maundy at St George's Chapel on 29 March 2018, a tiny figure amid the bishops in their mitres. As ever she timed her walks to sit down at the exact moment that *Zadok The Priest* ended. The occasion was memorable for a female recipient in the south nave aisle who suffered from a nose bleed. Elderly people tend not to remember what happened three days before, but the Queen did. As she left the cloisters after church on Easter Sunday, she swung round. 'Was that you the other day with that woman with the nose bleed?'

I said: 'No, Ma'am, that was Dr Briscoe.'

She said: 'I longed to tell her it wasn't the first time it happened,' and gave an amusing imitation of the recipient holding her nose with one hand, with the other hand outstretched for the Maundy money, and 'a pool of blood'. Then the Queen headed out to face the crowds, the Cambridges following in her wake.[1]

Two days after the Queen celebrated her ninety-second birthday at a concert at the Royal Albert Hall, the Cambridges' third child, Prince Louis, arrived, an intelligent and perceptive scamp in the making.

An unattractive feature of much press comment was that the reign was in its last phase. Every time the Queen missed an engagement, or Prince Philip went to hospital (as he did for a bad hip in April

2018), the worst was anticipated. The Queen no longer walked down the hill in the Garter Procession. In June 2018 she travelled to the North Door by car. A rumour circulated that she was determined to go on living as she deeply disliked the influence of Michael Fawcett on Prince Charles.[2] She discussed dying with her friend Prue Penn. Both had been born in 1926 so both were ninety-two. They agreed that death held no fear. The Queen told her she did not think she would live to be a hundred. Of dying, she said: 'At least you don't have to do it as publicly as me.'[3] When Barbra Streisand sang in concert in Hyde Park on 7 July 2019, the singer commended the best qualities of Britain and got an enormous cheer when she said: 'You still have your lovely Queen.'[4] On 14 November Prince Charles reached the age of seventy.

2019

Prince Philip spent most of his time at Wood Farm but came over to Sandringham for the Christmas holiday. On the afternoon of 17 January he drove out of the estate, unaccompanied, in his Land Rover. The sun was low. He failed to see the traffic coming from the Dersingham direction at the Babingley crossroad. He hit a car and his vehicle overturned dramatically. As a crowd began to gather, a local policeman advised him to leave the scene and return to Sandringham. He passed Edward Young's office and, without explaining why, asked for a plaster. The next day he was back behind the wheel of a new vehicle on the estate. However, he agreed not to drive on the open road again. He was ninety-seven at the time.

A passenger in the hit car suffered a broken wrist. The Duke wrote to her: 'I am deeply sorry about this injury. I wish you a speedy recovery from a very distressing experience.'[5] The best postscript was Gyles Brandreth at an *Oldie* lunch joking about Prince Philip taking part in a speed-awareness course.[6]

The incident was a diversion from endless speculation about Brexit. Soon afterwards the Queen paid her traditional annual visit to the Sandringham WI meeting and made a speech asking for tolerance and seeking common ground, which was immediately interpreted as relating to Brexit.

Prince Philip was at Windsor for Easter 2019, but did not join her for Easter matins (also her ninety-third birthday). Communion was brought to him privately. Sir William Heseltine came over from Australia and lunched with the Queen. He told the Duke he was surprised to see him. 'I'm always here in April,' he snapped. Heseltine thanked him for replying to a recent letter. 'Did I?'[7] On 7 May the Duke made a rare appearance at the Order of Merit lunch at Windsor Castle. Despite his various ailments he remained fit, walking for miles. Inevitably, the Queen worried about him.

The Queen and Prince Philip were as upright as ever as they attended the wedding of Lady Gabriella Windsor to Tom Kingston in St George's Chapel on 18 May 2019, another happy event, which contrasted sharply with the tensions of the Harry-Meghan wedding. The bride was exceptionally beautiful and her stylish wedding dress floated as in a Hollywood film. After the service Prince Philip strode unaided from the chapel* and returned to his carriage-driving at Wood Farm.

* * * * *

On 3 June 2019 US President Donald Trump arrived at Buckingham Palace with a host of his relations to enjoy a state visit to London. The Queen had met him the previous July at Windsor Castle. Reporters had made much of him walking in front of the Queen as he inspected the guard of honour, but this was the first time that Prince Philip had not been there to escort a visiting Head of State. The Queen entertained him to tea, and kept him with her longer than was scheduled. It was a great chance to examine him. He went away saying he was her favourite president. No doubt she sent away every president thinking that.

Trump was on his best behaviour during his 2019 state visit. In his speech he praised the Queen as 'a great, great woman'. On 5 June he further joined the Queen at D-Day anniversary celebrations in Portsmouth. The state visit was considered a success. It had a subtle twist. When the Royal Household discovered that Trump drank no alcohol, they served the finest wines from the Palace cellars.

---

* This was the last time I ever saw Prince Philip.

Theresa May was still (just) Prime Minister during the Trump state visit. She had failed to deliver Brexit and so, on 24 May, she announced her intention to step down, 'the second female Prime Minister, but certainly not the last'. She resigned as Leader of the Conservative Party on 7 June, but remained Prime Minister until 24 July.

While the Conservative Party set about selecting a new Leader, the Queen had a few days at Sandringham. She returned to Windsor early in July. She visited the new summer exhibition at Buckingham Palace on 17 July, shown round by Tim Knox, the new Director of the Royal Collection, who was particularly good with her. Contrary to the perceived view, the Queen took a great interest in her collection, not just in dogs and horses.

For the next week she had no outside engagements. She had to delay her holiday in Scotland while the Tory Party sorted itself out. She was able to ride her pony, Emma, and to spend time with her budgerigars, which lived just below the terrace steps to the right of the George IV Gate (as seen from the Long Walk). At last the party elected Boris Johnson. Theresa May assured the Queen that Johnson commanded the confidence of the House of Commons. She stepped down on 24 July. She went to the Palace to take leave of the Queen, departing emotionally but unseen by the media.

Boris Johnson

The new Prime Minister, the Queen's fourteenth, was Boris Johnson. He came back from the Palace to deliver a bombastic speech on the steps of 10 Downing Street, then went in with his partner, Carrie Symonds. There followed a veritable slaughter in the Cabinet, as ministers were sacked or resigned. The Queen had to make a further visit to London the next day to swear in new Privy Counsellors and the new ministers as they took up their new Cabinet posts.

Only at the end of July was the Queen able to get up to Scotland, arriving with the traditional Royal Guard at Balmoral on 6 August. While she was able to entertain her family and the guests who traditionally came for stalking, politics intervened once more. On 28 August Johnson asked the Queen to prorogue Parliament and sent Jacob Rees-Mogg, Lord President of the Council, to Balmoral to approve this at a specially convened meeting of the Privy Council. A huge constitutional and political muddle ensued. The Queen approved the prorogation to last from 10 September until 14 October.

In the midst of this came the traditional visit of the Prime Minister. Times were changing. The Court Circular announced that Johnson 'and Ms Carrie Symonds' had arrived at the castle on 6 September. The Queen's view was that she was sure many of her Prime Ministers had had mistresses, but she had never had to entertain them. However, Edward Young thought she would look old-fashioned if she did not entertain the pair.

Nicola Sturgeon, First Minister of Scotland, stayed a night at Balmoral on 16 September, enjoying the evening barbecues and the relative informality. Writing later, she claimed not to be a monarchist 'by instinct', adding: 'The private time I spent with the Queen ranks as one of the great privileges of my life. It was clear from my first meeting that she was an extraordinary woman.'[8] She reported that the Queen wanted to know about the misconduct claims against Alex Salmond. Naturally she liked to be well informed and Nicola Sturgeon could enlighten her. Who else could she ask?[9] Sturgeon made the perceptive remark that Princess Charlotte was very like the Queen. 'She lit up with a beaming smile, clearly thrilled that the resemblance had been noted.'[10]

Balmoral bored Prince Philip this year. He stayed for just ten days, before returning to Wood Farm. The Queen returned to London in early October.

Around the time that Prince Andrew gave his ill-fated interview to Emily Maitlis, there came serious rumours about Prince Philip's health at Wood Farm. The story was that it was 'just a matter of days'.[11] Though this was not published, Downing Street was alerted and a decision was taken that if the Duke died Boris's General Election would be postponed by five days. It was hard to get to the truth. None of the inner circle seemed to know what was happening and there were massive contradictions. A week before, Prince Charles had said his father was 'frustrated by inactivity'. Penny Mountbatten was said to be with him most of the time. He would exchange books and ideas about books with Lady Derby. A week before a letter had come that had upset her: it transpired he had been heavily on morphine. His ponies had been sent back to Windsor, so there would be no more carriage-driving, but this was normal in the winter. Even the other members of the Royal Family had not been informed of his condition. Everyone prepared for the worst. Sky TV and ITN presenters went round with black ties in their pockets. But then Prince Philip perked up and went to Broadlands for the weekend. Someone said he was being public-spirited and making an effort to survive so as not to upset the General Election.

In December he was in hospital for 'precautionary' tests for a 'pre-existing condition'. He came out in time to join the family for Christmas at Sandringham, looking 'pinched and rather haunted'.[12] At home he was looked after by David Berwick, who had served on *Britannia*. The Duke's health was monitored literally every day. He had a stent in his arm and they could pump steroids into him whenever they needed to. He was unwell over Christmas. It was said that it had been quite hard to keep him alive.

★ ★ ★ ★ ★

For the State Opening on 14 October 2019, the Queen did not wear the Imperial State Crown. Wisely she wore the George IV diadem as she had done in 1952, since she could not wear the crown before the Coronation. The crown was carried by the Lord Great Chamberlain and placed on a cushion beside her. As usual she had the Prince of Wales and the Duchess of Cornwall with her. It was to be the last time the Queen performed this ceremony in the full robes of state.

Johnson's act of proroguing Parliament had been proved illegal in the Supreme Court on 24 September. He tried to break the impasse several times, and eventually called a General Election for 12 December. From this he emerged with 305 seats, a majority of eighty. There was a further State Opening on 19 December, a low-key affair, the Queen in a pale blue-green day coat and hat, and the Prince of Wales in morning dress. The Lord Great Chamberlain wore his uniform and carried the Imperial State Crown. The few peers wore their parliamentary robes. There were no pages. The ceremony was pared to the minimum. In her speech the

Government had the Queen promising Brexit would be delivered on 31 January 2020. And on that date it was indeed delivered.

★ ★ ★ ★ ★

2020

The year started uncomfortably with issues relating to Prince Harry bowing out and settling in Canada. Apart from that, it was business as usual, the Queen coming down to London from Sandringham in early February. On 24 February she went to Whitelands House to present in person a hundredth-birthday card to her Mistress of the Robes, the Duchess of Grafton.

On 9 March she led the congregation at the Commonwealth Observance at Westminster Abbey. That morning there had been a large turnout of the Royal Household at the memorial service for Sir Malcolm Ross at St George's Chapel. Members of the Royal Family, including the Duke of York, the Duke and Duchess of Gloucester were there. In the afternoon attention focused on the Duke and Duchess of Sussex, because it was known that the Abbey Observance would be their last joint engagement in Britain before they set off for a new life in Canada (and later in California).

The Queen was a little stooped, but walked well. Prince Charles appeared to have thickened out. The Cambridges were tall and well-dressed. Prince Harry looked 'woolly and unimpressive' and his Duchess was 'smart in vivid green'. Much was made of the non-communication between the Cambridges and the Sussexes, with photos of them looking glum. While there was no communication, the atmosphere in the Abbey was not noticeably unpleasant.[13]

★ ★ ★ ★ ★

No one could have predicted the times into which the world would descend in the early months of 2020. Rumours of a Covid-19 pandemic began to spread and in March 2020 Britain was plunged into lockdown. At the time the Queen was almost ninety-four and the Duke of Edinburgh would turn ninety-eight in June. On 18

March someone dug up the 1988 quote from Prince Philip in which he had said: 'In the event that I am reincarnated, I would like to return as a deadly virus to contribute something to solving overpopulation.' This fuelled rumours on social media that the news of his death was being withheld. The Queen squashed them by issuing a statement to say he was to join her at Windsor Castle. She summoned him back from Wood Farm, Sandringham.

Just before the Queen left for Windsor a regular meeting between Sovereign and Prime Minister was scheduled for 18 March. Both had considered it their duty that it should take place. Edward Young later described the Queen's attitude as 'a sort of Blitz spirit, "Well, I've got to die sometime,"' but rightly he decided this was no time for the Queen to take risks. He contacted Martin Reynolds, the Prime Minister's Private Secretary. They agreed that Downing Street would be told that the Palace wanted to cancel, and the Queen would be told that Downing Street had got cold feet.[14] Dominic Cummings, Johnson's controversial adviser, told him not to go in person. He reported later: 'He rejected our advice. I was desperate and said something like "If you've got Covid and you kill the Queen you're finished." Cleo [Watson, his aide] said she would not let him get in the car.'[15]

No meeting took place, which was just as well as the Prime Minister was coughing. He tested positive for Covid, and by 6 April was gravely ill in hospital. Edward Young had to brief the Queen about the illness and to consider the ramifications should a Prime Minister die in office.[16]

The Queen left Buckingham Palace on 19 March, never to spend another night there. She moved into Windsor Castle, which was filled with memories of childhood, of her grandfather, of wartime with her sister, and of the park where she had so often ridden. The move was required since Boris Johnson was advising everyone over the age of seventy to avoid all non-essential contact and travel as part of unprecedented peacetime measures to control the spread of the pandemic. To have lost the Head of State to the pandemic would have been catastrophic. All of the Queen's public engagements were cancelled.

The Queen and the Duke were moved into four rooms in the castle, looked after by a skeleton staff, twenty-two in total. They entered a strict condition of isolation, jokingly nicknamed HMS *Bubble*, by the Master of the Household, Admiral Tony Johnstone-Burt. Nobody was allowed to enter the Upper Ward of the castle and there were no ladies in waiting in attendance. Later, when a lady in waiting came, she had to isolate for some days in the Lancaster Tower.

The Duke of Edinburgh needed injections. Simon Durnford, a Military Knight, was an oncologist and saw Prince Philip every day. They got on well due to a shared interest in naval history. Durnford told him he was giving him an injection and the last time he had done that it was to a bull.[17] Prince Philip laughed. The Military Knight found Prince Philip a likeable man, who expressed great concern for all those who were suffering from lockdown.[18] Durnford himself had to self-isolate. The Duke remained an avid reader, exchanging books with Tony Johnstone-Burt, and expecting a two-page analysis on completion. He had always been suspicious of novels but was greatly drawn to those of Robert Harris, especially the Pompeii ones.

Terry Pendry rang the Queen regularly and said she must use her muscles. Occasionally he brought her pony, Emma. She would drive out to meet him and ride for forty-five minutes.

The Prince of Wales and the Duchess of Cornwall caught Covid. When the clapping for the NHS started, a feature of every Thursday evening, the Prince and the Duchess were filmed clapping in separate rooms. Prince Edward made a statement, and the Cambridge children clapped together in unison – their first venture into public life. At the end of April, the beleaguered Yorks distributed hampers to regular worshippers at the Royal Chapel.

In Canada the Sussexes were criticised for departing to California. They flew there just before the borders closed. While in England everyone was working together, they were looking after themselves. The Queen took a dim view of her grandson: 'And now Harry has opted out, and *for what*? To be a carer for Archie.'[19]

On 5 April the Queen broadcast from Windsor Castle. Seven million or so tuned in on Christmas Day, but this time there were twenty-four million. The Queen looked well in her green dress with her hair done. Only one masked cameraman filmed her – in the White Drawing Room. During her speech she casually mentioned that she had broadcast from Windsor some eighty years before. She gave a reassuring message of hope, and reminded us all to stay together even while staying apart. There had been a lot of discussion as to whether she should include what became her most memorable line, 'We will meet again,' with its echoes of Vera Lynn in wartime. It worked.

On Easter Day, the Archbishop of Canterbury held a service in his kitchen. The Queen issued her own Easter statement, which proved popular, the idea of the Dean of Windsor. Presently Prince Philip also issued a message and was pleasantly surprised to find that he was not a forgotten figure. The Queen reached her ninety-fourth birthday on 21 April. Seven truckloads of birthday cards arrived at Windsor Castle.

On 8 May, to mark the seventy-fifth anniversary of D-Day, there was a virtual concert from Buckingham Palace, at the end of which the Queen appeared in pale blue with the aquamarine brooches given to her by her father on her eighteenth birthday in 1944. She delivered another speech with her ATS hat beside her.

It was important that the nation knew the Queen was well. She became proficient at Zoom. Her subjects could see her receiving an ambassador remotely or in discussion with charity workers. A photograph of her riding Fern in the grounds of the castle was published on 1 June. Another photograph, later used as the Queen's 2020 Christmas card, was released to mark Prince Philip's ninety-ninth birthday on 10 June. As a concession to age, he finally gave up carriage-driving.*

On 17 July Princess Beatrice married her Italian, Edoardo Mozzi. On the same day the Queen knighted Captain Tom Moore. He had caught the attention of the nation by walking up and down his drive for charity in his hundredth year. He had hoped to raise a thousand pounds for the NHS. By the time he reached his centenary on 30 April, he had raised an astonishing £30 million.

There was a final official appearance by the Duke of Edinburgh on 22 July when he handed over his colonelcy of the Rifles to the

---

* Prince Philip described carriage-driving as relaxation. Having watched him do it, I can but say that it required so much concentration that all other thoughts were expelled. During an Ascot week some years before, he took Christopher Balfour out with him. He said that normally they turned right, but this time he would make them turn left. 'They won't like it.' They did not. Both the Duke and Balfour were thrown off. 'See what I mean,' said Prince Philip.

Duchess of Cornwall. At ninety-nine, he emerged from the private apartments of the castle to take the salute, immaculately dressed, with a ramrod back, to mark the handover.

On 4 August the Queen and Prince Philip flew to Balmoral by private plane, she in a suit with headscarf and he in a yellow shirt and no tie. They stayed only until 14 September. Prince Philip had tended to go back to Wood Farm around then, and this time the Queen went with him. Prince Charles, who had now taken over Sandringham House, went to visit his parents in the much smaller Wood Farm, a strange reversal of roles. She returned to Windsor Castle in October and undertook a few engagements in London in the autumn. In November she was seen at the tomb of the Unknown Warrior, and on the Home Office balcony on Remembrance Sunday.

The Queen and the Duke spent Christmas at Windsor Castle, while other members of the Royal Family went to Sandringham. Her broadcast opened with the mounted band of the Household Cavalry in the Lower Ward of Windsor Castle, playing the National Anthem, and ended with the Lewisham and Greenwich NHS Choir singing and holding candles in St George's Hall. As she spoke, there were images of her and her family doing Zooms, knighting Captain Tom, and of the myriad ways her family had boosted people's spirits during that difficult year. The Queen looked robust, dressed in deep purple with her hair immaculate as ever. And she was inspirational. Where Ursula von der Leyen, President of the European Commission, quoted the Beatles, 'the long and winding road', the Queen quoted Tennessee Williams: 'the kindness of strangers'. Noting how the different religions celebrated their festivals, she appreciated that people could not 'gather as they would wish', but, ever positive, she added:

> Remarkably, a year that has necessarily kept people apart has, in many ways, brought us closer. Across the Commonwealth, my family and I have been inspired by stories of people volunteering in their communities, helping those in need.

She thanked nurses everywhere. She spoke of how some would be separated from friends and families 'when all they'd really want for Christmas is a simple hug or a squeeze of the hand'.[20]

48
PRINCE PHILIP

The hazard of a long life is that many friends die. On 11 April 2019 Jeanie, Lady Carnarvon, died. In March 2020, during lockdown, the Queen had a socially distanced meeting with her cousin Lady Elizabeth Anson in the garden at Frogmore and gave her a CVO. Lady Elizabeth died of cancer, aged seventy-nine, on 1 November 2020.

Prince Philip's short-term memory was deteriorating. He did not want to reach his hundredth birthday, particularly disliking the fuss attendant at such events.[1] Early in the new year it looked as though he might get his wish. On 17 February he was admitted to the Edward VII Hospital in London for tests. The gravity of the situation became apparent when Prince Charles came from Highgrove to see him, emerging looking forlorn. Prince Philip wanted to get back to Windsor Castle for his last days, but on 1 March umbrellas blocked the press cameras and he was moved to St Bartholomew's Hospital where he had an operation on his heart. They nearly lost him twice. On 5 March he was returned to the Edward VII. ITN had three entrances to Windsor Castle monitored in case Prince Philip came back or the Queen came out. I can think of at least four, excluding the possibility of a helicopter and there are surely more.

With no consideration for the stress under which the Queen was then living, and the precarious health of the Duke of Edinburgh, a much heralded interview between the Duchess of Sussex and Oprah Winfrey was screened on Sunday, 7 March, and available in the UK the following day. In this notorious exercise, the Duchess sat with Oprah Winfrey, wearing heavy mascara, dressed principally in black, in which she landed serious allegations against the Royal Family, several of which have since been successfully challenged. She accused members of the Royal Family of being racist and she played the mental-health card. Prince Harry was brought on at the end to show he knew what was going on. It was filmed in a sunny garden in California, a contrast to the cold winter of isolation in Britain.* After that the Queen issued her famous statement: 'Recollections may vary.'

Prince Philip was eventually well enough to go back to Windsor Castle, his return considerably delayed by the need to find nurses 100 per cent free of possible Covid infection. The press photographed him leaving the hospital by car on 16 March. He entered the castle grounds by the gate on King Edward VII Avenue (B470) – the road from Datchet to Windsor – one of the few entrances not monitored by the media. He never emerged again. However, during those last twenty-four days at Windsor he was up and about and one lady in waiting, ringing in, was surprised to get him on the telephone. Prince Philip loved the castle, the birthplace of his mother. There were surely elements of tranquillity in those last twenty-four days at Windsor.

Had the Duke been well enough, he might have been photographed going privately to church on his birthday. In a later interview, Prince Charles said he had discussed it with his father, who had barked back: 'Well, I have to be around for it.' During this time, his nephew was delighted to receive from him the foreword to a new book on Wolfsgarten. It arrived by post on the morning of 9 April, shortly before news came that the Duke had died. It showed that, in so far as he was able, Prince Philip was working till the end.

On the last night of his life, he gave his nurses the slip and went along the corridor on his Zimmer frame, helped himself to a beer and drank it in the Oak Room. The next morning, he got up, had a bath, said he did not feel well and quietly slipped away. The Queen was not there when he died. There had often been times in earlier days when the Queen had asked the staff to let her know when Prince Philip was leaving, only to be told 'His Royal Highness left twenty minutes ago.' She took the line that she was 'absolutely furious that, as so often in life, he left without saying goodbye'.[2]

---

* Kind friends in America made it possible for me to watch it on the Sunday night, their camera in front of the television. My verdict: 'sickening'.

Had the Queen retreated into Queen Victoria-style mourning, it might have been hard for her, at nearly ninety-five, to pick up the reins again. She pressed on, and in the days between the death and the funeral, spoke to the Prime Minister, bade farewell to Lord Peel, the retiring Lord Chamberlain, in person on 13 April, and the next day received the incoming Lord Parker of Minsmere. On 16 April the Governor-General of Australia (the Honourable David Hurley) and the Prime Minister of Canada (the Right Honourable Justin Trudeau) had telephone audiences of her. She attended to last-minute decisions about the funeral on Saturday, 17 April. Thoughtfully, she asked that the staff, including the chefs, should come out into the Quadrangle to witness the procession leave.

Prince Philip's Funeral

Nothing would have delighted Prince Philip more than that his funeral was so pared down. When it was arranged for London, he had reduced the ceremonial to the minimum – a procession between St James's Palace and Hyde Park Corner. At that point the coffin would be transferred into his specially designed Land Rover. Clearly there was no point in taking him to London and then back to Windsor.

On a perfect Saturday afternoon the military gathered in the Home Park and marched to the castle. Most areas of the Duke's naval, military and air-force life were represented in the castle precincts. A moving moment was the arrival in the Quadrangle of his driving carriage, a familiar sight in the Great Park for so many years, with two ponies, Storm and Nevis, led by the head coachman, Matthew Powers, and Kirsty Cox, the groom, with Michelle Maynard, another groom, seated on the carriage, holding the reins.

The Duke's coffin was conveyed on his Land Rover to the foot of the Great West Steps, with the Royal Family following on foot. He had chosen the music for the service. There was the *Jubilate in C* he commissioned from Benjamin Britten in 1961. He loved Psalm 104, and requested it be set to music, not so much in poetry but in poetic prose. This was done by William Lovelady in three movements and first performed for his seventy-fifth birthday. For his eightieth birthday service at St George's, it was adapted by the then organist, Jonathan Rees-Williams. It was more traditionally performed to a chant by William Hawes for his ninetieth, also at Windsor. The earlier version was sung at the funeral. The reading from Ecclesiasticus 43 – 'Look at the Rainbow' – he heard read at his ninetieth service by the Warden of St George's House.

The Queen restricted the mourners to thirty, in accordance with the guidelines for funerals across Britain. They sat distanced from one another in the Quire. She could have had another thirty in the Nave, but she did not. Unlike Boris Johnson's government, who were breaking the very guidelines they had introduced, she set an example. The thirty were the immediate family, with the Duke of Gloucester, the Duke of Kent and Princess Alexandra. Penny, Countess Mountbatten of Burma, his driving companion, represented the Mountbattens, and there was the Landgraf of Hesse, a Baden and a Hohenlohe. Sadly there was no room for Prince Michael of Kent (a page at their wedding) or Lady Pamela Hicks (bridesmaid and first cousin). Some other German relations were in the Cloisters.

The most poignant image of the day was of the Queen sitting alone, with her mask on. But her chosen relations were in view. As the Duke's coffin descended into the Royal Vault, which takes eight minutes, a lone piper played a lament walking up the North Quire Aisle and into the Dean's Cloister. The television cameras followed the piper, so the descent of the Duke's coffin remained private. There it rested until September 2022, alongside his maternal ancestors, George III and Queen Charlotte, and Prince Edward, Duke of Kent (father of Queen Victoria).

That evening, ever thoughtful to others, the Queen telephoned Lady Angela Oswald, whose husband Sir Michael* had died that morning. She spoke of how Prince Philip had been frustrated at not being able to make his normal contribution to life, a common

---

* Sir Michael Oswald (1934–2021), racing manager to the Queen Mother, 1970–2002, National Hunt racing adviser to the Queen, 2003–2021. The Queen had invested him with the GCVO at Sandringham in 2020. Although Sir Michael suffered from dementia towards the end of his life, the Queen had allowed him to think he was still running her horses. She did not make him retire. She told Lady Angela that that was on account of fifty years of friendship.

complaint from those who have striven actively to put things into life rather than take things out.

On Sundays during lockdown, an informal service of matins was zoomed from Cumberland Lodge. This the Queen watched regularly. It ended with some light music every week. On the day after the funeral, the music chosen was: 'You'll Never Walk Alone'.[3]

★ ★ ★ ★ ★

National mourning lasted until the day after the funeral, and family mourning until the following Thursday. The Queen was soon at the wheel of her car, inspecting Prince Philip's carriages in the Home Park at Windsor, and she undertook several Zooms. She dressed in pretty floral colours.

All eyes were on the Queen when she came to open Parliament on 11 May to read her sixty-seventh speech to Parliament. The ceremony was considerably reduced. She travelled in a rather modest four-by-four, with two vehicles following and an escort of four police motorcycles. Instead of the traditional train, the Queen was dressed in pale violet, wearing her mother's twin sapphire brooches, holding the hand of the Prince of Wales, who wore a morning coat with no stars or medals. A small procession of masked figures formed. Only thirty socially distanced peers occupied the chamber. There was one throne, and the speech was already waiting for the Queen. Only a handful of peers and the MPs present walked to the House of Lords in single file.

In a clear and calm, slightly piano voice, the Queen delivered the speech, reading it from a brochure, which she held with white gloves, turning the pages with care. The speech, written by the Prime Minister, was self-congratulatory in tone. Brexit had been done; Boris Johnson enjoyed a substantial majority in the Commons. He had done well in the recent council elections in Britain. The Queen returned to Windsor. In the House of Commons that afternoon, Katherine Fletcher, a Conservative MP (born 1976), described the Queen in a difficult year as 'still flipping ace'.[4]

The Queen had a busy summer. She invited Penny Mountbatten to the Windsor Horse Show. On 11 June she went to Cornwall to the Eden Project to meet world leaders attending the G7 Summit, arriving through beautiful foliage to be confronted by Boris Johnson. The following day there was a reduced Trooping the Colour in the Quadrangle of Windsor Castle. The Duke of Kent accompanied the Queen onto the dais. He had been given a new bearskin, which was too big, and the Queen had to guide him as he could not see where he was going.

The King's Troop and the Household Cavalry took part and the Queen clearly enjoyed it.[5] The next day she was back on the dais in pink, the Guards drawn up, as US President Joe Biden arrived by helicopter and then by car at the end of the G7 Summit. Relaxed and looking well, the Queen was having the time of her life. Thereced in the verdict of Charles Anson, her former Press Secretary, that her attitude to the next generation was: 'I've done my bit – get on with it.'[6]

Because the Colonels of the different regiments were not riding at Windsor, the issue of the Duke of York as Colonel of Grenadier Guards, was discussed behind the scenes. The Duke had been appointed on 1 December 2017, on the express wish of the Queen, to succeed Prince Philip. At the time the Grenadiers had not wanted him, but he proved a good Colonel, among other things entertaining warrant officers at Royal Lodge. After his fall from grace, the main concern of the Grenadiers was not to upset the Colonel-in-Chief. The solution was that the Queen resumed the colonelcy herself.*

The Queen had looked wonderful all summer, but less so after her return from Balmoral. It is likely that the inevitable grief had caught up with her, and anxiety over the Prince Andrew and Prince Harry situations, not to mention the Government. Picnics were cancelled or curtailed at Balmoral. It was probably then that she was diagnosed with cancer.

The Queen returned to Windsor on 6 October, looking drawn. She had opened Parliament in Scotland the previous Saturday (2 October) in a dark green outfit with a thistle brooch, but had then been made to stand for an hour and a half, on high heels, talking to people wearing masks. She could not hear a word they were saying, so she just smiled. Then the plane to London had had to

---

* After her death, the Duchess of Cornwall was appointed Colonel of Grenadier Guards (in December 2022).

land at RAF Brize Norton, some distance from Windsor. She met some soldiers in the castle. By then she was walking with a stick in private but not yet in public.

Soon came the cancellations. On 20 October she backed out of a visit to Northern Ireland and from a visit to COP 26. She went into hospital for an overnight stay. She recorded a moving address asking the COP 26 conference to rise above politics to statesmanship and to act for our children and our children's children. She wore green – not the bright, optimistic green of the April pandemic speech in 2020, but a more dusty shade. The press jumped on her 'None of us will live for ever' line, but it was one of her great speeches. The Queen did not come to the Cenotaph, due to 'a bad back', and just before Christmas she decided not to go to Sandringham.

On 30 November the Queen ceased to be Queen of Barbados. Prince Charles was sent out with apologetic words approved by the Foreign Office. He said: 'From the darkest days of our past, and the appalling atrocity of slavery, which forever stains our history, the people of this island forged their path with extraordinary fortitude.'[7] His words were widely commended, but they paved the way for demands for reparations.

The Queen lost two more close friends in December – her long-serving Mistress of the Robes, Fortune, Duchess of Grafton, on 3 December 2021, aged 101, soon to be followed by Diana, Lady Farnham (another lady in waiting) aged ninety, on 29 December. The Queen's family joined her at Windsor, the Prince of Wales and the Duchess of Cornwall, the Wessexes and the Gloucesters going to St George's Chapel for Christmas matins. Covid was in its last phase.

The Central Band of the Royal British Legion played the National Anthem on the terrace garden steps of Windsor Castle before the Queen's traditional Christmas broadcast. It opened with images of the Queen with Prince Philip and her 1997 tribute. Compared to the year before she was unquestionably weaker. Her red dress did not fit well and her features were pinched.

The Queen's voice was good but there was concern felt watching her. It was a more personal speech than usual. She began: 'Although it's a time of great happiness and good cheer for many, Christmas can be hard for those who have lost loved ones. This year, especially, I understand why.' She spoke of the comfort that the many tributes to her 'beloved Philip' had meant to her:

> His sense of service, intellectual curiosity and capacity to squeeze fun out of any situation – were all irrepressible. That mischievous, enquiring twinkle was as bright at the end as when I first set eyes on him. But life, of course, consists of final partings as well as first meetings; and as much as I and my family miss him, I know he would want us to enjoy Christmas.

For the second year running, Covid was keeping families apart. She looked forward to the Commonwealth Games in Birmingham and hoped that the year of her Platinum Jubilee would be 'an opportunity for people everywhere to enjoy a sense of togetherness; a chance to give thanks for the enormous changes of the last seventy years – social, scientific and cultural – and also to look ahead with confidence'.[8]

49
THE PLATINUM JUBILEE, 2022

The Platinum Jubilee was a remarkable anniversary – seventy years on the throne – and one never achieved by any previous British monarch. The Queen was not well, but she was determined to reach that anniversary.

The Queen's advisers were aware of the few issues that needed to be resolved. They were also concerned about the Queen's health. One such was the status of the Duchess of Cornwall when Prince Charles became King. She had been given the Royal Family Order in 2007, appointed GCVO in 2012, and made a Privy Counsellor in 2016, but the original statement that she would be Princess Consort still stood.

On New Year's Eve the Queen took the unprecedented step of bestowing the Order of the Garter on her. Tony Blair was also appointed, since it was easier if the Queen did this than Prince Charles later, along with Baroness Amos. The announcement was brought forward in case the Queen did not live until St George's Day, 23 April, the traditional date for appointments to be made.

The people of Windsor loved seeing the Royal Standard flying from the Round Tower, and knowing she was there. She decided to make Windsor her home, but even in the year of the Platinum Jubilee, she went to Wood Farm. She visited towards the end of January, which meant she could enjoy being with her horses and marked the day of her accession, 6 February, at Sandringham House.

The evening before, she performed her final act of generosity to her son and daughter-in-law by stating that she wished Camilla to be known as Queen Consort when Prince Charles became king. Signing herself: 'Your Servant, Elizabeth R', the Queen said: 'When, in the fullness of time, my son Charles becomes King, I know you will give him and his wife Camilla the same support that you have given me; and it is my sincere wish that, when that time comes, Camilla will be known as Queen Consort as she continues her own loyal service.'[1] After seventy years the Queen asked this small favour, and it was well received. The Queen returned to Windsor on Monday, 7 February.

The Platinum Jubilee

The Silver and Golden Jubilees (in 1977 and 2002) had started in an atmosphere of apathy, which soon changed to glorious enthusiasm. By the time of the Diamond Jubilee (2012), people knew what to expect. The Platinum Jubilee was different. It was a question of what the Queen might be well enough to take part in.

Sadly, at a time when the Queen should have been sailing into glorious sunlit uplands in the twilight days of the greatest reign in British history, she had much on her mind – family issues with Prince Andrew and Prince Harry, and an increasingly maverick Prime Minister in Boris Johnson. Prince Andrew had stepped down from royal duties in November 2019 'for the foreseeable future'. In January he dropped all his public appointments and ceased to use his HRH in public. In the course of the year, a considerable sum of money was donated to Virginia Giuffre and her charities, with no admission of liability conceded. This was done so as not to overshadow the Jubilee.

Prince Harry had gone to California. He was working on his ghosted memoir, *Spare*. Cynically publication was delayed lest it coincided with the Queen's death. Whenever Prince Harry called his grandmother, she asked her lady in waiting to stay with her. The distress the Sussexes caused the Queen in the last years of her life cannot be overestimated.

At the end of March the Queen came to London for the long-delayed memorial service for Prince Philip in Westminster Abbey. There were thirteen Kings and Queens in the Abbey, but the inept Lord Chamberlain's Office seated them many rows back behind the British Royal Family, which displeased the Queen. Princess Charlotte was greeted by the Archbishop of Canterbury who more or less knelt before her, and got in exchange the kind of look her great-grandmother sometimes gave people. The Queen travelled in the car with Prince Andrew, who escorted her through the south transept. Because he was so unpopular, he was castigated. It was seen not as the natural support a mother could expect from her son but pushing himself forward. The Queen and other royal ladies wore green, the colour Prince Philip favoured for his letter headings and staff ties. Inevitably, the service had a *fin de siècle* feeling to it. The Dean of Windsor, David Conner, gave his best ever address on the theme of service and sacrifice. He said of Prince Philip:

> There were times when he could be abrupt; maybe, in robust conversation, forgetting just how intimidating he could be. A kind of natural reserve sometimes made him seem a little distant. He could be somewhat sharp in pricking what he thought to be bubbles of pomposity or sycophancy. On the other hand, we should not forget that he himself was sometimes wounded by being unfairly criticised or misunderstood.[2]

The Queen did not disagree.

She went to Wood Farm for her ninety-sixth birthday and spent a week there. On 10 May she wanted to open Parliament but, rightly, it was decided unwise to have her read a convoluted speech under bright lights on live television. Prince Charles read her speech, with the Imperial State Crown placed beside him. The Queen did attend the Windsor Horse Show, though she arrived late, boosted by steroids. She toured the Chelsea Flower Show in a buggy. In May she spent some days at Craigowan, then prepared for the main Jubilee weekend.

The celebrations proved predictably successful, but the Queen's part was limited. The day of the Birthday Parade was Thursday, 2 June, the anniversary of the Coronation, a 'collar' day.* The Prince of Wales led the Birthday Parade on Horse Guards, but the Queen appeared on the balcony of Buckingham Palace to take the salute as the troops returned. At her side was her cousin, the Duke of Kent

---

* A collar day is when the collars of the Orders of Chivalry are worn. By tradition the riband of a lesser Order is worn. The Garter collar and riband are not worn together.

(as Colonel of Scots Guards). The Queen asked him if he was going to salute. He said he was. 'Well, don't knock my hat off,' she said.[3]

The effect of this was to give the Prince of Wales the chance to preside over the parade as he would when he became king. But the moment the Queen appeared, he dissolved into the background and the focus returned to her, a seamless balance. When she witnessed the flypast, she was joined on the balcony only by the so-called 'working Royals' – an idea cooked up to exclude Princes Andrew and Harry, and to honour those who supported her in her work. It was a particularly warm day and crowds thronged the Mall, way exceeding expectations. That night she lit the first of a series of beacons in the Quadrangle of Windsor Castle.

The Queen was disappointed to miss the National Service of Thanksgiving at St Paul's Cathedral on the Friday, at which again the working Royals sat in the front row. Nor did she attend the Derby on the Saturday. Prince Harry was at Frogmore Cottage with his wife and two children, the gate adorned with balloons to celebrate baby Lilibet's* first birthday. They visited the Queen with the children, again with a lady in waiting present.

The Queen was never planning to attend the pop concert outside Buckingham Palace. However, technology gave her an inspired presence, with the filmed vignette of her at tea with Paddington Bear. During the concert, extracts from speeches were broadcast. The enthusiasm of the crowd that evening proved once more that even if the Queen was not present she still galvanised the nation.

Nor did she attend the Pageant on the Sunday. But she decided at the last moment she could come and was driven to London from Windsor. The Union Flag came down the Palace flagpole and the Royal Standard went up, alerting the observant to her presence. At 5 p.m., the balcony doors opened and the Queen appeared, dressed in vivid green, accompanied by the Prince of Wales, the Duchess of Cornwall, the Duke and Duchess of Cambridge and their three children. She was there for three minutes. Here was a telling image of the future of the Royal Family – the Queen with three male

---

* To use the intimate family nickname of 'Lilibet', only used by close members of the family, was insensitive to say the least.

heirs in direct succession, in three generations. It was the last time she was seen in London.

Over those days, amid the adulation, there was a tinge of sadness, a hint of impending departure. When she went back into the Palace, it meant that four historic days were over. This was the tail end of a golden age. Were we sadly coming to the end of this glorious reign, or might she sail on to her century?

The Queen did not entirely disappear. The next day she was seen in a Zoom at Windsor Castle. She continued to fulfil her constitutional duties – to talk to the Prime Minister and to hold Privy Council meetings by Zoom, and sometimes to receive visitors in person. She attended to her red boxes as usual.

At the Order of the Garter ceremony, she invested the new Companions – the Duchess of Cornwall, Baroness Amos and Sir Tony Blair, the only concession being that she did not wear the heavy Garter robes and remained seated. She was able to do all the normal investing, except tying the ribbons to secure the collar (because she was seated). She lunched with the Companions and their spouses, but did not attend the Installation service in St George's Chapel, so the Prince of Wales installed the new Companions in her place.

In all these engagements, it was a question of the art of the possible – what the Queen could do, and what was best left to members of her family, principally the tiring public engagements, which involved walking and standing about. At the age of ninety-six, she was still very much at the helm, or 'in the saddle', as the Archbishop of York had put it in his sermon at the National Service of Thanksgiving. Unwittingly she broke some records. She became the longest holder in the Order of the Garter on 1 July, beating the record of the Duke of Connaught at more than seventy-five years. She just out-reigned the 70 years and 126 days of the King of Thailand – the Queen reigned 70 years and 214 days. Louis XIV of France held the record at 72 years 110 days, but he reigned under a minority and his early years were as a minor, so arguably she held that record too.

I had been afraid that I would never see the Queen again, but I was lucky. I had written the foreword to *The Queen and Windsor*, the handsome book sponsored by the Windsor Platinum Jubilee Committee, with photographs by Gill Heppell. On Friday, 24 June, the Queen had been riding with Terry Pendry for the second time that week, and said we could come and present her with a copy. Terry drove us through the Royal Mews, into the Long Walk area and through the George IV Gate. At a side door Annabel Whitehead and Matt Magee were waiting. The page, Stephen, took us up a small staircase, the walls covered with Topolski drawings of luminaries such as Edith Sitwell and E. M. Forster, into the large corridor, and along to the Oak Room, which is above the Sovereign's Entrance, and where we have seen many Zooms with the Queen on television.

I had never been into the Queen's private apartments before. There was a cut-out of a guardsman, many magazines neatly laid out, a great number of newspapers, boxes of chocolate, framed photos of the family, and the two Oswald Birley portraits of the Queen and Prince Philip in Garter robes at the time of their Installation.

The Queen came in slowly, walking with her big staff, which she put aside and did not use again. She was very small now, but bright-eyed and smiling, in a simple floral-patterned dress. We had tied a ribbon round the book, which she pulled off easily, looking for a while at some of the pictures. I ventured to say: 'I hadn't realised until researching this that you spent every Easter with your grandparents – the first visit recorded in the Court Circular in April 1928.' She said there was a photograph of her as a child saluting. The two friendly Corgis joined her.

There was discussion about St George's Chapel, the Queen pointing out that you could see the minarets on the chapel roof to the left of the Round Tower, because the castle curves. 'My lady in waiting thought it was on the other side.' Somehow we moved on to the fire restoration and I told her about walking round on the ceiling of the Grand Reception Room and how there were trays of rosettes and fleurs-de-lis and how happy the craftsmen were putting them up and the man who then tweaked these, creating perfect details which you can't see from ground level, but it is there. The Queen said: 'I went up with my sister, but halfway up she said she couldn't go up any higher.' She thought that amusing.

When it was time to go, Terry told the Queen about two of her horses that had come in second and another horse that had won a particular race. The Queen laughed: 'Bother. I sold him.' As we went out I looked round. The Queen was leaning over, looking at the book. That was my last sight of her – her white hair, her floral dress. She would then watch a race on television, and have dinner. I came away wondering if she might live to a hundred.

* * * * *

On the Sunday, the Queen took the overnight train to Edinburgh with the Wessexes to stay at Holyroodhouse in Edinburgh, a visit she considered important as it emphasised the monarch's links to Scotland. She was conspicuously present at the Ceremony of the Keys, and the parade of the Royal Company of Archers, but not the Thistle ceremony. When Nicola Sturgeon saw the Queen, she told her that she only got the point of the Paddington Bear sketch when she saw it on television. She found the Queen 'in great form'. Nicola Sturgeon was to come to Balmoral on 19 September.[4] The Queen then spent some days at Wood Farm before returning to Windsor Castle in July.

The last time she rode Emma was on 18 July. There was a final public engagement at the Thames Hospice, and then she flew to Scotland on 21 July, staying first at Craigowan and moving to Balmoral on 9 August. The weather was good for holidaymakers, less good for farmers. It was cooler than in the south. Her normal programme was somewhat moderated. There was no formal arrival at Balmoral, but most of her family came to stay with her at different times as they normally did. The traditional guests were entertained, and one night there was a dinner party for eighteen. Her bed was sent up from Windsor Castle. On 20 August she was described as 'the same as ever', though she told Prue Penn: 'I feel as if I'm in the departure lounge.'[5] She did not go to the Braemar Games. Myra, Lady Butter, a Wernher of Luton Hoo, and a key figure in Prince Philip's early life, died on 29 July aged ninety-seven.

The Moderator of the Church of Scotland came to stay on the weekend of 3 September. Katie Jerram-Hunnable had a win on First Receiver on 4 September, which delighted the Queen. First Receiver (aged five, trained by Sir Michael Stoute) qualified for the Horse of the Year prize, part of the Equestrian Championship.

50
THE LAST DAYS

On Monday 5 September, the long-drawn process of finding a new Conservative leader finally came to an end. Liz Truss won 81,000 votes over Rishi Sunak's 60,000. She was confirmed as the Queen's fifteenth Prime Minister. The Queen's first Prime Minister had been born in 1874. Her last was born in 1975.

The Queen had wanted to come south for the handover between the Prime Ministers, but she was advised that her health was too fragile. Instead the outgoing and incoming Prime Ministers had the unique experience of making their way to Balmoral Castle for this important ceremony, the only time it had ever happened there. The doctor came to see the Queen every morning during her Scottish holiday. He gave her a powerful boost to enable her to receive the two Prime Ministers.

The weather on Tuesday, 6 September, was inclement. Flights were delayed. Cameras recorded the arrival of Boris Johnson to be greeted by Sir Edward Young and an equerry. In his moving, beautifully crafted House of Commons tribute, Johnson gave a hint of what the Queen had said in private:

> ... that impulse to do her duty carried her through right into her tenth decade, to the very moment ... only three days ago, when she saw off her fourteenth prime minister and welcomed her fifteenth. And I can tell you in that audience, she was as radiant and as knowledgeable and as fascinated by politics as ever I can remember. And as wise in her advice as anyone I know, if not wiser.[1]

In his memoirs he elaborated. Edward Young warned him that the Queen had gone 'down a bit over the summer'. The Queen received him in her tartan skirt, grey blouse and grey cardigan. She was leaning on her stick and wearing spectacles. When he saw her, he found her frail but her mind 'unimpaired by her illness', and from time to time she 'flashed that great white smile in its sudden mood-lifting beauty'. They discussed Ukraine, and the Queen quoted Nehru telling her that India would always side with Russia. Johnson was determined not to be bitter at his downfall. 'There's no point in bitterness,' said the Queen.[2]

Johnson departed and Liz Truss arrived. Again the arrival was filmed. The Queen was also filmed by her long-serving cameraman, Peter Wilkinson, though that film has never been shown. But photographs were released, showing her smiling brightly for the camera. Her right hand was darkly bruised. Later Liz Truss revealed that the Queen had said how much she was looking forward to meeting her again. The new Prime Minister recalled: 'Although she was physically frail, she was alert mentally and absolutely determined to do her duty.'[3]

She, too, left, and Balmoral returned to its summer-holiday life. The Queen had her traditional house party staying. They were out stalking but returned in time for tea. David Bertie, a grandson of Jean Wills, recalled the Queen musing on the country's new leader. 'Liz Tough,' she said. The Queen stayed up for dinner while the stalkers willed her to go to bed as they were exhausted. Charles Richards had served her as equerry for twenty-three years. He escorted her to the stairs and told her he had cancelled an event due a few days later. 'I got a broad smile and a thank you before she headed upstairs,'[4] he recalled.

The next day the Queen did not come down. Her house party left as planned. The media had been so busy reporting the handover from Boris Johnson to Liz Truss that they had overlooked the fact that new Privy Counsellors had to be sworn in. The Queen had become a master of Zoom, and it would have been a straightforward procedure. She would have sat in front of her television screen and given her assent. A Zoom Privy Council meeting was planned for 6 p.m. Liz Truss and the Privy Counsellors assembled in the Cabinet Office. At 6.18 it was cancelled on doctor's orders. Liz Truss considered this 'a very ominous sign'.[5] It was the first time in her reign that the Queen had been unable to fulfil an important constitutional duty.

THE LAST DAYS

When I saw the newsflash, I panicked. I then received a text from a friend who had sources at Balmoral. It came through just after 7 p.m. on 7 September: 'Just to let you know that Her Majesty isn't very well and had been ordered by her doctor to rest ... The Prince of Wales will be going to Balmoral.' I was at a book launch in Hatchards and apparently I went white. The next morning, 8 September, a further message came: 'I really don't think we will have the Queen for much longer so you need to be ready for what may happen in the next few weeks as it's not looking good at the moment ... look out for 4 October.'

I took 4 October to be the date when the Queen was expected back at Windsor Castle. At 12.48 came another warning: 'News from Balmoral isn't good.'

I had taken a train to Edenbridge to attend the funeral of Sir Simon Bland, who had died on 11 August. He was an old friend in every sense of the word. He was ninety-eight and I had known him since 1972. He was the Duke of Gloucester's Private Secretary and the Duke was attending the funeral. The Queen was represented at this funeral by Lady Elton, one of her ladies in waiting. All mobile phones were switched off during the service. Only at the reception did the news come of the statement to the House of Commons. I immediately took the train back to London and went to ITN.

Prince Charles flew from Dumfries House, went to Balmoral and then retreated to Birkhall to pick mushrooms. Princess Anne was at the castle with the Queen. Prince Charles personally called the Queen's cousins, the Duke of Kent and Princess Alexandra, to warn them that death was imminent.

Princess Anne was the only member of the family there when the Queen died peacefully in her bedroom that afternoon. This was announced at 6.30 p.m.* The Queen had performed her last constitutional duty two days before. She died peacefully in a place she loved.

---

* I was sitting in the ITN studio, having been interviewed, when Mary Nightingale made the announcement at 6.30 p.m.

London Bridge

On the day after the Queen's death the new King made an inspirational speech. If on earlier such occasions he had been prone to self-pity, in this address he looked outwards. We should have been comforting him, but he comforted us. He commended 'a life well lived; a promise with destiny kept'. He said: 'She made sacrifices for duty. Her dedication and devotion as Sovereign never wavered, through times of change and progress, through times of joy and celebration, and through times of sadness and loss.' In turn he promised to uphold the constitutional principles at the heart of the nation, and to serve with loyalty. He laid aside any concerns that might have lingered. He would step back from his charities. He would make no controversial speeches. His words were well received.[6]

The new King was greeted with warmth when he arrived at Buckingham Palace. Contingency plans had been put in place in case he was greeted by a hostile crowd. No one had planned for the generous reception he got. He and the new Queen Camilla walked into the Palace. The next day there was the Accession Council and the Proclamation. Over the ensuing days the King addressed the Houses of Parliament in Westminster Hall and did likewise in the devolved parliaments in Edinburgh and Cardiff, then visited Belfast. He undertook a daunting schedule, buoyed by the warmth of the crowd.

The nation began the process of bidding farewell to the Queen. It had been seventy years since the last change of reign. Operation London Bridge had been put in place and developed since 1978 by the late Earl Marshal, Miles, Duke of Norfolk, and many others. Hundreds of hours were devoted to it, Duke Miles telling one briefing: 'I will probably be dead by the time it happens.' He was. There were meetings every five years, then every two and a half years. Some of the operational instructions stretched to sixty pages.[7]

On the day the Queen died, there happened to be a routine media recce with the BBC and ITN in Windsor. They were taking precautions for the Queen dying in Windsor Castle, how the coffin would be brought by train to Victoria Station and to the Lying-in-State in London. Members of the Household could be seen on telephones from as early as 9 a.m., but because the media representatives were there, they had to pretend that nothing was happening. However, the rehearsal was somewhat rushed.

At 12.20 p.m. the Brigade Major of the Grenadier Guards was telephoned. He asked 'Is everything quiet in the headquarters?' Out came a folder marked 'Brigade Major's Operation London Bridge'.[8] An emergency planning meeting took place in Whitehall at 2 p.m. No one remembered the King's funeral in 1952. The Major-General Commanding watched Pathé news clips for guidance.

News that the Queen had died at ten past three reached the various officials. Half of the King's Troop were on summer leave. They were summoned back and moved their operation from Woolwich to Wellington Barracks. They were to fire the Death Gun Salute of ninety-six guns. The State Trumpeters had flown to Canada on a visit, arriving twenty-four hours before. They were needed for the Proclamation. They were flown back and rehearsed at the Royal Exchange at 10 p.m. as revellers spilled out of pubs. The Queen's Company, Grenadier Guards, were serving on Operation Shader in Iraq. Back they came to act as bearer party and escort to their former Company Commander. The Garrison Sergeant-Major took one look at the men and commanded haircuts. He kept a comb on him at all times thereafter.

Brigadier James Stopford, a Gentleman at Arms, was in Corfu at his daughter's wedding. He was in the middle of his speech when his phone vibrated. He proposed a toast to his daughter, and to the memory of the Queen. He flew home the next day to take part in the Lying-in-State. Officers were recalled from Bangladesh, Iraq, Saudi Arabia and America, one from his honeymoon.[9]

There were rehearsals between 3 a.m. and 7 a.m., Beethoven's funeral marches were heard in the darkness. At Portsmouth 142 naval ratings prepared to pull the gun-carriage, and a hundred pipers kicked in with the slow march.

The Queen's present and former equerries gathered in London to act as pall-bearers. During the next days, the following words were seldom heard: 'No', 'Impossible', 'Too difficult' and 'Can't' as everyone rallied round to give a much-loved Monarch a spectacular farewell. One man worked out that by the time of the funeral he had marched seventeen thousand paces. The Major-General was conscious of how many played their part: 'They delivered the very best of the United Kingdom to the world and performed a magnificent final duty to the Queen.'

Four billion people across the world watched the events unfold. Because the Queen died in Scotland, Operation Unicorn was implemented. Her coffin was placed in the ballroom at Balmoral for tenants and staff to pay their respects. On the Sunday the hearse took it on its six-hour journey to Holyroodhouse in Edinburgh. Until a few days before, life at Balmoral had revolved around the Queen. There was a terrible finality as the hearse took her away for the last time. Many lined the routes, horses and even combine harvesters drawn up along the way.

During these days, the Princess Royal and her husband accompanied the Queen's coffin at every point of its journey. When it arrived at Holyroodhouse, there was a touching moment when the Princess Royal curtseyed to her mother's coffin. The next day there was a procession along the Royal Mile to St Giles' Cathedral and then twenty-four hours Lying-at-Rest there. The Royal Company of Archers and others brought a medieval feel to those days. Crowds were ten deep. Scotland enjoyed glorious weather but a strong wind. This whisked the bonnet off the head of one of the Guard of Honour. It was flattened under the wheel of the hearse.

The new King and his siblings mounted vigil at the side of the coffin in St Giles' Cathedral. Thirty-three thousand people walked past in twenty-four hours.

The Queen's coffin was flown from Scotland in an RAF Globemaster C-17, leaving Edinburgh in a lowering sky. During the flight the Scottish royal standard was changed to the English. The hearse was floodlit as it brought the Queen to Buckingham Palace on a dark and rainy night. The next day was gloriously sunny as the procession marched down the Mall to Westminster Hall for the Lying-in-State. Resting on the coffin were the Imperial State Crown and the Orb. Some three hundred officers mounted vigil over the next days, and mourners queued for miles and for long hours, often through the night, to pay their respects. The Queen's four children and later all of her grandchildren mounted vigil.

On the night of Thursday, 15 September, the procession from Westminster Hall to the Abbey, and on to Wellington Arch, was rehearsed between 12.30 a.m. and 7 a.m., with 3,314 troops on parade. On the Saturday there was a further rehearsal at Windsor with 1,100 troops on parade. This was described as 'an eerie experience moving in the dark along the rural roads and the Long Walk'. Sir Alexander Matheson, one of the pall-bearers, wrote of a particular problem: 'Marching in the dark removed all chance of avoiding the obstacles left behind by the Household Cavalry horses in front of us. What had they been eating?'[10]

More Heads of State than ever previously seen in London arrived for the State Funeral in Westminster Abbey. It was a magnificent service, one mourner noting in particular how the sunlight caught the diamonds on the Imperial State Crown. The service over, there was a procession to Hyde Park Corner, at which point the coffin was transferred to a hearse for the journey to Windsor.

The procession formed up at Shaw Farm Gate. The Brigade-Major noted that because so many had watched all the way from London it left late at 14.07. The Long Walk was packed, and there were flowers in profusion within the private grounds of Windsor Castle. Terry Pendry brought out the Queen's pony Emma to pay her respects, one of the Queen's headscarves on her saddle, a gesture that resonated with the general public.

When the procession reached the Quadrangle, the two Corgis were on leads to bid farewell. The hearse made its way down the hill to the West Steps of St George's Chapel. Under different circumstances I could have been on duty in the chapel helping to seat the congregation, many of whom I would have recognised. Or I could have been in the ITN studio. I was alone on the guardroom roof.

I saw a group of men and women walk down. They were still in the distance, when I spotted a Knight of the Garter in naval uniform. Could it be Lord Boyce?* As they hove into view, I recognised the King of Sweden and the other kings and queens of Europe heading to the South Door.

I must have seen the Queen walk or drive down that hill between fifty and a hundred times in life – fifty-four Garter processions to start with. I was acutely aware that I was witnessing the last time. This was final.[11]

The service in St George's Chapel was more emotionally moving

---

* Lord Boyce was too ill. He died from cancer on 6 November.

than the Abbey service had been. The Quire was filled with the Queen's close relations and the foreign Kings and Queens. At the end of the service, the Crown and the Orb were removed from the coffin and placed on the altar. The King put the camp colour of Queen's Company of the Grenadier Guards (until lately in Iraq) on the coffin. The Lord Chamberlain broke his wand. Garter King of Arms read out the Queen's styles and titles, and her coffin gradually disappeared from view in that eight-minute descent into the Royal Vault.

There was a short break while the mourners departed. Then the new King and Queen and the immediate Royal Family returned for the Committal. The Queen and Prince Philip's coffins had been brought up from the Royal Vault and placed side by side in the tomb. Beneath them were King George VI and Queen Elizabeth and also in the tomb the ashes of Princess Margaret. The Dean said some prayers and the King threw in some earth. The other members of the family went into the tomb house and did likewise. In due course the modest black marble stone was replaced. It bore their names and dates. Us Four were together again, with the 'suitable addition'.

The final curtain had fallen on a golden age.

PERSONAL POSTSCRIPT

A few weeks later, there was another funeral at St George's Chapel – of a Military Knight. For that I was able to stand alone outside the King George VI Memorial Chapel while the choir sang the sentences: 'I am the Resurrection and the Life …'

I had invested so much of my life in following the Queen. When she died, it was as though the Last Post sounded. I found myself floundering in the dread dark of night, fearful of the abyss into which I would stare when Reveille came.

Acknowledgements

A great number of people were keen for me to write about The Queen and it would take many pages to list them all. I would in particular like to thank Sir William Heseltine, the late Lady Penn, and the late Oliver Everett for their considerable encouragement.

A book such as this is the result of sixty years of observation and research. I have relied very heavily on my own documentation, including more than 500 books of concisely filed press cuttings made by me between 1963 and 1994 (and folders thereafter) for a timeline, and my own copious private diaries from 1975 to the present day, in which much was recorded. These diaries may never be made publicly available but have the advantage that much that was told to me was recorded at the time. The source notes sometimes refer to specific dates and sometimes list specific conversations many years ago. Where appropriate I have given the exact sources, but sometimes I have relied on the device of 'private information.'

Many people told me things over the years, and whilst I was not writing a book at the time, they were aware that I was a biographer and had written other books on royal subjects. Over many years I have had the advantage of conversations with certain members of the Royal Family, the Royal Household, and some of the Queen's friends, some of whom knew her in childhood. Many of these are no longer living.

I have in the past worked in the Royal Archives, and for this book undertook copious research in the National Archives, as well as at Churchill College, Cambridge and the Hertfordshire Archives and Local Studies Library (for this book), many others in the course of earlier research, and in various private papers.

I do not propose to give a long bibliography but direct quotations are concisely given in the source notes at the end of this book.

ACKNOWLEDGEMENTS

My agent, Clare Alexander, has guided me through the long process of this book and I am immensely grateful for her support and advice.

This book was originally commissioned by Rowena Webb and finally edited by Susannah Otter. I would like to thank her along with Lucy Buxton, Hazel Orme and Anna Hervé for bringing it to fruition.

Furthermore I would like to thank Mark Hollingsworth for obtaining copies of correspondence between the Queen and her uncle, the Duke of Windsor.

Hugo Vickers

Copyrights

The letters from HM Queen Elizabeth II and HRH The Duke of Edinburgh are the copyright of His Majesty The King.

The letters of Dame Daphne du Maurier are reproduced with permission of Curtis Brown Ltd, London, on behalf of The Chichester Partnership. Copyright © 1938 The Chichester Partnership.

Extracts from the Diaries and Letters of Sir Alan Lascelles are included in this book and published with grateful acknowledgement to and permission of the Estate of Sir Alan Lascelles.

I am literary executor to the Countess of Avon, Sir Cecil Beaton and Sir Charles Johnston and therefore give myself permission to quote from their letters and diaries.

I would like to thank the following for their permission to quote from copyright material:

The Hon Mrs Pearson for the letters of Lord Charteris of Amisfield.

Charles Duff for the letters of Sir Michael Duff and Lady Juliet Duff.

The Lady Thomas of Swynnerton for the diaries of Cynthia, Lady Gladwyn.

Anne, Lady Glenconner for the letter from Colin Tennant (Lord Glenconner).

The Hon Mrs Cullen for the letter from Lady Hartwell.

The Hon Mark Lascelles for the note by Patricia, Countess of Harewood.

Mr Clive Irving for his quote about The Crown.
Christopher Penn, David Penn & Fiona Wemyss for the diaries of Sir Arthur Penn.
&
Michael Mallon for the letter from James Pope-Hennessy.

Photographs

I am very grateful to Brigadier Andrew Parker Bowles for the use of three of his private photographs, also to my son George Vickers for the photograph of The Queen which he took when he was eight, and to Lara Arnott for the 2018 photograph of me with The Queen in the garden of Buckingham Palace. I am also grateful to Ian Brunskill, Deputy Editor of *The Times* for permission to use the signed Coronation photograph of 1953.

Copyrights for the remaining images are credited as follows:

First photographic inset:
Page 1: © Royal Collection Enterprises Limited 2026 | Royal Collection Trust
Page 2, above: Author's collection
Page 2, below left: Getty Images / Popperfoto / Bob Thomas
Page 2, below right: Bridgeman Images / Look and Learn / Valerie Jackson Harris Collection
Page 3, above: Getty Images / Topical Press Agency
Page 3, below left: Alamy / Chronicle
Page 3, below right: Getty Images / Popperfoto
Page 4: Getty Images / The Print Collector
Page 5, above left: Getty Images / Popperfoto
Page 5, above right: Getty Images / Hulton Archive / Studio Lisa / Lisa Sheridan
Page 5, below: Getty Images / Popperfoto
Page 6: Getty Images / Popperfoto
Page 7, above: Getty Images / Popperfoto / Paul Popper
Page 7, below left: Getty Images / AFP
Page 7, below right: Author's collection
Page 8: Getty Images / Fox Photos

ACKNOWLEDGEMENTS

Second photographic inset:
Page 1: Photograph by Stirling Henry Nahum (known as Baron)
Page 2, above left: Getty Images / Popperfoto
Page 2, above right: Alamy / Superstock / Associated Press Photo / Sydney Morning Herald
Page 2, below: Author's collection
Page 3, above: Getty Images / AFP / Intercontinentale
Page 3, below left: Getty Images / Hulton Archive / Studio Lisa / Lisa Sheridan
Page 3, below right: Alamy / Smith Archive
Page 4: Author's collection
Page 5, above: Getty Images / Hulton Archive / Express / Ron Gerelli
Page 5, below: Author's collection
Page 6, above: Alamy / PA Images
Page 6, below: Alamy / Smith Archive
Page 7, above and below: Author's collection
Page 8, above right: Getty Images / Keystone / Stringer
Page 8, centre left: Author's collection
Page 8, below right: Alamy / Keystone Press

Third photographic inset:
Page 1: Courtesy of *The Times*
Page 2, above and below right: Author's collection
Page 2, below left: Photograph taken by Andrew Parker Bowles
Page 3, above and below: Photographs taken by Andrew Parker Bowles
Pages 4, 5 and 6: Author's collection
Page 7: © Lara Arnott
Page 8, above: Getty Images / WPA Pool / Jane Barlow
Page 8, below: Getty Images / WPA Pool / Aaron Chown

Images integrated within the text:
Page 35: Getty Images / Hulton Archive / Studio Lisa / Lisa Sheridan
Page 36: Getty Images / Hulton Royals Collection / Central Press
Page 38: Getty Images / Bettmann
Page 41: Getty Images / Hulton Royals Collection / Central Press
Page 69: Getty Images / Hulton Archive / Studio Lisa / Lisa Sheridan

Page 107: Author's collection
Page 114: Author's collection
Page 167: Alamy / PA Images
Pages 178 and 474: Photographs by Cecil Beaton
Page 335: Getty Images / Central Press / Roger Jackson
Page 349: Alamy / Sydney Morning Herald / Paul Popper

Source Notes

INTRODUCTION

1. Sky News, 3 June 2022.
2. HV diary, 9 April 1999.
3. Princess George of Hanover to author, Buckingham Palace, 20 May 1997.

1. THE ROYAL HOUSE OF WINDSOR

1. Simon Heffer (ed.), *Henry 'Chips' Channon: The Diaries (Volume 2) 1938–43* (Hutchinson, 2021), p. 211.
2. Hugo Vickers, *Elizabeth: The Queen Mother* (Hutchinson, 2005), p. 92.
3. *Daily Express*, 28 January 1926.
4. *Daily Telegraph*, 29 January 1926.
5. *The Times*, 22 April 1926.
6. John Wheeler-Bennett, *King George VI: His Life and Reign* (Macmillan, 1958), p. 209.
7. Ibid.
8. Lady Cynthia Asquith, *The King's Daughters* (Hutchinson, 1937), p. 10.
9. Mabell, Countess of Airlie, *Thatched with Gold: The Memoirs of Mabell, Countess of Airlie*, (Hutchinson, 1962), p. 180.
10. Rosemary Olivier to author, 26 January 1984.
11. William Tallon to author, 5 July 2005.
12. Anne Ring, *The Story of Princess Elizabeth and Princess Margaret* (John Murray, 1932), p. 6.
13. James Pope-Hennessy, *Queen Mary: 1867–1953* (Allen & Unwin, 1959), p. 35.
14. Mabell, Countess of Airlie, *Thatched with Gold: The Memoirs of Mabell, Countess of Airlie* (Hutchinson, 1962), p. 197.
15. Sir Alan Lascelles to Nigel Nicolson, [January 1967] (LASC CA).

16 Miles Jebb (ed.), *The Diaries of Cynthia Gladwyn* (Constable, 1995), p. 171.
17 Lord Stamfordham to Rt Hon A. J. Balfour, Buckingham Palace, 19 July 1917 (courtesy of Somerset Herald).
18 Hugo Vickers, *Elizabeth: The Queen Mother* (Hutchinson, 2005), p. 7.

2. CHILDHOOD, 1926–30

1 Jane Marguerite Tippett, *Once a King: The Lost Memoir of Edward VIII* (Hodder & Stoughton, 2023), p. 77.
2 John Wheeler-Bennett, *King George VI: His Life and Reign* (Macmillan, 1958), p. 210.
3 *Daily Telegraph*, 11 October 1935.
4 *Daily Telegraph*, 29 May 1926.
5 *Daily Telegraph*, 31 May 1926.
6 *Daily Telegraph*, 17 November 1927.
7 Derived from the *Daily Telegraph*, 25 August 1928.
8 Anne Ring, *The Story of Princess Elizabeth and Princess Margaret* (John Murray, 1932), p. 13.
9 Derived from the *Daily Telegraph*, 25 August 1928.
10 Anne Ring, *The Story of Princess Elizabeth and Princess Margaret* (John Murray, 1932), p. 30.
11 Jane Ridley, *George V: Never a Dull Moment* (Chatto & Windus, 2021), p. 346.
12 *The Tongs and the Bones: The Memoirs of Lord Harewood* (Weidenfeld & Nicolson, 1981), p. 14.
13 HM The Queen to author, Windsor Castle, 24 June 2022.
14 *The Times*, 9 April 1928.
15 *Daily Telegraph*, 3 January 1931.
16 Winston Churchill to Clementine Churchill, Balmoral, 25 September 1928, quoted in Martin Gilbert, *Winston S. Churchill: Companion Volume V, Part 1: The Exchequer Years 1922–1929* (Heinemann, 1979), p. 1349.
17 Kenneth Rose, *King George V* (Weidenfeld & Nicolson, 1983), p. 389.
18 *Hail and Farewell: The Passing of King George V* (The Times, 1936), p. 5.
19 John Gore, *King George V: A Personal Memoir* (John Murray, 1941), p. 380.
20 St John Ervine to Lyon Phelps, quoted in the *Daily Telegraph*, 8 May 1937.
21 Herbert Hensley Henson, *Retrospect of an Unimportant Life* (Oxford University Press, 1943), p. 336.

22 John Gore, *King George V: A Personal Record* (John Murray, 1941), p. 405.
23 *The Times*, 5 April 1960.
24 Lady Cynthia Asquith diary, 11 July 1927, quoted in Nicola Beauman, *Lady Cynthia Asquith* (Hamish Hamilton, 1987), p. 289.
25 Lady Cynthia Asquith, *Haply May I Remember* (James Barrie, 1950), p. 192.
26 Lady Cynthia Asquith, *The King's Daughters*, (Hutchinson, 1937), p. 19.
27 *The King's Daughters*, pp. 10–11.
28 *Daily Telegraph*, 28 June 1928.
29 *Daily Telegraph*, 19 September 1929.
30 *Daily Telegraph*, 19 September 1929.
31 *Daily Telegraph*, 7 January 1930.
32 *Mail on Sunday*, 28 July 2014.

3. AND THEN THERE WERE TWO, 1930–6

1 Derived from Mabell, Countess of Airlie, *Thatched with Gold: The Memoirs of Mabell, Countess of Airlie* (Hutchinson, 1962), pp. 183–6.
2 Anne Ring, *The Story of Princess Elizabeth and Princess Margaret* (John Murray, 1932), p. 112.
3 *Daily Telegraph*, 28 August 1930.
4 Lady Cynthia Asquith, *The King's Daughters* (Hutchinson, 1937), p. 24.
5 *Daily Telegraph*, 23 January 1933.
6 Loelia, Duchess of Westminster, to author, 1983.
7 Anne Glenconner, *Lady in Waiting* (Hodder and Stoughton, 2019), p. 12.
8 *Daily Telegraph*, 17 May 1933.
9 Lady Cynthia Asquith, *The King's Daughters* (Hutchinson, 1937), p. 107.
10 *The King's Daughters*, p. 28.
11 *Daily Telegraph*, 19 November 1930.
12 Lady Helen Graham broadcast, *The Listener*, 27 April 1944.
13 Ibid.
14 Ibid.
15 *Daily Telegraph*, 17 March 1932.
16 Sister Catherine Black, *King's Nurse, Beggar's Nurse* (Hurst & Blackett, 1939), p. 167.
17 Winifred Murray, *Glimpses of a Happy Life* (Silverdart Publishing, 2009), p. 34.
18 *Daily Telegraph*, 3 June 1933.

19 A. N. Wilson introduction to Marion Crawford, *The Little Princesses* (Duckworth, 1993), p. vii.
20 *Daily Telegraph*, 21 April 1933.
21 Louis Wulff, *Queen of Tomorrow* (Sampson, Low, 1946), p. 34.
22 Lady Cynthia Asquith diary, quoted in Janet Dunbar, *J. M. Barrie: The Man Behind the Image* (HarperCollins, 1970), p. 375.
23 Lady Cynthia Asquith, *Portrait of Barrie* (James Barrie, 1954), p. 193.
24 Lady Cynthia Asquith, *The King's Daughters* (Hutchinson, 1937), p. 64.
25 *The King's Daughters*, p. 78.
26 *Daily Telegraph*, 27 July 1934.
27 Lady Mary Whitley interview, *You Magazine*, 24 January 1988.
28 *Daily Telegraph*, 7 May 1935.
29 *Daily Telegraph*, 18 May 1935.
30 *Daily Telegraph*, 13 May 1935.
31 *The Memoirs of Princess Alice, Duchess of Gloucester* (Collins, 1983), p. 104.
32 *The Memoirs of Princess Alice, Duchess of Gloucester* (Collins, 1983), p. 108.
33 Ibid.
34 *Daily Telegraph*, 6 July 1935.
35 Lady Cynthia Asquith, *The King's Daughters* (Hutchinson, 1937), pp. 72–3.

4. THE YEAR OF THREE KINGS, 1936

1 James Pope-Hennessy, *Queen Mary: 1867–1953* (Allen & Unwin, 1959), p. 537.
2 *Daily Telegraph*, 18 January 1936.
3 *Daily Telegraph*, 20 January 1936.
4 Marion Crawford, *The Little Princesses* (Cassell, 1950), p. 32.
5 *Daily Telegraph*, 29 January 1936.
6 Lady Cynthia Asquith, *The King's Daughters* (Hutchinson, 1937), p. 95.
7 *The King's Daughters*, p. 94.
8 *Daily Telegraph*, 2 March 1936.
9 HRH The Duchess of York to Lord Dawson of Penn, 9 March 1936 (Francis Watson, *Dawson of Penn* (Chatto & Windus, 1951), p. 285).
10 Hugh Cecil to author.
11 Joan Woollcombe, *The Toronto Star Weekly*, 16 May 1936.
12 Joan Woollcombe, *The Toronto Star Weekly*, 16 May 1936.
13 Included in the film of *A King's Story* by Jack Le Vien, 1965.

14 J. G. Lockhart, *Cosmo Gordon Lang* (Hodder and Stoughton, 1949), p. 397.
15 Stuart Ball (ed.), *Parliament and Politics in the Age of Churchill and Attlee: The Headlam Diaries 1935–1951* (Cambridge University Press, 1999), pp. 101–4.
16 Marion Crawford, *The Little Princesses* (Cassell, 1950), p. 39.
17 Lady Cynthia Asquith, *Haply May I Remember* (James Barrie, 1950), p. 201.
18 Lady Helen Graham broadcast, *The Listener*, 27 April 1944.
19 Lady Cynthia Asquith diary, 11 December 1936, quoted in Nicola Beauman, *Lady Cynthia Asquith* (Hamish Hamilton, 1987), p. 290.
20 *Daily Telegraph*, 12 and 14 December 1936.
21 Lady Cynthia Asquith, *The King's Daughters* (Hutchinson, 1937), p. 10.

5. THE PRE-WAR YEARS, 1937–9

1 *Daily Telegraph*, 13 May 1937.
2 *Daily Telegraph*, 12 May 1937.
3 *Daily Telegraph*, 13 May 1937.
4 *Daily Telegraph*, 13 May 1937.
5 Mrs Henrietta Bell, volume 205: 'How I saw the Coronation in Westminster Abbey, 12 May 1937' (Bell papers, Lambeth Palace Library).
6 *Daily Telegraph*, 27 May 1937.
7 Anthony C. Deane, *Time Remembered* (Faber & Faber, 1945), p. 222.
8 *Daily Telegraph*, 28 August 1957.
9 Horace Smith, *A Horseman Through Six Reigns: The Reminiscences Of A Royal Riding Master* (Odhams Press, 1955), pp. 144–5.
10 *Daily Telegraph*, 9 June 1938.
11 *Daily Telegraph*, 9 December 1938.
12 *Daily Telegraph*, 2 January 1939.
13 *Daily Telegraph*, 8 May 1939.
14 Harold Nicolson to Vita Sackville-West, 23 June 1939, quoted in Nigel Nicolson (ed.), *Harold Nicolson: Diaries and Letters 1930–39* (Collins, 1966), p. 405.
15 *Daily Telegraph*, 23 June 1939.
16 *The Times*, 24 July 1939.

6. THE WAR, 1939–45

1. Fisher Papers, George VI, Silver Wedding Service, 26 April 1948 (Lambeth Palace Library).
2. HM King George VI diary, 3 September 1939, quoted in John Wheeler-Bennett, *King George VI: His Life and Reign* (Macmillan, 1958), p. 405.
3. John Wheeler-Bennett, *King George VI: His Life and Reign* (Macmillan, 1958), pp. 406–7.
4. Conrad Russell to Lady Diana Cooper, 23 December 1939, quoted in Georgiana Blakiston (ed.), *Letters of Conrad Russell 1897–1947* (John Murray, 1987), p. 176.
5. HM The Queen's Broadcast, 11 November 1939, quoted in William Shawcross (ed.), *Counting One's Blessings: The Selected Letters of Queen Elizabeth the Queen Mother* (Macmillan, 2012), p. 283.
6. *The Times*, 18 January 1940.
7. Ben Pimlott, *The Queen: Elizabeth II and the Monarchy* (HarperCollins, 2001), p. 57.
8. HRH The Princess Margaret to author, Sutton Courtenay, 31 December 1993.
9. Albert Victor Baillie, *My First Eighty Years* (John Murray, 1951), p. 200.
10. Sir Edward Ford to author, 5 July 2006.
11. Albert Victor Baillie, *My First Eighty Years* (John Murray, 1951), p. 239.
12. Pamela Cooper, *A Cloud of Forgetting* (Quartet, 1993), p. 199.
13. *A Cloud of Forgetting*, p. 202.
14. *A Cloud of Forgetting*, p. 206.
15. *A Cloud of Forgetting*, p. 209.
16. Albert Victor Baillie, *My First Eighty Years* (John Murray, 1951), pp. 200–1.
17. Alathea Fitzalan Howard, *The Windsor Diaries: A Childhood with the Young Princesses Elizabeth and Margaret* (Hodder & Stoughton, 2020), p. 44.
18. *The Windsor Diaries*, p. 100.
19. *The Windsor Diaries*, p. 115.
20. *The Windsor Diaries*, p. 129.
21. *The Windsor Diaries*, p. 36.
22. *The Times*, 14 October 1940.
23. J. G. Lockhart, *Cosmo Gordon Lang* (Hodder & Stoughton, 1949), p. 433.
24. John Colville, *The Fringes of Power: Downing Street Diaries, 1939–55* (Hodder & Stoughton, 1985), pp. 265–6.
25. Marion Crawford letter to Queen Mary, 23 February 1941 (Lambeth Palace Library).

26 Marion Crawford to HM Queen Mary, 23 February 1941 (Lambeth Palace Library).
27 Duff Hart-Davis (ed.), *King's Counsellor: Abdication and War – The Diaries of Sir Alan Lascelles* (Weidenfeld & Nicolson, 2006), p. 85: diary, 11 December 1942.
28 Duff Hart-Davis (ed.), *King's Counsellor: Abdication and War – The Diaries of Sir Alan Lascelles* (Weidenfeld & Nicolson, 2006), p. 208.
29 Frances Towers, *The Two Princesses: The Story of the King's Daughters* (National Sunday School Union, 1941), pp. 127–8.
30 HRH The Princess Elizabeth to Winston Churchill, Windsor Castle, 23 April 1941 (Churchill papers, 20/29), quoted in Martin Gilbert, *The Churchill Documents, Volume 16: The Ever Widening War, 1941* (Hillsdale College Press, 2011), p. 536.
31 J. G. Lockhart, *Cosmo Gordon Lang* (Hodder & Stoughton, 1949), p. 442.
32 HM Queen Mary to HRH The Princess Alice, Countess of Athlone, quoted in *For My Grandchildren: Some Reminiscences of Her Royal Highness Princess Alice* (Evans Bros, 1966), p. 260.
33 Winston Churchill to Lord Simon, 25 June 1943 (Churchill papers, 20/29), quoted in Martin Gilbert, *The Churchill Documents, Volume 18: One Continent Redeemed, January–August 1943* (Hillsdale College Press, 2015), p. 1715.
34 Alex Danchev and Daniel Todman (eds), *War Diaries, 1939–1945: Field Marshal Lord Alanbrooke* (Weidenfeld & Nicolson, 2001), pp. 513–4.
35 Eleanor Roosevelt, *This I Remember* (Harper Brothers, 1949), p. 209.
36 Audrey Withers to Cecil Beaton, 1 January 1941 (Cecil Beaton papers, St John's College, Cambridge).
37 Cecil Beaton diary, 23 October 1942 (Cecil Beaton papers, St John's College, Cambridge).
38 Cecil Beaton diary, 20 November 1943 (Cecil Beaton papers, St John's College, Cambridge).
39 Cecil Beaton diary, 9 March 1945 (Cecil Beaton papers, St John's College, Cambridge).
40 Anthony Buckley (1912–93) to author, 26 July 1972.
41 HRH The Princess Elizabeth to Winston Churchill, Buckingham Palace, 23 April 1944, quoted in Gilbert, *The Churchill Documents, Volume 19: Fateful Questions, September 1943–April 1944* (Hillsdale College Press, 2017), p. 2552.
42 Mark Pottle (ed.), *Champion Redoubtable: The Diaries and Letters of Violet Bonham Carter 1914–45* (Weidenfeld & Nicolson, 1998), p. 301.
43 Vicki Stroeher, Nicholas Clark and Jude Brimmer (eds), *My Beloved Man:*

The Letters of Benjamin Britten and Peter Pears (The Boydell Press, 2016), letter, 10–11 May 1944, p. 72.
44 Interview with Godfrey Talbot, 8 May 1984.
45 The Dowager Marchioness of Salisbury to author, 9 November 2011.

7. ENTER PRINCE PHILIP, 1941–6

1 Alathea Fitzalan Howard, *The Windsor Diaries: A Childhood with the Young Princesses Elizabeth and Margaret* (Hodder & Stoughton, 2020), p. 282.
2 *The Windsor Diaries*, p. 71.
3 HM The Queen to author, 9 April 1999.
4 HRH The Duke of Edinburgh to author, Buckingham Palace, 20 May 1997.
5 HRH The Prince Philip note on George Baker typescript.
6 Memorandum by HRH The Duke of Edinburgh for Hugo Vickers, 27 April 2000.
7 Queen Alexandra of Yugoslavia, *Prince Philip: A Family Portrait* (Hodder and Stoughton, 1960), p. 63.
8 Note by HRH The Prince Philip on Queen Alexandra typescript (*Prince Philip: A Family Portrait*), p. 86 (HV collection).
9 *San Francisco Examiner*, 28 December 1940.
10 *St Louis Globe-Democrat*, 21 November 1940.
11 *El Paso Times*, 21 July 1939.
12 *Daily News*, 16 January 1940.
13 Simon Heffer (ed.), *Henry 'Chips' Channon: The Diaries (Volume 2) 1938–43* (Hutchinson, 2021), pp. 502–3.
14 Basil Boothroyd, *Philip: An Informal Biography* (Longman, 1971), p. 12.
15 *Evening Standard*, 1 April 1940.
16 HM King George VI to Victoria Milford Haven, 31 October 1941 (Broadlands Archives).
17 Alathea Fitzalan Howard, *The Windsor Diaries: A Childhood with the Young Princesses Elizabeth and Margaret* (Hodder & Stoughton, 2020, p. 75.
18 Simon Heffer (ed.), *Henry 'Chips' Channon: The Diaries (Volume 2) 1938–43* (Hutchinson, 2021), p. 774.
19 Alathea Fitzalan Howard, *The Windsor Diaries: A Childhood with the Young Princesses Elizabeth and Margaret* (Hodder & Stoughton, 2020, p. 203.
20 Simon Heffer (ed.), *Henry 'Chips' Channon: The Diaries (Volume 2) 1938–43* (Hutchinson, 2021), p. 1012.

21 Simon Heffer (ed.), *Henry 'Chips' Channon: The Diaries (Volume 2) 1938–43* (Hutchinson, 2021), p. 1047.
22 Simon Heffer (ed.), *Henry 'Chips' Channon: The Diaries (Volume 3) 1943–57* (Hutchinson, 2022), p. 38.
23 HRH The Princess Elizabeth to Diana Bowes-Lyon, 30 November 1943 (Dominic Winter Book Auctions catalogue, 8 March 2006, p. 42).
24 Ibid.
25 Sir Michael Duff to Lady Desborough, Vaynol, 12 July [1944] (Desborough papers, HALC).
26 HRH The Princess Elizabeth to Diana Bowes-Lyon, Windsor Castle, 15 February 1945 (Dominic Winter Auctions catalogue, 8 March 2006.
27 HRH The Princess Elizabeth to Diana Bowes-Lyon, Buckingham Palace, [22?] November 1945 (*Daily Mail*, 3 August 2013).
28 *The Philadelphia Enquirer*, 20 May 1945.
29 *The Mirror* (Perth, Australia), 15 December 1945.
30 *Daily Telegraph* (Sydney, Australia), 7 April 1945.
31 *The Inverell Times* (New South Wales, Australia), 8 April 1940.
32 *The Truth* (Sydney, Australia), 21 June 1942.
33 *The Mirror* (Perth, Australia), 15 December 1945.
34 Judy Fallon, 'A Gentleman rang and said it was Philip', unidentified press cutting, 1 January 1954.
35 Ibid.
36 *New Idea*, Australia News, 19 April 2021.
37 *Daily Telegraph* (Sydney, Australia), 15 September 1946.
38 *Daily Telegraph* (Sydney, Australia), 21 October 1941.
39 *Brisbane Telegraph*, 6 January 1940.
40 *The Rutherglen Sun and Chiltern Advertiser* (Victoria, Australia) 18 December 1945.
41 HV diary, Brisbane, 10 October 2005.

8. SOUTH AFRICA AND ENGAGEMENT

1 *Daily Mail*, 14 July 1960.
2 Victoria Milford Haven to Lord Mountbatten, Kensington Palace, 2 April 1944.
3 HRH The Princess Alice to HRH The Prince Philip, [Athens], 10 June 1944.
4 Victoria Milford Haven to Lord Mountbatten, Broadlands, 8 February 1945.

5 Lady Kennard to author, 3 March 1999.
6 The Countess of Avon to author, 9 March 1999.
7 James Pope-Hennessy to John Pope-Hennessy, 28 August [1955], citing an interview with Lady Buxton (then aged ninety-one) (Sir John Pope-Hennessy papers, Getty Museum, Los Angeles).
8 HRH The Princess Elizabeth to Betty Spencer Shew, 1947, quoted in the *Daily Telegraph*, 1 July 1996.
9 *Sunday Mirror*, 8 December 1946.
10 Mabell, Countess of Airlie, *Thatched with Gold: The Memoirs of Mabell, Countess of Airlie* (Hutchinson, 1962), p. 227.
11 HRH The Prince Philip to HM Queen Elizabeth, 14 September 1946, quoted in William Shawcross, *Queen Elizabeth The Queen Mother* (Macmillan, 2009), p. 625.
12 Lady Penn to author.
13 HM Queen Elizabeth to Sir Alan Lascelles, 7 July 1947 (a draft letter), quoted in William Shawcross, *Queen Elizabeth The Queen Mother* (Macmillan, 2009), p. 626.
14 HM Queen Elizabeth to Sir Arthur Penn, 9 July 1947, quoted in William Shawcross, *Queen Elizabeth The Queen Mother* (Macmillan, 2009), p. 626.
15 Ibid.
16 Lady Penn to author.
17 Prince Michel de Bourbon to author, South of France, 27 August 1989.
18 Lady Butter to author, 6 March 1999.
19 Lady Kennard to author, 3 March 1999.
20 Private information.
21 Hugo Vickers, *Alice: Princess Andrew of Greece* (Hamish Hamilton, 2000), p. 318.
22 Alathea Fitzalan Howard, *The Windsor Diaries: A Childhood with the Young Princesses Elizabeth and Margaret* (Hodder & Stoughton, 2020), p. xv.
23 Mabell, Countess of Airlie, *Thatched with Gold: The Memoirs of Mabell, Countess of Airlie* (Hutchinson, 1962), p. 225.
24 *The Times*, 31 January 1947.
25 Sir Alan Lascelles to Hon Lady Lascelles, *Vanguard*, 12 February 1947 (LASC CAC).
26 *The Times*, 21 April 1947.
27 *The Times*, 21 April 1947.
28 Sir Alan Lascelles to Hon Lady Lascelles, Government House, Bulawayo,

Southern Rhodesia, 14 April 1947 (Lascelles papers, Churchill College, Cambridge, GBR/0014), LASL 11/1.

29 Sir Alan Lascelles to Hon Lady Lascelles, April 1947 (Lascelles papers, Churchill College, Cambridge, GBR/0014), LASL 11/1.

30 Sir Alan Lascelles to Dermot Morrah, White Train, 10 March 1947 (Lascelles papers, Churchill College, Cambridge), quoted in Graham Viney, *The Last Hurrah* (Robinson, 2019), p. 274.

31 Frank Gillard, 'The First Post-War Royal Tour' from Caroline Elliot (ed.), *The BBC Book of Royal Memories 1947–1990* (BBC Books, 1991), pp. 32–3.

32 *The Times*, 22 April 1947.

33 Sir Alan Lascelles to Hon Lady Lascelles, *Vanguard*, 30 April 1947 (Lascelles papers, Churchill College, Cambridge, GBR/0014), LASL 11/1.

34 Marion Crawford, *The Little Princesses* (Cassell, 1950), p. 106.

35 *The Times*, 24 April 1947.

36 *The Times*, 6 July 1947.

37 Recalled by Commander Patrick Hoare, quoted in *Wiltshire Times*, 9 April 2021.

38 Sir Michael Duff to Lady Desborough, Six Apple Tree Yard, Duke of York Street, 14 July [1947] (Hertfordshire Archives and Local Studies).

39 HRH Princess Andrew of Greece to HM Queen Mary, 10 July 1947 (Royal Archives, GV/CC 45/15190).

40 HRH The Princess Elizabeth to Betty Spencer Shew, 1947, quoted in *Daily Telegraph*, 1 April 1996.

9. THE WEDDING, 1947

1 HM Queen Mary to Lord Hardinge of Penshurst, Marlborough House, 22 November 1947.

2 John Colville, *The Fringes of Power: Downing Street Diaries, 1939–55* (Hodder & Stoughton, 1985), p. 620.

3 The Countess of Avon to author, 18 October 1980.

4 Sir Michael Duff to Cecil Beaton, 10 December 1947 (Cecil Beaton papers, St John's College, Cambridge).

5 Alathea Fitzalan Howard, *The Windsor Diaries: A Childhood with the Young Princesses Elizabeth and Margaret* (Hodder & Stoughton, 2020), p. 335.

6 Sir Charles Johnston unpublished diary, 11 November 1947 (Johnston papers).

7 Sir Charles Johnston unpublished diary, 30 November 1947 (Johnston papers).
8 Sir Charles Johnston unpublished diary, 30 November 1947 (Johnston papers).
9 Alden Hatch, *HRH Prince Bernhard of the Netherlands* (George G. Harrap and co, 1962), pp. 253–4.
10 John Wheeler-Bennett, *King George VI: His Life and Reign* (Macmillan, 1958), pp. 754–5.

10. MARRIED LIFE, 1948

1 Private information, 18 September 2011.
2 Private information, March 2023.
3 Address by Lord Fellowes at Sir Edward Ford's memorial service, The Guards' Chapel, 28 February 2007.
4 John Julius Norwich (ed.), *Darling Monster: The Letters of Lady Diana Cooper to Her Son John Julius Norwich, 1939–1952* (Chatto & Windus, 2013), p. 263.
5 Sir Charles Johnston unpublished diary, 26 January 1948 (Johnston papers).
6 Sir Charles Johnston, unpublished diary, 1980 footnote to 26 January 1948 (Johnston papers).
7 Daphne du Maurier to Ellen Doubleday, 10 Whitelands House, Chelsea, 6 March 1948 (Doubleday correspondence, pp. 153–6, Princeton University).
8 Derived from Daphne du Maurier to Ellen Doubleday, Menabilly, 18 March 1948 (Doubleday correspondence, pp. 159–62, Princeton University).
9 Dermot Morrah, *Princess Elizabeth* (Odhams Press, revised edition, 1950), p. 142.
10 Sir Oliver Harvey to Rt Hon Ernest Bevin, British Embassy, Paris, 3 March 1948 (FO 372/6915, National Archives).
11 Jacques Dumaine, *Quai d'Orsay 1945–51* (Chapman & Hall, 1955), p. 167.
12 Derived from Cynthia Gladwyn unpublished diary: Prince Philip's visit, 1954 (Churchill College, Cambridge, GBR/0014), CGLA 2/8.
13 Sir Oliver Harvey to Rt Hon Ernest Bevin, British Embassy, Paris, 20 May 1948 (FO 372/6915, National Archive).
14 Jacques Dumaine, *Quai d'Orsay 1945–51* (Chapman & Hall, 1955), p. 170.
15 Cynthia Gladwyn unpublished diary: The Queen's State Visit, 1957 (Churchill College, Cambridge, GBR/0014), CGLA 2/8.
16 Sir Oliver Harvey to Rt Hon Ernest Bevin, British Embassy, Paris, 20 May 1948 (National Archives: FO 372/6915).
17 Jacques Dumaine, *Quai d'Orsay 1945–51* (Chapman & Hall, 1955), p. 171.

18 John Julius Norwich (ed.), *Darling Monster: The Letters of Lady Diana Cooper to Her Son John Julius Norwich, 1939–1952* (Chatto & Windus, 2013), pp. 277, 279, 280–1.
19 Elizabeth Longford, *Elizabeth R: A Biography* (Weidenfeld & Nicolson, 1983), p. 123.
20 *The Times*, 20 May 1948.
21 John Colville, *The Fringes of Power: Downing Street Diaries, 1939–55* (Hodder & Stoughton, 1985), pp. 625–6.
22 John Colville, *The Fringes of Power: Downing Street Diaries, 1939–55* (Hodder & Stoughton, 1985), p. 713.
23 William Shawcross, *Queen Elizabeth The Queen Mother* (Macmillan, 2009), p. 636.
24 HRH The Princess Elizabeth to Lady Mary Cambridge, Buckingham Palace, 1 December 1948 (illustrated in the *Daily Telegraph*, 30 March 2011).
25 *The Times*, 17 November 1948.

11. ANXIOUS YEARS, 1949–51

1 Peter Townsend, *Time and Chance* (Collins, 1978), p. 182.
2 *The Times*, 23 November 1948.
3 Sir Alan Lascelles to Lord Hardinge of Penshurst, Winchester Tower, Windsor Castle, 30 November 1948.
4 Cecil Beaton, *Strenuous Years: Diaries, 1948–55* (Weidenfeld & Nicolson, 1973), p. 17.
5 Miles Jebb (ed.) *The Diaries of Cynthia Gladwyn* (Constable, 1995), pp. 91–2.
6 *Sunday Express*, 3 July 1949.
7 HM Queen Elizabeth to Mrs Roosevelt, 21 July 1949 (Franklin D. Roosevelt Library).
8 HM Queen Elizabeth to Marion Crawford, Buckingham Palace, 4 April 1949 (copy in Princeton University Library).
9 Bruce Gould to Dermot Morrah (Manuscripts Division, Department of Rare Books and Special Collections, Princeton University Library).
10 Derived from Tom Harvey to Bruce Gould, 24 September 1950 (Gould papers, Princeton University, Box 8).
11 Robert Hardman, *Queen of Our Times* (Macmillan, 2022), p. 110.
12 Sir Alan Lascelles to Hon Lady Lascelles, Sandringham, 17 January 1950 (Lascelles papers, Churchill College, Cambridge, GBR/0014), LASL 11/1.

13 The Duchess of Grafton to author, 31 March 2012.
14 Jacques Dumaine, *Quai d'Orsay 1945–51* (Chapman & Hall, 1955), pp. 250–2.
15 Cecil Beaton, *Photobiography* (Odhams Press, 1951), p. 151.
16 *Photobiography*, p. 154.
17 Brigadier Sir Ivan de la Bere, *The Queen's Orders of Chivalry* (Spring Books, 1964), p. 130.
18 *The Times*, 26 May 1951.
19 *The Times*, 8 June 1951.
20 Richard Davenport-Hines (ed.), *Letters from Oxford: Hugh Trevor-Roper to Bernard Berenson* (Weidenfeld & Nicolson, 2006), p. 82.
21 *Daily Telegraph*, 19 September 1951.
22 *Sunday Express*, 16 September 1951.
23 CAB 128/20 – CM 60 (51), 27 September 1951 (National Archives).

12. DEMISE OF THE CROWN, 1951–2

1 Winston Churchill to Clement Attlee, Chartwell, 23 September 1951 (NA PREM 8/1513).
2 John Hartley, *Accession: The Making of a Queen* (Quartet, 1992), pp. 47–8.
3 *Accession*, p. 53.
4 Lady Charteris of Amisfield to author, London, 28 September 1989.
5 *Accession*, p. 62.
6 *Accession*, p. 2.
7 *Accession*, p. 64.
8 *Accession*, p. 68.
9 Edward Carpenter, *Archbishop Fisher: His Life and Times* (The Canterbury Press, Norwich, 1991), p. 270.
10 Lord Moran, *Winston Churchill: The Struggle for Survival 1940–1965* (Constable, 1966), pp. 372–3.
11 *The Times*, 12 February 1952.
12 HM The King to Sir Miles Thomas, *Daily Telegraph*, 1 February 1952.
13 *The Memoirs of Lord Chandos* (The Bodley Head, 1962), p. 425.
14 Aubrey Buxton, *The King in His Country* (Longmans, Green and co, 1955), p. 138.
15 HV diary, 7 January 2010.

13. ACCESSION, 1952

1. John Hartley, *Accession: The Making of a Queen* (Quartet, 1992), p. 2.
2. HM The Queen diary, quoted by HM King Charles at the state banquet in Nairobi, 31 October 2023.
3. Jim Corbett, *Tree Tops* (A Go Wild publication, Kenya, reprinted 1976), p. 11.
4. John Colville, *The Fringes of Power: Downing Street Diaries, 1939–55* (Hodder & Stoughton, 1985), p. 640.
5. Sir Charles Johnston unpublished diary, 10 February 1952 (Johnston papers).
6. Sir Arthur Penn, *The Death of King George VI* (Lady Penn collection).
7. Daphne du Maurier to Ellen Doubleday, 16 February 1952.
8. Sir Arthur Penn, *The Death of King George VI* (Lady Penn collection).
9. Daphne du Maurier to Ellen Doubleday, 16 February 1952.
10. CAB 129/150 – CC 52 (12), 6 February 1952 (National Archives).
11. Harold Macmillan, *Tides of Fortune: 1945–1955* (Macmillan, 1969), p. 371.
12. Evelyn Shuckburgh, *Descent to Suez: Diaries 1952-56* (Weidenfeld & Nicolson, 1986), p. 34.
13. James Pope-Hennessy, *Queen Mary: 1867–1953* (Allen & Unwin, 1959), p. 619.
14. *The Times*, 8 February 1952.
15. *The Memoirs of Lord Chandos* (The Bodley Head, 1962), p. 425.
16. Harold Macmillan, *Tides of Fortune 1945-55* (Macmillan, 1969), pp. 372–3.
17. Vincent Massey, *What's Past is Prologue – The Memoirs of Vincent Massey* (Macmillan, Canada, 1963), pp. 459-60.
18. Sir Charles Johnston unpublished diary, 10 February 1952 (Johnston papers).
19. Sir Arthur Penn, *The Death of King George VI* (Lady Penn collection).
20. Sir Arthur Penn to Prudence Penn, 4 March 1952 (Lady Penn collection).
21. Daphne du Maurier to Ellen Doubleday, 16 February 1952.
22. The Duke of Abercorn to author, 26 January 2010.
23. *The Times*, 15 February 1952.
24. Speech by HM The Queen, Unveiling of the King George VI statue, The Mall, 21 October 1955.

14. THE NEW REIGN, 1952–3

1. Sir Arthur Penn, *The Death of King George VI* (Lady Penn collection).
2. Daphne du Maurier to Ellen Doubleday, 16 February 1952.
3. Sir Alan Lascelles unpublished diary, quoted in the *Financial Times*, 3 June 2022.

4 *The Times*, 12 February 1952.
5 Susan Mary Alsop, *To Marietta from Paris, 1945–1960* (Doubleday, 1975), p. 200.
6 HRH Princess Andrew of Greece to HRH The Prince Philip, Drake Hotel, Chicago, 6 February 1952.
7 Simon Heffer (ed.), *Henry 'Chips' Channon: The Diaries (Volume 3) 1943–57* (Hutchinson, 2022), p. 755 (diary, 26 February 1952).
8 Simon Heffer (ed.), *Henry 'Chips' Channon: The Diaries (Volume 3) 1943–57* (Hutchinson, 2022), p. 784 (diary, 21 May 1952).
9 HRH The Prince Philip, *Selected Speeches 1948–1955* (Oxford University Press, 1957), pp. 26–7; *Daily Herald*, 9 August 1951.
10 Peter Catterall, *The Macmillan Diaries: The Cabinet Years 1950–57* (Macmillan, 2003), diary, 9 August 1951, p. 93.
11 Peter Catterall, *The Macmillan Diaries: The Cabinet Years 1950–57* (Macmillan, 2003), diary, 6 March 1952, p. 150.
12 John Colville, *The Fringes of Power: Downing Street Diaries, 1939–55* (Hodder & Stoughton, 1985), p. 641.
13 John Colville, *The Fringes of Power: Downing Street Diaries, 1939–55* (Hodder & Stoughton, 1985), p. 642.
14 CAB 129/51 – CC 52 (114), 7 April 1952 (National Archives).
15 'The Name of "Windsor"', memorandum by the Lord Chancellor, 7 April 1952 (CAB 129/51 – CC (52), 53, National Archives).
16 'The Royal Style and Titles', memorandum by the Lord Chancellor, 26 February 1952 (CAB 129/50 – CC (52), 53, National Archives).
17 Prime Minister's statement to Cabinet, 6 March 1952 (CAB 128/24 – CC (52), 53, National Archives).
18 Peter Catterall, *The Macmillan Diaries: The Cabinet Years 1950–57* (Macmillan, 2003), diary, 1 April 1952, p. 155.
19 *Daily Telegraph*, 10 July 1952.
20 *Daily Express*, 23 July 1952.
21 William Shawcross, *Queen Elizabeth The Queen Mother* (Macmillan, 2009), p. 660.
22 Ibid.
23 Michael Bloch (ed.), *The Secret File of the Duke of Windsor* (Bantam Press, 1988), p. 265.
24 Simon Heffer (ed.), *Henry 'Chips' Channon: The Diaries (Volume 3) 1943–57* (Hutchinson, 2022), p .755 (diary, 26 February 1952).
25 Archbishop Fisher Coronation diary, 6 November 1952 (Lambeth Palace Library).

26 John Colville, *The Churchillians* (Weidenfeld & Nicolson, 1981), pp. 120 and 121.
27 Lord Moran, *Winston Churchill: The Struggle for Survival 1940–1965* (Constable, 1966), p. 400.
28 *Winston Churchill: The Struggle for Survival 1940–1965*, p. 403.
29 *Winston Churchill: The Struggle for Survival 1940–1965*, p. 607.
30 John Colville, *The Fringes of Power: Downing Street Diaries, 1939–55* (Hodder & Stoughton, 1985), p. 644.
31 The Earl of Kilmuir, *Political Adventure* (Weidenfeld & Nicolson, 1962), p. 200.
32 Elizabeth Longford, *Elizabeth R: A Biography* (Weidenfeld & Nicolson, 1983), p. 157.
33 James Pope-Hennessy, *Queen Mary: 1867–1953* (George Allen & Unwin, 1959), p. 619.
34 Simon Heffer (ed.), *Henry 'Chips' Channon: The Diaries (Volume 3) 1943–57* (Hutchinson, 2022), p. 809 (diary, 30 July 1952).
35 *The Times*, 12 March 1953.
36 Simon Heffer (ed.), *Henry 'Chips' Channon: The Diaries (Volume 3) 1943–57* (Hutchinson, 2022), p. 867 (diary, 1 April 1953).

15. THE CORONATION, 1953

1 Derived from James Wilkinson, *The Queen's Coronation: The Inside Story* (Scala Publications, 2011), p. 31.
2 James Wilkinson, *The Queen's Coronation: The Inside Story* (Scala Publishers, 2011), p. 23.
3 Hugo Vickers, *Alice: Princess Andrew of Greece* (Hamish Hamilton, 2000), p. 348.
4 Ibid.
5 Archbishop Fisher Coronation diary, 6 November 1952 (Lambeth Palace Library).
6 Ibid.
7 James Wilkinson, *The Queen's Coronation: The Inside Story* (Scala Publishers, 2011), p. 5.
8 Archbishop Fisher to the Duke of Edinburgh, 22 May 1953 (copy in Lambeth Palace Library).
9 The Archbishop of Canterbury, *I Here Present Unto You ...* (SPCK, 1953), p. 14.

10 Ven F. H. House to Rt Rev Alan Don, 28 July 1952 (Westminster Abbey Archives).
11 The Duke of Norfolk to Rt Rev Alan Don, 4 August 1952 (Westminster Abbey Archives).
12 *Sunday Telegraph*, 9 January 1983.
13 Norman Hartnell, *Silver and Gold* (Evans Brothers, 1955), p. 124.
14 Ibid.
15 Norman Hartnell, *Silver and Gold* (Evans Brothers, 1955), p. 129.
16 *Daily Sketch*, 2 June 1953.
17 Archbishop Fisher Coronation diary (Lambeth Palace Library).
18 Ibid.
19 Ibid.
20 Ibid.
21 Ibid.
22 Ibid.
23 Lady Diana Cooper to Patrick Leigh Fermor, 15 June 1953, quoted in Frank and Anita Kermode (ed.), *The Oxford Book of Letters* (Oxford University Press, 1995), p. 528.
24 Robert Rhodes James (ed.), *'Chips': The Diaries of Sir Henry Channon* (Weidenfeld & Nicolson, 1967), pp. 476.
25 Hon Margaret Wyndham to James Pope-Hennessy, August 1956 (Sir John Pope-Hennessy papers, Getty Museum, Los Angeles).
26 Cecil Beaton unpublished diary, 31 May 1952.
27 Rt Rev Alan Don, 'The Coronation – 63189' (Westminster Abbey Archives).
28 L. G. Wickham Legg, *English Coronation Records* (Constable, 1901), p. 25.
29 Archbishop Fisher Coronation diary (Lambeth Palace Library).
30 Ibid.
31 Ibid.
32 L.E. Tanner, Recollections of a Westminster Antiquary, p. 152 (Westminster Abbey Archives).
33 *Guardian*, 3 June 1953.

16. THE CORONATION SUMMER

1 Simon Heffer (ed.), *Henry 'Chips' Channon: The Diaries (Volume 3) 1943–57* (Hutchinson, 2022), p. 884 (diary, 20 and 21 May 1953).

2 Simon Heffer (ed.), *Henry 'Chips' Channon: The Diaries (Volume 3) 1943–57* (Hutchinson, 2022)p. 895 (diary, 18 June 1953).
3 Hon Colin Tennant to Clarissa Eden, 6 William Mews, London SW1 (postmarked 30 June 1953) (Avon papers, Birmingham University).
4 Philip Reed, Mervyn Cook and Donald Mitchell (eds), *Letters from a Life: The Selected Letters of Benjamin Britten 1913–1976*, volume four, 1952–1957 (The Boydell Press, 2008), letter, 6 October 1952, p. 90.
5 John Colville, *The Fringes of Power: Downing Street Diaries, 1939–55* (Hodder & Stoughton, 1985), p. 716.
6 *The Tongs and the Bones: The Memoirs of Lord Harewood* (Weidenfeld & Nicolson, 1981), p. 138.
7 Ibid.
8 Lady Pamela Berry to Clarissa Eden, 3 Barton Street, Westminster, SW1, 17 June [1953] (Clarissa Avon papers, Birmingham University).
9 Ann Fleming to Clarissa Eden, Dover, 20 June [1953] (Clarissa Avon papers, Birmingham University).
10 Lady Juliet Duff to Clarissa Eden, Bulbridge House, Wilton, 26 June [1953] (Clarissa Avon papers, Birmingham University).
11 The Viscountess Monckton of Brenchley to Clarissa Eden, 2 Harcourt Buildings, Temple, London EC4, 9 July [1953] (Clarissa Avon papers, Birmingham University).
12 *The Times*, 18 June 1953.
13 *The Tongs and the Bones: The Memoirs of Lord Harewood* (Weidenfeld & Nicolson, 1981), p. 138.
14 Neil Powell, *Benjamin Britten: A Life for Music* (Hutchinson, 2013), pp. 409–10.
15 Neil Powell, *Benjamin Britten: A Life for Music* (Hutchinson, 2013), p. 410.
16 James Lees-Milne, *Through Wood and Dale: Diaries 1975–1978* (John Murray, 1998), p. 135.
17 Norman Barrymaine, *The Story of Peter Townsend* (Peter Davies, 1958), p. xiv.
18 *Evening Standard*, 10 June 1953.
19 'Royal Romance – the Inside Facts', *Vancouver News-Herald*, 15 December 1952.
20 Peter Townsend, *Earth, My Friend* (Hodder & Stoughton, 1959), p. 17.
21 John Colville, *The Fringes of Power: Downing Street Diaries, 1939–55* (Hodder & Stoughton, 1985), 13 June 1953.
22 Peter Townsend, *Time and Change* (Collins, 1978), p. 203.

23 Duff Hart-Davis (ed.), *King's Counsellor: Abdication and War – The Diaries of Sir Alan Lascelles* (Weidenfeld & Nicolson, 2006), p. 399.

17. THE COMMONWEALTH TOUR, 1953–4

1 The London Declaration, 26 April 1949, quoted in *The Royal Tour* (Royal Collections Publications, 2009), p. 6.
2 Ann Fleming to Clarissa Eden, Goldeneye, Oracabessa, Jamaica, 28 February 1954 (Clarissa Avon papers, Birmingham University).
3 Sir Geoffry Scoones, High Commissioner, 'Report on the Visit of Her Majesty The Queen and His Royal Highness The Duke of Edinburgh, December 1953–January 1954', Commonwealth Relations Office Print, 14 March 1954 (DO 35/5141, National Archives).
4 'New Zealand Fortnightly Summary, Part 1 – 18th–31st December 1953', UK High Commissioner to Commonwealth Relations Office No 137 (DO 35/5141, National Archives).
5 Sir Geoffry Scoones, High Commissioner, 'Report on the Visit of Her Majesty The Queen and His Royal Highness The Duke of Edinburgh, December 1953–January 1954', Commonwealth Relations Office Print, 14 March 1954 (DO 35/5141, National Archives).
6 Scoones, 14 March 1954 (DO 35/5141, National Archives).
7 Scoones, 21 January 1954 (DO 35/5141, National Archives).
8 John Quinn in *News*, 26 March 1954.
9 *The Macleay Argus*, 12 February 1954.
10 Sir Robert Menzies, *Afternoon Light: Some Memories of Men and Events* (Cassell, Australia, 1967), pp. 256-7.
11 Ronald Lewin, *Slim: The Standardbearer* (Leo Cooper, 1976), p. 298.
12 'Visit of H.M. The Queen and H.R.H. The Duke of Edinburgh to Australia – Report of the UK High Commissioner to Secretary of State for Commonwealth Relations', Commonwealth Relations Office print, 22 April 1954 (DO 35/5139, National Archives).
13 *Sun News Pictorial*, 8 February 1954.
14 Private information.
15 'Visit of H.M. The Queen and H.R.H. The Duke of Edinburgh to Australia – Report of the UK High Commissioner to Secretary of State for Commonwealth Relations', Commonwealth Relations Office print, 22 April 1954 (DO 35/5139, National Archives).

16 Ibid.
17 Cabinet minutes, 22 March 1954 (CC 54, National Archives).
18 *Newcastle Morning Herald and Miners Advocate*, 3 April 1954.
19 'Visit of H.M. The Queen and H.R.H. The Duke of Edinburgh to Australia – Report of the UK High Commissioner to Secretary of State for Commonwealth Relations', Commonwealth Relations Office print, 22 April 1954 (DO 35/5139, National Archives).
20 C. G. Syers, High Commissioner, 'Ceylon: The Royal Visit', Commonwealth Relations Office Print, 21 May 1954 (DO 35/5144, National Archives).
21 The Marquess of Salisbury, Commonwealth Relations Office to UK High Commissioner, 4 September 1953 (DO 121 213 – Cypher 534, National Archives).
22 Winston Churchill to Dudley Senanayake, 29 December 1952 (DO 121 213, National Archives).
23 Lord Soulbury to Viscount Swinton, Secretary of State for Commonwealth Relations, 1 February 1954 (DO 121 213, National Archives).
24 Aide Memoire by J. L. Kotelawala, 27 January 1954 (DO 121 213, National Archives).
25 Marquess of Salisbury to Viscount Swinton, 6 February 1954 (DO 121 213, National Archives).
26 *Yorkshire Post*, 8 April 1954.
27 C. G. Syers, High Commissioner, 'Ceylon: The Royal Visit', Commonwealth Relations Office Print, 21 May 1954 (DO 35/5144, National Archives).
28 C. G. Syers, High Commissioner, 'Ceylon: The Royal Visit', Commonwealth Relations Office Print, 21 May 1954 (DO 35/5144, National Archives).
29 HM The Queen to author, 9 April 1999.
30 *The Memoirs of Lord Chandos* (The Bodley Head, 1962), p. 418.
31 Colonial Secretary, 'Report to Cabinet – April 1954' (CC 26(54), National Archives).
32 Governor of Uganda to Oliver Lyttelton (Secretary of State for the Colonies), telegram no. 359 – to the Cabinet – 7 April 1954 (CAB 129/167 – CC54/146, National Archives).
33 *The Memoirs of Lord Chandos* (The Bodley Head, 1962), p. 422.
34 Ibid.
35 Wynford Vaughan-Thomas, *Royal Tour 1953–4* (Hutchinson, 1954), pp. 108–10.
36 Sir John Balfour, *Not Too Correct an Aureole: Recollections of a Diplomat* (Michael Russell, 1983), p. 159.

37 Hugo Vickers, *The Coronation* (The Dovecote Press, 2023), p. 293.
38 Paul Preston, *Franco: A Biography* (HarperCollins, 1993), p. 629.
39 Sir John Balfour, *Not Too Correct an Aureole: Recollections of a Diplomat* (Michael Russell, 1983), pp. 160–1.
40 Anthony Eden, Foreign Office, to Sir John Balfour, 12 January 1954 (FO 371/113037, National Archives).
41 Sir John Balfour, *Not Too Correct an Aureole: Recollections of a Diplomat* (Michael Russell, 1983), p. 162.
42 Governor of Gibraltar's Speech, February 1954 (extracted in CAB 129/66, Cabinet Memorandum – 1 March 1954 – C (54) 80 126, National Archives).
43 Telegram, Secretary of State for the Colonies to Governor of Gibraltar, 24 February 1954 (CAB 129/66, Cabinet Memorandum – 1 March 1954 – C (54) 80 126, National Archives).
44 Cabinet Notebook – The Queen's Tour to Gibraltar (CAB 195/111, National Archives).
45 Sir John Balfour to John Cheetham, British Embassy, Madrid, 17 February 1954 (FO 371/113079, National Archives).
46 Derived from memorandum, T. F. C. to J. Colville, 23 April 1954 (DO 121/213, National Archives).
47 Sir John Balfour to John Cheetham, British Embassy, Madrid, 20 April 1954 (FO 371/113079, National Archives).
48 Draft note by David Muirhead for the Foreign Secretary's reply to a parliamentary question by George Jeger, 29 April 1954 (FO 371/113079, National Archives).
49 Wynford Vaughan-Thomas, *Royal Tour 1953–4* (Hutchinson, 1954), pp. 112.
50 HM The Queen to author, 9 April 1999.
51 HM The Queen to Anthony Eden, Balmoral Castle, 21 May 1954 (Avon papers, Birmingham University).

18. CHURCHILL AND EDEN, 1952–7

1 Charles Wilson (Lord Moran), *Winston Churchill: The Struggle for Survival 1940–1965* (Constable, 1966), pp. 555–6.
2 John Colville diary, 7 July 1954, *The Fringes of Power: Downing Street Diaries, 1939–55* (Hodder & Stoughton, 1985), p. 701.

3   John Colville diary (undated but April 1955), *The Fringes of Power: Downing Street Diaries, 1939–55* (Hodder & Stoughton, 1985), p. 708.
4   Martin Gilbert, *Winston S. Churchill: Volume VIII: Never Despair, 1945–1965* (Heinemann, 1988), p. 1121.
5   John Colville, reminiscences, Stour, 8 June 1965, quoted in Martin Gilbert, *Winston S. Churchill: Volume VIII: Never Despair, 1945–1965* (Heinemann, 1988), p. 1124.
6   *Winston S. Churchill: Volume VIII*, p. 1124.
7   *Winston S. Churchill: Volume VIII*, p. 1125.
8   *Winston S. Churchill: Volume VIII*, p. 1126.
9   *Winston S. Churchill: Volume VIII*, p. 1127.
10 *Winston S. Churchill: Volume VIII*, p. 1128.
11 Countess of Avon diary, 6 April 1955 (Avon papers, Birmingham University).
12 The Countess of Avon to author, 10 January 2007.
13 HM The Queen to Anthony Eden, Balmoral Castle, 21 May 1954 (Avon papers, Birmingham University).
14 HM The Queen to Anthony Eden, Balmoral Castle, 6 October 1954 (Avon papers, Birmingham University).
15 Valentine Lawford to author, 31 May 1981.
16 The Countess of Avon to author, 26 May 2012.
17 The Duchess of Buccleuch to Alan Pryce-Jones, 8 November 1960 (Pryce-Jones papers, Beinecke Library, Yale).
18 *New Statesman*, 22 October 1955.
19 Hugo Vickers, 'Twenty-Five Years a Queen' in *Burke's Guide to the British Monarchy* (Burke's Peerage, 1977), pp. 29–30.
20 Harold Macmillan, *Riding the Storm: 1956–1959* (Macmillan, 1971), p. 747.
21 D. R. Thorpe, *Supermac: The Life of Harold Macmillan* (Chatto & Windus, 2010), p. 393.
22 Countess of Avon diary, 9 January 1957 (Avon papers, Birmingham University).
23 A private note written between 29 April and 26 September 1964, in Lord Avon's diary (Avon papers, Birmingham University).
24 HM The Queen to Sir Anthony Eden, Sandringham, 16 January 1957 (Avon papers, Birmingham University).
25 Sir Anthony Eden to HM The Queen, Chequers, 17 January 1957 (copy in the Avon papers, Birmingham University).

19. THE FAMILY IN THE 1950s

1. The Countess of Avon to author, Alvediston, 25 March 1980.
2. Fiametta Rocco interview, *Independent*, 13 December 1992.
3. *Report and Proceedings: His Royal Highness the Duke of Edinburgh's Study Conference on the Human Problems of Industrial Communities within the Commonwealth and Empire*, volume one (Oxford University Press, 1957), pp. 35–6.
4. Graham F. Thomas, *The Last of the Proconsuls: The Letters of Sir James Robertson* (The Radcliffe Press, 1994), p. 98 (letter, 14 May 1967).
5. HRH The Prince Philip speech, 25 February 1953, in HRH The Prince Philip, *Selected Speeches 1948–1955* (Oxford University Press, 1957), pp. 59-60
6. Fiametta Rocco interview, *Independent*, 13 December 1992.
7. *The Times*, 27 February 1957.
8. *The Times*, 27 February 1957.
9. *The Baltimore Sun*, 8 February 1957.
10. *The Baltimore Sun*, 9 February 1957.
11. *The Times*, 23 February 1957.
12. HRH The Prince Philip's speech to the Mansion House, London, *The Times*, 27 February 1957.
13. Hugo Vickers (ed.), *The Quest for Queen Mary* (Hodder & Stoughton, 2018), p. 222.
14. James Pope-Hennessy to John Pope-Hennessy, 26 August 1957 (Sir John Pope-Hennessy papers, Getty Museum, Los Angeles, Box 124).
15. HRH The Prince Philip to Jim Orr, Buckingham Palace, 4 March [1957].
16. HM The Queen to Sir Anthony Eden, Sandringham, 16 January 1958 (Avon papers, Birmingham University).
17. Cecil Beaton diary, March 1960 (Cecil Beaton papers, St John's College, Cambridge).
18. *Daily Telegraph*, 1 November 1955.
19. *Daily Telegraph*, 15 October 1955.
20. *Daily Telegraph*, 1 November 1955.
21. *Daily Telegraph*, 1 November 1955.
22. Hugo Vickers, *Elizabeth: The Queen Mother* (Hutchinson, 2005), p. 366.
23. Peter Townsend, *Time and Chance* (Collins, 1978), p. 285.
24. HRH The Princess Margaret, Countess of Snowdon, to author, 1996.

20. DIPLOMACY, 1954–9

1. Memorandum from Head, East African Department, J. N. O. Curle, Protocol & Conference Department, 21 September 1973 (FCO 31/1695, National Archives).
2. Ibid.
3. Confidential briefing notes on Iran, January 1961 (FO 372/7600, National Archives).
4. First draft of Speech for HM The Queen at Banquet given by the Shah in Tehran, February 1961 (FO 372/7600, National Archives).
5. George R. McRobert, Medical Adviser, CRO, to Sir Charles Dixon, Constitutional Adviser, CRO, 1 December 1960 (FO 372/7547, National Archives).
6. HM The Queen to author, 9 April 1999.
7. Clarissa Eden diary, 14 October 1954 (Avon papers, Birmingham University).
8. Ibid.
9. Clarissa Eden diary, 22 April 1956, quoted in Hugo Vickers, *Clarissa* (Hodder & Stoughton, 2024), p. 186.
10. Anthony Eden, *Full Circle* (Cassell, 1960), p. 423.
11. *The Times*, 22 October 1958.
12. Ibid.
13. Maurice Michael, *Haakon: King of Norway* (Allen & Unwin, 1958), p. 191.
14. *The Times*, 23 September 1957.
15. Hon Sir Robert Hankey, British Embassy, Stockholm, to Selwyn Lloyd, Foreign Office, 20 June 1956 (PREM 11/1554, National Archives).
16. Ibid.
17. Ibid.
18. Sir Roderick Barclay to Selwyn Lloyd, 7 June 1957 (PREM 11/2061, National Archives).
19. Anthony Meyer, *Stand Up and Be Counted* (Heinemann, 1990), p. 20.
20. Sir Gladwyn Jebb to Selwyn Lloyd, 23 April 1957 (PREM 11/2052, National Archives).
21. Ibid.
22. Ibid.
23. Ibid.
24. Simon Heffer (ed.), *Henry 'Chips' Channon: The Diaries (Volume 3) 1943–57* (Hutchinson, 2022), p. 1090 (diary, 10 April 1957).

25 Cynthia Gladwyn, Royal Visits diary, The Queen's State Visit, 8–11 April 1957 (Churchill College, Cambridge).
26 Cecil Beaton to Clarissa Eden, 8 Pelham Place, 26 April 1957 (Clarissa Avon papers, Birmingham University).
27 Miles Jebb (ed.), *The Diaries of Cynthia Gladwyn* (Constable, 1995), p. 206.
28 Cynthia Gladwyn, Royal Visits diary, The Queen's State Visit, 8–11 April 1957 (Churchill College, Cambridge).
29 Ibid.
30 A. J. Tyrell, Government Coastal Agency, Apapa, Nigeria, to R. W. Cook, Crown Agents' Office, London, 24 November 1955 (CA06 10/172, National Archives).
31 *The Queen's Tour of Nigeria* (Pitkin Pictorials, 1956), p. 7.
32 Brigadier Stanley Clark, *Palace Diary* (George G. Harrap, 1958), p. 182.
33 Sir James Robertson, *Transition in Africa: From Direct Rule to Independence* (C. Hurst and Co, 1974), p. 196.
34 *The Queen's Tour of Nigeria* (Pitkin Pictorials, 1956), p. 12.
35 The Duchess of Grafton to author, London, 31 March 2012.
36 *The Times*, 23 February 1956.
37 Graham F. Thomas, *The Last of the Proconsuls: The Letters of Sir James Robertson* (The Radcliffe Press, 1994), p. 69 (letter, 4 March 1956).
38 *The Times*, 23 February 1956.
39 *The Times*, 22 October 1957.
40 Sir Harold Caccia to Foreign Office, 22 October 1957 (CAB 21/3122, National Archives).
41 Ibid.
42 Sir Harold Caccia to Harold Macmillan, 23 October 1957, quoted in Harold Macmillan, *Riding the Storm: 1956–1959* (Macmillan, 1971), p. 319.
43 HM The Queen to Sir Anthony Eden, Sandringham, 16 January 1958 (Avon papers, Birmingham University).
44 F. E. Cumming-Bruce to Commonwealth Relations Office, 4 September 1959 (DO 35/7923, National Archives).
45 Ibid.
46 Ibid.
47 Claude Bissell, *The Imperial Canadian: Vincent Massey in Office* (University of Toronto Press, Canada, 1986), pp. 264–8.
48 Christopher McCreery, *The Order of Canada: Its Origins, History, and Developments* (University of Toronto Press, Canada, 1985), p. 106.

49 Claude Bissell, *The Imperial Canadian: Vincent Massey in Office* (University of Toronto Press, Canada, 1986), pp. 264–8, 293.

21. HAROLD MACMILLAN, 1957–63

1 Harold Macmillan, *Riding the Storm: 1956–1959* (Macmillan, 1971), p. 184.
2 *Riding the Storm: 1956–1959*, p. 185.
3 *Riding the Storm: 1956–1959*, p. 184.
4 *Riding the Storm: 1956–1959*, p. 344.
5 Harold Macmillan diary, 1 September 1957, quoted in Charles Williams, *Harold Macmillan* (Weidenfeld & Nicolson, 2009), p. 293.
6 Andrew Duncan, *The Reality of Monarchy* (Heinemann, 1970), pp. 4–5.
7 Charles Williams, *Harold Macmillan* (Weidenfeld & Nicolson, 2009), p. 471.
8 Alistair Horne, *Macmillan: 1957–1986* (Macmillan, 1989), p. 170.
9 Harold Macmillan diary, 7 September 1959, quoted in Harold Macmillan, *Riding the Storm: 1956–1959* (Macmillan, 1971), p. 750.
10 Kwame Nkrumah, *Towards Colonial Freedom: Africa in the Struggle Against World Imperialism* (Farleigh Press, 1947), p. 42.
11 Cabinet notebook, 2 November 1961 (CC (61) 59 – CAB 195, National Archives).
12 Hugo Vickers, 'Twenty-Five Years a Queen', *Burke's Guide to the British Monarchy* (Burke's Peerage, 1977), p. 48.
13 Harold Macmillan to Sir Winston Churchill, 19 October 1961, quoted in Martin Gilbert, *Winston S. Churchill: Volume VIII: Never Despair, 1945–1965* (Heinemann, 1988), p. 1331.
14 Commonwealth Secretary for Cabinet and [Sir Michael] Adeane, 7 November 1961 (CAB 21/4504, National Archives).
15 Cabinet notebook, 8 November 1961 (CC (61) 60 – CAB 195, National Archives).
16 Harold Macmillan diary, 13 November 1961, quoted in Peter Catterall, *The Macmillan Diaries: The Premiership 1957–66* (Macmillan, 2011), p. 425.
17 Audrey Russell, *A Certain Voice* (Ross Anderson Publications, 1984), p. 129.
18 Quoted in Alistair Horne, *Macmillan: 1957–1986* (Macmillan, 1989), p. 398.
19 Quoted in *Macmillan: 1957–1986*, p. 399.

20 Harold Macmillan diary, 3 November 1961, quoted in Harold Macmillan, *Pointing the Way: 1959–61* (Macmillan, 1972), pp. 471–2.
21 Sir Hilton Poynton to Sir Walter Coutts, 11 May 1962 (CO 822/2963, National Archives).
22 HM The Queen to author, The Mall, 2 June 2003.
23 Record of a Meeting held at Buckingham Palace at 9.45am on Wednesday 6 April 1960 (FO 371/153914, National Archives).
24 Sir Gladwyn Jebb, British Ambassador in Paris, to Rt Hon Selwyn Lloyd, Foreign Secretary, Paris, 8 April 1960 (FO 371/153914, National Archives).
25 The Countess of Avon to Cecil Beaton, 23 June 1963.
26 *The Times*, 23 March 1963.
27 *The Times*, 23 March 1963.
28 The Countess of Avon to Cecil Beaton, 23 June 1963 (Avon papers, Birmingham University).
29 *The Times*, 6 June 1963.
30 Charles Williams, *Harold Macmillan* (Weidenfeld & Nicolson, 2009), p. 380.
31 Harold Macmillan, *At the End of the Day* (Macmillan, 1973), p. 515.
32 Alistair Horne, *Macmillan: 1957–1986* (Macmillan, 1989), p. 565.
33 Harold Macmillan, *At the End of the Day* (Macmillan, 1973), p. 516.
34 The Countess of Avon to Cecil Beaton, 23 June 1963 (Avon papers, Birmingham University).
35 Harold Macmillan, *At the End of the Day* (Macmillan, 1973), p. 519.
36 Alec Douglas-Home (Lord Home), *The Way the Wind Blows* (William Collins, 1976), p. 201.

22. THE FAMILY IN THE 1960s

1 Lord Mountbatten diary, 14 November 1973, quoted in Philip Ziegler (ed.), *From Shore to Shore: Final Years Diary, 1953–1979* (William Collins, 1989), p. 273.
2 Sir Charles Johnston diary, Canberra, February 1966 (Johnston papers, p. 222E).
3 Michael Parkinson BBC interview, Australia, 13 October 1983.
4 James Pope-Hennessy to Sir John Pope-Hennessy, 27 October 1961 (Sir John Pope-Hennessy papers, Getty Museum, Los Angeles).
5 Derived from the Duchess of Buccleuch to Alan Pryce-Jones, 28 January 1962 (Pryce-Jones papers, Beinecke Library, Yale).

6   Quoted in Judith Campbell, *Anne: Portrait of a Princess* (Cassell, 1970), p. 91.
7   *The Tongs and the Bones: The Memoirs of Lord Harewood* (Weidenfeld & Nicolson, 1981), p. 295.
8   *The Memoirs of Princess Alice, Duchess of Gloucester* (Collins, 1983), p. 188.
9   Rt Hon Sir Angus Ogilvy to author, 25 January 2001.
10 Note from Philip de Zulueta to the Prime Minister, 26 April 1963 – Royal Family file, Princess Alexandra's Wedding (National Archives – PREM 11/4434).
11 Harold Macmillan diary, 7 March 1965, quoted in Pater Catterall (ed.), *The Macmillan Diaries: The Premiership 1957–66* (Macmillan, 2011), p. 657.
12 HM The Queen to HRH The Duke of Windsor, 26 February 1969; 5 August 1970.
13 HRH The Duke of Windsor to HM The Queen, 26 February 1970.
14 Ibid.
15 HM The Queen to HRH The Duke of Windsor, 5 August 1970.
16 Prince Philip to author, 20 May 1997.

23. DIPLOMACY, 1960–9

1   A. C. B. Symon to Sir Alexander Clutterbuck, Commonwealth Relations Office, Dacca, Pakistan, 17 February 1961 (DO 161/75, National Archives).
2   Ibid.
3   Sir Paul Gore-Booth to Secretary of State, Commonwealth Relations Office, Bombay, 23 February 1961 (DO 161/75, National Archives).
4   G. F. Hillier to Mr Samuel, 15 February 1961 (FO 372/7600, National Archives).
5   HM The Queen to Most Rev Geoffrey Fisher, quoted in Edward Carpenter, *Archbishop Fisher: His Life and Times* (Canterbury Press, 1991), p. 710.
6   Derived from the Duchess of Buccleuch to Alan Pryce-Jones, 15 June 1961 (Pryce-Jones papers, Beinecke Library, Yale).
7   Robert Menzies speech, Canberra, 15 February 1963.
8   British Embassy telegram to Foreign Office, 11 May 1963 (HO 325/6, National Archives).
9   *The Times*, 10 July 1963.
10 *The Times*, 11 July 1963.
11 *The Times*, 13 July 1963.
12 Queen Frederica of the Hellenes, *A Measure of Understanding* (Macmillan, 1971), p. 245.

13 *The Times*, 13 July 1963; also derived from reports in FO 953/2121, National Archives.
14 Private information.
15 High Commissioner H. Lintott to Commonwealth Relations Office, 21 October 1964 (FO 372/7902, National Archives).
16 Ibid.
17 Ibid.
18 Ibid.
19 HM The Queen to Sir Alec Douglas-Home, 15 October 1964, quoted in D. R. Thorpe, *Alec Douglas-Home* (Sinclair-Stevenson, 1996), p. 361.
20 Michela Wrong, *I Didn't Do It For You: How the World Betrayed a Small African Nation* (Fourth Estate, 2005), p. 156.
21 *The Memoirs of Princess Alice, Duchess of Gloucester* (Collins, 1983), p. 177.
22 Sir Lees Mayall, *Fireflies in Amber* (Michael Russell, 1989), p. 142.
23 Sir John Russell to Sir Edward Ford, Addis Ababa, 6 January 1965 (FO 2043/57, National Archives).
24 Ibid.
25 Sir Ian Scott to Ronald Scrivener, Foreign Office, 17 December 1964 (FO 371/178822, National Archives).
26 *Illustrated London News*, 5 June 1965.
27 R. A. Butler to the Prime Minister, 23 April 1965 (FO 372/7902, National Archives).
28 Sir Frank Roberts, *Dealing With Dictators* (Weidenfeld & Nicolson, 1991), p. 242.
29 Sir Frank Roberts, *Dealing With Dictators* (Weidenfeld & Nicolson, 1991), p. 244.
30 *Illustrated London News*, 29 May 1965.
31 Sir Frank Roberts, *Dealing With Dictators* (Weidenfeld & Nicolson, 1991), p. 245.
32 HRH Princess Andrew of Greece to HRH The Prince Philip, Munich, 1 August 1966.
33 HM The Queen to Ian Smith, 24 October 1965, reproduced in [Sunday] *Express*, 1965.
34 Dr Robin Tattersall, OBE, to author, Tortola, British Virgin Islands, 9 November 2016.
35 *Illustrated London News*, 12 March 1966.
36 *Illustrated London News*, 12 March 1966.

37 Godfrey Smith, notes for a 'Profile of a Prince', *Sunday Times* magazine, c. 1966.
38 Sir Charles Johnston unpublished diary, 19 July 1966 (Johnston papers).

24. HOME POLITICS, 1965–6

1 Martin Gilbert, *Winston S. Churchill: Volume VIII: Never Despair, 1945–1965* (Heinemann, 1988), p. 1256.
2 *Winston S. Churchill: Volume VIII*, p. 1364.
3 Douglas Brown (1917–2003), 'The Queen faces her Forties', *Sunday Telegraph*, 17 April 1966.
4 *The Times*, 24 March 1976.
5 Andrew Duncan, *The Reality of Monarchy* (Heinemann, 1970), p. 5.
6 Harold Wilson, *Memoirs: The Making of a Prime Minister 1916–64* (Weidenfeld & Nicolson, 1986), pp. 2–6.
7 *Evening Standard*, 24 May 1974 (26 November 1974; 27 September 1975).
8 Harold Wilson, *Memoirs: The Making of a Prime Minister 1916–64* (Weidenfeld & Nicolson, 1986), pp. 2–6.
9 Sir Charles Johnston unpublished diary, p. 410, entry for 25 June 1975 (Johnston papers).
10 Richard Crossman, *The Diaries of a Cabinet Minister*, vol. 1 (Jonathan Cape/Hamish Hamilton, 1975), p. 29.
11 *The Diaries of a Cabinet Minister*, vol. 1, p. 44.
12 *The Diaries of a Cabinet Minister*, vol. 1, p. 194.
13 *The Diaries of a Cabinet Minister*, vol. 1, pp. 132–3.
14 *The Diaries of a Cabinet Minister*, vol. 1, p. 534.
15 *The Diaries of a Cabinet Minister*, vol. 1, p. 544.
16 *The Diaries of a Cabinet Minister*, vol. 1, p. 953.
17 Evidence to the Committee on Ministerial Memoirs, Wilson papers, box 104, quoted in Philip Ziegler, *Wilson: The Authorised Life* (Weidenfeld & Nicolson, 1993), p. 454.
18 William Whitelaw, *The Whitelaw Memoirs* (Aurum Press, 1989), pp. 229–30.
19 Michael Orger to author, Windsor, 1 February 2004.

25. CHANGING TIMES

1. Hugo Vickers (ed.), *The Quest for Queen Mary* (Hodder & Stoughton, 2018), p. 304.
2. The Duke of Beaufort, *Memoirs* (Country Life Books, 1981), p. 103.
3. Tim Fitzgeorge-Parker, *The Field*, 18 February 1984.
4. 'Off the bit' by Loriner, *Horse and Hound*, 10 February 1984.
5. *Dictionary of National Biography*, Duke of Norfolk article by Michael Maclagan.
6. Andrew Duncan, *The Reality of Monarchy* (Heinemann, 1970), p. 7.
7. Sir Edward Ford to author, 5 July 2006.
8. *Daily Telegraph*, 20 May 2006.
9. Sir William Heseltine to author, 30 May 2015.
10. Brigadier Andrew Parker Bowles to author, 18 November 2025.
11. *Fool Britannia*, 1963.
12. *Daily Express*, 21 April 1970.
13. Tim Heald, 'Sniping after a royal best seller', *Daily Express*, 21 April 1970.
14. The late Anne Hawkins (Anne Wall) to author.
15. Andrew Duncan, *The Reality of Monarchy* (Heinemann, 1970), p. 101.
16. Andrew Duncan, *The Reality of Monarchy* (Heinemann, 1970), p. 202.
17. William Heseltine to HM The Queen, 26 February 1968.
18. Sir William Heseltine, extract from unpublished autobiography.
19. *The Times*, 10 November 1969.
20. Sir William Heseltine, extract from unpublished autobiography.
21. *The Times*, 6 June 1969.
22. Sir Charles Johnston unpublished diary, July 1969 (Johnston papers).
23. Ibid.

26. THE EARLY 1970s

1. HM The Queen to HRH The Duke of Windsor, 5 August 1970.
2. HM The Queen to James Orr, Windsor Castle, 1 March 1970.
3. *Daily Telegraph*, 12 March 1970.
4. *Daily Telegraph*, 1 May 1970.
5. *Daily Telegraph*, 14 March 1970.
6. HM The Queen to HRH The Duke of Windsor, 5 August 1970.
7. *Daily Telegraph*, 1 May 1970.

8   Michael Parkinson BBC interview, Australia, 13 October 1983.
9   Ibid.
10 *Daily Telegraph*, 24 April 1970.
11 *The Times*, 27 April 1970.
12 *Daily Telegraph*, 18 March 1970.
13 *The Times*, 27 January 2000.
14 Edward Heath, *The Course of My Life: The Autobiography of Edward Heath* (Hodder & Stoughton, 1998), p. 308.
15 Hugo Young, *One of Us* (Macmillan, 1989), p. 490.
16 Edward Heath, *The Course of My Life: The Autobiography of Edward Heath* (Hodder & Stoughton, 1998), p. 318.
17 Ronald Allison to author, 28 September 1997.
18 HIM The Emperor of Japan to HM The Queen, The Palace, Tokyo, 19 February 1971 (FCO 57/330, National Archives).
19 HRH Princess Alexandra to author, Kensington Palace, 29 October 2021.
20 Ibid.
21 Sir John Pilcher to Sir Alec Douglas-Home, 5 November 1971 (TNA FCO 21/926 FEJ/26/4 nos26/8).
22 *Private Eye*, 8 October 1971.
23 Quoted in Antony Best's article in Matthew Glencross, Judith Rowbotham and Michael D. Kandiah (eds), *The Windsor Dynasty 1910 to the Present* (Palgrave Macmillan, 2016), p. 245.
24 D. C. Walker to Mr Leahy, 19 October 1971 (FCO 26/664, National Archives).
25 Sir John Pilcher to Sir Alec Douglas-Home, 5 November 1971 (TNA FCO 21/926 FEJ/26/4 nos26/8).
26 Quoted in Simone Warner, Hugh Cortazzi (ed.) *Japan Experiences* (Japan Library, 2001), p. 562.
27 Sir Fred Warner to the Secretary of State for Foreign Affairs, Confidential report on the State Visit of Her Majesty The Queen, 12 June 1975, paragraph 5 – (National Archives – Diplomatic Report 249/75 – FCO 160/171/17).
28 HRH The Prince Philip's speech to the National Press Club in Washington, 18 May 1990.
29 *The Times*, 10 November 1969.
30 Harold Wilson, *Final Term: The Labour Government, 1974–1976* (Weidenfeld & Nicolson, 1979), p. 274.
31 Harry Brind to Lees Mayall, 7 January 1972 (FO 57/401, National Archives).
32 Ibid.

33 Annex 2 – Personality Notes – East African Department, Foreign Office, 9 July 1971 (PREM 15/707, National Archives).
34 Note by East African Department, Foreign Office, 9 July 1971 (PREM 15/707, National Archives).
35 Eastafco telegram to Savidge, Guidance Department, Foreign Office, 21 July 1971 (FCO 31/1073, National Archives).
36 William Heseltine to Mrs M. Drummond, 21 September 1972 (FO 57/401, National Archives).
37 S. Y. Dawbarn to Foreign Office, 4 October 1972 (FO 57/401, National Archives).
38 All preceding references are FO 57/401, National Archives.
39 Sir Martin Charteris, at Kuala Lumpur, to John Graham, Foreign Office, 25 February 1972 (FCO 57/412, National Archives).
40 Cecil Beaton diary, 11 April 1972, in Hugo Vickers (ed.), *The Unexpurgated Beaton,* (Weidenfeld & Nicolson, 2002), p. 244.

27. THE STATE VISIT TO PARIS, 1972

1 Sir Christopher Soames, British Embassy, Paris, to Sir Alec Douglas-Home, 2 June 1972 (FCO 57/404, National Archives).
2 Sir Christopher Soames, British Embassy, Paris, to Sir Alec Douglas-Home, 2 June 1972 (FCO 57/404, National Archives).
3 Sir Denis Greenhill, Foreign and Commonwealth Office, to Sir Christopher Soames, 5 January 1972 (FCO 57/404, National Archives).
4 William Heseltine to G. W. Harding, 21 January 1972 (FCO 57/404, National Archives).
5 R. W. H. du Boulay, British Embassy, Paris, to Lees Mayall, 4 February 1972 (FCO 57/404, National Archives).
6 C. M. James memorandum to Lees Mayall, 30 March 1972 (FCO 57/404, National Archives).
7 Speech by HM The Queen at President Pompidou's Banquet at Versailles, Monday, 15 May (FCO 57/404, National Archives).
8 Sir Martin Charteris to John Graham, 28 April 1972 (FCO 57/404, National Archives).
9 Draft speech by HRH The Duke of Edinburgh – State Visit to France – Joint Chamber of Commerce Luncheon, Paris, for 16 May 1972 (FCO 57/404, National Archives).

10 Memorandum by W. J. Adams, European Integration Department (2), Foreign Office, 11 May 1972 (FCO 57/404, National Archives).
11 Sir Christopher Soames, British Embassy, Paris, to Sir Alec Douglas-Home, 10 May 1972 (FCO 57/404, National Archives).
12 Hugo Vickers, *Behind Closed Doors: The Tragic, Untold Story of the Duchess of Windsor* (Hutchinson, 2011), p. 19.
13 State Visit – A confidential brief on France, 5 May 1972 (FCO 57/404, National Archives).
14 Sir Christopher Soames, British Embassy, Paris, to Foreign Office and William Heseltine, 12 May 1972 (FCO 57/404, National Archives).
15 Sir Christopher Soames, British Embassy, Paris, to Sir Alec Douglas-Home, 2 June 1972 (FCO 57/404, National Archives).
16 Ibid.
17 Ibid.
18 Ibid.
19 Ibid.
20 Ibid.
21 D. J. Swan, Marseilles, to Sir Christopher Soames, 25 May 1972 (FCO 57/404, National Archives).
22 Ibid.
23 Edward Heath to Sir Robert Armstrong, 7 November 1971 (PREM 1184, National Archives).
24 Sir Martin Charteris to author, 1980s.
25 The Duchess of Grafton to author, 1980s.
26 Sir Christopher Soames, British Embassy, Paris, to Sir Alec Douglas-Home, 2 June 1972 (FCO 57/404, National Archives).
27 Ibid.
28 *The Times*, 17 May 1972.
29 Sir Christopher Soames, British Embassy, Paris, to Sir Alec Douglas-Home, 2 June 1972 (FCO 57/404, National Archives).

28. POLITICS AND FAMILY, 1972–6

1 John Utter to the author, Paris, 11 September 1972.
2 Cecil Beaton diary, 5 June 1972, in Hugo Vickers (ed.), *The Unexpurgated Beaton* (Weidenfeld & Nicolson, 2002), p. 256.
3 *The Memoirs of Princess Alice, Duchess of Gloucester* (Collins, 1983), p. 194.

4 *Daily Telegraph*, 21 November 1972.
5 HM The Queen to the Earl of Avon, Buckingham Palace, 14 November 1972 (Avon papers, Birmingham University).
6 *The Times*, 7 July 1973.
7 Robin Ludlow to author.
8 Lady Diana Cooper to author, April 1981.
9 Jonathan Dimbleby, *The Prince of Wales: An Intimate Portrait* (Little, Brown, 1994), p. 191.
10 Philip Ziegler (ed.), *From Shore to Shore: Final Years Diary, 1953–1979* (William Collins, 1989), p. 273.
11 *From Shore to Shore*, p. 273.
12 Michael Parkinson BBC interview, Australia, 13 October 1983.
13 Jonathan Dimbleby, *The Prince of Wales: An Intimate Portrait* (Little, Brown, 1994), p. 210.
14 Philip Ziegler (ed.), *From Shore to Shore: Final Years Diary, 1953–1979* (William Collins, 1989), p. 290.
15 Harold Macmillan diary, 3 December 1960, in Peter Catterall (ed.), *The Macmillan Diaries: The Premiership 1957–66* (Macmillan, 2011), p. 340.
16 Confidential Memorandum from the Assistant Comptroller, Lord Chamberlain's Office, to the Lord Chamberlain, St James's Palace, 28 December 1973 (FCO 31/1695, National Archives).
17 Thomas Brimelow, FCO, to Philip Moore, Buckingham Palace, 5 February 1974 (FCO 31/1695, National Archives).
18 Edward Heath, *The Course of My Life: The Autobiography of Edward Heath* (Hodder & Stoughton, 1998), p. 520.
19 HM The Queen to James Orr, Buckingham Palace, 13 June 1975.
20 Christopher Balfour, *A Memoir* (privately printed, 2025), p. 170–4.
21 Cecil Beaton unpublished diary, mid 1960s (Cecil Beaton papers, St John's College, Cambridge).
22 Philip Ziegler, *Wilson: The Authorised Life* (Weidenfeld & Nicolson, 1993), p. 486.
23 *Wilson: The Authorised Life*, p. 490.
24 The Countess of Avon to author, 1980.
25 Elizabeth Longford, *Elizabeth R: A Biography* (Weidenfeld & Nicolson, 1983), p. 278
26 *Daily Express*, 7 April 1976.
27 HV diary, 22 June 1976.
28 Andrew Marr, *The Diamond Queen* (Macmillan, 2011), p. 268.

29. AUSTRALIA, 1975

1. Sir Martin Charteris to Sir John Kerr, Buckingham Palace, 5 November 1975, quoted in Paul Kelly and Troy Bramston, *The Truth of the Palace Letters: Deceit, Ambush and Dismissal* (Melbourne University Press, 2020), p. 209.
2. Sir Martin Charteris to Sir John Kerr, Windsor Castle, 19 June 1975 (NAA: AA1984/609, Part 1).
3. *The Canberra Times*, 4 July 1975.
4. Sir John Kerr to Sir Martin Charteris, Government House, Canberra, 3 July 1975 (NAA: AA1984/609, Part 1).
5. Sir Martin Charteris to Sir John Kerr, Balmoral Castle, 2 October 1975 (NAA: AA1984/609, Part 1).
6. Sir John Kerr to Sir Martin Charteris, Government House, Canberra, 17 October 1975 (NAA: AA1984/609, Part 2).
7. Sir Martin Charteris to Sir John Kerr, Buckingham Palace, 4 November 1975 (NAA: AA1984/609, Part 2).
8. Sir Martin Charteris to Sir John Kerr, Buckingham Palace, 5 November 1975 (NAA: AA1984/609, Part 2).
9. Statement by the Governor-General, included in a letter to Gough Whitlam, 11 November 1975 (NAA: AA1984/609, Part 2).
10. Sir John Kerr to Sir Martin Charteris, Government House, Canberra, 17 November 1975 (NAA: AA1984/609, Part 2).
11. Sir Martin Charteris to Sir John Kerr, Buckingham Palace, 17 November 1975 (NAA: AA1984/609, Part 2).
12. Sir Robert Menzies to Sir John Kerr, 95 Collins Street, Melbourne, 19 November 1975 (NAA: AA1984/609, Part 2).
13. Gough Whitlam, *The Whitlam Government 1972–1975* (Penguin, Australia, 1985), pp. 146–7.
14. David Smith, *Head of State: The Governor-general, the Monarchy, the Republic and the Dismissal* (Macleay Press, Sydney, 2005), p. 258.
15. Peter O'Brien, *Villain or Victim?: A Defence of Sir John Kerr and the Reserve Powers* (Connor Court Publishing, 2022), p. 43.
16. Jenny Hocking, *The Palace Letters: The Queen, the Governor-general and the Plot to Dismiss Gough Whitlam* (Scribe, 2020), p. 230.
17. Paul Keating foreword, in Paul Kelly and Troy Bramston, *The Truth of the Palace Letters: Deceit, Ambush and Dismissal* (Melbourne University Press, 2020), p. v.

30. THE SILVER JUBILEE, 1977

1. The Earl of Drogheda to author, 26 July 1977.
2. The Duke of Beaufort, BBC2 interview, 21 July 1977.
3. Mike Lawn, photographer, to author, 12 February 2021.
4. HM The Queen's speech in Westminster Hall, 4 May 1977.
5. Sir Michael Parker to author; Michael Parker, *It's All Going Terribly Wrong: The Accidental Showman* (Bene Factum Publishing, 2012), pp. 993–4.
6. Lord Mountbatten diary, 7 June 1977, quoted in Philip Ziegler (ed.), *From Shore to Shore: Final Years Diary, 1953–1979* (William Collins, 1989), p. 366.
7. HM The Queen's speech, Guildhall, 7 June 1977, quoted in many newspapers, 8 June 1977.
8. Idi Amin to Secretary-General, Shridrath S. Ramphal, 23 February 1977 (HO 290/159, National Archives).
9. *The Times*, 23 February 1977.
10. Cabinet Conclusions (CM (77) 20 – CAB 128/61/20, National Archives).
11. Sonny Ramphal to author.
12. Lord Mountbatten diary, 7 June 1977, quoted in Philip Ziegler (ed.), *From Shore to Shore: Final Years Diary, 1953–1979* (William Collins, 1989), p. 367.
13. Charles Wintour to author, 22 August 1977.
14. Sir Martin Charteris to Sir Alan Lascelles, Windsor Castle, 13 June 1977 (Lascelles papers, Churchill College, Cambridge).
15. Norman Lloyd-Jones to author, Cardiff, 20 July 1977.
16. Anne Wall to author, 18 July 1977.
17. Private information, recorded in HV diary, 25 August 1977.
18. Sir Martin Charteris to author, 1 November 1977.
19. Ibid.
20. Private information.
21. *Daily Telegraph*, 16 November 1977.

31. THE LATER 1970s, 1978–9

1. *Sunday Telegraph*, 26 March 1978.
2. Philip Ziegler (ed.), *From Shore to Shore: Final Years Diary, 1953–1979* (William Collins, 1989), p. 383.
3. *The Times*, 3 July 1978.
4. Foreign Office report prior to the visit (FCO 28/3437, National Archives).

5. Quoted in Robert Hardman, *Queen of Our Times* (Macmillan, 2022), p. 260.
6. Note by James Callaghan, National Archives (FCO 28/3436).
7. Lord Goronwy-Roberts, Foreign and Commonwealth Office, 15 June 1978, to Eric Deakins, 15 June 1978 (FCO 28/3436, National Archives).
8. R.L. Secondé, British Ambassador, Confidential report of the state visit, Bucharest, 4 July 1978 (FCO 28/3437, National Archives).
9. Sir John Johnston to author, 27 February 1994.
10. Robert Hardman, *Queen of Our Times* (Macmillan, 2022), pp. 260–2.
11. Anne Wall to author, 14 June 1978.
12. R.L. Secondé, British Ambassador, Confidential report of the state visit, Bucharest, 4 July 1978 (FCO 28/3437, National Archives).
13. David Owen, *Time to Declare* (Michael Joseph, 1991), p. 371.
14. Ben Pimlott, *The Queen: Elizabeth II and the Monarchy* (HarperCollins, 1996), p. 460.
15. Kenneth Harris, *The Queen* (Weidenfeld & Nicolson, 1994), p. 238.
16. Princess Josephine Loewenstein to author.
17. Humphrey Carpenter, *Robert Runcie* (Hodder & Stoughton, 1996), p. 214.
18. Charles Moore, *Margaret Thatcher – The Authorized Biography – Volume One* (Allen Lane, 2013), p. 757.
19. Humphrey Carpenter, *Robert Runcie* (Hodder & Stoughton, 1996), p. 168.
20. Ben Pimlott, *The Queen: Elizabeth II and the Monarchy* (HarperCollins, 1996), p. 467.
21. Lusaka Declaration, 7 August 1979.
22. HM The Queen to General Sir Desmond Fitzpatrick, 27 March 1980.
23. Lady Diana Cooper to author, 13 July 1979.
24. Andrew Duncan, *The Reality of Monarchy* (Heinemann, 1970), p. 114.
25. Private information.
26. HM The Queen to HRH The Duke of Windsor, 5 August 1970.
27. HV diary, 9 December 1978, for 7 December.
28. Audrey Russell to author (having witnessed it).
29. Timothy Knatchbull, *From a Clear Blue Sky: Surviving the Mountbatten Bomb* (Hutchinson, 2009), pp. 175–8.
30. Charles Smith, *Fifty Years with Mountbatten* (Sidgwick & Jackson, 1980), p. 170.
31. *Daily Telegraph*, 21 December 1979.
32. National Archives, PREM 19/68.
33. *The Times*, 17 November 1979.
34. MI5 papers, National Archives, released January 2025.

35 *Daily Telegraph*, 21 November 1979.
36 Derived from Lord Charteris of Amisfield to author, 23 August 1993.

32. ROYAL ENGAGEMENT AND WEDDING, 1980–1

1 Nigel Duncan, 'The Queen should abdicate at 60', *Now* magazine, 8 February 1980.
2 HV diary, 19 October 2004.
3 *The Times*, 2 May 1980.
4 Frank Law, CBE (d. 2009), to author, Marrakech, 1 January 1992.
5 Moroccan State Visit (FCO 160/207/12, National Archive).
6 Jonathan Dimbleby, *The Prince of Wales: An Intimate Portrait* (Little, Brown, 1994), p. 205.
7 *The Prince of Wales*, p. 182.
8 *The Prince of Wales*, p. 278.
9 Quoted by A. L. Rowse, Windsor Festival, 27 September 1975.
10 Jonathan Dimbleby, *The Prince of Wales: An Intimate Portrait* (Little, Brown, 1994), p. 265.
11 Dame Frances Campbell-Preston to author.
12 Lady Diana Cooper to author, February 1981.
13 Private information.
14 Sir Charles Johnston unpublished diary, 29 July 1981 (Johnston papers).
15 HV diary, 28 October 2018.
16 BBC, *The Reunion*, 30 April 2006.
17 Confirmed in conversation with India Hicks, a bridesmaid on the day, 9 April 2005.
18 Jonathan Dimbleby, *The Prince of Wales: An Intimate Portrait* (Little, Brown, 1994), p. 294.
19 Private information.

33. ENTER WILLIAM AND HARRY, 1981–6

1 Christopher Andrew, *The Defence of the Realm* (Allen Lane, 2009), p. 694.
2 Frank Pakenham (Lord Longford), *Diary of a Year* (Weidenfeld & Nicolson, 1982), p. 127.
3 Private information, 15 March 2021.

4   William Whitelaw, *The Whitelaw Memoirs* (Aurum Press, 1989), p. 213.
5   Brigadier Andrew Parker Bowles to author.
6   Frank Pakenham (Lord Longford), *Diary of a Year* (Weidenfeld & Nicolson, 1982), p. 214.
7   Koo Stark to author, 10 November 2020.
8   Sir William Heseltine to author, Perth, Western Australia, 8 October 2013.
9   Loelia, Duchess of Westminster, to author, autumn 1983.
10 Private information, 15 March 2021.
11 The Earl of Carnarvon to author, 11 June 1999.

34. CRITICAL TIMES, 1986–8

1   Philomena Adams (1924–2009) to author, 2 November 2008.
2   Private information, 11 October 2013.
3   *The Sunday Times*, 20 July 1986.
4   *The Sunday Times* ('The African Queen'), 20 July 1986.
5   *The Times*, 22 July 1986.
6   *The Times*, 21 July 1986.
7   Andrew Morton, 'Clues point to man at the Palace', *News of the World*, July 1986.
8   *The Times*, 28 July 1986.
9   Margaret Thatcher, *The Downing Street Years* (HarperCollins, 1993), p. 18.
10 Charles Moore, *Margaret Thatcher: The Authorized Biography*, vol. 2 (Allen Lane, 2015), p. 584.
11 Noreen Taylor review of a Shea book.
12 Michael Shea, *A View from the Sidelines* (Sutton Publishing, 2003), p. xvii.
13 *The Times*, 23 October 1986.
14 Letter from Christopher White, Northwestern University, Xian, *The Times*, 22 October 1986.
15 HV diary, 22 February 2000.
16 Private information, 15 March 2021.
17 Lynda Lee-Potter article, *Daily Mail*, April 1987.
18 *Daily Mail*, 20 May 1987.
19 *The Times*, 18 December 1987.
20 *Daily Mail*, March 1988.

35. DARK DAYS, 1987–90

1. *The Times*, 26 September 1987.
2. *The Times*, 2 July 1990.
3. *The Sunday Times*, 1 July 1990.
4. *The Times*, 2 July 1990.
5. *Daily Telegraph*, 28 December 1987.
6. Private information, 1988.
7. Sir Peter Gillett to author, 13 November 1988.
8. *The Times* and *Daily Telegraph*, 15 November 1988.
9. Private information, 8 February 1989.
10. *The Sunday Times*, 22 January 1999.
11. Peter Kornicki, Anthony Best and Sir Hugh Cortazzi, *British Royal and Imperial Relations 1868–1918* (Renaissance Books, 2019), p. 192.
12. *The Sunday Times*, 19 March 1988.
13. The Earl of Carnarvon to author, London, 22 January 1992.
14. *Daily Telegraph*, 18 January 1992.
15. Terry Pendry to author, 15 July 2025.

36. THE EARLY 1990s, 1989–91

1. Quoted in *Hello*, 7 July 1990.
2. *Daily Mail*, 4 April 1989.
3. Dickie Arbiter to author, 10 June 2025.
4. *Daily Telegraph*, 1 September 1989.
5. *Evening Standard*, 31 August 1989.
6. *The Times*, 1 September 1989.
7. *Daily Telegraph*, 25 September 1989.
8. *Independent*, 18 March 2003.
9. *The Times*, 8 November 1990.
10. Margaret Thatcher speech, 12 November 1990.
11. Lord Wigram to author, 19 April 1991.
12. *The Sunday Times*, 10 February 1991.
13. HV diary, 23 April 1991.
14. *Daily Telegraph*, 24 April 1991.
15. *The Times*, 26 April 1991.
16. *Daily Telegraph*, 17 May 1991.

17 Reuters report, 16 May 1991, 16.50.
18 Ibid.
19 'The Thorn at her Side', Profile of Prince Philip, *Independent*, June 1991.
20 HRH Princess Alice, Duchess of Gloucester to author, Barnwell, 4 November 1991.

37. ANNUS HORRIBILIS

1   *Daily Telegraph*, 27 December 1991.
2   *The Sunday Times*, 19 January 1992.
3   *The Sunday Times*, 22 March 1992.
4   *The Sunday Times*, 3 May 1992.
5   John Julius Norwich to author, 2 April 1992.
6   The Marquess of Abergavenny to author, 23 April 1995.
7   HV diary, 23 February 1992.
8   Sir Robert Southey (1922–98) to author, Melbourne, 12 March 1992.
9   Jenny Hocking, *The Palace Letters* (Scribe, 2020).
10 HV diary, London, 19 March 1992.
11 Mark Simpson to author, New York, 17 February 1992.
12 Oliver Everett to author, Windsor Castle, 24 January 1992.
13 HV diary, Windsor, 19 April 1992.
14 *Daily Mail*, 30 May 1992.
15 *The Times*, 13 May 1992.
16 *The Spectator*, 6 June 1992.
17 Anthony Holden, 'Prince Charles should read this book and learn about his wife', *Evening Standard*, June 1992.
18 HV diary, 20 November 2002.
19 Private information to HV, diary 24 July 1992.
20 HV diary, 4 August 1992.
21 Sarah Ferguson, The Duchess of York, with Jeff Coplon, *My Story* (Simon & Schuster, 1996), p. 4.
22 'Andrew's trouble and strife', *Evening Standard* magazine, c. November 1992 (press cutting, vol. 408).
23 Sally Bedell Smith, *Diana in Search of Herself: Portrait of a Troubled Princess* (Times Books, 1999), p. 201.
24 *The Times*, 25 November 1992.
25 *Sunday Telegraph*, 13 December 1992.

26 HV diary, 2 February 2009.
27 HV diary, 1 May 1993.
28 General Sir John Waters, GCB (1932–2025), to author, Wiltshire, 12 February 1993.

38. THE MID 1990s, 1993–6

1 HV diary, 19 April 1993.
2 Lord Irvine of Lairg to author, 31 January 2013.
3 Geoff Crawford to author, St James's Palace, 30 September 1993.
4 HV diary, 17 January 1993.
5 HM The Queen to author, Windsor, 24 June 2022.
6 *Daily Mail*, 12 May 1993.
7 HV diary, 14 June 1993.
8 HV diary, 16 June 1993.
9 Sir Ralph Anstruther to author, 4 September 1993.
10 *The Times*, 11 September 1993.
11 *The Times*, 20 September 1993.
12 Sir Robert Fellowes to author, St James's Palace, 30 September 1993.
13 Paul Keating foreword, in Paul Kelly and Troy Bramston, *The Truth of the Palace Letters: Deceit, Ambush and Dismissal* (Melbourne University Press, 2020), p. vi.
14 Private information, 17 October 1993.
15 HRH The Princess Margaret, Countess of Snowdon to author, Oxfordshire, 31 December 1993.
16 *The Times*, 22 October 1993.
17 *The Times*, 10 December 1993.
18 *The Times*, 10 December 1993.
19 HRH The Princess Margaret, Countess of Snowdon to author, Oxfordshire, 31 December 1993.
20 Private conversation, in HV diary, 31 May 2000.
21 Dame Barbara Cartland to author, 16 November 1994.
22 *The Resident*, Christmas 2004.
23 *The Times*, 8 April 1989.
24 HV diary, Highclere, 21 January 1995.
25 Sir Robert Fellowes to author, Highclere, 21 January 1995.
26 HV diary, reporting 5 May 1995.

27 *Daily Telegraph*, 11 October 1991.
28 Steve Hewlett obituary, *Daily Telegraph*, 20 February 2017.
29 HV diary, London, 30 January 1997.

39. THE DEATH OF DIANA, 1997

1 HV diary, 9 March 1997.
2 Tony Blair, *A Journey* (Hutchinson, 2010), p. 14.
3 HV diary, 14 May 1997.
4 HV diary, 14 June 1997.
5 HV diary, 17 May 1997.
6 HV diary, 14 May 1997.
7 HV diary, 1 June 1997.
8 Personal observation on several visits to the house between 1989 and 1997.
9 HV diary, 11 August 1997.
10 Raine, Countess Spencer, to author, London, 20 August 1997.
11 Oscar Wilde, *The Ballad of Reading Gaol*, 1904.
12 HV diary, 31 August 1997.
13 Viscount Norwich to author, September 1997.
14 Tony Blair, *A Journey* (Hutchinson, 2010), p. 133.
15 HRH The Princess Margaret, Countess of Snowdon to author, 1 January 1998.
16 Ibid.
17 Sir Malcolm Ross to author, 28 April 1998.
18 Tony Blair, *A Journey* (Hutchinson, 2010), p. 133.
19 Lady Angela Oswald to author, 25 November 2023.
20 Very Rev Patrick Mitchell to author, 21 September 1997.
21 Private information.
22 Private information, 16 September 2006.
23 Sir Malcolm Ross to author, 28 April 1998.
24 Sir Robert Fellowes to author, 9 May 2001.
25 Alastair Campbell, *The Blair Years: Extracts from The Alastair Campbell Diaries* (Hutchinson, 2007), p. 234.
26 Lord Charteris of Amisfield to author, 18 December 1997.
27 Private information.
28 Nigel Jaques to author, 26 July 2004.

29 'The Queen to Lady [Henriette] Abel Smith, Balmoral Castle, 12 September 1997.'

40. REGROUPING, 1998–2000

1 HM The Queen's televised address to the nation, 5 September 1997.
2 Alastair Campbell, *The Blair Years: Extracts from The Alastair Campbell Diaries* (Hutchinson, 2007), pp. 245-6.
3 HM The Queen to author, 9 April 1999.
4 Quoted retrospectively in *The Times*, 30 May 2012.
5 HV diary, 1 October 1997.
6 HV diary, 17 October 1997.
7 Private information.
8 HV diary, 10 February 1998.
9 HRH Princess George of Hanover to author, 23 November 1997.
10 HRH The Princess Margaret to author, 1 January 1998.
11 *The Times*, 14 May 1998.
12 The Earl of Longford to author, 15 July 1998.
13 *The Times*, 7 January 1999.
14 HV diary, 19 June 1999.
15 Sir Sherard Cowper-Coles (quoted in Vox.com, 23 January 2015).
16 Hansard, 17 November 1999.
17 *Daily Telegraph*, 18 November 1999.
18 Simon Lewis to author, 10 February 2000.
19 John Howard, *Lazarus Rising: A Personal and Political Autobiography* (HarperCollins, 2011), p. 334.
20 HV diary, 1 November 1999.
21 Sir Brian McGrath to author, Buckingham Palace, 8 December 1999.
22 Private information.

41. THE GOLDEN JUBILEE, 2002

1 HV diary, 14 June 2001.
2 Prince Karl of Hesse to author, 10 June 2001.
3 HV diary, 31 December 2001.

4 HV diary, 11 February 2002.
5 Private information, 2002.
6 Gyles Brandreth, diary, 21 February 2002.
7 Ibid.
8 Private information.
9 Private information.
10 Dame Frances Campbell-Preston to author, 1 June 2006.
11 'In the long run they said "The Best of British luck to you"' review by Alastair Forbes, *The Spectator*, October 1981, pp. 409–10.
12 Patricia, Countess of Harewood, private account of Her Majesty The Queen's Golden Jubilee Celebration, 11 July 2002.
13 Ibid.
14 *The Times*, 14 October 2002.
15 HV diary, 30 November 2002.
16 Sir Miles Hunt-Davis to author, 24 October 2003.

42. RESOLUTION, 2003–7

1 Lord Luce to author, 11 November 2003.
2 HV diary, 7 April 2004.
3 HV diary, 6 July 2004.
4 *The Times*, 3 November 2004.
5 HV diary, 24 February 2005.
6 HV diary, 1 January 2006.
7 William Feaver, *The Lives of Lucian Freud: Youth 1922–1968* (Bloomsbury, 2020), p. 406.
8 William Feaver, *The Lives of Lucian Freud: Youth 1922–1968* (Bloomsbury, 2020), p. 407.
9 Brigadier Andrew Parker Bowles to author, 5 September 2025.
10 HV diary, 17 June 2006.
11 HV diary, 10 May 2006.
12 Private information, 8 April 2006.
13 Private information.

43. CHALLENGING TIMES, 2007–11

1. Gordon Brown, *My Life, Our Times* (The Bodley Head, 2017), p. 197.
2. Gordon Brown, *My Life, Our Times* (The Bodley Head, 2017), p. 198.
3. Private information, 9 September 2009.
4. HV diary, 31 August 2007.
5. *Guardian*, 1 September 2007.
6. HV diary, 31 August 2007.
7. *The Times*, 9 April 2008.
8. New Vision, quoted in *Daily Telegraph*, 21 November 2007.
9. Sir Michael Hobbs to author, 9 April 2008.
10. Sir Brian McGrath to author, Buckingham Palace, 16 April 2008.
11. HV diary, 23 April 2008.
12. HV diary, 16 June 2008.
13. Prince Karl of Hesse to author, 28 December 2008.
14. HV diary, 19 May 2009.
15. *The Times*, 12 December 2009.
16. HV diary, 15 April 2010.
17. Gordon Brown, *My Life, Our Times* (The Bodley Head, 2017), p. 372.
18. *My Life, Our Times*, p. 384.
19. David Cameron, *For The Record* (William Collins, 2019), p. 21.
20. *For The Record*, p. 12.
21. HV diary, 25 May 2010.
22. Lord Rothschild to author, 23 February 2011.
23. David Cameron, *For The Record* (William Collins, 2019), p. 310.
24. BBC, *Last Word*, 16 June 2017.
25. HM The Queen's speech at the State Banquet for the President of Ireland, 8 April 2014.
26. HV diary, 9 April 2014.
27. HV diary, 10 June 2011.
28. HV diary, 10 June 2011.
29. The Countess of Airlie to author, 9 April 2015.
30. HV diary, 17 January 2012.
31. Sir Michael Oswald to author, Buckingham Palace, 15 May 2012.

44. THE DIAMOND JUBILEE, 2012

1. HM The Queen's speech in Westminster Hall, 20 March 2012.
2. HV diary, 28 October 2018.
3. HV diary, 28 May 2012.
4. HV diary, 3 June 2012.
5. HV diary, 3 June 2012.
6. HV diary, 4 June 2012.
7. The Earl of Airlie to author, St Paul's Cathedral, 5 June 2012.
8. *Daily Telegraph*, 16 August 2012.
9. Her Majesty's most gracious speech to both Houses of Parliament at the State Opening of Parliament, 8 May 2013.
10. Dame Frances Campbell-Preston to author, 19 September 2013; and Lord Charles Fitzroy to author, 7 May 2014.
11. *Daily Telegraph*, 8 June 2013.
12. HV diary, 7 March 2014.
13. Dame Frances Campbell-Preston to author, 30 January 2015.
14. *The Times*, 15 September 2014.
15. David Cameron, *For the Record* (William Collins, 2019), p. 556.
16. Lord Young of Old Windsor, 'The Mysteries of the Golden Triangle', *Heywood Quarterly*, 2024.
17. Nicky Haslam to author, 7 September 2015.
18. HM The Queen's banquet speech, Malta, 27 November 2015.
19. HV diary, 25 December 2015.

45. FICTIONAL REPRESENTATIONS

1. Giles in the *Daily Express*, 22 March 1962.
2. Stephen Frears to author, 8 July 2016.
3. Peter Morgan, *The Audience* (Faber & Faber, 2013), p. 4.
4. Clive Irving to author, 22 September 2021.
5. Private information, 1 February 2016.
6. HV diary, 20 April 2016.
7. HV diary, 27 March 2016.
8. HV diary, May 2016.
9. Sir Brian McGrath to author, Buckingham Palace, 16 January 2012.
10. HV diary, 4 June 2016.

11 HV diary, 13 June 2016.
12 HV diary, 12 August 2017.
13 HV diary, 23 February 2017.
14 Tim O'Donovan to author, 21 February 2017.
15 BBC lunchtime news, 16 June 2017.
16 HV diary, 18 June 2017.
17 HV diary, 27 October 2017.

46. PRINCE HARRY AND PRINCE ANDREW

1 *The Times*, 9 November 2016.
2 *Vanity Fair*, September 2017.
3 *The Times*, 1 May 2018.
4 HV diary, 9 June 2018.
5 HV diary, 18/21 April 2019.
6 Private information, 12 October 2018.
7 Cecil Beaton, private diary, 21 May 1964 (St John's College, Cambridge). Also published in Hugo Vickers, *Cecil Beaton: The Authorised Biography* (Hodder & Stoughton, 2020), p. 568.

47. THE ROAD TO COVID

1 HV diary, 1 April 2018.
2 Private information, 26 July 2018.
3 Lady Penn to author, Scotland, 23 October 2018.
4 HV diary, 7 July 2019.
5 HRH The Duke of Edinburgh to Mrs Fairweather, 21 January 2019, quoted in *The Times*, 28 January 2019.
6 Gyles Brandreth Speech, *Oldie* lunch, 29 January 2019.
7 Sir William Heseltine to author, London, 23 April 2019.
8 Nicola Sturgeon, *Frankly* (Macmillan, 2025), p. 254.
9 *Frankly*, p. 400.
10 *Frankly*, p. 400.
11 HV diary, 24 November 2019.
12 HV diary, 24 December 2019.
13 HV diary, 9 March 2020.

14 Speech by Lord Young of Old Windsor, House of Lords, Hansard, 24 November 2024.
15 Covid Inquiry – Dominic Cummings, quoted in *The Times*, 4 November 2023.
16 Speech by Lord Young of Old Windsor, House of Lords, Hansard, 24 November 2024.
17 Simon Durnford to author, 2 July 2021.
18 Simon Durnford to author, 23 November 2023.
19 Lady Penn to author.
20 HM The Queen's Christmas broadcast, 25 December 2020.

48. PRINCE PHILIP

1 Lady Penn to author, 7 January 2021.
2 Private information.
3 HV diary, 18 April 2021.
4 *The Times*, 12 May 2021.
5 HV diary, 12 June 2021.
6 HV diary, 7 July 2021.
7 HRH The Prince of Wales's speech, Barbados, 30 November 2021.
8 HM The Queen's Christmas broadcast, 25 December 2021.

49. THE PLATINUM JUBILEE, 2022

1 HM The Queen's message, 5 February 2022, *Mail on Sunday*, 6 February 2022.
2 Address by Rt Revd David Conner, Dean of Windsor, Westminster Abbey, 29 March 2022.
3 HRH The Duke of Kent to author, June 2022.
4 Nicola Sturgeon, *Frankly* (Macmillan, 2025), pp. 401–2.
5 Lady Penn to author, 20 August and later, 2022.

50. THE LAST DAYS

1 Boris Johnson, Tribute to HM The Queen, House of Commons, 9 September 2022.

2 Boris Johnson, *Unleashed* (William Collins, 2024), pp. 725–7.
3 GB News interview, Liz Truss with Cameron Walker, 7 September 2023.
4 *Melton Times*, 8 December 2023.
5 GB News interview, Liz Truss with Cameron Walker, 7 September 2023.
6 HM The King's speech to the nation, 9 September 2022.
7 William Kenyon, 'Artillery Row', *The Critic*, 24 January 2024.
8 Lt Colonel J. N. E. B. Shaw, 'Operation London Bridge', *The Guards Magazine*, no. 206, Winter 2022, p. 58.
9 'Summoned from Corfu', *The Guards Magazine*, no. 206, Winter 2022, p. 82.
10 'The Pall Bearers', *The Guards Magazine*, no. 206, Winter 2022, pp. 94–5.
11 HV diary, 19 September 2022.

Index

The names are usually those borne in the reign of The Queen – e.g. Prince Edward is Earl of Wessex. Some Kings and Presidents (but not all) are listed under their countries:

Abbott, Tony (b. 1957), 515
Abel Smith, Colonel Sir Henry (1900-93), 33n
Abel Smith, Lady May (1906-94), 33 & n
Abergavenny, 5th Marquess of (1914-2000), 420
Adair, Major-General Sir Allan (1897-1988), 156n
Adams, Noel, 192-3
Adams, Sir James (1932-2020), 318
Adeane, Hon Edward (1939-2015), 444
Adeane, Lord (Michael) (1910-84), 204, 205, 212, 244, 253, 263, 275, 281, 286-7, 292-3, 368
Afghanistan, HM King Amanullah of (1892-1960), 23n
Afghanistan, President Hamid Karzai of (b. 1957), 493
Agnew, Sir Godfrey (1913-95), 285-6
Aird, Sir Alastair (1931-2009), 430
Airlie, 12th Earl of (1893-1968), 261
Airlie, 13th Earl of (David) (1926-2023), 419, 421, 507
Airlie, Mabell, Countess of (1866-1956), 11, 52n, 102-3, 261
Airy, Major-General Sir Christopher (1934-2025), 476
Akintola, Chief Ládòke (1910-66), 239-40, 239n
al Khalifa, Shaikh Isa bin Salman (b. 1933-99), 360
al-Said, Nuri (1888-1958), 231
Alanbrooke, Field Marshal 1st Viscount (1883-1963), 79, 120
Albert, Harold (1909-97), 87, as Helen Cathcart, 295-6, 297

Albert, HRH Prince (Prince Consort) (1819-61), 14, 78n, 121, 157, 237
Alderson, Maggie (b. 1959), 426
Alderton, Rt Hon Sir Clive (b. 1967), 532
Alexander of Tunis, 1st Earl (1891-1969), 120, 136, 138
Alexandra, HM Queen (1844-1925), 13, 14, 56n, 60, 234
Alexandra, Hon Lady Ogilvy, HRH Princess (b. 1936), 16, 53, 54, 57, 60, 63, 73, 103, 182, 211, public duties, 226-7, 241, 261-2, 270, 356; 308, 350, 374, 382, 412, 442, 460, 473, 475n, 478-9, 480, 521, 549, 563
Algeria, President Chadli Bendjedid of (1929-2012), 371
Allendale, 2nd Viscount (1890-1956), 22, 132
Allendale, Viscountess (1892-1979), 61
Allfrey, Phyllis Shand (1908-86), 278n
Allison, Ronald (1932-2022), 307, 328
Althorp, Viscount – see Spencer
Altrincham, Lord (John Grigg) (1924-2001), 210, 294
Ambatielos, Antonis (1919-95), 270, 271 &n
Ambatielos, Betty (1917-2011), 270-1, 271n
Amies, Sir Hardy (1909-2003), 471
Amin, President Idi (1928-2003), 197n, 312-4, 330, 351-2, 352n
Amos, Baroness (b. 1954), 554, 558
Andrew, HRH The Prince (now Andrew Mountbatten-Windsor) (b. 1960), 5, 156n; birth, 247, 250, 256; 257n, 359, 372, 374, 383, marriage, 388, 390, 392, 393-4; 427, 428, 429, 470, 472, 486 &n, 508, 525; travails of, 532, 533-4, 535, 539, 551, 555; 556, 557

Annaly, Lavinia Lady (1899-1955), 10
Anne, HRH The Princess (The Princess Royal) (b. 1950), 1, 5, birth, 132, in London (1952), 140, at Sandringham (1952), 141, 150; & Mountbatten name, 157, 256; in Libya (1954), 197-8, in Gibraltar (1954), 200-1; fearless, 221-2; at Shah of Iran lunch, 231; at Benenden, 257; & Princess Andrew, 265; at Greek Royal Wedding (1964), 272; portrayed fictionally, 295; emerges into public life, 297-9; In New Zealand & Australia, 303-5; as an equestrian, 306, 326, 340; in Washington (1970), 307; on Emperor Hirohito, 310; on SE Asia tour, 314; & Mark Phillips, 328-30; & kidnap attempt (1974), 330-1; on Pacific Islands tour (1974), 334; In Montreal Olympics (1976), 340; & her son Peter, 354; given the title, Princess Royal, 400; & Monty Roberts, 407; separates from Mark Phillips, 409-10; & Tim Laurence, 410; divorced, 421; marries Tim Laurence, 428; at Dome for millennium, 464; appointed Lady of the Thistle, 465; & Diamond Jubilee. 503; with the Queen at her death, 563; accompanies the Queen's coffin, 566; mentioned, 28, 208, 225, 240, 260, 290, 296, 365, 372, 380, 405, 429, 466, 494, 500, 501, 508, 517
Anson, Charles (b. 1944), 418, 441, 551
Anson, Lady Elizabeth (1941-2020), 494, 546
Anson, Viscount (1913-58), 59
Aosta, HRH Princess Irene, Duchess of (1904-74), 113
Argyll, Margaret, Duchess of (1912-93), 295n
Armstrong-Jones – see Snowdon
Armstrong-Jones, Hon Frances (b. 1979), 337
Armstrong-Jones, Lady Sarah (later Chatto) (b. 1964), 258, 262, 355 &n, 469
Armstrong-Jones, Ronald (1899-1966), 225
Ascroft, Eileen (1914-62), 182
Ashmore, Vice-Admiral Sir Peter (1921-2002), 104
Asprey, Helen, 493
Asquith of Yarnbury, Baroness (1887-1969), 81
Asquith, H.H. – see Oxford & Asquith
Asquith, Lady Cynthia (1887-1960), 19, 28-29, 28n, 33, 40&n, 43, 47, 52, 53, 128
Astor, Viscountess (Nancy) (1879-1964), 40
Athlone, HRH Princess Alice, Countess of (1883-1981), 33n, 37n, 44, 53, 60, 65, 119, 160, 176, 278 &n, 307, 350
Athlone, Major-General the Earl of (Alexander) (1874-1957), 13, 33n, 44, 53, 119, 160, 176, 213, 215, 374
Attlee, 1st Earl (Clement) (1883-1967), 111, 113, 119, 125, 134, 139, 147, 159, 212n, 230, 262, 282
Attlee, Countess (Violet) (1895-1964), 262
Auric, Georges (1899-1983), 238
Auriol, President Vincent (1884-1966), 122, 132, 163
Austin, Ven George (1931-2019), 435
Avedon, Richard (1923-2004), 278n
Avon, 1st Earl of (Anthony) (1897-1977), as Prime Minister, 206-7, 211-4; 147, 201, 202-5, 221, 223, 227, 231, 242, 245, 251, 252, 270, 278, 282, 327, 338
Avon, the Countess of (Clarissa) (1920-2021), 112, 207, 215, 223n, 230, 238, 245, 251, 252, 254, 259n, 278, 325, 327
Aylard, Commander Richard (b. 1952), 436, 442

Baden, HRH Prince Ludwig of (b. 1937), 524
Baden, HRH The Margravine of (Theodora) (1906-69), 84, 168, 276,
Bahrain, Crown Prince of (b. 1969), 532
Baillie, Rt Rev Albert (Dean of Windsor) (1864-1955), 49, 70, 71n, 72, 76
Baillieu, Mrs John (Elizabeth) (1918-2007), 97
Bainimarama, Commodore Frank (b. 1954), 400
Baker, Kenneth (Lord) (b. 1934), 339
Baldwin of Bewdley, 1st Earl (Stanley) (1867-1947), 58
Balfour, 1st Earl (A.J.) (1848-1930), 16, 212n
Balfour, Christopher (b. 1941), 337, 544n
Balfour, Serena (b. 1944), 494
Balfour, Sir John (1894-1983), 199
Balmain, Pierre (1914-82), 322
Bandaranaike, Sirimavo (1906-2000), 195n
Bandaranaike, Solomon (1899-1959), 194, 195n
Barber, Rt Hon Anthony (Lord) (1920-2005), 311
Baring, Sir Evelyn (Lord Howick of Glendale) (1903-73), 196
Barlow, Gary (b. 1971), 507
Baron (1906-56), 209

INDEX

Barrantes, Hector (1939-90), 388
Barrantes, Susan (1937-98), 388
Barrie, J.M. (1860-1937), 40 &n
Barrymaine, Norman (1900-91), 223 &n, 224-5
Barwick, Sir Garfield (1903-97), 343
Bassey, Dame Shirley (b. 1937), 507
Battenberg, Prince Louis of – see Milford Haven
Bavadra, Dr Timoci (1934-89), 399
Beales, Peter (1936-2013), 504n
Beaton, Inspector James (b. 1943), 331
Beaton, Sir Cecil (1904-80), 1, 43, 64, 80-1, 112, 127, 132, 165, 166, 168, 173, 209, 221, 226, 237-8, 254, 294, 315, 325, 534
Beatrice, HRH The Princess (1857-1944), 256
Beaudette, Palmer (1914-68), 89
Beaufort, 10th Duke of (1900-84), 58, 68, 172, 290-1, 292, 306, 347, 501
Beaufort, 11th Duke of (1928-2017), 290n
Beaufort, Duchess of (Caroline) (1928-95), 290n
Beaufort, Mary, Duchess of (1897-1987), 132, 290-1
Beaumont, Hon Ela (Countess of Carlisle) (1925-2002), 22 &n, 63
Beaverbrook, 1st Lord (Max) (1879-1964), 134, 223n, 297, 518
Beaverbrook, Lady (1910-94), 406n
Bedford, 11th Duke of (1858-1940), 68
Beerbohm, Sir Max (1872-1956), 208, 290n
Belgians, HM King Albert II of the (b. 1934), 479
Belgians, HM King Baudouin of the (1930-93), 432
Belgians, HM King Leopold III of the (1901-83), 47, 59
Bell, Henrietta (Mrs George Bell) (d. 1968), 56
Bellew, Sir George (Garter King of Arms) (1899-1993), 166, 170, 171-2
Bennett, Alan (b. 1934), 518
Benning, Osla (later Henniker-Major) (1921-74), 99 &n
Berlin, Sir Isaiah (1909-97), 285, 437n
Berry, Lady Pamela (Lady Hartwell) (1914-82), 180
Berry, Sir Anthony (1925-84), 386
Bertie, David (b. 1963), 562
Berwick, David, 540
Bessborough, 10th Earl of (1913-93), 122, 123, 124n

Betjeman, Sir John (1906-84), 369n
Bevan, Ian, 190
Bevin, Rt Hon Ernest (1881-1951), 121
Bhutto, Benazir (1953-2007), 434
Bidault, Georges (1899-1983), 121
Biden, President Joe (b. 1942), 551
Bigge – see Stamfordham
Bigland, Eileen (1898-1970), 19
Binswanger, Dr Ludwig (1881-1966), 85-6
Black, Dorothy (1893-1987), 129
Black, Sister Catherine (1878-1949), 37 &n
Blair, Cherie (b. 1954), 443, 488, 489
Blair, Sir Tony (b. 1953), as Prime Minister, 443, 446-9, 453, 455, 456, 461, 463-4, 464n, 465, 471, 472, 481, 482, 483, 488, 499; mentioned 489, 518, 554, 558
Bland, Lt-Colonel Sir Simon (1923-2022), 563
Bliss, Sir Arthur (1891-1975), 181, 301
Blum, Maître Suzanne (1898-1994), 165n, 326, 389, 513
Blunt, Anthony (1907-83), 368-9, 369n, 518
Boardman, Harry, 175
Bocelli, Andrea (b. 1958), 532
Bodley-Scott, Sir Ronald (1908-82), 259 & n
Boe, Alfie (b. 1973), 507
Boling, Dulcie (b. 1936), 430
Bolland, Mark (b. 1966), 444, 458
Bonas, Cressida (b. 1989), 532
Bonham Carter, Lady Violet – see Asquith of Yarnbury
Bonham Carter, Lord (Mark) (1922-94), 81
Bonnet, Madame Georges (Odette) (1891-unknown), 61
Boothroyd, Basil (1910-88), 90
Bordes, Pamella (b. 1961), 409-10
Bourbon, HRH Prince Michel de (1926-2018), 101
Boussac, Marcel (1889-1980), 238
Bowes-Lyon, Anne (later Anson, & Princess George of Denmark) (1917-80), 59
Bowes-Lyon, Diana (later Somervell) (1923-86), 91, 121
Bowes-Lyon, Hon Sir David (1902-61), 12, 17, 63
Bowes-Lyon, Sir Simon (b. 1932), 514
Bowlby, Hon Mrs Geoffrey (Lettice) (1885-1988), 68
Boyce, Admiral of the Fleet Lord Boyce (1943-2022), 567 &n
Boyd-Rochfort, Sir Cecil (1887-1983), 176n
Boyd, Sir Harry (1876-1940), 31
Boyle, Andrew (1919-91), 368

Brabourne – see Mountbatten
Brabourne, 7th Lord (1924-2005), 103, 298, 365-6, 367 &n
Brabourne, Doreen, Lady (1896-1979), 103n, 365, 366
Bradby, Tom (b. 1967), 532
Bradman, Sir Donald (1908-2001), 191
Bramall, Field Marshal Lord (1923-2019), 440
Brand van Zyl, Hon Gideon (1873-1956), 105, 106
Brandreth, Gyles (b. 1948), 469, 536
Bratby, John (1928-92), 406
Braye, 5th Lord (1849-1928), 346
Brazil, President Ernesto Geisel of (1907-96), 339
Brennan, Sarah, 397n
Brewer, Sir David (1940-2023), 520
Briscoe, Dr John (b. 1933), 535
Britten, Benjamin (Lord) (1913-76), 130 -1, 178-81, 180n, 548
Brockway, Fenner (Lord) (1888-1988), 141n
Brooke, Peter (Lord) (1934-2023), 427
Brooke, Rear-Admiral Sir Basil (1876-1945), 68
Brookes, Sir Norman (1877-1968), 191
Brooks, Lady (1904-88), 192
Brooks, Sir Dallas (1896-1966), 192
Brooksbank, Jack (b. 1986), 532
Brooksbank, Jack (b. 1986), 532
Brown, Douglas, 283
Brown, Fraser (b. 2006), 496
Brown, Harold (b. 1952), 467-8
Brown, Rt Hon Gordon (b. 1951), 472, as Prime Minister, 488-90, 495, 496; 515
Browning, General Sir Frederick (Boy) (1896-1965), 119, 139, 146, 153
Bruce of Crionaich, Major-General Alastair (b. 1960), 7
Bruce, Alice (1895-1960), 70 &n
Bruce, Fiona (b. 1964), 500-1
Bruni, Carla (b. 1967), 491 &n
Bryan, John, 419, 425, 426
Bryce, Dame Quentin (b. 1942), 515
Buccleuch & Queensberry, 7th Duke of (1864-1935), 15, 42, 44
Buccleuch & Queensberry, 8th Duke of (Walter) (1894-1973), 208
Buccleuch & Queensberry, 9th Duke of (1923-2007), 208
Buccleuch & Queensberry, Mary Duchess of (1900-93), 12, 176, 208, 258, 262, 270n

Buckley, Anthony (1912-93), 81
Buganda, King Freddie of – see Mutesa
Buist, Commander Colin (1896-1981), 10
Bulganin, Nikolai (1895-1975), 207 &n, 231
Bulgarians, HM King Simeon of the (b. 1937), 505
Burns, George (1896-1996), 383
Burrell, Paul (b. 1958), 424n, 475-6
Bush, President George H.W. (1924-2018), 405, 416
Bush, President George W. (b. 1946), 479, 482
Buthlay, Major George (1893-1977), 128, 129n
Butler of Saffron Walden, Lady (Mollie) (1907-2009), 254n
Butler, R.A (Lord Butler of Saffron Walden) (1902-82), 159, 185, 212, 253-4, 254n, 275
Butter – see Wernher
Buxton, Aubrey (Lord Buxton of Alsa) (1918-2009), 141, 216
Buxton, Countess (1866-1955), 100

Caccia, Sir Harold (Lord) (1905-90), 242
Callaghan of Cardiff, Lord (James) (1912-2005), 202, 283, as Prime Minister, 339, 346, 351-3, 357, 361; 389, 453
Cambridge, 2nd Marquess of (1895-1981), 28, 44
Cambridge, HRH Prince Adolphus, 1st Duke of (1774-1850), 13
Cambridge, HRH Prince George of (b. 2013), 512, 543, 557
Cambridge, HRH Prince George, 2nd Duke of (1891-1904), 78n
Cambridge, HRH Prince Louis of (b. 2018), 512n, 535, 543, 557
Cambridge, HRH Princess Charlotte of (b. 2015), 512n, 515, 539, 543, 555-6, 557
Cambridge, HRH The Duchess of (Catherine) (b. 1982), 498, 508, 509, 512, 515, 529, 531, 535, 541, 557
Cambridge, HRH The Duke of (Prince William) (b. 1982), 266, 380, birth, 382; 389, 442, 445, 450, 451, 457, 463, 477, 479, 486n, 488, 489-90, 493, wedding, 497-8; 508, 511, 512, 514, 515, 519, 520, 526, 529, 531, 535, 541, 557
Cambridge, Lady Mary – see Beaufort
Cambridge, Lady Mary (later Whitley) (1924-99), 28 &n, 33n, 41, 43, 53, 125

INDEX

Cambridge, Lady May – see Abel Smith
Cameron of Chipping Norton, Lord (David), (b. 1966), 495-6, as Prime Minister, 496, 499, 514-6, 522-3
Campbell-Preston, Dame Frances (1918-2022), 375, 498, 510-11, 510n
Campbell, Alastair (b. 1957), 449, 453
Campbell, Sir Harold (1888-1969), 142
Canterbury, Archbishop of – see Lang – Fisher – Ramsey – Coggan – Runcie – Carey – Williams - Welby
Carey, Lord (George), Archbishop of Canterbury (b. 1935), 466, 470, 481, 482
Carisbrooke, the Marchioness of (1890-1956), 216
Carisbrooke, the Marquess of (1886-1960), 216
Carnarvon, 7th Earl of (1924-2001), 5, 387, 406-7, 429, 459, death, 465
Carnarvon, Jeanie Countess of (1935-2018), 5, 459, death, 546
Carr, Harry (1916-85), 177
Carrington, 6th Lord (1919-2018), 486
Carrington, Lady (1920-2009), 486
Carson, Willie (b. 1942), 406n
Carter, President Jimmy (1924-2024), 347, 349, 360, 370, 419
Carteret-Carey, Mrs Florence (1864-1949), 71
Cartland, Dame Barbara (1901-2000), 374, 436
Case, Simon (Lord) (b. 1978), 532
Casey, Lord (Richard) (1890-1976), 140, 244n
Cassidy, Sir Maurice (1880-1949), 45-6
Casson, Sir Hugh (1910-99), 460
Cathcart, Helen – see Albert, Harold
Cavendish, Lady Elizabeth (1926-2018), 225
Cawston, Richard (1923-86), 298-9
Ceauçescu, Madame Elena (1916-89), 357
Ceauçescu, President Nicoleae (1918-89), 357-9, 359n
Cecil, Lord David (1902-86), 48
Cecil, Robert – see Salisbury
Chagall, Marc (1887-1985), 321
Chamberlain, Rt Hon Neville (1869-1940), 59, 62, 119, 161
Chandos, 1st Viscount (1893-1972), 140, 148, 196, 197, 200
Channon, Sir Henry (Chips) (1897-1958), 9, 89, 90, 91, 155, 160, 164, 172, 176, 177, 236
Chappell, Leslie, 469

Chaput, Dr Marcel (1918-91), 272
Charteris of Amisfield, Lady (Gay) (1919-2017), 432
Charteris of Amisfield, Lord (Martin) (1913-99), 1, 94n, 130, 137, 145-6, 155, 195, 210, 218, 251, 259n, 292, 293, 295, 313, 314, 316-7, 320, 323, 327, 328, 333, & Australian crisis (1975), 341-4, 348n; 346, 351, 353, 354, 368-9, 373, 424, 432, 450, death, 463; 470
Chatto, Arthur (b. 1999), 467
China, Emperor Pi-Yu of (1906-67) 394
China, President Jiang Zemin of (1926-2022), 461
China, President Li Xiannian (1909-92), 394
Cholmondeley, 6th Marquess of (1919-90), 335
Chowdhurry, President Abu Sayeed, 384
Church of Scotland, Moderator of (Dr Iain Greenshields) (b. 1954), 560
Churchill, Clarissa - see Avon
Churchill, Hon Randolph (1911-68), 205
Churchill, Lady (Clementine) (Baroness Spencer-Churchill) (1885-1977), 113, 200
Churchill, Rt Hon Sir Winston (1874-1965), 25 & n, 57, 77, 78-9, 81, 82, 103, 111, 113, 118n, 120n, 124n, 125, 134, 136, 139, 140, 141n, & death of George VI, 144, 147-8, 148n; praises new Queen, 154-5; & Windsor name, 157-8; 160, as Queen's Prime Minister, 161-2, 163, 202-6; & Coronation, 170: boosts Queen Mother, 181, & Townsend drama, 184-5; & Commonwealth tour, 188, 193-4, 199&n, 200, 214; 210, 212&n, 227, 230, 245, 261, 270n, death, 281-2, 282n, 331, 338, 506, 509
Clapton, Eric (b. 1945), 491
Clarendon, 4th Earl of (1800-70), 13
Clarendon, 6th Earl of (1877-1955), 163
Clark, Petula (b. 1932), 355
Claudel, Paul (1868-1955), 61
Clayton, Lady Mary (1917-2014), 513 &n
Clayton, Michael (1934–2022), 408
Clegg, Rt Hon Sir Nick (b. 1967), 495-6, 515-6, 522
Clifford, Max (1943-2017), 410
Clough, Major H.K. (1876-1970), 513
Clynes, Rt Hon J.R. 1869-1949), 31
Cobbold, 1st Lord (1904-87), 292-3, 297
Cockcraft, Louise (later Nickson) (1930-2012), 72 &n

Cocteau, Jean (1889-1963), 238
Coggan, Lord (Donald), Archbishop of Canterbury (1909-2000), 354
Cohen, Samantha, 487
Cohen, Sir Andrew (1909-68), 196
Cole, Cheryl (b. 1983), 507
Cole, Michael (b. 1943), 402, 423, 446, 489
Collins, Dame Joan (b. 1933), 252n, 326n, 389, 518
Collins, Phil (b. 1951), 404
Colville, Commander Sir Richard (1907-75), 219, 295
Colville, Lady Cynthia (1884-1968), 112 & n
Colville, Lady Margaret (1918-2004), 119
Colville, Sir John (Jock) (1915-87), 75, 119, 121, 124 &n, 144, 157, 161, 162, 170, 179, 204, 205
Connaught, HRH Prince Arthur of (1883-1938), 62 &n,
Connaught, HRH Princess Arthur of (1891-1959), 215
Connaught, HRH Princess Margaret of (1882-1920), 234
Connaught, HRH The Duke of (Arthur) (1850-1942), 1, 27, 34, 58, 62n, 77, 91, 120, 234, 558
Conner, Rt Rev David (Dean of Windsor) (b. 1947), 516, 544, 556
Cook, Rt Hon Robin (1946-2005), 443, 445 &n, 455
Cooper, Dame Jilly (1937-2025), 482
Cooper, Lady Diana (1892-1986), 94n, 118, 123-4, 172, 329, 363, 375
Cooper, Pamela – see Ruthven
Cooper, Rt Hon Duff (1st Viscount Norwich) (1890-1954), 118
Corbett, Colonel Jim (1875-1955), 143-4
Cornwall, HRH The Duchess of (Camilla) (b. 1947), early relationship with Prince Charles, 372-3, 375; marries Andrew Parker Bowles, 372; & Diana's suspicions, 375, 378; at wedding (1981), 377; & renewed relationship with Prince Charles, 386, 421, 423-4, 435; & taped conversation, 430; & Prince Charles's admission on camera, 436; & unpopularity, 442; & Bolland's promotion of, 444, 458; at Golden Jubilee concert, 473; at Angus Ogilvy funeral, 480-1; engagement to Prince Charles, 481-2, 481n; wedding, 483; & the press warm to, 483; at Diamond Jubilee celebrations, 506n, 507-8; & increased prominence of, 510; in Malta, 517; fictional portrayal of, 519; at Prince Harry wedding, 530; at state opening (2019), 540; catches COVID, 543; becomes Colonel of the Rifles, 544-5; becomes Colonel of Grenadier Guards, 551n; at Christmas at Windsor (2021), 552; & Queen's decision she should be Queen Consort, 554-5; at Diamond Jubilee. 557; invested as Lady of the Garter, 558; as Queen 564; mentioned, 485, 489
Cosgrove, General Sir Peter (b. 1947), 515
Costa e Silva, President Artur da (1899-1969), 296n
Cottrell, Most Rev. Stephen (Archbishop of (b. 1958), 558
Coward, Sir Noël (1899-1973), 92
Cowdrey, Sir Colin (1932-2000), 211n
Cowie, Colonel Mervyn (1909-96), 144
Cox, Kirsty, 548
Craig, Daniel (b. 1968), 508
Cranborne, Lady – see Salisbury
Cranko, John (1927-73), 179
Crawford, 28th Earl of (1900-75), 208
Crawford, Geoffrey (1950-2017), 446, 455
Crawford, Marion (1909-88), as governess, 38-9, 47, 51, 52 &n, 68, 73, 75, 76, 106, 109: & the saga of her books, 128-30, 129n; mentioned, 124n, 209, 210
Crawley, Canon Stafford (1876-1948), 71, 75
Crichton, Anne (later Cole) (1927-2004), 72
Crookshank, Harry (1st Viscount) (1893-1961), 204
Crossman, Rt Hon Richard (1907-74), 285-8
Curry, Bishop Michael (b. 1953), 530

d'Ormesson, Jean (1925-2017), 322
Dalton, Robin (1920-2022), 96
Daly, Amy (1873-1956), 60
Damaskinos, Archbishop (1891-1949), 97
Dashwood, Sarah (later Lady Aberdare) (1924-2007), 72
Davenhill, William, 199
Davidson, Lady Rachel (later Pepys) (1905-92), 155
Davies, Clara Novello (1861-1943), 25&n
Dawkins, Lady Bertha (1866-1943), 112 &n
Dawnay, Oliver (1920-88), 73
Dawson of Penn, Lord (1864-1945), 26, 44-6, 46n, 48

INDEX

de Bellaigue, Vicomtesse de (1904-96), 41, 121-2
de Brunhoff, Jean (1899-1937), 9
de Gasperi, Alcide (1881-1954), 202
de Gaulle, Yvonne (1900-79), 491
De L'Isle, 1st Viscount (1909-91), 296
de la Bigne, Comtesse Andrée (1903-89), 100
de la Billière, General Sir Peter (b. 1934), 5
de la Rochefoucauld, Edmée Duchesse de (1895-1991), 238n
de Labilliere, Paul (1879-1946), 59
de László, John (1912-90), 183
de Manio, Jack (1914-88), 300
de Rouet, William (b. 1971), 467
Deakins, Eric (b. 1932), 358
Deane, Canon Anthony (1870-1946), 58, 71 &n
DeBakey, Michael (1908-2008), 370
Dening, Sir Esler (1897-1977), 308
Denmark, HM King Christian X of (1870-1947), 47
Denmark, HM King Frederik IX of (1899-1972), 133, 234, 272, 282, 314
Denmark, HM Queen Ingrid of (1910-2000), 33n, 234, 272
Denmark, HM Queen Margrethe of (b. 1940), 217n-218n, 314 &n, 336
Denmark, HRH Prince Axel of (1888-1964), 217n
Denmark, HRH Prince Henrik of (1934-2018), 217, 314 &n, 336
Denmark, HRH Princess Axel of (1899-1977), 217n
Derby, Countess of (b. 1963), 539
Devonshire, 9th Duke of (1868-1938), 58, 245
Devonshire, Deborah, Duchess of (1920-2014), 482
Devonshire, Mary, Duchess of (Mistress of the Robes) (1895-1988), 173, 180, 293
Diefenbaker, John (1895-1979), 244
Dilhorne, 1st Viscount (1905-1980), 98n-99n
Dimbleby, David (b. 1938), 443
Dimbleby, Jonathan (b. 1944), 329, 372, 436
Dimbleby, Richard (1913-65), 120n, 172
Don, Very Rev Alan (1885-1966), 167, 169
Donoughmore, 7th Earl of (1902-81), 365
Donoughmore, Countess of (1906-95), 365 &n
Douglas-Home – see Home
Douglas-Home, Hon William (1912-92), 72
Douro – see Wellington

Draper, Derek (1967-2024), 463 &n
Drogheda, 11th Earl of (1910-89), 346-7
Druon, Maurice (1918-2009), 322
du Cros, Sir Arthur (1871-1955), 26n
du Maurier, Dame Daphne (1907-89), 119, 145, 146, 150, 153
Dudley Ward, Freda (1894-1983), 15
Dudley, 3rd Earl of (1894-1969), 165, 226-7
Dudley, 4th Earl of (1920-2013), 384n
Dudley, Countess of (Maureen) (1932-2011), 384n
Duff, 3rd Bt, Sir Michael (1907-80), 92, 110, 112-3, 165, 301 &n
Duff, Lady Juliet (1881-1956), 113, 180
Duffy, Mrs Gillian (b. 1935), 496
Dugdale, Rt Hon Sir Thomas (Lord Crathorne) (1897-1977), 158
Duke-Elder, Sir Stewart (1898-1978), 262
Dumaine, Jacques (1897-1953), 121, 122n, 123, 132
Dumbrell, Dougie, 328
Duncan Smith, Rt Hon Sir Iain (b. 1954), 465
Duncan, Andrew, 245-6, 283, 291, 296-8, 297n, 364
Duncannon, Viscount – see Bessborough
Dunne, Dominick (1925-2009), 476
Dunne, Lady (Henrietta) (b. 1937), 481
Dunne, Sir Thomas (1933-2025), 492
Dunning, John (1731-83), 77 &n
Durnford, Colonel Simon, 543
Dyer, Brigadier-General Reginald (1864-1927), 454

Eccles, 1st Viscount (David) (1904-99), 158
Eden – see Avon
Edinburgh, HRH Prince Philip, Duke of (1921-2021),
For State Visits to & from Britain, and four joint tours of the Commonwealth, see under Queen Elizabeth II – as Prince Philip always accompanied her. Only specific references will be made here to what he did individually on certain tours.
Character, 3-4; relationship with his parents, 5, 84-5, 86, 265-6; & Princess Marina, 16, 41, 91, 94; at Kent wedding (1934), 41; lunches with Queen Mary (1937), 57 &n; & Dartmouth meeting with Princess Elizabeth, 64-66; & early relationship with Princess Elizabeth, 83, 89-90, 91-3, 98-102; background, 83-4; early life, 84-90; in line to be King of

Edinburgh, HRH Prince Philip, Duke/ character (contd)
Greece, 86n; & Cobina Wright, 87-9, 87n; & Queen Alexandra of Yugoslavia's biography, 87, 87n-88n; in Athens (1941), 89; in Australia, 94-7; & the Fallons, 95 &n, 112, 191-2; & Sue Other-Gee, 96 &n; & Sandra Jacques, 96-7, 96n; at Corsham, 98; & Mountbatten's plans, 98-9; & Olsa Benning, 99 7n; at Princess Sophie's wedding (1946), 100; at Balmoral (1946), 100-1; & difficult relationship with Queen Elizabeth, 100-1; & beastliness of courtiers, 101; & engagement, 110-1; wedding, 112-5; & early married life, 115-20, 127; invested in the Garter, 120; in Paris (1948), 121-4; & birth of Prince Charles, 125; goes on half pay in navy, 126; in Malta, 131-3; in Canada (1951), 136-9; in Kenya (1952), 143-6; returns to Britain, 146n;

Early days of the Queen's reign, 149, 155; & end of naval career, 155; rejected as Colonel, Grenadier Guards, 156 &n; & Mountbatten name issue, 156-8, 246 & n, 256; & Civil List, 159; & move to Buckingham Palace & Windsor Castle, 162; appointed Admiral of the Fleet, etc, 163; & shooting in France, 163; & the Coronation (1953), 167-9, 171-5; & *Gloriana*, 179; & Benjamin Britten, 180-1; & Townsend, 184, 185; appointed Regent-designate, 185; at funeral mass in New Zealand (1953), 190; taught to march by Lord Slim, 191; slips out to parties in Australia, 192; dines with Churchill (1955), 204; Churchill on, 206; & Edens at Balmoral, 207; & Muggeridge & Altrincham attacks, 210; at Duchess of Norfolk ball, 211; & Queen's awareness of his sacrifices, 216; & Award scheme, 216; & his dislike of chairmen, 217-8; & his solo Commonwealth trip (1956-7), 217-20; appoints Jim Orr, 220-1; & relationship with Prince Charles & Princess Anne, 221-2; & Russian leaders, 207, 231; & World Wildlife Fund, 235; Gladwyn Jebb's view of

(Paris, 1957), 236; Lady Jebb's view of, 237; & his annoyance at workers with wire microphones, 238; & his views on Canadian liquor laws, 243; & Vincent Massey Garter issue, 243; at Kennedy funeral (1963), 254; & Prince Charles & Princess Anne's education, 257; on Princess Margaret, 258; on the family monarchy, 259; & tiger shoot in Jaipur (1961), 267; at King Constantine's wedding, 272; & visit to Germany (1965), 275; upsets the press in BVI (1966), 278; & controversial interview in New York, 279; visits Aberfan, 288; & opening of St George's House, 288; & fictional representations, 295, 518-9; & Andrew Duncan, 296-8; & *Royal Family* film, 298-300; at Prince Charles Investiture, 300; on Australian walkabout (1970), 304; & Hirohito state visit (1971), 309-10; & his tact during 1975 state visit to Japan, 310; & royal finances, 311; & Foreign Office concerns over his speech to the Chamber of Commerce in Paris (1972), 317-9, 321-2; & the Duke of Windsor's papers, 325; at Munich Olympics (1972), 326; & speech at Princess Anne's wedding, 330; on Princess Anne kidnap attempt, 331; at inauguration of King of Spain (1975), 336; & problems with Mountbatten, 365; & Mountbatten's assassination, 366-7; & his advice to Prince Charles over Diana, 375; on Sarah Ferguson, 388, 425; & his 'slitty eyes' comment in China, 394; & reservations about the young royals, 395; & 40th wedding anniversary, 401; volunteers to attend Hirohito funeral, 405-6; at 70, 416; & change in perception of his achievements, 416-7; & letters to Diana after the Morton book, 423-4, 424n; at St George's House, 428; barbecues for Keating, 433; & dismissive of Australia, 434; berated by Prince Charles in Dimbleby book, 436-7; visits Aunt Ella's convent in Moscow, 437; at Prince William's confirmation, 442; & Fayed accusations, 446 & 446n; reacts to press response to Diana's death, 448, 449;

INDEX

responds to the crowd at the Palace, 450; offers to walk in the procession with William & Harry, 450-1, 451n; & deemed gaffe in India (1997), 454n; & conclusion on press in India, 455; Queen praises in Golden wedding speech, 456; on Emperor Akihito's Garter, 457; at Dome on Millennium eve, 463-4;

80th birthday, 465, 467; & death of his sister Sophie, 465-6; at Princess Margaret's funeral, 468; & death of the Queen Mother, 470; on Prince Charles at Birkhall, 472; Lady Harewood on, 475; considers litigation over Burrell book, 477; at Charles and Camilla wedding, 483; on Lucian Freud, 485; at Diana's 10th anniversary service, 490; insulted by Fayed, 490; & 60th wedding anniversary, 490-1; & his health, 491-2, 493; & his working methods, 492; berates Cyril Taylor, 497; at Cambridge wedding, 498; reaches 90, 500-1; in hospital (2011), 501-2; & Diamond Jubilee, 503-4, 505; hospitalised after Jubilee pageant, 506-8; at Cowes (2012), 509; abdominal operation, 511; & Irish state visit, 513; at Lady Mary Clayton funeral, 513-4; appointed Knight of Australia, 515; & his impatience, 516-7; & Queen's 90th birthday, 520, 522; & loss of triumvirate of Household, 521-2; & grave illness (2016), 523-4; retires from royal duties, 524-5; & last public duties, 526-7; at Wood Farm, 527, 536, 539; on Meghan Markle, 529; at Harry wedding, 530; at Eugenie wedding, 532; & car accident (2019), 536; at OM lunch, 537; at Gabriella Windsor wedding, 537; & health scare (2019), 539-40; at Windsor during lockdown, 542-5; last public appearance, 544; in hospital (2021), 546-7; last days at Windsor, 547; death 547; funeral, 548-9; & Queen's mention in Xmas broadcast, 553; memorial service, 555-6;

mentioned, 1, 6, 28, 103, 103n, 104, 118, 135, 160, 182, 227, 255n, 262, 264, 270, 303, 322, 338 &n, 371, 374, 397, 407, 411, 421, 427, 432n, 476, 479, 486, 490, 531, 534, 551, 552, 559, 568.

Edward VIII, HM King – see Windsor, Duke of
Edward, HRH The Prince - see Wessex
Egerton, Lady Alice (1923-77), 131
Egypt, HM King Farouk of (1920-65), 292
Egypt, President Anwar El-Sadat of (1918-81), 377-8, 378n
Egypt, Princess Fazile of (1941-2024), 231
Eisenhower, Mrs Dwight D. (Mamie) (1896-1979), 164
Eisenhower, President Dwight D. (1890-1969), 164, 203, 204, 211, 242, 282
Eldon, 4th Earl of (1899-1976), 101, 217

ELIZABETH II, HM QUEEN (1926-2022):

As Princess Elizabeth:

record-breaker, 1; approach to work, 1-3; as conciliator, 2; modesty & humour, 3; comparison to Queen Mother, 4; author's meetings with, 4-8; Princess George of Hanover on, 7; Birth, 9-10; seen by George V & Queen Mary, 10-11; blissful childhood, 13, 18, 37-8, 40; Queen Mary's interest in, 14; relationship with her paternal uncles and aunts, 15-16; & her maternal grandfather, 16-17; & her maternal uncle, David Bowes-Lyon, 17; christening, 18-19; & use of her name for hospitals, 19-20; with her nurse, Alah, 20-1; left with grandparents for six months, 21-2; at 145 Piccadilly, 21-2; at Naseby Hall, 22-3; strong relationship with George V, 23-7, 33, 34, 43; & the Lascelles brothers, 24, 25; at Bognor with George V, 26-7; & her cousins, 27-8; Lady Cynthia Asquith on, 29-30; given dog by Prince of Wales, 30; & Sonia Graham-Hodgson, 30, 48; & birth of Princess Margaret, 31-2; closeness to sister, 32-3; Lady Helen Graham on, 34-5; at Royal Lodge, 36; & Welsh house, 36; with Marion Crawford as governess, 38-9; ticked off by Queen Mary, 39; with J.M. Barrie, 40; as bridesmaid to Princess Marina, 4; & George V;'s Silver Jubilee, 42; as bridesmaid to the Duchess of Gloucester, 42-3; at Sandringham, 1935-6, 44-6; & death of George V, 46-7; attends funeral, 47; & effect of George V's death, 47-8; at Eastbourne (1936), 48;

QUEEN ELIZABETH II

ELIZABETH II, HM QUEEN/As Princess Elizabeth (contd)
10th birthday, 49; & peoples' hopes she would be Queen, 49-50; warned by Crawfie that the Abdication would change her life, 51; accepts her destiny as heir to the throne, 52; conclusions on her childhood, 53;

At christening of Prince Edward of Kent, 54; at the Coronation (1937), 55-7; & Coronation summer engagements, 58-9; & death of Countess of Strathmore, 60; as a Girl Guide, 60; esrly riding, 60-1, 79; & the Paris dolls, 61-2; at launch of *Queen Elizabeth*, 62; 13th birthday, 63: & parents trip to Canada, 63-4; & meeting Prince Philip at Dartmouth (1939), 64-6; at Balmoral & Birkhall as war is declared, 67-8; at Sandringham Xmas (1939), 68; at Windsor in wartime, 68-82; Alathea Fitzalan Howard on, 73-4, 83; & wartime broadcast (1940), 74-5; & Queen Mary's involvement in her education, 75-6; & wartime pantomimes, 76-7; becomes Colonel of Grenadier Guards, 77-8; confirmed, 78; as Counsellor of State, 78-9; & Mrs Roosevelt, 79-80; photographed by Cecil Beaton, 80-1; 18th birthday, 81; joins ATS (1945), 82; early relationship with Prince Philip, 83, 91-3, 97, 98, 102; & speculation about Prince Philip as future husband, 89-90; & Earl of Euston, 90-1, 93, 99; & plans for Prince Philip, 97, 98-101, 103; & post-war engagements, 102-3, 110, 127, 131; on South African trip, 104-9; & 21st birthday broadcast, 106-8; & engagement (1947), 110-1;

Wedding (1947), 112-6; & early married life, 116; 117-9; appointed Lady of the Garter, 118; & move to Windlesham Moor, 119; & her early Household, 119; & move to Clarence House, 120, 130; at Silver Wedding of King & Queen (1948), 120-1; visits Paris (1948), 121-4; & birth of Prince Charles (1948), 124-5; & King's illness, 126; & Crawfie revelations, 128-30; at Harewood wedding (1949), 130-1; in Malta with Prince Philip, 131, 132, 133; at Auriol state visit, 132; & birth of Princess Anne (1950), 132; deputises for ill King, 133-4; presides at King Haakon state visit, 133; & King's operation (1951),134-5; & visit to Canada (1951), 136-9; & last days of the King, 140; departs for Commonwealth tour (1952), 140; in Nairobi (1952), 143-4, 145-6; not aware of King's death, 145-6; told of King's death, 146; returns to London, 146.

As Queen:
Cabinet discusses titles, 146-7; arrives in London, 147; hailed by Churchill, 148, 154-5; at Accession Council, 148-9; proclaimed, 149; at Sandringham, 149-50, 153; & Lying-in-State, 150; at King's funeral, 151; on her father, 151-2; Daphne du Maurier & Lascelles impressed by, 153-4; early engagements (1952), 155-6; & colonelcy of Grenadier Guards, 156; & Mountbatten name issues, 156-8, 256 &n; & Civil List, 159; & Duke of Windsor issues, 159-60, 227; & Churchill as 1st Prime Minister, 161-2, 202-6; & her approach to being Queen, 162-3; & summer engagements (1952), 163; & death of Queen Mary (1953), 164-5;

Coronation, 166-75; & Coronation summer, 176-80, & Aureole at the Derby (1953), 176-7, 176n; & *Gloriana*, 177-80; & dealings with Benjamin Britten, 180-1; & role of the Queen Mother, 181, 222; & Princess Margaret – Townsend drama (1953), 182-5, & (1955), 222-3.

Commonwealth tour (1953-4), 187-201; plans 187-8; in New Zealand, 189-90; in Australia, 190-3; in Ceylon, 193-5; in Aden, 195-6; in Uganda, 196-7; in Libya, 197-8, in Malta, 198; in Gibraltar, 198-201; reunited with children, 197;

& Eden as Prime Minister, 206-7, 211-4; & Duke of Buccleuch appointment, 208; & criticism by Malcolm Muggeridge, 208-210: criticism by Lord Altrincham, 210; & Duchess of Norfolk's ball, 211; & Suez crisis, 211;

& Macmillan as Prime Minister, 213, 245-50, 252-4;

& Royal Family deaths, 215-6; & Prince Philip's work, 216-7; & his Commonwealth tour (1956-7), 217-8; & rumours of a rift, 219; creates him a Prince, 219-20; & children's education, 221-2; & support of the Royal Family, 226-7; visit of Shah of Iran (1955), 230-1; visit of the Russian leaders (1955), 207, 231;

& attempt to give the Garter to Vincent Massey, 243-4; & Profumo crisis, 251-3; & Alec Douglas-Home as Prime Minister, 254-5; & Harold Wilson as Prime Minister (1966-70), 255, 283-5, 286-7, 305, & (1974-6), 334-5, 337-9;

& birth of Prince Andrew (1960), 256; & of Prince Edward (1964), 257; creates Prince Charles Prince of Wales (1958), 257; creates Armstrong-Jones Earl of Snowdon (1961), 258; & death of The Princess Royal (1965), 259-60; & Lord Harewood divorce, 259-60, 260n; at Duke of Kent's wedding (1961), 261; & Princess Alexandra's wedding, 261-2; & Duke & Duchess of Windsor, 262-4; & Lord Mountbatten, 264-5; & Princess Andrew of Greece, 265; entertains President & Mrs Kennedy (1961), 269;

& Independence of Rhodesia, 277; & visit to Northern Ireland (1966), 280; death & state funeral of Churchill, 281-2; & assessment of the Queen at this time, 282-3; sends Prince Charles to Harold Holt funeral, 284-5; & Richard Crossman, 285-8; & Aberfan disaster (1966), 288; & St George's House, 288-9; & the Duke of Beaufort, 290-2; & the Duke of Norfolk, 291-2; & early Private Secretaries, 292-3; & other Royal Household, 293-4; & Sir John Miller, 293-4; & satirical attacks, 294-5; & Press Secretaries, 295-6; & Andrew Duncan's book, 296-7; & emergence of Prince Charles & Princess Anne into public life, 297-8; & *Royal Family* film (1969), 298-300; & Investiture (1969), 300-1; & first walkabouts, 303-4;

& Edward Heath as Prime Minister, 286, 305-6, 327, 334; summons Prince William of Gloucester home from Japan, 307; & Select Committee on Civil List, 311; & President Amin's invitation, 312-3; visits ailing Duke of Windsor (1972), 319, 323; & death of Duke of Windsor, 325-6; & death of Prince William of Gloucester, 326; Silver Wedding, 317; & entry into Common Market, 327; & marriage of Princess Anne (1973), 329; & kidnap attempt on Princess Anne, 331; & Prix de Diane, 336; & death of Patrick Plunket, 336; & Princess Margaret's separation, 337; 50th birthday, 339;

& James Callaghan as Prime Minister, 339, 361; & Australian crisis (1975), 341-3, 345; Silver Jubilee (1977), 346-54; & possibility of Amin coming, 351-2; & Northern Ireland visit, 353; & 1st grandchild, 354; & Prince Michael's marriage, 356;

& Margaret Thatcher as Prime Minister, 361-4, 368-9, 400, 413-4; & Commonwealth disagreements, 262-3; at Sir Robert Mayer's centenary concert, 363; & assassination of Lord Mountbatten (1979), 364-7; & Anthony Blunt exposure (1979), 368-9; & abdication of Queen Juliana, 370; refuses to get involved in Charles-Camilla relationship, 373; & King of Spain boycotting Charles & Diana wedding, 377; & attitude to Diana, 378; & danger from assassination, 379; & gun shots at Birthday Parade (1981), 379-80; takes sanctuary in Cross Hands hotel, 380; & Michael Fagan intrusions, 380-1; & resignation of Michael Trestrail, 381; & IRA bombs in royal parks, 381; invites editors to discuss excessive interest in Diana, 382; & birth of Prince William, 382; & Prince Andrew in the Falklands (1982), 382-3; at Heinz ball (1983), 384-5; in Kentucky (1984), 387; & Sarah Ferguson, 388, 389; 60th birthday, 388-9; & Duchess of Windsor's funeral (1986), 390; & Michael Shea affair, 390-3; ceases to ride at Trooping the Colour (1986), 395; hears of death of Major Lindsay, 397-8; & crisis in Fiji (1987), 399-400; bestows Princess Royal title on Princess Anne, 400;

ELIZABETH II, HM QUEEN/As Queen (contd)
40th wedding anniversary (1987), 401; Christmas message after Enniskillen bomb, 402; criticised for not visiting Lockerbie disaster site, 405; & Dick Hern saga, 406-7; & Monty Roberts, 407-8; & poor relations with Prince Charles, 409; & Queen Mother at 90, 412-3; gives Princess Margaret the Royal Victorian Chain, 413;

& John Major as Prime Minister, 414, 421, 422, 427-8, 443; broadcasts about Iraq war, 415; allows hair to go grey, 417; & 40th anniversary of accession (992), 418; Annus Horribilis, 418-28; in Mirzoeff documentary, 419-20; & death of Lord Southesk, 421; remains neutral over Diana & Morton book, 422, 423; & family in disarray, 425; & fury over Sarah Ferguson scandal, 425; & fire at Windsor Castle (1992), 427; & Annus Horribilis speech, 427; & to pay income tax, 427; & Wales separation, 427-8; at Princess Anne's 2nd wedding, 428; described as 'tired', 428; & investitures, 429; & Windsor fire restoration, 431; tries to persuade Queen Mother to slow down, 431; & wet Garter procession, 431-2; & Paul Keating visit to Balmoral, 433-4; & death of Bobo MacDonald, 434; & the Way Ahead group, 436; & Robert Fellowes, 439; & VE Day 50th anniversary, 439-40; & Diana *Panorama* interview, 440-1; & Charles Anson, 441; at Prince William's confirmation (1997), 442;

& Tony Blair as Prime Minister, 443, 446-9, 461-2, 463-4, 483, 488; & reactions after Diana's death (1997), 446-9, 451; & broadcast about Diana, 450; & Diana's funeral, 451; & new ideas after Diana's death, 453; Golden Wedding, 456; & decommissioning of *Britannia*, 456; on Camilla relationship, 458; worries over health of Queen Mother & Princess Margaret, 458-9; & Prince Edward's wedding, 460; drives Crown Prince of Saudi Arabia, 460; & Australian referendum, 462; & loss of friends, 463; at Millennium Dome evening, 463-4;

& reaction to 9/11, 465; & death of Lord Carnarvon, 465; & Queen Mother's 100th birthday, 466-7; & death of Princess Margaret (2002), 467-8; & Golden Jubilee, 468-9, 472-5; & death of the Queen Mother (2002), 469-70; & new style of dressing, 470-1; & increased reliance on Countess of Wessex, 471-2; Lady Harewood on, 473-5; & Burrell trial, 476-7; in hospital (2003), 478; unveils Diana fountain, 479; & death of Princess Alice, Duchess of Gloucester, 479-80; & of Sir Angus Ogilvy, 480; & marriage of Prince Charles & Camilla Parker Bowles, 481-3; & poor relations with Clarence House. 484; & Lucian Freud portrait, 484-5; 80th birthday, 485, 486; & Western Isles cruise, 487;

& Gordon Brown as Prime Minister, 488, 489, 495-6; at Diana 10th anniversary service, 490; & 60th wedding anniversary, 490; becomes longest serving monarch, 491; & Prince Philip's health, 492; becomes great-grandmother, 493; & Prince Charles at 60, 493-4; at Castle of Mey party (2009), 494-5;

& David Cameron as Prime Minister, 496-7, 499, 515-6, 522-3; at Cambridge wedding (2011), 498; meets Martin McGuinness, 499; & Prince Philip at 90, 501; & Prince Philip in hospital (2011), 501-2; & Diamond Jubilee, 503-8; & Sovereigns lunch, 505; & River Pageant, 505-6; & Prince Philip in hospital again, 506-7; & London Olympic Games, 508-9; & her bad knee, 509-10; at Baroness Thatcher's funeral, 510; visits *Today* show (Radio 4), 511; wins Gold Cup at Ascot, 511-2; sees Prince George, 512; at Cumberland Lodge (2104), 513-4; & advice over Scottish referendum, 514-5; becomes longest reigning monarch, 517; & fictional representations, 518-20; 90th birthday, 520, 522; at Terry Pendry fundraiser event, 521; & Brexit, 522-3, 541;

& Theresa May as Prime Minister, 523, 525, 538; & death of Margaret Rhodes, 523; ill at Christmas (2106), 523-4; & Prince Charles as future Head of the Commonwealth, 524-5;

INDEX

& Christpher Geidt & Prince Philip's retirement, 524-5; visits Grenfell Tower, 525-6; at Lady Mountbatten's funeral, 526; & last public duty with Prince Philip (2017), 526; lets Prince Philip live at Wood Farm, 527; private 70th wedding anniversary, 527; advises Prince Harry to wait a year before marrying, 529; at Prince Harry's wedding, 530; dislikes Meghan Markle's dress, 531; photographed with Sussex baby, 531; & Prince Harry's departure as working royal, 532; enjoys Princess Eugenie's wedding, 532; & distress over Prince Andrew, 534; at Royal Maundy & Easter (2018), 535; & attitude to dying, 536; worried about Prince Philip, 537; & Trump visit to Windsor (2019) 537;
& Boris Johnson as Prime Minister, 538-40, 562-2; & Nicola Sturgeon, 539, 560; does not wear crown at State Opening (2019), 540; at Commonwealth Observance (2020), 541; at Windsor for lockdown, 541-50; & COVID broadcast, 543-4; & Easter message, 544; at Princess Beatrice's wedding, 544; knights Captain Tom Moore, 544; at Balmoral (2020), 545; & Prince Philip's hospitalisation (2021), 546-7; issues her 'Recollections may vary' statement after Oprah Winfrey interview, 547; not with Prince Philip when he died, 547; & Prince Philip's funeral, 548-9; opens Parliament (2021), 550; & busy summer, 550-1; at Balmoral (2021), 551; returns to Windsor (2021), 551; decline in health, 552-3; last Christmas broadcast, 552-3.
Platinum Jubilee (2022), 554-8; appoints Duchess of Cornwall to Garter, 554; asks that Camilla be Queen Consort, 554-5; continuing anxiety over Prince Andrew & Prince Harry, 555; at Prince Philip's memorial service, 555-6; 96th birthday at Wood Farm, 556; on balcony for Birthday Parade, 556-7; misses service of thanksgiving, 557; last appearance on Palace balcony, 557-8; invests new Garter companions, 558; last meeting with author, 558-60; in Edinburgh, 560; at Balmoral (August 2020), 560; sees Johnson out, 561-2; & Liz Truss as last Prime Minister, 562; cancels Privy Council zoom, 562; dies peacefully at Balmoral, 563.
New King's tribute to, 564; preparations & rehearsals for funeral, 564-5, 567; Operation Unicorn in Scotland, 566; London Bridge procession 566-7; Lying-in-State, 566; State Funeral, 567; Windsor procession & Committal in St George's Chapel, 567-8; interment in King George VI Memorial Chapel, 568.

Principal State Visits to Britain after 1952:
Nature of such visits, 228-9; visits from: King of Sweden (1954), 230; Emperor of Ethiopia, (1954), 230; King of Iraq, 231; President Heuss of Germany (1958), 232-3; President de Gaulle of France (1960), 250-1; King of Greece (1963), 270-1; King of Jordan (1966), 279-80; President Saragat of Italy (1969), 280; Emperor of Japan (1971), 307-10; Denmark (1980), 314; Queen of the Netherlands (1972), 315; Grand Duke of Luxembourg (1972), 326; President of Zaire (1973), 331-3; President of France (1976), 339-40; President of Romania (1978), 357-9; President of Indonesia (1979), 367-8; President of Poland (1991), 415-6; Emperor Akihito of Japan (1998), 457-8; President Jiang Zemin of China (1999), 461; President Sarkozy of France (2008), 491 &n; President Obama of the USA (2009), 494; President Higgins of Ireland (2014), 499-500, 514; & President Trump of USA (2019), 537;

Principal State Visits overseas after 1952:
Nature of such visits, 229-30; visits to: King of Norway (1955), 233; King of Sweden (1956), 233-4; King of Denmark (1957), 234; Queen of the Netherlands (1958). 234-5; President Coty of France (1957), 235-9;
Emperor of Ethiopia (1965), 273-5; Sudan (1965), 275; President Lübke of Germany (1965), 275-6; Emperor of Japan (1975), 310; President Pompidou of France (1972), 316-24;

639

QUEEN ELIZABETH II

ELIZABETH II, HM QUEEN/As Principal State Visits overseas after 1952: (contd)
President Scheel of Germany (1978), 359; Arabia (1979), 360-1; President of Switzerland (1980), 371; King of Morocco (1980), 371-2; King of Jordan (1984), President of China (1986), 394; King of Spain (1988), 403; President Bush of USA (1991), 416; France (1992), 422; Germany (1992), 426; Cyprus (1993), 434-5; President of Russia (1994), 437-9; President of Ireland (2011), 498-9; & Italy (2014), 514;

Principal Commonwealth visits after 1954:
Visits to: Nigeria (1956), 239-41; Canada (1957), 241-2; Canada (1959), 242-3; Ghana (1961), 247-50; Pakistan, India & Iran (1961), 267-8; Italy (1961), 269; New Zealand, Tasmania & Australia (1963), 269-70; Canada (1964), 272-3; the Caribbean (1966), 278-9; New Zealand & Australia (1970), 303-5; Canada (1970), 307; Canada (1971), 307; South East Asia (1971), 314; Canada (1973), 328; Pacific Island Territories (1974), 334-5; Canada (1976), 340; Australia (etc) (1977), 347-8; Canada etc (1977), 353-4; Canada (1978), 359; Jamaica, California etc (1983), 383; Kenya & Bangladesh (1983), 383-4; 384; Canada (1990), 401; Australia (1992), 420-1; Malta (1992), 422; President of South Africa (1995), 440; the Caribbean (1994), 436; Pakistan & India (1997), 453-5; Australia etc (2002), 469; Canada (2005), 483-4; Australia (2006), 485; Uganda (CHOGM) (2007), 490-1; Australia (2011), 501; & Malta (CHOGM) (2015), 517

Elizabeth The Queen Mother, HM Queen (1900-2002):
As Duchess of York:
Childless, 10 &n, background & character, 11-13, 16-7, & birth of Elizabeth, 18, & hospitals, 19-20, Australian trip, 20-1, at 145 Piccadilly, 21-2, & Lady Cynthia Asquith, 28-9, 47, 52n, on Elizabeth as a child, 29, & birth of Margaret, 31-2, relations with Duke of York, 33, & raising her children, 39, & J.M. Barrie, 40, & her image, 43, & death of George V, 45-6, in Eastbourne (1936), 48, at Royal Lodge (1936), 48-9, at Birkhall (1936), 50-1, & Abdication, 51-3;

As Queen Consort:
at Windsor, 54, & the 1937 Coronation, 55-7, & Coronation summer engagements, 58-9, & death of her mother, 59, & state visit to Paris (1938), 61-2, launches *Queen Elizabeth*, 62, & Canadian tour (1939), 63-4, Harold Nicolson praises, 64, & Dartmouth visit, 64-5, at Glamis (1939), 67, on the effects of war, 68, at Windsor in wartime, 70, 73, 79, & her approach to the children's education, 75, invites Mrs Roosevelt to Britain, 79-80, on VE Day (1945), 82, on Prince Philip, 93, 100-1, & Dermot Morrah, 105n, 106, & South African tour (1947), 104-9, at Royal Wedding (1947), 113, Silver Wedding (1948), 120, & birth of Prince Charles, 125, & King's illness, 126-8, 134-5, & Crawfie saga, 128-9, at Harewood wedding, 131, her 'plumpness', 132, & Princess Elizabeth's departure for Kenya, 140-1, & King's last day at Sandringham, 141-2, & King's death (1952), 145, 150, 155;

As Queen Mother:
presses for Windsor name, 157, & Duke of Windsor, 159-60, still at Buckingham Palace, 162, at 1953 Coronation, 172, at Ward ball, 176, & *Gloriana*, 179, & new life at Clarence House, 181, 183, & Rhodesia visit, 185-6, visible presence in the Queen's life, 222, & Townsend saga, 223, & state visits, 228, & Shah of Iran's visit, 231, & de Gaulle state visit, 250, & 1963 lunch party, 252, & appendix operation, 259n, & relations with Prince Charles, 265, 436, at Churchill's funeral, 282, 70th birthday, 306, at Duke of Windsor's funeral, 326, as Counsellor of State, 334n, on Harold Wilson, 338, 80th birthday, 371, & Prince William's christening, 382, at Duchess of Windsor's funeral, 390, & Monty Roberts, 407, her popularity, 409, 90th birthday, 412-3, on badly behaved Prime Ministers,

420-1, 92nd birthday, 425, & Bomber Harris statue, 426, at Princess Anne's second wedding (1992), 428, health issues, 429, & Garter ceremony (1993), 431, & death of Sir Martin Gilliat and Lady Fermoy, 432, eclipses her daughter, 439, 508, at VE Day celebrations (1995), 439-40, at Prince William's confirmation, 442, reaction to Diana's death (1997), 448, at Queen's Golden wedding party, 456, & concerns for her health (1998), 458-9, 99th birthday, 459, 100th birthday, 465-7, at Sandringham (2001), 467, & death of Princess Margaret (2002), 467-8, death, 469-71, funeral,470, on Cherie Blair, 488, & fictional representations, 518;

mentioned, 4, 9 & n, 22, 28, 34 & n, 36, 42, 61, 66, 76, 80, 81, 102, 103, 115, 118, 133, 139n, 188, 201, 211, 215, 217, 236, 259, 261, 274, 293, 372, 374, 377, 427, 463, 478, 479, 483, 502, 568

Elliot, Annabel (b. 1949), 458
Elliot, Roger, 279
Elphinstone, 16th Lord (1869-1955), 208
Elphinstone, Hon Andrew (1918-75), 91-2, 103
Elphinstone, Hon Elizabeth (1911-80), 32
Elphinstone, Hon Jean – see Wills
Elphinstone, Hon Margaret – see Rhodes
Elphinstone, Hon Mrs Andrew (Jean) (1923-2017), 103, 119
Elphinstone, Mary, Lady (1883-1961), 17
Elton, Lady (Richenda), 563
Emerson, Ralph Waldo (1803-82), 416
Engelson, Trevor (b. 1976), 528
Epstein, Jeffrey (1953-2019), 533
Erhard, Dr Ludwig (1897-1977), 276
Erskine, Caroline (1928-2024), 184n
Erskine, Sir Arthur (1881-1963), 60-1
Ethiopia, HIM Emperor Haile Selassie of (1892-1975), 228, 230, 273-5, 274n
Euston – see Grafton
Evans, Sir Horace (later Lord) (1903-63), 164, 259 &n

Fabre, Francis (1911-90), 322
Fagan, Michael (b. 1948), 380-1
Fairbanks, Jr, Douglas (1909-2000), 295n, 384
Fairbanks, Mary Lee (1912-88), 384
Fallon, Joseph (1911-71), 95-6, 95n, 112, 192
Fallon, Judy (1916-67), 95-6, 95n, 112, 191-2

Farebrother, Michael (1920-87), 72
Farish III, William S. (b. 1939), 416, 487 &n
Farish, Sarah Sharp (1942-2025), 487 &n
Farnham, Diana Lady (1931-2021), 507, 552
Fawcett, Michael (b. 1962), 477, 485, 536
Fayed, Dodi (1955-97), 445, 481n, 490
Fayed, Mohamed (1929-2023), 402, 423, 444-6, 446n, 489-90, 518
Fellowes, Robert (Lord) (1941-2024), 388, 405, 416 &n, 433, 436, 438-9, 441, 449, 453, 456, 484
Fellowes, Sir William (1899-1986), 142
Ferguson, Major Ronald (1931-2003), 388, 396, 412, 430
Ferguson, Sarah (b. 1959), 388-9, 393, 395-6, 397, 403 &n, 405, 415, 418-9, 422, 425, 429, 433, 532, 533, 543
Fermoy, Ruth Lady (1908-93), 432
Festing, Andrew (b. 1941), 419
Field, Albert Patrick (1910-90), 341n
Fife, HRH The Princess Louise, Duchess of, 400
Fisher of Lambeth, Lord (Geoffrey) (1887-1972), 67, 103n, 111, 116, 138, 160, 168, 210, 217, 223, 224, 269
Fisher, Graham and Heather, 297
Fitzalan Howard, Alathea (1923-2001), 69 &n, 73-4, 82, 83, 90-1, 102, 115
Fitzalan of Derwent, 1st Viscount (1855-1947), 69n, 73, 79
Fitzalan-Howard, General Lord Michael (1916-2007), 443
Fitzalan-Howard, Lady Anne (1938-2014), 211 &n
Fitzpatrick, General Sir Desmond (1912-2002), 443
Fitzroy, Lord Oliver (1923-44), 92 & n
Fleming, Mrs Ian (Ann) (1913-81), 180, 188
Fleming, Peter (1907-71), 230
Fleming, Renée (b. 1959), 507
Fleming, Tom (1927-2010), 389
Fletcher, MP, Katherine (b. 1976), 550
Fonteyn, Dame Margot (1919-91), 350
Forbes, Alastair (1981-2005), 473
Forbes, Bryan (1926-2013), 395
Ford, General Sir Robert (1923-2015), 364n
Ford, Mrs Lionel (May) (1875-1957), 71, 75
Ford, President Gerald (1913-2006), 310, 347
Ford, Sir Edward (1910-2006), 71 &n, 117-8, 144, 170, 292-3, 427, 468, 487
Fortescue, 5th Earl (1888-1958), 133
Fowler, Isabelle, 171
France, President Valéry Giscard d'Estaing of (1926-2020), 284, 339-40, 358, 360

France, King Louis XIV of (1638-1715), 1, 558
France, President Charles de Gaulle of (1890-1970), 229n, 250-1, 282, 316, 320, 322, 331, 432,
France, President Félix of (1841-99), 284 &n
France, President Jacques Chirac of (1932-2019), 479
France, President René Coty of (1882-1962), 235, 238
Francis, HH Pope (1936-2025), 514
Franklin, Olga (1895-1087), 98
Fraser, Malcolm (1930-2015), 341-4
Frazier, Alice, 416
Freeman, Simon, 381n
Freud, Lucian (1922-2011), 484-5
Friberg, Marie (1852-1934), 234n

Gaddafi, Colonel Muammar (1942-2011),197n, 329n, 352
Gage, 6thViscount ('George')(1895-1982), 9, 10
Gailey, Dr Andrew, 457
Gaitskell, Rt Hon Hugh (1906-63), 251, 262
Gale, George (1927-90), 405
Gallacher, Willie (1881-1965), 57 &n, 125
Ganilau, Ratu Sir Penaia (1918-93), 399
Gardner, Andrew (1932-99), 376
Geidt, Christopher (Lord) (b. 1961), 487, 524-5
George III, HM King (1738-1820), 242, 346, 549
George V, HM King (1865-1936), 11, 13, & Windsor family name, 14, 16, 156-8; Lord Harewood on, 24, Silver Jubilee, 42, & death of Princess Victoria, 44, last Christmas at Sandringham, 44-6, death, 46, 47-8, funeral, 47; relationship with Princess Elizabeth, 14, 23, 24, 26, 33, 42, 47; mentioned, 9, 26n, 30, 41, 54, 55, 62n, 77, 102, 124-5, 267, 437, 470, 498
George VI, HM King (1895-1952),
As Duke of York:
Childless, 10, background & character, 11-13, & birth of Elizabeth, 18, Australian trip, 20-1, at 145 Piccadilly, 21-2, at Naseby, 22-3, & birth of Margaret, 31, relations with wife & children, 33, & Welsh cottage, 36, & J.M. Barrie, 40, & death of George V, 45-6, in Eastbourne (1936), 48, at Royal Lodge (1936), 48-9, at Birkhall (1936), 50-1, & Abdication, 51-3;

As King:
shock on becoming King, 52, at Sandringham (1936), 53, assumes role, 54-5, & Coronation (1937), 55-7, & civil list, 57-8 & 57n, & 1937 summer engagements, 58-9, & death of Countess of Strathmore, 59, & state visit to Paris (1938), 61, & impending war crisis, 62-3, & Canada tour, 63-4, & Dartmouth visit (1939), 64-5, & declaration of war (1939), 67-8, & Windsor in wartime, 70, 72, 73, 75, 76, 78-9, 82, & Regency Act (1937), 78-9, & VE Day (1945), 82, 102, & Prince Philip in the navy, 86, 90, & Princess Elizabeth's wish to marry, 100, & South African visit, 104-9, & Princess Elizabeth engagement, 110-1, at the royal wedding (1947), 113, 116, & relationship with Princess Elizabeth, 117, & his gnashes, 117-8, bestows Garter on Princess Elizabeth, 118, 120, & Silver Wedding, 120, agrees Princess Elizabeth's visit to Paris, 121, & royal titles, 125, 156, 158, & health concerns, 126-8, 132, 133-5, 136, 139, & Harewood wedding, 130, 131, bids farewell to Princess Elizabeth (1952), 140, last days at Sandringham, 141-2, death, 142, 144-8, 153, funeral, 149-51, Queen's tribute (1955), 151-2; mentioned, 9, 14, 17, 22, 28, 34, 42, 46, 47, 61, 67, 81, 103, 105n, 142, 155, 159, 164, 181, 183, 231, 264, 279, 282, 293, 325, 347, 390, 412, 470, 508, 568
Germany, President Heinrich Lübke of (1894-1972), 275-6
Germany, President Richard von Weizsäcker of (1920-2015), 426
Germany, President Theodor Heuss of (1884-1963), 232
Germany, President Walter Scheel of (1919-2016), 359
Gibbs, Mrs Vicary – see Elphinstone
Gibbs, Sir Humphrey (1902-90), 277
Gilbey, James, 426
Giles, Carl (cartoonist) (1916-95), 518
Gillard, Frank (1908-98), 107
Gillard, Julia (b. 1961), 501
Gillett, Major-General Sir Peter (1913-89), 404
Gilliat, Lt-Colonel Sir Martin (1913-93), 432, 439

INDEX

Giuffre, Virginia Roberts (1983-2025), 533, 555
Gladwyn, 1st Lord (1900-96), 127, 235-6, 351
Gladwyn, Lady (Cynthia) (1898-1990), 16, 127, 235-8
Glenconner, 3rd Lord (Colin) (1926-2010), 177, 459
Glenconner, Anne, Lady (b. 1932), 32, 459
Gloucester, HRH Prince William of (1941-72), 15, 307, 308, killed in air accident, 326-7, 364, 449; 358
Gloucester, HRH Princess Alice, Duchess of (1901-2004), 15, 33n, 42-3, 44, 53, 131, 132, 140, 176, 211, 226, 233, 261, 263, 269, 273-4, 283, 295, 306, 326-7, 327n, 417, 467, 468, 480, 518
Gloucester, HRH The Duchess of (Birgitte) (b. 1946), 327, 458, 541, 552
Gloucester, HRH The Duke of (Henry) (1900-74), 15, 42-3, 44, 53, 95, 111, 131, 132, 133, 139, 140, 147, 165, 172, 174, 176, 194, 226, 227n, 231, 233, 241, 246, 249, 257&n, ill health, & death, 261; 263, 273, 283, 306, 307, 308, 374, 388, 390
Gloucester, HRH The Duke of (Richard) (b. 1944), 15, 307, 327, 424, 458, 495, 503, 541, 549, 552, 563
Gluck (1895-1978), 22
Gopallawa, William (1897-1981), 195n
Gordon-Lennox, Lady Algernon (1864-1945), 14
Gordon-Lennox, Lt-Colonel Sir George (1908-88), 155-6
Gordon, John (1890-1974), 134
Gordon, Lord Adam (1909-84), 96 &n
Goronwy-Roberts, Lord (1913-81), 358
Gorton, John 1911-2002), 305
Gosling, Sir Donald (1929-2019), 533n
Gould, Beatrice Blackmer (1898-1989), 128-9, 129n
Gould, Bruce (1898-1989), 128-9, 129n
Gove, Michael (Lord) (b. 1967), 522-3
Gowrie, 1st Earl of (1872-1955), 70 &n, 71
Grafton, 11th Duke of (1919-2011), 69, 90-91, 90n, 92, 93, 100, 293, 338, 510
Grafton, Duchess of (Fortune) (1920-2021), 90n, 91n, 131-2, 240, 293, 320, 323, 510 &n, 541, 552
Graham-Hodgson, Sir Harold (1890-1960), 30
Graham-Hodgson, Sonia (1925-2012), 30, 48, 73n, 102
Graham, Joan (1917-2012), 219
Graham, Kathini (1929-2012), 146

Graham, Lady Helen (1879-1945), 34-5, 34n, 52, 63
Granville, 5th Earl (James) (1918-96), 24n
Granville, Rose, Countess (1890-1967), 17
Greece, HM King Alexander I of (1893-1920), 87
Greece, HM King Constantine II of (1940-2023), 86n, 265, 272, 282, 370, 382, 442, 500
Greece, HM King George I of (1845-1913), 83, 379n
Greece, HM King George II of (1890-1947), 84, 86
Greece, HM King Paul I of (1901-64), 86, 270-1, 272 &n
Greece, HM Queen Anne-Marie of (b. 1946), 86n, 272, 442
Greece, HM Queen Frederika of (1917-81), 86, 165, 168, 270-1, 275, 356n,
Greece, HRH Crown Prince Pavlos of (b. 1967), 4
Greece, HRH Prince Andrew of (1882-1944), 26n, 83, 84-5,100
Greece, HRH Prince George of (1869-1957), 86, 122 & n
Greece, HRH Prince Peter of (1908-80), 86n
Greece, HRH Princess Andrew of (Alice) (1885-1969), 5, 26n, character, 84-5; 89, 99, 110-1, 123n, 155, 168, death, 265-6; 276, 466n
Greece, HRH Princess Aspasia of (1896-1972), 87
Greece, HRH Princess Cécile of (1911-37), 25-6, 57
Greece, HRH Princess George of (1882-1962), 84, 122 & n
Greece, HRH Princess Irene of (1942-2026), 270
Griffin, Richard (Dick), 3
Griffiths, Dame Anne (1932-2017), 522
Grigg, John – see Altrincham
Grosvenor, Lady Tamara (b. 1979), 481
Grove, Valerie (b. 1946), 435
Guérin, Georgina &n, 68
Guinness, Lady Brigid (1920-95), 90 &n, 91

Habgood, Dr John (1927-2019), 435
Hadow, Sir Michael (1915-93), 251
Hague, William (Lord) (b. 1961), 465
Hahn, Kurt (1886-1974), 85, 216
Hailsham of St Marylebone, Viscount (1907-2001), 248, 254
Hajby, Kurt (1897-1965), 234n

Halifax, Countess of (Dorothy) (1885-1976), 63
Hall, John, 441
Hall, Sir Peter (1930-2017), 437n
Hamilton, 14th Duke of (1903-73), 312
Hamilton, Alan (1943-2013), 394
Hamilton, Lord Claud (1889-1975), 26
Hamilton, Rt Rev Eric (Dean of Windsor) (1890-1962), 70, 71n
Hamilton, Willie (1917-2000), 305 &n, 311
Hanbury-Williams, Gwladys (1889-1979), 71
Hanbury-Williams, Major-General Sir John (1859-1946), 71
Hankey, Sir Robert (Lord) (1905-96), 234
Hanover, HRH Prince Ernst August of (1914-87), 157
Hanover, HRH Prince Ernst of (b. 1954), 482
Hanover, HRH Prince George of (1915-2006), 6, 100, 123, 466
Hanover, HRH Princess George of (1914-2001), 6, 84, 100, 168, 266; death, 465-6, 466n, 495
Hardinge of Penshurst, 2nd Lord (Alec) (1894-1960), 37, 63, 69, 70
Hardinge of Penshurst, Lady (Helen) (1901-79), 19, 70
Hardinge, Hon Elizabeth (Lady Johnston) (1927-95), 63, 70 &n, 487
Hardinge, Hon George, 3rd Lord Hardinge of Penshurst (1921-97), 63, 69
Hardinge, Hon Winifred (Lady Murray) (1923-2019), 63, 70, 79
Hardman, Robert (b. 1965), 492, 520
Harewood, 6th Earl of (1882-1947), 12, 16, 125 &n
Harewood, 7th Earl of (George) (1923-2011), 1st wedding, 130-1; & *Gloriana*, 177-80; & death of the Princess Royal, 259-60, 259n-260n; divorce, 260, 337, 411;
& Golden Jubilee visit to Harewood, 473-5, 475n; mentioned, 9, 16, 23-4, 23n, 24, 25, 27, 47, 58, 60, 78, 125 &n, 296, 389, 473n
Harewood, Countess of (Marion) (later Mrs Jeremy Thorpe) (1926-2014), 130-1, 260
Harewood, Patricia, Countess of (1926-2018), 260, 389, 473-5, 473n, death, 475n
Harlech, Lady (Beatrice) (1891-1980), 104
Harlech, Pamela, Lady (b. 1934), 337
Harrington, Illtyd (1931-2015), 346
Harris, Dr C.R.S. (1896-1979), 105n-106n
Harris, Kenneth (1919-2005), 361
Harris, Marshal of the RAF Sir Arthur (1892-1984), 426
Harris, Robert (b. 1957), 418, 543,
Harris, Rolf (1930-2023), 484
Harris, Sir William (1883-1973), 58
Hartley, John, 136-8
Hartley, Sir Harold (1878-1972), 216
Hartnell, Sir Norman (1901-79), 43, 170-1, 170n, 238
Harvey, Lady (1893-1970), 123
Harvey, Major Thomas (1918-2001), 129-30
Harvey, Sir Oliver (Lord Harvey of Tasburgh) (1893-1968), 121, 123
Hasluck, Sir Paul (1905-93), 244n, 348n
Hastings-Bass, William (17th Earl of Huntingdon) (b. 1948), 406
Hastings, 21st Lord (1882-1956), 171, 174
Hattersley, Roy (Lord) (b. 1932), 465
Hawes, William, 549
Hawkins, Anne (later Anne Wall) (1928-2016), 43, 295-6, 297, 299, 328, 360n, 395
Hay, Lady Margaret (1918-75), 119, 239, 336
Hay, Sir Philip (1918-86), 119, 226, 262, 308 &n
Hayward, John, 144
Headlam, Sir Cuthbert (1876-1964), 51
Heald, Tim (1944-2016), 295, 296
Healey, Denis (Lord) (1917-2015), 433
Heath, Rt Hon Sir Edward (1916-2005), 283, as Prime Minister, 287, 305-6, 312, 323, 324, 327, 334, 368; 338, 361, 419-20, 420n
Heenan, John (Archbishop of Westminster) (1905-75), 151 &n
Heinz, H.J. (1908-87), 384
Heinz, Mrs Drue (1915-2018), 384, 483
Helena Victoria, HH Princess (1870-1948), 48
Henderson, Sir Nicholas (1919-2009),
Henniker-Major, John (8th Lord Henniker) (1916-2004), 99
Henry, Dr Leigh, 25
Henson, Bishop Herbert Hensley (1863-1947), 27
Henson, Leslie (1891-1957), 19
Heppell, Gill (b. 1963), 558
Herbert – see Pembroke
Herbert, Lady Patricia (later Viscountess Hambleden) (1904-94), 12
Herbert, Lady Penelope (1925-90), 93
Hern, Dick (1921-2002), 406 &n
Heseltine, Michael (Lord) (b. 1933), 414

INDEX

Heseltine, Sir William (b. 1930), 294, 296, 298-9, 303, 319, 320, 328, 341, 343, 357, 390, 392-3, 397-8, 399, 537
Hesse, HRH Prince Ludwig of (1908-68), 276
Hesse, HRH Prince Moritz of (1902-2013), 365 &n
Hesse, HRH The Grand Duchess of (Alice) (1843-78), 84
Hesse, HRH The Grand Duke of (Ernst Ludwig) (1868-1937), 84, 86
Hesse, HRH The Hereditary Grand Duke of (George Donatus) (1906-37), 57
Hesse, HSH Prince Karl of (1937-2022), 365, 375n, 493
Hesse, Landgraf of (Donatus) (b. 1966), 549
Hesse, Princess Victoria of – see Milford Haven
Hewett, Sir Stanley (1880-1954), 45
Hewitt, James (b. 1958), 396
Hewlett, Stephen (1958-2017), 441, 523 &n
Heycock, Lord (1905-90), 300
Hicks, David (1929-98), 215
Higgins, President Michael D. (b. 1941), 499-500, 514
Hillary, Sir Edmund (1919-2008), 244n, 268, 350, 440, 492 &n
Hindlip, 6th Lord (1940-2024), 485
Hitler, Adolf (1889-1945), 5, 46, 62, 64n, 130, 232, 234n, 270, 276
Hobbs, Major-General Sir Michael (b. 1937), 492
Hobson, Valerie (1917-98), 252 &n
Hobson, Valerie (Profumo) (1917-98),
Hocking, Jenny, 345
Hohenlöhe-Langenburg, HRH Princess Margarita of (1905-81), 66, 84, 155, 168, 276
Holden, Anthony (1947-2023), 403-4, 423
Holland, Sir Sidney (1893-1961), 188, 189-90, 514
Holmes, Sir Stephen (1896-1980), 193
Holt, Harold (1908-67), 284
Holyoake, Sir Keith (1904-83), 244n
Home of the Hirsel – see Douglas-Home
Home of the Hirsel, Lady (1909-90), 320
Home of the Hirsel, Lord (Alec) (1903-95), as Prime Minister, 253-5; 268, 273, 283, 312, 313, 319, 320
House, Ven Francis (1908-2004), 169
Howard-Johnston, Captain Charles (1903-96), 122
Howard-Johnston, Lady Alexandra (1907-97), 122

Howard, John (b. 1939), 462, 485
Howe, Geoffrey (Lord) (1926-2015), 399, 413-4
Humphrys, John (b. 1943), 511
Hunt-Davis, Brigadier Sir Miles (1938-2018), 521
Hunt, Peter, 526
Hurd, Douglas (Lord) (b. 1930), 414
Hurley, Hon David (b. 1953), 548
Hussein, President Saddam (1937-2006), 419
Hussey, Lady Susan (b. 1939), 382, 442, 485, 487
Hyde, Marion, Lady (1900-70), 142

Imperial, Louis-Napoléon, Prince (1856-79), 292
Indonesia, President Suharto of (1921-2008), 367-8
Indonesia, President Sukarno of (1901-70), 367
Ingham, Sir Bernard (1932-2023), 390
Iran, HIM Empress Farah Diba of (b. 1938), 229
Iran, HIM The Shah of (1919-80), 2, 229 &n, 230, 267, 268, 370 &n
Iraq, HM King Faisal II of (1935-58), 113, 164, 216, 231-2, 379n
Iraq, HRH the Crown Prince of (1913-58), 164, 231
Irvine of Lairg, Lord (b. 1940), 429
Irving, Clive, 519
Ismay, General Lord (1887-1965), 141n
Italy, President Alessandro Pertini of (1896-1990), 371
Italy, President Giorgio Napolitano of (1925-2023), 514
Italy, President Giovanni Gronchi of (1887-1978), 269
Italy, President Giuseppe Saragat of (1898-1988), 280
Italy, President Luigi Einaudi of (1874-1961), 133
Ivanov, Yevgeny (1926-94), 252

J., Jessie (b. 1988), 507
Jackson, General Sir Mike (1944-2024), 509
Jacques, Sandra (1922-2004), 96 &n
Jagger, Dr Walter (1871-1929), 18
Jagger, Sir Mick (b. 1943), 491
Jaipur, the Maharajah of (1912-70), 4
Janvrin, Robin (Lord) (b. 1946), 405, 447-8, 453, 456, 461, 481, 487, 508, 519
Japan, HIH Princess Chichibu of (1909-95), 308

Japan, HIM Emperor Akihito of (b. 1933), 405, 457-8, 457n, 505
Japan, HIM Emperor Hirohito of (1901-89), 46, 307-10, 308n, 310n, 323, 336, 405
Japan, HIM Empress Michiko of (b. 1934), 405, 505
Jarman, Major Norman, 145
Jebb, Sir Gladwyn & Lady – see Gladwyn, Lord & Lady
Jeffreys, Field Marshal the Lord (1878-1960), 156 &n
Jenkins of Hillhead, Lord (Roy) (1920-2003), 346
Jephson, Patrick, 429, 482
Jerram-Hunnable, Katie (b. 1963), 560
John Paul II, HH Pope (1920-2005), 371, 482
John XXIII, HH Pope (1881-1963), 269
John, HRH The Prince (1905-19), 478
John, Sir Elton (b. 1947), 451, 507 &n
Johnson, Paul (1928-2023), 431
Johnson, Rt Hon Boris (b. 1964), 523, as Prime Minister, 538-40, 542, 549, 551, 555, 561-2
Johnston, Lady (Natasha) (1914-84), 115&n, 116, 118
Johnston, Lt-Colonel Sir John (1922-2006), 70n, 358-9, 377, 486, 487
Johnston, Paul (1928-2023), 431
Johnston, Sir Charles (1912-86), 115-6, 115n, 118, 144-5, 257, 280, 301, 302, 376
Johnstone-Burt, Vice-Admiral Sir Tony (b. 1958), 543
Jones, Grace (b. 1948), 507
Jones, Sir Tom (b. 1940), 507
Jordan, HM King Hussein of (1935-99), 231, 279, 384
Jordan, HM Queen Noor of (b. 1951), 384
Jordan, Princess Muna of (b. 1941), 279-80
Judge, Robert, 25
Junor, Penny (b. 1949), 397

Kaunda, President Kenneth (1924-2021), 362-3
Kavanagh, General Sir Charles (1864-1950), 71
Keating, Paul (b. 1944), 345, 420-1, 420n, 433-4
Keatley, Patrick (b. 1971), 352n
Keeler Christine (1942-2017), 251-2
Kelantan, Sultan of (1897-1960), 168
Kelly, Angela (b. 1957), 471, 493
Kelly, Autumn (b. 1978), 493
Kelly, Sir Gerald (1879-1972), 76

Kennard – see Wernher
Kennedy, Joseph (1888-1969), 59
Kennedy, Jr., John F. (1960-99), 255n
Kennedy, Mrs John F. (Jackie) (1929-94), 255n, 269
Kennedy, President John F. (1917-63), 249, 254 &n, 269, 304
Kent, HRH Prince Michael of (b. 1942), 16, 78, 140, 166, marriage, 356-7; 384, 424, 475n, 513, 526, 549
Kent, HRH Princess Marina, Duchess of (1906-68), 16, 33, 41, 43, 44-6, 53, 63, 64 &n, 79, 89 &n, 91, 92, 94, 113 &n, 115, 118, 132, 140, 149, 176, 211, 226, 248, 260, 263, 264, 272 &n, 283, 301, 327n, death, 364, 449 & n; 374
Kent, HRH Princess Michael of (b. 1945), 356-7, 384 &n, 395, 424
Kent, HRH The Duchess of (Katharine) (1933-2025), 261, 283, 411
Kent, HRH The Duke of (Edward) (b. 1935), 16, 43, 44, 51, 60, 73, 140, 174, 211, 226, 250, 261, 272, 283, 332, 350, 356, 374, 411, 458, 511, 549, 551, 556-7, 563
Kent, HRH The Prince George, Duke of (1902-42), 9, 14, 16, 25, wedding, 33, 41; 43, 44-6, 63, 73, killed, 78; 364
Kenya, President Daniel Arap Moi of, 384
Kenyatta, President Jomo (1897-1978), 272
Kerr, Sir John (1914-91), 341-5, 341n, 348n
Khan, HH Aga (1877-1957), 177
Khan, President Ayub (1907-74), 267
Khashoggi, Adnan (1935-2017), 410
Khrushchev, Nikita (1894-1971), 207 &n, 231, 248, 251
Kilmuir, 1st Earl of (1900-67), 162, 185, 212
Kime, Robert (1946-2022), 472
Kingston, Tom (1978-2024), 537
Kinnock, Neil (Lord) (b. 1942), 421
Kipling, Rudyard (1865-1936), 45
Kissinger, Dr Henry (1923-2023), 370
Knatchbull, Hon Amanda (b. 1957), 373-4
Knatchbull, Hon Nicholas (1964-79), 365-6
Knatchbull, Hon Timothy (b. 1964), 365-6, 526
Knight, Andrew (b. 1939), 422n
Knight, Barbadee (later Lady Meyer) (1921-2006), 72
Knight, Clara ('Alah') (1879-1946), 20-1
Knox, Tim (b. 1962), 538
Köhler, President Horst (1943-2025), 480
Kotelawala, Sir John (1897-1980), 193
Kuenssberg, Laura (b. 1976), 217

INDEX

Lacey, Robert (b. 1944), 211, 282
Lambart, Lady Elizabeth (later Longman) (1924-2016), 72
Lamport, Sir Stephen (b. 1951), 442
Lang Lang (b. 1982), 507
Lang of Lambeth, 1st Lord (Cosmo Gordon), Archbishop of York, & of Canterbury (1864-1945), 18, 41, 49-50, 53, 55, 68, 75, 78, 138
Larkin, Philip (1922-85), 251
Lascelles, Andrea, 474
Lascelles, Charlotte, 474
Lascelles, Hon Benjamin (b. 1978), 474
Lascelles, Hon Gerald (1924-98), 9, 16, 23, 24, 25, 27, 47, 55, 125n, 260n, 279, 389, 411n, 463
Lascelles, Hon Mark (b. 1964), 259 &n, 260, 474
Lascelles, Hon Mrs Gerald (Elizabeth) (1924-2006), 260n
Lascelles, Lady Emily (b. 1975), 474
Lascelles, Martin (b. 1962), 260n
Lascelles, Mary (Mollie) – see Buccleuch
Lascelles, Mrs Mrs Gerald (Angela) (1919-2007), 260n
Lascelles, Rt Hon Sir Alan (Tommy) (1887-1981), 70, 76, 77, 100, 101, & South African trip, 104-9; 125, 126, 127, 128, 131, 134, 138, & King's death, 144, 145, on Elizabeth II as Queen, 154; 160, 165, 177, & Townsend saga, 184-5, 224; 185n, 202, 203, 292, 330n, 353
Lascelles, Viscount (later 8th Earl of Harewood) (b. 1950), 474
Laurence, Vice-Admiral Sir Timothy (b. 1955), 398, 410, 428, 566
Leadsom, Rt Hon Andrea (b. 1963), 523
Lee-Potter, Lynda (1935-2004), 397
Lees-Milne, James (1908-97), 181
Legh, Diana (later Kimberley & Colville) (1924-2000), 72
Legh, Sir Francis (1919-84), 72
Legh, Sir Piers (Joey), 72
Leicester, Countess of (Elizabeth) (1912-85), 293
Lennox, Annie (b. 1954), 507
Leonard, Dr Graham (1921-2010), 362
Levin, Bernard (1928-2004), 358
Lewin, Admiral of the Fleet Lord (1920-99), 6
Lewinsky, Monica (b. 1973), 458
Lewis, Simon (b. 1959), 453
Liberia, President William Tubman of (1895-1971), 250

Libya, HM King Idris I of (1890-1983), 197 &n
Lichfield, Edward Woods, Bishop of (1877-1953), 127
Liddell, Alice (later Hargraves) (1852-1934), 37 &n
Liechtenstein, Prince Franz Joseph II of (1906-89), 371
Liechtenstein, Princess Gina of (1921-89), 371
Lifar, Serge (1905-86), 235-6, 235n
Lindbergh, Captain Charles (1902-74), 24 &n
Lindsay, Hugh (1953-88), 396, 397 &n, 398
Linley, Viscount (David) (later 2nd Earl of Snowdon) (b. 1961), 258, 415, 459, 468, 509
Linley, Viscountess (Serena) (b. 1970), 509
Llewellyn, Sir Roderick (Roddy) (b. 1947), 336, 355, 504
Lloyd George, David (1ST Earl) (1863-1945), 212n, 300
Lloyd, Rt Hon Selwyn (later Lord Selwyn-Lloyd) (1904-78), 237
London, Bishop of (Richard Chartres) (b 1947), 490
Longford, 7th Earl of (1905-2001), 458, 466
Longford, Elizabeth, Countess of (1906-2002), 380, 466
Loughborough, Sheila, Lady (1895-1969), 11 &n
Louise, Princess – see Sweden
Lovelady, William, 548
Low, Valentine, 523n
Loyd, Zelda (later Dunlop) (1923-2014), 72
Luce, Lord (b. 1936), 478, 492
Ludlow, Robin (1931-2016), 320, 321, 328
Lumumba, President Patrice (1925-61), 331
Lutyens, Sir Edwin (1869-1944), 148n
Luxembourg, HRH Grand Duchess Josephine Charlotte of (1927-2005), 217n, 326
Luxembourg, HRH Grand Duke Jean of (1921-2019), 217n, 326
Luxembourg, HRH Princess Marie-Astrid of (b. 1954), 373 &n
Lynn, Dame Vera (1917-2020), 544
Lyttelton, Oliver – see Chandos

MacColl, René (1905-71), 56
Macdonald, Margaret (Bobo) (1904-93), 434
Macdonald, Rt Hon Ramsay (1866-1937), 32
Macdonald, Ruby, 145
Mackenzie-King, William (1874-1950), 79
Maclagan, Eric (1879-1951), 14
MacLeod, Colonel Roderick Robertson- (1919-89), 93 &n

MacMillan of MacMillan, Sir Gordon (1897-1986), 199-200
Macmillan, Lady Dorothy (1900-66), 245
Macmillan, Rt Hon Harold (1894-1986), 147, 148n, 149, 157-8, 179, as Prime Minister, 212-3, 245-54; 212n, 217, 220, 242, 252n, 254n, 262, 263, 282, 284n, 331, 379, 389
Magee, Matt, 559
Magnani, Anna (1908-73), 133
Maitlis, Emily (b. 1970), 533
Major, Rt Hon Sir John (b. 1943), 414, 421,422, 428, 443, 456, 519
Makarios, Archbishop (1913-77), 267
Malan, Dr D.F. (1874-1959), 141 &n
Mallaby, Sir Christopher (1936-2022), 471
Malley, Professor Bernard, 200
Malta, President Vincent Tabone of (1913-2012), 421-2
Malyam, Mama, 312
Mandela, President Nelson (1918-2013), 187n, 247, 440 &n, 441
Mandelson, Peter (Lord) (b. 1953), 496
Mann, Rt Rev Michael (Dean of Windsor) (1924-2011), 388-9, 390, 424
Mannakee, Barry (1947-87), 385-6, 394, 396
Margaret, Countess of Snowdon, HRH The Princess (1930-2002), bullied by the Lascelleses, 24; birth, 30, 31-2; character, 32-3, 37, 40; at Windsor Castle (1931), 34; with J.M. Barrie, 40; & George V Silver Jubilee, 42; & last illness of George V, 46; witnesses funeral procession of George V, 47; at Birkhall (1936), 50; reaction to Abdication, 52; at 1937 Coronation, 56-7; & lack of rapport with Queen Mary, 59; as a Brownie, 60; at Dartmouth (1939), 64-5; at Windsor Castle in wartime, 68-77, 79-80, 82; comments on Prince Philip's photo, 83; & South African tour (1947), 104, 106, 109; at Sandringham Xmas (148), 127; condemns Crawfie, 130; at Harewood wedding, 131; 21st birthday, 134; & King's last days, 140-1; bereft after King's death, 145, 155, 172; still at the Palace (1952), 162; at Coronation (1953), 172; at Ward ball, 176; living at Clarence House, 181-2; & resentment of her mother, 181-2; & Townsend affair (1953), 182-6; (1955), 222-5, 224n; & Rhodesia trip, 185; dropped as potential Regent, 185; at Duchess of Norfolk ball, 211; in Caribbean, 225; & wedding, 225-6, 246 &n; & marriage difficulties, 258; & separation (1976), 336-7; at Silver Jubilee, 350; & Roddy Llewellyn, 355; & divorce, 355-6; on Margaret Thatcher, 362; in trouble in Chicago, 367; & 50th birthday party, 374; on Charles & Camilla, 375; & dislike of Princess Michael, 384 &n; & 60th birthday, 413; cancels Mustique visit during Gulf War, 415; & Prince Charles's separation, 428; at Princess Anne's 2nd wedding, 428; & close relationship with the Queen, 429; & restoration of Windsor Castle, 431; on Paul Keating, 433-4; on Diana after separation, 435-6; at VE Day 50th anniversary, 439-40; At Balmoral after Diana's death, 447-8; & concern for the Queen, 450; at Sandringham (1997), 457; & decline in health, 458, 459-60, 467; & Prince Philip's 80th birthday, 467; death & funeral, 467-8; memorial service, 471; & 10th anniversary service, 504;
mentioned, 20, 22, 27, 103, 120n, 126, 128, 139, 160, 177, 188, 201, 209, 216, 233, 250, 283, 296, 308, 334n, 339, 353n, 372, 411, 421, 479, 480, 568
Marie Louise, HH Princess (1872-1956), 112, 127, 179, 215
Markle, Meghan (Duchess of Sussex) (b. 1981), 528-32, 537, 541, 543, 546, 555
Markle, Thomas (b. 1944), 529-30
Marten, Commander Toby (1918-98), 73
Marten, Sir Henry (1872-1948), 75, 77, 202, 210
Martin, Kingsley (1897-1969), 208
Martin, Paul (b.1938), 484
Mary, HM Queen (1867-1953), & birth of Princess Elizabeth, 11, ancestry, 13, character, 14, looks after Princess Elizabeth, 21, 25, 27, 33, 36, 42, rebukes Princess Elizabeth, 39, & dislike of Princess Victoria, 44; & death of George V, 46-7; stays at Royal Lodge (1936), 48-9; at Sandringham (Christmas 1936), 53, at 1937 Coronation, 55-7; & Princesses' education, 58-9, 63, 75; at Badminton in wartime, 68, 75; & Princess Elizabeth's marriage, 100, 112-3;80th birthday, 109-10; & Prince Charles, 131-2; &

INDEX

King's operation, 134; at Sandringham (1951), 140; & death of George VI, 144, 150; greets new Queen, 147; & Proclamation, 149; & Mountbatten name issue, 157; & Duke of Windsor feud, 159-60; death, 162, 164-5, 215, 227; memorial (1967), 263, 479; mentioned, 9n, 12, 16, 18, 29, 32n, 37, 52, 54, 62, 77, 78, 102, 103, 121, 130, 133, 172, 237, 238, 292, 301, 460
Mary, Princess – see Royal, Princess
Massey, Vincent (1887-1967), 149, 243-4
Massingberd, Hugh Montgomery (1946-2007), 406
Massingham, Hugh (1905-71), 297n
Matheson of Matheson, 8th Bt, Sir Alexander (b. 1954), 567
Maud, Princess – see Southesk
Maudling, Rt Hon Reginald (1917-79), 254
Mauriac, François (1885-1970), 238
Maurois, André (1885-1967), 238 &n
Maxwell Fyfe, David – see Kilmuir
Maxwell, Paul (1965-79), 365-6
May, Brian (b. 1947), 473
May, Theresa (Baroness) (b. 1956), 523, 525, 538
Mayall, Sir Lees (1915-92), 274
Mayer, Sir Robert (1879-1985), 58, 363
Maynard, Michelle, 548
McAleese, President Mary (b. 1951), 498-9
McCartney, Sir Paul (b. 1942), 507
McCreary, Alf, 297n
McDonald, Sir Trevor (b. 1939), 442, 458, 492 &n
McGrath, Sir Brian (1925-2016), 463, 521
McGregor of Durris, Lord (1921-97), 430
McGregor, Stuart, 304
McGuinness, Martin (1950-2017), 499, 500
McKinnon, Don (b. 1939), 491
Meakin, Jacqui, 469
Meighen, Arthur (1874-1960), 342 &n
Mendès France, Pierre (1907-82), 207
Menzies, Rt Hon Sir Robert (1894-1978), 164, 188, 191, 192 &n, 212, 257, 269, 270 &n, 282, 296, 344
Messel, Oliver (1904-78), 179, 225, 226
Metcalfe, Lady Alexandra (Baba) (1904-95), 365
Metcalfe, Major Edward (Fruity) (1887-1957), 227
Mexico, President Luis Echeverrria Àlvarez of (1922-2022), 327
Mexico, President Miguel de la Madrid of, 383
Meyer, Bt, Sir Anthony (1920-2004), 235, 413

Middleton, James (b. 1987), 498
Middleton, Michael (b. 1949) 498
Middleton, Mrs Michael (Carole) (b. 1955), 498
Middleton, Pippa (b. 1983), 498
Miéville, Sir Eric (1896-1971), 80
Milford Haven, 1st Marquess of (1854-1921), 14, 86n, 155
Milford Haven, 2nd Marquess of (George) (1892-1938), 65-6
Milford Haven, 3rd Marquess of (David) (1919-70), 96, 103n
Milford Haven, Dowager Marchioness of (Victoria) (1863-1950), 14, 57, 66, 84, 85, 86, 99
Milford Haven, Nada Marchioness of (1896-1963), 103n
Miliband, Rt Hon Ed (b. 1969), 516
Millar, Sir Oliver (1923-2007), 368-9
Millard, Sir Guy (1917-2013), 99 &n
Miller-Bakewell, Brigadier Archie (b. 1954), 522
Miller, Sir John (1919-2006), 274, 294 &n, 407, 487
Milnes-Gaskell, Lady Constance (1885-1964), 112 &n
Milošević, Slobodan (1941-2006), 5
Mirren, Dame Helen (b. 1945), 518, 519
Mirzoeff, Edward (b. 1936), 415, 416n, 419
Mitchell, Sir Philip (1890-1964), 143, 146
Mitchell, Very Rev Patrick (Dean of Windsor) (1930-2020), 442, 448
Mitchell, Vyrell B. (1929-72), 326
Mobutu, Bobi Ladawa (b. 1945), 333n
Mobutu, Marie-Antoinette (1941-77), 333n
Moch, Jules (1893-1985), 123
Monaco, HSH Prince Rainier III of (1923-2005), 482
Monaco, HSH Princess Grace of (1929-82), 329, 375
Monckton of Brenchley, Viscountess (1896-1982), 263
Montagu of Beaulieu, Belinda Lady (1932-2022), 460
Montalva, President Eduardo Frei (1911-82), 296n
Montefiore, Bishop Hugh (1920-2005), 362
Montgomery of Alamein, Field Marshal 1st Viscount (1887-1976), 120, 151, 282, 283, 338 &n
Moore of Etchingham, Lord (Charles) (b. 1956), 393, 428
Moore of Wolvercote, Lord (Philip) (1921-2009), 293, 354, 463

Moore, Captain Sir Tom (1920-2021), 544
Moore, General Sir Rodney (1905-85), 4
Moran, 1st Lord (1882-1977), 134, 161, 202, 203
Morgan, Peter (b. 1963), 519
Morgan, Piers (b. 1965), 463, 479
Morley, Sir Godfrey (1909-87), 160, 264
Mornington, Lord (b. 1978), 431-2
Morocco, HM King Hassan of (1929-99), 371-2
Morrah, Dermot (1896-1974), 105-7, 105n-106n, 109, 120, 126, 128-9, 297n, 298
Morrison of Lambeth, Lord (1888-1965), 262
Morrison, Hon (Dame) Mary, 487
Morshead, Lady (Paquita), 71
Morshead, Mary, 72
Morshead, Sir Owen (1893-1977), 71, 75
Morton, Andrew (b. 1953), 392, 418, 422-3, 422n, 423n, 424, 452
Moses, Robert (1888-1981), 243
Mountbatten of Burma, 1st Earl (1900-79), at Dartmouth, 65-6; steers Prince Philip to navy, 86; in SE Asia, 91; machinates for Prince Philip, 98, 99n, 101; in Malta, 131, 198; & Mountbatten as family name, 156-8, 246 &n, 256 &n, 257n; at Coronation, 168, 172; & Suez, 211, & Edwina's death, 215; & Prince Charles education, 257; interfering, 264-5; & Rhodesia, 277; 70th birthday, 306; snubs Emperor Hirohito, 309-10; & Duchess of Windsor, 325-6; & Princess Anne's wedding, 330; at Silver Jubilee, 350, 352; & Prince Michael's marriage, 356-7; assassinated, 364-6, 364n, 379n, 366n, 499; advice to Prince Charles, 372-3, 436, 529; mentioned, 85, 89, 103 &n, 110, 115, 118, 125, 155, 283, 297, 298, 314, 331, 335, 367 &n, 374, 388, 449
Mountbatten of Burma, 3rd Earl of (Norton) (b. 1947), 367, 382
Mountbatten of Burma, Countess (Edwina) (1901-60), 84, 85, 99, 113, 115, 118, 125, 131, 180, 198, death, 215
Mountbatten of Burma, Countess (Patricia) (1924-2017), 103, 366, 367 &n, 499, 500, 526
Mountbatten of Burma, Countess (Penelope) (b. 1953), 367, 442, 527, 539, 549, 550
Mountbatten-Windsor, Archie (b. 2019), 531
Mountbatten-Windsor, Lilibet (b. 2021), 557 &n

Mountbatten, Lady Pamela (later Hicks) (b. 1929), 103, 215, 549
Mowatt, Marina (b. 1966), 460
Mowbray, Segrave and Stourton, 25th Lord (1895-1965), 174 &n
Mozzi, Edoardo (b. 1983), 544
Mugabe, Robert (1924-2019), 363, 482
Muggeridge, Malcolm (1903-90), 208-10, 224n, 294, 305
Muldoon, Robert ('Piggy') (1921-92), 362
Mulele, Pierre (1929-68), 331-2
Mulholland, Hon Mrs John (Olivia) (1902-85), 132
Mulroney, Brian (1939-2024), 401
Murdoch, Rupert (b. 1931), 5, 395, 430
Murray, Sir Anthony (1921-2002), 79
Mussolini, Benito (1883-1945), 46
Mutesa II, Sir Edward (Kabaka) (1924-69), 196, 312n
Muzorewa, Bishop Abel (1925-2010), 363

Napier, Elma (1892-1985), 278
Nasser, President Gamel Abdul (1918-70), 211
Nehru, Jawaharlal (1899-1964), 562
Neil, Andrew (b. 1949), 391-2, 409
Nepal, HM King Birendra of (1945-2001), 341n
Nepal, HM King Mahendra of (1920-72), 267
Netherlands, HM Queen Beatrix of the (b. 1938), 370, 479
Netherlands, HM Queen Juliana of the (1909-2004), 113 & n, 163, 234-5, 282, 294, 307, 315, 370
Netherlands, HRH Prince Bernhard of the (1911-2004), 116, 163, 234
Netherlands, HRH Prince Claus of the (1926-2002), 217
Nevill, Lady Rupert (1925-2023), 296
Newley, Anthony (1931-99), 252n, 518
Nicholson, Max (1904-2003), 216, 352
Nicolson, Hon Sir Harold (1886-1968), 64, 230
Nigeria, President Yakubu Gowon of (b. 1934), 327
Nightingale, Mary (b. 1963), 563n
Nixon, President Richard M. (1913-94), 243, 307, 370
Nkomo, Joshua (1917-99), 362
Nkrumah, President Kwame (1909-72), 211, 226, 247-9
Norfolk, 16th Duke of (Bernard) (1906-75), 58, 150, 163, 166, 167, 170, 177, 204,

INDEX

211, 282n, 286-7, 291, 292, 300, 301, 501
Norfolk, 17th Duke of (Miles) (1915-2002), 461, 564
Norfolk, Lavinia Duchess of (1916-95), 171, 204, 211, 292, 414
Norrie, Lt-General the Lord (Willoughby) (1893-1977), 190, 201n
Northumberland, 10th Duke of (1914-88), 262
Northumberland, Duchess of (Elizabeth) (1922-2012), 262
Norway, HM King Haakon of (1872-1957), 47, 133, 233
Norway, HM King Harald V of (b. 1937), 479
Norway, HM King Olav V of (1903-91), 27n, 179, 282, 379
Norway, HM Queen Maud of (1869-1938), 47, 233
Norwich, 2nd Viscount (John Julius) (1929-2018), 446
Nureyev, Rudolf (1938-93), 350

O'Dea, Sir Patrick (1918-2010), 303
O'Dwyer, Lt-Colonel Sean (b. 1941), 396
O'Mara, Michael, 422
O'Toole, Peter (1932-2013), 394
Obama, Michele (b. 1964), 494, 520
Obama, President Barack, 269n (b. 1961), 494, 520
Obermeyer, Nesta (1893-1984), 22
Obote, Milton (1925-2005), 197n, 352n
Ogilvy, James (b. 1964), 262, 480
Ogilvy, Marina (b. 1966), 262, 412
Ogilvy, Rt Hon Sir Angus (1928-2004), 261, 296, 412, 424, 442, 480
Ollard, Canon Sidney (1875-1949), 71
Ormsby-Gore - see Harlech
Orr, James (1917-2008), 220-1, 220n, 303, 336, 367
Osborne, John (1929-94), 418
Osborne, Rt Hon George (b. 1971), 523
Oswald, Lady Angela (b. 1938), 6, 549 &n
Oswald, Sir Michael (1934-2021), 6, 448, 549 &n
Other-Gee, Sue (1916-80), 96 &n, 112
Ovenden, Canon John, 448
Owen, David (Lord) (b. 1938), 357-8, 359
Owen, H., 60
Owen, Nick (b. 1947), 455

Paget, Lady Caroline - see Duff
Paget, Lady Elizabeth - see von Hofmannsthal
Pakenham, Lady Antonia - see Fraser

Palmer-Tomkinson, Patricia, 397
Palmer, General Sir Patrick (1933-99), 447n
Pandit, Madame Vijaya Lakshmi (1900-90), 267, 366
Papagos, Alexandros (1883-1955), 270
Paravicini, Lisa - see Glendevon
Parker Bowles, Brigadier Andrew (b.1939), 363, 372, 374, 381, 396, 485, 494, 495
Parker of Minsmere, Lord (b. 1962), 548, 568
Parker, Commander Michael (1920-2001), 95, 119, 131, 144, 146, 192, 218, 219, 220, 350,
Parker, Major Sir Michael (1941-22), 350, 466
Parker, Suzy (1932-2003), 278n
Parkinson, Sir Michael (1935-2023), 304, 330
Parris, Matthew (b. 1949), 495
Patten, Chris (Lord) (b. 1944), 443
Patterson, Hunter (1882-1963), 218
Paul VI, HH Pope (1897-1978), 357
Paul, Henri (1956-97), 446, 490
Paul, Maury (1890-1942), 88 &n
Pears, Sir Peter (1910-86), 81, 131, 179, 180n, 181
Pearson, Lester (1897-1972), 127
Peat, Sir Michael (b. 1949), 432, 473, 477, 484
Peel, 3rd Earl (b. 1947), 548
Peet, PC Steven, 386
Pembroke, 16th Earl of (1906-69), 92 &n, 225
Pembroke, Countess of (Mary) (1903-95), 92 &n
Pendry, Terry (b. 1950), 408, 521, 543, 559, 567
Penn, Lady (Prudence) (1926-2023), 486, 517, 536, 560
Penn, Sir Arthur (1886-1960), 101, 145, 148n, 149-50, 153, 181n
Perkins, Canon Jocelyn (1870-1962), 54
Pethick-Lawrence, Frederick (1871-1961), 58 &n
Philip, Prince - see Edinburgh
Philipps, Lady Joan (1900-2001), 72 & n
Philipps, Sir Grismond (1898-1967), 72 &n, 90
Phillips, Captain Mark (b. 1948), 256, 328-31, 334, 409-11, 411n, 421
Phillips, Harold (Bunny) (1909-80), 99
Phillips, Isla (b. 2012), 493
Phillips, Major Peter (1920-98), 329, 410 &n
Phillips, Mrs Peter (Anne) (1926-88), 329, 410n
Phillips, Nicholas (1947-91), 401 &n
Phillips, Peter (b. 1977), 354, 493, 511

Phillips, Savannah (b. 2010), 493
Pilcher, Lady (Delia) (1916-2003), 309
Pilcher, Sir John (1912-90), 308-9
Pimlott, Ben (1945-2004), 254, 393n
Pinsent, Sir Matthew (b. 1970), 506
Piper, John (1903-92), 179
Pipinelis, Panagiotis (1899-1970), 271n
Pius IX, HH Pope (1876-1958), 133
Player, Lesley, 430
Plomer, William (1903-73), 178-9
Plumer, Field Marshal Lord (1857-1932), 19
Plunket, 7th Lord (Patrick) (1923-75), 293-4, 320, 336
Poignand, Beryl – see Ring, Anne
Poklewska, Zoia (1896-1976), 115
Poland, President Lech Wałęsa of (b. 1943), 415-6, 415n
Pollard, Lt-General Sir Reginald (1903-78), 304
Pompidou, Claude (1912-2007), 320, 322n, 323
Pompidou, President Georges (1911-74), 316, 319-21, 322n, 323
Ponsonby, Sir Frederick (later Lord Sysonby) (1867-1935), 32
Pope-Hennessy, James (1916-74), 15, 44, 100, 164, 220, 227n, 290, 292
Portal of Hungerford, Marshal of the RAF Viscount (1893-1971), 120, 171, 281-2
Poulenc, Francis (1899-1963), 238
Powell, Rt Hon Enoch (1912-98), 392
Powers, Matthew, 548
Prescott, John (Lord) (1938-2024), 453, 466
Profumo, John (1915-2016), 251-3, 295
Profumo, Philip (1919-86), 72
Prussia, HRH Prince Frederick of (1911-66), 90n
Pryce-Jones, Alan (1908-2000), 258
Putin, President Vladimir (b. 1952), 479

Qasim, Brigadier Abdul-Karim (1914-63), 231

Rabuka, Lt-Colonel Sitiveni (b. 1948), 399-400
Radziwill, Prince Stanislas (1914-76), 269
Radziwill, Princess Lee (1933-2019), 269
Ragland, Doria (b. 1956), 530, 531
Ramphal, Sir Shridath (Sonny) (1928-2024), 351-2, 362-3, 399
Ramsay of Mar, Captain Alexander (1919-2000), 27, 58
Ramsay, Admiral Hon Sir Alexander (1881-1972), 326n
Ramsay, Lady Patricia (1886-1974), 326n

Ramsey of Canterbury, Lord (Michael), Archbishop of Canterbury (1904-88), 329-30, 330n
Randolph, Nancy, 88
Rankin, Lady Jean (1905-2001), 183
Reagan, Nancy, 383, 393
Reagan, President Ronald, 383
Redgrave, Sir Steven (b. 1962), 506
Redhead, Brian (1929-94), 430n
Reed, Jr, Joseph Verner (Joe) (1937-2016), 416
Rees-Mogg, Sir Jacob (b. 1969), 539
Rees-Williams, Jonathan (b. 1949), 549
Renton, Major Leslie (1868-1947), 23
Reynolds, Frank, 31
Reynolds, Martin (b. 1969), 542
Rhodes, Hon Mrs (Margaret) (1925-2016), 50, 469, 479, 523
Rhys-Jones, Sophie – see Wessex
Richard, Sir Cliff (b. 1940), 507
Richards, Sir Charles (b. 1953), 562
Richards, Sir Gordon (1904-86), 177
Ridley, 3rd Viscount (1902-64), 148n
Ridley, Ursula, Viscountess (1904-67), 148n
Ring, Anne (Beryl Poingand) (1887-1965), 13&n,
Rippon, Angela (b. 1944), 376
Roberts, Monty (b. 1935), 407-8, 408n
Roberts, Sir Frank (1907-98), 232, 275-6
Robertson, Sir James (1899-1983), 216-7, 240-1, 504
Robey, George (1869-1954), 40n,
Rocco, Fiametta, 216, 218
Rockefeller, Nelson (1908-79), 243
Romania, HM King Carol II of (1893-1953), 62
Romania, HM King Michael I of (1921-2017), 62, 505
Romania, HM Queen Helen of (1896-1982), 98, 113
Romsey – see Mountbatten
Roosevelt, Alice (later Longworth) (1884-1980), 373
Roosevelt, Mrs Franklin D. (Eleanor) (1884-1962), 79-80, 127-8
Roscoe, Dame Ingrid (1944-2020), 475n
Rose, General Sir Michael (b. 1940), 5
Rose, Kenneth (1924-2014), 46n, 148n, 413
Rosebery, 6th Earl of (1882-1974), 177
Ross, Lt-Colonel Sir Malcolm (1943-2019), 448 &n, 449, 479n, 484, 541
Rosse, Anne Countess of (1902-92), 225, 337
Rothschild, Baron Guy de (1909-2007), 336

INDEX

Royal, HRH The Princess - see Anne, Princess
Royal, HRH The Princess (Mary) (1897-1965), 9 &n, 12, character, 16; 109, 125 &n, 130, 237, death, 259; 400
Runcie, Lord (Robert), Archbishop of Canterbury (1921-2000), 377
Russell, Audrey (1906-89), 173, 249
Russell, Earl (Bertrand) (1871-1970), 271
Russell, Sir John (1914-84), 274-5
Russia, HI & RH Grand Duchess Elisabeth of (1864-1918), 84, 89, 265, 437
Russia, HIM Tsar Nicholas II of (1868-1918), 84, 379, 437
Russia, HIM Tsarina Alexandra of (1872-1918), 84, 89, 379
Russia, President Boris Yeltsin of (1931-2007), 5, 437-8, 438n
Russia, President Mikhail Gorbachev of (1931-2022), 437
Ruthven, Pamela, Viscountess (1910-2006), 71-2
Rutland, 10th Duke of (1919-99), 93-4, 94n, 174n

Salisbury, 5th Marquess of (Bobbety) (1893-1972), 124n, 150n, 163, 171, 193, 194, 199, 202, 203-4, 212, 213, 245
Salisbury, 6th Marquess of (1916-2003), 72, 83, 505
Salisbury, 7th Marquess of (b. 1946), 505
Salisbury, Marchioness of (Betty) (1897-1982), 150n, 155, 180, 230
Salisbury, Marchioness of (Mollie) (1922-2016), 82
Salmond, Alex (1954-2024), 539
Sandys, Duncan (Lord) (1908-87), 248
Sarawak, Ranee of (Sylvia) (1885-1971), 96
Sargent, Sir Malcolm (1895-1967), 58
Sarkozy, President Nicolas (b. 1955), 491
Sassoon, Sir Philip (1888-1939), 48, 60
Sassoon, Sir Victor (1881-1961), 176n
Saudi Arabia, HM King Abdullah of (1924-2015), 460
Saudi Arabia, HM King Faisal of (1906-75), 379
Saudi Arabia, HM King Khalid of (1913-82), 360
Scales, Prunella (1932-2025), 518 &n
Scarbrough, 11th Earl of (1896-1969), 292
Scarbrough, Countess of (Katharine) (1899-1979), 230
Schmidt, Chancellor Helmut (1918-2015), 360
Scholes, Gordon (1931-2018), 343

Schwarzkopf, General Norman (1934-2012), 416
Scoones, Sir Geoffry (1893-1975), 189
Scott, Brough (b. 1942), 406
Scott, Selina (b. 1951), 409
Scott, Sir Kenneth (1931-2018), 398, 419
Secombe, Sir Harry (1921-2001), 301
Sellers, Peter (1928-80), 252n, 518
Senanayake, Dudley (1911-73), 193
Sénard, Jacques (1919-2020), 319
Serato, Massimo (1917-89), 133
Severn, James Viscount (b. 2007), 472, 491
Sewell, Brian (1931-2015), 368
Seymour – see Hay
Shand Kydd, Hon Frances (formerly Roche) (1936-2004), 374
Shattock, Lady (d. 1984), 387
Shaw, Ben, 174
Shaw, George Bernard (1856-1950), 49
Shaw, Sandie (b. 1947), 300
Shea, Michael (1938-2009), 373, 383, 390-3, 393n, 394-5, 405
Shew, Betty Spencer (1915-71), 100 &n, 128
Shore, Rt Hon Peter (Lord) (1924-2001), 324
Short, Rt Hon Clare (b. 1946), 453
Shuckburgh, Sir Evelyn (1909-94), 147
Shuttleworth, 5th Lord (b. 1948), 520
Simmons, Simone (b. 1955), 424n
Simonds, 1st Viscount (1881-1971), 158, 204
Simpson, Dawn (later Fahey) (1929-84), 72 &n
Simpson, Ernest (1897-1958), 50
Simpson, Wallis – see Windsor
Simson, Sir Henry (1872-1932), 10 &n, 31
Sinatra, Frank (1915-98), 383
Sinclair, Sir Archibald – see Thurso
Slim, Field Marshal 1st Viscount (1891-1970), 164, 191, 201n, 244
Slim, Viscountess (Aileen) (1901-93), 164, 191
Smith, Charles, 367
Smith, Graham (b. 1974), 497n
Smith, Horace (1881-1975), 79 &n
Smith, Ian (1919-2007), 277
Smith, Sir David (1933-2022), 343, 345
Smuts, Field Marshal Jan (1870-1950), 55, 79, 89n, 104-6, 112
Snowdon – see Margaret, Princess
Snowdon, 1st Earl of (1930-2017), 225-6, 246 &n, 258, 283, 288, 296, 300, 301n, 302, 336-7, 355, 356, 436, 468
Snowdon, Lucy, Countess of (b. 1941), 337, 356
Soames, Lady (Mary) (1922-2014), 282n
Soames, Lord (Christopher) (1920-87), 316-7, 319-24, 363

653

Soulbury, 1st Viscount (1887-1971), 163, 193-4, 201n
South Africa, President F.W. de Klerk of (1936-2021), 435
Southesk, 11th Earl of (1893-1992), 421
Southesk, Countess of (Maud) (1893-1945), 421
Spain, General Francisco Franco, Caudillo of (1892-1975), 198-9, 200, 336, 403
Spain, HM King Juan Carlos I of (b. 1938), 336, 377, 389, 403, 432
Spain, HM Queen Sofia of (b. 1938), 377, 389, 505
Spain, HM Queen Victoria Eugenie of (Ena) (1887-1969), 113, 379n
Spanton, Tim (b. 1957), 485
Spencer, 7th Earl (1892-1975), 198, 374
Spencer, 8th Earl (1924-1992), 198, 374, 377, 421
Spencer, 9th Earl (b. 1964), 451, 479, 490
Spencer, Countess (Raine) (1929-2016), 374, 423n, 445
Spencer, Lady Sarah (Later McCorquodale) (b. 1955), 373 &n, 374
Spry, Constance (1886-1960), 179
St Laurent, Louis (1882-1973), 136, 244
Stack, Air Chief Marshal Sir Neville (1919-94), 308n
Stack, Robert (1919-2003), 89
Stamfordham, 1st Lord (1849-1931), 16, 292
Stancer, Rosie (b. 1960), 513
Stark, Koo (b. 1956), 383
Steinheil, Marguerite (1869-1954), 284n
Sterling of Plaistow, Lord (Jeffrey) (b. 1934), 347, 473, 505
Stevens, Janie (1937-2022), 459
Stevens, Marti (b. 1933), 270 & n
Stewart, Alastair (b. 1952), 495
Stewart, Rt Hon Michael (Lord Stewart of Fulham) (1906-90), 141n
Stoneman, William H., 183
Stopford, Brigadier James, 565
Stoute, Sir Michael (b. 1945), 560
Strachey, Lady Mary (later Gore) (1920-2000), 119
Strathmore, 14th Earl of (1855-1944), 9, 10n, 16-7, 20, 33, 58, 59, death, 92
Strathmore, Countess of (1862-1938), 9, 10n, 12, 17, 20, 21, 29, 33, 51, 52n, death 59-60, 61
Streisand, Barbra (b. 1942), 536
Strong, Sir Roy (b. 1935), 444
Stuart of Findhorn, 1st Viscount (James) (1897-1971), 12, 208 &n

Sturgeon, Rt Hon Nicola (b. 1970), 517, 539, 560
Suchet, John (b. 1944), 440
Sudan, President Ferik Ibrahim Abboud of (1900-83), 275
Suharto, Madame Siti Hartinah (1923-96), 367-8
Sunak, Rt Hon Rishi (b. 1980), 561
Sweden, HM King Carl XVI Gustaf of (b. 1946), 336, 364, 567
Sweden, HM King Gustaf V of (1858-1950), 234 &n
Sweden, HM King Gustaf VI Adolf of (1882-1973), 228, 230, 233-4, 314
Sweden, HM King Oscar II of (1829-1907), 234n
Sweden, HM Queen Louise of (1889-1965), 5, 168, 230, 233-4
Sweden, HM Queen Silvia of (b. 1943), 364, 374
Sweden, HRH Prince Bertil of (1912-97), 217n
Swinton, 1st Earl of (1884-1972), 204
Syers, Sir Cecil (1903-81), 193, 195
Symonds, Carrie (b. 1988), 539

Talbot, Godfrey (1908-2000), 82
Tallon, William (1935-2007), 466, 485
Tannar, Hubert (1896-1948), 76
Tanner, Lawrence (1890-1979), 175
Tattersall, Dr Robin (b. 1930), 278 &n
Taylor, Noreen, 393
Taylor, Sir Cyril (1935-2018), 497
Taylor, Timothy (b. 1963), 425
Te Kanawa, Dame Kiri (b. 1944), 376, 485
Tebbit, Margaret (Lady) (1934-2020), 387
Tebbit, Norman (Lord) (1931-2025), 387
Teck, HH The Duke of (1837-1900), 13
Teck, HRH Princess Mary Adelaide, Duchess of (1833-97), 13
Teitgen, Pierre-Henri (1908-97), 123
Templer, Field Marshal Sir Gerald (1898-1979), 364 &n
Tennant, Hon Colin – see Glenconner, Lord
Tensing, Norgay (1914-86), 268
Thailand, HM King Bhumibol of (1927-2016), 1, 317n, 558
Thatcher, Baroness (Margaret) (1925-2013), 212n, 277, 306, 311; as Prime Minister, 361-3, 369, 381n, 400, 404; & Anthony Blunt, 368; & Falklands, 382-3; & Brighton Bomb, 387; & Shea affair, 390-3; & fall from power, 413-4; death,

INDEX

Thatcher, Bt, Sir Denis (1915-2003), 361, 414, 510; mentioned, 389, 394, 402, 428, 437, 440, 454n, 494, 497

Thomas, J.H. (1874-1949), 25

Thompson, Cort, 137

Thompson, Major W.L. (Tommy) (1915-2006), 6

Thorpe, Jeremy (1929-2014), 311, 334

Tindall, Mike (b. 1978), 501

Tindall, Zara (b. 1981), 410, 501

Titchmarsh, Alan (b. 1949), 500

Tito, President Josip Broz (1892-1980), 207

Toms, Carl (1927-99), 301

Tonga, HM King Tāufa 'āhau Tupou IV of (1918-2006), 5

Tonga, HM Queen Salote of (1900-65), 168, 189

Tonkin, Heather (b. 1950), 411n

Towers, Frances (1885-1948), 77 &n

Townend, Colonel H. Stuart (1909-2002), 221

Townsend, Group Captain Peter (1914-95), 73, 104, 126, & Princess Margaret, 182-6, 207, 209, 223-5; his memoirs, 355; 389, 428

Townsend, Marie-Luce (1939-95), 225, 492

Townsend, Mrs Peter (Rosemary) (1921-2004), 183

Townsend, Sue (1946-2014), 518

Toynbee, Polly (b. 1946), 447

Trelford, Donald (1937-2023), 409-10

Trestrail, Commander Michael, 380, 381 &n

Trevor-Roper, Hugh (Lord Dacre of Glenton) (1914-2003), 134

Troubridge, Thomas (1939-2015), 356

Trudeau, Justin (b. 1971), 517, 548

Trudeau, Margaret (b. 1948), 307

Trudeau, Pierre (1919-2000), 307, 328, 340, 359, 517

Truman, President Harry S. (1884-1972), 138

Trump, President Donald (b. 1946), 537-8

Truss, Rt Hon Liz (b. 1975), 561, 562

Tryon, Brigadier 2nd Lord (1906-76), 264

Tunisia, President Habib Bourguiba of (1903-2000), 371

Turnbull, Malcolm (b. 1954), 515

Tutt, Julian, 443

Utter, John (1905-80), 322n, 325, 326

Vacani, Madame Marguerite (1885-1955), 40, 72, 73

van Cutsem, Edward (b. 1973), 481

van Cutsem, Mrs Emilie, 481n

van der Kemp, Gérald (1912-2001), 321

van der Post, Sir Laurens (1906-96), 378, 382

van der Woude, Gerrit (1920-99), 93

van Duzer, Winifred (d. 1951), 93

Vaughan Williams, Sir Ralph (1872-1958), 180

Vaughan-Thomas, Wynford (1908-87), 120n

Venables, Terry (1943-2023), 473, 475

Vervoerd, Hendrik (1901-66), 247

Vickers, Arthur (b. 1999), 507n

Victoria, HM Queen (1819-1901), 1, 2, 13-14, 24, 25, 37n, 71, 81, 84, 121, 154, 156, 256, 346, 400, 419, 517, 520, 548

Victoria, HRH The Princess (1868-1935), 41, death, 44, 45, 47

Viney, Graham, 107

Vitiello, Cory (b. 1979), 528

von der Leyen, Ursula (b. 1958), 545

Von Reibnitz, Baron Günther (1894-1983), 356

Votichenko, Sacha (1888-1971), 65

Wade, Judy (1939-2020), 438

Wagner, Sir Anthony (1908-95), 300

Wakeham, Anne (1938-84), 386-7

Wakeham, John (Lord) (b. 1932), 386-7

Wales, Diana, Princess of (1961-97), early relationship with Prince Charles, 373-5, engagement, 375-6; wedding, 377; honeymoon, 377-8; & press reaction to, 378, 382; & birth of Prince William, 382; & birth of Prince Harry, 385; & affair with Mannakee, 385-6; & Queen's opinion of, 388; & Sarah Ferguson, 388-9, 394, 395-6, 429; & Hewitt affair, 396; & AIDS work, 396-7; & Lindsay skiing tragedy, 397-8; & crumbling marriage, 402, 409, 411, 421; upset by Holden book, 403; & death of her father, 421; & Andrew Morton book, 422-4, 423n; & Squidgygate tape, 426; & separation from Prince Charles, 427-8; & feeding the press, 430; steps down from public life, 432; Princess Margaret on, 435-6; & *Panorama* interview, 440-1; & divorce, 441; & early 1997 engagements, 442; & sale of her dresses, 444; & Dodi Fayed affair, 444-5; & death in Paris, 445-6; & week of grieving, 446-52, 450n; & funeral, 450-1; & aftermath of the tragedy, 453-6, 482, 493; & Burrell's involvement, 475-7;

Wales, Diana, Princess of (contd)
& memorial fountain, 479; & 10th anniversary of her death, 489-90; & inquest, 490; mentioned, 198, 256, 264n, 392, 394, 405, 411, 425, 458, 467, 471, 481 &n, 484, 488, 498, 512, 518

Wales, HRH The Prince of (b. 1948), birth, 125, 126; at Clarence House, 130; left at Sandringham, 131-2, & birth of Princess Anne, 132, at Balmoral, 132-3; & parents return from Canada (1951), 139 &n; & death of George VI, 140-1, 149-50; at 1953 Coronation, 174; reunited with parents in Libya (1954), 197; in Gibraltar, 200; at school, 221, 257; & Mountbatten name, 256; at Cambridge, 257; installed as Knight of the Garter, 257; relationship with Mountbatten, 265, 329, 364; at Churchill funeral, 281; & Holt funeral in Australia, 284-5; & cherry brandy incident, 295 &n; & Andrew Duncan, 296; emerges into public life, 297-8; & *Royal Family* film, 298-9; & the Investiture, 300-2; in New Zealand & Australia (1970), 303-5; in House of Lords, 306; in Washington, 307; in Japan, 308; & state visit to France (1972), 322-3; & Duke of Windsor's funeral, 325; & shock at Princess Anne's engagement, 329; & Princess Anne kidnap attempt, 330-1; in the Royal Navy, 340, 372; & Silver Jubilee, 347, 349; & impending marriage, 355, 360 &n, 372; in Rhodesia, 363; & murder of Mountbatten, 366-7; his popularity, 370; & Camilla Parker Bowles, 372-5; & Diana Spencer engagement, 374-6; & wedding, 377, on honeymoon, 377-8; & move to Kensington Palace, 378; overshadowed by Diana, 382 &n; & birth of Prince William, 382: & birth of Prince Harry, 385; & Diana's infidelity, 386, 396; worn down, 388; unhappiness, 396; & Lindsay skiing tragedy, 397-8; in Northern Irelands, 402; 40th birthday (1988), 403-4; at Lockerbie, 404-5; & his frustration, 409, 421, 425; & later Camilla relationship, 421, 423, 435, 441-4, 458, 481 &n; & Morton book, 422-4; & separation from Diana, 427-8, 435; & the press, 429; & taped conversation with Camilla, 430; & polo accident (1993), 432; & Dimbleby book & film, 436; & divorce, 441; in Hong Kong, 443; & death of Diana, 447, 449, 450n, 451; & his children at Christmas, 457; refuses to attend Chinese banquet, 461; his suitability as future king questioned, 463; & death of Princess Margaret, 467; & death of the Queen Mother, 469-70; Moves into Clarence House & Birkhall, 472; & Burrell case, 476-7; at Diana memorial in Hyde Park, 479.

Wedding to Camilla, 481-3; & bad vibes at Clarence House, 485; insults Nicholas Witchell, 486; & Diana anniversary, 489-90; & Commonwealth, 491, 517, 525, 552; & 60th birthday, 493-4; & Diamond Jubilee speech, 507; takes more prominent role, 508, 510, 511, 526, 527, 540, 550; & fictional portrayals, 518-9; & illness of parents (2016), 524; & Geidt dismissal, 525; & Prince Harry marriage, 529-30; & reluctance re Prince Andrew, 534; & 70th birthday, 536; catches COVID, 543; takes over Sandringham, 545; visits Prince Philip in hospital (2021), 546; & death of Prince Philip, 547; in Barbados, 552; & more prominent role in 2022, 554, 556-8; & the Queen's death, 563; as King 564; mounts vigil in Scotland, 566; at the Queen's committal, 568; mentioned, 5, 9, 31n, 157, 231, 233, 240, 266, 272, 278, 293, 294, 296, 327, 334, 341, 357, 378n, 388, 389, 394, 396, 411, 417, 429, 439, 442, 444, 512, 517n, 521, 526, 539, 541, 552

Walker, Jim (b. 1967), 503
Wall, Anne – see Hawkins
Wallace, Anna, 373 &n
Wallis, Mary Levena (1839-1939), 65
Warburg, S.G. (1902-82), 232
Ward, Dr Stephen (1912-63), 252
Ward, Elizabeth (1935-88), 176 &n
Ward, Hon Lady (Jean) (1884-1962), 176 &n
Ward, Lt-Colonel John (1909-90), 176n
Ward, Mrs John (Susan) (1915-81), 176 &n
Warner, Sir Christopher (1895-1957), 224
Warner, Sir Fred (1918-95), 310
Warren, John (b. 1960), 512

INDEX

Warwick, Daisy, Countess of (1861-1938), 26n
Waterhouse, Hugo (1918-2007), 72
Watson, Cleo, 542
Watson, Francis (1907-88), 46n
Wavell, Field Marshal 1st Earl (1883-1950), 91
Weeks, Romilly, 491n
Weir, Sir John (1879-1971), 126, 134
Welby, Justin, Archbishop of Canterbury (b. 1956), 544, 555-6
Wellesley, Lord Gerald – see
Wellington, 1st Duke of (1769-1852), 78 &n
Wellington, 7th Duke of (1885-1972), 16, 133
Wellington, 8th Duke of (1915-2014), 91 &n, 431, 486
Wellington, Duchess of (Diana) (1922-2010), 486
Wernher, Georgina (Gina) (1919-2011), 99, 101
Wernher, Lady Zia (1892-1977), 91, 99
Wernher, Myra (later Butter)(1925-2022), 91, 101, 560
Wernher, Sir Harold (1893-1973), 91, 99
Wessex, HRH The Countess of (Sophie) (b. 1965), 429, 460, 471-2, 491, 508, 513, 520, 522, 552, 560
Wessex, HRH The Prince Edward, Earl of (b. 1964), 4, 254, 256, 257&n, 261n, 262, 272, 327, 359, 366, 383, 395, 429, 437, 459, 460, 466, 471, 472, 486 &n, 492n, 496, 534, 543
West, Dame Rebecca (1892-1983), 128
West, Mrs George (Hazel), 396
Westminster, 6th Duke of (Gerald) (1951-2016), 442
Westminster, Anne, Duchess of (1915-2003), 385
Westminster, Dean of – see Don
Westminster, Loelia, Duchess of (1902-93), 204
Westminster, Natalia, Duchess of (b. 1959), 382, 442
Wheatcroft, Geoffrey (b. 1945), 406
Whitaker, William (Billy) (1910-88), 91
Whitehead, Dame Annabel (b. 1943), 559
Whitehead, Sir John (1932-2013) 405
Whitelaw, William (1st Viscount) (1918-99), 381
Whitlam, Gough (1916-2014), 341-5, 341n
Whitley, Lady Mary – see Cambridge
Whitley, Peter (1923-2003), 28n
Whitney, John Hay (1904-82), 252
Whybrew, Paul (b. 1959), 508
Wigram, 1st Lord (Clive) (1873-1960), 55, 70
Wigram, Captain Hon Francis (1920-43), 72
Wilcock, Reg (1934-2000), 467
Wild, Rev R.D.F. (1910-95), 281n

Willans, Sir Frederick (1884-1949), 45
William, Prince – see Cambridge
Williams of Elvel, Lord (1933-2019), 246
Williams of Oystermouth, Lord (Rowan), Archbishop of Canterbury (b. 1950), 486, 507
Williams, Naomi (b. 1968), 532
Williams, Robbie (b. 1974), 507, 532
Williams, Sir Rodney (b. 1947), 517n
Williamson, Dr John (1907-58), 197
Wills, Hon Mrs (Jean) (1915-99), 32, 459, 463, 562
Wilson of Rideaux, Lord (Harold) (1916-95), 251, 253, 262, 271, as Prime Minister, 255, 277, 283-7, 284n, 287, 305-6, 334-5, 337-9; 340, 453
Wilson, A.N. (b. 1950), 39, 398
Wilson, Gordon (1927-95), 402
Wilson, Lady (Mary) (1916-2018), 337, 339
Winchester, Bapsy Marchioness of (1902-95), 439 &n
Windsor, Dean of – see Baillie – Hamilton – Woods – Conner
Windsor, HRH The Duke of (1894-1972), As Prince of Wales, 9, & Elizabeth Bowes-Lyon, 12; strained, 15, on George VI, 18, at Sandringham Xmas (1935), 44, & death of George V, 46;
As King, 48-51, abdicates, 51;
As Duke of Windsor, 52, sends present to Princess Elizabeth, 53, 63, not invited to Queen Mary's 80th birthday, 110, worries the Queen, 159-60; & death of Queen Mary, 164-5; & death of the Princess Royal, 259-60; & declining health, 262-4; visited by Emperor Hirohito, 308; final illness, 319-20, Queen visits, 323; death & funeral, 325-6, 328;
mentioned, 11, 16, 30, 33n, 54, 64, 160n, 165n, 194, 215, 227, 300, 303, 304, 322n, 364, 365, 370, 395, 402, 424n, 444, 445, 459, 474, 479
Windsor, Lady Gabriella (b. 1981), 357n, 537
Windsor, Lady Helen (later Taylor) (b. 1964), 262, 425
Windsor, Lady Louise Mountbatten- (b. 2003), 256n, 472, 522
Windsor, Lord Frederick (b. 1979), 357n
Windsor, the Duchess of (1896-1986), 15, 50-1, 159, 160n, 165n, 227 & n, 259, 260, 262-4, 308, 323, 325-6, 364, last years & death 389-90; 395, 402, 444, 445, 447n, 449n, 459, 474, 479, 513

Winfrey, Oprah (b. 1954), 546
Winn, Godfrey (1906-71), 209
Wintour, Charles (1917-99), 353
Witchell, Nicholas (b. 1953), 486
Withers, Audrey (1905-2001), 80
Wollaston, Sir Gerald Woods (1874-1957), 51
Wonder, Stevie (b. 1950), 507
Woods, Rt Rev Robin (Dean of Windsor) (1914-97), 257, 288, 389
Woollcombe, Joan (1904-93), 49
Woolton, 1st Earl of (1883-1958), 147, 158
Worsley, Bt, Sir William (1890-1973), 261
Worsthorne, Sir Peregrine (1923-2020), 356
Wright, Cobina (1921-2011), 87-9, 87n, 89n
Wrong, Michela (b. 1961), 273, 275n
Wulff, Louis (1905-82), 39
Wyatt, Steve, 418, 425-6

Yelland, David (b. 1963), 463
York, Archbishop of – see Lang
York, HRH Princess Beatrice of (b. 1988), 397, 403, 513, 520, 521, 544
York, HRH Princess Eugenie of (b. 1990), 403n, 520, 532
York, Sarah Duchess of – see Ferguson
Young of Old Windsor, Lord (Edward) (b. 1966), 500, 504n, 516, 525, 532, 536, 539, 542, 561
Yugoslavia, HM Queen Alexandra of (1921-93), 87-8, 87n-88n, 474
Yugoslavia, HRH Prince Alexander of (1924-2016), 57n, 89n
Yugoslavia, HRH Prince Paul of (1893-1976), 57n, 64 &n, 89n, 165
Yugoslavia, HRH Princess Paul of (1903-97), 57n, 64 &n, 89n, 149, 165, 272n

Zaire, President Mobutu Sese Seko of (1930-97), 331-3, 333n
Ziegler, Philip (1929-2023), 338

RAISING READERS
Books Build Bright Futures

Dear Reader,

We'd love your attention for one more page to tell you about the crisis in children's reading, and what we can all do.

Studies have shown that reading for fun is the **single biggest predictor of a child's future life chances** – more than family circumstance, parents' educational background or income. It improves academic results, mental health, wealth, communication skills, ambition and happiness.[1]

The number of children reading for fun is in rapid decline. Young people have a lot of competition for their time. In 2024, 1 in 10 children and young people in the UK aged 5 to 18 did not own a single book at home.[2]

Hachette works extensively with schools, libraries and literacy charities, but here are some ways we can all raise more readers:

- Reading to children for just 10 minutes a day makes a difference
- Don't give up if children aren't regular readers – there will be books for them!
- Visit bookshops and libraries to get recommendations
- Encourage them to listen to audiobooks
- Support school libraries
- Give books as gifts

There's a lot more information about how to encourage children to read on our website: **www.RaisingReaders.co.uk**

Thank you for reading.

---

[1] OECD, '21st-Century Readers: Developing Literacy Skills in a Digital World', 2021, https://www.oecd.org/en/publications/21st-century-readers_a83d84cb-en.html

[2] National Literacy Trust, 'Book Ownership in 2024', November 2024, https://literacytrust.org.uk/research-services/research-reports/book-ownership-in-2024